A Life Rew

Memoirs of a Freelance Producer and Director

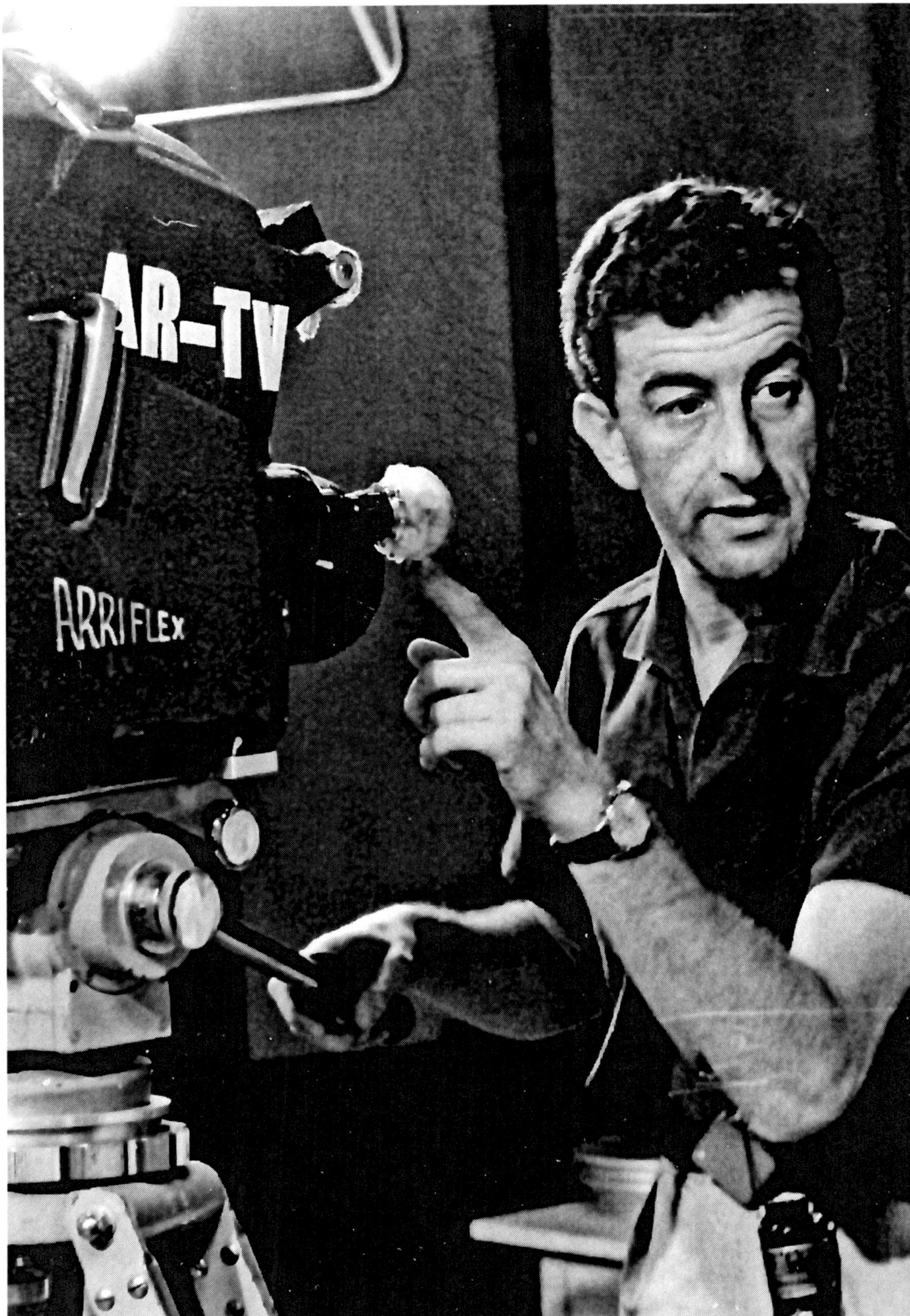
AR-TV
ARRIFLEX

A Life Rewound

Memoirs of a Freelance Producer and Director

to. Jim Doyle

with best wishes

and memories of Only Yesterday

Peter Morley

Peter Morley

BANK HOUSE BOOKS

First edition published online by
the Royal Television Society and the British Academy of Film and Television Arts, November 2006

Second expanded edition published in the United Kingdom in 2010 by
Bank House Books
PO Box 3
New Romney
TN29 9WJ

www.bankhousebooks.com

British Library Cataloguing in Publication Data
A catalogue record for this book is available from the British Library

ISBN 9781904408772

Typesetting and origination by Bank House Books

Contents

Acknowledgements

I owe a huge debt of gratitude to my family, and especially to Jane, for her patient and constructive support during my long absences at the computer keyboard and, of course, for her valiant proofreading of this narrative.

A special vote of thanks to my editor at Bank House Books, Simon Fletcher — and I am also grateful to Ann Parry for her expertise in compiling the index.

I want to pay tribute to everyone who has assisted in the task of helping to identify photographs, and wish to stress that every effort has been made to establish the owners' rights. If there are any regrettable omissions or mistaken attributions I will be pleased to rectify them.

The photographs reproduced in these memoirs, except for those taken from my private collection, are by courtesy of the following:

Rediffusion Television
BBC Television
British Academy of Film and Television Arts
The Broadlands Archive
EMI Films
Granada Television
Imperial War Museum
Royal Television Society
Yorkshire Television

Introduction

When I first started on this project in 2003, with two overworked index fingers searching for letters on the keyboard, I had misgivings about it. Who was it aimed at? Would it turn out to be solely for the family or for the world at large? Or was it merely an act of gross self-indulgence? I decided that the best way to proceed was to get things down on paper, or in this case the hard disk, and then see what would happen.

Over the years it has been my experience that the moment one starts on a new film or television programme it takes on a soul of its own, making its own unexpected and often positive contributions to the final result. And, once again, as month by month the word-count grew, this new project also began to have a mind of its own – it began to tell me that the film and television archives would probably be the most logical targets and depositories for this narrative. I hope that media students today and in years to come may find these recollections by a freelance director – dating back to a time before the birth of Independent Television in the UK – readable and maybe useful.

Sadly I have never kept a diary – but I have an attic full of letters, scripts, press cuttings, brochures and tons of photographs. This motley collection, plus a fairly crisp memory of the years gone by, have made it possible for me to catalogue – I trust with not too many inaccuracies – the main incidents of what might be called a fairly eventful life. I must confess that some anecdotes which I have lunched out on over the years have, in the act of retelling them, suffered a degree of embellishment that have surprised me, and I have taken this opportunity to unembellish them. I have tried to track down these misdemeanours and put matters right.

On 22 September 1955, when Associated-Rediffusion first went on the air, I joined a keen band of fellow ITV adventurers who shared with me the good fortune to be there right from the very start – and together, in the early years of this amazing medium, we embarked on this great adventure. I have recalled my early formative years: family background, schooling, wartime service – the ingredients that eventually shaped me, and influenced my career – and occasionally I had to ask myself: 'Who do I think I am?' I must confess that I have some difficulty in providing a sensible answer; I must leave that to others.

My family – my wife Jane and sons Jonathan and Benjamin – might think that they have drawn the short straw, because I have only included major family landmarks covering the past eighty-plus years. I think they will understand.

And if anyone should think that I have been journeying on a long-extended ego-trip – rewinding my life – I must plead guilty.

1: Family Break-Up

During the night of 27 February 1933 the Reichstag went up in flames. Goering and Goebbels had allegedly caused the building to be torched, subsequently claiming it as a communist plot. I clearly recall the next day when my elder brother, Tommy, aged eleven, announced with great excitement that he had seen the whole building ablaze on the way home from school. Just a few days before, leaning over the parapet of the balcony of our fourth-floor Berlin flat in the Kaiserallee, I was mesmerised, as only an eight-year-old could be, at the sight and sound of an endless parade of 'brownshirts' strutting in step to their military music, with the standard bearers flaunting their swastika flags and banners.

There is very little else I remember about Berlin. I was born in 1924, and occasionally trivial happenings from my very early days appear from nowhere, ring their little bell and then slip away again. But in 1933 incidents were firmly stamped on my memory: everything was about to change. The Reichstag fire had triggered events that were to spell the break-up of our family.

My father ran a small company, wholesaling and exporting women's fashion (the rag trade). He spent a good part of every year in London, where he had opened an office in the early '20s. He had developed a great affection for England and loved London, which had become his second home.

On 30 January 1933 Hindenburg offered the Chancellorship of Germany to Hitler, signalling the birth of the Third Reich. My parents, both Jewish, had already decided that we should leave Germany as soon as arrangements could be made, and England became the obvious choice. My mother, Alice, had located a school in Ulm, in Germany, which was to relocate to Kent later that year, and Tommy and I, with our elder sister Anne, had been accepted. In April my father happened to be in London when the boycott of Jewish businesses was set in motion, and he learnt that his premises in Berlin had been burned down by a Nazi mob. He decided to remain in London, and in a panic our mother arranged for us to leave Berlin immediately, without so much as closing up the flat or storing its contents. For Anne, Tommy and for me it was to mean much more than saying goodbye to a family home.

Anne, five years older than me, had sensed the coming crisis in our parents' relationship. Our mother was artistic, extrovert and fun loving, all the things that our father was not. She had collected a circle of friends around her: artists, actors and writers. Theatre-going and parties were her passion. She was also conducting a long-standing and not very secret affair with Harry Kahn. Our father, to whom her life style was alien, painfully accepted all this, and for the sake of keeping the family whole he suffered this hopeless situation in silence.

'Uncle' Harry, as we knew him, had been a frequent visitor to our home. He was a journalist, author, playwright and scriptwriter. He had long stints in Hollywood, adapting scripts and overseeing foreign language version films. And it was on one of his trips back to Berlin that he presented me with a packet of pure magic – Wrigley's chewing gum from America. This persuaded me that I wanted to get into films – long before I ever saw one. Anyway, I like to think that this was the motivation.

In April 1933, just two months after Hitler became Chancellor, with our father in London and our school places not yet finalised, our mother took us, via Frankfurt, to Switzerland. There was a scheduled stop for the train in Frankfurt, and I remember stepping down onto the platform to be greeted by my grandmother, uncles, aunts and cousins (my mother's family hailed from Frankfurt). They plied us with food and drink to sustain us for the rest of the journey. It was to be the last time I saw them. They were all to perish in Theresienstadt concentration camp.

When we arrived in Bern we boarded with a Swiss family, arranged by our mother, who then set off for Paris to plan a new life with Harry Kahn. I remember having to endure a fearsome teacher at our new school who rapped me over the knuckles with a ruler every time my handwriting did not come up to his liking. In spite of that I enjoyed the next six months. The novelty of a different country, with its magical mountain scenery, made the break from Berlin easy for me to accept. The three of us were now, for the first time, on our own.

The break-up of our home hardly affected me: I was too young to appreciate its significance. I cannot recall any pain at the separation from our parents. There was little closeness between my mother and me. She had different priorities and concentrated on her own pursuits, having handed over the normal motherly duties and functions to our nanny. As my father spent half of his time in London I had become used to his absences. In any case I was now preoccupied with the upheaval and the excitement of starting a new life in a new country, and as it turned out I was to be with a lot of other children who had also said goodbye to their parents and their homes.

In the late summer of 1933 we travelled by train to Paris on the way to England. I remember my mother and Harry meeting us and taking us to a hotel near the Eiffel Tower. It was in the evening, and I was much impressed by a glittering Citroën advertisement, which ran up and down each side of that huge tower. The next day our mother accompanied the three of us to England. She deposited us, temporarily, in a school for girls near Walmer in Kent, which took on holiday children during the long summer break. My memories of this short stay are vague, except that I can clearly recall my introduction to cornflakes. Kellogg's is a name that never fails to remind me of this interlude. And on 5 October the three of us travelled down to Dover, each with one suitcase containing our modest possessions, to meet the arrival of the ferry that was carrying a strange cargo – our new school. The new life was about to start.

2: Bunce Court School

Bunce Court School, in Kent, was unique. It was labelled 'progressive', and was a rarity in England at the time as it was a non-denominational, co-educational boarding school. And its arrival, lock, stock and barrel from Germany, was entirely thanks to the prescience of one person.

In the early '20s Anna Essinger returned to Germany from the United States. She had been there to finish her degree course and had then joined the academic staff of the German Department of the University in Wisconsin. While she was in the States she was influenced by a new philosophy that some schools were developing; it became known as 'progressive education'. She was also deeply influenced by her Quaker friends and adopted their beliefs; and it was with a Quaker mission that she returned to Germany to help bring relief to those who had suffered the ravages of the First World War.

In 1925 Anna founded and became head of a boarding school in Ulm. Based on her experiences in America, she put into practice her enthusiasm for the new progressive pedagogy. She created a family atmosphere within the school, promoting mutual respect for fellow pupils and staff, with a shared sense of responsibility towards each other and a pride in sharing the day-to-day running of the school. Her boarding school catered for all children, regardless of religious background, but with the rapid rise of anti-Semitism in Germany she began to accept more and more children from Jewish homes. And when Hitler came to power in 1933 this farsighted and brave woman raised funds in England, mainly from Quaker sources, that enabled her to purchase a large country property with ample grounds; it was to become the new home for her school in the heart of Kent, and she named it Bunce Court. She then shipped the staff and all the children from Ulm: it was a stupendous organisational feat.

From the Dover ferry quay my sister, brother and I travelled with the rest of the pupils in a convoy of buses to the school's new location near the village of Otterden. It was to become my home for the next seven years.

The youngest in the party, and I was one of them, were accommodated in 'The Cottage'. This was in a field, a quarter of a mile away from the main building. There were about twenty of us and it was pretty spartan, with no electricity at first, but we soon turned it into a comfortable new home for us. A month later, in November, our parents came down to check that the three of us had settled in and were well looked after. Our father had taken up residence in London, in the King's Court Hotel, off Bayswater, while our mother had come over from Paris and stayed there for this brief period. Months before, on leaving Berlin, she had made up her mind to abandon our father – and the three of us – and go her own way. She chose this moment to make the final break, and the morning after their return from the school to the King's Court Hotel he found a letter from her, stating that she was leaving him for good and was going to live permanently in Paris with Harry Kahn. She also took £200 in cash, the last of his money. From London he begged her not to desert the family but to join him back in England. He made desperate last-minute appeals to her by letter, telephone and telegram, but of no avail. They would never meet again and he would never forgive her.

Years before, our parents had acquired a Renoir and a Holder (I don't know how) which hung in the living and dining room of our Berlin home. Max, one of my father's two brothers, an American citizen living in New York, had agreed that in the event of the family leaving Germany he would undertake the task of closing down the Berlin flat and then oversee the sale of the paintings to raise the funds to pay our school fees. This was done.

I recall my seven years at Bunce Court with great affection. It was a happy time. Teachers were known by their first names, or by nicknames thought up by the pupils. The essence was teamwork. Formal lessons and study went hand in hand with the running of the school. All of us cheerfully shared the duties of bed-making, washing-up, cleaning and polishing, gardening, mending clothes, carrying out furniture repairs, tending to the orchard, looking after the chickens and the rest of it.

Music, art and sport occupied much of our spare time. For those who were self-motivated and keen to learn the chances were there to grasp. The standard of teaching was exceptional. I must admit I was more interested in practical pursuits: carpentry, making electrical repairs, building radios, laying telephone lines connecting some of the school's outbuildings. I enjoyed art classes, especially when engaged in design work. Maths was anathema, although geometry, because of its tangible shapes, had some appeal. I had violin lessons, but abandoned them. I couldn't bear the sound of my playing: I was too fond of music.

My mother came over from Paris for a brief visit to London and to Bunce Court. It was my tenth birthday, and she presented me with a tennis racquet and a punnet of strawberries. It would be eleven years before we were to meet again.

We were in the heart of the country, with few outside distractions. Contact with the outside world was sparse. In the summer, at weekends, the Wall's ice-cream man came up on his tricycle from Lenham, a small town a few miles away. On the front of his contraption was the slogan 'Stop me and buy one'. I did, if I could spare a penny from my monthly pocket money allowance of 1*s* 6*d*.

When school holidays came round I went up to London to stay with my father in the small King's Court Hotel in Leinster Gardens, off the Bayswater Road. He could not afford to put me up for any length of time, so I just spent the first few days with him. Then I went off to Sussex to stay with a large family, the Corbett-Fishers, who had 'taken me on'. That was a true stroke of luck. They were liberal, public-spirited, generous and what we would now call very laid back. Cicely Corbett-Fisher had given financial support to the school, and offered an open house to a pupil for holidays. Although Bunce Court had become a substitute home, with a special bond between children and staff, it was the Corbett-Fishers who provided a true family home. I was to spend all my holidays with them, and during those formative years that the happy-go-lucky and warm atmosphere must have had a great influence on me. It must have helped to shape my attitude to other people, the way I think and speak, my sense of humour and all the other idiosyncrasies that I am both blessed with and burdened by.

One of 'Ma' Corbett-Fisher's passions was motor racing. She had a racing car, an MG K3 Magnette, which had previously been owned by Tazio Nuvolari. The highlights of my holidays were meetings at Brooklands and Crystal Palace, where I used to help with the timekeeping in the pits. It was wildly exciting, and it gave me an appetite for the sport which has never left me – although I do miss the old-style racing cars with their distinctive designs, and drivers with leather helmets and goggles, sitting up so that you could see their expressions as they grappled with the steering wheel. Sadly the sport has lost a lot of its character.

It was at the start of the summer holiday in 1935 that my father treated me, together with my sister and brother, to a visit to the Marble Arch Pavilion. I was very excited as it was to be my first visit to a cinema. My first film was *The Camels Are Coming*, with Jack Hulbert and Cicely Courtneidge; it was also my first exposure to a newsreel and a Disney cartoon. After that, down in Sussex, we used to go at least once every holiday to a cinema in East Grinstead. I recall having an embarrassing accident out of sheer fright when we saw the horror movie *The Old Dark House* with Boris Karloff; but rich musicals with Fred Astaire and Ginger Rogers made up for all that.

Anne left Bunce Court for London in 1936 to take up secretarial training, and two years later Tommy left the school and started as an apprentice chef at the Dorchester Hotel. They lived

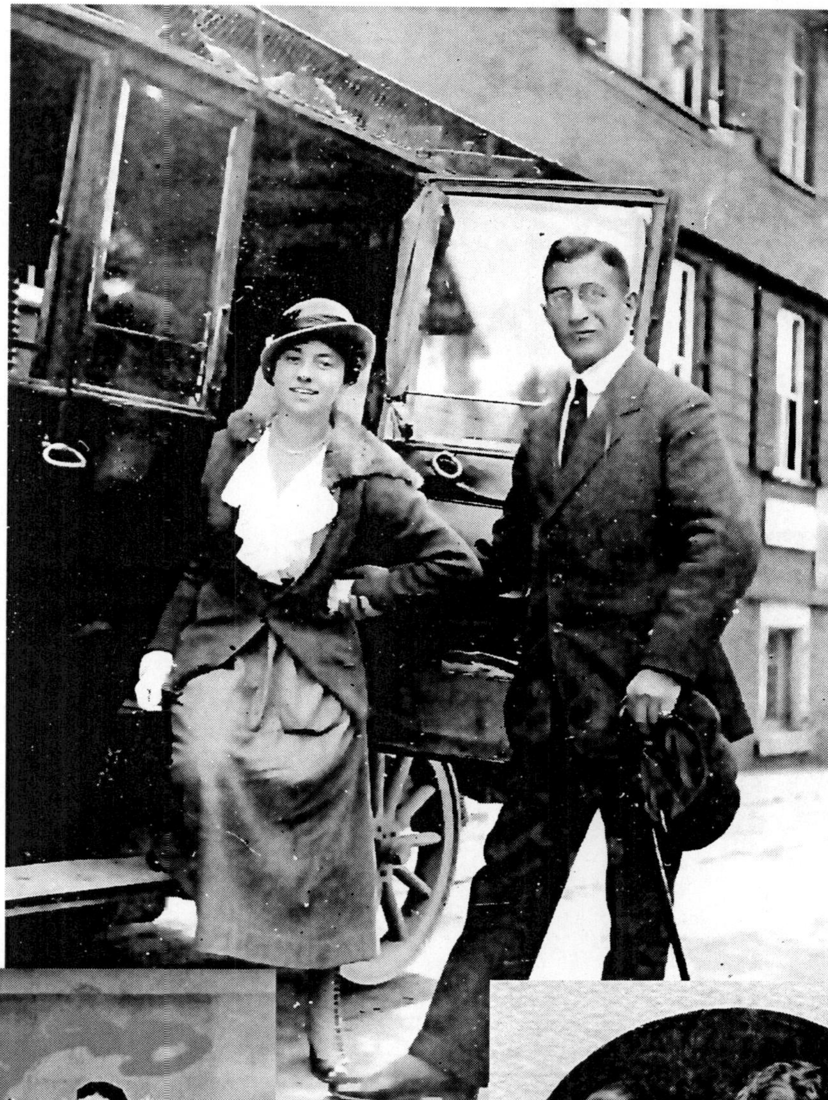

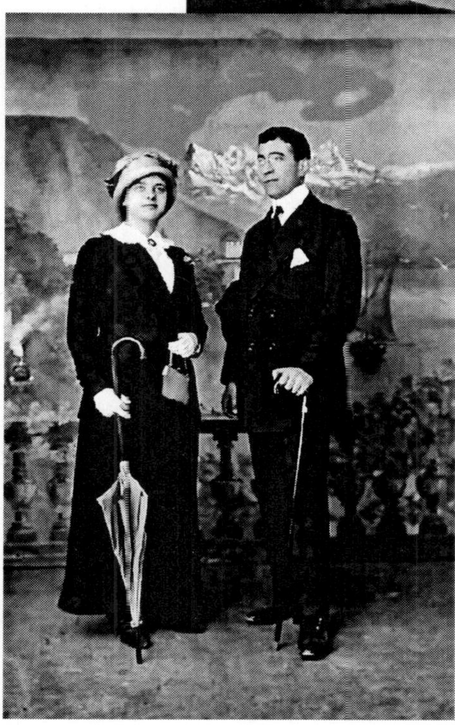

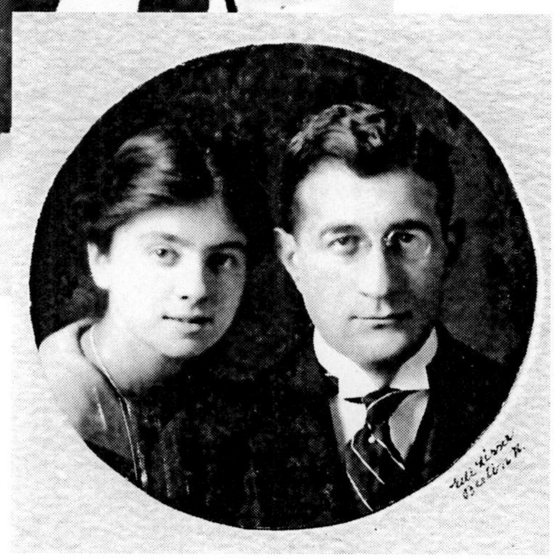

My parents, Willy and Alice, married in 1913. (PM)

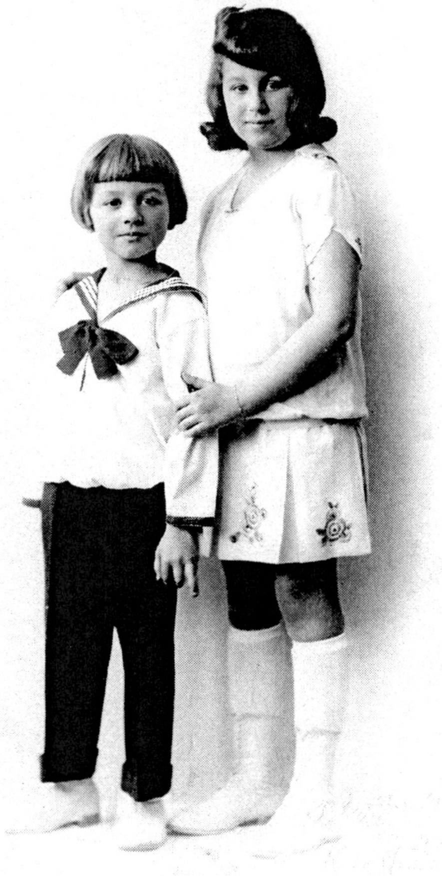

My brother Tommy (aged five) and my sister Anne Marie (aged eight). (PM)

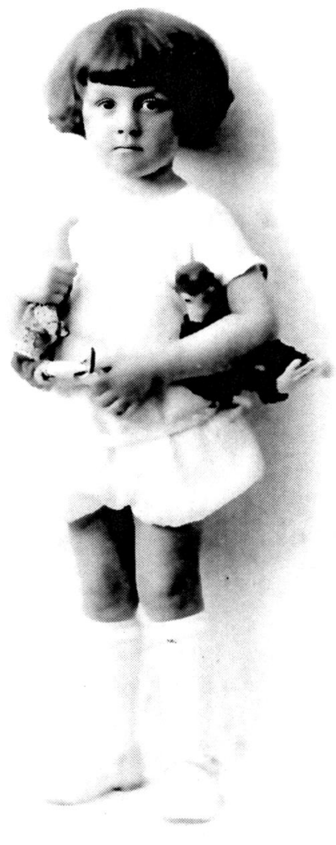

Me aged three. (PM)

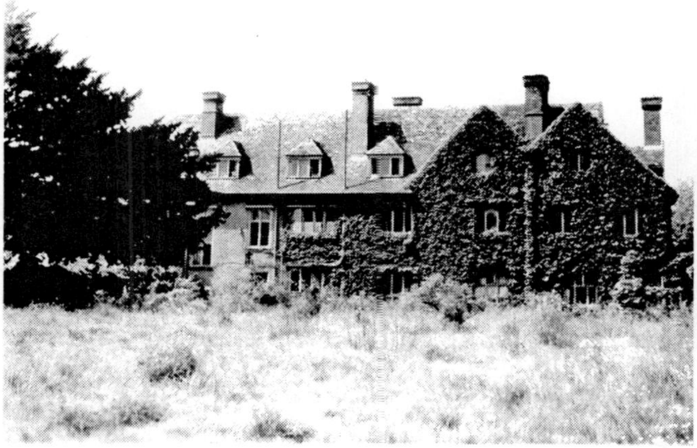

Bunce Court School. (PM)

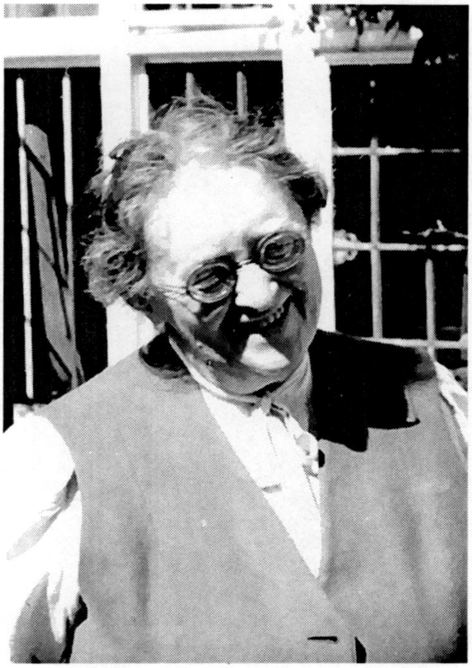

Headmistress Anna Essinger MA. (PM)

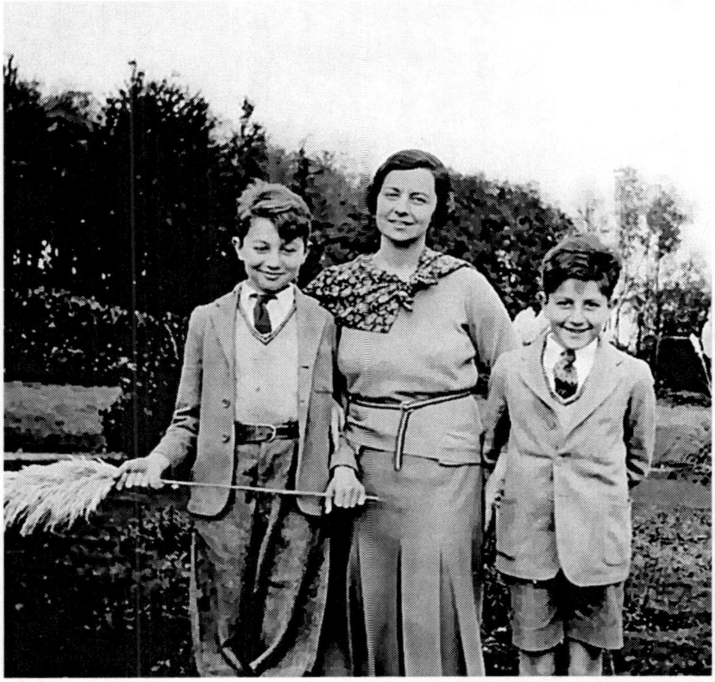

My mother visits Tommy and me at Bunce Court on my tenth birthday, 1934. It would be eleven years before we were to meet again. (PM)

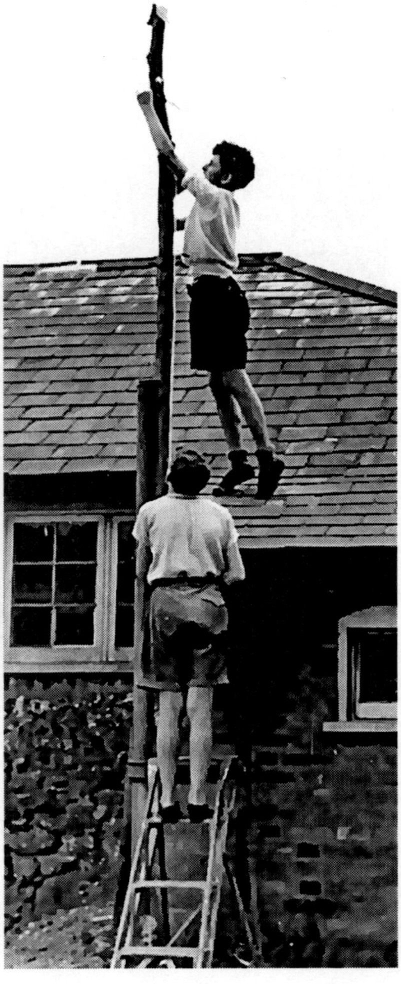

Stringing telephone cables to the Bunce Court cottage. (PM)

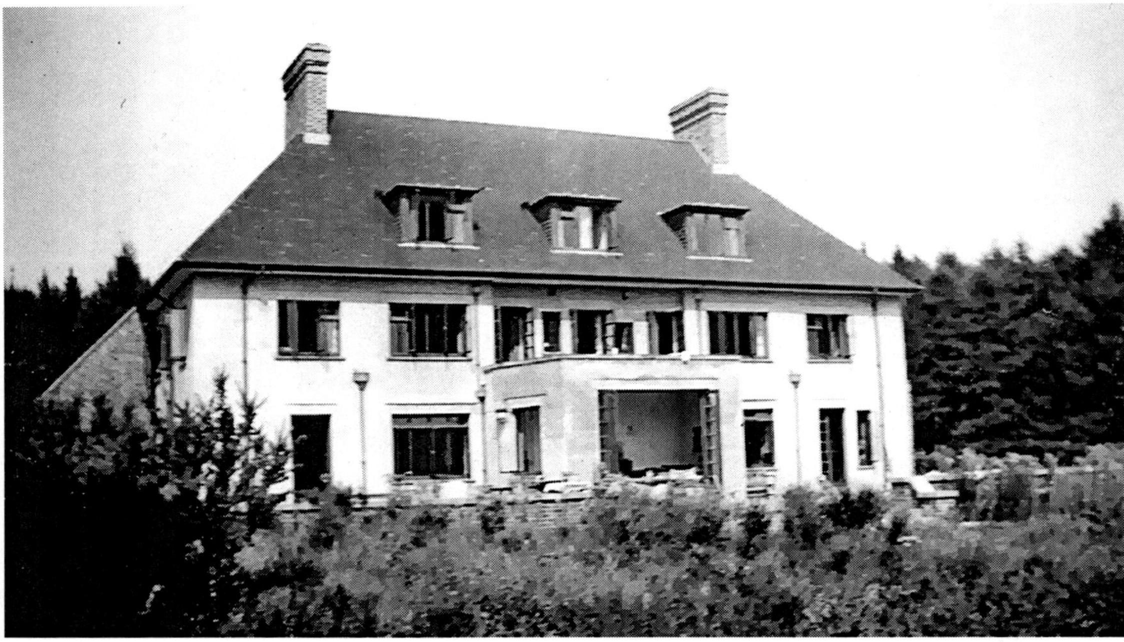

Newnham's Rough in Sussex, the Corbett-Fishers' home. (PM)

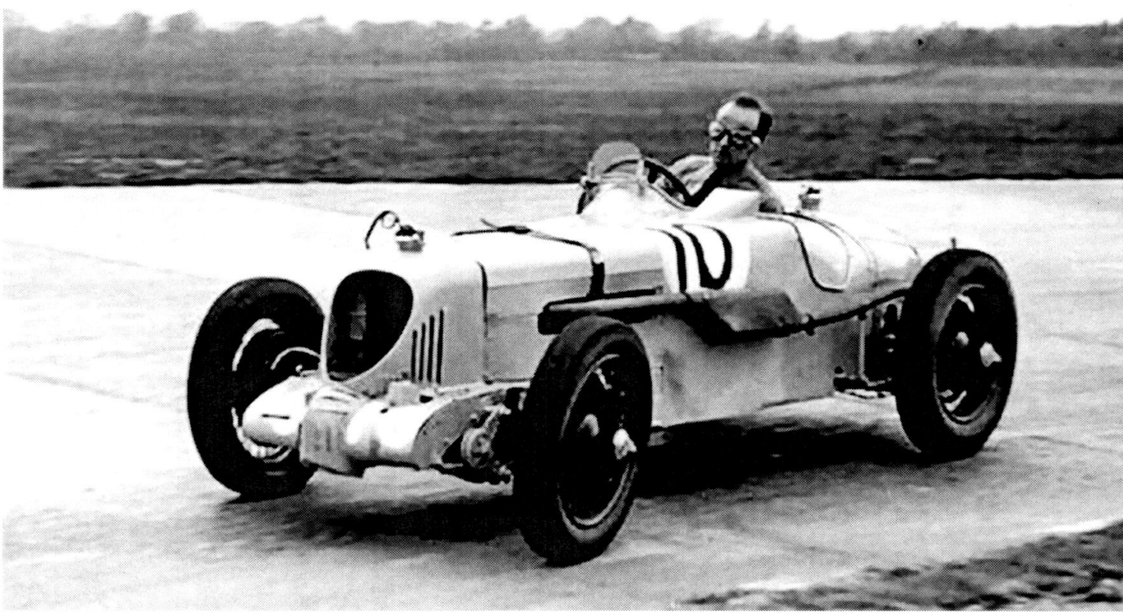

The ex-Nuvolari MG K3 Magnette owned by Cicely Corbett-Fisher at Brooklands, with Stuart Wilton at the wheel. (PM)

in rented rooms in Clarendon Road, near Holland Park, and saw a great deal of our father. By 1937 he had opened an office with a small showroom in Hanover Street, off Regent Street. Clients came up to the fourth floor by lift to see his various lines of imported women's wear. As he could no longer afford to stay at the King's Court Hotel he installed a bed in his small stock-room, and (quite illegally) made his office his home. This was where I stayed during those few days in London at the start of each holiday. I spent most of my time, hours, in the News Theatre in Oxford Street, just round the corner. It screened newsreels, cartoons, travelogues and general interest shorts. Quite often I stayed to see the whole programme a second time round. The magic of the movies, the silver screen as it was called, had got under my skin.

In 1937 I had a most distressing experience. For the first time in my life I found myself facing something that I simply could not comprehend. As I record it now, many decades later, I admit that I have always felt reluctant to share this episode with others. It concerns the Jewish ceremony of confirmation, the *bar mitzvah*. Both my parents came from fairly prosperous families in Germany, which observed the accepted traditional rituals associated with well-ordered, middle-class Jewish homes. My mother, so she told me years later, reluctantly joined in, merely paying lip service to it all. I have no childhood memories of this, but I was told that our father had a strong sense of duty and took the lead to ensure that his children would perpetuate the Jewish tradition. When the family home broke up in January 1933 and he remained in London to live on his own he must have found it very hard to adjust to his new and rather lonely life.

I had travelled up, as usual, from Bunce Court to spend a week with my father, before going down to Sussex to stay with the Corbett-Fishers. I had now reached the age of thirteen and he had made arrangements for my confirmation. He took me to see a rabbi in a local synagogue off the Bayswater Road for tuition and preparation for the *bar mitzvah* ceremony. The date was set and I was to spend an hour a day for the next five days with the rabbi for tuition. I felt very apprehensive. Although the great majority of children in Bunce Court were Jewish we lived in a non-denominational environment, so there was no personal Jewish experience to draw on.

Looking back on it now, it is not surprising that going to see a rabbi for tuition, and what's more to learn enough Hebrew to be able to participate in the ritual of the ceremony, was a daunting prospect. But as the whole experience was going to be over in a week, for my father's sake I would do my best.

The rabbi turned out to be a man with a very short fuse. During the second session, when he realised that I had failed to learn the Hebrew alphabet overnight, he went into a rage and slapped my face. He then tried to get me to repeat after him, letter by letter, word by word, the passage I was due to read at the ceremony. Every time I hesitated or stumbled he brought a ruler down on my hands. I was simply at a loss to know what to make of this. My father always looked forward to my return from these sessions, and I was too frightened and too ashamed to let on. On the last day of these painful visits the rabbi made me write down the passage phonetically. He had not only failed to beat Hebrew into me but, what is worse, he had not devoted any time to explain to me the solemnity or the significance of the *bar mitzvah*.

My father had asked a handful of his friends to the synagogue. I recall feeling scared, but I managed to utter the words on cue and somehow got away with it. In short, it was a ceremony that had not been properly explained to me with words that, for me, were gibberish. It was a total farce. Anne reminded me years later that there was a modest celebratory meal in a restaurant afterwards, but all I remember is that I felt so ashamed that I did not want to tell anyone about this humiliating experience. And I didn't. I escaped to the Corbett-Fishers in Sussex and tried to forget the past week. Fortunately there was the August Bank Holiday Brooklands meeting, and I could concentrate on my passion for racing cars.

With hindsight I don't think this traumatic episode at the age of thirteen unduly influenced my concept of being Jewish, or, as it turned out, of feeling totally non-Jewish. I believe it merely added to a subconscious process which was in any case evolving. I had been brought up in a religious void, and I was naturally much influenced by and identified with the Corbett-Fisher's liberal attitudes and agnosticism. I was made to feel part of that family, and spent three glorious holidays every year in a relaxed and freewheeling atmosphere. Being a close member of that family not only made me feel thoroughly 'English', but I also adapted to a way of life in which religion played no part. As a result I have never thought of myself as a Jew. Of course I have

Jewish blood in my veins, but I don't know what it is like to 'feel Jewish'. I have always found Jewish beliefs and especially the rituals intriguing, often baffling, sometimes exasperating, but as foreign to me as those of other religions. This has always proved to be a most difficult concept to explain to family members and Jewish friends. When I married Jane in 1962 it did not even occur to me that others might think that I was 'stepping out of my religion'. Jane and I happily accepted the co-existence of her Church of England upbringing and my agnosticism. Our boys, Jonathan and Ben, have always accepted this situation, and have been free to make up their own minds about their religious leanings.

3: War

I have memories of 3 September 1939 that to this day remain crystal clear. I was now fifteen and, as usual, I was spending the summer holidays down in Sussex with the Corbett-Fishers. We were crowded round the big radiogram in the living room and heard Chamberlain's famous declaration: 'This morning the British Ambassador in Berlin handed the German Government a final note stating that unless we heard from them by eleven o'clock that they were prepared at once to withdraw their troops from Poland a state of war would exist between us. I have to tell you now that no such undertaking has been received and that consequently this country is at war with Germany . . .' Immediately after the broadcast we went outside and heard the wail of distant air-raid sirens drifting across the Downs from the direction of Brighton. Then suddenly a low-flying RAF Beaufighter roared over the treetops close to the house and disappeared. Apart from the shock, it dramatically punctuated the impact of Chamberlain's speech.

The Home Office had ruled that anyone born in Germany was classed an 'enemy alien', and all German-born males over the age of sixteen were interned. Early in 1940 both my father and my brother Tommy went to Huyton, near Liverpool, and then to an internment camp on the Isle of Man. I was lucky to escape this because I was just under sixteen. And they were lucky too, as they were spared the fate of a great number of internees who were shipped to Canada and Australia. Some did not make it: U-boats were claiming their early victims.

Back at Bunce Court the drama unfolded. Evacuation. In June 1940 Kent was deemed to be a protected area, too close to the potential action: air attacks and invasion were the threat. Once again Anna Essinger had to find a new location for her school; but this time she was given a mere seven days' notice. Using her organisational genius, she found a suitable new site. It was a mile outside the small town of Wem, in Shropshire. Being fifteen, I was one of the senior boys, right in the middle of swotting for the Cambridge School Certificate, the equivalent of today's GCSEs. We became members of the advance party. There was little time to adapt a large country house. We had to use our carpentry skills to make dozens of bunk beds, build cupboards and generally provide the basic necessities. It was both exciting and exhausting, albeit at the expense of getting one's head down for revision work.

One of my subjects was Art. Apart from painting and 'design & decorative composition' there was also a paper on the History of Art. Owing to an oversight the latter had not been taught. It was May and we were three weeks away from sitting the exam. In a panic our art teacher gripped the situation and gave us a crash course on the Parthenon, as she was convinced that there was going to be a question on it. We boned up on it, quickly learning how to draw up architectural plans and memorise names like pediment, architrave and entablature. And sure enough, of the two questions set in the paper one was on the Parthenon. As luck would have it I was able to handle the second one as well. It read: 'Describe a modern building, draw a sketch, explain its use and why you have chosen it.' It so happened that in the holidays, when we drove down to Sussex from the Corbett-Fishers' London home, we passed over Chelsea bridge. Across the Thames on the left stood the majestic Battersea Power Station. It then boasted only three huge chimneys, which always impressed me. What's more, I was an avid collector of De Reske cigarette cards, and had just started on their 'Famous Buildings' series. One of my first swaps with a fellow collector was a splendid picture, in colour, of the power station, with some brief text on the reverse side. It was hardly detailed enough for a PhD, but adequate for my exam. To my surprise I passed.

It was July 1940. I had just turned sixteen, and mercifully the internment rules had been relaxed so I escaped that fate. The question now was what should I do. The school had been my home for seven years, and I was ill-prepared to face the wartime reality of the outside world. My father had been released from his camp on the Isle of Man and had returned to live in his showroom off Regent Street. He did his duty as an air raid warden. London was experiencing very heavy bombing and he rented a basement flat in Earls Court, which he believed to be as safe as anywhere else. He did not relish the thought of spending nights in air-raid shelters, or on the Underground platforms of the Piccadilly Line.

There seemed to be little point in my joining him from the relative safety of the countryside, and my father decided that I should remain where I was. I became a lodger in my old home, the school, and found a job in Wem. The school provided me with a pack of sandwiches for my lunch and a hearty meal when I returned from town in the evening.

In reality my job was several rolled into one, and all for the same boss. Mr Huxley owned the local radio and bicycle shop, the coal yard down at the railway station and the local tennis club, with six grass courts. The two men who worked for him had been called up to the services, and he hired me to replace them. I was paid the princely sum of 12*s* 6*d* a week, of which 10*s* went to the school for my keep. The rest I spent on the odd Mars bar, some Woodbine cigarettes and postage stamps.

To get to work I rode into Wem on a bicycle – about 2 miles. But that had to be negotiated. As I was officially classed as an enemy alien, special police permission had to be sought for riding a bike. Likewise, one had to have permits for travelling anywhere outside a 5-mile radius of one's registered address; and it was mandatory to report to the police on arrival at the new destination.

I started work at 8 a.m. My duties were manifold. The first job was always to wash down the pavement outside the premises and clean the shop window. Then I had to see to the accumulators, which had been on charge overnight: many domestic radios in those days were battery operated and used low voltage accumulators. I disconnected these from the charging panel and cleaned off the corrosion from the terminals. The ones left on the doorstep by customers the previous night had to be topped up with distilled water and put on charge. Usually there were some bikes to repair as well: punctures, new brake blocks (these were now getting scarce) and messy adjustments to chains and so on.

Serving in the shop behind the counter was a novel experience. I had to teach myself how to handle money and give the correct change; not easy, as Mr Huxley kept all the shop cash in small biscuit tins under the counter. He also contributed hugely to my education by explaining in a bizarrely convoluted way what condoms were used for. Apparently the small chemist shop in Wem did not stock these items, and he was the High Street's sole supplier, satisfying the demands of the male population from the town and surrounding countryside. His instructions were quite clear. 'Only serve men', he said, 'when they ask for a special valve rubber for their bike.'

I thought Mr Huxley was rather odd. I had never met anyone like him before. He was unmarried, had plucked eyebrows, lacquered fingernails and introduced me to a small library of books at the back, which today would be described as the worst examples of hard-core pornographic literature. It was an eye-opener for a sixteen-year-old. Instinctively I kept my distance from him.

One of his predilections was to invite the pretty publican's wife over from the pub across the road (her husband was abroad in the army) to bring comfort to one of his soldier lodgers who was staying upstairs in the spare bedroom while stationed in the vicinity. Mr Huxley was thus able to indulge in a most curious sport. He tied a long piece of string to the mattress of the spare bed upstairs, fed it through a small hole he had drilled in the ceiling of his living room below, then attached a small handbell to it – the sort of bell that, in a slightly more refined home, was used to summon people to lunch, tea or dinner. When the newly acquainted visitors retired upstairs – usually in the afternoon – he waited downstairs for the bell to start its joyous ringing, then came into the shop, his face flushed, rubbing his hands and proclaiming, 'They're at it!'

It was during one of these diversions that my History teacher stepped into the shop to congratulate me on passing my School Certificate exam. I was both surprised and delighted at this news, and quickly came to the conclusion that exams were a rather inadequate preparation for life beyond school.

Down at the Wem station coal yard work took on a different meaning, especially through the severe winter of 1940 when we had a great deal of snow. I had to unload literally tons of coal from a railway wagon into a wheelbarrow and take it to Mr Huxley's coal pen a few yards away. This sometimes took two backbreaking days. One hundredweight sacks had to be filled, weighed and loaded onto a horse-drawn dray for delivery to customers' homes, and often to farms outside Wem. Carrying these sacks on my back, sometimes up steep steps, taught me at an early age to have great respect for those who earn their living by hard physical toil. It certainly did no favours to my back.

Looking after the tennis lawns was a great relief. How Mr Huxley obtained petrol for his motor mowers remained a mystery, but he did, and I spent many late evenings of the summer of 1940 manicuring his six courts with a short cut and marking them up with white lines.

It was a strange existence. In 1941 I felt like moving on. I knew that I could not join the services until I reached the age of seventeen and a quarter, and I was keener than ever to 'get into films'. I had absolutely no idea on how to set about this. I did not know anybody in the film industry I could approach and had no friends to advise me. My father, whom I had not seen for well over a year, still did not want me to join him in London because of the bombing, so I opted to go to Birmingham instead. The school arranged for me to stay in a hostel for young people, so at least I had an address to go to.

My first job in Birmingham was with an engineering company making and repairing armatures and rotors for electric motors, some destined for use in submarines. I had to sweep the shop floor and clear tons of swarf from the lathes. I lasted a week, because this was war-work and I was refused the necessary permit. Back I went once more to the labour exchange, resulting in a job with a small building firm. By now Birmingham was on the Luftwaffe's target list, and bomb damage repairs kept builders in business. My job was with a small team that repaired chimneys, and the work was precarious. I had to climb up very long ladders, which reached right up to the chimneys, carrying a heavy hod of bricks. Half-way up, my weight and that of the bricks made the ladder bow in and out: I don't think I have ever been so scared. I was very thankful when this torture came to an abrupt end. It happened like this. One night there was a heavy raid, and a few yards away from my hostel a similar building received a direct hit, leaving a huge gap in the line of houses. I wrote to my father, suggesting that as we were both being bombed it made no sense for me to be on my own in Birmingham. He wrote back to say that he would come up to have a look for himself, gave the train arrival time and asked me to meet him. That night we had another heavy raid, and New Street Station was so badly damaged that the trains had to stop about a mile outside it. I walked along the track to the train, and helped my father down from the carriage. We walked past the wrecked station to my hostel, where he took just one look at the gaping void three houses up before saying that we might as well be bombed together, and agreeing that I should join him in London. After just one month I was very glad to say goodbye to Birmingham.

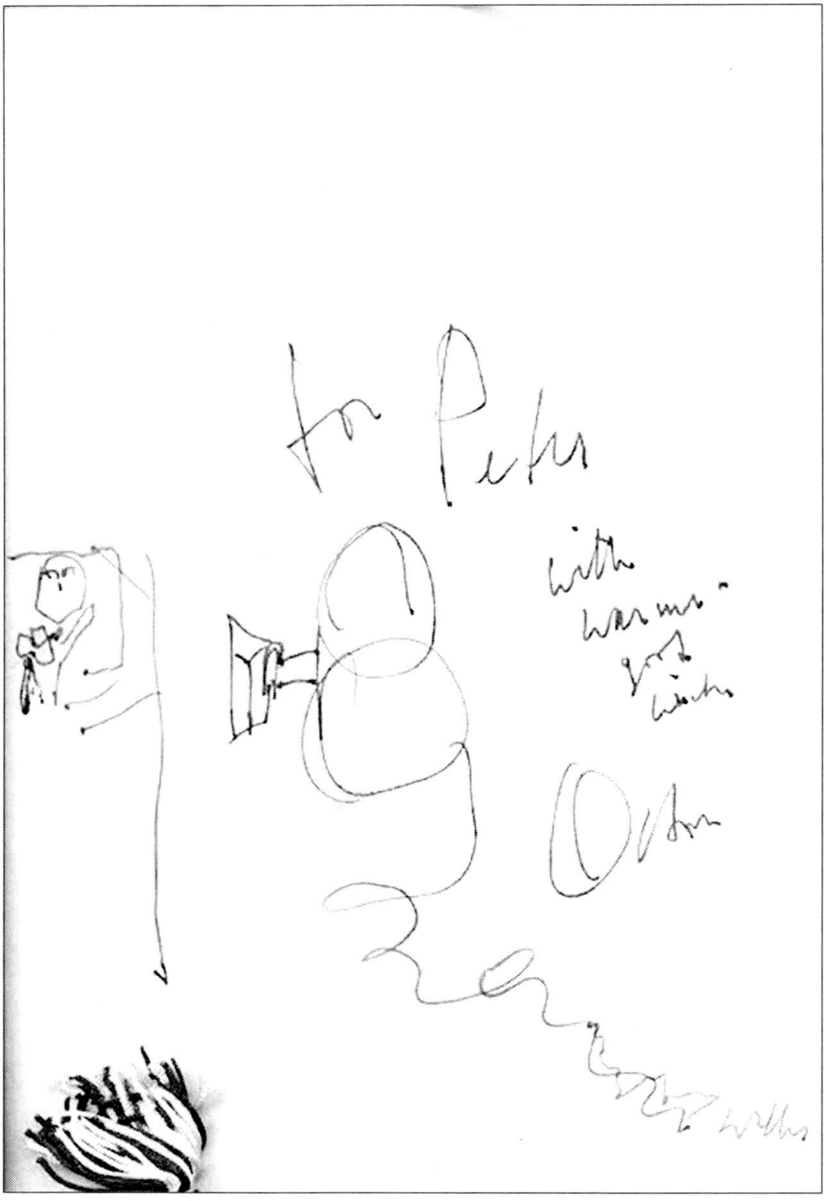

Lightning cartoon drawn by Orson Welles at the fiftieth anniversary of the British Film Institute.

4: Rewind-Boy

I was now installed in my father's basement flat opposite Earls Court station. It seemed rather strange at first to live under the same roof as him; it was, after all, the first time since I was eight years old. But we got on well, and soon discovered how best to share and eke out our food rations.

My sister was living on her own in London, having joined the staff of the Warburg Institute in 1937. The Institute specialises in the history of the classical tradition, and in 1944 it was incorporated into the University of London. After the war Anne became the Secretary and Registrar of the Institute, and was recognised by her colleagues as being its main pillar of strength, right up to and even after her retirement in 1984. She was made an Honorary Fellow of the Institute and appointed MBE. Anne died in 2004, aged eighty-five.

Tommy, my brother, secured his early release from internment by volunteering for the army, and left London to do his primary training. I felt very frustrated. I was so keen to have something to do with film, but had no idea how to go about it.

Instead I settled for a job with a fur-dressing company in Bermondsey – which was a pretty revolting experience. The furs, mostly rabbit, were pickled in large vats filled with a foul-smelling caustic brine. After this pickling process had taken place, my job was to pull the furs out of the vats, with bare arms, and throw them into a 12 foot high wooden drum that I had half-filled with clean sawdust. An electric motor then slowly spun the drum, cleaning and drying the tumbling furs. After several hours I unlocked a small hatch cover and climbed inside the drum, threw out the furs and bagged up the sawdust, which was now filthy and reeked of decayed flesh; then I lifted the bags out through the hatch. I soon developed rampant impetigo, which covered most of my body, and I welcomed a doctor's advice to change job.

Off again to a labour exchange, but the one I was registered with at the corner of Poland Street and Great Marlborough Street (near Carnaby Street) had been flattened. A notice tied to the stump of a lamp-post outside it referred 'customers' to another branch in the City. The night before I was due to report there, the Luftwaffe carried out yet another of its destructive raids over London, and the City, as usual, had borne the brunt. The next morning I had to walk most of the way, as London Transport often ceased to operate in the City. Nearly all the buildings and churches around St Paul's Cathedral stood in ruins.

One had to be careful walking in this wasteland because of all the debris, broken glass and fire hoses. For good reasons I could not find my labour exchange: it too had been obliterated. But I did find another job.

Nurdin & Peacock was a large wholesale food distributor with premises in Wells Street, just off Oxford Street, near Tottenham Court Road. Most of the produce that arrived for onward distribution was imported. It arrived in London's docks, was unloaded there and brought to Wells Street in lorries and drays. Little did we realise at the time the perilous voyages of the Atlantic convoys that kept us alive in Britain: the public was kept ignorant of the huge cost in ships and men, and it was only some time later that the newsreels showed the disastrous losses caused by U-boats hunting in packs. My job was to unload these cargoes from the docks, so once again I was humping heavy loads and not enjoying it. This was July 1941 – a very hot summer. When a huge shipment of Chinese frozen eggs (in liquid form) arrived at the docks, stored in large tins the size of orange crates and wrapped in sacking that acted as insulation, they had to be lifted off the lorries and carried on the shoulder into cavernous cold storage rooms in Wells Street. Stepping out of the hot sun into this arctic temperature simply took your breath away.

But there were compensations. On Fridays we were given a bonus in the shape of a tin of either pineapple slices or peaches, which I used to bring home in triumph. Sometimes Anne joined us in Earl's Court for lunch at the weekend to participate in these rare treats.

I decided to make up for my poor showing in Maths at school and signed up for a course with a Correspondence Learning Institute in Oxford Street. That brought my first bit of good luck. When the parcel of textbooks and other literature arrived there was also an invitation to come and discuss my career prospects. The institute's offices above Lilly & Skinner opposite Bond Street station turned out to be a very small but useful labour exchange. When I went for an interview, for the first time in my life somebody actually asked me what I wanted to do. The interviewer was not really able to give me detailed advice on the film industry, but suggested that a good start would be to take on a rare job vacancy on their books – for a trainee cinema projectionist, known in the industry as a rewind-boy. I felt I had arrived!

The Dominion cinema in Tottenham Court Road was opened in 1929 as part of the huge Gaumont-British chain. Designed as a theatre and cinema, it was the largest in London's West End. It could seat about three thousand, had a deep stage with revolves and lifts, a full complement of artistes' changing rooms and a giant Wurlitzer organ. Unfortunately the architect failed to incorporate the projection box in his plans, so it had to be constructed as an afterthought and stuck high up on the outside vertical wall at the back of the auditorium. You can still see it today if you stand on the other side of Tottenham Court Road and look up through the big marquee ironwork.

I was interviewed by the manager, and after a quick once-over from the chief projectionist was engaged at a salary of £1 5*s* a week. The 'chief' took me up to the box. Many stairs later a door led to a flat roof, and then the real climb started. This was an exterior iron fire escape, which eventually reached the projection box. I was shown the box, the rewind room and the lime room, with its powerful limelights which were often used for stage shows. Outside, half-open to the elements, was a passage where there stood four upright, narrow steel cabinets for coats – except that the fourth had a different purpose. I soon discovered its secret. When I opened the door there was a bucket *in situ*, known as the 'chief's piss bucket'. It was as disgusting as it was essential, because the nearest toilets – and there were many in the Dominion – were a steep climb down the fire escape and a long march away. It was explained to me that my duties included the emptying of this bucket, which meant carrying it down the fire escape to the flat roof and disposing of the contents down a rain gutter. This precarious journey, with the bucket full to its brim and the wind blowing, was not much fun. Nevertheless, it was this rewind-boy's introduction to film.

There were two 35mm projectors in the box and a spool of film ran for about twenty minutes, after which we had to change over to the other projector and the old spool had to be rewound. This was done with great care, with the film passing between forefinger and thumb to feel for torn sprocket holes or damaged splices where reels had been joined together.

There were two programme changes every week, on Thursdays and Sundays. A programme consisted of two feature films, a newsreel, a cartoon and often a 'short' or a travelogue. There were also brief Central Office of Information films, known as food flashes, including a series called 'Potato Pete' that implored us to plant and to eat more potatoes; and trailers for the next tranche of feature films. The live part of the programme consisted of the cinema organist letting fly with a popular medley of tunes. Occasionally he treated the audience to a simulated air raid, using a special array of keys to produce sound effects and making up his own commentary. It usually ended with a German bomber being hit, with an ear-splitting crescendo as it spiralled down to earth.

Sometimes at the weekend there was a stage show as well, usually a big band with popular singers, like Anne Shelton. This kept us busy in the lime room, following performers with the limelights.

The films came in 1,000 foot reels, each in its own can. These were stored in heavy steel transit boxes which held ten cans each: we had to carry them all the way from the street up to the box. In any one week we humped over sixty cans of film. As each reel ran for about ten minutes, two had to be joined together to make up the twenty-minute spools for the projectors. Splicing film was quite an art. At its head each reel has a standard lead-in, called the Academy leader (it was instituted by the American Academy of Motion Pictures) and at the end there is the tail leader. When joining two reels together you wound the first one onto the projector spool and cut off its tail leader. Then you cut off the leader from the head of the second reel and spliced the last picture frame of reel one to the first picture frame of reel two.

The chief was a stickler for tradition. Although the rewind room was equipped with a mechanical splicer he insisted on using the traditional hand-splicing method. This was really tricky. 35mm film consisted of a celluloid nitrate base – highly inflammable – with a layer of emulsion that carried the photographic image. In order to join the two bits together the emulsion had to be removed from one piece, exposing the nitrate base. You then ran your tongue along the cut you have made – just like licking a Rizla cigarette paper – and with a razor blade gingerly removed the wet emulsion to expose the base, which you then coated with film cement. Then you matched up the sprocket holes with the other piece, pressed the two together and held the splice in your hand for about ten seconds for it to 'take'. To this day I can clearly smell the intoxicating vapour of the cement, which was made up of amyl acetate and acetone – reminding me of old-fashioned pear drops.

Twice a week, when the next programme change came, the spools were broken down into single reels again and the head and tail leaders had to be spliced back. Because the sprocket holes had to overlap, with every splice made you shortened the movie by two frames! Just imagine the state of these pristine West End prints by the time they ended their run in a host of cinemas across the country, smudged with the fingerprints of the nation's rewind-boys.

The distance from the projector's lens to the screen, known as the throw, was 180 feet. The Dominion claimed to have the longest throw in the country, and for focusing we had to look at the screen through the glass porthole, using binoculars to ensure a really sharp picture.

At the base of the Dominion's massive screen was an illuminated box which displayed one of two messages: 'All Clear' or 'Alert': the manager phoned through instructions for us to switch from one to the other. Regardless of the severity of the air raid, the tradition of 'the show must go on' was observed. When the noise of exploding bombs and the racket of the anti-aircraft guns sounded a bit close, we found ourselves marooned in the projection box screening films to an almost empty auditorium. At moments like this one of us had to stand in the passage outside the box and watch the flat roof in case incendiary bombs landed on it. On one occasion we hurried down the fire escape and extinguished two of these with buckets of sand and the standard issue stirrup pump. Luckily we had just changed over to the other projector; even so, we barely got back in time from this distraction for the next changeover.

Once a week we had to stay overnight on fire-watching duties. This was the time to have a bit of fun. One of the dressing rooms had a small electric hob for my ritual fry-up: for supper I blew my weekly ration of one egg and two rashers of bacon, and added some fried bread. Sometimes we switched on the giant Wurlitzer in the orchestra pit, rode it up and down, and experimented with the dozens of stops, keys and buttons.

But the real sport was shooting rats. One of the projectionists had a .22 rifle – highly illegal. Our hide was the lime room. We removed the big glass portholes, raised the Dominion's safety curtain, opened the screen tabs, struck the arcs on the limes, pulled open the dowser and floodlit the stage. There they were, as big as cats. Hitting them from that great distance was another matter, but this sport certainly gave a different meaning to fire-watching.

Call-up to the services was taking its toll on the cinema's staff and as a result there were glittering career prospects and rapid promotion. To reach the dizzy heights of second projectionist in the West End in peacetime normally took about twenty years, but there was a war on – so I achieved that status in nine months. Sitting on a high stool next to the projector and being in charge was both exciting and a bit frightening, with the knowledge that there could be about three thousand people watching the screen.

As the nitrate 35mm film was extremely inflammable, the threat of a serious blaze was always present. The arcs provided a high intensity and powerful light source, but at the cost of generating enormous heat. If for some reason there was a tear in the film, usually caused by a broken sprocket hole, and a small piece of it got trapped in the gate of the projector, it would instantly melt and catch alight. One had to react very quickly by dowsing the arc, thus shutting off the light beam. After removing the debris one pulled down about 6 feet of film from the top spool box and quickly laced up the projector again for the show to continue. I remember hearing the howls of the audience's derision through the thick glass of the porthole.

By studying films, albeit through a porthole, I was beginning to get ideas about how they were made and the many talents employed in the production process. When a film particularly intrigued me I turned up on my weekly day off and sat at the back of the balcony to see it properly. One day Orson Welles's *Citizen Kane* arrived. It instantly made a deep impression on me; in fact it was a turning point, because it made me see quite clearly what I wanted to learn and what I wanted to be. I was stunned by Greg Toland's deep-focus photography, a craft that he pioneered and which had never been achieved before in such style. But it was the film editing, the cutting, which fired me most. Robert Wise was responsible for that, and he became my hero. I promised myself that one day I would find a way into a film cutting room.

Over forty years later I was to meet Orson Welles. The occasion was the BFI's fiftieth anniversary, elaborately celebrated in the Guildhall, with Prince Charles presenting Welles with a BFI Fellowship. After the feast and the ceremonies he was taken to a side room where he held court, his immense bulk having been lowered into a gigantic chair. His fans were able to pay their respects. I was introduced to him as the ex-projectionist whom he had inspired. I told him that seeing *Citizen Kane* at least twenty times through a small porthole paved the way to my career and that I was eternally grateful to him. He had already taken my posh BFI souvenir programme out of my hand, and without looking up at me he drew a lightning cartoon. I am seen at the porthole next to a projector with the film coming off the take-up spool, curling all over the floor and spelling out 'Welles', with the inscription 'for Peter with warmest good wishes, Orson'.

There was not much of a social life to be enjoyed when working at the Dominion; the working hours of a projectionist conspired against it. Usually we had one day off during the week; otherwise the day started at 10 a.m. and the safety curtain did not come down till shortly before midnight. Travelling home to Earls Court was erratic. Often I had to walk because air raids were apt to bring the Underground to a halt. At sunset the station entrances swallowed up an endless procession of Londoners – whole families carrying their bedding, food and thermos flasks for the nightly escape from the bombs. By the time I set off for home most of them were fast asleep on the platforms. Later, double bunks were provided, which meant that one was less likely to trip over sleeping bodies when getting onto or alighting from a tube train. The odour on the platforms was often overpowering.

In the autumn of 1941, aged seventeen and a quarter – the minimum age for acceptance to the services – I went to Adastral House, the Air Ministry in Kingsway (which years later was Television House, the home of ITV's Associated-Rediffusion), and they sent me off to the RAF recruiting office opposite Euston station, where I volunteered to join up. I wanted to be a fighter pilot. I passed my aircrew medical and ability test, but was told to call back in six months as there was a flood of applicants and the training facilities in Canada could not cope. Then a letter arrived to tell me that my status as an enemy alien barred me from joining the RAF. I refused to believe it.

When I took this news to the Corbett-Fishers on one of my visits to their London home, Cicely Corbett-Fisher's sister, Lady Marjorie Corbett-Ashby, happened to be there. She was a leading member of the Liberal party and knew the Air Minister, Sir Archibald Sinclair, very well. She offered to contact him to see whether he could smooth my way into the RAF. I got a reply six months later saying that my application was being 'looked into'. A few months afterwards, having heard nothing more, I volunteered all over again. It was now early 1943. Again I passed all the tests, but was told that because I was not a member of the Air Training Corps my name would go to the bottom of the applicants' list. I had very much wanted to join the ATC, because as part of the training programme teenagers were taught to fly gliders; but it relied on evening and weekend commitments, which I could not manage because of my job. So off I went to the Army recruiting office, also opposite Euston station, and volunteered my services. No problems there.

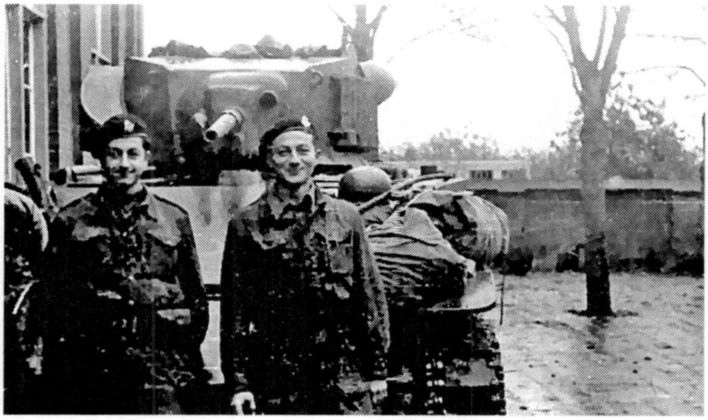

With Tommy in the Nijmegen Corridor, Holland, September 1944. (PM)

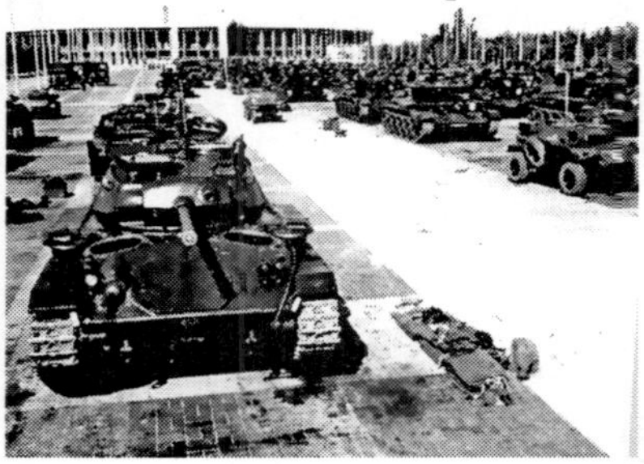

The 8th Hussars' tank park in front of Berlin's battered Olympic Stadium, 4 July 1945. (PM)

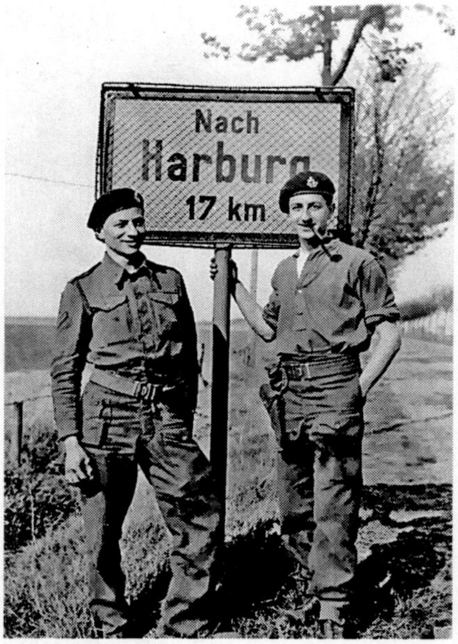

With Tommy on the way to Harburg, closing in on Hamburg, April 1945. (PM)

Winston Churchill takes the salute with Field Marshal Montgomery and Clement Attlee, 21 July 1945. (IWM)

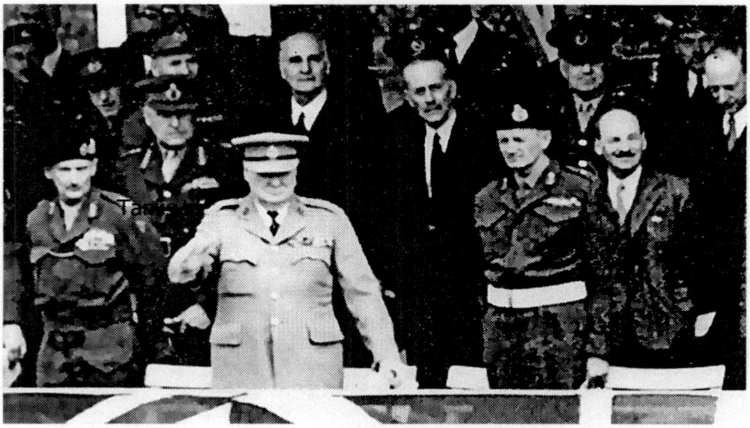

The Berlin Victory Parade, 21 July 1945. Tommy is in his tank on the extreme left and I am in mine on the right. (IWM)

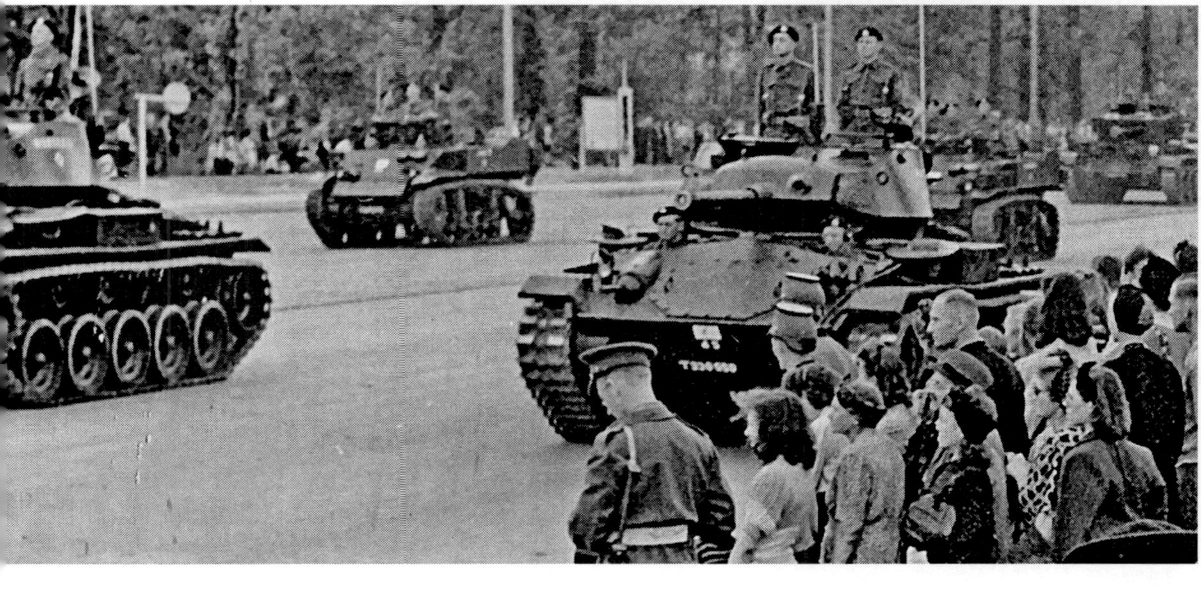

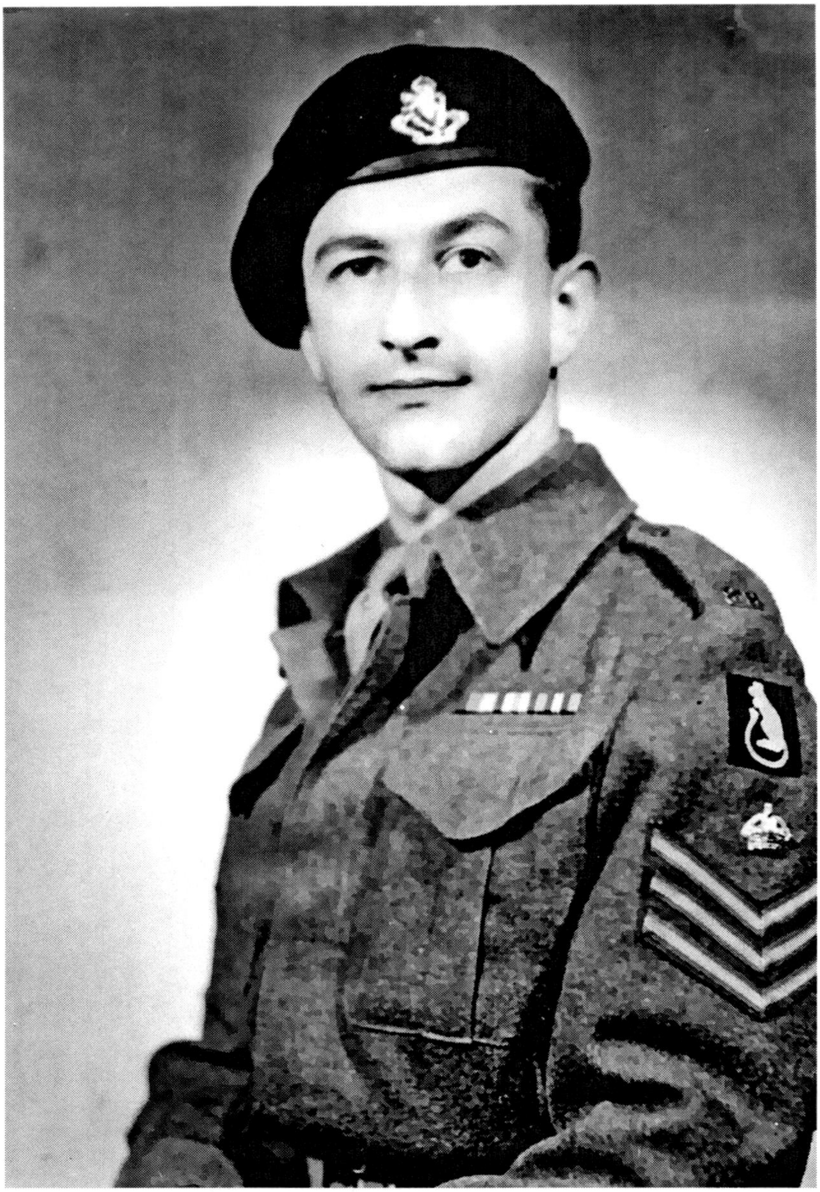

Special leave to Switzerland. (PM)

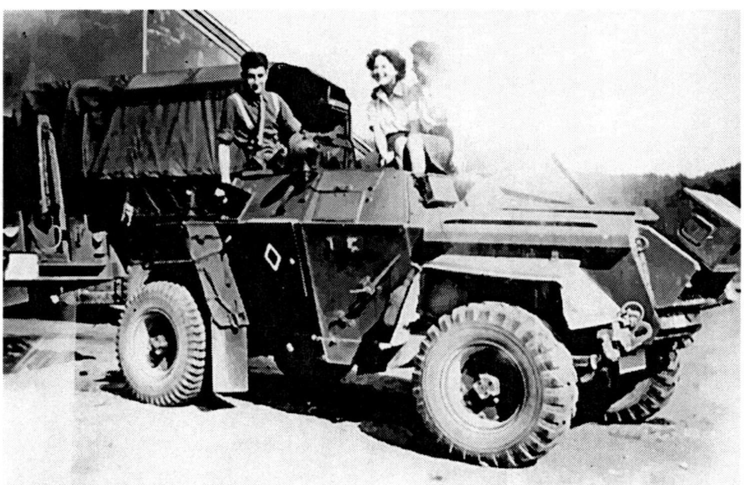

Arriving to a friendly reception at the Osnabrück RAF Gliding Club in the Colonel's Scout car. (PM)

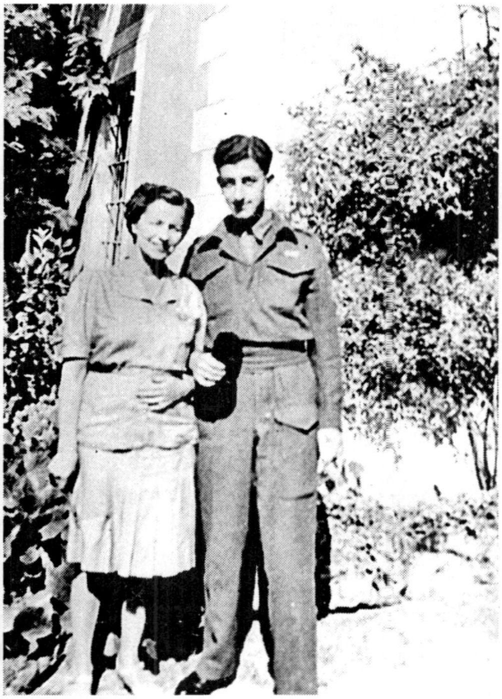

Meeting my mother after eleven years. (PM) .

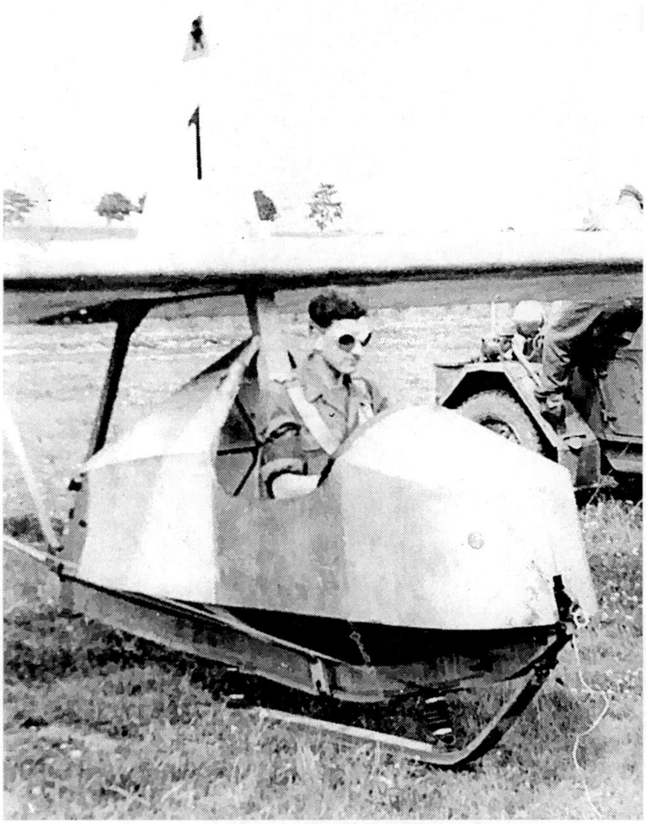

Solo in the 'broomstick'. (PM)

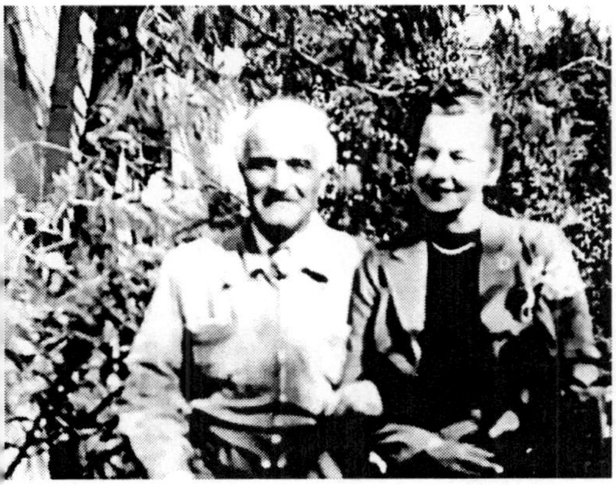

My mother and Harry. (PM)

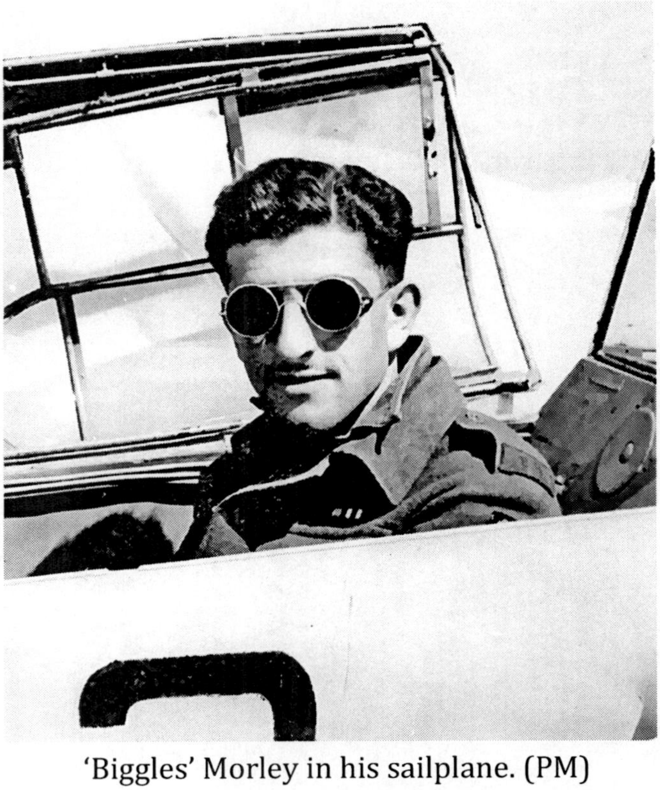

'Biggles' Morley in his sailplane. (PM)

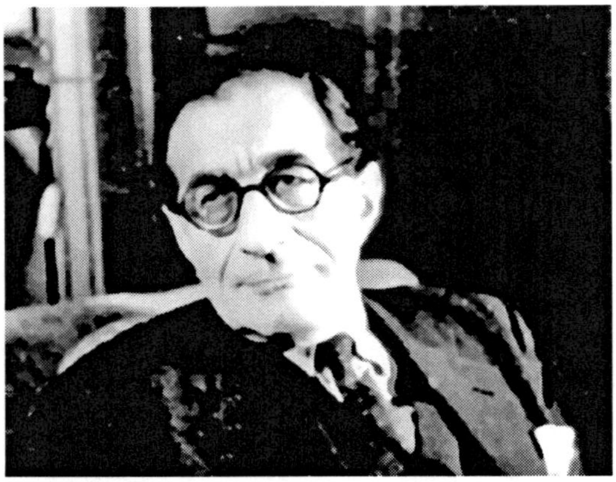

My father, aged sixty-eight. (PM)

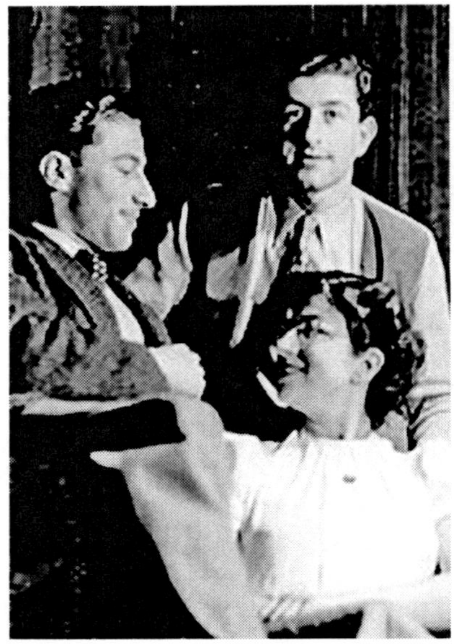

With Anne and Tommy, 1950. (PM)

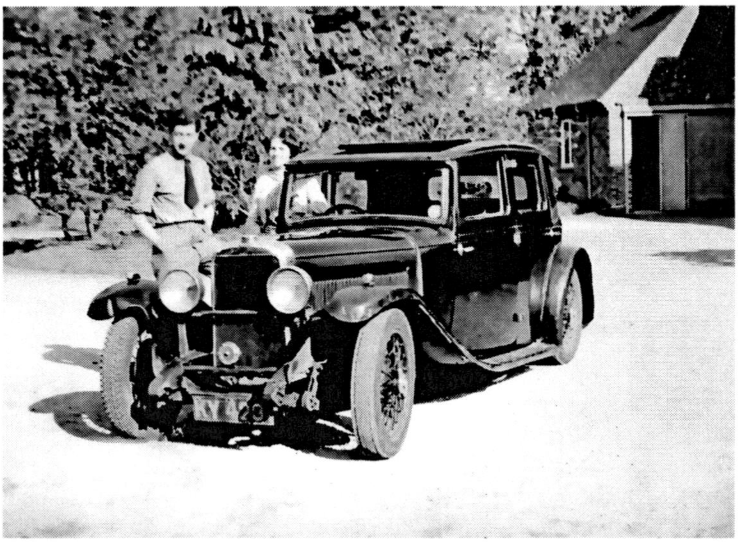

My first car, 1950. It was a 1932 Alvis Firefly. (PM)

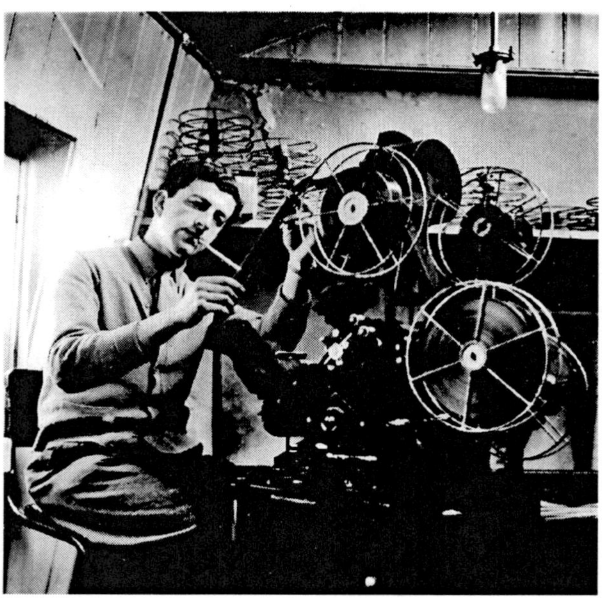

Film Editor – at last, 1950. Here I am in my cutting room over the exclusive James Smith & Sons umbrella shop in New Oxford Street. (PM)

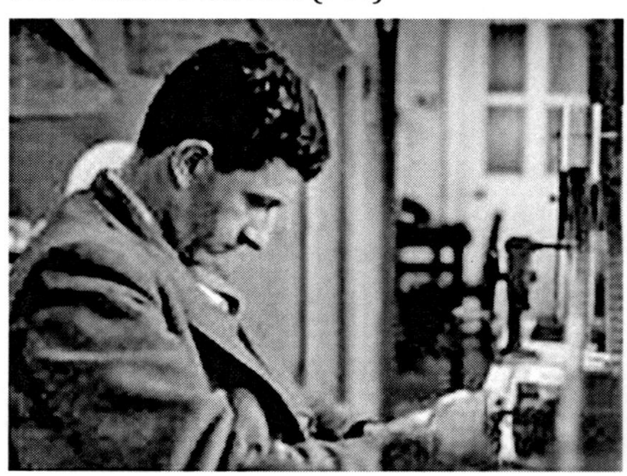

5: The Royal Armoured Corps

Brother Tommy had chosen to join the Royal Armoured Corps (he wanted to ride into battle and not walk!), and he was stationed at Farnborough for his tank training. Because of our family background he was made to change his name – a wise precaution in case of capture by the Germans. He told the story of a fellow recruit blindfolding him, and how he stuck a pin into an open telephone directory. He landed on Morley. Now it was my turn, and it just seemed too silly to think of yet another name for the family to remember. That is how between us we started a modest Morley dynasty, which consisted of two 'stateless enemy aliens' serving King and Country.

There was a rule in the army that an elder brother could claim a younger brother to join him in the same regiment. It seemed a good idea at the time, although we deeply regretted it later. I volunteered for the Royal Armoured Corps and started my primary training in Glasgow's Maryhill Barracks. This was a pretty bleak place, and had been condemned after the First World War. At the first uniform inspection the sergeant major yelled at me, 'You may be standing to attention, you scruffy shower, but your uniform is standing at ease. To the Regimental tailor, at the double. Dismiss.' It was two weeks before we were considered smart enough to qualify for a pass to explore Glasgow.

After six weeks came the first posting. And having volunteered for the RAC, true to form I was sent to the infantry – the Royal Fusiliers. The training was tough: assault courses, live ammunition and endless route marches. It took several weeks to extricate myself from all this, and I was finally posted to the RAC training regiment at Farnborough. Tommy had already finished his training there and had joined his regiment: the 8th King's Royal Irish Hussars. This was a senior cavalry regiment that had come home from its campaigns in North Africa and Italy to prepare for the invasion of mainland Europe. The regiment had been in the Middle East since the start of the war, having exchanged its horses for tanks, and was part of the 7th Armoured Division – Montgomery's Desert Rats.

I was told that I was going to be a gunner/wireless operator. The training was very concentrated, with little free time. We had to learn gunnery, navigation, operating wireless sets, mastering a fast Morse-code speed, the workings of the internal combustion engine and so on. Every member of a tank crew had to be able to drive, and so we had intensive instructions learning to handle a variety of tanks, including Cromwells, Shermans, Churchills and Grants. I soon realised that they were the most uncomfortable means of transport ever invented – smelly, oily and very noisy. They rattled and lurched and, with little to hang onto, one was forever painfully knocking against bruising steel projections inside the turret.

Two memories come to mind from these intensive eight months. The camp's tank park was next to the Royal Aircraft Establishment's runway at Farnborough, and we witnessed the very early experimental flights of Frank Whittle's jet-powered prototype fighter. The other was a rare

ENSA concert for the troops, when the infant daughter of a sergeant instructor performed on stage, impersonating Carmen Miranda. Her name was Petula Clark.

Half-way through this training regime I was picked out to go to an officer-training unit. Although the thought of a commission in the army had some appeal, I turned the opportunity down when I was told that it would add another ten months to my training course. I wanted to get to the 8th Hussars as soon as possible: we knew that the invasion and liberation of mainland Europe could not be far off, and I wanted to be part of it. Looking back now, almost seventy years later, it is salutary to reflect on this decision and to try to recall my feelings and motivations. There was, of course, a natural sense of duty, to 'do your bit'. It would not have occurred to me to question that. After all, people of my age were being conscripted – I got a clear sense of that when I was at the Dominion – and in any case the air raids seemed to unite everyone in their resolve to win the war. But there was more to it: there was a tangible cause – something to believe in.

With my background, and with the tales from fellow Bunce Courtians about the parents they had left behind in Germany, the threat of Nazism had become plain to see. I was also much influenced by the Corbett-Fishers, who were very active in supporting various refugee organisations. In addition the media, limited as they were in those days, made one more or less aware of Hitler's ambitions. The annexation of the Rhineland and the Austrian Anschluss were quite well reported, and anyone with a radio was moderately well informed. But it took one particular edition of *The March of Time* (these American newsreels were produced by Time, Inc.), which I clearly remember seeing in a newsreel cinema, to give me a jolt. It dealt in the clearest and starkest terms with the threat Hitler was imposing on the world, and was unequivocal about his anti-Semitism. Many years later, when I was making documentaries dealing with this period, one of my film researchers dug up this very same edition, and I realised that this hard-hitting film journalism was for its time unique in its outspoken opinions and warnings. In comparison our newsreels were as insipid as they were jingoistic.

For those who cared to look, the cause was there to see. To put it simply, we knew what we were fighting for and what we were fighting against, although I don't suppose that we were able to articulate it in such bald terms. To explain, and to justify this today to the post-war generations, who have enjoyed the longest peacetime period since the last world conflagration, is to say the least difficult.

Tommy had finished his training as a gunner/wireless operator and had joined the Recce Troop of the 8th Hussars. This was part of the Regimental HQ squadron, equipped with American light tanks, the Mk 5 Stuart, known in the British army as the Honey. Its job was to undertake the forward reconnoitring of enemy positions ahead of the other squadrons with their battle tanks. While I was finishing my training at Farnborough the 8th Hussars were going through their final tactical training in Norfolk. And then on 8 June 1944, D-Day+2, they went across to land on the Normandy beaches, the biggest amphibious operation ever. I was posted to a reinforcement unit in the Essex woods near Hatfield Peverel. We were under canvas, and we eagerly waited for the latest invasion news, impatient to cross the Channel to join our allocated regiments. To keep us busy, some hastily conceived manoeuvres were organised, and one of these I remember very clearly. I was driving a Cromwell, the lead tank in a troop of tanks making its way through Chelmsford. The sergeant who was acting as tank commander instructed me, through the intercom, to turn sharp right. I did, and as a Cromwell driver only had restricted forward vision I did not see the rear of the tank uproot a pillar-box, right in front of a café. We stopped and dismounted to clear up the mess, having brought Chelmsford successfully to a standstill. The café proprietor appeared with a huge tray with mugs of tea: a minor example of the Dunkirk spirit.

Another occasion was an exercise in convoy-driving at night. I was driving a 15cwt truck, the second vehicle in a long convoy of thirty trucks. Because of the blackout, vehicles had to travel without lights, except for the convoy light – a small lamp that illuminated the white differential box on the rear axle of the vehicle in front of you. If you could keep sight of that weak light source you were observing the correct convoy distance. It was a pitch-dark night, and after about 100 miles fatigue set in. I found it hard to keep up, and when the convoy leader in the truck in front of me took us onto minor roads with their twists and turns I lost contact with him altogether. And that's when it happened. I could just make out a fork in the road in front of me:

which one should I take? Panic set in, and knowing that there were twenty-eight trucks following me I quickly made the choice. To my huge relief I saw the light in the distance, and put my foot hard down to catch up. Then I felt a change in the road surface. The ride was getting bumpy, and then, as if in a bad dream, the faster I drove the weaker and smaller the light got – until it rose above the horizon and disappeared. I had followed a Tiger Moth taking off. And that is how twenty-nine army trucks fetched up on the grass runway of an RAF training aerodrome, wrecking the night-flying exercises of a whole squadron of Tiger Moths.

I obtained a forty-eight-hour leave pass and went home to Earls Court. It was going to be my last leave for two years. On my first night my father and I heard the distinctive sound of the rocket engine of a V1 flying bomb. The engine cut out, and we held our breath waiting for the explosion. It found its random target – the nurses' home of St Mary Abbot's Hospital, half a mile away on the other side of the Cromwell Road. There were many casualties.

It was an odd feeling being on leave, with all hell let loose in Normandy. We naturally worried about Tommy, and my father and Anne knew that I would be joining him very soon.

6: Eighth Hussars

It was some time before I finally stepped off an American infantry landing craft onto the floating Mulberry harbour at Arromanches on the Normandy beaches. I was with a small group of reinforcements, and we had to make our own way to find and join our allocated regiments. The 7th Armoured Division (the Desert Rats) had broken out of the Normandy beachhead and catching up with it was not easy. I had to cadge a lift on all sorts of transport, and often I was held up because of anti-tank mines and blown up bridges. It was for me the first realisation of the real horror of war: unburied German corpses, wrecked field guns and lorries, masses of dead cattle with their rigid limbs pointing skywards – and the sickening pervasive stench of decomposing flesh. And then, in a ditch, I came across a burned-out tank. The regimental number '45' just visible on its blackened hull told me that the 8th Hussars had been here. Looking through the front port I saw a crewmember's charred remains. My first thought: was it Tommy I was looking at? Luckily I remembered that he was in a Honey tank and this was a Cromwell. This made me realise that being 'claimed' by an elder brother into his regiment was a thoroughly bad idea. There was quite enough going on without being constantly preoccupied with your brother's safety.

By the time I had caught up with the 8th Hussars the Division was fighting its way north, to Belgium and on to Holland. I found the Recce Troop tanks overnighting by a canal. When I first glimpsed Tommy – with great relief – he was roasting a 'liberated' chicken over an open fire: his crew was lucky to have an expert cook as gunner/wireless operator. The crew I joined had different methods. The driver pitched a hand grenade into the canal, and shortly afterward a rich selection of fish popped up to the surface – my first supper with my new comrades-in-arms.

In September 1944 the great airborne operation was launched that famously failed to capture the bridge across the Rhine at Arnhem. We were fighting our way up north from Eindhoven, half-way up the Nijmegen corridor, in an attempt to bring relief to the airborne army, which was surrounded by the Germans in the battle for the bridge. We were able to prevent the Germans from cutting through the corridor. This was bad tank country, crisscrossed with dykes and polders that made us visible and vulnerable. It was very unpleasant.

As winter approached the 7th Armoured Division took up position in East Brabant in what was called 'The Watch on the Maas'. It really came as a shock to us. This turned out to be a bitterly cold winter, with thick ice and snow, and we were told to assume the role of infantry, with our tanks remaining in the rear area. We had already adorned them with their winter camouflage – we had painted them white.

We had to go on forward night patrols on foot into no-man's land, facing German SS troops and parachutists. It was not a happy time. On one of my patrols we found some abandoned German slit trenches and occupied them for the night to observe what their patrols were up to. Often they passed us not more than 20 yards away. We had taken a field telephone with us on the end of a long cable, so we could report back and keep in touch with our tanks in case of trouble. We took it in turns to lie down in the trench to rest, and on one occasion the temperature was so low that I found myself frozen into the slush at the bottom of the trench and had to be hacked out of the ice. The regiment was positioned in the small mining town of Geleen, in East Brabant; we were billeted with miners' families and shared our rations with them. They were in a bad way. The Germans had stripped Holland, and there was a grave shortage of everything. These poor people showed their gratitude with their friendliness and their efforts to make us as comfortable as possible. I was particularly lucky, as the family that sheltered my crew had a delightful seventeen-year-old daughter who helped to ease the tensions of war.

We were to spend several weeks of that awful winter in Geleen, with many night patrols and sporadic fighting. But there was a hiatus on both sides caused by the weather. Amazingly short leave passes were issued for trips to Brussels. That was an eye-opener, and left me with an impression of Belgium that has coloured my feelings toward that country ever since. Unlike its neighbour, Belgium did not appear to have been plundered by the Germans. We were in the middle of a war, yet the shops were stuffed with items I had not seen for some years. The restaurants made one forget army rations. In a very smart shop dedicated to marzipan goodies I found a treat to send home to Anne.

Also, I was able to buy her some fur-lined gloves without having to surrender clothing coupons. But it was the attitude of the people towards us that was so surprising. We had been wildly cheered when our tanks entered Belgian towns and villages just a few weeks before, when we were showered with flowers and bottles of wine. I noticed that this mood had changed, and we were now treated with indifference. As a contrast, the Dutch had nothing to give other than friendship and a genuine show of gratitude.

Mid-December 1944 marked Hitler's last desperate military gamble, with the counterattack in the Ardennes and huge casualties on both sides. Over Christmas we were heavily raided (it must have been the last fling of the Luftwaffe) with a strange assortment of aircraft, including some Mustangs that they had captured and rebuilt. On New Year's Day, using our turret-mounted machine guns, we brought down a Focke-Wolf 190, and every tank crew in the Regiment claimed to have bagged it.

January saw the beginning of what turned out to be the last big push to defeat the Germans. It was still bitterly cold. On our front we started our progress to the German frontier. There was fierce resistance and the going was rough and slow. There were many small-scale battles and casualties. Place names spring to mind: Echt, Sustern, Schildberg, Heide, St Joost, Montford. Also etched into the memory is a close shave when one of our deadly RAF Typhoons launched a rocket salvo, and narrowly missed us. Today they call it 'friendly fire'. What a crass description. At last, on 23 March, we crossed the Rhine and found ourselves in Germany. For me it was a mixed feeling of elation and fear. We had been told about Hitler's order to all Germans, military and civilian, to fight to the last. Not only did we have to face crack Panzer and Infantry divisions, but now the enemy included a motley array of hastily trained civilians, especially young boys. Children.

This was our first introduction to the deadly Panzerfaust. This lethal anti-tank weapon (we knew it as a bazooka) was fired from the shoulder. Its hollow-charge projectile cut a small hole through the tank's armour, allowing the explosive charge to go off inside the tank. Unlike the desert, which was ideal for tank warfare, we were fighting in close country, and forests, narrow lanes, hedges and ditches provided ample opportunities for ambushes. Young boys would hide in a ditch, and at the last moment pop up and fire their Panzerfaust at close range. We had to be very alert, simply firing at anything that moved or could be a hiding place for the enemy. As we advanced, self-preservation made us shoot up farmhouses, buildings and shops. I remember that in one small town we encountered snipers firing from the top windows of the local bank. We loaded explosive rounds into our main gun and blew the place up. Soon thousands of Mark notes were fluttering through the air, an amazing sight. The same treatment was meted out to the local jeweller, with his choice stock blown into the street. I hope that our infantrymen, who were following us on foot, benefited.

On one occasion, when we lost contact with the infantry, we had to dismount in order to flush out some enemy troops who were hiding in the basement of a villa. I had to break the glass of a large window to climb into the living room, slipped and badly lacerated my wrist. I'm afraid that this is going to be a bit of a Walter Mitty story. I made my own way to our field dressing station. Our medical officer had been killed and a brand new second-lieutenant doctor, who had just arrived from England, straight out of medical school, was in charge. The gash right across my wrist had luckily missed the main vein by a whisker. He started to stitch up the wound, threading a length of catgut into the eye of a big curved needle and, with the aid of medical pliers, inserting the sharp end of the needle into one side of the gash for it to come out again at the other side. Then he clicked the pliers onto the protruding end and pulled it out – but his hands were shaking so badly that he also pulled the length of catgut right through the gash. He tried this twice more with the same result, so I asked him to let me have a go. He got his corporal to thread the needle, and I did the actual sewing. Nine stitches were required; then the corporal knotted the ends together. I was able to rejoin my crew. Had my sons ever asked, 'What did you do in the war, Daddy?' that would have been my prize story.

The weapon most feared by tank crews was the infamous '88'. In the North African campaign Rommel's troops discovered that their powerful 88mm anti-aircraft guns could play a devastating part in desert fighting. When armed with armour-piercing rounds they were capable of penetrating the thickest armour of all types of Allied tanks. By the time of the Normandy invasion this lethal gun had become the main armament of German battle tanks, and we only had to spot one, or hear on the regimental wireless net that an '88' was in the vicinity, for our hearts to miss several beats. Tigers, King Tigers, Leopards and Panthers were their names; they were absolutely terrifying. One of our Troop's Honey tanks was knocked out by an '88'. The round penetrated the side armour in the rear, went straight through the two side-by-side V8 Cadillac engines and out through the side armour on the far side. The crew escaped. Later we inspected the hulk of that Honey, and when we looked through the hole in the side it was like looking through a barrel of a gun, with the clear imprint of the spiral rifling marks left by the armour-piercing shell.

We crossed the Rhine at Wesel and on the next day there was a massive airdrop of the 6th Airborne Division, with 3,000 aircraft and gliders. They established a 6 mile deep bridgehead, the launch pad for the British 2nd Army's final thrust to Hamburg and beyond. I discovered many years later that my future brother-in-law, Colonel John Tillett, was in one of those gliders. He played a vital and courageous part in the now famous capture of Pegasus Bridge in Normandy on the eve of D-Day. Again, memory conjures up place names, each adding details to a long-forgotten campaign: the river Elbe, Osnabrück, the Dortmund/Ems canal, and especially Fallingbostel. Here we stumbled across a massive prisoner of war cage, waiting to be liberated. Stalag XIB housed mainly British servicemen, many of whom had been captured during the recent ill-fated airborne assault on Arnhem; others had been captured years before in the desert and others more recently in Normandy. We were overjoyed when we were able to free a contingent of 8th Hussars. It was a great day for the Regiment, and I remember relieving our tank of all its cigarettes, chocolates and the remainder of some bottled Calvados, which had been hidden in our tank turret since Normandy.

But this feeling of euphoria was short lived. Soon after, beyond Fallingbostel, we approached Soltau, and came across an appalling scene. In spite of all our training, together with the experiences we had acquired fighting the Germans, we were totally unprepared for this. At first we thought it was another PoW camp, but when we saw emaciated skeletons shuffling around among corpses lying all over the place we simply did not know what to make of it. I remember being very relieved when the infantrymen of the 1/5th Queens were summoned to sort things out, and our Recce Troop was ordered to press on.

The words 'extermination' and 'final solution' had not yet entered our vocabulary. It was only a few days later that we heard reports about the discovery of Belsen. Representatives from our Division had been summoned to this huge concentration camp so that they could report back to all the regiments. We were too preoccupied for any of this to sink in; it was only weeks later, when we were exposed to the newsreel footage of Belsen, that it began to dawn on us what we ourselves had witnessed. And for those who needed convincing, it became very clear what it was we had been fighting for, and what many of our comrades had laid down their lives for.

We crossed the Elbe on 24 April and shortly afterwards took Harburg, where we came to a halt on high ground overlooking Hamburg. Surrender negotiations now commenced. The local military commander, Major-General Woltz, had been told by the German High Command to surrender to the 'Desert Rats' (7th Armoured Division), which was just as well, as Hamburg had been threatened with yet more bomber raids. On 3 May, in pouring rain, we entered Hamburg, a city flattened by the RAF. I had seen devastation before – the sight of London and the area around St Paul's in 1941 was still fresh in my mind; but this was different. From driving through the streets, with a grandstand view from the top of the tank, clear impressions have remained with me. I could not spot a single building that had escaped damage. Many of those still standing were burnt-out shells. I nearly had my head cut off by a tram cable that was dangling loosely at tank turret height. And then there was that awful stink of death. Civilian casualties had been enormous, with thousands buried in the mountains of the rubble we were passing. Naturally we felt a sense of bravura. We were the victors, proudly riding in our tanks – the conquerors. But these jubilant feelings were soon tempered by the reactions from the Hamburgers who lined the streets. After all, the RAF had flattened Hamburg, its inhabitants had suffered the fire storm with its massive casualties, and now we were entering their city. We expected a hostile reception.

Hamburg had been one of the great Hanseatic ports, with a thriving trade with the rest of the world; the population of this maritime region of Germany was well disposed towards the British. And now we watched them as they watched us, some looking on dazed and resigned, others smiling, while a few threw flowers at our tank, and on one street corner a group actually applauded. They were expressing their sense of relief that it was all over – no more bombing, no more fire storms, no more casualties. For us this was rather difficult to take. It was an anti-climax.

Our Recce Troop set up temporary residence close to the Alster near the Gauleiter's house, with our tanks neatly parked in the street. German troops were surrendering to the Allies in droves and we knew that the end of fighting was imminent. We behaved fairly outrageously; from the naval barracks, which housed the 400 German Wrens who had surrendered to us, we liberated heavy navy roll-neck sweaters, standard issue for U-boat crews; and on our first morning all of us wore them, much to the consternation of our divisional commander and commanding officer as they stopped their half-track vehicle to inspect this curious addition to the British army. Our Troop leader got a suitable rocket. I have treasured that sweater ever since, and the next severe cold weather will, no doubt, see it on parade again.

We managed to find something stronger than tea to drink in the cellar of a rowing club a few yards away on the Alster. Thus reinforced, we went into Gauleiter Kaufmann's magnificent villa, where I spotted a bronze bust of Hitler. Two of us carried this outside and put it on a plinth next to the villa's flagstaff, draped a swastika round its shoulders and rammed an enamel chamber pot on its head. It was all very childish, maybe, but we were young and had been through a lot together; now, moderately inebriated, we savoured the excitement of victory. Twenty years later I came across this bust in the United Services Museum, then still in Whitehall, with a small plaque saying that it had been found and presented to the museum by the 8th Hussars.

We moved out of Hamburg two days later to do some mopping up of German troops in Schleswig-Holstein, north-east of Hamburg. A mass of humanity was on the move. In addition to the tens of thousands of German soldiers and naval personnel, only too ready to be disarmed, we were quite overwhelmed by hordes of Hungarians, Romanians, Austrians, non-combatants, refugees from the east, slave workers and so on. Only the SS arrogantly marched towards us with heads held high. Our infantry soon changed their demeanour.

Although we knew that fighting had stopped, we were very much on our guard. I came across this passage in a journal written by an officer from the 5th Royal Tank Regiment, which was on our flank: 'As the leading tank was nearing a T- junction, it was met by a small ten-year old boy. He stood alone defiantly, armed with a Panzerfaust with his finger on the trigger. The sergeant tank commander dismounted quickly and disarmed the boy. When he had made the anti-tank weapon safe, he bent the boy over his knee and gave his arse a good spanking, then before he sent him back to his mother, gave him a bar of chocolate.'

On 7 May we were in our tanks near Pinneburg when the news came through on our regimental wireless net with the order to cease fire, and that the next day, 8 May, had been declared VE Day. I tore off my headset and shouted to the crew that it was all over, and that we had the order to clear live rounds from our main guns. Another order came from our troop leader, telling us to dismount and gather round him. In my euphoria I stupidly jumped off the top of the tank and broke my leg. Some war wound! The regimental medical officer took one look and got his orderly to strap up the suspected break with tough elasticised bandages, and told me to soldier on. I did, in great pain. A week later I was X-rayed in a German naval hospital, confirming the break. The bandage stayed on for another month, and luckily the break healed with no ill effect.

The Regiment now bivouacked near Itzehoe, well north of Hamburg, and my crew was issued with the new M-24 Chaffee Light Tank. I wished that it had been sooner, as the new 35mm main gun packed a lot more punch. But, mercifully, we were never going to fire anything in anger again. We were at a loss to guess what would happen next. The war had come to a sudden end and thoughts of going home, and what it would be like being a civilian again, became a preoccupation.

In early June the order came through that the 7th Armoured Division must stand by to move to Berlin. At the same time a big load of battleship grey paint arrived, lifted from German naval stores in Kiel. That caused a painting frenzy. Our tanks, scout cars and other vehicles bore the dirt and scars of twelve months' campaigning, and now we had the order to make them look as good as new, not only to impress the Russians in Berlin but also to outdo our fellow armoured regiments. Even the new Chaffees did not escape this treatment. We embarked on the bullshit regime with gusto. The regimental tailor's sewing machine worked overtime to make our uniforms parade-worthy again, and to embellish them with newly issued medal ribbons. Our barber had a field day too. It was my twenty-first birthday that month. I am sure that it was duly celebrated; alas, I cannot remember anything about it.

At the Yalta Conference in February 1945 the Allied leaders, Stalin, Churchill and Roosevelt, decided on the division of Germany, or carve-up as it was called, once hostilities had ceased. Berlin, which was going to be slap bang in the middle of the Russian Zone, was itself divided into Russian, American, British and French sectors. And so on 4 July 1945 our Division, acquainting itself for the first time with Hitler's famed Autobahn, progressed through the Russian zone and, via Magdeburg, entered Berlin.

Over twelve years had elapsed since I had last seen the city – the place of my birth. I was rather bemused by this curious coincidence; the irony that I should be in Berlin of all places to savour the end of the war. I had been too young to form any attachments to the place, and so much had happened since 1933 that my memories of it were extremely hazy. Probably this was just as well: what we experienced beggars description. It was far worse than Hamburg. Two months earlier the Russians had stormed the city, street by street, in the most ferocious fighting to date. What Allied bombers had failed to flatten suffered the onslaught of murderous Russian artillery. More than half of all the buildings had been destroyed. There was no electricity, water or drainage. The weather was hot, and the stench of bodies in the ruins was overwhelming. And yet here we were, the victors, occupying the capital of the defunct Third Reich, being received by Berliners more as liberators than conquerors. We soon realised why.

In the final battle for Berlin the Russians had thrown in a force of over one million troops, a large proportion being infantry made up of men from remote Mongolia. They had never travelled outside their homeland before, and they were promised that when Berlin fell they would get a few days' immediate leave plus the army pay that was owing to them. They had never set eyes on a 'western' city before, let alone white women. As a result, when the end came tens of thousands went on the rampage. Anyone wearing a skirt, regardless of age, was in grave danger of being raped; those who resisted were often murdered. This went on for about four weeks, before the Allied sectors were properly established. The statistics are appalling. The historian, Antony Beevor, in his book *Berlin The Downfall, 1945* writes: 'Some two million German women were raped, 120,000 were hospitalised, while 10,000 died.' No wonder we were looked upon as liberators.

We were stationed in Berlin's Olympic stadium, a gigantic Nazi showpiece made famous by the 1936 Olympic Games. Russian troops had just moved out, and we got an instant insight into how they lived. The place was unspeakably filthy. Toilets had been shunned, and there was excrement all over the place. Our medical officer would not allow us in until the whole area had been cleaned up, fumigated and disinfected, so we bivouacked outside for the first few nights next to our tanks. A vast parade ground that marked the entrance to the stadium, flanked by dozens of tall flagpoles, became our tank park, and we did all of our maintenance work there.

The Russian Commander of Berlin asked for the British army's help to round up a mass of deserters; their few days' leave on conquering Berlin had expired weeks before. We saw these hordes roaming the streets, sometimes with a dozen watches taken from their victims strapped to their arms, checking that they were all ticking. Our Military Police helped the Russians clear them from the streets in our sector.

In April, shortly after we had crossed into Germany, Field Marshal Montgomery had issued his non-fraternisation order to all troops. It simply said that we were forbidden all contact with German civilians, unless in the course of duty. On the very day we entered Berlin Montgomery issued a new order:

> TO ALL MEMBERS OF THE BRITISH FORCES IN GERMANY
>
> Great progress has been made in the de-Nazification of the British Zone and in removing Nazis from all responsibility in German life. Further, the Germans have shown themselves willing to obey my orders and to co-operate in the reconstruction of their country on non-Nazi lines. I have already modified my orders about non-fraternisation and allowed you to speak and play with little children. I now consider it desirable and timely to permit a further modification of these rules. You may now engage in conversation with adult Germans in the street and in public places. You will not for the present enter the homes and houses of the Germans nor permit them to enter any of the premises you are using except for duty or work. I know the non-fraternisation policy has been a strain upon many of you who have to live and work in close contact with Germans, and I appreciate the loyal way in which you have honoured it.
>
> Signed: B.L. Montgomery
> Field Marshal
> Commander-in-Chief
> British Zone

If ever there was an open invitation for soldiers to find comfort in people's homes, this was it!

Each morning a troop of tanks took it in turns to go on what was called a flag-waving drive. With Union Jacks fluttering from the aerials and sirens blaring, we travelled at a good speed through the main thoroughfares all the way to the Brandenburg Gate, and parked for an hour by the Tiergarten before returning to the Olympic Stadium. I don't know what Berliners made of it; I think they were too busy to take much notice. I carry a picture in my mind of people, mostly women, working in the ruins – beginning to clear away the debris with spades and bare hands, and still discovering bodies. At the same time, miraculously, some sort of city life was emerging. Trams were starting to operate, and when we went on our runs in the early morning the Berlin rush hour was beginning to make itself felt again.

Tommy was busy doing some interpreting for the Regiment, so I did not see a lot of him. His German was still very fluent, whereas mine was rusty. I began to explore Berlin on foot in the evenings. Tommy had told me the address of our old apartment in the Kaiserallee at the corner of the Güntzelstraβe. The blue enamelled plate with the house number 36A was still fixed to the entrance porch, but all that was left was the façade, precariously upright, waiting to be demolished. The old baker round the corner had survived and was still in business. Anne had sent some names and addresses for me to try and trace, and that was how I was able to find our old nanny, Frau Müller. She had survived the years of bombing and the final street battles, and could hardly believe her eyes when I told her who I was. She was living in a small room on pathetic rations, with no one to help her forage on the black market – which was now a thriving institution, partly financed by a ready supply of cigarettes and coffee, which sustain armies. While I was in Berlin I was able to make her life a little more bearable with provisions she had not seen for some years. Tommy was also able to visit her and provide her with items that she considered luxuries, no doubt.

It was on one of my walks exploring the city that I was approached by a woman and her daughter and asked whether I was interested in acquiring a camera. She explained that it was a ciné camera: would I like to see it? What better reason for disobeying Montgomery's orders, I thought, as they took me to their flat. They showed me a 16mm ciné Kodak magazine camera. I felt that Christmas had come early. We agreed a price: a 7 lb tin of concentrated soup, 2 lbs of coffee, 400 Senior Service cigarettes and a few bars of chocolate. It was all highly illegal, but very exciting. We made a rendezvous at the Tiergarten, where on my daily 'waving the flag' run my tank usually stopped for an hour before returning to the stadium. I told her exactly where, and the following day she waited for me in the bushes. When we arrived at our rendezvous she came forward, I reached across my tank turret and the great barter exchange took place. I was the proud owner of a ciné camera, and I did not realise how useful it was going to be once I was demobbed.

At a brigadier's inspection on our parade ground outside the Olympic Stadium I was picked with six others to act as one of Churchill's guards at the Potsdam Conference – with little insight into the significance of this historical event.

On 15 July the conference delegates began to arrive in Berlin, as the Regiment girded itself for the great victory parade scheduled for 21 July. Bullshitting our gear took on a new meaning. Tanks and vehicles were endowed with yet another layer of paint, and all brass fittings, buckles and belts out-sparkled each other.

The 21st was going to be a day to remember. On the saluting base stood Churchill, Montgomery, Attlee and a host of cabinet ministers and high-ranking brass from all the allied services. The route started at the Grosse Stern at the foot of the Franco-Prussian War Memorial and went all the way to the Charlottenburger Chaussee, as far as the Brandenburg Gate. Regimental bands struck up, and for twenty minutes tanks and armoured cars roared past the base, led by the 3rd Regiment, Royal Horse Artillery, the senior regiment on parade, and the 8th Hussars, the senior cavalry regiment. It was going to be the last time that Tommy and I were alongside each other in our respective tanks. I know that both of us felt, in the middle of this jubilation, a great sense of relief, not having to worry any more about each other's safety.

Soon afterwards Tommy left Berlin as a liaison interpreter, having been seconded to the Royal Engineers, who were responsible for getting the German rail network to function again.

The Potsdam Conference took place in the Cecilienhof Palace, to the west of Berlin. It was in the Russian sector, and the delegates were accommodated nearby in Babelsberg, the Beverly Hills of Berlin, near the UFA film studio. The whole delegation area was sealed off by Russian troops, and the streets were lined every 30 yards by Russian officers (none below the rank of colonel) with tommy-guns at the ready. This had been the wealthiest part of Berlin, with opulent film stars' villas to match. Churchill's villa was in the Ringstraβe, its grounds sloping down to the waters of the Havel. Our job was to protect the house and prevent incursions from the Havel.

The villa next door housed a high-ranking Russian general, a delegate to the conference, and I got to know one of his guards. He was a colonel, aged seventy, with a long white beard tucked into his belt. We managed to converse in halting German, and I remember swapping cigarettes with him: he enjoyed my Senior Service and I sampled his army issue cigarettes – long tubes half-filled with what I assumed was tobacco. Mary Churchill (Lady Soames), WSC's youngest daughter, a captain in the ATS (Auxiliary Territorial Service), was her father's aide-de-camp, and she used to come out of the villa and bring us cups of tea. At one point we heard Churchill bellowing from a window at the top of the house that his bath water was not hot enough, and Mary rushed back inside to attend to her father's needs.

Outside the villa a ceremonial guard, mounted by Coldstream Guardsmen, countermarched on the pavement, but the noise made by their army boots deeply disturbed Churchill. Someone at the War Office in London was detailed to go to Woolworth's and buy a consignment of screw-on rubber heels – a wartime expedient to save leather. A Dakota was flown from Berlin to England to pick them up, and the problem was solved. There was a photocall for the world's press in another villa, and I stood in the bushes together with Russian and American soldiers guarding Churchill, Stalin and Truman. It's odd to think that we referred to Stalin as Uncle Joe, a term of affection. Churchill, as we now know, regarded him in a very different light.

Churchill and Truman acknowledged Soviet predominance in Eastern Europe by accepting Polish and Soviet administration of certain German territories, and agreed to the transfer of the

German population (over ten million people) to Germany. Plans were agreed to introduce democratic principles of government in Germany; deal with reparations; outlaw the Nazi Party; and so on. The Potsdam Declaration (26 July 1945) also demanded from Japan the choice between unconditional surrender or total destruction. Stalin was told about the atom bomb.

I got to know a civilian whom I took to be one of the team of Churchill's Special Branch officers. He used to come into the garden at the end of each day for his constitutional stroll, puffing away at his pipe. He was very friendly, much concerned about our welfare and keen to find out what we were going to do after demobilisation. A few days later, on 25 July, Churchill left for London to hear the dramatic results of the first post-war general election. He was no longer prime minister, and his successor returned to Potsdam. It was Clement Attlee, my pipe-smoking acquaintance. Politics had not played any part in my life, and although I probably knew that Attlee was wartime deputy prime minister I did not know what he looked like. I felt suitably chastened. Twenty-one years later, when I was filming the Mountbatten series, I met him again as one of many eyewitnesses who told the story of how he appointed Mountbatten to be India's last viceroy. ('I needed a change of bowling at the top in India and Dickie was the man for the job.') We talked about the Potsdam Conference, and he clearly remembered his strolls in the grounds after work.

After the conference the Regiment stayed on in Berlin, and we were able to relax a bit more. PT was once more part of the routine and, being keen on hockey, I played several Divisional matches in the Olympic Stadium.

7: Gliding to Naturalisation

It was in June 1945 that my sister was able to make contact with our mother. We learned that she and Harry Kahn had been rounded up by the French police in Paris and shipped to separate camps in Marseilles. In 1943, with the help of an escape organisation, they managed to cross into Switzerland on foot, and after initial internment they lived with a family in Winterthur and then settled in Massagno, overlooking the Lake of Lugano. They had escaped from France in the clothes they were wearing, plus a small bag with a few personal possessions that my mother had been able to hang onto since Paris. They had to start all over again, setting up home in an old rented farm cottage; the Swiss government and a charity provided a small living allowance for refugees. Harry was able to organise the odd contract with Swiss publishers and started earning modest fees translating books from English into German. My mother had to master a life-style totally foreign to her. She had been used to a pampered life, and had never needed to go out and work: cooks, nannies and other servants had been at her command. But like so many others she managed to adapt and run a household for Harry on a very tight budget.

Tommy was the first to manage to get to Switzerland, and visited them when they were still in Winterthur. I was able to wangle special leave some months later. This turned out to be quite an adventure. I was given a seven-day leave pass, and with the rail network still largely in ruins it took that many days just to get to Paris. There I was delayed for five very enjoyable bonus days, while rail bridges were repaired further down the line. Finally I got to Basel and found the platform for the train to Lugano. To my surprise I ran into Lady Marjorie Corbett-Ashby, who was on one of her high-powered political missions – this time to Switzerland. I had not seen her since I joined the army, and she told me she was relieved that her intervention to get me into the RAF had failed, or we might not have met that day. The other surprise was the station fruit stall, on which I spotted a rare sight, something I had not seen for five years – bananas. They became my sustenance for the four-hour train journey to Lugano. I got some curious looks from some of my fellow passengers, who had probably never seen a banana-eating British soldier in uniform before.

My mother and Harry were at the station to meet me, but in spite of my uniform they did not spot me, and I failed to recognise them. After all, eleven years had elapsed since we had last seen each other and a great deal had happened in between, while the memories of a nine-year-old were a bit hazy. I asked for directions to their house, and with my kitbag over my shoulder climbed up the steep slope to Massagno. It was a hot August day, and by the time I made it to the house I was exhausted. Slumping down on a small patch of grass outside their front door, I fell fast asleep. Voices woke me up, and there they were. It must have been quite an emotional experience for my mother, because in 1944 she had picked up a *Swiss Illustrated* magazine and had been convinced that a photograph of a badly wounded British soldier, taken prisoner by the Germans at Arnhem, was me.

She had missed my formative years, and must have been intrigued to find out what sort of person her youngest child had grown into. For my part I was rather amused by it all. I was certainly not aware of close ties or maternal love, but we got on very well. There was a lot of family banter, and although it was all very light-hearted and superficial a relationship slowly evolved which made it congenial for me to visit them for many summer holidays to come.

In the autumn of 1945 the 8th Hussars moved into German barracks in Lingen, not far from the Dutch border. By now I had the rank of Squadron quartermaster sergeant and had to endure some peacetime soldiering while I waited for my demob number to come up. The rule was 'first in, first out', regardless of whether you were a conscript or, like me, had volunteered, so I knew that it would mean at least another six months in uniform. I was determined to make this period as agreeable as possible and I had a bit of luck. Soldiers were able to join a newly formed RAF gliding club near Osnabrück, which was about two hours' drive away. The RAF personnel staffing the club, especially the WAAFs, made everyone very welcome. The club was equipped with a fleet of different types of German gliders and sailplanes, and the instructors were German. It was democratically run: rank was ignored and we were all on first name terms. On an early visit I met our Brigade commander who had also just joined. I told the brigadier that I might have a transport problem and might find it difficult to journey to the club at weekends. He told me that he was due to carry out one of his feared regimental inspections and that he would fix things. The following week we were on parade in our smartest kit. As our CO, Colonel (Cuthy) Goulburn, led the brigadier past the recce troop he stopped and said, 'Ah, it's Morley from the gliding club. Tell me, do you have problems getting there?' 'Yes, sir', I replied. He turned to the CO and said, 'Please see to it that this quartermaster sergeant is given decent regimental transport.' And that is how I was able to enjoy the permanent use of the colonel's Daimler scout car on my weekly trips.

Gliding is a wonderful sport, and I was able to make the most of it. The *ab initio* flying training was to say the least primitive, but it worked. There was no question of sitting next to or behind an instructor in a training glider. The contraption I was strapped into was a huge pair of wings attached to a narrow wooden beam; there was a small seat at the end of it with a joystick and rudder pedals. It was appropriately named the 'broomstick'. There was a short lesson when the instructor got hold of the wing and tilted it up and down, so that I learnt how to counteract these movements with the joystick controlling the ailerons. Then he went round the back, lifted up the tail or pressed it towards the ground, and I had to correct this to begin to master the functions of the elevator. End of lesson. Next he attached a rope from the nose of this contraption to the back of his car, and while someone else held the wings level I was towed across the airfield, fast enough for the ailerons to react but not enough for the 'broomstick' to take off. There were several tows, each one getting slightly faster, and on one of them I spotted a large molehill ahead. As we skidded over it I actually took off. I was airborne! I was actually flying – albeit for only about 3 yards and only inches above ground.

Now a much longer rope was used, hooked onto a special ring. To my right was a small lever that released this towrope. And off we went, this time much faster. When we had reached what I felt was flying speed I gently pulled back on the stick, and hey presto I was seriously airborne. I pulled the release lever, the instructor did a smart turn to the right to get his car out of the way, and I made my first solo landing. And so we progressed, reaching a height of about 80 feet and learning how to make turns and decent landings.

Then came the next stage, when I was promoted to an advanced training glider, in fact a sailplane. It was called a Grunau Baby, with a proper cockpit and equipped with an array of flying instruments. A powerful winch was positioned several hundred yards away on the edge of the airfield, its huge drum housing hundreds of feet of towing cable. The end of the cable was attached to a Jeep, which then tore across the field to bring it to the launch area. The cable was attached to the nose of the glider, and with hand signals from the instructor to the far edge of the field the winch operator took up the slack in the cable. As it tightened we moved forward, and when flying speed was reached we quickly took off. By pulling the stick hard back into my stomach the glider shot up into the sky at an alarming angle. I was literally lying on my back and could only see the clouds above me. As the winch rapidly hauled in the cable the glide path flattened out, and the horizon mercifully came back into view. That was the crucial time to pull the release lever, and I was free. From then on I progressed to making circuits of the field and practised making accurate landings, which meant coming to a halt with the sailplane's skid resting on a 6 foot by 2 foot bright orange piece of canvas. (These were the Allies' recognition panels, which were tied to all our vehicles to avoid 'friendly fire'.)

Learning the art of thermal soaring came next. This was real flying. Thermals are rising bubbles of warm air, and the needle on the variometer, the instrument that measures the rate of climb or descent, tells you whether you have sniffed one out; you also feel by the seat of your pants that you are being pushed up. The trick is to find the centre of this invisible bubble and with tight turns to circle around that point, to stay within it and to rise with it. A barograph records the height gain. One day, after a lot of practice flights, I managed to climb to a height of over 3,000 feet, and clocked up an entry for my Silver 'C' Certificate.

My most memorable adventure was on my first cross-country flight. This means finding and climbing within a thermal until it peters out and then pressing on, losing height in the process but hoping to find another one, and so on. I was about 30 miles away from my airfield when luck ran out. Thermals were getting scarce as it was getting late in the afternoon, and the heat of the sun was no longer triggering the formation of thermals. For obvious safety reasons the drill was that at 1,000 feet you had to pick out a suitable landing spot; obviously it had to be a field, ideally without cattle or power cables. You then had just enough time to pick the exact spot, work out wind direction and the best approach for a safe landing. Unfortunately the only open space I saw was a football field, with lots of buildings, tall trees and huts around its edges. The trouble was that a game was in progress. I approached the field by making several circuits round it, getting lower all the time. Luckily the players realised that I was going to attempt a landing and cleared off the pitch. I flew in, just clearing the top of one goal, and came to a safe halt at the other end of the pitch in front of the other goal. Before I was able to undo my harness a couple of British military policemen came up and welcomed me to a prisoner of war camp. The German POWs helped to manhandle the glider off the pitch, and they resumed their game.

In spite of the huge kick I got out of these exciting gliding weekends, many miles away from my boring duties back in the barracks, I was eagerly awaiting news of my demob date, which I had been told would probably be towards the end of 1946. I had my first home leave in the autumn – ten days in which I was able to catch up on all the home and family news. Tommy had just been demobbed (he had volunteered a year before me), which just increased my wish to go home for good as soon as possible. On my return to the regiment I learnt that this would not happen until 1947.

June 1947 marked a very British ceremony. I had to report to the CO's office, where Colonel Goulburn announced that my naturalisation papers had come through. He told me to swear the oath of allegiance, and I was more than happy to oblige: 'I, Peter Morley, swear by Almighty God that I will be faithful and bear true allegiance to His Majesty King George the Sixth, His Heirs and Successors, according to law.' The colonel shook my hand, wished me well and offered me a drink to mark the occasion. At last I had British citizenship, but it did not escape our notice that we do have the most bizarre ways of going about things. After all, I had served 'King and Country' for four years, seen action with the 8th Hussars, guarded two prime ministers at Potsdam, and all that time I was officially classed as an enemy alien. It's a funny old life.

8: Demobilisation and Documentaries

At last, in September 1947, my number came up. There was a lot of drinking in the mess the night before my departure, with the words 'Civvy Street' and 'dear old Blighty' figuring largely in the noisy alcoholic singing. Trains had now resumed almost normal service, and the channel port Ostend was not far away.

Like many servicemen I had fallen prey to a particularly stupid venture. During our advance through Germany it had become an act of great prestige to claim the proud ownership of a Luger pistol. One had, of course, acquired it from a German prisoner or taken it from a dead soldier, usually an officer. When the army realised that troops coming home on leave or demobilisation were bringing these lethal souvenirs into the country, a strict order was issued to stamp this out. If you were caught there were very serious consequences. The challenge was to beat the system and to invent foolproof smuggling methods. Mine was to cut open my army issue water bottle, and to stuff it with the dismantled parts of my Luger. I then soldered it up again and replaced the webbing holder.

On the way across on the ferry there was a Tannoy announcement warning everyone that military police were waiting at Harwich with the special task to search for illegal arms. I took fright and tossed my Luger overboard into the channel. Mine was not the only splash in the water on that day.

The demob centre was in York, and the train journey from Harwich marked the last time I was going to be in uniform. We were kitted out with basic clothes to make civilians of us again. I chose a double-breasted grey pin-striped suit, my one and only 'whistle' for the next ten years. My gratuity payment, based on rank and length of service, was all of £90.

Back in London I joined my father in his basement flat in Hogarth Place. The winter of 1947 presented a challenge to us all. It was incredibly bitter, and coal for the fireplace was not only severely rationed but often unavailable. We had a small paraffin Valor stove, and we huddled around it trying to keep warm. I used to queue for several hours with our 1 gallon paraffin can to get our ration of the wretched stuff. This was not an easy time, especially for the elderly. I gave my miserly sugar ration to my father, so that at least one of us could enjoy a cup of tea. As a result, to this day I find sweetened tea undrinkable.

My four years in the army had not blunted my desire to pursue a career in films, and film editing was on top of the agenda. But how to go about it still remained a mystery. I wrote to all the studios and small film companies and got identical replies: that there were no vacancies, as so many ex-servicemen from the film industry who had joined up for the duration were now returning to their old jobs. In any case, what has since become a classic Catch 22 syndrome prevailed: no job without a union ticket; no union ticket without a job.

With hindsight, I often regret that it never occurred to me to seek a university education: as an ex-serviceman I would have qualified for a grant. But my family and friends never mentioned this possibility, probably because they knew that I was totally obsessed with a career in films. I realised some months later that my old Bunce Court classmates had all chosen the university route. Sometimes I wish that I had done things differently – maybe taken a degree in architecture, which had always intrigued me. I would have enjoyed the camaraderie of college life, and I am sure that it would have helped me to overcome a natural shyness, and encouraged greater confidence. Subsequently I could have decided whether to pursue a film career or not.

I was so angry about the hopeless union situation that I decided to fight it. I had an idea on which I was to gamble my gratuity. If I could produce a privately financed film, surely I could then apply for a ticket. I had struck up a pub friendship with a demobbed squadron leader who had opened a small television retail shop very close to our flat, opposite Earls Court station. At that time there was only one channel – BBC TV. I noticed that at night the six TV receivers in his shop window all showed the same programme. Passers-by stopped and watched these magical new moving pictures in silence, as my friend had not rigged up a speaker outside to relay the sound. My idea was to place a seventh TV set in his window showing a different programme, and I hoped that this might cause a bit of a stir. I persuaded him to let me film an advertising feature, proclaiming his wares, hire purchase offers and after-sales service. The first move was to set up a company, and with the help of my father's accountant P.J. Morley Film Production Limited was born. This, I felt sure, would vouchsafe my acceptance for union membership – after all, I was now a film producer!

My prized magazine ciné Kodak camera, bartered for and procured in Berlin in the shadow of the Brandenburg Gate, now came into its own. As this was a silent film, I drew and then shot the title cards pinned to my bedroom wall. The small cast was made up of the shop owner's family, representing the public visiting the shop and being shown the various television receivers, with prices and so on. The film's running time was seven minutes, which I thought was long enough to hold the attention of passers-by. I enjoyed working out how to show it in the shop window. The owner gave me a defunct television set, which I gutted. I had bought a small 16mm projector, and asked a local engineering company to manufacture, from a drawing I had made, a film loop device, which I attached to the take-up spindle of the projector. This was crucial to the whole enterprise, as my masterpiece could now play continuously on a seven-minute loop. With my bedroom as a workshop I squeezed all this into the confined space inside the TV cabinet. A thick sheet of tracing paper replaced the cathode-ray tube, ready for the back-projected picture. A series of small mirrors bent and enlarged the image to fill the false TV screen. It worked. My friend was delighted and we installed it in the shop window, ready for the big switch-on that night.

But there was a totally unexpected problem. As darkness fell, crowds started to gather to have a look at this extra television programme. This was repeated the next night. The following morning the police arrived in the shop and told the owner to remove the television set with the 'other' programme, as the crowd it was attracting was causing an obstruction on the pavement. So that was the end of that. The owner and I licked our wounds. He paid his share of the cost, but I had blown my gratuity and my new National Provincial Bank account looked very sick. Even so, full of optimism, I applied to the union for a ticket; I was a producer whose company had made a film. As a condition of being accepted they asked for the impossible: proof that my company had employed a full-size unionised film crew and film editor and paid standard union rates. Disaster. The whole scheme had failed, and I was back to no job, no ticket; no ticket, no job.

Luckily, during this period I had met and become friendly with Geoff Hughes, who was a director with the Shell Film Unit, making mostly scientific films. He had also had problems getting into the industry and recognised my plight. The Shell Film Unit, which had been set up in 1934, was still not unionised, and he arranged for me to be interviewed by his boss, the Unit's head. Sir Arthur Elton had taken on its leadership after the war, and I was given fair warning that he was not the easiest person to talk to – correctly, as it turned out. He quickly summed me up: 'You will never make a career in the film industry as I cannot detect one spark of talent.' He made me very angry, and more determined than ever to get into films and prove him wrong.

Geoff Hughes tried again. He arranged for me to be interviewed by one of the bosses of the Film Producers Guild. This was a collective of documentary film companies with offices and preview facilities in Guild House, Upper St Martin's Lane, just off Cambridge Circus. We thought that if I had the good luck to land a job there in any capacity I would at least be working in a film environment, and who knows what that might lead to: anything to get a union ticket. They did have a vacancy, but to my dismay it was as an assistant projectionist in the preview theatre. I had had my fill at the Dominion, and had never thought that I would have to go back into a projection box. I persuaded myself that this was a necessary ruse to achieve my aims and accepted the job. The weekly wage was a princely £5. Projectionists were looked after by a different union (NATKE), which did not prescribe a closed shop policy, so I still had to overcome the vexed hurdle of somehow joining the main film union, the ACT.

As it turned out, this proved to be the best move I could have made. The Guild's array of film companies produced a wide range of documentaries, mostly sponsored by industry, the government, charitable foundations and so on. They also owned Merton Park Studios in south London, which made 'B' movies to support main feature films in cinemas. I was determined to exploit this situation.

At the Guild I got an introduction to the basic processes of film-making, both technical and creative. It was my job to screen rushes, first assemblies, rough cuts, fine cuts, voice tracks, music tracks, dubbed tracks, animation roughs, grading prints and so on. I was able to follow all the stages from first ideas to the final show print. And, equally important, I got to know the Guild's producers, directors, writers, cameramen and film editors – always game for a chat when they came round to the projection box after a screening. Luminaries like Humphrey Jennings, John Grierson, Jill Craigie and Paul Rotha hired the preview theatre on occasions, and I felt that I had become a small speck of dust on the wheel of the British post-war documentary movement. Of course it was very frustrating to screen other people's work all day long, when I was aching to have a go myself.

It was during this time that I grasped the opportunity to make my first amateur film. My old school had returned after its wartime evacuation in Shropshire to its home in Kent. Bunce Court was destined to close down in 1948, having fulfilled its role of giving both sanctuary and education to its pupils, most of whom had been engulfed by the tyranny of Nazism. It had accomplished its mission in the most admirable way, and the time had come for it to bow out. In 1947 I went down to Kent for the first peacetime reunion, and Anna Essinger agreed that I could make a little film in advance of the school's closure. Bunce Court paid for the film stock, and I dusted down my precious magazine ciné Kodak, bought some cheap lights, wrote a script and spent three weekends shooting it. I called the film *Once upon a Time,* and to my surprise it earned a special commendation from the magazine *Amateur Cine World.* Over fifty years later I was able to provide some archive footage clips from it for historical documentaries that were being made in the USA and Germany, dealing with subjects such as the 1939 Kindertransport.

There were numerous attempts to talk myself into an opening in one of the Guild's many cutting rooms, which were always thwarted by the union's mad closed shop dictum. It was not merely 'jobs for the boys' that drove this policy, but resistance to letting new blood enter the industry. To the ACT the word 'merit' had little meaning. It was now 1949 and I could hardly believe that I had spent almost two years in my quest to 'get in'. By now my salary had increased to £7, and I was still sharing the basement flat in Hogarth Place with my father. Neither of us had much spare cash, but we managed to keep our heads above water. Food rationing – four years after the war – seemed to have become a permanent way of life. Today it sounds almost too absurd when reminiscing about this period to realise that we had to wait till the mid-1950s for rationing to be finally abandoned.

In 1950 rescue came in the guise of one of the Guild's ace producers, Ronald Riley, the head of a small and very successful company, Verity Films. He took me under his wing, recognising my frustration and realising that I was not cut out to be a projectionist for the rest of my life. He found a classic opening for me – as a tea-boy. Technical & Scientific Films, a small Guild production company, was on the lookout for someone and he put me up for the job. There was no interview: I just started the following Monday. Accepting the demotion from assistant projectionist to tea-boy was not a problem, but the drop in wages to £4 a week was very painful. T&S was located up the road from Guild House, and was therefore removed from the constant glare of the ACT. In any case, the grade of tea-boy was not recognised by the union. The company had a staff of ten and was housed in a Victorian building at the corner of New Oxford Street and Shaftesbury Avenue, above James Smith & Sons, London's oldest manufacturer of sticks and umbrellas – with its original large and ornate brass plates announcing its name and business still intact in the twenty-first century. Whenever I pass it now it reminds me of the very first car I owned, bought for £70. It was a 1932 Alvis Firefly, and I used it to travel every morning from Earls Court to New Oxford Street, where masses of parking places were always available!

My job was ill defined, and that suited me well. The brief I got from the managing director, Dr Denis Ward, an ex-ICI chemist, was to lend a hand wherever I could make myself useful. He was impressed that I could work the ancient 35mm projector, and relished the possibility of film screenings to some of his clients. He also told me to run errands for the resident film editor, Pam Bosworth, and I felt that this could turn out to be the golden opportunity I had been waiting for. Pam, who some years later became a top-flight BBC film editor, gave me great encouragement. I spent my time watching her in the cutting room, and helped her to file film trims and other more menial tasks when they were required. When a wrong cut was made in an optical soundtrack in those days it could not be unmade, unlike the later magnetic sound tapes, which were joined with a special Sellotape that could be unpicked. A new print of the section had to be made overnight from the original 35mm negative, which was held by Humphries Film Laboratories in Whitfield Street, just off Tottenham Court Road. I used to fetch and carry cans of film on foot (up New Oxford Street and past my old Dominion Theatre), but charge 2*d* for the bus fare. This boosted my weekly wage by the odd shilling.

Soon Pam let me assemble rushes for her, and quite quickly I got the feel of handling 35mm film – with the thrill of making my first decisions about joining one scene to another. And then I had some real luck. Denis Ward came up to the cutting room, proudly announcing that T&S had just been commissioned to make a cinema appeals film for the British Legion's Poppy Day. I had already told him about my amateur Bunce Court film when I joined T&S, and he was prepared to try me out as film editor. Pam backed me up, and at last I was able to get my teeth into something tangible. This was the first of a number of films I was to edit. The small team over the umbrella shop knew perfectly well that I was blacklegging, but they were very understanding and helped to protect me from prying eyes. The documentary convener for the union was famous for being both very charming and quite ruthless – so when Bessie Bond announced that she was coming round to check out the union status at T&S I was given the day off. But I knew that sooner or later I would be rumbled, and I got some helpful advice on what tactics to adopt.

One of my sister's close friends was Oswald Hafenrichter, who was considered to be one of the ace feature film editors; his credits include such classics as Carol Reed's *The Third Man*. I met him, and he introduced me to another editor, Rex Endsleigh, a member of the ACT union committee representing editors. He explained to me that film companies were obliged to inform head office when they wanted to fill vacancies covered by the union's many technical grades. If the ACT books showed that an unemployed technician in that grade was available he or she had to be offered and given the job. Merit played no part. But if the union was unable to provide such a person the company was free to employ anyone they wished, even a non-cardholder. He then planned to let me know the moment the books showed that there were no unemployed assistant editors available. I got his call some months later, and my T&S boss immediately declared a vacancy for that grade. As the union could not fill it Rex Endsleigh told them that he was going to give the job to me, and that I was coming over to their office in Soho Square for official membership papers. And that is how, more than three long years after demobilisation, I acquired my ticket. By the time the various committees had accepted my membership application I had already been promoted to full editor.

The company slowly expanded and I soon found myself scripting and then directing a variety of films. I can recall two titles with great clarity because they gave me a useful grounding in styles and techniques, which I would be able to exploit later on in my television work. The first was a colour film for the British & Foreign Bible Society, celebrating its centenary and dealing with social issues in Ruanda and Burundi. The only material at my disposal was a large collection of contemporary indigenous paintings and sketches, so I had my first experience in what is now rostrum camera work. In the early 1950s it was no more than pinning a picture on the wall and carefully panning with the camera to achieve smooth movements over the selected area – some of the close-up details being merely half an inch wide. I began to learn the value of exploiting the still image. By lingering on it for quite some time and adding appropriate music, I realised one could highlight important visual details and create a desired mood with an eloquence that the moving image often finds difficult to achieve. A perfect example of this is Ken Burns's hugely successful American documentary series *Civil War* (1990).

The other title was a ciné magazine for the industrial steel giant Richard, Thomas & Baldwin Ltd, largely aimed at their huge workforce. These quarterly editions of *Ingot Pictorial* were forerunners of television magazine programmes, and each consisted of two or three specially filmed items covering training, safety, personnel issues and morale boosting and recreational stories. All of us at T&S contributed to these, and the variety of subjects and their treatment of them was the best sort of training for budding writers, editors and directors. For example, I learnt how to cut a number of these short magazine items to music, eschewing the spoken word – again, something I was able to put to good use later on in television. I was unaware that I was going through a period of unstructured but intense learning, of a kind that was not available elsewhere: film schools had not yet become fully established. I suppose that I really ought to think about this period as my attendance at a rather special university.

I have always believed that the magical atmosphere within a cutting room creates the finest training ground for anyone who seeks a career in film or television. It is, after all, the focal point of the production process, bringing together the expertise and talents of writers, producers, directors, editors, cameramen, sound recordists and all the other crafts that contribute to the final product. When I am asked by young people to help them get into the industry, I urge them not to be afraid of starting as a cutting room tea-boy, runner or sweeper, because it is here, after a few months, that you begin to discover whether you are developing that magical facility – that invisible small screen embedded in your forehead – which automatically triggers your visual senses and translates thoughts and words into pictures. If you have made a cut, joining two shots together, but think better of it by trimming three frames from the outgoing shot, you can picture the effect in your mind's eye before you do it. Or you wish to start music one or two beats before the picture cut – you hear, see and feel the effect as the thought comes to you. Honest assessment of all this should tell you something about your potential: whether you are blessed with the necessary talent; whether you have 'got it'. This, of course, applies equally to the other crafts, whatever they are, and in the cutting room they all come together, opening up the options whether to stick to editing or to pursue a career as a cameraman, recordist, director, animator, even writer. Today, when digital picture editing is becoming the norm, and would-be editors look for training in the many video facility houses, I would still recommend a solid grounding in a film cutting room. Its unmatched tranquillity beats the busy hustle of video editing. The ever-changing technology of video editing (linear and non-linear) makes it enormously expensive, with the cost of using the latest gizmos being many hundreds of pounds per hour. The last time I worked in a facility house I reckoned that saying good morning to the editor cost £3, and falling out for a quick pee used £20 of editing time. The meter is remorselessly ticking all the time, whereas the tranquillity of the film cutting room provides the luxury of time – to be able to sit down and reflect. Try a sequence one day, sleep on it, tear it all up the next morning and have another go.

Something else that was important for me, and presumably for others too, is the tactile property of film: the feel of it between your fingers; holding it up to the light to spot a frame; laying soundtracks in a synchroniser; feeding film into a Moviola; rolling up out-takes and so on. Somehow, magically, these sensations stimulate that special visual sense: the ability to see it in your mind's eye. Editors brought up solely on video will probably have a problem in understanding this.

The relentless march of technology has changed everything. The video facility houses are strongly challenged by digital non-linear picture and sound editing, now available to all on desktop computers – and you can work from your home.

* * * *

Back in our basement flat my father had little concept about my work, and I think he regretted that I had not taken up what he would have described as a proper job. We got on very well, sharing the household chores, but life was pretty frugal. By now he made his modest living dealing in rabbit skins, and had his pitch on the pavement outside Smithfield Market, standing there in all weathers. His earnings had always been minimal and my contribution, small as it was, managed to keep us afloat. There was just enough for him to afford a short annual holiday with his close friend Madeleine Adcock, and I saved enough to stay for two weeks in the summer with my mother in Lugano. I could never mention my destination to my father, but he knew well enough. Mother and Harry Kahn eventually married and took on Swiss citizenship. I managed several sorties from Lugano into Italy, and got my first introduction to Florence, Venice, Rome and Naples. One year I managed to explore Sicily, long before it became today's tourist attraction.

Anne was totally absorbed by her intensive work at the Warburg Institute. She devoted a lot of her spare time to helping our father with his purchase tax returns and typing. Most weekends she came to Hogarth Place, so we saw a lot of each other.

Tommy had married Molly Jermyn, a teacher from Ipswich. At first they lived near Holland Park and then bought a house in Camden Town, which became the family home. They produced three sons: Anthony, David and Richard. Tommy started in the catering business after the war, and in the '70s he bought a hotel near Bovey Tracey, in Devon, which he and Molly ran. Sadly she succumbed to cancer. He remarried, and later retired in Devon. Tommy died in 1997.

In September 1954 we had to move our father to a nursing home in Osterley, Middlesex. He was now seventy-two and had been unwell for quite some time; the family doctor had diagnosed lung cancer. He had been an extremely heavy smoker all his life. He died peacefully in his sleep a month later, and we felt that the doctor had mercifully minimised his suffering. My father was a kind man, generous to a fault, and a great optimist, always believing that tomorrow was going to be better than today. He never forgave our mother for deserting the family twenty-one years earlier, but he never talked about it. The three of us were to miss him very much.

9: The Launch of ITV

The following year things turned round. ITV was to launch its national television service in September 1955. Associated-Rediffusion (A-R) had successfully applied for the London weekday franchise. All the new ITV companies were feverishly recruiting staff and quite a number were enticed away from the BBC. Others came from the film industry and the theatre, and hurried training programmes were set up to meet the huge demand that the launch of this new enterprise was going to make.

Bob Evans, one of my colleague directors at the Film Producers Guild, had joined A-R early that year to start his television training. He felt that television was going to be good news, and wondered whether I had thought about moving over. I hadn't, but he persuaded me to have an interview, which he volunteered to set up. And that is how I came to face Lloyd Williams, an ex-BBC floor manager, who had joined A-R as their production chief in charge of hiring and firing staff. Bob had told him about me, and came round to see me at T&S to brief me. He said that as long I expressed a belief in television, and had an enthusiastic desire to be part of it, I shouldn't have problems with Lloyd Williams.

On entering his office, he said, 'Sit down, Peter, and tell me why you want to be in television.' The informality came as a bit of a shock, but I felt confident, and with Bob's advice fresh in my mind I launched into my eulogy of the new challenge. I told him what a magnificent medium it was; that it was here to stay; that it would revolutionise communications; that I wished to play a part in it; that I would bring my documentary experience to it; and so on. He wanted to know a bit about the films I had made, and then asked me how much television I watched. I told him that my job prevented me from viewing a lot of the programmes I wanted to see, as I worked long hours (true) and got home rather late in the evenings. 'Do you own or rent a television set?' I replied, 'As a matter of fact I don't have a set at home, but I have unlimited access to the one in my friend's flat upstairs.' 'What is your favourite programme?' came the next question, and I thought to hell with it: I had better own up. 'Mr Williams, the only programme I have ever seen was the Coronation, and I thought it was absolutely splendid.' 'Right,' he said, slamming his palm down on his desk, 'when can you start?' I was almost speechless.

We briefly discussed the terms of employment. I declined the invitation to join the company as a staff employee and opted for a short-term contract. I proposed that the contract should be between A-R and my company, P.J. Morley Film Productions Limited, which was lying dormant after my doomed attempt to use it as a ruse to acquire a union ticket. In turn, my company would contract me to work for A-R. This was a useful employment arrangement (with obvious income tax advantages) that I used forever after. I was now a freelance, a status I was to enjoy for the rest of my career. Instinctively I thought I would be happier if I was able to preserve a certain amount of freedom and individuality in this new exciting environment. I was hoping that the day would come when I could direct programmes of my own choice and, if necessary, thump a table when disagreeing with a programme controller or head of a department. Lloyd Williams found it difficult to understand this, and was a little hurt when I refused his staff offer. Nevertheless he proposed a three-month contract at £24 per week. I accepted, and he wanted me to start the next day, which was impossible as I was just finishing a film for the British Productivity Council and was due to take it into the dubbing theatre in a fortnight. We agreed a starting date, and as I got up to thank him he opened up his production schedule and said, 'You're on the air with a live programme three weeks into your contract.' And that is how I got into television.

It is really quite amazing the risks that these new television companies were prepared to take in order to start up and sustain a mainstream television service. But all that pressure created great excitement for those of us who felt compelled to take the plunge. We were about to embark on a great adventure.

A-R had taken over Adastral House, the wartime Air Ministry building at the bottom end of Kingsway where it meets the Aldwych. It was now named Television House, and it was my place of work for the next twelve years. The building had been pretty well gutted to make room for three small studios, and for the modernisation of the offices that occupied six floors. It was total bedlam, and it continued to be so for months after A-R went on the air, with the new lifts not yet working and builders' rubble and dust everywhere: female staff had to be given a stocking and hairdressing allowance. And yet, somehow, the station was made to function, propelled by the enthusiasm of all of us who were lucky enough to be in at the start.

I had been promised some intensive training sessions to help me master the technical side of live television production, but the moment I arrived I had to concentrate on my first programme, and there simply wasn't time to attend these. In fact, the only training I can boast about was a red ring binder that arrived on my desk entitled 'How to Control Budgets for Television Programmes'. A fat lot of help.

All directors were allocated production assistants, and my PA was Margaret Balfrey, a repertory actress who had joined A-R some months earlier. She had attended a training course and was at least able to answer some of my queries. Together we went to A-R's main production complex in Wembley, and that was my first introduction to a television studio. As a fly-on-the-wall observer in a director's control gallery, I looked over the studio floor down below and watched camera rehearsals. I had to come to grips with live television's multi-camera technique, and had just one day to do it in. I stood behind the director, a lady wearing a large hat, facing a bewildering bank of monitors. She called out ceaseless instructions through the talkback microphone to the cameramen, floor manager, boom operator, and, clicking her fingers, cued the vision mixer sitting next to her. Her PA added to all this by calling out shot numbers and timings, and clearing cameramen to move to their next positions. When it was over I introduced myself to the owner of that splendid hat – it was Joan Kemp-Welch, herself on a training mission for her first programme. She had been a stage and film actress, and became a brilliant, award-winning television director for A-R. Her many TV dramas included Harold Pinter's early works, including *The Lover* (1962), and Bucchi's ballet *Laudes Evangelii* (1962), specially choreographed by Massine for its first television production.

By now I had installed a rented television set in Hogarth Place, and it became my mentor by proxy. While I was frantically preparing my first programme – a dreadful advertising magazine – I got a chance to fly solo. A-R put out a nightly epilogue to mark the end of the day's transmission called *And so to Bed*. It was very simple (and cheap), with a pianist and his grand piano in a small studio in Television House. There was a duty roster for directors responsible for these late-night epilogues, which were considered to be a bit of a chore, but I was very keen to have a go. From a creative point of view there was not much one could do, other than find interesting angles from which to shoot the pianist; the excitement was in going on the air. As Margaret counted down from ten seconds to the start of the programme, the flow of adrenalin increased by several knots. When she reached 'three' it was my turn to observe the ritual of saying 'Good luck, studio' over the talkback microphone . . . and we were on. In the control gallery you face a bank of monitors. There is one for each camera, showing its output, and another to display the picture you have selected to go to the transmitter. And then there is one, usually placed on top of the others, which shows your chosen picture coming back from the transmitter as broadcast. That was most salutary because here, for the first time, there was proof that millions of people might be watching you, and that you are entirely responsible for everything they see and hear, no matter how brilliant or awful your programme.

There now followed a string of these advertising magazines. The only thing to be said for them was that they made it possible for me to learn – to get to grips with the grammar of live television programme making. With no one around to use as a sounding board, to give help or advice, I looked upon each one of these transmissions as an essential tutorial. The scripts for these twenty-minute offerings were pretty dire. They often revolved around a corny home situation in which the actors, while engaged on some domestic routine, had to handle dialogue like, 'While I remember, did you know that Gladys next door has lent me her new vacuum cleaner to try out? Here, I will show it to you. Maybe you would like to have a go – it's called a Goblin.' And so on . . . I will say no more.

These admags were the closest that advertisers were allowed to get to programme sponsorship: this was one of many rules laid down by the Independent Television Authority. The ITA, established by Act of Parliament when ITV started in September 1955, was the regulator and controller of the network, embracing all the regional television franchise holders; and they kept very close to the minutiae of programme contents. All the admag scripts had to be submitted, and it is not surprising that we often had to accommodate last-minute changes. I really enjoyed making these awful programmes, as the thrill of being in charge and the excitement of going on the air was stimulating; but I soon felt that I needed to get my teeth into something more taxing.

In the next few months there was a variety of afternoon and early evening programmes, including my first all-filmed adventure. I can't remember why I was chosen for this project: maybe my film background counted for something. But A-R took a huge risk when they flew me with a commentator to Rome, to pick up two Italian camera crews and shoot the World Bantam Weight Boxing Championship – and I had never been to a boxing match in my life. In those days the only way to get pictures back to the UK was to go and film an event, bring the negative back, edit the rushes and then go on the air. Satellites still had to be invented.

Then I was allocated to the remotes unit – a life-changing moment if ever there was one. I was asked to devise and direct an outside broadcast from No. 1 London, Apsley House, the home of the Duke of Wellington, one of a series of outside broadcasts called *Afternoon Out*. The unit provided me with one of their production assistants. Her name was Jane Tillett, and she was very pretty, cheerful and extremely efficient. We got on well, but in the confines of a windowless office the size of a cupboard she announced that she could not work with me because of the awful fug caused by my heavy smoking habit. I grasped this opportunity to give up and was successful; I have not touched a cigarette since. Little did I realise at the time that within two years we would be married and now, over half a century later, she is the mother of our two sons and grandmother of six granddaughters.

* * * *

This was to be my only outside broadcast for the remotes unit, as Caryl Doncaster had clapped her eyes on me. Caryl was a highly regarded, fiery, no-nonsense producer who had come over from the BBC and was put in charge of the features department. She bubbled with programme ideas and surrounded herself with film directors, journalists and actors to pioneer television documentaries and what became known as current affairs programmes. This turned out to be a lucky break: I was able to call on my past directing and editing experience and apply it to this new television grammar. Caryl had thought up a series called *People are Talking*, half-hour investigations into topical subjects. I teamed up with Elkan Allan, a journalist, and our first contribution was called *On the Firm*. It dealt with business expense accounts.

Peter Black in the *Daily Mail* wrote: 'This new kind of Journalism which substitutes for words the direct impact of faces, voices and pictures, made a lively feature of the expense account lark last night. The interviews and the fourhanded discussion afterwards produced a number of talking points which were valuable in themselves, doubly so through the sharp impact of television on the audience.' This was the first opportunity I had to integrate film clips with the live studio pictures, and I am sure that my film editing past played a role in this; the manipulation and juxtaposition of pictures has always held a fascination for me.

Altogether I directed four programmes in the *People are Talking* series: one dealt with the British motor industry, another with the commercialisation of Christmas, but it was the third that caused a big stir. It was an investigation into a new phenomenon that had crossed the Atlantic, the mass hysteria of young girls when they attended their pop idols' concerts, and we called it *Fan Fever*. The girls were oblivious of the film camera in the orchestra pit of the Coventry Theatre, not more than 3 feet away from their faces, and I captured what at the time was considered sensational material. Dickie Valentine was the artist a few feet behind on the other side of the footlights. Even before he started singing these young girls were in a frenzy; and when his performance started one of them, so innocent looking when she came to take her seat, went wild, tore off her bra and threw it on the stage. I treasure the following cutting from *The People*, which says as much about the times we lived in as it does about me:

> ITV SCRAP 'TEENAGE' FRENZY FILM. Parts of a film showing the reactions of an audience of teenage girls to crooner Dickie Valentine has been destroyed by order of Independent Television bosses. The decision never to show these scenes to viewers was taken because the film showed girls in frenzies while Valentine was singing. According to ITV producer Peter Morley, who made the film: 'Some of the girls got completely out of control. They became very emotional. I will not give any details, but they were things which should not be seen in a public place.'

Fan Fever got huge ratings and became a talking point in the media. Dilys Powell, the doyenne film critic, wrote to me: 'I looked in at *Fan Fever* last night and thought it really excellent. I do hope you will get the chance to do more work of this kind.'

The *Observer* television critic Maurice Richardson wrote:

> Associated-Rediffusion's *Fan Fever* programme last Tuesday was an excellent piece of reporting, and a bold one coming as it did on the eve of Liberace's advent day. You saw crooners themselves: one, Dickie Valentine, expressed his satisfaction that his organised fan-mass now totalled 8,000. You saw fans en masse in screaming ecstasies. You saw fans interviewed individually. A girl who was tattooed with 'I Love Johnnie Ray'; a girl who had cut out, and wore on her dress, a piece of carpet on which Johnnie Ray's foot had trod; a girl who dreamed of him constantly 'very unpleasant dreams in which Johnnie always dies.' We saw bewildered parents who 'simply don't understand,' parents, who were shocked, a father who had finally come to the conclusion that it kept his daughter out of mischief. We saw a very amiable woman psychiatrist whose sympathy with adolescents appeared to be boundless. We also saw Liberace's manager. He launched a sharp attack on the tempestuous Elvis Presley – the ultimate Rock and Roller – as an undesirable influence on youth, put in a plea for a clean family life 'and no running around with single women.' Altogether this was one of the most fascinating TV half-hours for some time.

Tom Driberg wrote in the *New Statesman*:

> Such is the prestige of the BBC's Special Inquiry series that Associated-Rediffusion essayed on Tuesday night an experiment in the same genre 'a special hard-hitting report,' as they called it, 'on a burning issue of the day'. The burning issue in question was 'fan fever' – the behaviour of the teen-age girls who worship singers of popular songs: 'what turns ordinary girls into a social phenomenon?' The hard hitting was the impact on our eyes and ears of some really first-rate documentary recording of the girls' behaviour: oblivious of the camera,

> they screamed, writhed, gasped, beat their pretty but clammy brows, suffered the delicious agonies of divine possession common to all the lower mystery religions. All this made vital television. It was refreshing to see on commercial television so vigorous and objective a social document.

In the *News Chronicle* Philip Purser wrote: 'Documentary is a word brought into disrepute by television. Too often it has meant dreary and portentous reports on the one hand, novelettish 'true life', playlets on the other. Documentary can be television at its most stimulating and informative. A shining example was *Fan Fever* last night, ITV's inquiry into mass-adulation of the popular singers of the day. The ingredients, whether on film or from the studio, were assembled with the quick sure strokes of a master draughtsman.'

Some people thought that we were experimenting, except I did not feel that these programmes were experimental. We were simply trying to throw light on something new and intriguing, using cameras in an untried manner, and also breaking some of the traditional film editing rules. And in so doing, without any conscious awareness, we helped fresh thoughts and images to emerge. That really was the excitement at the time. There was no yardstick to measure our work by: it was all so new.

The pressure to make programmes to help feed the voracious hunger of the broadcasters' schedules meant that we simply got on with it. My score for 1956, my first full year, was twenty-four programmes. There was no time to reflect or analyse, let alone indulge in esoteric discussions and arguments about the new medium's purpose and style. With some relish I have always told younger people who are new to the industry that in those early days it was really quite difficult to be unoriginal. No matter how good or awful the programme turned out to be, the chances were that nothing like it had been attempted before. Today it is infinitely more difficult to create something that is truly original.

Looking back on this period, with *Fan Fever* being transmitted barely a year after the inauguration of ITV, one can trace the first glimmer of recognition that the upstart 'commercial boys' – that is how BBC insiders referred to us – were making a mark. Dramas, documentaries and news coverage started to have an impact on the BBC, causing television historians and pundits to declare some time later that the competition presented by ITV at this early stage motivated and inspired the BBC to develop and achieve its worldwide reputation as the leading purveyor of television.

* * * *

I had by now relinquished my mole-like existence in the old basement flat in Earls Court that I had shared with my father, and moved south of the river to Lambeth. My new landlord was Prince Charles. As the Duke of Cornwall he had inherited the huge Duchy of Cornwall estate, comprising vast tracts of land in Devon and Cornwall, and also a large chunk of Lambeth, close to the Thames. Mostly residential, with some fine Georgian housing, it was a hotchpotch of styles and included the Oval cricket ground and Kennington Park. In 1955 the Duchy of Cornwall built London's first – and now politically incorrectly named – bachelor flats. Today they would be classified as studio flats, with one bedroom, kitchenette and bathroom – ideal for this bachelor. Named Rothesay Court, the block was close to the Oval and to the Houses of Parliament the other side of the Thames; the flats were popular as convenient *pieds-à-terre* for MPs wanting to live within division-bell distance of the House of Commons. It took me no time in the mornings to drive to the National Film Theatre car park, and then stroll across Waterloo Bridge to the Aldwych and Television House. The daily unfolding of the rich panorama of London's riverside frontage, always seen in a different light and in all weathers, was exhilarating.

In January 1957 I started my own weekly series, called *Members' Mail*. This was village pump politics at its most basic and MPs were the stars; this was long before BBC television cameras were allowed into the House so that MPs could be seen in action. Every week this filmed fifteen-minute programme showed an MP coping with a local constituency problem. There were twenty-three of these, all filmed on location. It was a tight schedule, having to find and organise locations, film and edit each episode ready for transmission every Tuesday night. We had to observe strict guidelines laid down by the ITA regarding political balance – in this case the correct proportion of Tory, Labour and Liberal MPs. Recruiting these good people posed no problems; they were only too keen to be seen on their constituents' television screens doing a valuable job. All of a sudden I found myself quite popular with our MPs, and it sharpened my judgement of politicians. Journalist and writer Dan Farson travelled to the locations in advance to winkle out potential participants, find interviewees and reduce the story to its bare essentials to suit the fifteen-minute format.

I will never forget Colonel Bromley-Davenport. He was the Tory member for Knutsford in Cheshire, a very colourful figure in the House of Commons, referred to by another Tory MP in the series as 'our resident buffoon'. He had just solved a very malodorous problem in Goostrey, a small village in his cabbage patch. The *Yorkshire Post* wrote as follows:

> Drains sound an uninspiring subject for a TV programme, but drains it was on Tuesday when Rediffusion's vigorous feature department presented their latest *Member's Mail.* The village of Goostrey, in the Colonel's constituency, is a pretty place, but sanitation is primitive. The film cameras left viewers in no doubt about that. The long struggle for improvement was packed into a short time with considerable skill. Rapid interviews over the stable door, in the local and by an offending stream, had an encouraging vitality. Rediffusion's documentary team deserve every praise for their work.

Antonia Fraser wrote in the *Evening Standard*: 'Colonel Bromley-Davenport, MP for Knutsford, came on the screen in *Member's Mail.* Apparently his constituency stinks. Or rather stank. Now, thanks to the gallant colonel, the gurgle of its new drains is music to the ears of its inhabitants.'

As always we got reactions from viewers – but in this case there was an uncanny consistency of language in a large pile of identical postcards, which stated: 'Could we please see more of Colonel Bromley-Davenport on TV, he is such a brilliant man and comes over so well.' They were all written in the same hand, and they all shared the same dated Knutsford postmark!

During the six months it was on air *Members' Mail* covered a wide spectrum of local problems, including Teddy boys, old people's homes, wrongful conviction, air pollution, hooliganism, industrial disease, pensions, Zebra crossings, the mentally handicapped, cat stealing and gypsies. Nothing has really changed.

I began to notice during this early period of programme making that I was somewhat ambivalent about the role of the interviewer. I felt that if possible one should try to establish the closest link between the person imparting information and viewers at home, treating them as participants rather than just onlookers. Interviewers, important as they are to so many programmes, change that relationship. I first tried this approach with *Fan Fever.* Elkan Allan used his journalistic flair for sniffing out good stories and whittling them down to their essential ingredients, but when it came to interviewing the fans I asked him to rephrase his questions so they would elicit statements rather than straight answers. Then I coaxed the hapless fans to speak directly into the camera lens, so I took on the role of an invisible interviewer. I stood right behind the camera, out of their direct sightline, and chipped away at them until I was happy with their statements. Even though these contributions sometimes sounded a bit stilted and awkward, they provided a direct link with the viewing audience, demanding their attention. For members of the public to be grabbed in the street and then asked to speak into the camera for television was, of course, a total novelty, and it certainly sorted out the shy from the extrovert. I recall a hilarious moment when a Petticoat Lane stall-holder, only too eager to boast about winning a long-running argument with the council overseer concerning his market trading permit, said, 'This was the biggest and most exciting thing I have ever had in my wife.' The gathered throng that had accumulated to listen gave him a standing ovation. At first this rather artificial technique did not make me very popular with interviewers, but as these programmes began to attract attention, and there were encouraging press reviews, I persevered – and my colleagues slowly accepted this strange style.

Derek Knight wrote in *Film*:

> One of the main innovations of Associated-Rediffusion's team of film-workers has been the successful development of the speaking-to-camera technique applied to non-actors, and the consequent discarding of the interviewer. It says much for the ability and skill of directors like Michael Ingrams of *Look In On London* and Peter Morley who directed *Fan Fever* and *Members' Mail*, that people in fact do not dry up, do not stammer, but say what's on their minds calmly, where necessary with good humour. No easy feat. The direct speaking-to-camera by people in all walks of life has an impact which we filmgoers are not used to. It is documentary with the gloves off, and the laurels for virile and aggressive film-making are being seized by the team at Associated-Rediffusion.

Early in 1957 I had a call from the BBC. It was from Andrew Millar-Jones, one of the founders of the Guild of Television Producers and Directors. I had not heard of it before, but soon realised that it was an exclusive and elitist group of practitioners who had got together at the BBC to pursue mutual interests. I was told that as 'Commercial Television' (their name for ITV) was now a fact, they wished to extend an invitation for me to join the Guild. I was thrilled by this; the prospect of being able to meet people from the great British Broadcasting Corporation and to talk with them about television was hugely exciting, and I looked forward to my first Guild meeting. When I arrived I realised that I was one of only three directors there representing ITV, and became aware that I would have to work hard to lose the 'outsider' label. To my surprise, after a short period they elected me to serve on the Guild's Council.

Right from my first days at ITV I had been aware of people like Grace Wyndham Goldie, the head of the BBC's talks department. She had launched *Panorama* and recently created the ground-breaking BBC *Tonight* programme. Grace discovered, employed and then provided creative leadership for a clique of director/producers who were pioneering documentary and current affairs programming. In fact most of 'Grace's young men', as they became known, rose to the highest ranks in British television.

The Guild organised valuable evening sessions, usually held on the premises of the English Speaking Union in Mayfair and sometimes with Grace in attendance. I tried to go to these as often as I could – as there was a lot to absorb and learn. I also made the acquaintance of Huw Wheldon, who was rapidly rising to the higher echelons of the BBC as a master communicator and programme maker. At one of these Guild meetings the expansion of television was discussed, and the effect this might have on the creative freedom of writers, producers and directors. His words ringing in my ears to this day, and often quoted, Huw told us: 'We must never forget that Television is a business that massproduces handmade objects'. This is truer today than ever, when you consider the burdening commercial pressures on programme makers.

The Guild's other activity was to organise the annual Television Awards Ball. The trophy presented to winners was a bronze mask that the Guild commissioned from the sculptress Mitzi Cunliffe. In 1958 the Guild amalgamated with the British Film Academy, and became the Society of Film and Television Arts (SFTA). In 1976 it emerged as the British Academy of Film and Television Arts – BAFTA. The Guild's trophy was retained, and became known as the BAFTA mask.

10: Years of Adventure

Altogether I directed over thirty-five programmes in 1957 to help satisfy the relentless hunger of the transmission schedule. Within a week of the last transmission of *Members' Mail* I was on the air with my fourth, *People are Talking*. Entitled rather grandly *The Future of Britain,* it indulged in periodic navel-gazing when the economic news was dire: export orders cancelled, growing strike threat, BOAC buys US jetliners, hire-purchase deposits on cars up again, another fares shock, and so on. This was a studio-based programme with filmed inserts. It was the first time we used Kenneth Harris, industrial correspondent of the *Observer*, who subsequently collaborated with me on several other programmes. In the studio we had Frank Cousins, Dr Donald Soper and J.B. Priestley. The highlight for me was filming an excerpt of Richard Pasco delivering a characteristic Jimmy Porter outburst from John Osborne's *Look Back in Anger* to illustrate the lacklustre attitude of the then younger generation.

This was followed by a short season of magazine programmes called *On Stage*, reporting on the live theatre, with the participation of many names to conjure with: Donald Wolfit, Anthony Quayle, Yvonne Arnaud, A.E. Matthews, Robert Morley, Elizabeth Seal, Dame Sybil Thorndike, Sir Lewis Casson, Evelyn Laye – one could go on name-dropping for ever. One of the highlights was the re-opening of the Theatre Royal, Windsor. The Royal Family came across from the castle to enjoy *The Rivals*, and I produced the outside broadcast of this event. I was then asked to go on stage and join the cast after curtain down to meet the Queen, Prince Philip, the Queen Mother and the rest of the royal party. It was my first encounter with them.

Jane stayed on as my production assistant for the next extraordinary and slightly bizarre adventure. Controller of Programmes John McMillan decided to throw a huge party to mark A-R's second birthday. It was called *Salute to Show Business* and it attracted over eight million viewers. John felt that A-R had something to shout about, and not just its programmes. The company was beginning to turn the financial corner, having lost £3 million by their first anniversary, and the high profile party would help to restore the City's confidence and please the advertising industry. Peter Hunt was the overall producer, and Joan Kemp-Welch and I were co-directors, sharing the various elements that made up this two-hour spectacular. She made a film about the life of Dickie Valentine, while I shot *The Margaret Lockwood Story* in St John's Wood Studios, starring Margaret's daughter Toots, playing the part of her mother. I also made another film, which told the story of John Buxton, the legendary ghost who resided at the Theatre Royal, Haymarket. The ghost was played by that great comic actor James Hayter, and I filmed it all in the Theatre Royal with a cast of bit-players to break the bank: Dame Edith Evans, Leslie Arliss, Felix Aylmer, Fay Compton, Sir John Gielgud, Celia Johnson, Michael Redgrave, Sir Carol Reed, Sir Ralph Richardson, Athene Seyler, Diana Wynyard – to name but a few.

It was then that I witnessed a dazzling demonstration of the curious ways of big business. The night before the celebratory broadcast A-R threw a big party for the great and the good on board the *Royal Sovereign*, one of those floating fun palaces on the Thames. This was an extravagant moonlight river trip with champagne and music for 'a thousand stars of stage and screen', as the brochure said. I had already filmed some hilarious sequences with Peter Sellers and Kenneth Connor on board the ship to set the tone for the main programme, and that night I shot scenes of the party itself, which were to be included in a short opening sequence to the main broadcast the following night. This meant getting the film rushes to Humphries, the film laboratory, for overnight processing as soon as the *Royal Sovereign* had docked, so that we could edit the footage in the morning. As the rushes would not arrive at the labs until after midnight, Humphries said that they could not handle them unless they called in an extra nightshift, which they refused to do. I reported this to Captain Brownrigg, A-R's general manager, and he told me he would come back to me within a couple of hours. Apparently he then had a telephone conversation with Harley Drayton, the chairman of British Electric Traction as well as Associated Newspapers, the owners of A-R. Within the hour he popped his head round my office door: 'Go ahead as planned. Our film will be processed. Harley Drayton has just bought Humphries Film Laboratory Limited!'

* * * *

A-R was making its mark. It was being talked about and its programmes were attracting decent viewing ratings. Proof of this came towards the end of 1957, when the BFI commissioned Derek Prouse, its programme editor, to mount a short season of A-R documentaries to be shown on the large screen at the new National Film Theatre on the South Bank. In the brochure for this event, he wrote:

> We have called the programme CAPTIVE CINEMA for the following reasons. The TV director's means are narrowly controlled; he is beset by inhibiting pressures: pressure of time; pressure imposed by the need to capture the widest possible viewing audience. It is therefore particularly impressive that in spite of all these conditions the TV directors should succeed so often in incorporating that rare quality in British documentary today – a friendly and unpatronising attitude to ordinary people, which can persuade them to reveal themselves fully and naturally before the demanding camera. But in the best TV work there is something more; a quality almost disturbingly new – an urgency, an instinct for the timely reportage which catches its people when feelings are still running high, when resentments or a sense of injustice are burning and eager to communicate. The impact is nearly always irresistible and almost shockingly true. CAPTIVE CINEMA is selected from the work of the Features Department of Associated-Rediffusion, which is under the leadership of Miss Caryl Doncaster.

And in the same BFI brochure Caryl introduces her team:

> The films the National Film Theatre have chosen to show on December 11th are representative of programmes – many of them live and therefore lost – which Associated-Rediffusion have been transmitting four or five times a week for the last two years. During this period a strong 'Features' team has grown up in A-R. It has drawn its talent from many sources. Peter Hunt and John Rhodes left the BBC when its documentary department was disbanded. Directors like Geoffrey Hughes, Michael Currer-Briggs and Peter Morley, and our capable manager Deborah Chesshire, came to us from the documentary film world. Writers like Elkan Allan, Cyril Bennett and Daniel Farson joined us from Fleet Street and Michael Ingrams came from the theatre. This mixture of skills and points of view have given our output

> a virility which I hope we will not lose when our techniques become more polished and a routine develops.

On the opening night of the Captive Cinema season at the NFT each one of us introduced our programmes to the audience, and it was fascinating to see them on the large screen for the first time, let alone to read reactions in the film press. Penelope Houston wrote in *Sight and Sound*:

> For the most part these programmes are concerned to report on life and people, to let the implicit social comments emerge from the material itself rather than to state them openly. The longest and most hard-hitting of the films in the Captive Cinema programme follows this principle, but its material has been selected to brutal effect. *Fan Fever*, directed by Peter Morley, written by Elkan Allan and first shown on the day of Liberace's overpowering arrival in London, has to do with mass hysteria, with the idolaters who mob the stage doors, rip their hero's clothing to pieces. As a contemporary document, *Fan Fever* conveys less an atmosphere than an impression of personality exposed, trapped, caught in the act of self-revelation. Television, and not merely television documentary, has made no discovery more valuable for itself than the simple one that people are interesting.

By 1958 ITV had become a fixture in the nation's homes. Its role *vis-à-vis* the BBC was manifest; all the regional franchise holders were in place, and A-R was well in profit. My initial three month contract had been changed to a one year rolling contract, and that worked well for me. It gave me a good deal of independence, and a certain amount of security. A-R had by this time launched its weekly current affairs magazine programme, *This Week*, and that gave our features department a high profile. Peter Hunt produced it and I made one or two filmed contributions to it. It was considered by the press to be a minnow compared with the BBC's *Panorama*, but the challenge, even in this field, was taken very seriously by the Corporation.

In the late '50s and early '60s a great number of programmes were original in content and technique: innovation was the order of the day, as I have said. When recalling these times I often find myself saying that a particular programme of mine was the first of this or the first of that – and I feel a bit self-conscious about making such extravagant sounding claims – but it was really like that.

It is too easy to label this period as the golden years of television. I have never subscribed to that, because I believe that young people entering the media today will in fifty years' time consider this to have been their golden years. I like to describe the late '50s and early '60s as our years of adventure, when we were exploring something entirely new, with the excitement of being allowed to experiment and to be paid for it. We were even allowed to fail. I believe that it was not until the late '60s that television metamorphosed into the full-blooded industry that we know today.

In attempting to recall these times I keep on diving into my own archive, stored haphazardly in the attic: a jumble of press cuttings, articles, camera scripts, letters and photographs, preserved in odd boxes, old suitcases and plastic bags. It harbours memories of a prolific and eclectic portfolio of work; and it was here that I discovered that my tally of programmes for 1957 totalled thirty-five. Needless to say, some were better than others.

Early in 1958 I started a weekly series with Wolf Mankowitz in conversation with an 'opponent' of his choice. He picked them from all walks of life and relished having red-hot arguments. We called this thirteen-episode series *Conflict*, and it was transmitted live. Cyril Bennett was the programme editor. The episode I remember with great fondness focused on comedy, and the guest was Spike Milligan.

I opened each programme with a top shot looking down on Wolf Mankowitz and his guest, silhouetted against a chequerboard painted floor. I superimposed the title and then a second caption gave the name of Wolf's contestant. But this time, on the ten-second countdown to the start of the transmission, Spike leapt out of his chair and ran off the set, and I had to go on the air with Wolf on his own. I looked down to the studio set from the control gallery and saw Spike grabbing one of the cameramen, trying to bite his ear. At that point the opening music stopped, the lights came up, and as I cut to one of the floor cameras Spike came running back onto the set, hitching up his trousers. I knew we were in for an exciting thirty-minute programme.

Surprisingly, it was a fascinating discussion about comedy and how comedians were adapting to television. However, on two occasions it was briefly punctuated by Spike, in mid-flow, looking straight into his camera to produce a rich repertoire of 'Goon' noises and catchphrases. Thirty seconds before the end of the programme, as usual, I went back to the top shot, cued the end music and released the floor cameras to their caption stands for the end credit routine. At this point Spike took off once again. Before the show started he must have grabbed a piece of chalk from the floor-manager, and as I cut to the first caption, which read '*Conflict* with Wolf Mankowitz', a hand appeared, quickly scribbling on the caption card 'Who he?' Cutting to the other camera with the caption 'Spike Milligan', he raced across to it and again a disembodied hand wrote 'Yippee!' Back to the first caption, which read 'Programme Editor Cyril Bennett', Spike chalked in '8 out of 10', and lastly, on the caption 'Directed by Peter Morley', appeared the simple words 'Oh dear'. All of us fell about, having savoured, once again, the hazards of live television.

After *Conflict* I embarked on a new weekly series of twenty-six episodes called *Only Yesterday*. Again these were live studio-based productions, but this time they had an important filmed element. Each programme was dedicated to an historical event, which was illustrated with archive film, with eyewitnesses and survivors recalling their experiences in the studio. It was a very simple and effective formula, which at the time was considered innovative, and it attracted a large viewer following. A diverse range of subjects included the R101 airship disaster, the Reichstag fire, the Jarrow hunger march, Amy Johnson, the submarine *Thetis* disaster, Lenin's death and so on. What fascinated me most was discovering the richness of our film archives – not just the newsreel resources of Gaumont British, Pathé and Universal, but also the archives of the BFI and the Imperial War Museum.

Only Yesterday whetted my appetite for visual history, and for the next twenty years I had many opportunities to get to know the world's archives really well, and many times asked film researchers to raid them for a host of programmes.

Fan Fever, 1956

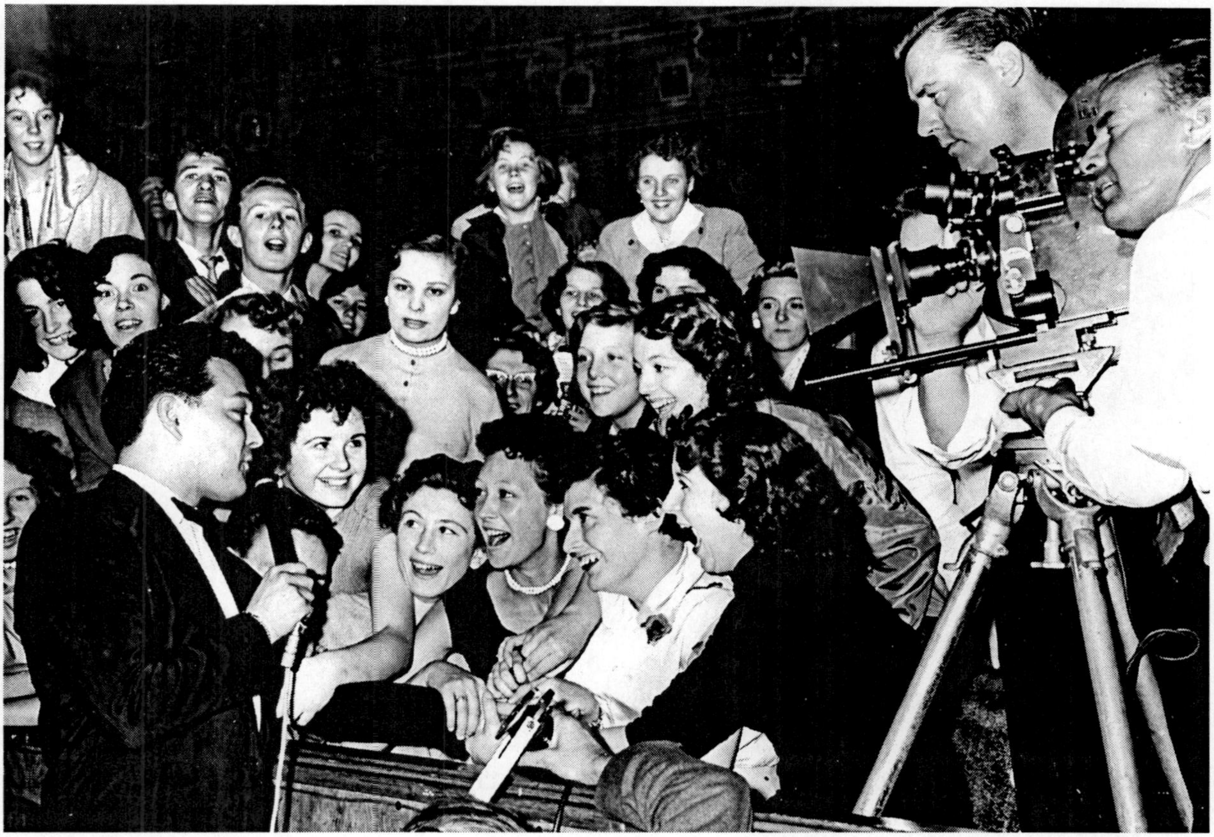

Dickie Valentine with fans at the Coventry Theatre. (Rediffusion Television)

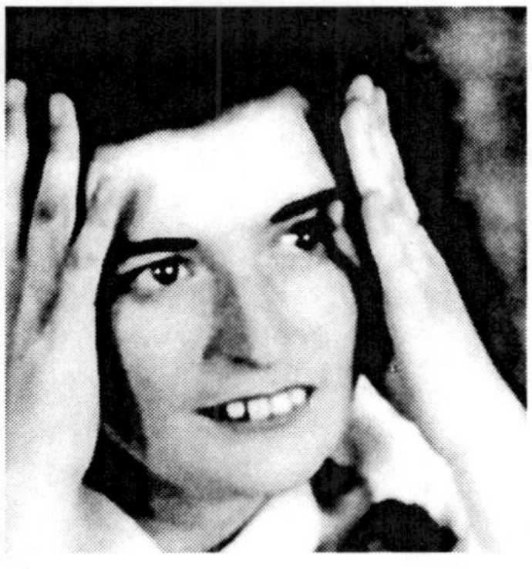

Tom Driberg wrote in the *New Statesman*: 'Oblivious of the camera, they screamed, writhed, gasped, beat their pretty but clammy brows, suffered the delicious agonies of divine possession. All this made vital television.'

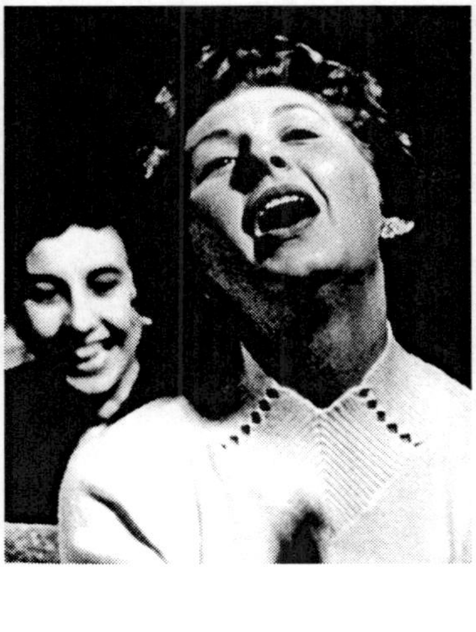

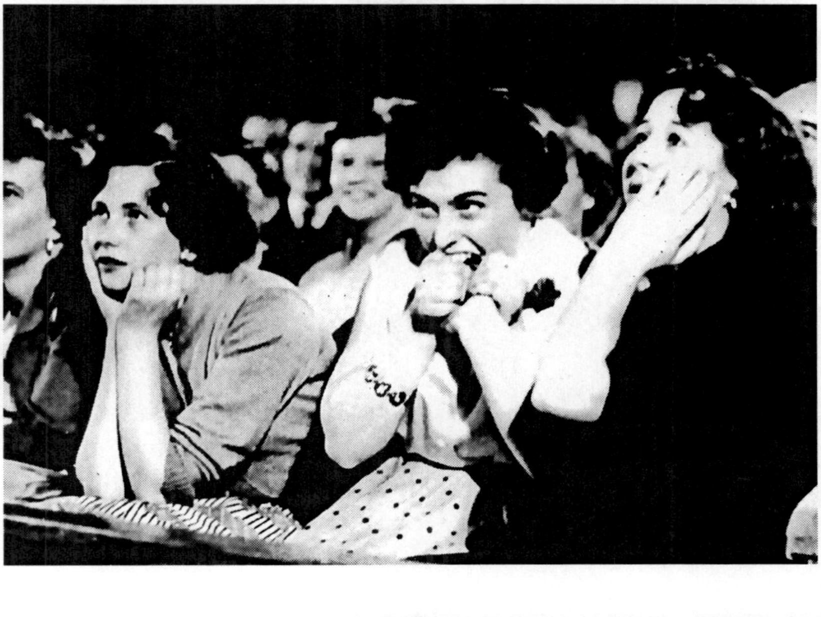

Members' Mail, 1956

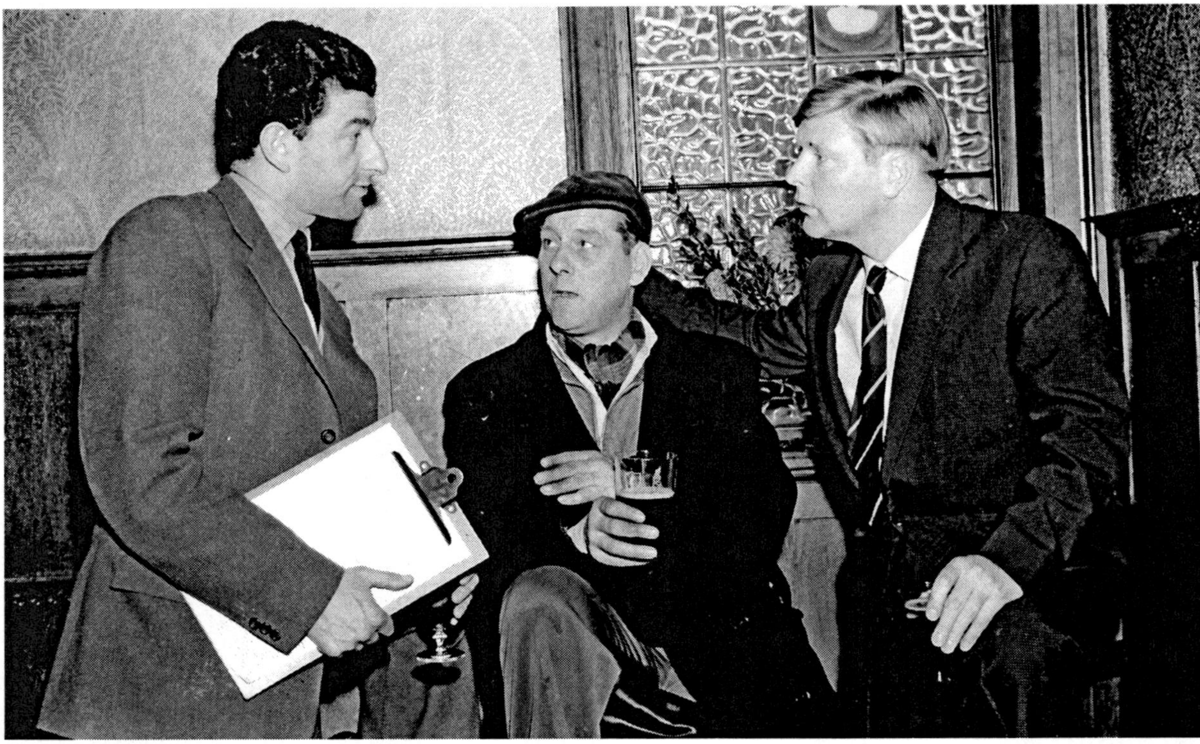

Robert Mellish MP: the problem was the wrongful conviction of a dockworker. Here we are planning the victim's 'to camera' statement with Dan Farson. (Rediffusion Television)

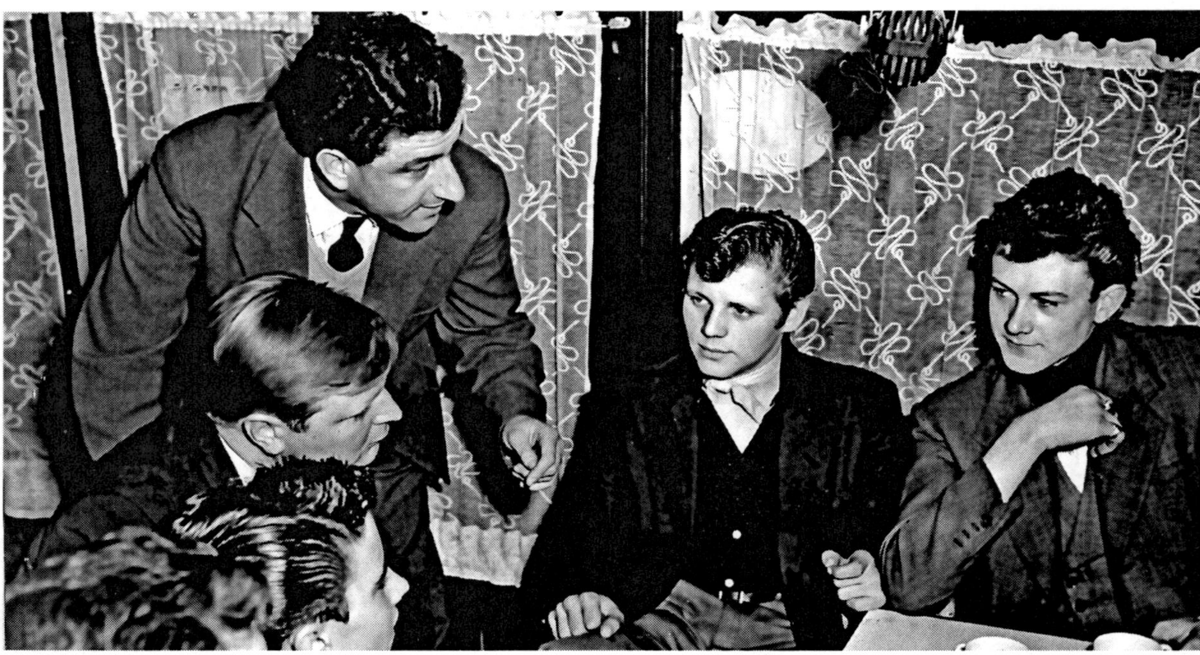

Graeme Finlay MP: the problem was the behaviour of Teddy boys. Dan Farson and I soften up our participants. (Rediffusion Television)

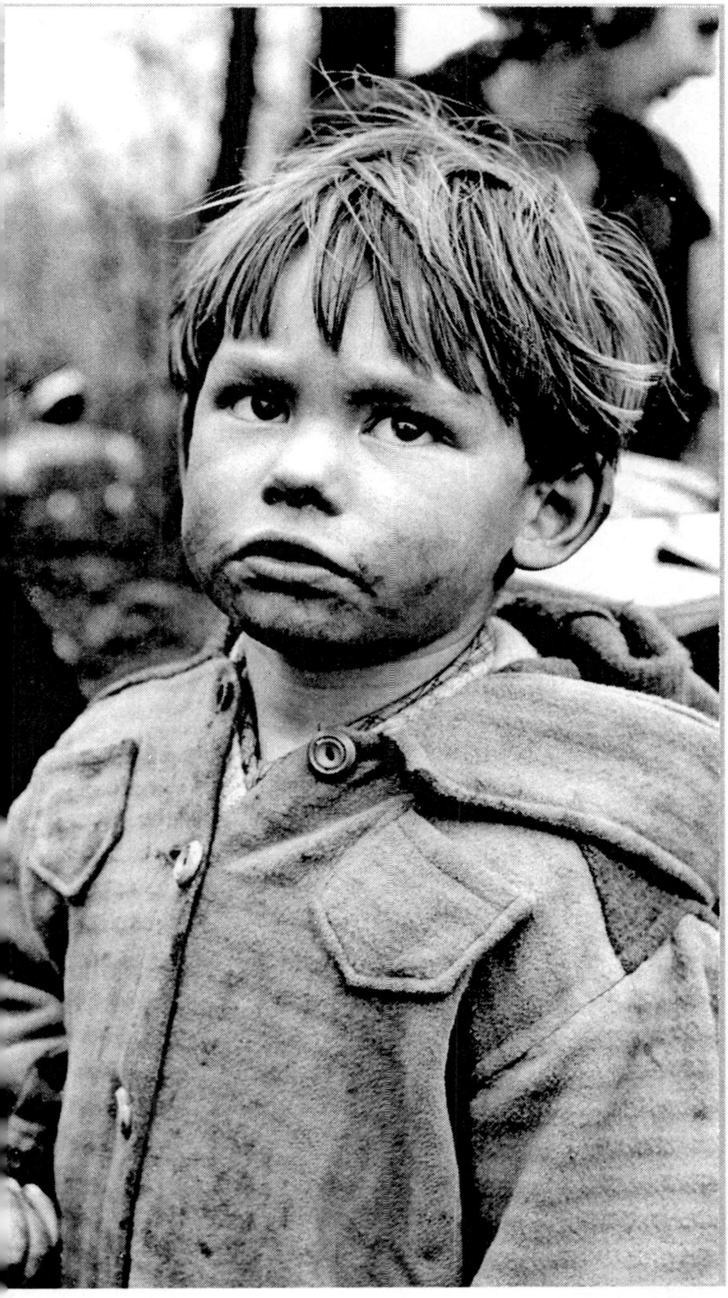

Norman Dodds MP: the problem was rights for gypsies. (Rediffusion Television)

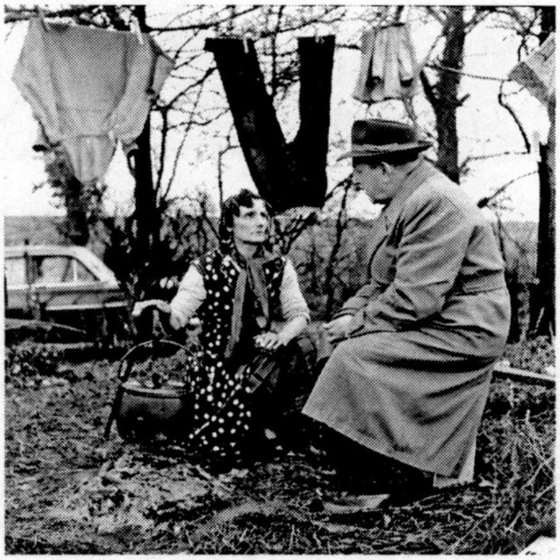

Norman Dodds MP and a complainant. (Rediffusion Television)

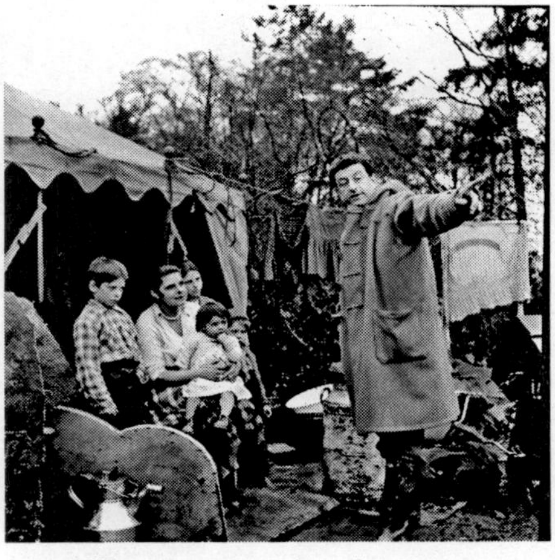

Duffle coats were *de rigueur*. (Rediffusion Television)

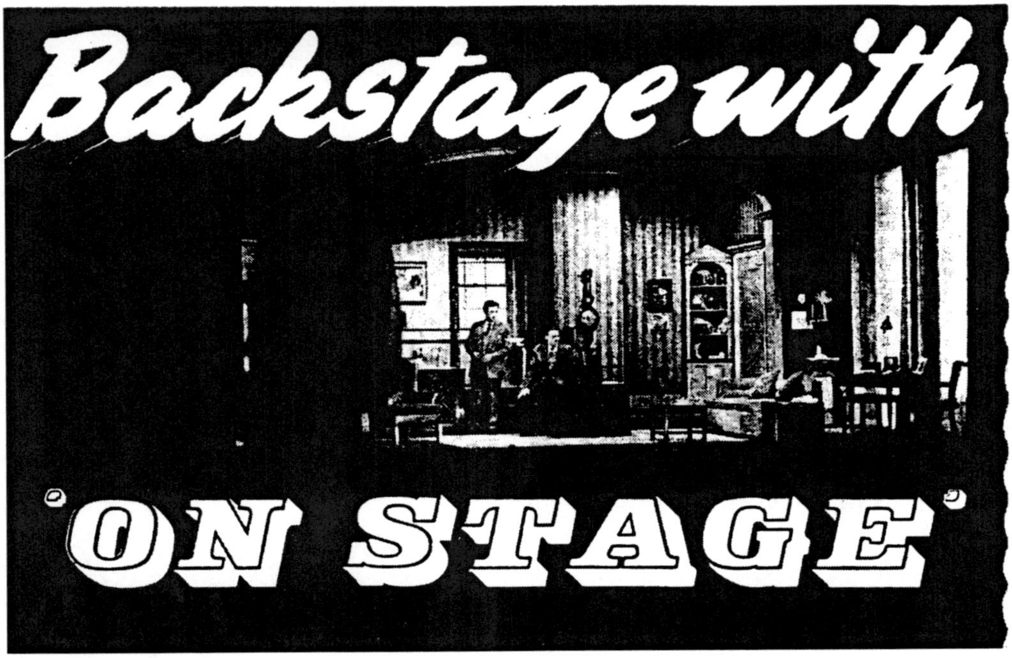

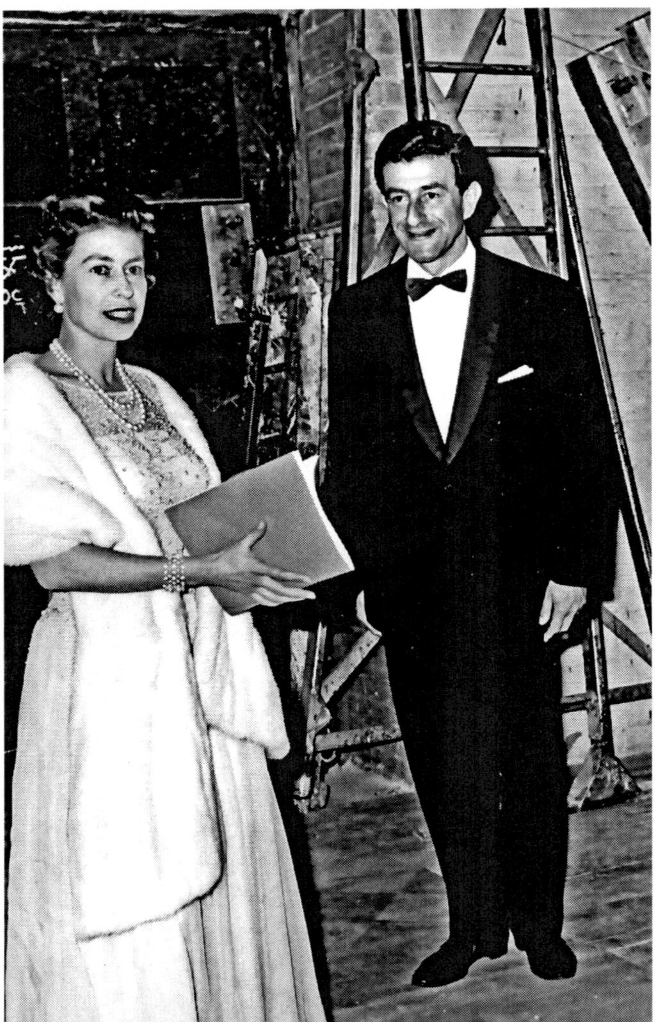

After curtain-down at the Theatre Royal, Windsor, 1957. A production of *The Rivals* marked the re-opening of the royal family's neighbourhood theatre. (Rediffusion Television)

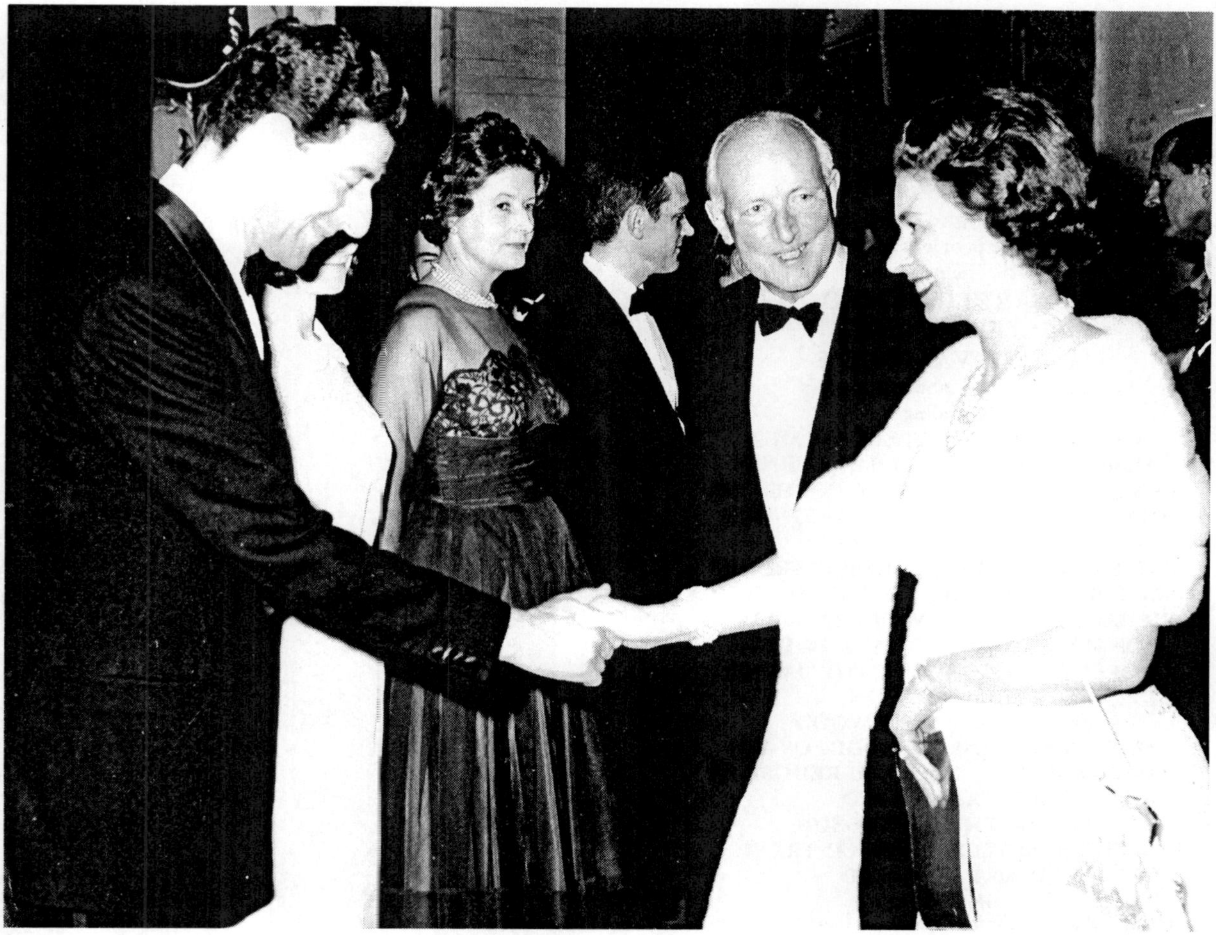

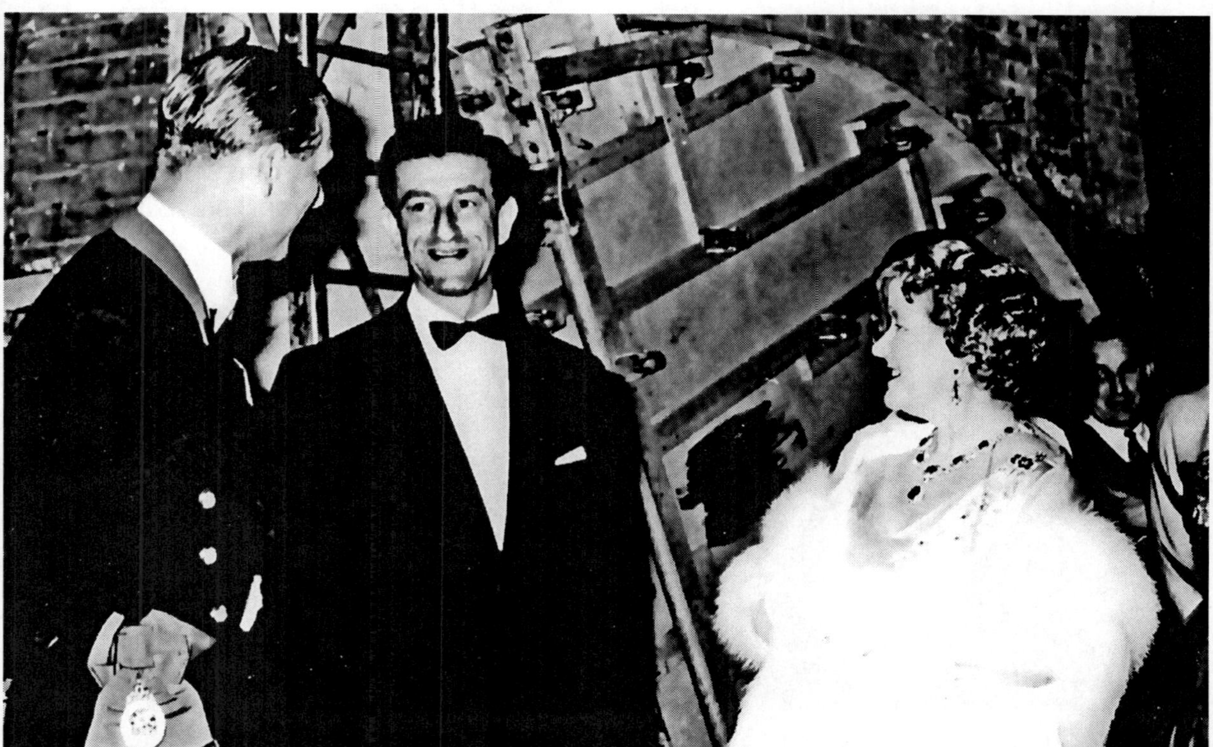

8.0 SALUTE

to

SHOW BUSINESS

Independent Television's second year ends with a story about the people who entertain you

with

MARGARET LOCKWOOD
PETER SELLERS
DICKIE VALENTINE

and a host of other great stars

including

LESLIE ARLISS   FELIX AYLMER
ALBERT BURDON   SUSAN BURNET
PHYLLIS CALVERT   PEGGY COCHRANE
FAY COMPTON   KENNETH CONNOR
HERBERT DE LEON
DAME EDITH EVANS   LESLIE FREWIN
SIR JOHN GIELGUD   JAMES HAYTER
RICHARD HEARNE   WILLIAM HOLDEN
RONALD HOWARD   JACK HYLTON
DOROTHY HYSON   JIMMY JAMES
CELIA JOHNSON
JULIA (Toots) LOCKWOOD
MARY MALCOLM   PADDIE O'NEIL
VAL PARNELL   MICHAEL REDGRAVE
SIR CAROL REED
SIR RALPH RICHARDSON
ATHENE SEYLER   BRUCE TRENT
DIANA WYNYARD

Written by
Hazel Adair   Cyril Bennett   David Freeman
Theme music composed by
Peggy Cochrane
Arranged and conducted by
Laurie Johnson
with his concert orchestra
Studio orchestra conducted by
Geoff Love
*Designed by **Michael Yates***
*Studio director **Joan Kemp-Welch***
*Programme directed by **Peter Morley***
Produced by
PETER HUNT
Presented by
JOHN McMILLAN
An Associated-Rediffusion Network Production

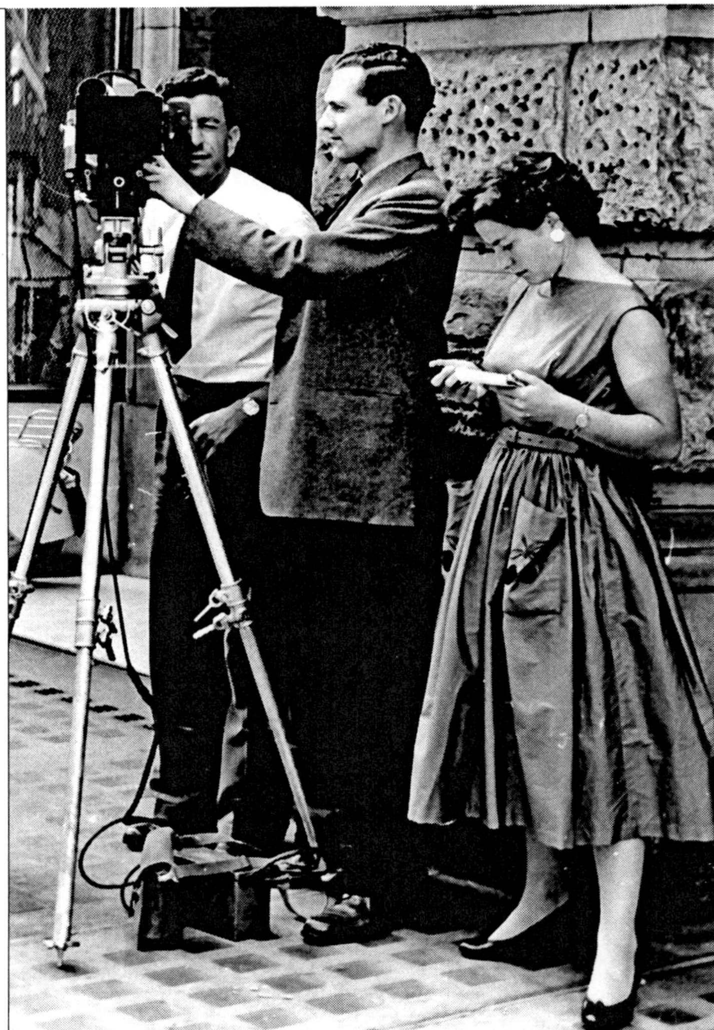

Checking a shot with assistant cameraman Mike Rhodes and production assistant Jane Tillett – my wife to be. (Rediffusion Television)

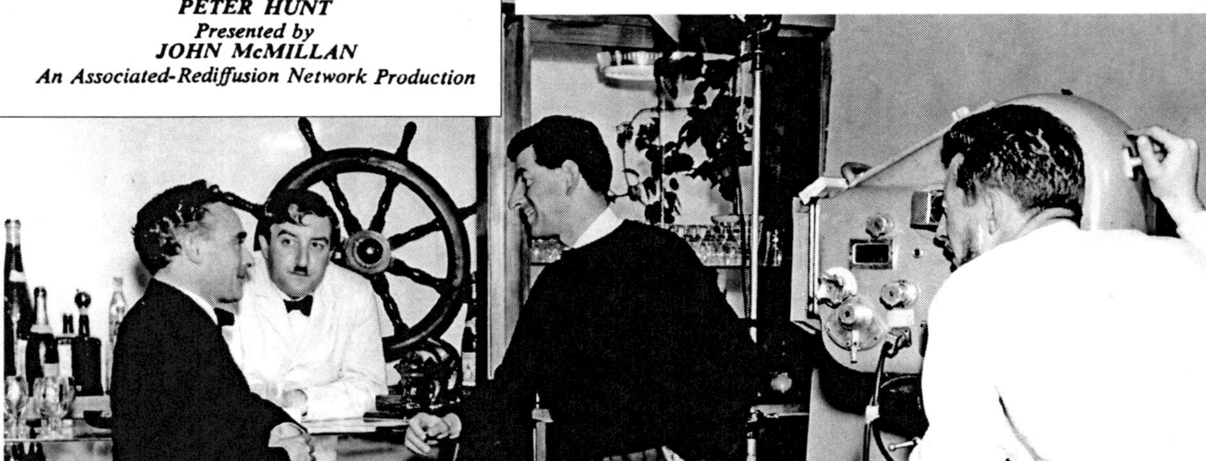

Shooting a sketch with Peter Sellers and Kenneth Connor. (Rediffusion Television)

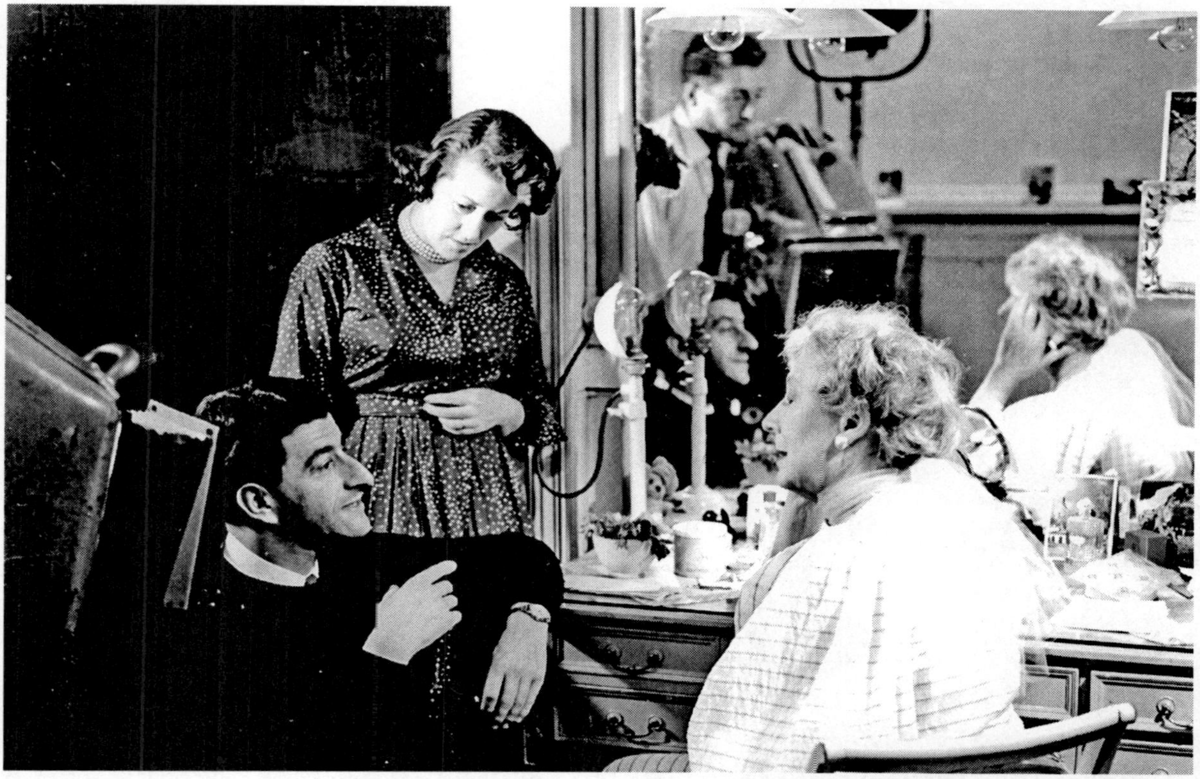

In Dame Edith Evans's dressing room with writer Hazel Adair. (Rediffusion Television)

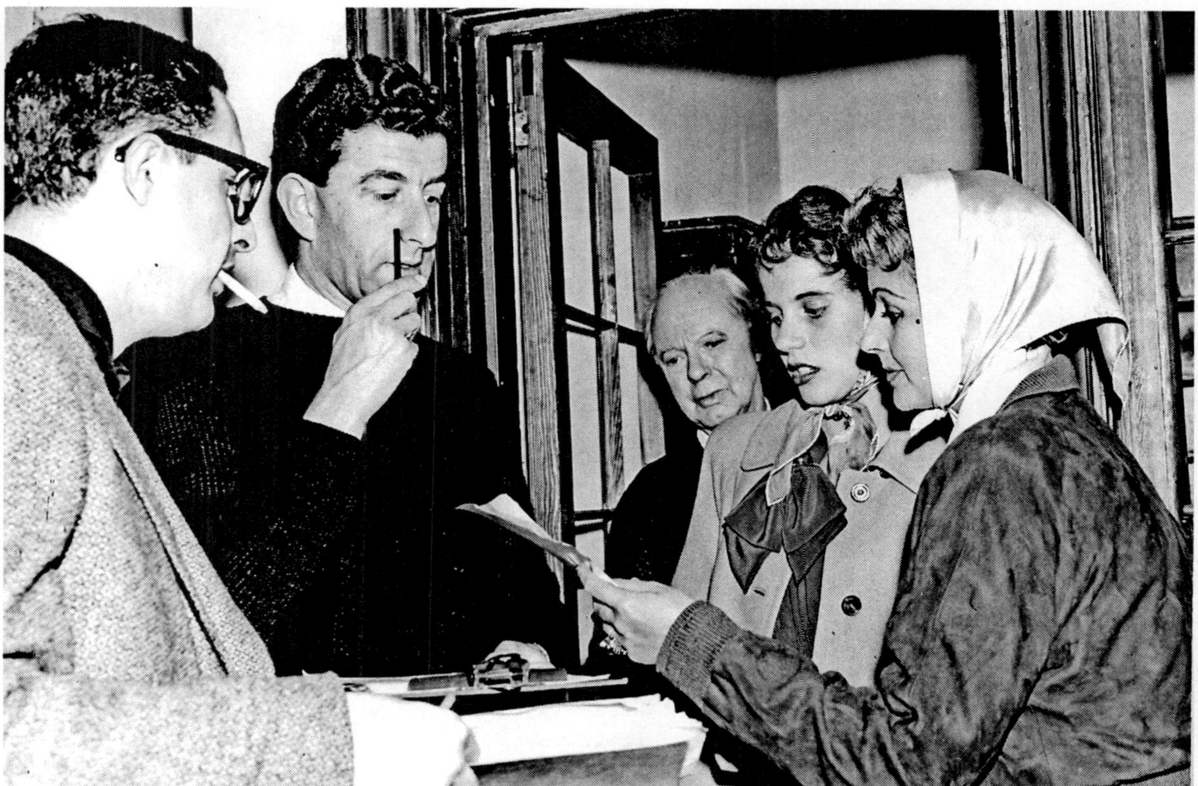

My first collaboration with Cyril Bennett: discussing the script with Margaret Lockwood and her daughter Toots. (Rediffusion Television)

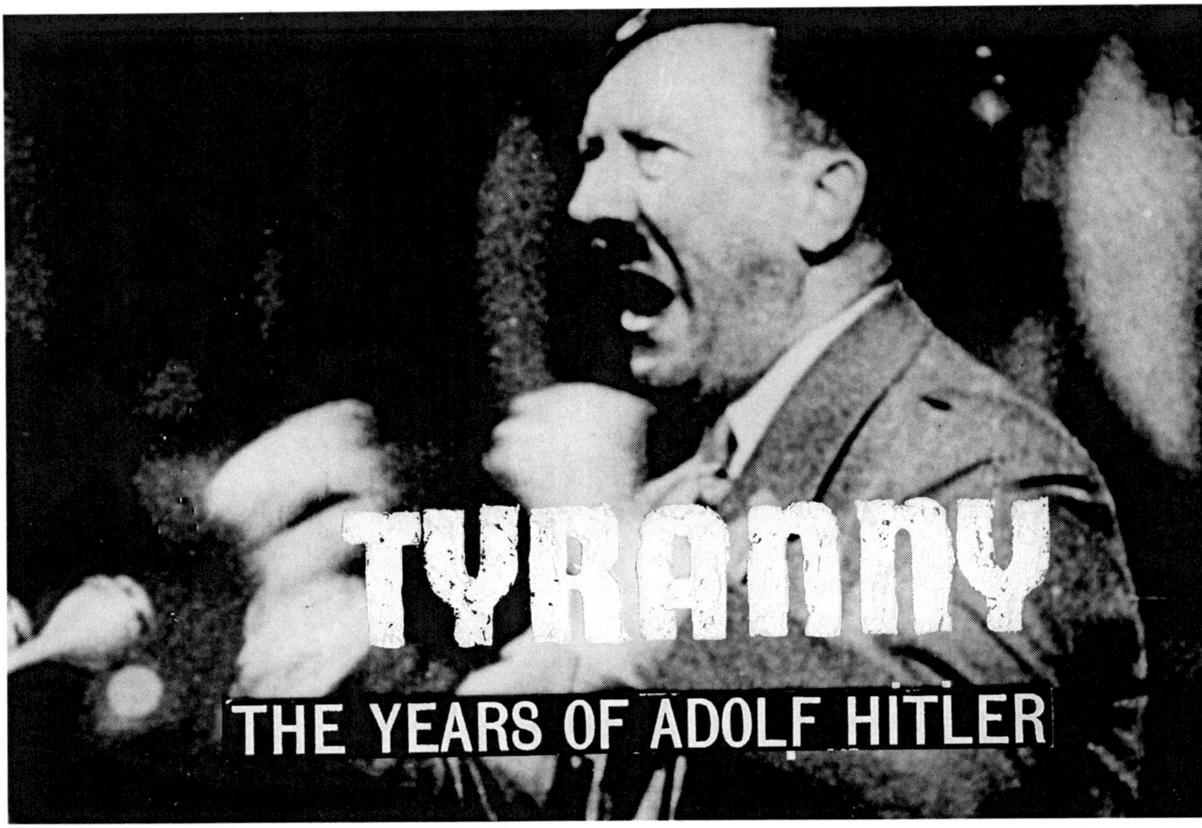

The main title caption card used in the 1959 live transmission. (Rediffusion Television)

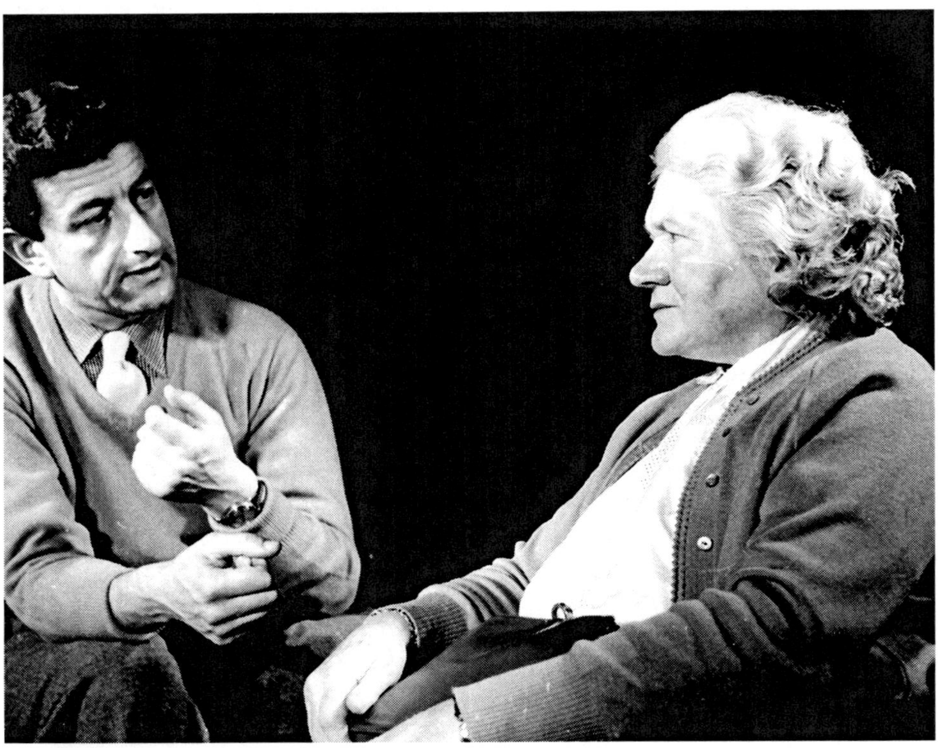

Warming up Hitler's sister, Paula Wolf. (Rediffusion Television)

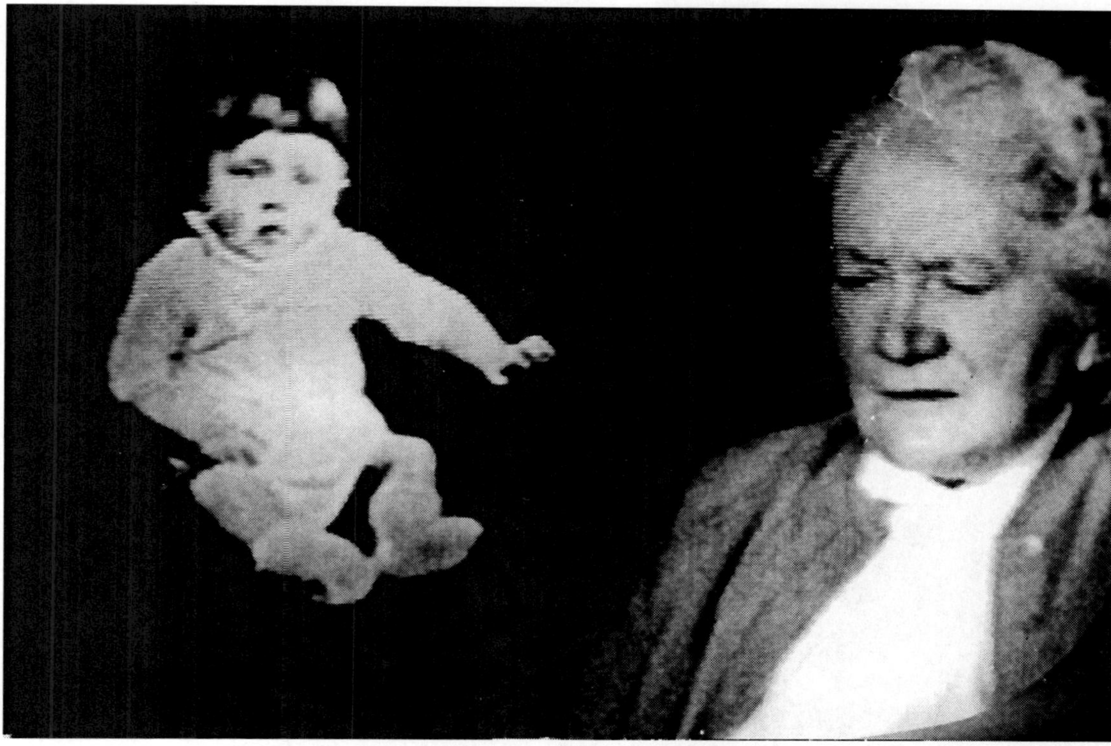

'When we children played Red Indians, my brother Adolf was always the leader.' (Rediffusion Television)

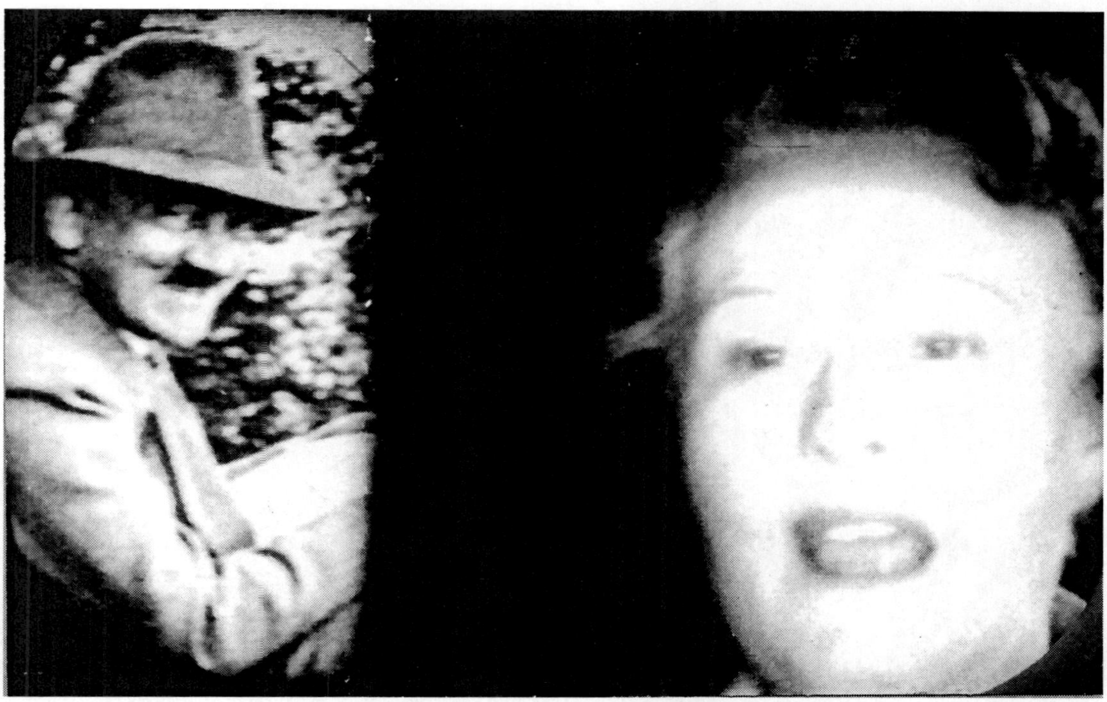

Frau Wilma Schaub (wife of Hitler's adjutant). 'Those rumours that Adolf Hitler was supposed to be abnormal over women are false.' (Rediffusion Television)

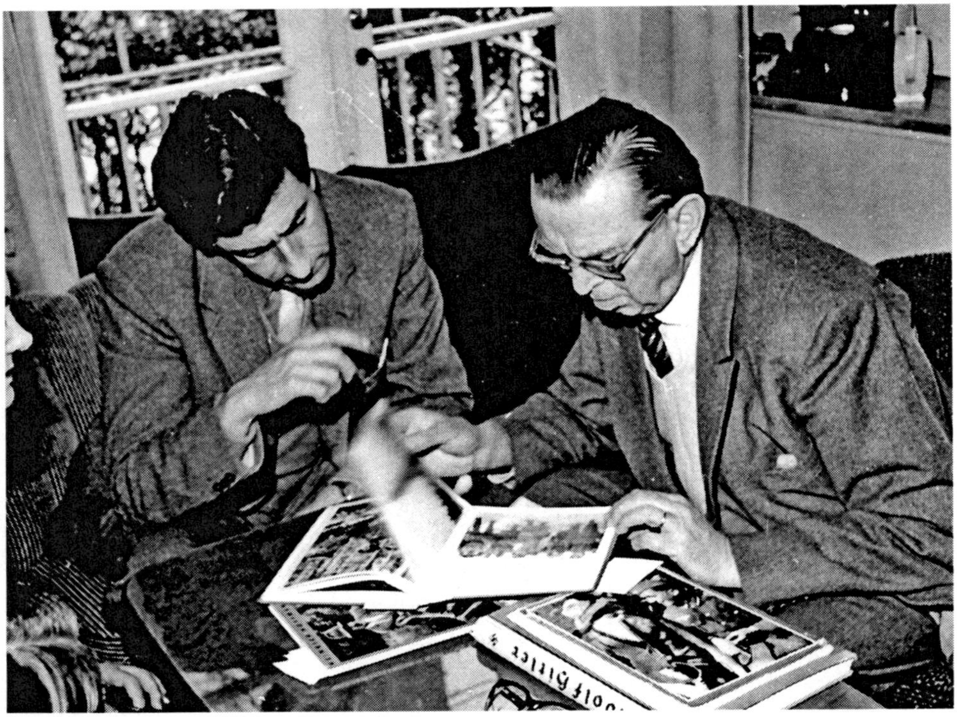

Obergruppenführer Julius Schaub, Hitler's adjutant, proudly shows me his photo collection, including pictures of himself with 'der Führer'. (Rediffusion Television)

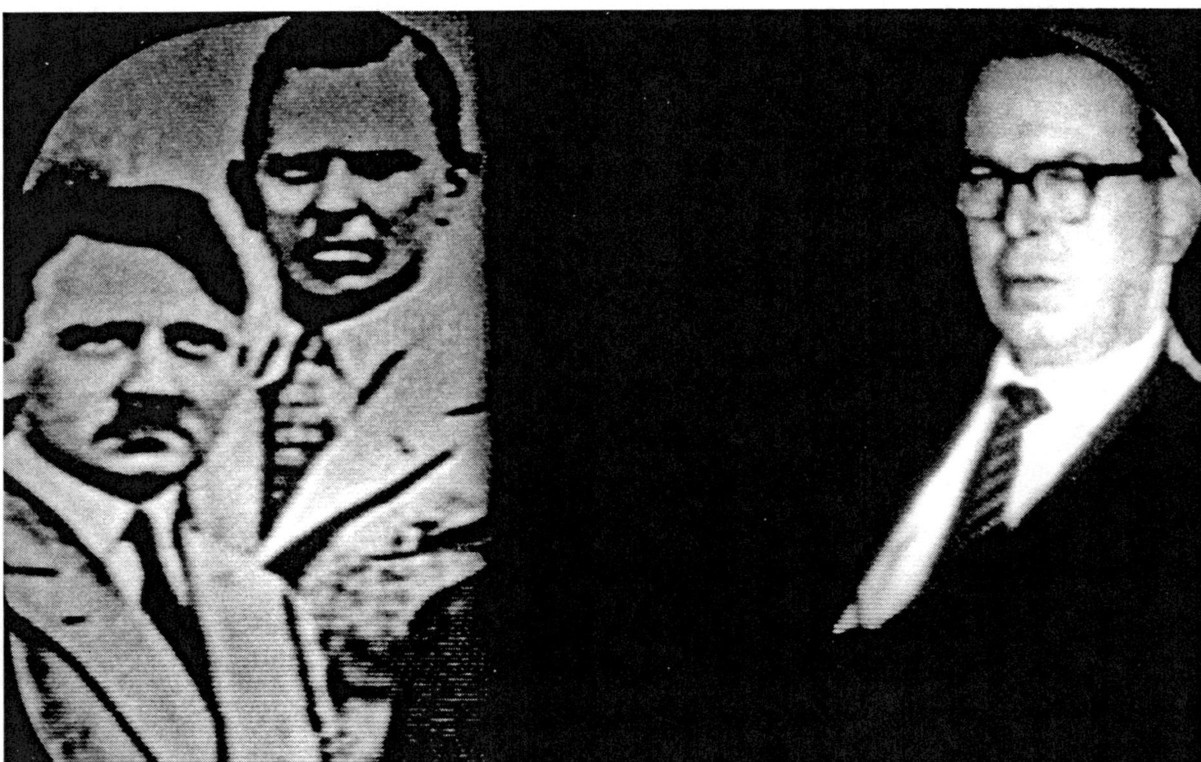

'I entered his bedroom in the bunker with him. On the table there was a 7.5mm pistol. He was only making sure that it was loaded.' (Rediffusion Television)

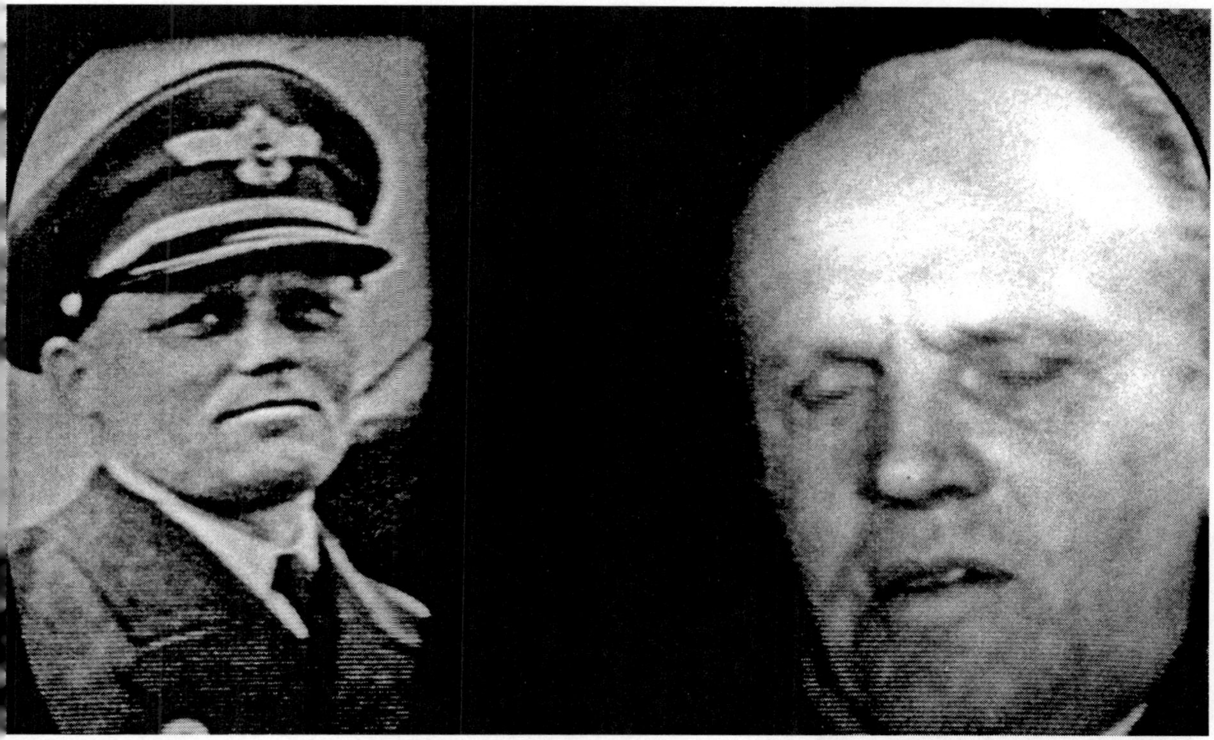

Flug Kapitän Hans Bauer, Hitler's personal pilot. 'I make you personally responsible for burning the corpses of my wife and me.' (Rediffusion Television)

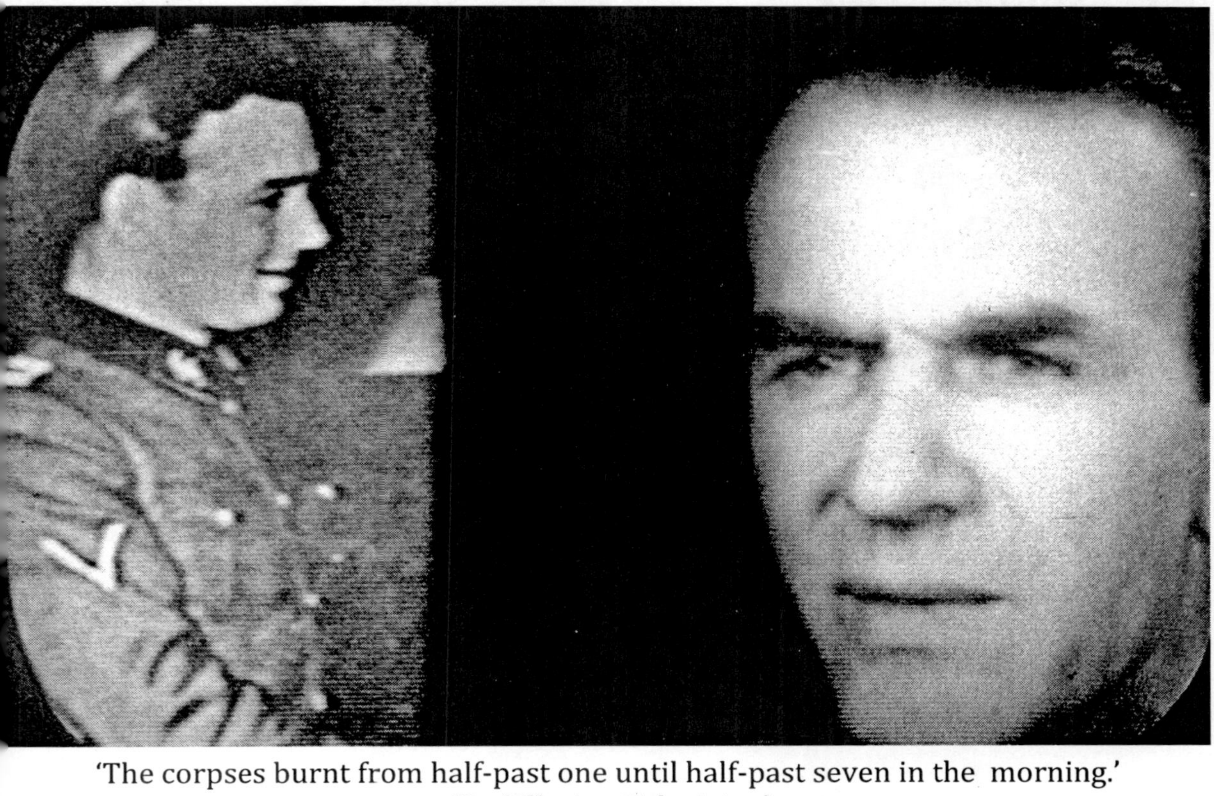

'The corpses burnt from half-past one until half-past seven in the morning.' (Rediffusion Television)

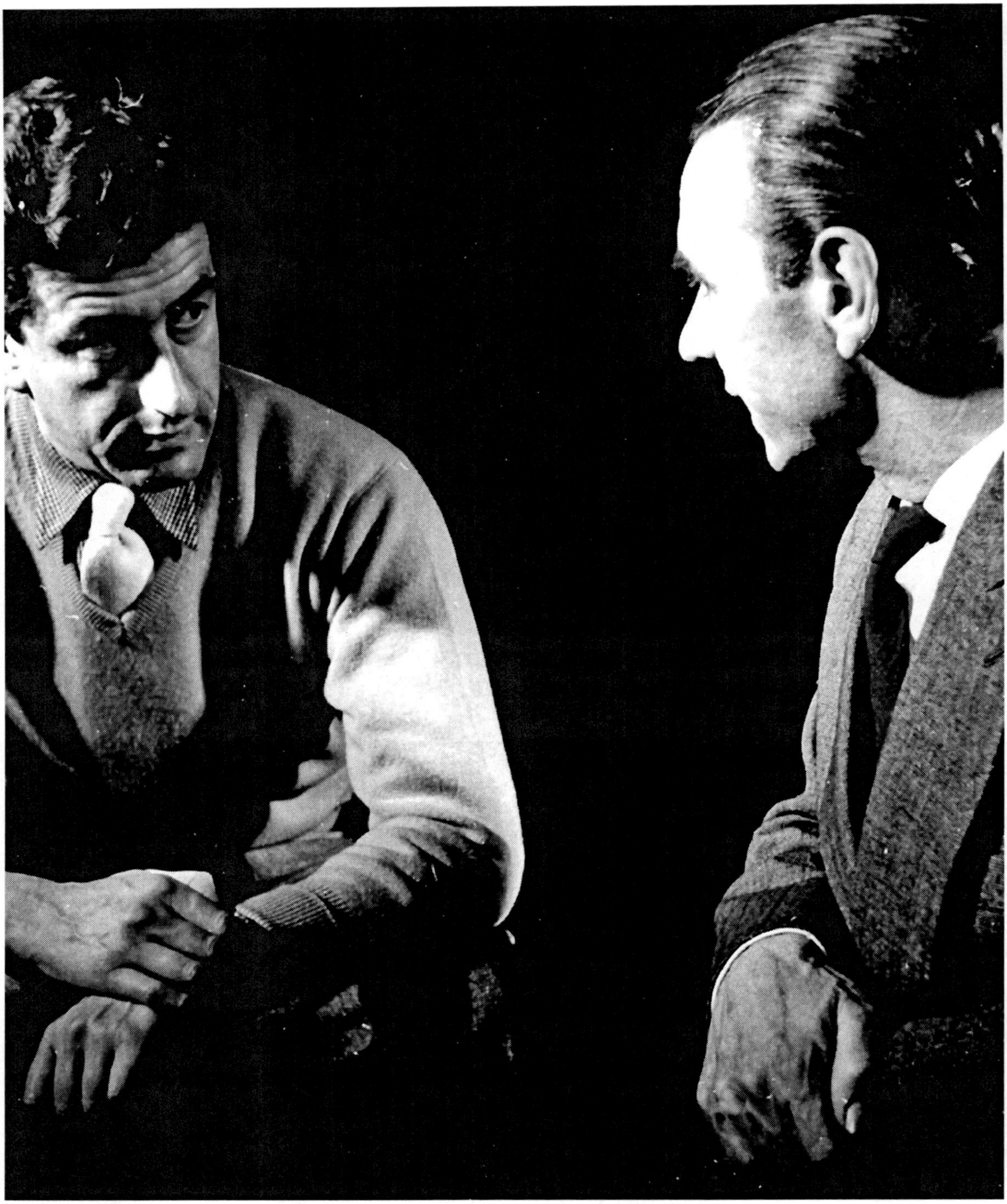

Erich Kempka, Hitler's chauffeur, sharing some grisly statistics with me.
(Rediffusion Television)

11: Hitler and Israel

I had now teamed up with Cyril Bennett, and for the next few years we collaborated on several programmes; we became known as A-R's writer/director team. I first met Cyril on *Conflict* and we hit it off straight away, sharing similar ideas about the sort of programmes that would be exciting to make. He came to television from journalism, writing for *Illustrated* and other papers. The reason we got on so well was that we readily accepted each other's strengths and weaknesses in journalism and film-making. His repertoire of hysterically funny Jewish jokes became a byword in Television House. We became good friends.

Cyril and I came up with the idea of a full-length programme on Adolf Hitler. The motivation was to remind those who had forgotten, or were too young to remember, of the events of the recent past; to try to find out how it was possible for an enlightened nation to be seduced by this monster. The opportunity came when, early in 1959, I was asked to choose a subject for the next major project for A-R's features department. Cyril and I went to John McMillan, Controller of Programmes, with our idea. At that time it was a novel idea for ITV to tackle such a large subject. We asked for and were given a one-hour slot, and it turned out to be ITV's first documentary of that length. We had the naïve notion that we could tell the story of the rise and fall of Hitler in sixty minutes, and soon learnt that there were limitations to how much one could crowd into one hour. But we had a go – and it became frantic when we realised that transmission was only four weeks away.

By the end of that first day we had blocked out the ingredients for the programme and set the production in motion. We called it *Tyranny – The Years of Adolf Hitler*. We recruited Kenneth Harris from the *Observer* to be the presenter, met him for dinner that night to discuss his role, and also to select an authoritative historian/consultant and potential experts or eyewitnesses to take part in the programme.

We were lucky to recruit historian Alan Bullock (later Lord Bullock) to be the consultant. Author of the internationally renowned biography *Hitler: A Study in Tyranny* (1952), he also agreed to appear on the show and helped us to persuade Lord Strang to take part. Lord Strang had been permanent under-secretary of state at the Foreign Office, had accompanied Anthony Eden and later Neville Chamberlain on their missions to Germany, and had observed Hitler at close quarters. He raised the interesting point in the programme of whether the existence of television in the '30s might have altered the course of history. Sefton Delmer also agreed to take part. As a young man he became the *Daily Express* bureau chief in Berlin. In Germany's 1932 general election he travelled with Hitler on his private aircraft; he was also with Hitler when he inspected the 1933 Reichstag fire, and in his presence Hitler said, 'This is a God-given signal! If this fire, as I believe, turns out to be the handiwork of Communists, then there is nothing that shall stop us now crushing out this murder pest with an iron fist.'

Archive film research for the programme became a priority. I wanted to use as much German footage as possible and was surprised at the avalanche of material. It was fascinating to see how the German film industry had been geared to Hitler's propaganda machine. Leni Riefenstahl (personally appointed by Goebbels for the production of documentary films, and still sitting pretty in Germany at the time – with all the rights to her films restored to her) was responsible for the epics that made such sickening viewing for us. Technically these films were brilliant. Twenty sync units were under her command for her film of the 1934 Nuremberg Rally, *The Triumph of the Will*. I tremble to think of the shooting ratio. Copies of these films were lodged with the Imperial War Museum, and as all that material was classed as war booty no fees were paid to Riefenstahl. With all this footage from Movietone, Gaumont British, Pathé and others, as well as German newsreels, we set to work. I learned from the archivist in the Imperial War Museum that throughout the war there was a weekly exchange between British and German newsreels, which was orchestrated in neutral Lisbon.

Cyril Bennett quickly produced a script outline, and from this it became clear that we had to find some personal testimony: all the millions of feet of film failed to reveal anything of the man behind the public image. A quick telephone call was made to a young Austrian journalist in Innsbruck who had unique contacts with all sorts of famous and infamous people in Europe, and I made a date to meet him in Munich the following day. Reg Courtney-Browne, our chief researcher, came with me as a 'strong man' because I was unsure of what I was letting myself in for. It was also my first visit to Germany since my army days: twelve years had elapsed, and I was intrigued to find out how I would react on seeing Germans of my age or older, especially those in uniform such as customs officials and police – and whether I would speculate what their role might have been in the war. This became a preoccupation that was to last for several years.

We arrived in Munich on the last day of *Fasching*, a six-week carnival ending in a day of national merrymaking: people went about their business wearing false noses, funny hats, and grotesque make-up. (The mechanic refuelling our aircraft in Frankfurt wore a bandaged false nose dripping with 'blood'.) In this bizarre atmosphere of beer and sausages we met Gunter Peis, our Austrian contact, and through him an extraordinary collection of Hitler's 'nearest' – who were to make their public debut on worldwide television.

I hired a preview theatre and turned it into a studio, complete with a German cameraman and sound recordist, both sworn to secrecy, and spent six days coaxing, persuading and finally filming Hitler's sister, pilot, chauffeur, his adjutant and his adjutant's wife. They were secretly smuggled into the preview theatre by Peis, and agreed to cooperate provided I restricted the interviews to personal questions about Hitler. I did not expect to hear anything new about him, but what really surprised me was that they were willing to talk at all – and fourteen years since his defeat they showed undiminished respect and adoration for him. His sister referred to him simply as *mein Bruder* and the others as *der Chef* or *der Führer*. Here are some extracts from the interviews. They don't amount to much today, but in 1959 they grabbed the headlines.

Paula Wolf (seven years younger than her brother Adolf):

> When my brother, Adolf, was about two years old he once climbed up a ladder to the top rung. Mother heard that he was up there on the ladder and was frightened to death. She coaxed him to come down. She said, 'Be a good boy, come down.' He didn't move but stayed up and was very pleased with himself that no one could get at him.
>
> We had a very good mother. My brother loved Mother especially. When Mother said anything he obeyed, and when father said anything he always went against it.
>
> He had a real dislike of the female sex, up to the moment when he was grown up. And when Mother wanted him to get up in the morning, she only had to say to me, 'Go and give him a kiss.' She said it not very loud but still for him to hear, and as soon as he heard the word 'kiss' and that he was to get one from me, he was out of bed in a flash, because he just couldn't stand that. When we children played 'Red Indians' my brother Adolf was always the leader. All the others did what he told them. They must have had an instinct that his will was stronger than theirs. I next saw my brother Adolf in 1921, after twelve

years, and there I was face to face with a man who knew exactly what he wanted.

Frau Wilma Schaub (wife of Hitler's adjutant):

> Those rumours that Adolf Hitler was supposed to be abnormal over women are false. As the wife of the man who was his Adjutant for twenty years, I often had occasion to watch him in private and when in the company of ladies. I can assure you that he was definitely a very normal man. He loved women and loved to be in the presence of feminine beauty. I knew all about the relationship between him and Eva Braun from 1931 right up to the end. I also knew about many other love affairs.

Obergruppenführer Julius Schaub (Hitler's adjutant):

> (1924) While we were prisoners together at Landsberg, Adolf Hitler spent the mornings working on his book Mein Kampf. After supper he used to read out several chapters from his book. There were discussions; for us that was an education, because at that time we hadn't realised just what Adolf Hitler was planning to do.
> (1933) Adolf Hitler came in and joined us in the room in the Reich Chancellery. He came from seeing the President. And of his own accord, he said, 'Friends, no power in the world will ever get me out of this place alive.' Maybe it was a premonition of the bitter end in 1945. He also said, 'There's no more private life for me. From now on, all my work is going to be for my people.' And that was the reason why he never entered into matrimony.
> (1938) I made a lot of journeys with the Führer in the car. I never saw Adolf Hitler moved like he was on our triumphal entry into Linz. The crowd went mad with joy. As we entered the Town Hall he said to me, 'And now a lifelong dream has been fulfilled.'
> (1943) 'Adolf Hitler's state of health got a lot worse because of the set-backs on the front, especially after the battle of Stalingrad. He couldn't sleep, his nerves got worse and he had to take to medicine. But I must kill all those rumours – his brain was clear right up to his death.
> (1945) I entered his bedroom in the bunker with him. On the table there was a 7.5mm pistol. He went up to it. I got a terrible shock. He cocked the gun – but no, it wasn't the last hour yet. He was only making sure it was loaded.

Flug Kapitän Hans Bauer (Hitler's personal pilot):

> (1945) Approximately one-half to three-quarters of an hour before Hitler's death on 30 April he sent for me. When I reported, he took both my hands in his and said to me, 'Bauer, I want to say goodbye to you.' I was so stupefied I could not speak. This parting took twenty minutes. He said, 'Bauer, I have two more orders for you. The first is, I make you personally responsible for burning the corpses of my wife and me. The second is, see to it that Bormann gets through to Doenitz. Doenitz will become my natural successor. I have given Bormann large numbers of orders and documents to take with him to Doenitz.' All the time I was struck by Hitler's clear way of speaking. I couldn't believe that this was to be the finish.

Obersturmbannführer Erich Kempka (Hitler's chauffeur):

> (1945) When I saw the Chief for the last time, I definitely had the feeling that the end was near. But there was no change in him that you could see – not in his character, nor anything else. He said goodbye and dismissed me. Next day, when the Chief was dead, I went to the bunker just as they were carrying out the corpse. Then came Martin Bormann with Eva Braun in his arms. I took her body away from him and carried her along behind Adolf Hitler. We placed these two bodies side by side in the garden. I had placed on me the exceptionally difficult moral duty of pouring petrol on them and setting fire to them. The corpses burnt from half-past-one until half-past seven in the evening.

This last sentence sounded like a well-rehearsed, if rather bizarre, statistic. But it was during the preliminary softening-up discussions with these people that I heard some unfamiliar stories about Hitler. How, for instance, he learned to mistrust his own press soon after becoming chancellor. Once he ordered a certain article to be suppressed. When he went through his own editions of the morning papers he saw that the order had been obeyed. But, by pure chance he picked up his chauffeur's paper while he was being driven to a reception. It happened to be a later edition, and it carried the banned article. From that day onwards he cancelled the chancellery's subscription for papers and magazines, insisting that they should be bought in the street from different newspaper kiosks each morning.

I was told that Hitler was a great believer in England and her parliamentary system, and that he was convinced the future of Germany and Britain was closely linked; together they would be the world power bloc and dictate to the other nations. He had, in fact, completed a manuscript of a new book, which he called *My Alliance with England*. But on the day our ambassador handed him the note that declared war, Hitler, in a blind fury, stormed out of the room into his private study, threw his manuscript on the carpeted floor and set fire to it.

One of Hitler's habits, I was told, was that during the war he only went to bed after the last Allied aircraft had left German air space. He must have had many sleepless nights. I also learned that he was the 'dictator without a bank account'. He did not draw one pfennig from the state in the form of salary or expenses, but lived entirely on the royalties of *Mein Kampf*.

The Eher-Verlag, publishers of the *Völkischer Beobachter* (the Nazi Party newspaper) handled this book and his royalties. Whenever Hitler required cash his adjutant, Schaub, rang up the publisher and drew out the necessary amount. They, in turn, made a huge profit from the interest on Hitler's money, which grew to a large fortune; when he killed himself he was worth 5 million marks.

For me, those six days in Munich were both fascinating and nauseating: fascinating because of these new stories I heard, and nauseating because I heard them from the mouths of people who revered Hitler as much then as they had ever done. It was hard to suppress my thoughts; but I forced myself to concentrate solely on the end product – an interesting and I hope worthwhile programme.

Back in London the physical work of getting the programme on the air was in full swing. I had brought back a case full of original photographs, documents and gramophone records – to the extent that we were embarrassed by the abundance of good material. Now had to face the agony of deciding what to exclude. The midnight sessions started: writing commentary, translating the German dialogue, editing the film elements to be inserted into the live programme, and recording and dubbing the final soundtrack. Cyril and I frequently met Kenneth Harris to tie up the contents of the studio side, and with my PA, Joan Jarratt, feverishly typing the camera script (which she got far too late from me, as usual), we were ready to move to Wembley Studios. The 12 foot blow-up of Hitler's face dominated Studio 2, and his baleful, piercing eyes followed us everywhere.

I thought up a technique of integrating the live studio elements with the film clips to make these transitions both logical and seamless. The set designer made large photographic blow-ups of the very first frame of each of the film clips, and these were framed and hung from the lighting gantry: it made the studio look like an art exhibition. When Kenneth Harris turned to camera after a live studio interview to introduce the next bit of film, I cued the camera to track past him to the appropriate picture frame, cued the operator to start the telecine machine and, as the film started, cued the vision mixer to cut to the clip – making the still picture come to life. It was all very primitive but it worked. Looking back on it now, it is a graphic reminder of the many opportunities we were able to exploit in those early days by trying something that had never been done before.

On 4 March 1959, with headlines from the tabloids screaming, for example, 'Hitler's Sister Breaks Her Silence On ITV Tonight', we went on the air. *Tyranny – The Years of Adolf Hitler* attracted a huge audience. It was number two in that week's top ten, with close to 10 million viewers. It also sparked off an avalanche of press cuttings, of which these are a small selection:

James Thomas, *Daily Express*: 'As a TV documentary on Hitler it was one step ahead of anything before: documentary which did not rant, which did not spark off phoney argument, which handled its subject with sober authority and careful good language.'

Peter Black, Daily Mail: 'The editing was brilliant. The programme stands comparison with any of the similar films made by the NBC Twentieth Century series.'

Television Today: 'More documentaries like this from A-R and they will well rival the BBC in this important field.'

Most live programmes, like *Tyranny*, were not telerecorded 'off-air' but were sadly lost into the ether. By 1959 A-R had acquired the first two Ampex video recording machines from the States, with their extremely costly 2 inch Quad videotapes. These were mainly used for recording programmes in advance of transmission and then for their playback. The film elements of these programmes, clips as they are called, which would have been simple to archive, were also disposed of. Nevertheless I always assumed that the interviews I had made with Hitler's cronies had survived, because I was told that they were sold to American Television soon after our transmission.

Twenty-seven years later, in 1986, a seminar was about to be staged at BAFTA, the subject being Programme Preservation, and I was on the panel. This caused me to have a belated search for my German footage, as this would have been the only remains of the *Tyranny* programme. I failed, however, and came to the sad conclusion that this historical material had really disappeared. A-R had lost its franchise in 1968, and I could not find a survivor from the rump of the company who might have known where to find long-forgotten records that would have helped to trace the missing film. I told the story of this lost material to the assembled audience, and at the end of the afternoon session Richard King came up to me with some news. He was a regional executive of the Independent Broadcasting Authority, a mere schoolboy when *Tyranny* was transmitted. That year, 1959, he had been given an open-reel quarter-inch audio tape recorder, and thanks to his growing interest in history he decided to record the programme. Richard graphically described his method. He tied his microphone to the back of a chair and pushed it up against the side of the television set that housed the loudspeaker. He asked his mother to put down her knitting, as his mike was picking up the clicks of the needles. Then he made a remarkably good audio recording of the whole programme – including, of course, the German interviews. He let me make a copy from his master tape and I was able to marry up the audio of the interviews with stills taken during the filming sessions in Munich all those years ago. I have put this film to good use as part of my portfolio of programmes for seminars, colleges and museums.

In January 2005, as I was gathering the photographs for these pages and as Jane was proofreading this chapter, a call came out of the blue from a Munich-based documentary film company that was making a programme about Hitler's private life for the German ZDF Television network. They had scoured the world's archives for footage of Paula Wolf, and their research had led them to a documentary called *Family Hitler*, which was made in the United States in 1960 and contained all my material of Hitler's cronies as they had appeared in *Tyranny* the year before. The company invited me to Munich to identify the lost material, and it was quite spooky to view it again after forty-six years. They interviewed me, then and there, for their film, and recorded my impressions, especially of Paula Wolf. It just goes to show that one must never give up looking for lost treasures.

* * * *

Immediately after *Tyranny* we were given the opportunity to make another sixty-minute documentary. This time Cyril Bennett chose the subject – a programme we called *Israel Rises – The Birth of a Nation*. The link between this and our last documentary became even more obvious the moment we started our three weeks of location filming, as we met many people who were tragic witnesses to Hitler's regime of extermination. As we travelled from Galilee in the north to Negev in the south, we never ceased to be amazed at the surprisingly arrogant confidence, happiness and sense of achievement written on the faces of the younger Israelis. Although it is no larger than Wales, Israel is a long, narrow country and our two camera cars travelled over 3,000 miles to many fascinating locations. But this was first and last a story about people. Instead of handling the programme as a straight objective historical analysis as in *Tyranny,* we were faced with a wealth of human material to capture and record. I enjoyed hearing the story of the Canadian reporter who, after touring the country for several weeks, told his guide: 'Fine! Now take me to the Jewish quarter.' This shows the impact that Israel makes on the first-time observer – transforming the Jew into an Israeli, adding to the traditional ethnic and religious awareness a new national identity. Filming in a kibbutz brought this home to this first-timer. I became aware of the many cultural problems stacking up that had to be solved, so that the many Jews seeking a home in Israel from places as diverse as Yemen and Morocco could be successfully integrated. At that time one was barely aware of the build-up to continuing strife that the future had in store for this new nation.

We managed to arrange an interview with Prime Minister Ben Gurion, who led the struggle to establish the state of Israel in 1948. As we had to be ready for filming in his office at eight in the morning, Cyril and I and the crew rose very early in the apartment we had rented in Tel Aviv and motored to Jerusalem. As the prime minister's office was lit and ready by half past seven, with the camera in position, we went to a café opposite his office building for breakfast. It was a beautiful sunny morning and we occupied a long trestle table on the pavement with benches on each side; I sat on a stool at one end. Then a small elderly man with flowing white hair and open-necked shirt came up to us: 'You must be the television team from England who have come to see me. Can I join you for coffee?'

Ben Gurion swung his legs over the bench next to me, I ordered some coffee and we had an interesting conversation. 'What sort of things do you show on television?'

I told him that we had just transmitted a programme about the rise and fall of Hitler.

'Surely people in England wouldn't be that interested to look at such a thing?'

I explained that it happened to be the second most popular programme that week. In fact, nearly 10 million people had viewed it.

'Nearly 10 million people?' asked the prime minister of an eleven-year-old country with a population of under 2 million – and without a television service. 'Nearly 10 million people? Have they nothing better to do?'

As with *Tyranny* this was a live studio-based broadcast, and Kenneth Harris was the presenter again. With him in the studio were experts on Israel: Ambassador Abba Eban, Lady Megan Lloyd George, whose father had signed the Balfour Declaration, and Professor Laurence Rushbrook Williams.

The 'morning-after press' was mixed. Maurice Wiggin wrote in the *Sunday Times*: 'In the not-overcrowded field of solid information, ITV had a very good week with Associated-Rediffusion's massive, searching study of a nation nascent, "Israel Rises".' In the *Daily Mail* Peter Black commented: 'The director, and scriptwriter compiled a picture, which despite some curious omissions gave a stirring impression of a country vibrating with a sense of purposeful destiny. The historical record, the interviews, the final analyses were cool and informative. The programme most commendably kept a level head amid emotional tugs.' The *Jewish Chronicle* was more critical:

> Israel Through A Clouded Lens. Mr Morley's Mistake.
>
> Are Israelis to be simply divided into the category of pathetic immigrant, bearded rabbi or trigger-happy youth? Is Kenneth Harris gleefully looking forward to Israel's early demise? Was this the best

> that producer Peter Morley and his ITV team could do? Using nearly every technical trick in the box, the production mixed film shot with studio interview to the point of irritation and irrelevance. But, basically, the major mistake was the attempt to stuff the history of Israel into one hour, less several minutes of commercials. The programme was rescued from complete inconsequence only by the interview with Ben-Gurion and the display of diplomatic patience presented by Abba Eban under a barrage of loaded questions delivered by Kenneth Harris with the bite of a prosecuting counsel. And yet it was the same ITV team, which only recently dealt so magnificently with the story of Hitler's Germany. Perhaps Mr Morley should be given the benefit of the doubt, and *Israel Rises* set aside as 'just one of those things'.

This rather skewed view at least highlighted the limitations of television as a purveyor of detailed information. In order to hold an audience with its notoriously short attention span, there is just so much one dares to pile into sixty minutes. The conflict, as I have said before, between what to include and what to leave unsaid is frustrating. If one prints out every word uttered in a non-fiction film or programme it results in the thinnest of pamphlets. *Israel Rises,* in spite of these limitations, was appreciated by a large television audience, which stayed with it to the end. But the contribution it made to a deeper understanding of Israel's role in the Middle East, and what the future might hold for the country, was modest.

12: ITV's First Opera

What with *Tyranny* and *Israel Rises,* the first half of 1959 had been pretty hectic. The next six months were an adventure of a totally different kind.

In 1954 Benjamin Britten had completed his opera *The Turn of the Screw,* which is based on Henry James's novella, written in 1898. Together with the librettist Myfanwy Piper, Britten created what some connoisseurs consider to be his finest opera. It had its inaugural performance at the Teatro la Fenice in Venice in September 1954 and opened at London's Sadler's Wells Theatre three weeks later. I didn't know anything about opera, other than listening to the odd radio performance from Covent Garden, and I was totally unfamiliar with Britten's music; but my sister Anne had been his ardent fan for a number of years and managed to drag me, somewhat reluctantly, to the London premiere of *The Turn of the Screw* (my first visit to an opera house), with Benjamin Britten conducting. I was totally captivated, so much so that I went to the next three performances, this time standing at the back of the stalls – which was still possible at Sadler's Wells in those days. It was an extraordinary experience for me and left a lasting impression.

Five years later, with a fair amount of programme-making under my belt, it occurred to me that Britten could have written this opera for television. It is a story that is intimate, claustrophobic, haunted and haunting, with a small cast and small orchestra. In the original novella Henry James deliberately sets out to force his readers to apply their imaginations to a number of situations, which he only indicates in a most tantalising way. Indeed, it is the individual interpretation that one is compelled to make that adds to the excitement of the story. Benjamin Britten and Myfanwy Piper transformed this into a most thrilling and satisfying experience on the stage. I was convinced that the intimacy of its atmosphere and the scale of the relationship between the characters were ideally suited to television, and I harboured a desire to bring it to the small screen one day. I knew that many problems would have to be resolved, in addition to the obvious technical ones, such as the balance between the real and the abstract, and preserving the ambiguity of who was haunting whom; also, how to present the ghosts without the intrusion of the mechanics of television. The guiding principle from the outset had to be the production's simplicity, so that the richness of the score and the conflicts of the characters could predominate.

At this point I must recall the hoops Associated-Rediffusion had been through in its first four franchise years, having been awarded, in 1955, what was considered the plum contract – London, Monday to Friday. A-R's initial investment was heavy, and as I have mentioned by its first anniversary of going on the air the company had lost £3 million. At that time Associated Newspapers wanted to get out of the partnership and sold 80 per cent of its shares to Rediffusion. 'Associated' was soon to be dropped from the company's name. By 1959 things were very different. The annual profits had reached £2.7 million, and senior management began to think about the company's future, girding itself for the dreaded franchise renewal five years on in 1964. To this end they went on a mission to score 'brownie points' by backing programmes that were out of the ordinary, that might bring prestige and chalk up some plus marks on the ITA's franchise scorecard. Support of the arts was on the agenda, with both the London Symphony Orchestra and the Hallé Orchestra benefiting from this largesse, not only with financial support but also with a spate of outside-broadcast concerts finding a place in the television schedules.

When, early in 1959, I decided to put in a plea for A-R to back me in staging a television version of *The Turn of the Screw,* I was unaware of ITV franchise politics, as I was far too busy making programmes, but with hindsight I realise that my timing was fortuitous. I had a very good relationship with John McMillan, the Programme Controller, boosted by the success of the Hitler and Israel documentaries, which enjoyed a good press and high viewer ratings: I was, temporarily, a blue-eyed boy on A-R's executive floor. With fingers crossed, I went to see McMillan.

'John, you owe me,' I said.

'All right, Pete [he was the only person ever to call me that]. What are you selling?'

'I want to do *The Turn of the Screw.*'

'What is it?'

'It's a ghost story by Henry James.'

'But you're not a drama director. You've never directed a play in your life.'

'John, it's not a play.'

'What is it then?'

'It's an opera.'

He nearly fell off his chair. 'You must be out of your mind. Who wrote it?'

'Benjamin Britten.'

I feared he was going to throw me out of his office. Instead he glanced up at the ceiling and I could see his mind ticking over fast: John McMillan was no slouch. 'Come and see me next week. I can't promise anything.'

When we met again he wanted further details. I said that there were hurdles to cross, the main ones being Britten's approval and his collaboration. There were also other conditions that I knew were going to be very unpopular, but which I had to clear before I approached Britten. The first was that I wanted to make it clear to Britten that I would not allow one note to be cut from his score. John agreed after I explained that the work was in two acts, each lasting approximately sixty minutes. And then I stipulated the really tough one: 'No commercial breaks.' I thought this would kill the whole project stone dead. To my surprise John saw the point, and said the two acts might have to be interrupted by the ITN news. As it turned out, the ITV network stipulated that the acts had to be separated and aired over two nights – possibly the longest commercial break in history!

'How about the budget?' I asked.

'Leave that to me. I'll take care of that,' came the reply, and I thought, what a wonderful way to run a shop.

This was typical John McMillan. He knew as little about opera as I did, yet he trusted me not to let him down. Tragically those exciting times, when it was possible for a brave entrepreneur like John to call all the shots, disappeared a long time ago. The bean-counters were destined to take over.

The time had arrived to sell the concept to Benjamin Britten. I arranged a date with his secretary and drove to the East coast, to Aldeburgh, a journey I was to repeat several times that year. I checked in at the Brudenell Hotel, on the edge of the North Sea, and set off for the Red House, which Britten shared with Peter Pears. I had been asked to be in time for lunch, and when they both appeared I was asked to join them for a drink; it took no time at all for the ice to break. I soon got the impression that Britten was intrigued by the idea of trying something new. Television was rather foreign to him, but he said that he liked experimenting, and seemed very open to ideas and new challenges. Peter Pears, who had created the role of Quint in *The Turn of the Screw,* was also excited by the thought of a television version. Sadly he was not able to take part, as he had other commitments in Switzerland that clashed with the crucial production dates.

I made it very clear to them from the start that I wished to retain the spirit, style and attitude, the very essence of the original production, but in order to achieve that for television there would have to be adaptations. This idea was well received.

After lunch I joined Britten on one of his constitutional walks along Aldeburgh's deserted beach. The noise of the sea breaking on the shingle must have inspired so much of his music, and I was aware of my good fortune to be in the company of this great composer. He probed me about ITV and the sort of programmes I had made. Then he asked what my opera experience was, and when I told him that I knew nothing about opera, and could not even read one note of music, he laughed and said that we would probably get on quite well with each other. The look of relief on my face must have been palpable, and I got the distinct feeling that he thought the enterprise was worth trying.

When we got back to his house Britten said that he wanted to discuss the project with his publishers, Boosey & Hawkes, and suggested a date for my next visit. He also wanted to consult Stephen Reiss, the general manager of the Aldeburgh-based English Opera Group, which would provide the know-how of the original production and, crucially, the cast, the orchestra, John Piper's stage and costume designs, and the consultancy services of Colin Graham, the Group's present producer. He hoped to persuade John Piper to come up to Suffolk for the next meeting, as there were design issues to be discussed. Piper had worked closely with Britten for a number of years and had created the designs for most of his operas. I was looking forward to meeting him.

I went back to London to continue to familiarise myself with the opera and to marshal my thoughts and reasoning for all the points that had to be resolved. Having purchased the Decca set of long-playing records of the original production, I spent many hours listening to them, and annotating the score with early ideas concerning visualisation. I had taken a couple of lessons to help me read the score, and that proved to be essential when it came to the final broadcast. There was now one major conundrum to be solved, as it had been worrying me for some time.

The opera is divided into two acts, with eight scenes to each act. The end of each of these scenes is linked to the next scene by musical 'Variations' which prepare you for the scene to come; the music helping you to anticipate the next turn of the screw. For me, this is some of the most magnificent music Britten has composed. In the original stage production the stage went black, the auditorium was in darkness and one was not aware of minor scene changes – in which some of John Piper's glorious gauzes that predominated the set were replaced. This device of creating total darkness achieved an atmosphere in which the audience was able to listen to the music undisturbed by stage distractions. That was my problem. One simply could not plunge a television network, let alone a commercial one, into screen blackout: some of the 'Variations' lasted two minutes! I was well aware that after three seconds the audience would expect a caption to come up stating that 'normal service will be resumed shortly'.

I was able to put forward a solution to this problem on my next visit to the Red House to meet Britten again, as well as John Piper – who also made me feel very much at ease. My proposal was for the cameras to explore specially created abstract paintings during the 'Variations'. They would be in harmony with the music and would enhance it, without causing a visual distraction. Britten was really intrigued, and asked Piper what he thought. He in turn suggested that I should meet him again to take the idea a stage further. I gladly accepted.

The following week Michael Yates accompanied me on this important visit. He had been head of television design at the BBC and took up this position with A-R when ITV started. He was a brilliant set designer and he was now going to interpret the original stage set for television, retaining John Piper's original Venice and Sadler's Wells concept.

Fawley Bottom, near Henley-on-Thames, was John and Myfanwy Piper's home. Now I was able to meet the opera's librettist as well. She acted as a very perceptive and enthusiastic sounding board as our ideas for the production evolved, and that was very encouraging. We were given a conducted tour of Piper's huge studio – which was a real eye-opener. I was struck by the prolific output from this great artist, including examples of what he called his 'experiments'. One was a huge galvanised tank filled with water. He picked up some tubes of oil paint and squirted their contents onto the water's surface, and gently created a strange pattern with a stick. Then he dragged a large sheet of paper across the surface and produced some stunning designs. 'One day I might master this,' he said.

John Piper was in the middle of his stained glass period, in which he was exploring the properties of stained glass and the effect of light on it and through it. He had been commissioned to create the baptistery window for Basil Spence's new Coventry Cathedral, which had been totally destroyed in the blitz. And there, on a trestle table, was the recently completed model he had made of the window. Some years later, while filming in Coventry, I went to the rebuilt cathedral and saw the window in its full glory. I recalled my good luck in having had this masterly work explained to me by its creator.

I had brought with me my set of Decca LPs, to try to explain to John Piper what I was after. We settled in front of his gramophone and by trial-and-error use of the pick-up I managed to find each of the sixteen 'Variations'. I attempted, in a fumbling way, to find the right expressions for what I was seeing in my mind's eye – and how it might look on the screen. He listened patiently and made some notes as I was talking, and then we had a long discussion. All this took several hours, after which he said, 'It sounds as though I'll have to come up with about twenty or thirty drawings or paintings. When do you need them by?'

'I'm due to be in the studio six weeks from now.'

'I thought you might give me at least six months – but I'll see what I can do.'

A week before going into the studio I received a huge bundle delivered by British Rail. I can't remember ever feeling such excitement in opening a parcel as – one by one – the most apt, surprising and brilliant illustrations were revealed. The problem set by the 'Variations' had been solved. There was a note attached, which simply said, 'Sorry I am a bit late with these. I hope they will do – if there are any you don't like, let me know and I will quickly send you alternatives. Good luck, John.' John Piper has been my hero ever since. (He later presented me with the signed illustration for Act 1, Variation III, which has hung over my fireplace ever since – a prized possession.)

The contracts department of A-R had completed the necessary agreement with the English Opera Group, and I was at last able to meet all the key people. The cast list included two singers from the original production: Jennifer Vyvian played the governess, and Arda Mandikian Miss Jessel. The role of Quint (created by Peter Pears) was played by Raymond Nilsson, and Judith Pearce was Mrs Grose, the housekeeper. The two children, Flora and Miles, were played by Janette Miller and Tom Bevan. David Hemmings had been the original Miles but now, five years later, his voice had well and truly broken. Charles Mackerras was engaged to conduct the English Opera Group Orchestra, and Paul Hamburger was the assistant conductor.

Basil Coleman, who had produced the original Venice version for the English Opera Group, had handed over the baton to his assistant, Colin Graham. For the five-year period, since 1954, he had been responsible for staging the opera in different venues here and abroad. And now, before I could start on my rehearsals, he trained the cast to make sure that musically they remained true to the original. I had never worked with artistes before, let alone opera singers, and it was with some trepidation that I welcomed them to our rehearsal rooms in the YWCA in Museum Street. I had spent the previous day there with my two stage managers, marking out the floor areas with coloured camera tape to show the outline of the studio sets, and we were ready to go. I think everyone felt a bit awkward at first, but coffee and sticky buns procured by my PA soon broke the ice. I asked them to gather round so I could explain the difference between a stage and a television production, and introduced them to some of the technical disciplines demanded by television. I got a very warm response from them all, and from that moment on an atmosphere developed that was based on hard work and friendly banter.

Paul Hamburger provided the piano accompaniment, and I found it particularly rewarding to work closely with Colin Graham in creating the cast's stage directions, which were quite different from those they had all mastered for the opera stage. My most important prop was my master camera script – a hugely heavy Twinlock A3 loose-leaf book. Each sheet had one page of the score pasted on the right-hand side, leaving the left for my annotations for the moves of the cameras, microphone booms and the artistes, together with all other instructions, both for me and my vision mixer.

Half-way through the rehearsal period Benjamin Britten came up to London to spend the day with us at the YWCA. He said that he simply couldn't stay away, and was very intrigued by the strange way that television went about portraying his precious opera. He made some very helpful suggestions, and remarked that he would really have liked to be able to conduct the orchestra. Sadly he couldn't spare the time, and in any case he was suffering from a painful shoulder ailment which would have made it impossible.

It is hard to remember the technical limitations we worked under in the late '50s. It is almost impossible now, for a generation grown up in front of a television set, to realise that studio productions were transmitted 'live': they were continuous performances – warts and all. The means of video recording were primitive, to say the least. Videocassette recorders for the home had yet to be invented. The previous year A-R had acquired the first two Ampex studio video recorders from America. These were huge machines that required a forklift truck to move them; heavy spools held the very costly 2 inch wide videotapes. Video editing as we know it today was still a thing of the future. When plays were transmitted millions of viewers witnessed the mishaps during transmissions. If a microphone boom came into shot, or a floor manager tripped over a camera cable, or an actor dried up it was seen by all. You simply pressed on: there was no going back, no means of 'doing that bit again'. Plays were often recorded in advance of transmission onto Ampex tapes for studio planning reasons, but it always had to be 'take one': there was no other choice. At the time video recording was merely a time-shift device, and we called it 'recording as for live'. The only exception was when something really dire happened during a recording and it had to be stopped half-way through, maybe a key camera breaking down, a power failure or a scenery flat falling over. The offending bit could be physically cut out from the tape before restarting the recording, but as the cost of the tapes was huge this was always an emergency operation. Watching the technician carry out this procedure was nail-biting. He had to spool the tape and stop on the exact frame where the cut had to be made. Then he pulled that section of the tape under a microscope and sprinkled what looked like very fine iron filings onto the section. These formed a visible magnetic pattern, and by looking through the microscope he could determine exactly where to make the cut with a razor blade. Next he had to find the point on the other piece of tape, do the same to that and join them together with some special agent. That expensive tape was then useless for future use. No wonder that 'editing' was discouraged. Naturally *The Turn of the Screw* had to go out 'live', but scheduling the studios presented a problem because I had to ask for two – one for the actual production and the second for Charles Mackerras and the orchestra. The only way A-R could make these available was to allow me to pre-record – 'as for live' – on two weekends, with Act I on the first and Act II on the second, using two of the largest studios in A-R's Wembley complex. On the Saturday we would have our first camera rehearsal and a 'stagger through', and on the Sunday a 'run through', a final camera rehearsal, and then in the evening the actual recording.

A camera was permanently trained on Charles Mackerras in his studio, and its output was relayed to an array of TV monitors carefully placed in the main studio, where possible within sight of the artistes as they moved around the sets. They sang to a low-level playback of the orchestra, which came from a set of speakers hung from the lighting gantries. Paul Hamburger hopped around the set, repeating the conductor's arm movements – taking his cues from the monitors. I was full of admiration for the cast, who took to this bizarre discipline with gusto.

At that time the cameras were huge and heavy; I used four of them, with three on wheeled pedestals and one on a crane. Zoom lenses only came into studios in the 1960s, and tracking in or out with fixed lens cameras was always tricky, especially when I attempted camera moves on John Piper's illustrations for the 'Variations'.

In the control gallery, which overlooked the studio floor, I had my PA, Rosemary Winckley, on my left calling the shot numbers, and Bridget Booth, my vision mixer, to my right. We faced a clutch of monitors displaying each camera's output, and immediately in front of us was my mammoth camera script. Colin Graham was also present, and whenever we broke the rehearsal we went down on the studio floor to give notes to the cast.

The set that Michael Yates realised from John Piper's original designs was quite magical, and as I walked around it I could sense the atmosphere of Henry James's ghostly novella. What a shame that we had to wait another eight years in the UK for colour television.

In October 1959, after four months' planning, five weeks' rehearsal, and now four days in the studios, we were about to commit *The Turn of the Screw* to videotape, including a short introduction to each act by Lord Harewood, President of the English Opera Group. A telegram arrived, addressed to me at the studio: 'Good luck to all. Ben Britten.'

The meticulous planning of every shot, every camera move, the cues to floor managers, lighting changes and so on were now put to the test – and all worked as planned. And then, shock and horror, half-way through the recording of the second act I lost one of my cameras. At a blow all the detailed planning became meaningless, and we had to act very quickly and improvise; luckily it sprang back to life after a few long minutes. The brilliance of the camera and boom operators, floor staff and vision mixer saved the day. Through their skill we managed to cover up so well that viewers were unaware of this disaster.

It was a huge relief when it was all done and I was able to say to the studio 'It's a wrap.' It was the first time that I had been in charge of a major television production – and with this came my great good luck to have had the privilege to produce an opera with the help and advice of those who created it for the stage.

A-R's press office now busily promoted the actual transmissions, which were scheduled across two evenings at Christmas that year. A press preview was arranged for 10 December 1959 at Television House in Kingsway, and when I studied the formidable list of invitees, including Benjamin Britten, John and Myfanwy Piper, Lord and Lady Harewood, Stephen Reiss and the cast, I clearly recall an attack of first-night nerves.

In addition to the usual roll-call of television critics and journalists, music and opera critics were present in force – Donald Mitchell, Desmond Shawe-Taylor, Edmund Tracey and many more. What a relief when the screening was over and cocktails were served. Britten and the Pipers were more than complimentary; all three were pleasantly surprised at how well the translation of the opera to television had worked, and felt that the adaptation had caught the spirit of the original production much better than they had thought possible.

It was sad to say farewell to the cast, especially to Jennifer Vyvian. She was vivacious and fun loving and we met again at the following year's Aldeburgh Festival. We kept in touch right up to her tragic early death.

Four days after the preview I received this hand-written letter:

> Dear Peter,
> I must write a note (only a note because other operatic matters press on me!) to congratulate you most sincerely on a really fine achievement. I thought the production of the Turn of the Screw most convincing. I am not very experienced in 'watching' T.V. but all the people I mind about who were there said that it was easily the best operatic T.V. production they had seen, & I can quite believe it. Anyhow you've quite convinced me that serious opera works on that screen, as long it is done with your taste & skill. Do let's talk sometime about the whole subject, & in the mean time many thanks for your endless trouble and patience.
> Yours, Benjamin B

Ten days later, over Christmas 1959, *The Turn of the Screw* was seen on the ITV network. It felt odd to sit back in the comfort of my home, instead of having to sweat it out in the studio, as a machine some miles away played back the results of my labours. Of course I was intrigued to watch my own work and, as always, wished that I had done certain things differently – perpetuating the programme-maker's mantra: 'If only I could do it all over again . . .'.

The reaction of the press over the next few days was extremely good, and I was very glad that a number of influential papers applauded A-R for being so adventurous. A lot of mail arrived at Television House, and this letter, sent to A-R's managing director, Paul Adorian, must have gone down well with his Board of Directors:

> THE ARTS COUNCIL OF GREAT BRITAIN,
> 4, St. James's Square, London, S.W.1
> Chairman: Sir Kenneth Clark, C.H. K.C.B, D.Litt, I.L.D.
> 31st December 1959.
>
> Dear Adorian,

> I feel I must write you a letter of congratulation on A-R's production of The Turn of the Screw. Programmes of this kind done for a minority very often don't come off, and succeed in pleasing nobody, but this was really a masterpiece of television, both as production, performance and photography.
>
> In fact, as a work of art I think it the best thing the medium has ever produced. I have seen the opera many times, and to tell the truth I thought it came off better on the T.V. than it had ever done in the opera house. I am quite sure that one or two productions of this kind do the medium an immense amount of good, and even from the commercial point of view, are money well spent. They are the sort of argument which the friends of commercial television will be able to use when the whole subject comes up for review.
>
> Please give my warmest congratulations to John McMillan and to everyone else concerned.
>
> Yours very sincerely,
> Kenneth Clark

And then the viewing figures were published. The TAM (Television Audience Measurement) ratings were the commercial yardstick for ITV's audience size, as well as the share of the overall audience with the BBC. These weekly statistics, which were avidly scrutinised by advertisers and broadcasters alike, were obtained by means of meters that were attached to television sets in several thousand homes. These meters looked like barographs, with a rotating drum covered with graph paper and an inked needle tracing the time the set was switched on and to which channel, BBC or ITV. It did not measure whether anyone was actually watching anything, but it was accepted as the best system available at the time. Years later this important data would be remotely accessed, but back in the late '50s a TAM representative used to call once a week on the selected homes to collect the graph paper and attach a fresh one. *The Turn of the Screw* broke a record: it registered a rating of precisely nil, the inked needles having failed to spring into action. I was not a bit surprised (neither was John McMillan) that ITV's excursion into an area even the BBC would class as esoteric programming failed to produce a measurable audience. However, McMillan bravely commissioned an independent research organisation to discover whether anyone at all had watched the programme.

Several months later interesting statistics came to light. Sadler's Wells Theatre (where the opera was first performed) seated an audience of 1,600. The research project established that the number of people who actually watched *The Turn of the Screw* would have filled Sadler's Wells for eight performances a week for sixteen weeks – an audience of just over 200,000 people. As a TAM rating, where audiences are measured in millions, this miserable total was an unmitigated disaster, but in terms of opera-going audiences it was an unprecedented and colossal triumph.

McMillan asked A-R's graphic design department to create a colour brochure to celebrate the opera. Our designers were well known in the industry for the company's in-house magazine, *Fusion*, which was winning a host of awards. They were able to draw on a rich selection of excellent production stills, but in addition they asked the main contributors for short comments; today these have become useful archival material, and are preserved in the Britten-Pears Library in Aldeburgh:

> Benjamin Britten: This is the first time in this country that an opera of mine has been specially produced on television, and I am extremely grateful to Associated-Rediffusion for its enterprise and courage in mounting THE TURN OF THE SCREW. I am particularly happy that it should have been this opera that was chosen because it is one of my works most close to me, and also the one I feel most suitable for television.
>
> Television can do an enormous amount to popularise opera in this country, especially if it avoids the spectacular Grand Opera so beloved by the eighteenth and nineteenth centuries and concentrates

on the intimate and concise, which seems to me to belong particularly to the present day.

I cannot praise too highly the skill, taste and knowledge shown in adapting this difficult opera for television, especially when coupled with a respect for the score which did not allow one note to be cut.

Myfanwy Piper: The work is a combination of strangeness and intimacy, and so for television, at its best in conveying both these, an obviously suitable subject. What surprises and delights is, that without distorting or adapting, the producer has made it seem as though it were specially created for the medium. It has illusion without apparent trickery, reality without realism, as it must in any presentation, but a new kind – so it is a new experience. It makes me realise how much can be done with the exuberant possibilities of television when they are used with tact and sensibility.

John Piper: This scenery is a matter of creating atmosphere, not of presenting facts. Scale, texture and a telling disposition of darks and lights are all-important. As to texture, I was surprised to find how well it could be realised by the television cameras, and how many new means of suggesting it are possible. The matter of lights and darks I found exciting, because the medium does not so much reflect light, as it allows light to pierce through darkness, as in stained glass. Here again the possibilities seem enormous. But it is in the matter of scale that I was most interested of all. You can move, for instance, from a small drawing, with some tiny scribbles or spots of darkness on it, to a full-sized theatre cloth with a figure in front of it without any jolt to the eye, so that scale momentarily disappears, and there is the thrill of being in a no-man's-land of dimension, which can be most helpful in a highly atmospheric work.

Stephen Reiss (General Manager of the English Opera Group): For many years we have been trying to produce vital English operas, but, mainly for financial reasons, the public has had very little chance of seeing the results. We therefore have every reason to be grateful to Associated-Rediffusion for putting one of our works onto television, and, in THE TURN OF THE SCREW, we feel that Peter Morley has chosen an opera ideally suited to the medium. The original production has inevitably had to undergo a complete metamorphosis, but, by his understanding of the opera and the style we have striven to create, he has made sure that the impact remains as strong as ever. The English Opera Group feels that, if just a handful of people, who have never seen opera before, make their acquaintance with it through the television medium, surely the effort which has gone into this production will have been justified many times over.

By now I had moved on to my next assignment – but I must recall some intriguing repercussions. A-R had to enter into a contract with Boosey & Hawkes, Benjamin Britten's publishers, before staging the television version. One of the clauses stipulated that if the production process entailed any form of recording, those recordings would have to be destroyed within two years of transmission. One must remember that the words 'video-piracy' and the means of carrying it out had not yet been invented. But B&H was afraid of possibly losing control of their material, and with hindsight they cannot be blamed. Depositing video tapes for posterity in the National Film and Television Archives was still in its infancy.

Almost two years later, in 1961, Lord Cottesloe, who had been chairman of the Arts Council, wrote to A-R's chairman asking whether he could come and have a playback of the opera, as he was an ardent Britten fan and had missed the transmission. As this was a valuable and timely opportunity for good PR, he was immediately invited to come to Television House to view it. Unfortunately the overworked Ampex machines could not be made available to play back the video recording. Instead engineers had to come to the studios at the weekend, when the machines were idle, to make a telerecording of the opera – to put the electronic image onto film. Apparently the first attempt was technically below standard and they threw it out. The next effort was successful, as I found out for myself when I was present at the screening. Soon afterwards, as per contract, the Ampex video tapes were wiped and the telerecording was destroyed. Under the heading of 'material wiped or lost forever', *The Turn of the Screw* was often quoted as a tragic example.

Twenty-five years later, however, I received a call from Pam Logan, assistant curator of the BFI's television archives in Berkhamsted, telling me that they had discovered an old crate filled with rusty cans of film that was marked *The Turn of the Screw*. This must have been the discarded 'take one' of the telerecording, and no one has been able to explain how it found its way to the archives. I was immediately given a VHS copy by the BFI for confirmation that it was my production, and it would be an understatement to say that I was thrilled and very happy to be reunited with the opera. In October 2000, four decades after its original transmission, the Britten-Pears Library in Aldeburgh held a *The Turn of the Screw* study weekend, and invited me to introduce and screen my tape. The audience was made up of senior musicologists and Britten experts – most of whom had not seen the production. What pleased me most about their very warm reactions was that of all the hundreds of interpretations over the last fifty years my television version was deemed to be the truest to the original production, as staged at the Teatro la Fenice and Sadler's Wells in 1954.

Subsequently I bequeathed my original camera script and production stills to the Britten-Pears Library. Then, in January 2002, an audience of 250 attended my introduction and screening of *The Turn of the Screw* (on the large screen) at the National Film Theatre on the South Bank. The inferior technical quality of both picture and sound did not seem to matter a bit; I believe that it actually adds to the historical value of the work. The question and answer sessions after these presentations are always interesting and rewarding, especially with the presence in the audience of an opera buff who was in Venice for the premiere in 1954 and was able to make some valuable comparisons.

That same year saw the publication of *Television Opera*, written by Jennifer Barnes, Assistant Principal and Dean of Studies at Trinity College of Music, London. Comparing stage productions with my version, she writes:

> The Turn of the Screw was adapted from a ghost story by Henry James, which revolves around a central conceit: 'Do the children see the ghosts or are they the product of the governess's imagination? Are Miles and Flora preyed upon by ghosts – or by the governess?' As Britten and Piper discovered, this particular element was problematic in the theatre; singing ghosts were clearly visible to the audience, if not to all the characters. However, five years after the opera's premiere, the televised production used camera techniques to reinstate some of James's ambiguity. From the moment Quint first 'appears', Morley directed the cameras to focus first on The Governess's eyes and then on the balcony. She looks to the empty balcony and sees his image materialize from nothingness. Thus when the ghost appears he does so specifically through her eyes. The ghosts in Morley's production are still singing ghosts, but the camera script ensures that they consistently emerge through the disturbed eyes and mind of The Governess.
>
> In 2001, Peter Morley contacted the Britten-Pears Library and offered to donate his production script, which includes his beautifully drawn story-board adjacent to his camera shot list. Combined with the film, this provides a complete cycle of investigation, from Britten's manuscript, to the camera script to an aural and visual record. With

> recent public screenings in both Aldeburgh and London, the Morley production is beginning to get the recognition it deserves.

A nice thought, after a mere forty-three years.

13: Outside Broadcasts Plus

The relentless pressure on programme-makers saw to it that any euphoria I felt after the successful airing of *The Turn of the Screw* soon evaporated – especially with the choice of subject for our next documentary. John McMillan asked Cyril Bennett and me to his office and said that he thought it would be a good idea for us to make a programme about alcoholism. He was aware of the importance for A-R to be seen to handle difficult social subjects, and I remember him saying to me, 'After all the fun you have had with your opera, this should make a nice change for you.' It certainly did.

At this time the general public did not consider alcoholism to be a disease, let alone that alcoholics could seek treatment. As part of the research I went to the World Health Organisation in Geneva and visited a number of hospitals and social welfare centres to see how the Swiss dealt with alcoholic aversion treatment. It was a depressing trip.

In May 1960 *Alcoholism – Study of a Disease* hit the screens. Philip Purser wrote in the *News Chronicle* :

> John McMillan, who is Controller of Programmes of Associated-Rediffusion, thought it would be a good idea to do a feature about the disease of alcoholism and handed this idea to director Peter Morley and scriptwriter Cyril Bennett, who had previously worked together on documentaries about Hitler and about Israel.
>
> They got down to some intensive research; discovered the rather alarming extent of alcoholism in this country; summarised medical opinion. They rounded up victims and redeemed victims of the disease (not cured victims, for there is no cure). They visited the lower-depths bombsite off the Commercial Road, London, where the meth-drinkers assemble in final degradation. They ended up with the informative, graphic, fully documented kind of thing which is the TV equivalent of a weighty piece of magazine journalism.

That definition 'magazine journalism' was a novelty. It had taken me a little while to realise that television was redefining the accepted definition of both documentary film-making and print journalism. The developing medium caused the blurring of these two traditional methods of communication. I had cut my teeth on the all-filmed and carefully crafted documentary, and realised now that filmed 'documentary' elements inserted into studio-based programmes created a different dimension because of the immediacy and urgency of being 'live'. One simply had to come to terms with it. There is, of course, a role for the traditional documentary on television fulfilling the classic definition of 'the artistic interpretation of reality'; but it has had to adapt to the grammar and the immediacy of the new medium. When the two traditions meet on the small screen the label 'factual television' seems as good as any. It adequately describes the communication of facts, the art of story telling and the exploration of ideas. *Alcoholism — Study of a Disease* is a classic example of this developing genre. My filmed elements included sequences illustrating the horrific hallucinations that were described most graphically by two of our participants, recalling their delirium tremens. But it was the filming with a group of alcoholics who had hit rock bottom and were now unable to find a way out of their dilemma that is so vivid in my memory. There were four men and one woman, barely sheltered from the elements and living a vagrant life in utter squalor in the ruins of a bombed-out East End church – with their killer drink, methylated spirit. It was both shocking and depressing to witness the depths plumbed by these wretched meth-drinkers. I spent a very cold night with my small crew trying to get to know them and to elicit some facts about the how and why of their situation. We had to be very patient. They sat or lay huddled close to a fire they had lit, using branches, old furniture and orange crates that they had harvested during the day. The strong, intoxicating presence of methylated spirit hung heavily in the cold air. This, somehow procured from chemist shops, was their staple diet. There were also bottles of cider and cheap wine — full, empty and smashed. We were walking on broken glass. The woman and one of the men, barely capable of speech, attempted to explain how the world had conspired to reduce them to this. Neither seemed to want their circumstances to change. In the early hours, in the middle of this painful conversation, I noticed one of the men, who had been lying close to the fire and totally comatose, roll over on his side into the red-hot embers. Harry Hart, my cameraman, and I made a dive and rolled him back onto his other side, beating glowing cinders from his ragged overcoat. He remained oblivious of what had just happened, and so did his friends; they did not bat an eyelid. What a night. It took a good week for the smell and taste of meths, which had penetrated my lungs, to leave me.

I cued these film sequences into the live programme, which I directed from our studio in Television House. The linkman was a doctor, a specialist in the treatment of alcoholism, and with him were two recovered alcoholics who were interviewed by him.

The reaction to the programme was subdued. The cold statistics it revealed and the fact that there is no cure for this disease were, to say the least, sobering. A letter sent to the *TV Times* by Alcoholics Anonymous after transmission spoke of the public reaction to the programme: 'The most remarkable response we have ever had to any publicity. Since the programme, the A.A. have had dozens of inquiries from heavy drinkers seeking advice.'

* * * *

1960 was a busy year and, looking back on it, a clear reminder of the risks A-R took with their directors.

While I was filming for *Alcoholism* I was planning, with my other hand, the outside broadcast of Princess Margaret's wedding to Anthony Armstrong-Jones. I was surprised when I was asked to direct this for the Independent Television Network. After all, the only outside broadcast experience I had was that modest afternoon programme in 1957 from Apsley House, when Jane was my PA. As it turned out, only twelve days before going into the studio to direct *Alcoholism* I was on air, live, for over two hours with the wedding. For the first time, ITV was covering a major national event in competition with the BBC.

There are two memorable images from that occasion which I shall always cherish. The first was during camera rehearsal, the day before transmission. One of my camera positions was on a scaffolding tower we had erected in Trafalgar Square, looking straight down Whitehall. Sitting in the control gallery in Studio 9 in Television House, Kingsway, I was eagerly awaiting the bank of monitors to come alive so that I could establish the repertoire of all the shots I could exploit, from the many cameras covering the procession from Buckingham Palace to those inside Westminster Abbey for the service. I could not believe my eyes when the very first picture to appear was a huge close-up of a man in a barber's chair being shaved with an old-fashioned cut-throat razor. We all fell about. It was only when the cameraman zoomed out that he revealed an open window of the first-floor barber's shop in the building on the corner of Northumberland Avenue and Whitehall.

The other vivid memory is a shot, after the ceremony, of a glamorous Princess Margaret processing out of the Abbey with her groom, the lights from inside the west door backlighting her train as it billowed in the breeze. All of us who played a part on this happy day were relieved that everything had worked.

Maybe it was because of this outside broadcast that shortly after its transmission I was asked to produce and direct the state funeral of Sir Winston Churchill for the whole ITV network – a huge outside broadcast with an unknown transmission date. It was to be a constant pre-occupation – but much more of that later.

* * * *

Cyril Bennett and I had been talking for quite some time about the idea of producing a one-hour documentary film on Japan, based on our fascination for that country and our ignorance of it. We were spurred on by Reg Courtney-Browne (our programme researcher on *Tyranny* and *Israel*) who was posted to Japan in 1945 while serving in the army, and stayed on for ten years. We were intrigued by his endless stories about his experiences, and the more we heard the more determined we were to make a peak-time documentary. He had married Kaye in Japan, a Canadian-born Japanese who was working as an interpreter for the US army, and his knowledge of the country and his command of the language were impressive. Cyril and I were not alone in being ignorant about that far-off country. Hardly any film about it had been shown on television, so the prospect of bringing back an unfamiliar story with unique footage became irresistible. We wanted to get away from the public image of Japan in Britain: an image based on the odd mixture of flower arrangements, Madame Butterfly, Pearl Harbor and prison-guard atrocities. Instead we hoped to explore the so-called 'Coca Cola Culture' brought in by the US military and its administrators, and to find out what sort of impact it was exerting on Japan – how much was rubbing off on that ancient culture. In other words, we wanted to see how far the Japanese had taken to the democracy that General MacArthur brought with him after Japan's surrender in 1945, and how profoundly the western way of life had altered this highly traditional and feudal people.

Once again a visit to John McMillan's office bore fruit. He was keen on the idea, and famously said, 'It had better be good – it's going to cost an arm and a leg.' It did. He gave us a one-hour peak-time transmission slot for early November and wished us luck. We thought of a working title for the project, *The Two Faces of Japan*, and we never felt the need to change it. For background briefing I spent every spare minute reading up on Japanese history and culture. I agreed with A-R's features department that I would take with me the smallest possible team to do the job: Cyril as writer, Reg as researcher and consultant, my PA Rosemary Winckley, Charlie Squires as film editor, and Deborah Chesshire, our unit manager. It was agreed that I would recruit and use a Japanese camera crew.

I flew out in advance of the team to find a crew and set up the technical facilities. Cyril and Reg were to come out a week later, with the other three joining us a few days before the start of shooting. A couple of days before my trip I had to fight a recurring back problem, so when I stepped into the cabin of the BOAC Comet I was distinctly below par. I suppose the excitement of the whole enterprise made it all just about bearable. This was my first long distance flight, with refuelling stops in Rome, Cairo, Karachi and Singapore before landing at Tokyo airport. The journey seemed to be never-ending. A fresh crew took over after every stop, joining distinctly unfresh passengers, and after each take-off they always served the same cooked breakfast. Fortunately, BOAC was famous at the time for its scrambled eggs, but I had had my fill on reaching Singapore and I was feeling distinctly ill. When we finally landed in Tokyo I was more than ready to crawl into my hotel bed – but that was not to be.

When I got to the top of the aircraft's steps, to my horror I saw a photographer on the tarmac and four identically suited men huddled under umbrellas in the pouring rain, forming Japan's Foreign Office press department's reception committee. As the Japanese BOAC official escorted me down the steps under his umbrella I was stunned by the hot, humid, steamy air, which made breathing quite difficult. Fortunately Reg had briefed me well on matters of etiquette, and although I just wanted to curl up and die I was able to fish some rather soggy business cards out of my raincoat pocket and go through the formal exchanges of cards. There was a short speech by their spokesman, declaring that it was a great honour to welcome me to their country, to which I replied by stressing my gratitude for being received in this generous way, and saying how much I was looking forward to the honour of having the opportunity to get acquainted with Japan. Reg would have been proud of me.

We set off in two chauffeur-driven limousines. I had been booked into the Maranouchi Hotel, right in the middle of Tokyo's business district. When we got out I was yearning for my escape to bed, and was about to thank them for meeting me and escorting me to my hotel, when their spokesman announced, 'Morley-san, now is the time for you to go up to your room to freshen up. We look forward to seeing you down here in reception in ten minutes.' Reg had also taught me never to make a Japanese lose face – so I showered quickly, gritted my teeth and reappeared downstairs. They were all looking at their watches, and it soon became clear what was in store for me for the rest of the evening. The cars took us to a theatre. My four well-meaning torturers showed me to my seat, handed me a seat cushion and pulled a wire with an earpiece from it; the cushion acted as the aerial. Thus I suffered the instantaneous translation of the longest and most boring play I have ever endured. And then, to my dismay, there was dinner in a typical Japanese teahouse: shoe removal on entering, four geishas in attendance and a bevy of kimono-clad waitresses. I was sharply reminded of my recent back condition when I attempted the agonising ritual of squatting down on the traditional tatami matting for the meal. I had not seen a bed for what seemed like a week and I felt like death, and knew I could only survive the ordeal by concentrating on some serious sake consumption. The soup was fine, but it was followed by my first true culture shock. A waitress brought on a long, slim dish which displayed an octopus tentacle. With a sharp knife she cut off thin slices, delicately placing them in my bowl with chopsticks. All eyes were on me. I learned later that the Japanese take great interest in how foreigners react to their first taste of raw fish. Once more I thought of Reg's instruction: 'Close your eyes and think of England.' I did, and swallowed. In spite of feeling so ill I was surprised that I rather liked the texture and the taste. There were a lot of courses to come, and speeches. Finally, and mercifully, I was brought back to my hotel, where I had just enough strength to get undressed and crawl into bed. I woke up fourteen hours later.

My first task was to make contact with an old friend of Reg – Ian Mutsu. We became good friends, and I was to meet him many times in Tokyo and London over the next forty years. He died in 2001, aged ninety-six. Ian's father, whose family belonged to high-ranking Japanese nobility, was a diplomat. In the '20s he was posted to London as first minister to the Japanese Embassy. He married an English woman and they produced a son. Ian, standing at 6 foot 3 inches, was unusually tall for a Japanese, his facial features carrying only the slightest Japanese trait. In his teens he went to school in England, and never lost his love and close ties to the old country. In the mid-'30s the family returned to Japan, where later Ian studied journalism. The war caused great personal difficulties for him. Apart from torn loyalties, and feeling closer to England than to Japan, his physical appearance made it difficult for him to be seen in public. He virtually went into hiding in the country some distance from Tokyo, but because of his family's wealth was able to survive the war in some comfort.

At the end of the war Ian returned to Tokyo, pursued journalism and then started his own small film company. In 1960, when I first met him, his company was making documentaries and instructional films. That was our good luck. He was able to present me with a camera crew, and all their gear: a location manager, an interpreter who had worked for Reg, and an all-round fixer who had the know-how for getting filming permits, finding locations and approaching potential participants. I don't know how we could have made that film without Ian Mutsu and his organisation.

Arriving in Japan for the first time is a breathtaking experience. It is so completely different from any other country I had been to that I might have landed on Mars. It was just as well that I did not come with preconceived ideas about what we were going to do or how we were going to do it. I felt disarmed, astonished, enchanted and rather intimidated by the thought of having to condense the thoughts, actions and feelings of this nation into a one-hour film. I could hardly wait for Cyril and Reg to join me, and to share my first experiences with them. I remember the night before their arrival when I was channel-hopping on my TV in my hotel room and was introduced to the Japanese baseball craze and traditional Sumo wrestling. The grotesque size and mountains of flesh of the wrestlers, coupled with the ancient ceremonial rituals observed by the sport, was an eye-opener; even more so when every so often, just at the moment when a gigantic posterior filled the screen in tight close-up, dressed in what I suppose today would be called a modest thong, a short message was superimposed cheek to cheek, which I assumed was something to do with the contestant's score. The next day I spoke to my contact at Fuji Television to see whether we could hire a studio for filming, should we require it. I asked him to translate the messages electronically pasted on the wrestler's rear end. 'Morley-san, the Japanese letters have little to do with wrestling. They are commercials for Johnson's Baby Powder.' How stupid of me not to have thought of that.

Cyril and Reg arrived in the hotel that afternoon, and by the next morning had recovered well enough for us to meet for breakfast and make plans. Cyril, always worried about his fibre diet, had telexed me to ask whether he should include a packet of All-Bran in his luggage, and I was able to assure him that every breakfast cereal God had thought of was on the hotel's menu. When the waiter came to take our orders, to Cyril's dismay and mine he sucked in his breath and said, 'Hhaa so sorry – Arr-Bran arr gone.' This became the unit's stock phrase when things conspired against us.

We had budgeted four weeks for the completion of the script and four weeks for shooting it. This was a tight schedule for television in those days, and we were not helped by the fact that 1960 produced the worst summer in Japan for fifty years – unbearably hot and humid, with typhoons that swept across the Pacific every few days and daily earthquake tremors in Tokyo. In Kyoto we were right in the centre of a typhoon that killed fifty people. One quickly became aware of the fatalism of the Japanese in the face of natural violence and disaster: the death toll of this typhoon barely rated a headline in the local press.

There was so much to see, so much to take in. In Tokyo we explored kabuki theatres, department stores, communal bathhouses, temples, pachinko saloons, geisha houses, massage parlours, parliament buildings and so on. In those days street names did not exist, and many an hour was lost finding our way around. When I handed a note with the written destination to a taxi driver he would look at it, smile and say '*Hi*', meaning 'yes'. I soon learnt that this meant he did not have the faintest idea where to go. If I got a '*Hi-hi*' the chance of reaching our goal was more favourable. Inevitably he would have to stop at various police kiosks and ask for directions. These smartly dressed cab drivers, always sporting white gloves, were known locally as *kamikaze* – for good reasons. I said to Cyril after our first morning that we must write a taxi journey into the script. I would shoot it, and with luck survive the trip. In our film's final cut that ride remains as a monument to a very scary moment.

We narrowed down our locations to certain specific areas of Japan that represented different social backgrounds: Tokyo itself; the Kansai region, including the shipyards of Kobe; Kyoto, the ancient capital of Japan; the industrial area of Osaka (the Manchester of Japan); and, of course, Hiroshima. We decided to tell our story through four representative people, and a lot of time during this research period was taken up in finding them and getting their approval and co-operation. In the end our cast consisted of a housewife near Osaka, married to a white-collar worker (he was an administrator with a film company that made commercials for Japanese television); a shipyard riveter in Kobe; a girl model; and a university student in Tokyo. These four people gave us our story-line. In the meantime Reg, together with Ian Mutsu, was negotiating agreements for us to interview the prime minister, Hayato Ikeda, and the leader of the socialist opposition, Inejiro Asanuma.

One surprising impression I got during this planning period – another graphic aspect of the 'two faces' – was the contrast between the beauty, simplicity and delicacy of the Japanese home, no matter how poor, and the hideous sprawling vulgarity of everything outside it. Town planning in the cities was piecemeal, loud advertisements hung untidily all over the street, the traffic and the driving were chaotic and often ruthless. All the signs of form and order expressed inside the home were blatantly disregarded. The instant rebuilding of Tokyo after the war had produced unspeakable ugliness. I was thrilled when I returned to the city twenty years later to see a huge change, with a display of some very fine architecture.

During these travels we met many European and American residents, and it was strange what little insight we got from them on Japan and its people. Foreigners in Japan lead a very secluded life in their isolated enclaves, and there seems nothing as insular as a Western mind resident in the East.

We had by now amassed so much potential material, so many contradictions with sharp conflicts between the traditional and the new, that to decide what to include in the film was overshadowed, as usual, by the problem of what to leave out. We wanted to show not just the manner in which the American 'Coca-Cola culture' was merging with Japanese tradition, but also the conflicts that this created in the Japanese mind – how traditional feudal family life, in spite of television sets and washing machines, seemed to have been completely untouched; how in the home the male still took precedence over the female, and found his entertainment and romance outside the home in the vast industry of bars, clubs and hostesses; how there still existed such a weight of formality and etiquette, and over-riding obligation to family and ancestry. All this, in one way or another, we hoped to reveal.

The time arrived for a final script discussion and, as there was no air-conditioning in the hotel, Cyril and I hired a chauffeur-driven Cadillac as our office for the day. We decided then and there to invite Tom Harrison, the anthropologist (founder of Mass Observation in 1937), to act as a linkman and to conduct the two political interviews. At the time he lived in Sumatra, and we flew him in from there. I cannot remember where the driver took us that day, but when we returned that evening we had a script.

The rest of the unit had checked into the hotel. The day before we started filming Ian Mutsu introduced us to the crew, who had brought the equipment for me to approve. We used a 35mm Arricord, which also recorded sound, and a hand-held Arriflex. I attempted to break the ice and, through our interpreter, briefed them about the film we were about to embark upon, and explained the very tight schedule I had organised. The cameraman, Sabura Iwamura, his assistant and the sound recordist listened without showing any reaction whatsoever. Once more I had to remind myself of Reg's wise words and warnings. Naturally I accepted the language barrier, which our splendid interpreter handled with ease. This is more than one can say about that much bigger barrier: the schism separating the western from the eastern mind; the great difficulty of understanding people whose thoughts, emotions and feelings are so hidden by conventions, traditional behaviour and etiquette. This became a real obstacle when I tried to establish a rapport with the cameraman, to make him appreciate the flavour and style I was trying to get into the film. What was new and exciting for us was commonplace to him. Why should he get enthusiastic about shooting scenes of a kamikaze taxi ride or the dense Tokyo rush hour crowds, so solid in their movement that they made London look under-populated, when he himself was normally part of the crowd? I had to learn to conceal my emotions too: if I had shown despair, impatience or anger this would have caused deep offence and humiliation. Filming with a crew who speak only Japanese, in a temperature of 97 degrees with maximum humidity, made it quite hard to remember these subtleties.

Before shooting started I had heard a story of an American producer working in a Japanese studio who had shouted at and bawled out a Japanese technician, a focus-puller, who had inadvertently ruined half a day's shooting. The producer found this technician in his office the following morning, vehemently protesting at having being humiliated in front of his own people. He then produced a knife, hacked off his little finger and flung it at the producer, not merely to show the depth of the insult he had been made to suffer, but also as a symbol of repayment of the debt of obligation to himself, his family and his ancestors. Mercifully I remembered this extraordinary anecdote, because two weeks into our shooting schedule the camera assistant accidentally loaded an exposed roll of negative film into a magazine, and when I received the rushes report the next morning announcing a double-exposure problem I could have killed him: in the UK that is about the worst crime a camera operator can commit. Instead I put my arm round his shoulder, thanked him for all his sterling work, told him that the technicians at the laboratory were highly amused when they screened the rushes, and that I would be really grateful if it did not occur again. At the end of that day Iwamura-san, the cameraman, came over to me, bowed, and simply said '*Domo arigato*', thank you very much.

They all turned out to be very charming, willing and hard working, but there was this ever-present strain of observing correct behaviour, even during the most difficult and trying moments. After every shot when I had said 'cut', there was always the ritual of the interpreter having to ask on my behalf whether the cameraman thought the shot OK, and as committal is taken very seriously by a Japanese, the time wasted in getting his considered opinion, with a tight shooting schedule hanging over us, needed an extra amount of self-control. I soon found out that whenever Iwamura-san turned to me after a shot with a smile on his face I knew that something had gone wrong – for in Japan you hide your sorrow behind a smile, and the greater the trouble the bigger the smile.

However informal the technicians appeared to be with each other during working hours, rank was always strictly observed. They must have found our speed as difficult to take as our informality, and the goodbyes in the evenings after shooting were always elaborate and formal, acting as a constant reminder to us of how crucial our observance of etiquette was to the success of the film.

Our first location was Hiroshima. This was the unit's introduction to the famous air-conditioned bullet train. We all enjoyed that ride, and were amazed that one could actually make telephone calls from the train to anywhere in the world. We arrived 500 miles later. I found it hard to believe that it was a mere fifteen years since the dropping of the bomb. Hiroshima was the first Japanese city to be rebuilt after the war. We shot a sequence in the atomic radiation sickness hospital; for all of us this was a deeply moving and very depressing experience. We saw patients who had languished there since 1945, their number dwindling as daily deaths from leukaemia and other radiation diseases occurred daily. When our crew was confronted with this tragedy of filming dying people I wondered how they would react, but there was no trace of emotion. Japanese know how not to show emotion, or evoke it in others. I got a graphic example of this from the local driver we had hired for the shoot. He was very friendly, and by the second day, as he took us to another location, I could not resist asking him through our interpreter where he was when the bomb fell on Hiroshima. He smiled and explained that he was lucky, because he was on a job 10 miles outside the city, but his wife, three children, parents and in-laws all perished. And he kept on smiling – which meant that he avoided the natural reaction from a Westerner, who would have expressed his deep sorrow. This would have placed him under an obligation to me, and to absolve him from this he would have had to find a way to repay me. There was a lot to learn.

We first met Seichi Kubota, our twenty-one-year-old student from Tokyo University, in a coffee bar – the Mozart coffee bar. We could just as well have met in the Chopin or Louis Armstrong coffee bar – each one with its dedicated musak. Kubota-san was a member of the militant and violently anti-American student organisation Zengakuren, which organised the riots against President Eisenhower's visit to Japan. In spite of the trouble these riots caused few of the Zengakuren members to whom we spoke appeared to take them very seriously. Most of them, like Seichi Kubota, regarded their student years as the last opportunity to let off steam before taking their place in the formal, ultra-conservative mainstream of Japanese life. He invited us to film him in the student dormitories of his university, which were deliberately kept filthy and untidy – a calculated act of defiance that perpetuated the traditional university ritual of a final fling before they had to face the 'discipline of the rest of my life', as he put it. Kubota-san saw nothing odd in this, or the fact that he discussed Marxism with his fellow students – and then, on his way to the tranquillity of his home, stopped off at a Shinto shrine to offer a prayer to his dead ancestors.

Kubota-san invited us to his home. This in itself was unusual, as foreigners were rarely given that opportunity, but he wanted us to meet his mother. His father had been killed in the battle for Okinawa, and by tradition he was now the master of the house. When we arrived by taxi, Kubota-san begged us to wait in the car. He went into the traditional small house, which had sliding doors and tatami matting throughout, and a few minutes later the delicate main door slid to one side. There was his kimono-clad mother facing us, kneeling, with her head bowed low touching the floor; standing behind her was the man of the house, who had quickly changed into his yukata – and now welcomed us to his home. His mother continued to bow, gracefully shuffled backwards, slid open another door and from the kitchen brought in small bowls of green tea and a platter with daintily arranged minute pastries. The title of our film seemed to me to be most appropriate.

Filming with our second cast member was a delight. Shigeko Yamasaki was a very beautiful and very funny twenty-two-year-old model. She had excellent English, or actually American; we discovered on our last day with her that she had mothered a US soldier's baby. Shigeko also neatly underlined the theme of our film. Like Kubota-san she invited us to her home, where she lived with her mother: her father had been a war casualty. Both in their kimonos, they introduced Cyril and me to the tea ceremony, observing all the traditional rituals. He hated drinking it, but I quite liked the taste of what looked like thick surface water from a rich pond. Inside the confines of her home there were no signs of the banter and the fun we were to have when we filmed her daily life free from these constraints. She went about her job as a successful model smartly dressed and expertly made up. She arrived at a Takashimaya department store in a taxi, smoking, to be met by senior staff for a photographic session modelling their latest French collection. Shigeko easily and happily combined the razzmatazz of jazz, baseball, the glamour of modelling beautiful clothes with the ritual of the tea ceremony. We did not expect to find a typical Japanese career girl: western ignorance on display once again.

Our third cast member was Uzuki Shoji, a riveter in a modern shipyard. It was through him that we were able to shed some light on the miraculous development of Japanese industry in merely fifteen years. Shoji-san had been a sailor in the Imperial Japanese Navy during the war and now worked in the Kawasaki shipyard in Kobe. We filmed him at work with his team of riveters, all helmeted and wearing identical uniforms, evoking unpleasant wartime imagery. But this time the threat was rather different. Very simply, his shipyard produced a 45,000-ton tanker every two and a half months, while in Britain we took ten months. His living standards were three times higher than pre-war, and he had a union to negotiate his wages. Shoji-san lived with his family in the traditional manner, but with a washing machine and six-channel TV. The company rented him a house, gave him cheap lunches, free medical treatment and cheap holidays with his family at a company hotel. We soon discovered that this level of prosperity was reserved for the industrial elite, working in major industries and living in company-owned suburbs. Of course we also filmed the other side of the story – oriental Japan, unchanged by Western modernisation, with 60 per cent of the working population labouring in back streets to provide cheap goods to the world. If I were to go back now, over forty years later, and make a follow-up of *The Two Faces,* the industrial story would be rather different.

Osaka was the hometown of our fourth cast member, Shizu Yamaoka, a suburban housewife and mother of two young boys. When she shopped in a supermarket, gossiped with her neighbours or cooked for her family, she seemed to be very like a housewife in the West. But Mrs Yamaoka – like most Japanese women at that time – had been trained for two years at a 'brides' school' and her parents had arranged her marriage. Within a family unit the ranks were prescribed – first the husband, then the eldest son and then the wife. She accepted her status because she had been brought up to do so, and was content to be addressed at all times not by her name but by her rank of '*oksan*' – wife. We filmed the family at home having dinner, which she had prepared for her husband and children, and also went on a shopping spree with her – which was another opportunity to juxtapose the old with the new. Shizu Yamaoka only wore kimonos, and there she was in the fur department of a very modern department store choosing a stole, while Beethoven was gently piped to all the floors. Back at home she was perfectly content to spend the evenings alone, while her husband, like most Japanese husbands, found his 'relaxation' outside the home amid the exotic pleasures of an abundance of bar girls in the world's most bizarre entertainment industry. No Western woman who hasn't been to Japan and studied the relationship within a typical family will ever understand this. To have a sequence in the film showing this extraordinary industry was, of course, irresistible. Cyril and I first came across an amazing example early on, when we were researching facts and looking for locations. We went and had dinner in a large and well-appointed restaurant, where a small group played the latest pop music from the US; the waitresses were friendly and the food excellent. Our conversation was, as ever, about the script and the many problems we had to solve before we could lock down the final shape of the film. We hardly noticed when our table was cleared after the meal, and it was only when the lights dimmed that we realised that some sort of floorshow was being prepared. I looked up and noticed that a searchlight was focused on a large birdcage that was slowly descending from the ceiling; then I realised that it was going to land on our table. A beautiful, nude young lady stepped out of the cage, and to applause from the other guests handed me a menu and asked what we would like to drink. The only thing she was wearing was a headband advertising Santori whisky. We were not able to include this particular venue in our 'bar sequence', but we discovered so many other establishments that we had no difficulty illustrating Tokyo's unique nightlife.

There were just two interviews to be shot. The first was Tom Harrison's interview with the prime minister, Hayato Ikeda, in his official Tokyo residence. He praised Japan's relationship with the United States, re-affirming that Japan's future was closely linked to America. He stressed that promotion of trade with China was desirable, but friendly relations with the United States were vital to the Japanese people. Inejiro Asanuma, the opposition leader, stated the opposite viewpoint in our interview with him at his Socialist Party headquarters. He said that economic dependence on America had not brought prosperity to many Japanese people, and that America was a danger to the freedom and independence of Japan. He worried about the likely re-emergence of the Japanese armament industry, and insisted on a peace economy, not one geared to war. Sadly this proved to be Asanuma's last ever interview, as just a few days later, at a political rally in Tokyo, he was assassinated by a right-wing student who ran onto the speaker's platform and stabbed him. Newsreel cameras recorded this grisly and tragic event – and we used that footage in the final cut.

There just remained one more sequence to get into the camera – an act of pure self-indulgence. I had spotted amongst the plethora of the Ginza's animated bright advertising lights, high up on a tower of the Asahi Shimbum building, an electric news bulletin – similar to the running ribbon in New York's Times Square, showing all the latest news in letters 6 feet tall. I asked Reg to negotiate permission for us to 'borrow it' for twenty minutes on the evening of our last day's filming. I don't know what the revellers in the Ginza might have made of it, but had they looked up to catch the news they might have been surprised to read 'Written by Cyril Bennett, Directed by Peter Morley, An Associated-Rediffusion Network Production'. These instant end credits for our film were paid for by Reg with a crate of beer, happily accepted by the operator of the facility.

In *The Two Faces of Japan* we tried to convey the mood of that complex nation – and tried to indicate the way it was likely to swing in the future. I have never ceased to be fascinated by the country. In the 1980s, when I was developing the first interactive video discs, I had the good luck to make several trips, learning more about its people and observing the fantastic changes that were taking place. In 1985 I was at last able to take Jane with me, and let her experience some of the many impressions that I had brought back to London over the years.

The Two Faces of Japan was transmitted on 2 November 1960. It got huge viewer ratings, attracting an 87 per cent share of the audience that night. The film was repeated three months later and was also shown worldwide, including in Japan, where it was broadcast by Fuji Television. The press reviews were fairly blush-making, but it was a letter from the BBC that meant most to me. I had never met Norman Swallow, their great documentary maker, although we became good friends later. This is what he wrote:

> BRITISH BROADCASTING CORPORATION 4th November 1960
>
> Dear Peter Morley,
> A brief line to say that I found your Japanese film to be quite magnificent; the best example of documentary television on an international theme that I have seen for a very long time – beautifully shot, edited with great style and force and with a commentary which was absolutely right. Many congratulations on a job of which you and your colleagues must surely be very proud.
>
> With regards,
> Yours sincerely,
> Norman Swallow
> Chief Assistant (Documentary & General)
> Talks, Television

14: Film versus Television

In 1960, with five years experience directing live and filmed television programmes, I agreed to have a go at answering some questions sent to me by Derrick Knight, the editor of *Film*. I first met him in 1951, when he came to interview me in my cutting room over the old umbrella shop in New Oxford Street. At the time he was writing a piece on British documentary film. Now, ten years later, his magazine embraced television, and these excerpts which I have found among my papers reflect some early thoughts – almost forty-five years ago:

> DK: Coming from Documentary Films to Television, did you find the transition difficult?
>
> PM: I joined Independent Television in its early chaotic days, and after four weeks went on the air with an all-live fifteen-minute programme. When it was over, I went down on the studio floor to thank the cast and technicians. Within a matter of minutes the studio had been cleared of all scenery. After all the effort that had gone into producing fifteen minutes screen time, all there was to show for it was this empty studio, and one or two people coming up and saying 'That was jolly good – went very smoothly'. Adjusting myself to accepting this new end-product was the most difficult part of the transition from film to television. Remember that the director of a live television programme does not see the final result of his efforts. Surrounded by a bank of TV monitors, he is so involved in conducting this giant electronic dubbing session, where production, performance, photography, cutting and dubbing take place simultaneously, that he has to ask an outsider after it is all over 'how did it go?' It is this adjustment to a very much shorter, and highly concentrated creative period, and having to be 'right first time', that presents the main difficulty. From the technical point of view, learning, or as I was, being plunged into this new medium, was frightening and exciting, but not difficult. I shall always be grateful for the years I spent hunched over a Moviola with scissors at the ready. I consider the cutting room to be the finest possible training ground for the television director, because it prepares one for the ultimate job in the control gallery: the composition, assembly and rhythm of the visual image in the course of a live production.
>
> DK: Does television require more talents than film?
>
> PM: No. Television is more complicated than film, therefore the television director's knowledge of the technical aspect of his craft has to be of a somewhat greater range, but the basic talents to be able to tell a story in picture and sound are shared by both.

DK: You have directed programmes that were either all-film, film and live or all-live. How long did it take you to make one of the 'Members' Mail' series, 'Tyranny – the Years of Adolf Hitler', and 'The Turn of the Screw'?

PM: 'Members' Mail' was a weekly fifteen-minute series, all shot on location. It allowed for two-and-a-half days shooting, the remainder of the week cutting, dubbing and preparing the next one. I remember years ago, spending six months cutting a one-reeler. Here, in the same length of time, the output was six and a half hours screen time. Sacrificing polish and finesse for urgency and topicality is one of the demands of television documentary. 'Tyranny' was a different type of programme. It ran for one hour and was a mixture of archive film, specially shot film and the live studio. From the moment the idea was accepted, I had four weeks to transmission. This meant day and night work for the writer, Cyril Bennett, Charles Squires, the film editor, and myself, and included a hurried trip to Germany for filming key interviews. Benjamin Britten's opera, 'The Turn of the Screw', was a two-hour live television production. It took nine months planning (part time only), five weeks rehearsing, and four days in the studio.

DK: By comparison with TV, film allows time far perfection. No doubt it would have been easier to film 'The Turn or the Screw' than produce it on live TV, but do you think it would have been any more effective?

PM: If you mean 'a film of the opera', using film technique and breaking it down shot for shot, it would have been laborious from a technical point of view, very hard on the cast, and an immensely long and expensive production. On the other hand, the Paul Czinner method, using his multi-film-camera technique, and recording on film an existing stage production for posterity, would have defeated the point of my television production. I did not aim to preserve 'The Turn of the Screw' the same way that the Bolshoi Ballet, and recently Margot Fonteyn have been recorded by that excellent method. I chose this opera because I felt that it would make 'good television'; that it was well suited to the small screen. Opera and television have found it difficult to be mutually compatible, in spite of some magnificent BBC productions by Rudolph Cartier. I felt that Benjamin Britten could have written 'The Screw' for television, and it was for that reason that Associated-Rediffusion agreed for me to direct it. Here we had all the advantages that television alone can offer. A special production, containing pure television technique, with the live sustained performances of the cast and orchestra. So the question of whether filming it would have been any more effective does not arise, as it would have been a totally different interpretation. In my view, it would have become another filmed opera, pleasing neither opera lovers on the one hand, nor filmgoers on the other.

DK: Are you influenced, and if so how, by the fact that the audience is millions of small separate family groups sitting in their own living rooms rather than large mixed audiences in cinemas or theatres?

PM: Whether the audience is a few hundred thousand or several millions, I never think of it in terms larger than a mass audience made up of one or two people. This is fundamental to the attitude a TV director has to have to his work. Balance, pace and timing have to be totally different for group audiences. I had proof of this when some of my programmes, like 'Member's Mail' and especially 'Fan Fever' were shown at the National Film Theatre's main cinema, on a large screen, for the 'Captive Cinema' season. The time I allowed for laughter reaction from a television viewer was not nearly long enough for a large audience, and a lot of dialogue got lost. Tony Hancock's success as a television comedian is largely due to the way he addresses and plays to an intimate family circle. Sir Kenneth Clark's magnificent lectures on revolutionary painters are a perfect example of how to speak to an audience of a few.

DK: Some film producers are ingenuous enough to think they are uninfluenced by the thoughts of the audience, is this self-delusion possible on TV?

PM: The TV director who is not influenced by his audience fails in his responsibility to it. 'Tyranny' was a peak-time programme, aimed at a mass audience. This meant that the production had to have ingredients that would make it compelling viewing to readers of, say, both the Daily Mirror and The Times. Presenting the facts clearly and simply, without talking down to the audience and underestimating their intelligence (it often happens) are the basic rules. Over nine million people watched this programme, the largest audience a documentary programme has ever attracted – one cannot but help being influenced by it. 'The Turn of the Screw', on the other hand, was aimed at a minority group – opera lovers. Here one could be quite uncompromising. I was free from the responsibility of attracting a large audience, a most refreshing and exciting experience, and of great credit to Associated-Rediffusion for making it possible.

DK: Finally, can you see any advance in television technique in the foreseeable future, which will widen the gulf between TV and film?

PM: The development of video-tape is bound to have a profound effect on both. How far it will bring the two together, or the opposite, is hard to tell. To the TV director this new device opens up great possibilities. The quality of the recorded picture is so good that he can use it as an additional picture source during a live studio production without anyone being able to tell that it has been pre-recorded. And who knows what future video-tape holds for the film-maker. Is film out? Will the amateur cinematographer with a small electronic camera be able to strap a pocket video-tape recorder round his waist, shoot, go home and play it back on a TV monitor? I am looking forward to reading FILM in 1965, I think, by then, we may have the answer.

Younger people working in the industry today, never having experienced a world without television, might find the excerpts from this interview rather quaint. But it all had to start somewhere, and those of us who had the great good luck to be involved in these early days look back with some pride on this period of unpredictability and excitement. I don't think any of us realised at the time that we were pioneering – we would have been even more impossible to live with if we had. It is only in looking back that we can recall the huge risks that the ITV bosses took, employing producers and directors with negligible experience and no yardstick to go by: it really was a step into the unknown. This was the age of adventure and exploration – before that adventure turned into a giant industry – and we marvelled at the fact that we were actually being paid for it. How things have changed.

* * * *

My next assignment was a follow-up to *The Two Faces of Japan*. A-R was on a roll with its documentaries, and it was not difficult to get John McMillan to back the 'Japan' team with our next idea. Little did we know that we were making a rod for our backs: we chose France. Japan was unfamiliar territory, so viewers simply had to take our word for everything in the film; but here we were going to explore a country a few miles across the Channel. We soon discovered a major tripwire – the danger of perpetuating clichés about that familiar neighbour of ours. We had to be on our guard all the time.

The press quoted me as saying before we left for France: 'We do not intend to do a highly topical programme, but rather one which if viewed in twelve months time will still be as balanced as on the day of the original transmission. We want to find out something about the French character and through that come to a better understanding of their problems – in short "what makes a Frenchman tick".' It was a tall order.

As with Japan we spent a month in France, travelling round, researching, meeting people, getting ideas, finding locations and allowing enough time for a script to emerge. We looked for participants who would act as points of focus. There was also the research for archive material for short historical sequences (French Indo-China, Algiers, elections, demonstrations and so on). Finally we settled for a peasant farmer and his family, a goldsmith, a young artisan family, a Dior model and a painter. I used a French film crew; mercifully this time the cameraman, Jack Curtis, was bilingual. The only bit of France that I could recall was Normandy and the 1944 fight north to Belgium and beyond; all of that had by now taken a back seat in my memory. Now television presented me with an opportunity to get to know the country. I found the pre-production month stimulating and very enjoyable. With Paris as our headquarters that was not difficult – going to one of Edith Piaf's famous performances being one of the high points.

We collected such a rich inventory of potential ingredients that the problem of deciding what to include stared us in the face. It was as important to show the squalor of Algerian immigrants surviving in their *bidonvilles,* the 'petrol can' shantytown slums of Nanterre, only 3 miles from the Arc de Triomphe, as it was to show the positive achievements of French industry, the country's infrastructure, and the changing face of the nation.

On our last night before shooting started, over a dinner that went on to the early hours, Cyril and I came to the final script decisions. The next day the four-week shoot started. Of the many locations and situations we filmed, all with their memories, I will recall just two.

France's *haute couture* and its influence on the rest of the world demanded inclusion in our story. We had persuaded the House of Christian Dior to let us film their famous Spring Collection. I got a second camera crew for this, because at the last moment I got permission to shoot inside the sacred changing room for a behind-the-scene sequence, in addition to the front-of-house catwalk. Dior had never allowed this before – so they took quite a risk. The camera captured total pandemonium in the overcrowded inner sanctum as the models came off the catwalk. They had to change into a new number at lightning speed, ready for their next entrance. There were about twenty of them in various stages of undress, some half-naked, some totally, with an army of hysterical dressers in a great panic ministering to them. And the international audience outside, closely seated around the catwalk, was aware only of gentle music and the serene appearances of models. It was a useful addition to our study of the French.

The other vivid memory concerns Yves Klein. We were keen to give a picture of the contemporary art scene in Paris in 1960 – with the accent on the avant-garde. Yves Klein was considered to be one of the most controversial artists of the twentieth century, a pioneer of performance and conceptual art who explored the 'poetic power of pure colour and space'. He was a leading member of the Neo-Dadaists in Europe, and with others founded *Nouveau Réalisme*, a movement in which elements that constitute everyday reality – such as junk metal or rubbish collected at random – are transformed into works of art. Klein was also a jazz musician and a black belt judoka. We found him committed to the use of his ultramarine blue, a glorious pigment that he claims to have invented, which he called International Klein Blue (IKB). He used this colour to make monochrome paintings and sculptures, often featuring sponges painted blue. Klein sought to 'free art from line and form, and rid it of its material dimension'. Cyril and I felt that we simply had to capture this man on film.

Klein had recently embarked on a series of 'living brush' exhibitions, public performances in which, under his direction, naked models covered themselves in his blue paint and used their bodies to make imprints on canvas laid out on the floor and on the walls. One such performance, which took place at the Galerie Internationale d'Art Contemporain in 1960, was accompanied by an orchestral rendition of Klein's Symphonie Monochrome, in which a chord, held for twenty minutes, was followed by a twenty-minute silence. Klein called his 'living brush' paintings *Anthropométries.* I feared that he would not want to co-operate, but I was wrong; he was only too willing. However, he said that he might have legal problems filming his 'living brush' paintings in France, and suggested we should go to a friend's photographic studio in Düsseldorf, Germany. There we were introduced to his ultramarine pigment and then to a very beautiful model, his 'living brush'. Klein had prepared the studio before we arrived, with huge sheets of white paper on the floor and others covering the walls. He asked his model to undress and to cover herself head to foot with his paint, while he went next door to put on his dinner jacket and black tie. When he reappeared he spotted a couple of small areas on the model that needed some more paint, which he applied himself by hand.

In the meantime we had set up the camera, and because I had no idea what to expect Klein agreed that we could have a rehearsal. He climbed up a tall stepladder, and using that as his director's chair instructed his 'living brush', telling her to take up her first position, with her back to the camera, then to kneel down and bend forwards until her head touched the floor in front of her. At this point Jacques Chotel, the non-English-speaking assistant cameraman, who was lining up the first shot, looked across to me and urgently called out, 'Peteur – Peteur'. He beckoned me to come over quickly, pointed at the camera's viewfinder and exclaimed, 'Oulala – lala – lala!' I soon spotted what was causing his great concern: our model had failed to apply paint to the most intimate part of her anatomy – it was like seeing a close-up of a rabbit (a blue one) from behind, with its conspicuous white tail. I explained this to Klein and he executed a quick repair.

The filming went well, with shots of the model writhing all over the floor, her movements directed by Klein, followed by a quick application of fresh paint. Then she stood up and was told which parts of her body to press against the paper, with quite complicated movements. It was a unique piece of filming.

Sadly Yves Klein died two years later, aged only thirty-four. An exhibition at London's Hayward Gallery in 1995 showed the impact this extraordinary artist made, with the lasting legacy of his work as proof.

At A-R Joan Elman, the resident company lawyer, had to vet the station's output. All scripts went to her as a matter of routine, and all pre-recorded programmes were scrutinised by her for possible legal infringements. *The Heartbeat of France,* she felt, needed to go up to the ITA for approval, because of the full-frontal nudity of Yves Klein's model. I was told to delete a particular scene, but good sense prevailed when I was able to persuade them that, in fact, she was not nude because she was dressed in the artist's paint!

Transmission was on 14 June 1960. The programme attracted good audience ratings, and press reaction was, on the whole, fairly positive:

> We saw a France awakening to new life, taking the Sixties as she finds them. This was a land with no time for yesterday; a land being inherited by a generation that recognized that the world is changing, and succeeding in giving their country a part in setting the direction.
>
> . . . glimpses of extremes, from the opulence of fashion and beauty salons to the misery of Algiers, civil disturbance, independent peasants, the abstract artist. A country of contrasts that no one would wish to alter. Yet a country of confusion that one hopes will find tranquillity.
>
> . . . delightfully conceived and presented, and was not without its crazy side – unless the shots of an artist on top of a ladder directing a paint-

> daubed girl as she rolled against a wall to produce his masterpiece were intended to be serious.
>
> As a reminder of the truth of the old adage, 'The situation in France is always critical but never serious' it could not have been more effective.

Were we any the wiser about the French? I doubt it, but I believe that at least we managed to portray their country in a different light, avoiding well-worn clichés.

15: This Week

You've both had your moments in Japan and in France – and now you owe me.' Once again John McMillan had called Cyril Bennett and me to his office. 'Good programmes, good press, good ratings, and the Board is delighted – but I have a big problem, and I'm counting on you to help me out.' I was at a loss to guess what would come next.

At that time *This Week* was ITV's flagship current affairs programme – in fact its only one. It had been launched by A-R in 1956, and after early teething troubles became the network's weekly prestige programme. The BBC's *Panorama* had been revamped that year, with Richard Dimbleby as its chief anchor, and for the next thirty-five years *This Week*'s strident opening title music, Sibelius's *Karelia Suite*, was to herald ITV's weekly challenge to the BBC.

But now, after a fairly uneven first five years, *This Week* was under threat. Although it was getting a peak-time audience of between 9 and 10 million viewers, it was regularly clobbered by Friday night BBC comedy (Tony Hancock). In spite of its long run it was never able to build up a following to compare with *Panorama*. By early 1961 it was struggling, and a drop in the ever-important ratings battle alarmed the ITA. The press often referred to it as the 'poor man's *Panorama*', while the other ITV network companies threatened to seek ITA ruling to make it no longer mandatory for the programme to be carried by the rest of the ITV network. For a company like A-R, with its eye on the next franchise allocation battle, this was very bad news.

'I want you boys to take it over immediately, and to make it sing again,' said John. 'You, Pete, to be its producer, and you, Cyril, its editor. After six months you can go away and do anything you like – just get me out of this hole.'

Cyril was delighted. After all, he was a journalist who had clocked up a lot of experience in Fleet Street. His nose for good news stories and politics, here and abroad, was well developed – and now he had the chance to be in the editorial driving seat. He relished the prospect, having been in television long enough to appreciate the finer points of the new visual journalism. What better way to show his mettle than to call the editorial shots for a major weekly current affairs programme. We recruited Elkan Allan (who had worked with me on *Fan Fever* five years earlier) to share the editor's function with Cyril for the first few months, before he went off to concentrate on his own programmes.

My reaction was, to say the least, muted. Of course I felt flattered to have been asked, but I left McMillan's office with trepidation. I was not a journalist, nor was I particularly interested in politics. I was a film-maker, a director – someone who cared very much about the style, look and feel of a programme – and I feared that I would have to compromise standards to meet the urgency and immediacy of current affairs. Once we got going, Cyril wallowed in the weekly transmission cycle, and his adrenalin flowed even more rapidly when, on the morning of transmission day, the contents of that night's programme were still in doubt. Every week he lived for that moment – and every week I nearly died.

There was another matter that worried me: the thought that we could hoist up a programme by its bootstraps and transform it in six months was ludicrous. After all, we were about to inherit a large team that had been with *This Week* for a very long time and had ambitious programme plans in the pipeline. I knew that it would take at least six months to absorb this inheritance factor, and probably another six for our proposed changes to begin to take effect – and to become discernible to the viewer. We kept on Brian Connell as our presenter and enlarged the reporting team to include Brian Magee, Jeremy Thorpe, Desmond Wilcox and Judith Jackson, and supplemented this list with the *ad hoc* use of well-known Fleet Street journalists, including Kenneth Harris, James Cameron, George Ffitch, Colin Legum, Paul Johnson, Ludovic Kennedy, Dan Farson, Robert Key, Alistair Burnett and John Morgan. Either Cyril or I chaired our weekly editorial meetings, but it was Cyril who supplied the impetus for the long and often heated debates, narrowing down the subjects that the programme should tackle. I took on the role of the long-stop, the filter, who on behalf of the viewers questioned the whys and hows of the plethora of subjects that emerged from the journalistic team.

Reg Courtney-Browne was our senior researcher. He had made contact with a most valuable spy in the *Panorama* unit, so we were pretty well informed about their plans – just as the BBC had their spy (unknown to us) in Television House. *Panorama* was transmitted on a Monday and *This Week* was traditionally on the air every Friday. The press took great interest in our rivalry.

My primary concern was to instil and maintain the highest possible production standards in an atmosphere where everything happened at breakneck speed, often sidelining the care and quality I cared about. I spent a great deal of my time in our four cutting rooms, where I was able to supervise the directing, shooting and editing of our output.

When we took over in 1961 all film was still shot on 35mm. Having cut its teeth in the amateur home movie business, 16mm was entering the professional field: Arriflex cameras from Germany were now becoming available, and the film laboratories were gearing up for 16mm processing. Professionals were very sniffy about 16mm and the *This Week* team, especially the cameramen and film editors, had to be persuaded to embrace this breakthrough. The great advantage was the mobility (weight and size) of the equipment, including the cost-saving in flying it all over the world; but what intrigued me most was the effect of lightweight hand-held cameras on our film-making style. We were trying out something new, and that was exciting.

Of course there were problems to solve. The 16mm editing equipment in the cutting rooms was still primitive and extremely fiddly. As an ex-editor I readily understood that our editors would hate it. The solution I came up with, bizarre as it might sound today, was to 'blow up' the 16mm negative film to 35mm positive working prints as part of the overnight laboratory routine for rushes. It was efficient, and kept the editors happy.

Up to now I had always created my own programmes for A-R, and I knew that as a producer in charge of a huge output I would find it very frustrating to be one step removed from the action. Right from the start, therefore, I decided that I would be responsible for the weekly live studio direction. This would not only keep my hand in but also give me a chance to set a coherent style for the 'on air' look of the programme.

I was to clock up over one hundred live *This Week* transmissions. This was my way of giving my adrenalin a weekly outing.

We went on the air with our first edition on 23 June 1961. A-R had put out a press release announcing *This Week's* new production team, and press coverage had been both flattering and scary; I have always preferred faint praise after a show rather than before.

> *Bristol Evening World*: One of Britain's most experienced programme directors is Peter Morley. So it is no surprise that he has been given the job of putting extra punch into *This Week*. Despite its excellence, it has been regularly losing viewers to the other channel, where a well-known comedian has been currently holding forth each week at the same time.

> *North Western Evening Mail*: *This Week* has inevitably been renamed as ITV's answer to the BBC's *Panorama*, and likewise has

> suffered by comparison with it. An impressive number of the famous have appeared in *This Week*, but in spite of this, and not always without justification, it has tended to be looked on as *Panorama*'s 'poor relation'. It has undergone many changes and tonight comes 'under entirely new management'. Brian Connell, ITV's Dimbleby, is still there to steer the programme, but there is a new behind the scenes team. It includes Peter Morley as producer, and Cyril Bennett and Elkan Allan as editors, three men who have been responsible for some successful feature programmes among them *Tyranny, The Two Faces of Japan* and *The Heartbeat of France*.

There was a huge sigh of relief all round when we came off the air that first night. The programme had worked and the *This Week* team seemed to approve the new style – but I well remember being in a cold sweat worrying about the next week's edition when I drove home that night.

So, week after week, under very close scrutiny both from the press and the ITA, we slowly hauled ourselves up the prestige and ratings ladder; but it became clear that John McMillan's 'just for six months, boys' was woefully inadequate. The changes we were instituting had to be gradual. Sometimes we chose single item editions: these were on film or in the studio or (often) a mixture of both. Sometimes we had magazine editions with two or three or sometimes even four items. The press began to take us seriously, which gave the team the 'wanted' feeling that Cyril and I built on. Soon the day of transmission was to change – and we all welcomed that.

> *Television Weekly*: The New Year has brought a revised time for TV's longest running current affairs programme, *This Week*. 'Now we are going on the air at 9.15 pm on Thursdays, directly after the nine o'clock news, we shall have to be even more careful that we are bang up to date,' explains Peter Morley. 'Topicality will become even more important than before and already we try to be as up to the minute as we can, sometimes still editing film for the programme after it has started.' Peter Morley started directing the programme that he has slowly but surely re-shaped into its present form.

McMillan's famous six months stretched to just over two years before he agreed to let us move on. The pace was hectic. A-R was generous with its programme budget, and we could afford to send directors, reporters and crews all over the world.

It would make a very heavy read indeed if I were to list all the stories and subjects we covered during that time – so I won't. It would also reveal an impossibly long name-dropping list of the good, bad, famous and infamous people I have met, usually in the green room before and after the programme. In over two years there could not have been a leading politician, prime minister past or present, or major figure from around the world who did not grace our studio. A history of *This Week* has recently been compiled by academics at Bournemouth University – now published by its author, Patricia Holland, who has called it *The Angry Buzz* – and this authentic and extremely well-researched account gives us more detail than my sketchy memory can deliver after all this time.

However, there are just a few highlights I would like to recall. The first is a one-item edition, and its subject is as relevant and urgent today as it was in 1962. Peter Black, that much-respected critic, set the tone in the *Daily Mail*:

> *This Week* has steadily improved since it was moved to its new day and time. Its interviews in particular have found increased vitality. Last night it had a terrific sequence of filmed interviews with young proletarian smokers (ages 11–15) who testified to their addiction in language that lost none of its horror through being drawn, as far as one could judge, from a total vocabulary of about 200 words. Even optimistic sociologists must have reflected that these children

> represented a poor return for all that orange juice and vitaminised milk. The talk between the doctor and the tobacco manufacturers' representative generated further heat. This is one subject that can stand the fullest debate, and TV is the most telling place for it. Associated-Rediffusion is to be congratulated on not ducking it, as it could easily have done.

Behind this particular edition is a story that I take some comfort in recalling now, because it shows how hopelessly wrong one can be. A-R's staff department had asked us to interview a young man, straight down from Cambridge, to see whether he would be acceptable as a trainee researcher on the team. Cyril and I thought that we should give him a chance – he seemed to have a good approach to current affairs television and also displayed a healthy sense of humour. Some weeks after he joined us we decided to do the young smokers edition, and I asked this trainee to do the research, find the school, lay on the participants and organise the shoot. Desmond Wilcox, who was so good with children, would have been the ideal reporter for this story, but unfortunately we had sent him abroad with a film crew – and there was no one else to call on at short notice. I discussed this with Randal Beattie, the director for the story, and asked him to use this trainee as the interviewer, and to make sure that his questions solicited statements from the kids rather than short answers. We would then delete the questions on the final cut – a technique I had developed since *Fan Fever* and *Members' Mail*, six years earlier. If this did not work out the trainee was to ask his questions in the standard form but off camera, as I did not think that he was good enough to be seen in shot – indeed, would never make it in television. His name was David Frost!

This press review by Pauline Richardson in the *New Daily* is a particularly apt reflection: 'One of the strengths of *This Week* is that its reporters take a back seat, as it were, in most of the interviewing they are called upon to do, and people questioned very largely are left to ramble on by themselves. *This Week* abounds in a delightful spontaneity and freedom which makes the interviewing methods of *Panorama* seem dull.'

Some months later David, soon known as 'Frostie', asked if I would release him for the odd afternoon as he had been asked to help in the development of a new BBC programme, a satirical show. With my earlier misjudgement of him in mind, I readily agreed to his request. The upshot was *That Was The Week That Was,* fronted by David Frost. We have often bumped into each other over the years, always with a good laugh about my prescient vision of him.

Another *This Week* highlight that is worth recalling goes under the heading of 'the one that got away'. Ever since the end of the war there had been speculation about the fate of top Nazis – who they were and how they escaped the Allies. One notorious escape route was known to military intelligence as the 'ratline'. This ran from numerous collection points in Central Europe through a series of monasteries and Catholic safe houses to St Gerolomos (a college in Vatican City) and then on to Genoa, from where the escapees sailed to South America. It was said that the Vatican organised and financed the 'ratline', and that it was partly funded by assets stolen from concentration camps and other victims. According to records uncovered in Argentina, President Peron's government, which was in power from 1946 to 1955, shepherded nearly 300 war criminals into his country. Besides such notorious figures as Adolf Eichmann, Josef Mengele, Klaus Barbie and other high-ranking Nazi fugitives, dozens of French, Belgian, Italian, Croatian and Slovak fascists, many of them Nazi collaborators sought in their home nations, were also admitted – some under aliases, others under their real names.

In 1960 Eichmann was tracked down to Argentina and spirited back to Israel by Mossad agents, tried and executed. Mengele, the murderous Auschwitz doctor who was perpetrator of the most horrific medical experimentation, died in Brazil in the '80s. In 1987 Barbie, the Butcher of Lyons, was extradited from Bolivia to France and convicted of war crimes; he died in prison in 1991. But it was the possibility of Martin Bormann's survival after the fall of Berlin that caused a continuing controversy right up to the 1970s. He was, after all, Hitler's closest colleague, and his possible escape spawned many wild stories.

Now, in 1961, sixteen years after the end of the war, I was given the opportunity to film the 'ratline'. It came about when the contact I had made two years earlier – leading to my secret interviews with Hitler's sister and other cronies – again approached me. He arranged for me to be met by a man at Munich airport who would be my guide. I was instructed to bring plenty of cash. John McMillan agreed to this venture, and told me to ring him at his flat in London should I need more than £500. He, Cyril and I decided that this story was potentially so hot that we should keep it under our hats until I returned.

My guide duly met me. He told me that he was a journalist and businessman, but withheld his name. He drove me south through Garmisch Partenkirchen and into the Austrian Tyrol – followed by the car belonging to the German film crew that I had previously booked from London. Our destination was the small town of Nauders, situated in the Austrian *Dreieck* – the triangle – the three-cornered meeting point of the borders of Austria, Switzerland and Italy. He had booked rooms in a small hotel, and over dinner (superb fresh trout from the river Inn) he told me the plan for the next day. We would climb up to a small, ancient homestead to meet its owner, the local mountain guide, also known as 'The Smuggler'.

We started our trek early, humping the camera gear up the steep slopes until we reached our destination. The mountain guide came out to meet us – an old man with a full beard and a gnarled face, who spoke a dialect that even my nameless German-speaking guide struggled with. He could have stepped straight out of Central Casting.

I had told the camera crew beforehand to shoot from the hip, as we called it, and cover this meeting, especially my attempt to interview the guide. He turned out to be amazingly frank. He clearly remembered giving shelter to a great number of high-ranking Nazis, recalling the names of Eichmann and Mengele. He also spoke of Martin Bormann, but was not certain of his identity, as all his clients (as he called them) were in some form of disguise. Each stayed a single night with him, and when I asked to see the room in which he hid his travellers he proudly let me film him heaving a huge wardrobe away from the wall, to reveal the door that led to their hide-out.

In the early hours he took his charges up the mountain to the *Dreieck* border point, crossed with them into Italy and handed them over to an Italian guide. The old man now led us along the same route, up the mountain to the *Dreieck*. There was no border sign, fence or even a post to mark the three frontiers, but with his spiked walking stick he pointed in turn to Switzerland and Italy. A few yards further on he announced that we were now in Italy – the point where sixteen years earlier he had handed over his charges. Then he led us back to his homestead. My Munich guide had agreed a fee with him in advance of our arrival and I parted with £50, which he gladly accepted.

The next morning I joined the camera crew in their car, and we set off for Italy. Our guide had arranged for me to meet a 'friend' in Merano to reveal the next stage of the 'ratline'. Merano is in the Trentino-Alto Adige Region of northern Italy, about 100 mountainous miles south-east of the Austrian *Dreieck*. Before the First World War this part of Italy belonged to the Austro-Hungarian Empire, part of a much larger Tyrol, but it was ceded to Italy in 1919. In 1945 it was a largely German-speaking region (as it still is), and became a haven to thousands of escapees from Nazi Germany, many of whose descendants still live there today.

My rendezvous with the new contact was at Merano railway station. He spotted us first, introduced himself in perfect German (again giving no name) and took us to the hotel he had booked for us near the station. At the check-in desk I became aware for the first time of a slightly strange atmosphere. It was the way the clerk took our details and scrutinised my passport, without the friendly greeting one normally gets on checking in. I also noted that the guide was in deep conversation with the hotel manager, in German. Later he took us to some locations he thought would be of interest. He pointed to the exterior of our hotel and a set of windows on the top floor, which he said were the overnight rooms for the German 'visitors'. From here they were handed over to the 'experts', as he called them, before they were escorted to their next temporary home. Then we walked to a couple of mansions that he said were safe houses, from which the 'visitors' would be put on a train the next morning to go further south. By the end of that day I had enough information to plan a shooting sequence, portraying Merano and the obvious landmarks and illustrating this part of the story. But over dinner there was some disappointing news. My guide told me that he had failed to get me an introduction to someone he knew well in a Vatican college in Rome, and that he had declined to be interviewed. He also said that it was highly unlikely that I would find anyone else in Rome who would be prepared to speak about the immediate post-war period. The Vatican's alleged involvement in the escape of leading Nazis was not new information – so I was not a bit surprised. Then there was some good news: my guide had managed to set up three interviews. He said that he would give me the names and addresses, but I would have to handle the filming on my own, as he was leaving Merano early the next morning. He then told me who they were. As the Russians approached Berlin in 1945, Bormann dispatched his wife, Gerda, and their ten children to northern Italy – not the only high-ranking Nazi who organised his family's escape from Germany at that time. In 1946 Gerda Bormann died of cancer, and a countess with an old Habsburg title, who lived in a large villa outside Merano, fostered the family. My guide had persuaded her to take part in an interview with me, as well as two of Bormann's daughters who were staying with her. That was a bit of luck, and I looked forward to the next day.

When I went up to my room I discovered that while we had been in the dining room someone had rifled my briefcase and been through my as yet unpacked clothes. This was not what I had expected.

While we were filming the exteriors the next morning I got the distinct feeling that we were being followed and observed. Later the cameraman told me that he had seen the same two men on several occasions, and that they were taking notes. I began to feel a bit uneasy.

In the afternoon I made contact with the countess and we set off to her villa for the interviews. She was in her seventies, very friendly and hospitable and willing to talk about the Bormann family. She only spoke German so I had quite a struggle, but we managed to communicate fairly easily. I was told in some detail how she coped with the Bormann children, that she had never met their father, and believed absolutely that he perished in Berlin, escaping from the bunker shortly after Hitler had shot himself.

Then it was the turn of the daughters. The eldest was teaching, and the youngest, aged eighteen, was studying. They spoke lovingly of their parents, especially their mother, and were adamant that their father was shot by Russian troops while he was trying to escape.

When I said that this was the *This Week* story 'that got away', I was not referring specifically to Bormann but to the whole story. On my return to London I screened the rushes and quickly assembled the material into a ten-minute item. Cyril and I then ran head-on into a brick wall. Brian Connell, our very conservative presenter, protested that because the veracity of my escape line story could not be proved, *This Week* could be accused of tabloid journalism. Of course we never intended to claim that this was the truth; we simply wanted to present a piece of speculative journalism – that it was quite possible that this could have been a section of the 'ratline', and that Bormann might have used it. In any case, we told him, we had planned to follow up the film with a discussion in the studio about possible Vatican involvement. And that did it. John McMillan (who was on our side) decided to sound out the ITA. The official verdict was that some viewers might be misled into believing that the programme had conclusively shown that Martin Bormann and other high-ranking Nazis had escaped to South America with the connivance of the Vatican, which would be harmful to *This Week*. Their consensus was that the project must be abandoned; its transmission was banned. Cyril and I were furious. We began to appreciate the immense power of the word 'Vatican' – and the reactions programmes like this could generate.

Ten years later, in 1972, a skeleton discovered in West Berlin not far from Hitler's bunker was identified as Bormann. Dental and DNA matches were established, and in 1973 he was officially declared dead by the West German authorities.

Sadly, when A-R lost its franchise in 1967 a considerable amount of its film library was lost as well – and in spite of many searches I have failed to track down my 'ratline' film. However, I still have a number of photographs, so at least I have a record of my Munich contact, the mountain guide, the climb to the *Dreieck* and pictures of the countess and the two Bormann daughters.

* * * *

Another highlight of 1962 was a *This Week* special. The Duke of Edinburgh had just set off on a two-month tour of South America. This was more than a flag-waving exercise; it was a journey to promote British trade, money and skills. Cyril and I put in a request to Buckingham Palace, inviting Prince Philip to present a personal report on his return from this ambitious trip. We went to the Palace to meet James Orr, his private secretary, who was quite keen on the idea, but he warned us that HRH would need some persuading. I spelt out in some detail what our plans entailed. The programme would be extended to forty-five minutes. We would script and assemble, using archive footage, historical sequences of all the countries of his visit, also including ITN newsreel material covering the journey. HRH would then come to Television House a day or so before transmission to record his own narration for the film clips (which Cyril would write). And I was keen for him to present the 'live' programme himself, ending with an interview with Brian Connell.

James Orr took a deep breath. He pointed out that HRH had never appeared on ITV before, and the Palace was always cautious about setting precedents. Also, up to now he had only ever agreed to a BBC interview, and might baulk at anything more ambitious. But James said he would put our request to HRH.

It's worth recalling that at the time ITA rules stipulated that programmes featuring royalty were not allowed to carry advertisements; not only that, they had to have 'neutral buffers' at the beginning and end to separate them from the commercials.

While we were waiting for news we started compiling the filmed elements – and after several approaches by James Orr, Prince Philip agreed to the project. We sent our narration scripts to Windsor Castle to await HRH's return, and were told by James to report there to discuss the programme. When we arrived we were told to wait outside his private quarters. I recall seeing a young Prince Charles playing with a toy glider in the grounds before HRH appeared and asked us into his study. He was very cold with us, castigating the script and telling us that he had never read such rubbish in his life. He said that we were to return the following day by which time he would have rewritten it. Inwardly I was furious and, even though I realised that I was putting the whole enterprise at risk, I replied that we were professionals with a lot of television programme-making experience, and that I would be surprised if the script could be improved. He showed us out.

We realised the following morning, when we once again entered the castle's inner sanctum, that this was Prince Philip's way of sizing up the people he deals with – finding out what they are made of and whether they can be trusted. He came out and gave each of us a beautifully typed copy (on crested heavy cream paper) of his rewrite. 'Come straight through to my study when you have finished reading.' We read it quickly, noting that he had hardly altered anything, and walked in. He greeted us with a smile, pressed a bell to order some coffee for us, and from that moment we got on like a house on fire.

A-R's managing director was Captain Tom Brownrigg RN (Ret'd). He took an intensive interest in *This Week's* foray into royal waters, having been the Mediterranean Fleet's navigating officer during the war, where he had made the acquaintance of the young Lieutenant Philip Mountbatten. Now he made sure that the prescribed royal protocol was followed to the letter. He issued 'orders of the day' to stage-manage the first royal visit to Television House, with detailed instructions about the official line-up in the foyer: 'The Chairman, Board of Directors, General Manager, Controller of Programmes and Morley to be in position at 11.00 hrs,' etc. There were detailed instructions about the food, drink and floral decorations in the green room; 'The "Gents" on the floor of the dubbing theatre to be re-decorated, with Morley to be the key holder,' and so on.

Prince Philip wanted to see the film clips before coming to Television House for the recording, and he asked whether this could be done at Windsor. I organised the temporary installation of a 35mm projector in the castle's glorious St George's Hall, and we made another trip to show the clips. All went well, and I took the opportunity to brief him about Captain Brownrigg's arrangement at TV House. 'Good God,' said Prince Philip, 'you don't mean Bugger Brownrigg?' We learnt that this was how he was known in the Navy, and enjoyed listening to some hilarious wartime anecdotes, some very indiscreet, about naval matters during the war. HRH said that he really hated overblown arrangements whenever he went anywhere, especially when he was on what he called a 'working visit'.

The day came for the recording. The line-up was in position, and when Prince Philip arrived with James Orr there was a perfunctory shaking of hands with Spencer Wills, the chairman, and the others. Then he quickly turned to me. 'Come on, Peter, let's go, we have work to do.' This, I was to learn over the years, was typical Prince Philip.

We went upstairs to our dubbing theatre, and I installed him in the commentary booth , sitting next to him. He readily took directions, and was prepared for any number of takes to get it right. I had booked an extra two hours of rehearsal time in the main studio, so that I could give some quick lessons on the use of the Autocue teleprompting system. It was a good day.

And then came transmission day. Prince Philip arrived early evening for another studio rehearsal, and then Cyril and I had dinner with him in the Green Room. At 9.15 p.m. we went on the air. He took to it like a seasoned reporter, not showing any nerves. About half-way through the programme, as we came out of a film clip and back 'live' to the studio, he ignored his autocue and said, 'Well, this seems to be rather like a natural break here. I wonder if could do a bit of advertising.' Turning to one of the cameramen, he asked, 'Would that be all right?' The whole crew corpsed, but he quickly returned to his script and continued, until finally, with great relief, I cued the end credits, the ringing tones of the *Karelia Suite* seeing us out.

* * * *

Without any doubt the most important and memorable event during my *This* Week stint occurred early in 1962. I finally did it: I married that delightful, pretty and young PA from Ipswich who had been my assistant for a short period in 1956 and again in 1957. Jane had been a senior drama PA these past years and was enjoying her work very much, and because *This Week* kept me in London we saw a great deal of one another, and enjoyed holidays in Scandinavia, Italy and Switzerland. Jane recalls with glee that I had been hopelessly reluctant to commit myself, clinging onto my confirmed bachelorhood; now, though, aged thirty-eight, I finally decided to settle down. We got married in London's famous register office, Caxton Hall, in Victoria Street, with both families and our friends on parade, except my mother, who did not come over from Switzerland.

John and Jackie McMillan had generously invited everyone to their flat in Bickenhall Mansions, by Regent's Park, for a sumptuous buffet luncheon. Afterwards we went to our brand new home, a small neo-Georgian house in Grange Grove, Canonbury, to get ready for our evening party. I had already moved in from my Kennington bachelor flat a month earlier for some serious do-it-yourself; and that very morning I was putting the last coat of paint to some bookshelves when I let in the caterers, who arrived with tables and chairs. I had the paintbrush in my hand as I opened the door, and was not surprised when they asked whether Mr Morley, the groom, was at home.

The small house nearly burst at the seams as our guests arrived that evening. Jane's parents, Arthur and Phyllis Tillett, her aunt, Marjorie Stevens, my sister Anne, my brother Tommy, his wife Molly and their three boys, Anthony, David and Richard; our closest friends, Thilde and Ernst Fraenkel, Shirley Nutten, Rosemary Peachment and many more; and from the television world Cyril and Shirley Bennett, the McMillans and Brian Connell.

It was a good party. Cinderella-like, at midnight our coach arrived to take us away to our short honeymoon in St Moritz. Jane had been on skis before, winter sporting in Austria, but I was a total novice. On our first day we signed up for lessons; surprisingly I was put into a more advanced class than Jane, and so on day one of our marriage I was separated from my bride. My group was taken up by ski-lift to a modest height (in my book it was the summit of a major peak), and the instructor shouted, 'See you all down below.' I was terrified, and, what's worse, totally humiliated when with yells of delight a large group of tiny children shot past me from much higher up the mountain. I came to two instant decisions: to slide down on my backside and, from that moment on, only to indulge in serious après-skiing. I arrived sore but safely in the valley and found Jane in her class of beginners. We came to the conclusion that this sport was not for us. Even so we had a good time, with excursions in cable cars to savour the views and to take in the air of this Alpine paradise. On the way back we stopped off in Lugano to look in on my mother and Harry Kahn.

* * * *

By September 1962 Cyril and I had been running *This Week* for well over a year and we were getting consistently encouraging press coverage and good audience ratings. The time had come for a heart to heart with John McMillan, and to put our 'six-months' on the table. We armed ourselves with some press cuttings. From the *Oxford Mail*: '*This Week* (9.15) has long since risen above the ignominious description once given to it as "poor man's *Panorama*" and now has a well-earned reputation for lucid and interesting presentation of current affairs.' And from the *Aberdeen Evening News*: '*This Week* is rapidly becoming one of the high spots of the week. Its simple forthright style combines the informality of "Tonight" with the searching eye of "Panorama" to provide one of the best ITV offerings.'

McMillan must have guessed our reason for wanting to see him, as on his desk was a large album also containing press cuttings. 'It's been an extremely long six months,' I said to John, 'and both of us want to move on.' I told him that from my point of view, as much as I relished the challenge of 'making it sing' (as he put it when he asked us to take on the programme), it would be better for A-R, and certainly better for me, if I could go back and do what I enjoyed most: making my own programmes. Cyril said that he was looking forward to a new challenge.

'Both of you have done me a huge favour, and the ITA and the Board are full of praise,' said John, 'and this is what I want you to do. Find a suitable successor to take over the show and you're free to do whatever you like.'

Little did we guess that it would take us another year to find the right person. We soldiered on, and in spite of the weekly grind of turning out a peak-time programme I almost enjoyed it, because *This Week* could hold its head up high. For a moment I thought that we might have sniffed out a successor when Reg's spy at the BBC suggested that *Panorama*'s very successful editor, Paul Fox, was looking for a change. I gave him a call, suggesting that it was about time we met and had a drink to toast our rivalry. He readily agreed, and we made the Old Bull and Bush, in Golders Green, our venue. Little did I realise that their spy in our camp had already told him that I was ready for a move away from *This Week*. We were much amused by the bizarre situation. Here we were, offering each other our jobs, and neither of us had the slightest interest: I wanted to go back to my own programme-making, while Paul had ambitions within the BBC. (He became Controller of BBC1, and some years later moved to ITV, as managing director of Yorkshire Television. I was to see quite a lot of him in both these roles.)

* * * *

We agreed with reporter Bryan Magee's suggestion to send a crew to the States to cover the 1962 mid-term elections. Having spent well over a year dispatching directors, reporters and crews all over the world, I decided that I would send myself to the other side of the pond as well, as I had never been to America. My PA, Rosemary Winckley, who had been brought up there, nobly volunteered to swap directors with Jane so that she could join me as my PA on this exciting trip. The plan was for us to fly over, take two weeks as holiday (a second honeymoon) and then meet Bryan Magee in Hollywood to cover Governor Pat Brown's stump around California. After that we planned to journey up to Michigan to do the same with Governor George Romney, then finish with Edward Kennedy in Massachusetts. A lot of preparations and planning had to be done, and as usual in a hurry. Because of American union rules I had to pick up local film crews in these locations.

I remember with some embarrassment an occasion during the planning of the trip when I was late in rushing across to the Savoy for a lunch date with an American embassy official. I pushed hard at that grand establishment's revolving door, not realising that someone was exiting at the same time. The poor man (he happened to be an American) was knocked to the ground; I apologised, helped him up, and he was very gracious about it all.

This was an exciting time. Jane and I could hardly wait to discover New York during the first week of the holiday. There were two aunts and six cousins to look up, none of whom I had seen since I was a small boy. We did all the tourist sights and more; and ever since I have cherished the thought of living and working in that amazing city for a year or so – an unfulfilled ambition – although I have been back very many times for short stays. Then we flew to Washington DC for a couple of days and were given an extensive tour, including Capitol Hill with the Senate in session. Our generous guide was Victor Sadd, a comrade-in-arms of Jane's father, who had served with him in the Suffolk Yeomanry at Gallipoli during the First World War.

After Washington we travelled to San Francisco, and after two days sightseeing we picked up a hire car to take us down to Los Angeles. I chose an open Chevrolet, white with red upholstery: it was just like being in the movies. We chose the coastal road, as I was keen to stay overnight near San Simeon. I simply had to see William Hearst's Xanadu; my early memories of *Citizen Kane* and Orson Welles made this mandatory. I was not disappointed.

Then on to Hollywood. We checked into the Washington Hotel, rising early the following morning for our last holiday treat – a drive out to Disneyland. I wanted to be back at the hotel by 2 p.m. to rendezvous with *This Week* reporter Bryan Magee, who was due in from London. The huge size of Disneyland's car park, almost deserted so early in the day, was most impressive. We sampled a great number of the attractions, and against expectations I was surprised that it was all staged in such good taste.

We left at noon to face a nightmare. The massive car park was a sea of cars, including hundreds of white Chevrolets with red upholstery. I panicked because I had failed to make a note of where we had left ours, and found myself having to try dozens of doors. We finally made it back to the hotel, just after 2 p.m. Then occurred one of those bizarre coincidences for which there is no explanation. I said to Jane that I would quickly pop in to see if Bryan had arrived, rushed to the entrance, pushed hard on the revolving door and, to my horror, knocked down an exiting man. It was the very same victim who had received my Savoy treatment a few weeks earlier. I was speechless, and all he could say was, 'Not you again!' Truth really can be stranger than fiction.

Just as we were organising the local film crew and getting ready to start filming with Pat Brown on his Californian re-election stump, the October 1962 Cuban missile crisis balloon went up. This was a piece of fortuitous timing for *This Week*. Telexes to and from Cyril in London soon established the line we were going to follow. Bryan's interviews with Governor Pat Brown reflected this world crisis, and we were right in the middle of it. It was fascinating for a non-journalist like me.

We spent about three days in and around LA and then flew to Detroit to do the same with Governor Romney and his cronies. We finished that assignment, and on 22 October we found ourselves at Detroit airport waiting to be called for a flight to Boston. I overheard a waiting passenger say that President Kennedy was about to address the nation, so I got out the pocket transistor radio that I had brought back from Japan – it always travelled with me whenever I left London in case there was any breaking news about Churchill's health. A crowd of passengers straining to hear JFK on my tiny radio pressed around me. It was a dramatic moment: the Soviet ships carrying missiles were nearing Cuba.

When we arrived at Boston airport we picked up the film crew and drove into the country to find Edward Kennedy, who was out on the stump. It was a memorable drive: we had heard about the display of New England's foliage with its fantastic colours in the fall, but never expected anything so spectacular. We found young Teddy Kennedy and his entourage coming out of a church in a small Massachusetts village and grabbed him for an interview. Bryan naturally asked him what he thought his brother the president should do, with the world on the brink of nuclear conflict. We were all astonished when he told Bryan that he hadn't really thought about it. More questions elicited similar responses. Whenever I saw him on television subsequently I was amazed at the way in which he developed to play such an important political role in the United States.

We packed up and flew to New York, having arranged with London to base ourselves at the UN headquarters and cover the crisis from the very centre of the storm. The next few days were nail-biting, and we managed to grab politicians as they flitted in and out of that building. We had booked accommodation at the Beekman Tower Hotel nearby, and I well remember that we got little sleep. Of the many interviews we shot the most impressive was with Senator Hubert Humphrey, later to become Lyndon Johnson's vice-president. We also filmed *vox pop* interviews in Time Square, and Bryan and I were surprised to record so many bellicose, gung-ho sentiments.

It was now 26 October – United Nations Day: always a cause for celebration. And in the middle of this unprecedented and frightening drama the Tel Aviv Symphony Orchestra performed a concert in the main UN chamber: even the Russian delegates attended.

Two days later, on the 28th, the world breathed again, with Kennedy and Khrushchev declaring a solution to the missile crisis in Cuba. We pulled up sticks and returned to London.

I found it quite hard settling down to the weekly programme pattern, but at least I knew that there would be an end to it once we had found the right person to take over. It took another ten months before we struck gold. Our saviour was Jeremy Isaacs, who was making his mark at Granada Television as editor of the popular *What the Papers Say* and other successful current affairs programmes like *World in Action*, and was keen for a move. Cyril and I could not have handed our baby over to a more talented pair of hands. He made many changes to the programme, and under his editorship it climbed to its highest peak.

On 15 August 1963 we went on the air for the last time; thanks to the press, our departure did not go unnoticed. Maurice Richardson wrote in the *Observer*: When you think what it used to be like, the improvement in A-R's *This Week* since Peter Morley and Cyril Bennett took over two years ago has been quite phenomenal.' In the *Sunday Times* Maurice Wiggin commented: Peter Morley and Cyril Bennett leave *This Week* in the highest point of renown. Their enterprise has made it a feature not to be missed.'

On 22 November, at the Guild of Television Producers and Directors annual award ceremony at the Dorchester Hotel, Cyril and I were presented with our masks (now known as the BAFTA masks) for the best Current Affairs programme. This was the first time that ITV had gained this award, and we were in good company: other award winners included Harold Pinter, Vivien Merchant, Joan Kemp-Welch, Morecambe and Wise, Alan Badel, Anthony Craxton and Bernard Braden. But our euphoria came to a sudden halt when awful news spread across the dance floor to the dining tables: John F. Kennedy had been assassinated in Dallas.

Many who had attended the evening's celebrations raced to their various news desks, leaving those of us who were left totally bewildered. Jane and I did not really take it in until the next morning, when all the lurid details began to emerge.

Two evenings later John McMillan phoned me. He wanted a fully networked live tribute programme the following night, 25 November, the day of Kennedy's funeral. I phoned Cyril, and we quickly decided on the style we wanted, taking into account that we had just under twenty-four hours before we went on the air. That evening we recruited Bernard Levin to write the tribute, and he gave us lists of books by American authors and poets that he needed first thing in the morning in order to compile a selection of appropriate readings. He would then write the linking material for whoever was conducted the tribute. I remember looking up the telephone number of Vivienne Moynihan, A-R's casting director, at midnight to give her some suggestions of American names to contact first thing, and to find out who was in town. I suggested to Cyril that Laurence Olivier would be right for the presenter's role; fortunately Vivienne knew him well. During the next hectic day we recruited the services of Eli Wallach, Anne Bancroft, Gary Merrill and Joseph C. Harsh as the readers. A quick call to Michael Yates, our head of design, and we settled for stark simplicity – four lecterns against a background of black drapes. By lunchtime Bernard Levin had produced a most moving and brilliant script, and Laurence Olivier had agreed to come to the studio two hours before transmission so that I could introduce him to the trick of reading from the teleprompter, which he had never done before.

We went on the air at 9.30 p.m., and it turned out to be a very moving programme. It was telerecorded, and at the request of the American Embassy copies were made available to be shown all over the world.

* * * *

This broadcast marked the end of my close four-year partnership with Cyril Bennett. It was an exciting adventure in which we explored the magic of television, learning about its power and its strengths, as well as its limitations.

Town magazine interviewed us, and came out with this embarrassingly flattering piece, which modesty compels me to quote:

> Peter Morley is the producer of *This Week*, Associated-Rediffusion's answer to *Panorama*, with Cyril Bennett as the editor beside him. Morley, 38, handsome, courteous and well-liked, is typical of this

> better type of ITV features producer – a skilled technician who pushes himself and others hard, and lives and breathes television. He joined A-R in 1956 after years in the film industry, directing and film-editing documentaries – and the experience he picked up there on the cutting floor is responsible for much of the polish and the often poetic quality of *This Week*'s film work. He and Bennett have worked as a team at A-R since 1957, first making documentaries, then building *This Week* into the best regular serious programme on ITV, with unusual autonomy. Their secret: they cancel out each other's limitations – Bennett, a journalist, is no expert in filming, and Morley is no authority on current affairs, which he leaves to Bennett. Now Bennett is being promoted to features director, and Morley too will get some new overlordship of features production. The tandem will continue at higher executive level and the next challenge will be colour TV.

Cyril and I had a good laugh over this – and went our separate ways. Cyril rose to head of A-R's features department, four years later emerging as the Controller of Programmes of the newly created London Weekend Television.

Israel Rises – The Birth of a Nation, 1959

ISRAEL RISES

ISRAEL RISES

Transmitted Thursday, June 4th, 1959

Those taking part in the programme:

KENNETH HARRIS

HIS EXCELLENCY ABBA EBAN

LADY MEGAN LLOYD GEORGE

PROFESSOR LAURENCE RUSHBROOK WILLIAMS

Script	**Cyril Bennett**
Script research	**Reg Courtney-Browne**
Film research	**John Mountford**
Cameraman	**Harry Hart**
Sound recordists	**Basil Rootes and Fred Slade**
Film editor	**Charles Squires**

Directed by **PETER MORLEY**

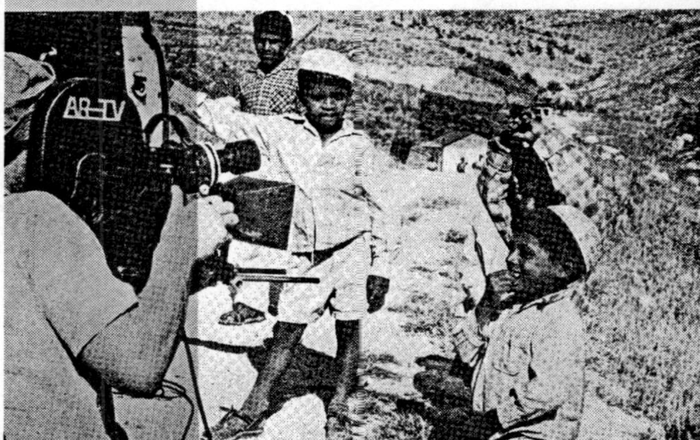

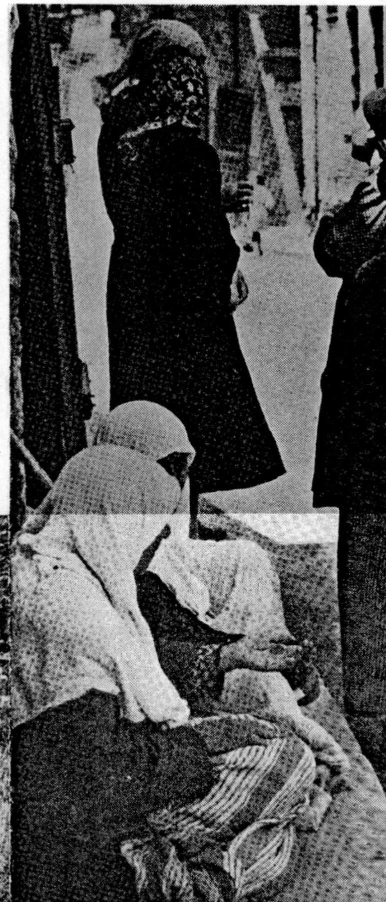

Associated-Rediffusion

TELEVISION HOUSE, KINGSWAY, LONDON, W.C.2

Printed in England, June 8th 1959

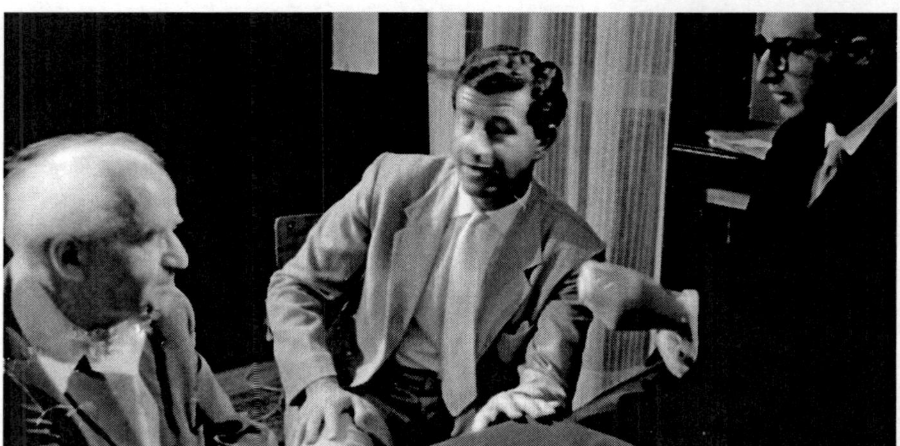

With Cyril Bennett, interviewing Prime Minister Ben Gurion.
(Rediffusion Television)

The Turn of the Screw, 1959

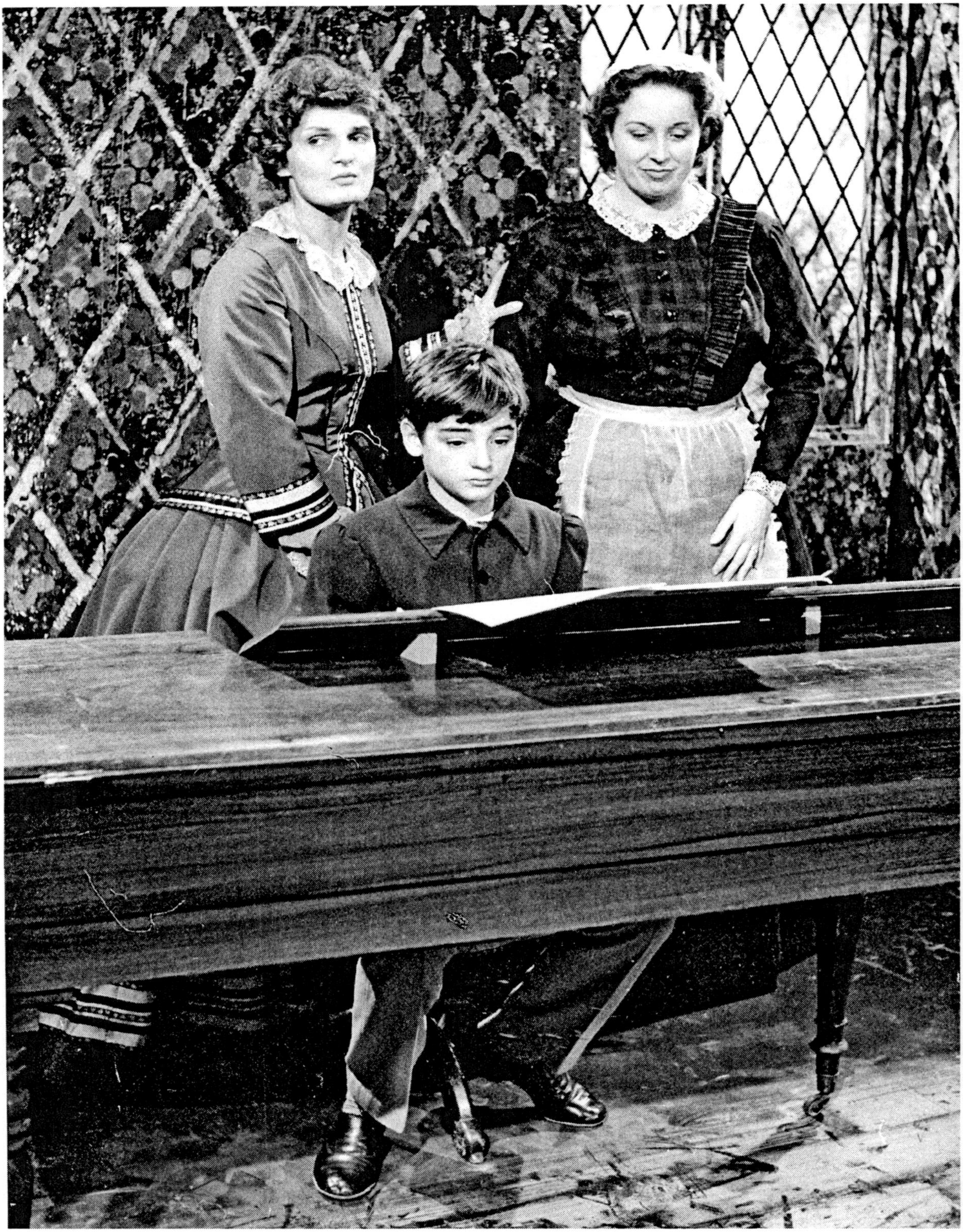

The Governess (Jennifer Vyvyan) and Miles (Tom Bevan) and The Housekeeper (Judith Pearce) (Rediffusion Television)

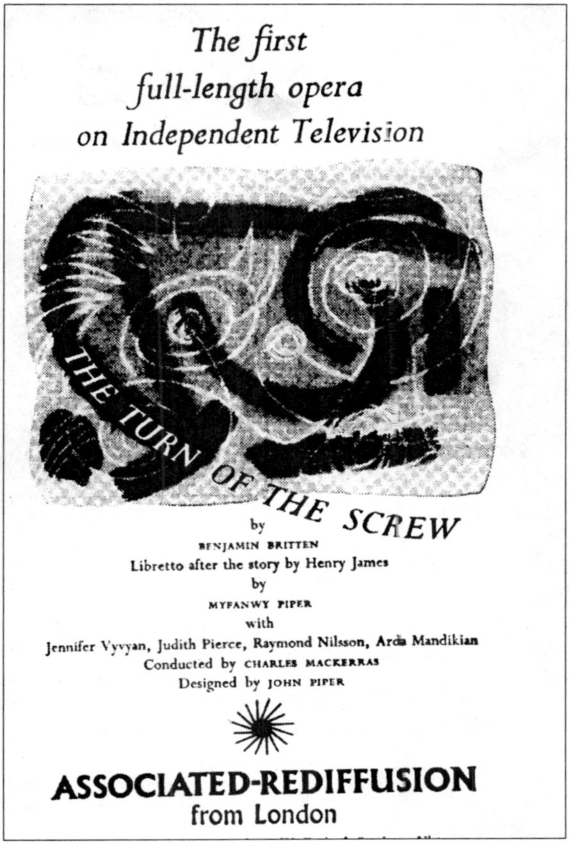

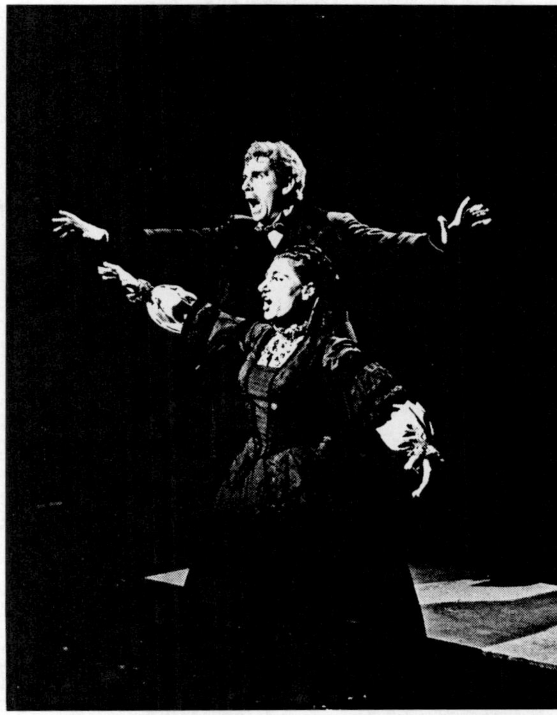

The Ghosts: Quint (Raymond Nilsson) and Miss Jessel (Arda Mandikian). (Rediffusion Television)

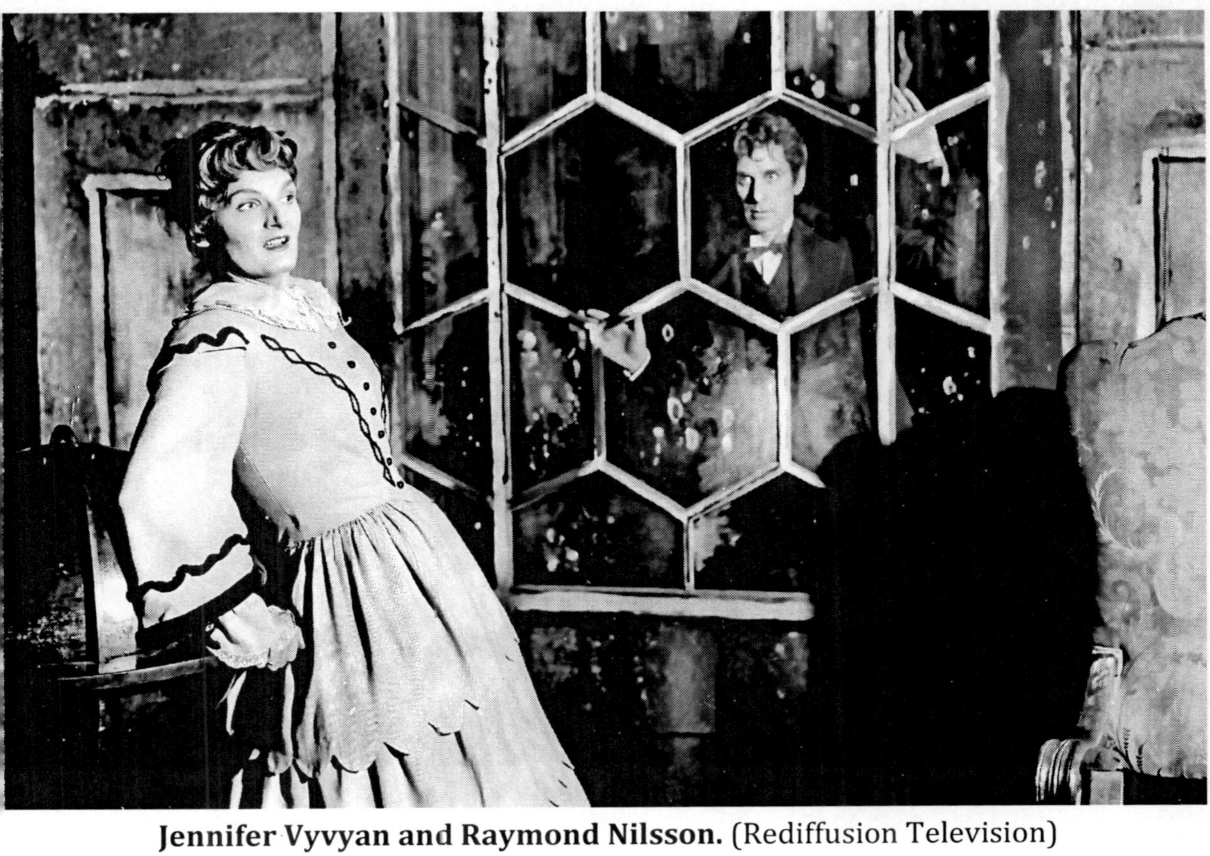

Jennifer Vyvyan and Raymond Nilsson. (Rediffusion Television)

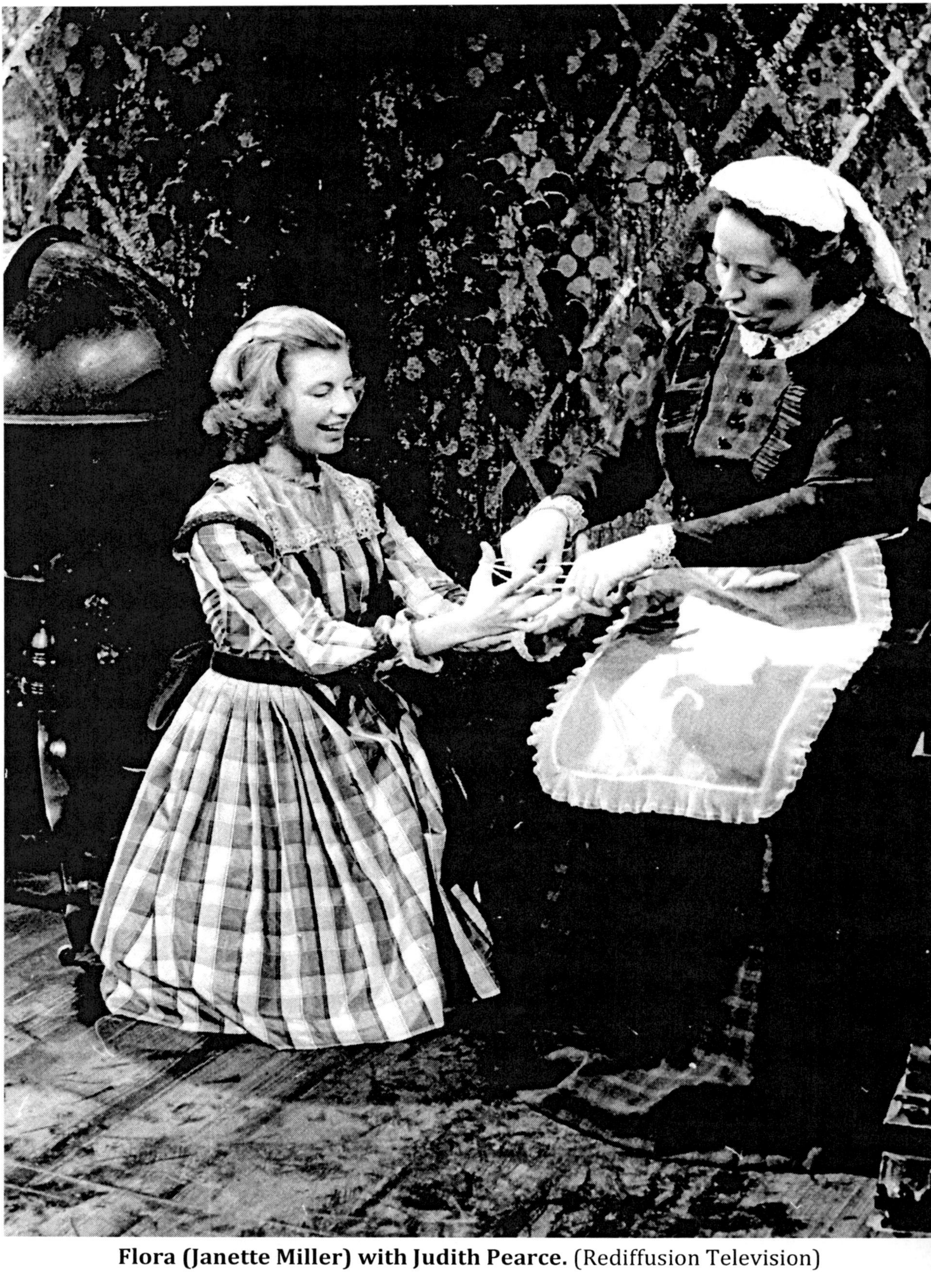

Flora (Janette Miller) with Judith Pearce. (Rediffusion Television)

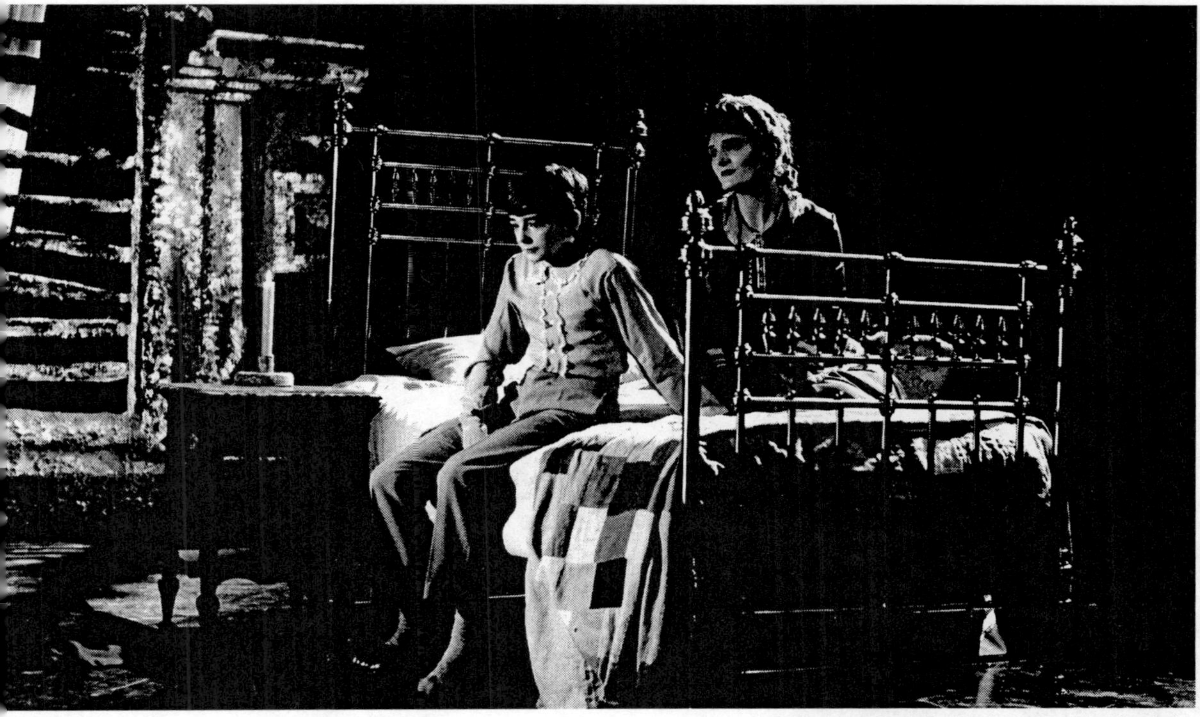

'Miles, dear little Miles, is there nothing you want to tell me?' (Rediffusion Television)

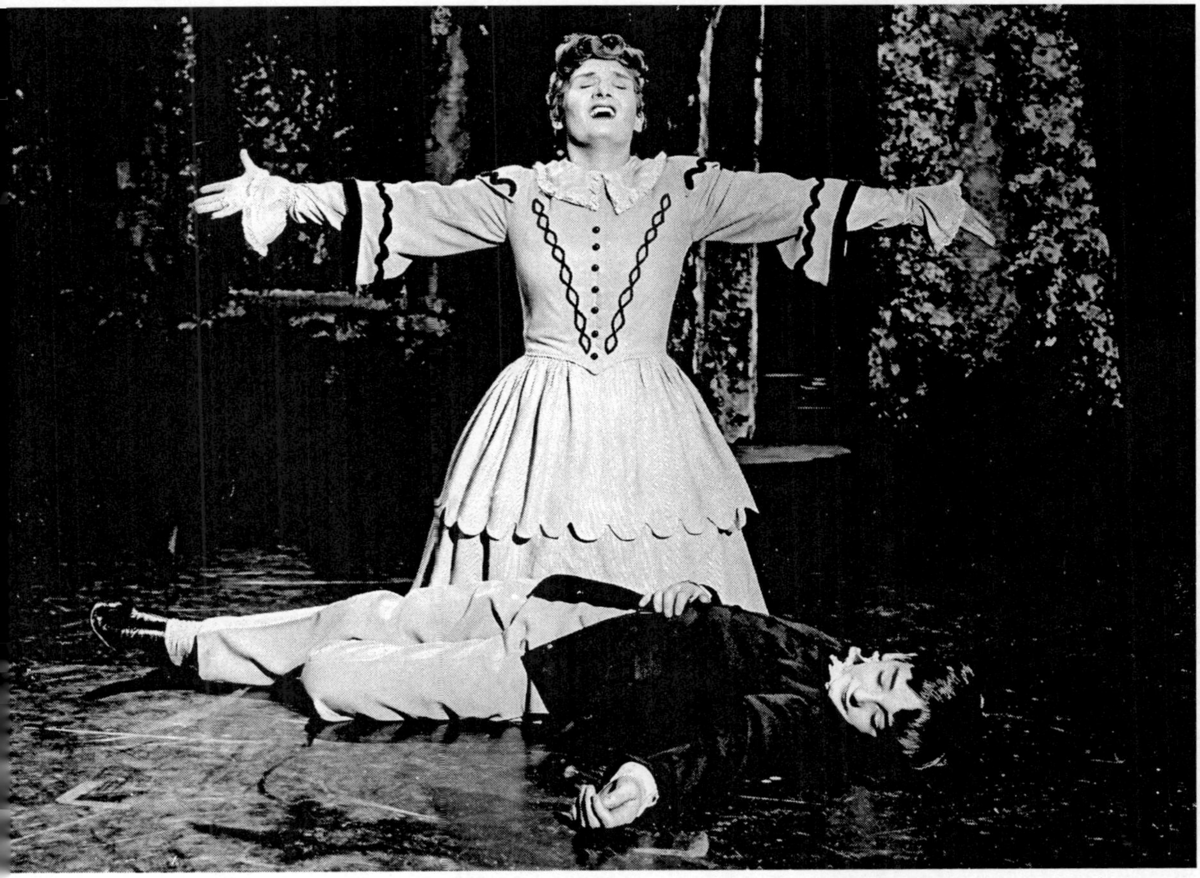

'What have we done between us?' (Rediffusion Television)

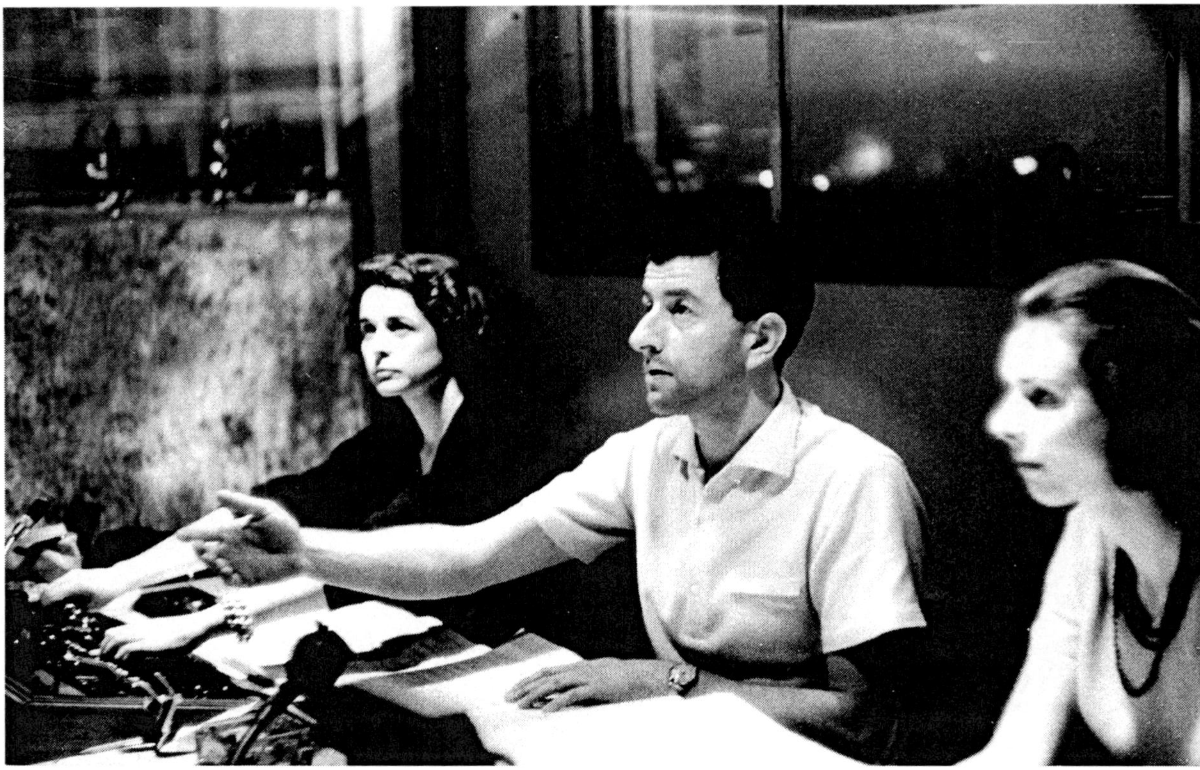

Directing the *Screw* in Studio 5, Wembley: Bridget Booth, vision mixer and Rosemary Winckley, production assistant. (Rediffusion Television)

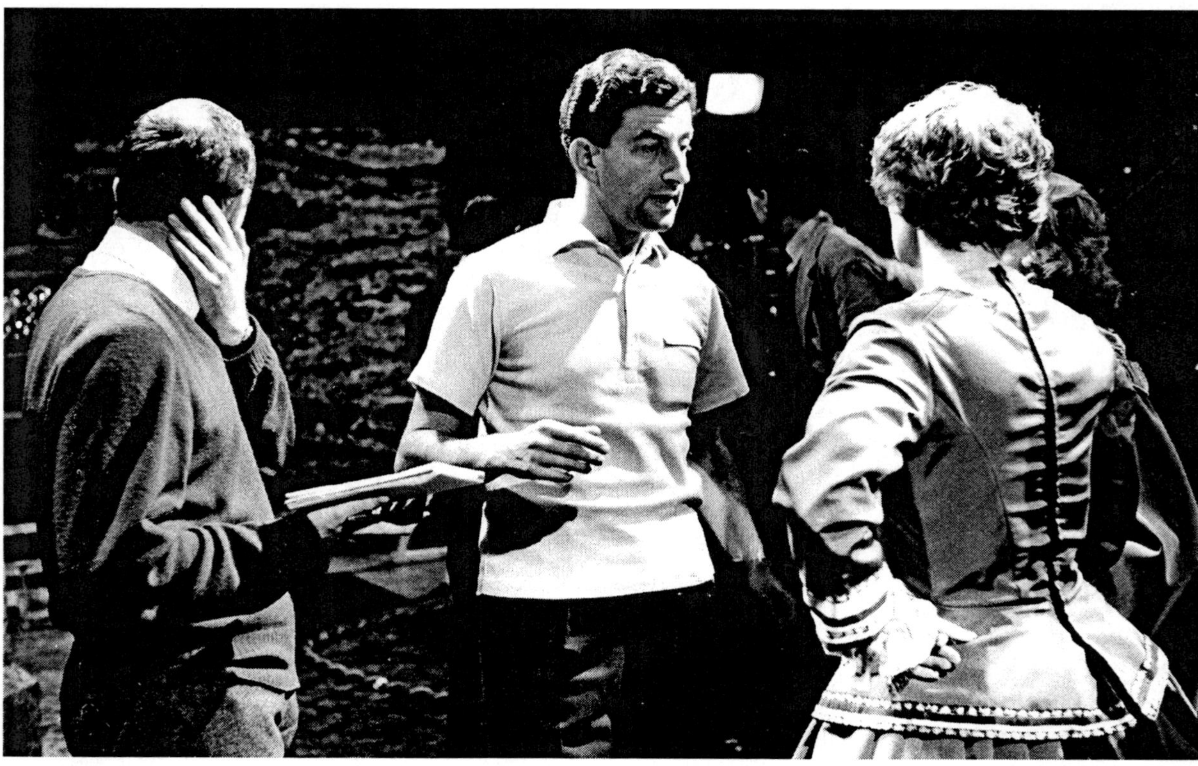

Final notes to Jennifer Vyvyan in a break before recording 'as for live'. Colin Graham is in attendance. (Rediffusion Television)

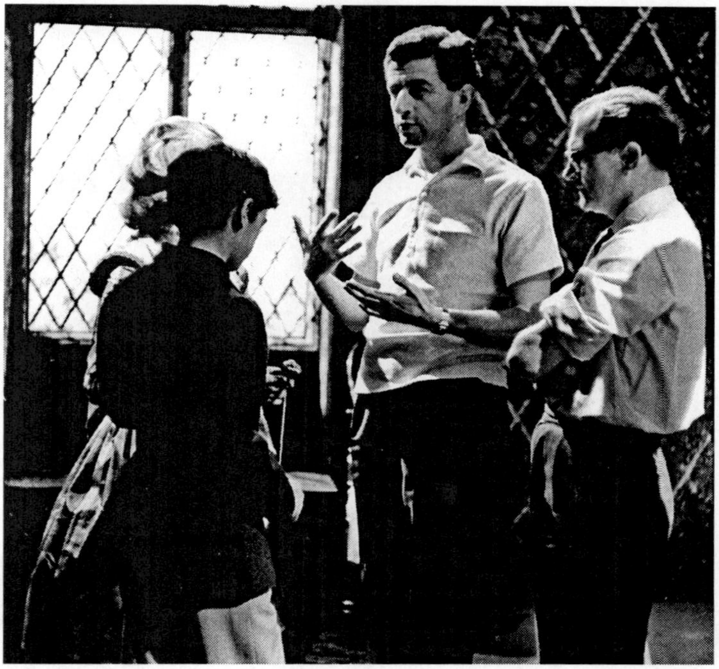

Miles and Flora receiving notes during a camera rehearsal. (Rediffusion Television)

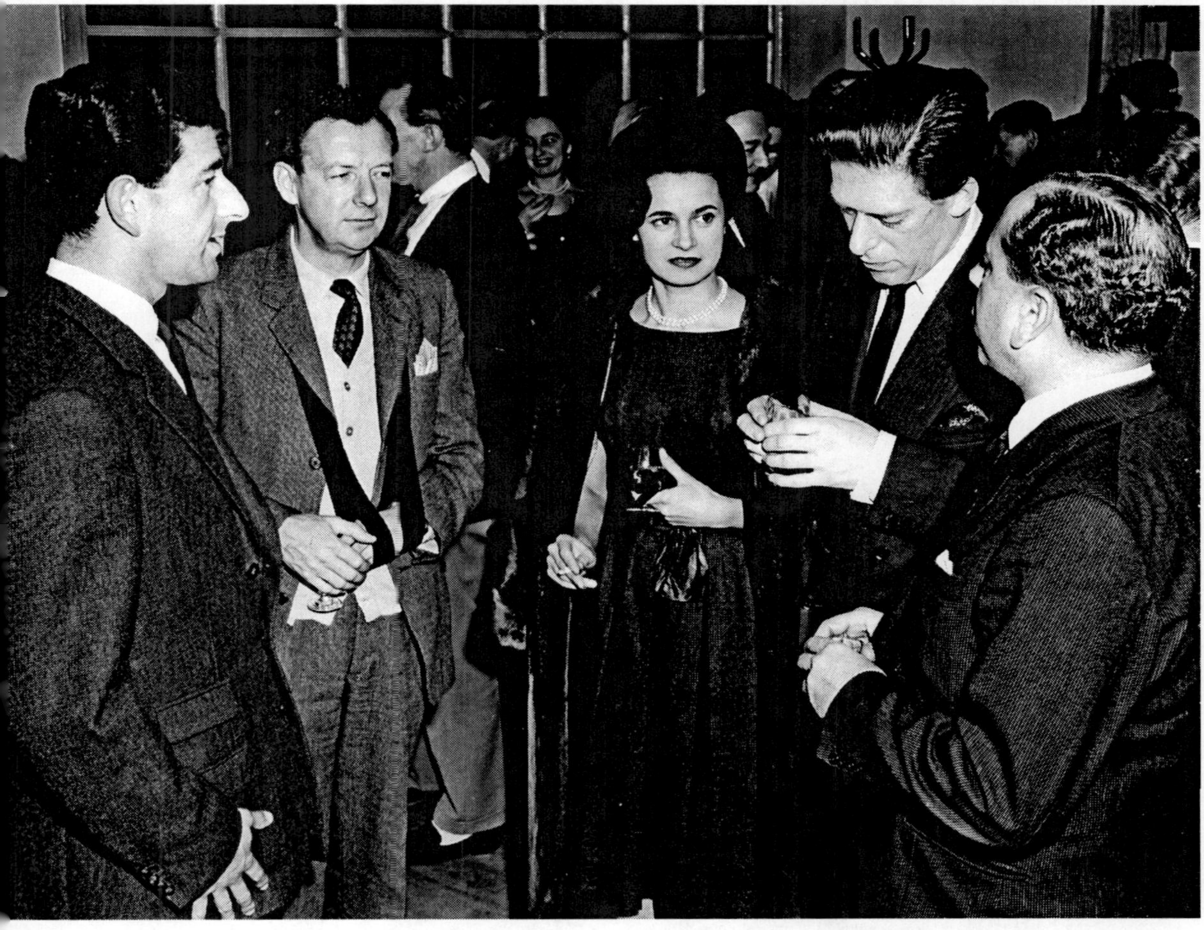

Feeling a bit nervous at Associated-Rediffusion's press preview, with Benjamin Britten, Lord and Lady Harewood and John McMillan. (Rediffusion Television)

The Two Faces of Japan, 1960

9.25 NEWS
The latest from the newsroom of ITN

9.35 THE TWO FACES OF JAPAN

Japan, 1960 . . . Fifteen years after the first atomic bomb exploded on Hiroshima and the surrender of the Imperial Japanese Army, it is at peace. But it is a country of extreme contrasts. Rock 'n' roll and the Geisha girl; baseball and arranged marriages; mob violence and Buddhism. Have the Japanese changed? Despite 15 years of democracy, the Japanese still believe in violent solutions to their problems. A few days after he was interviewed in Tokyo for this programme, the leader of Japan's Socialist Party, I. Asanuma was assassinated. An Associated-Rediffusion Features Unit spent two months travelling in Japan to picture, in human terms, the impact of Western modernisation on the unvarying ritual, the strict code of discipline that is the essential feature of the Japanese nation. The programme poses two major questions for Britain: Are we ever going to have to fight Japan again? Will Japan ever again be an economic threat to this country?

Introduced by **Tom Harrisson**

*Written by **Cyril Bennett***
*Research by **Reginald Courtney-Browne***
*Film editor **Charles Squires***
*Film cameraman **Saburo Iwamura***
Camera assistants
Takayoshi Sugiuchi, Hiroyasu Koitabashi** and **Goro Uchiyama
Sound crew
Chisato Ota** and **Michio Orimoto
*Directed by **PETER MORLEY***
An Associated-Rediffusion Network Production
(See Page 18)

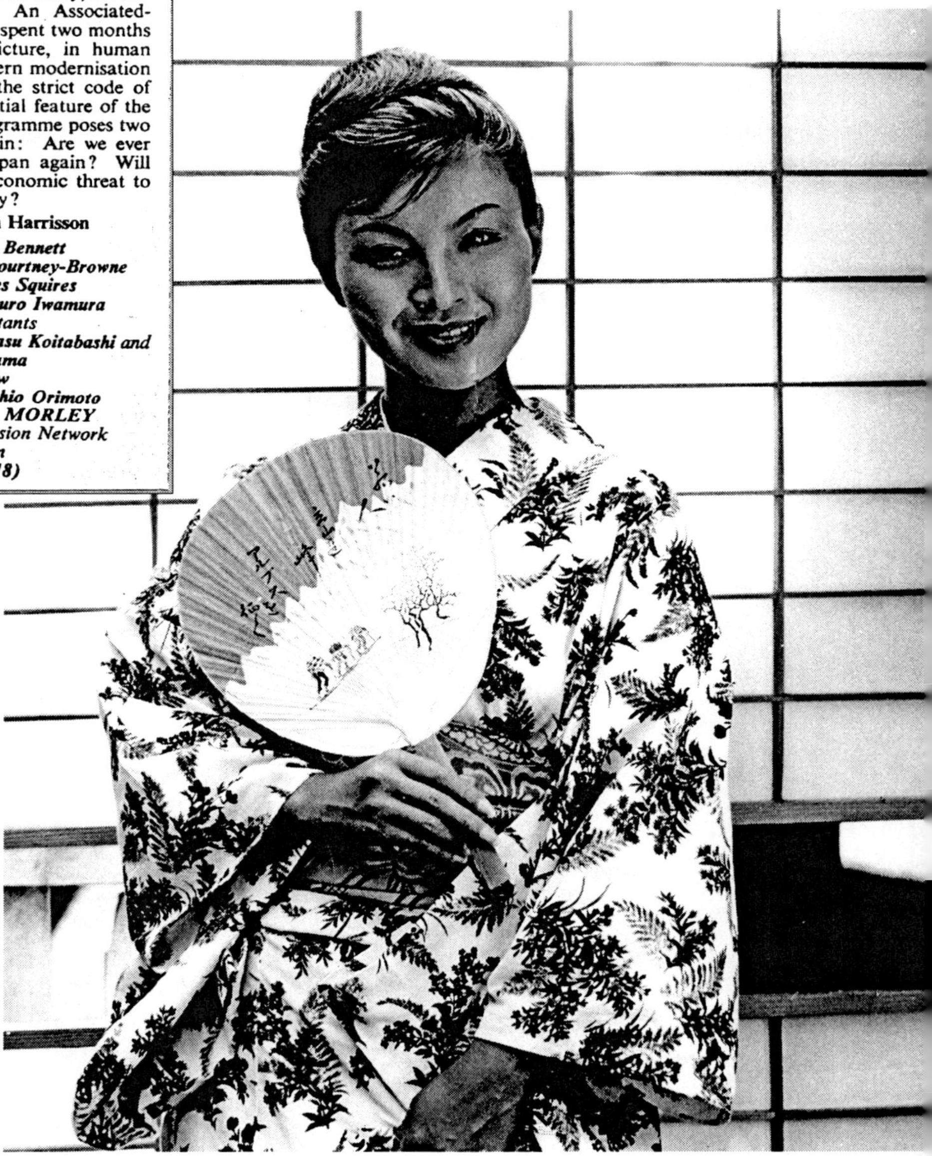

Shigeko Yamasaki: a twenty-two-year-old Tokyo model at home . . . (Rediffusion Television)

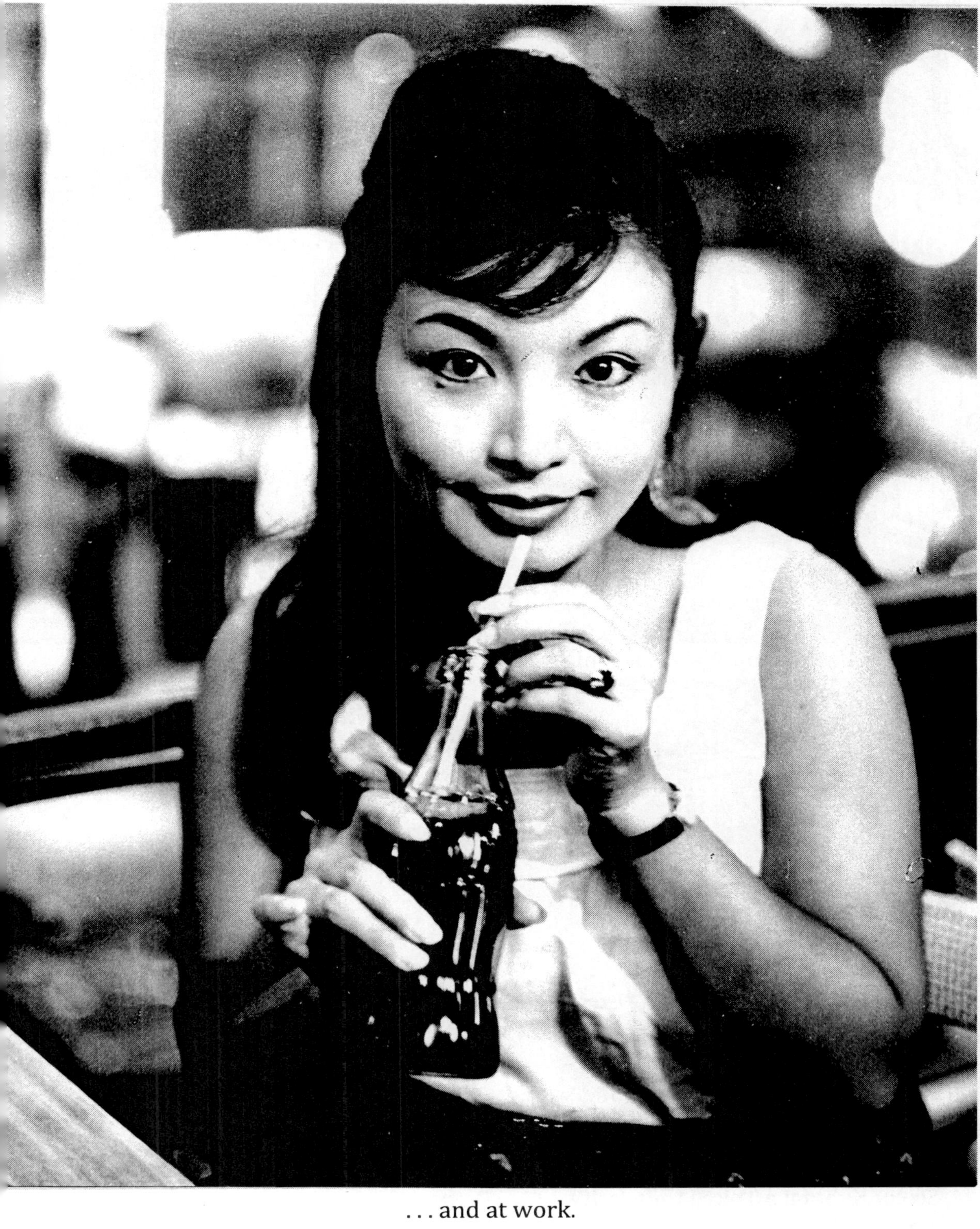

. . . and at work.

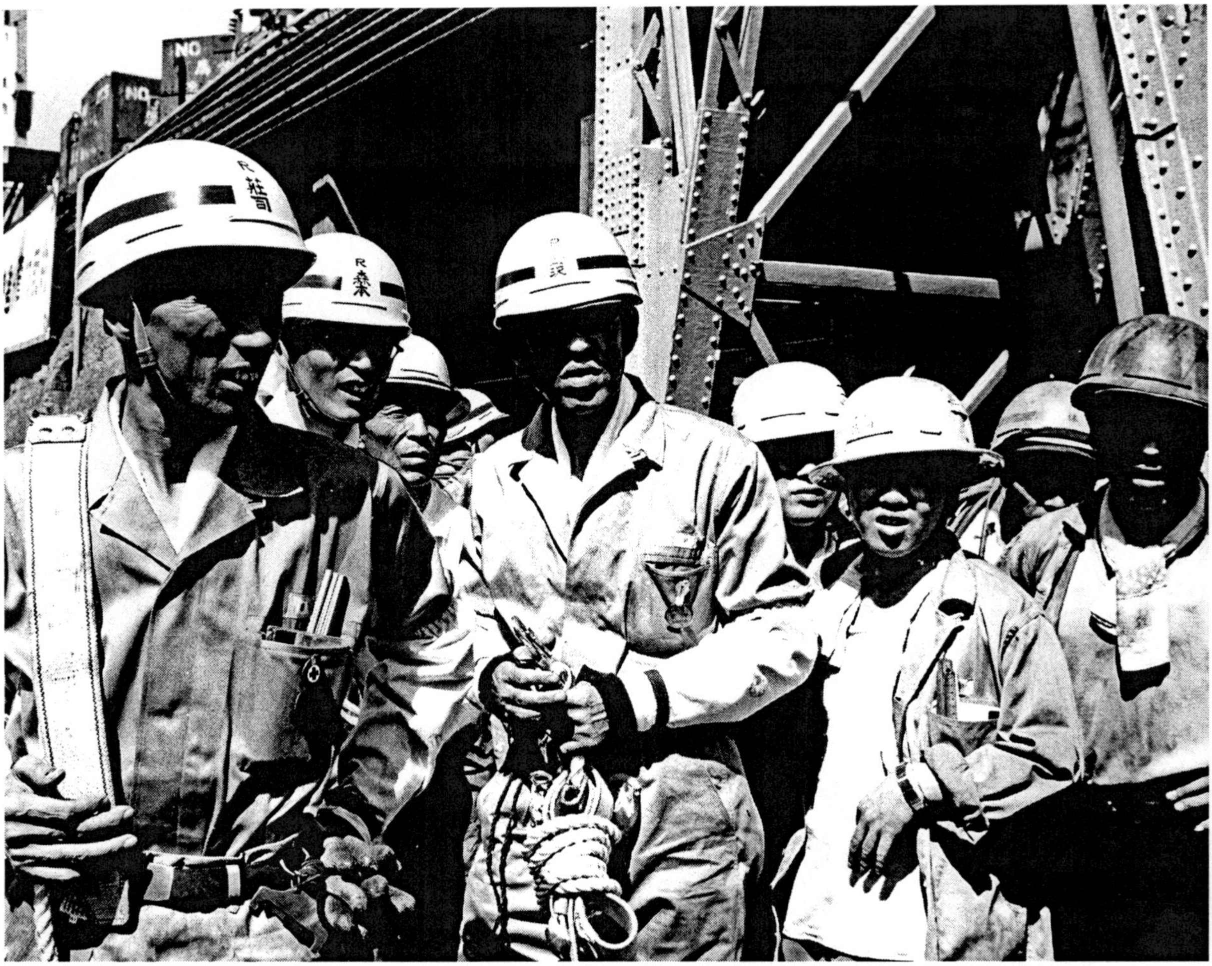

Uzuki Shoji: Kawasaki shipyard worker. (Rediffusion Television)

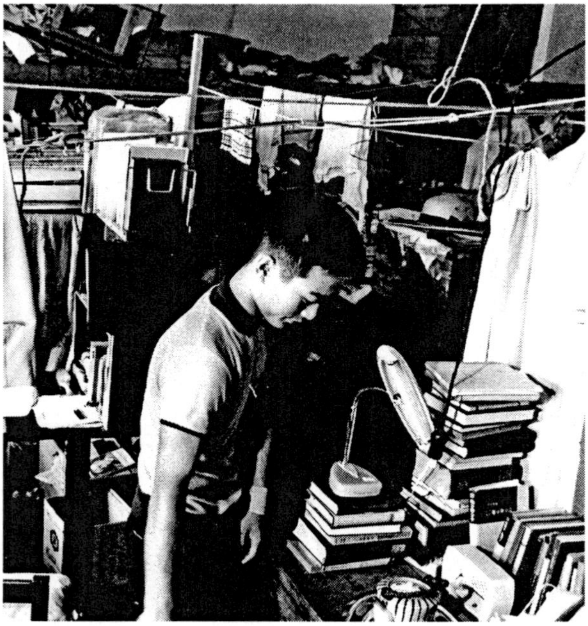

Seichi Kubota: a Tokyo University student. (Rediffusion Television)

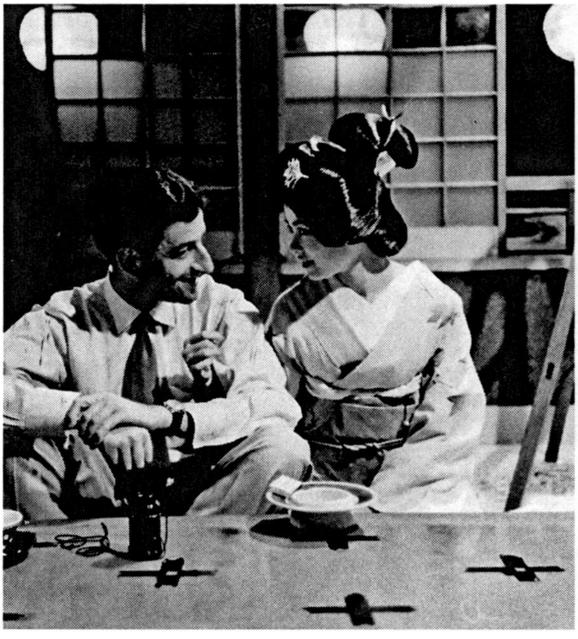

East meets West: research for the film was not unpleasant! (Rediffusion Television)

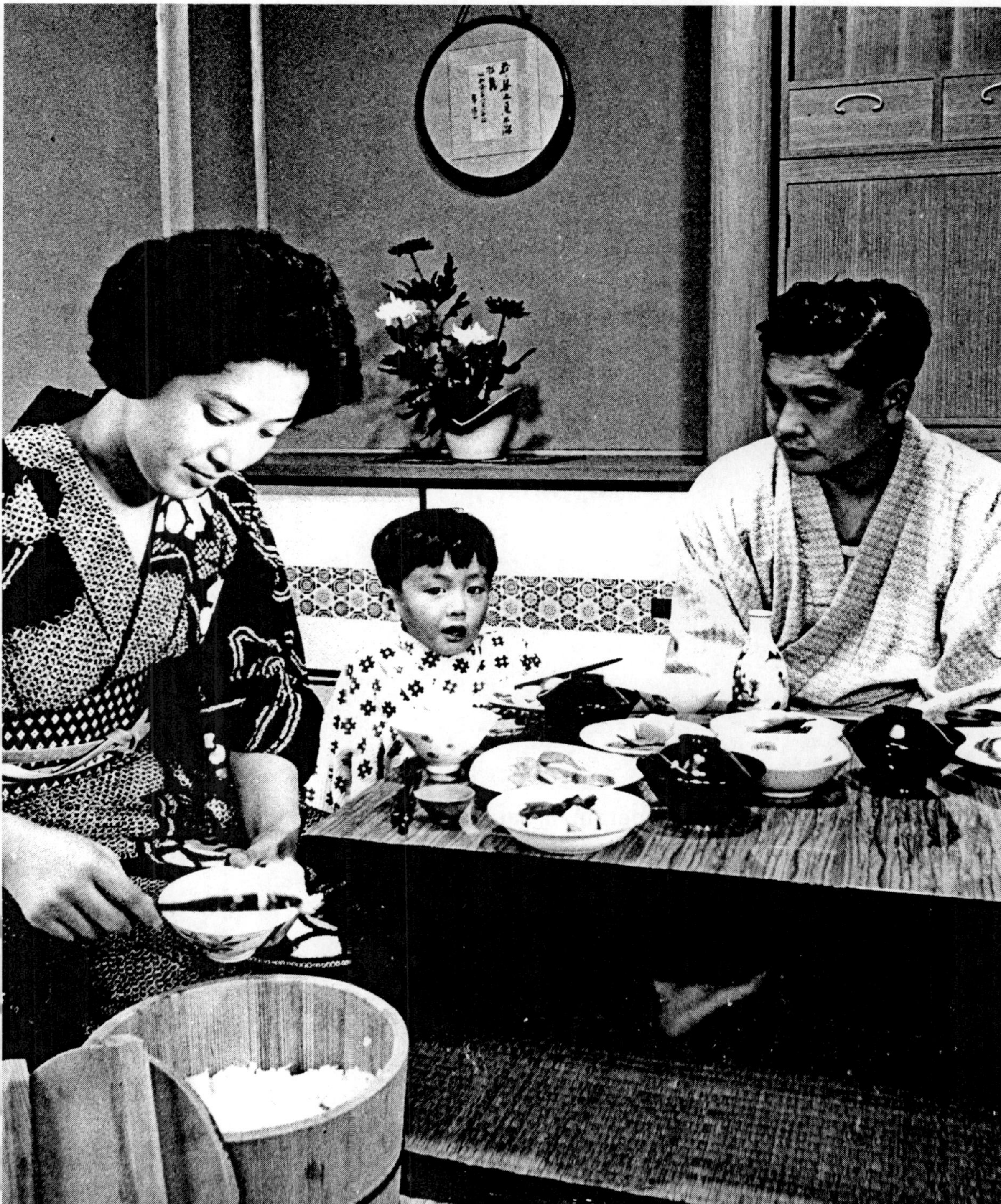

Shizu Yamaoka: housewife. (Rediffusion Television)

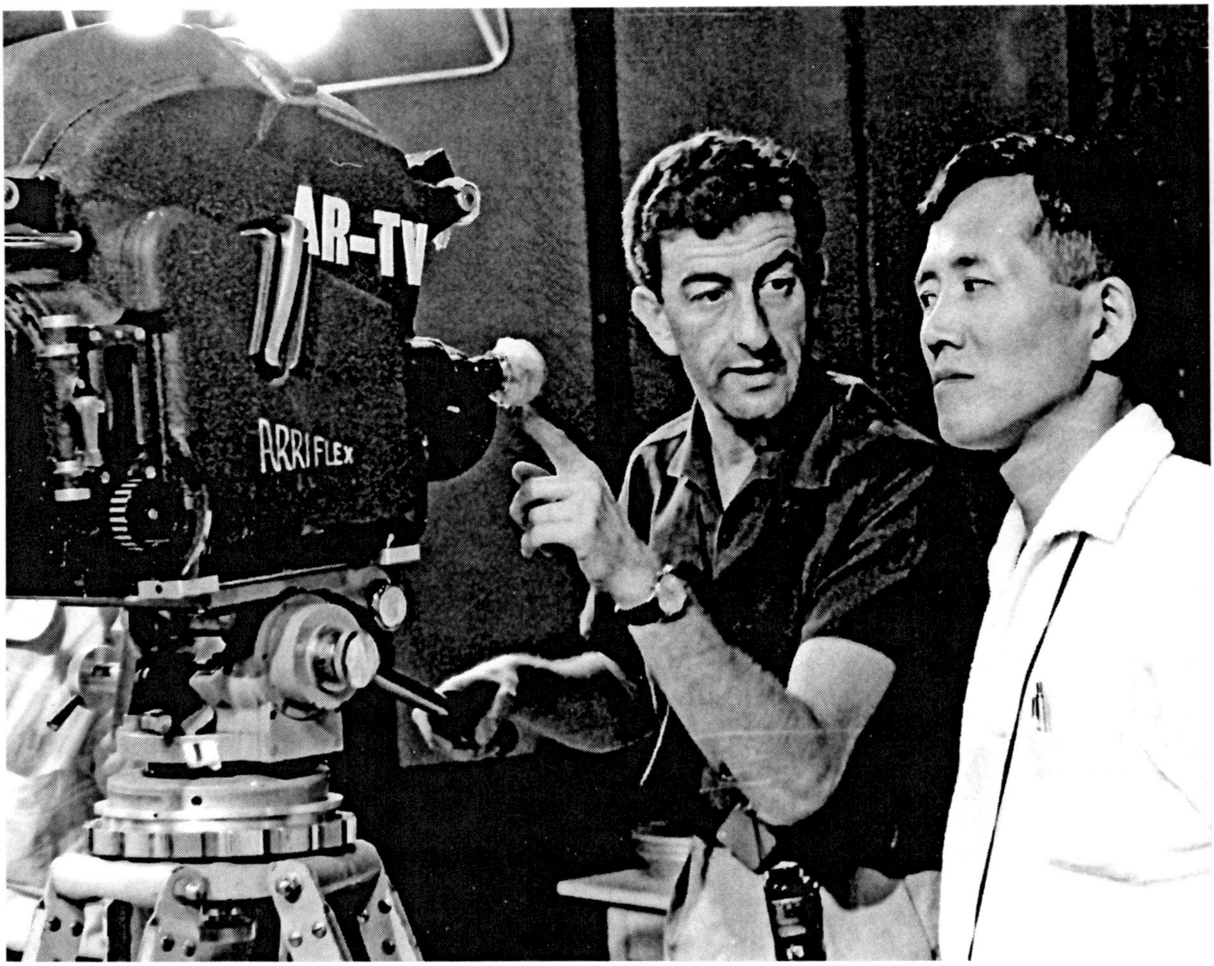

Breaking the ice with my cameraman, Sabura Iwamura. (Rediffusion Television)

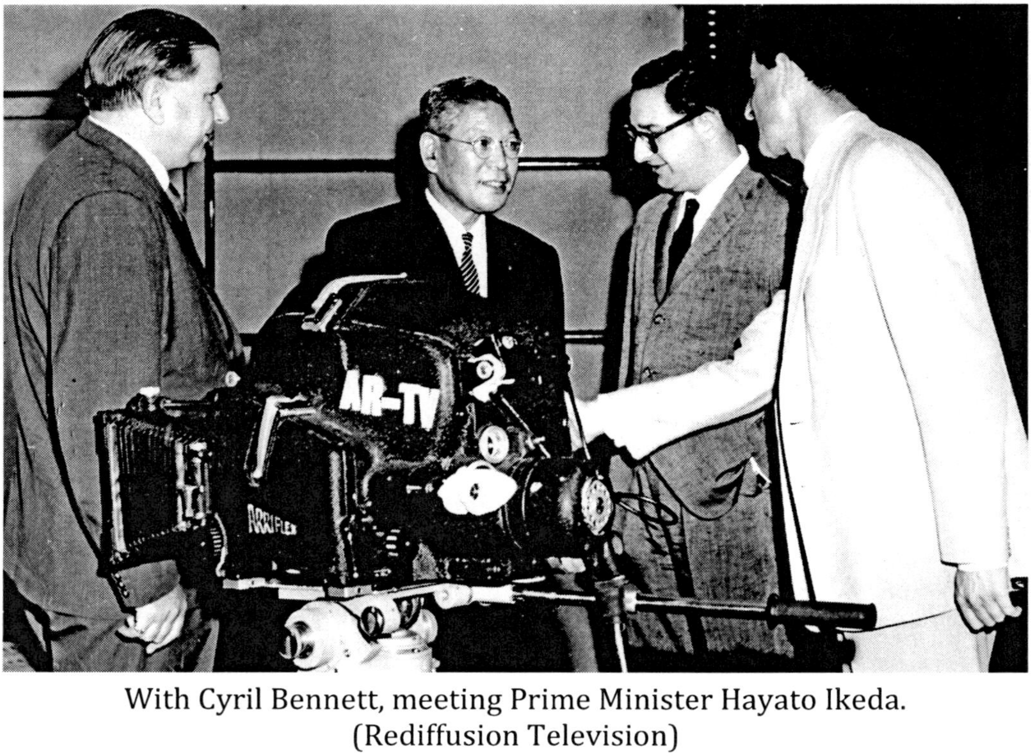

With Cyril Bennett, meeting Prime Minister Hayato Ikeda.
(Rediffusion Television)

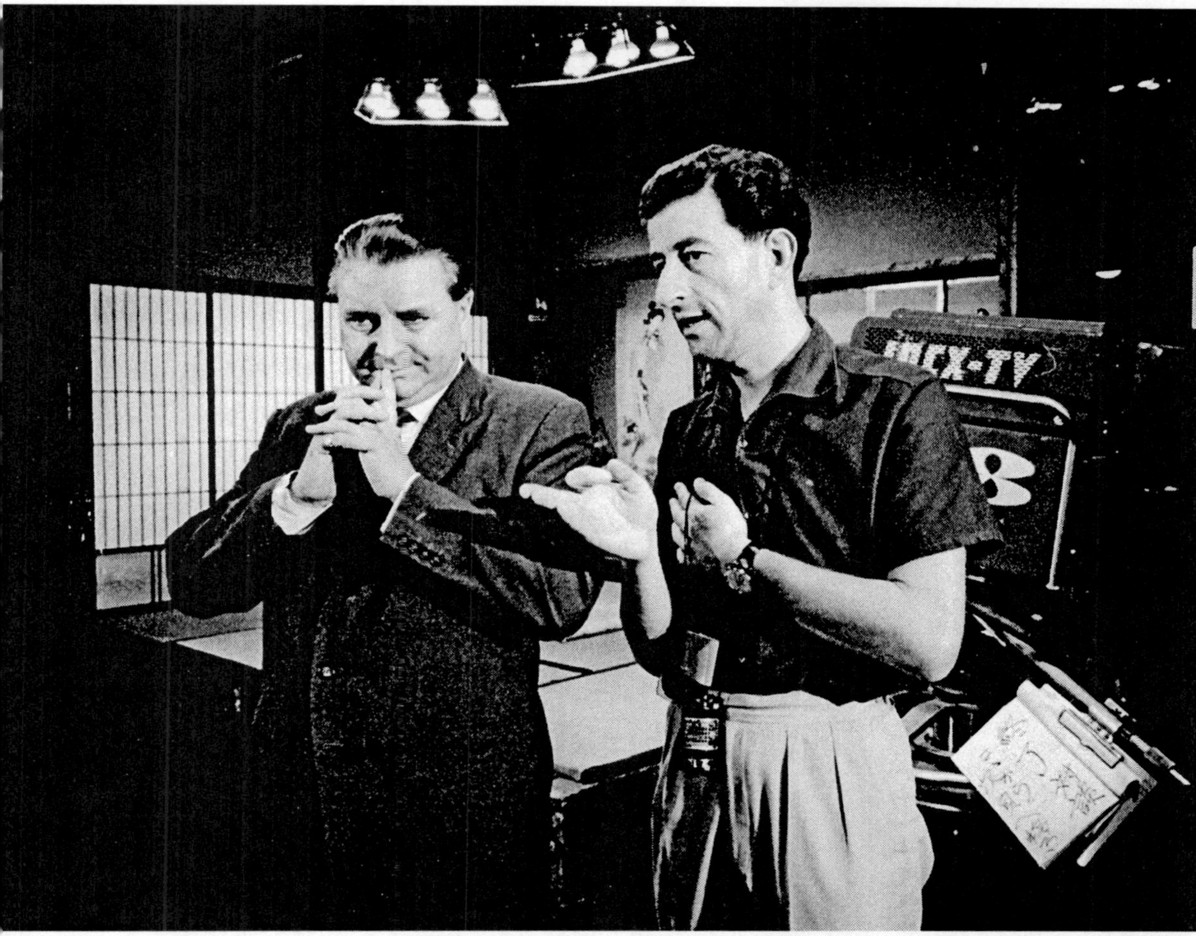

Finalising 'to camera' links with Tom Harrison. (Rediffusion Television)

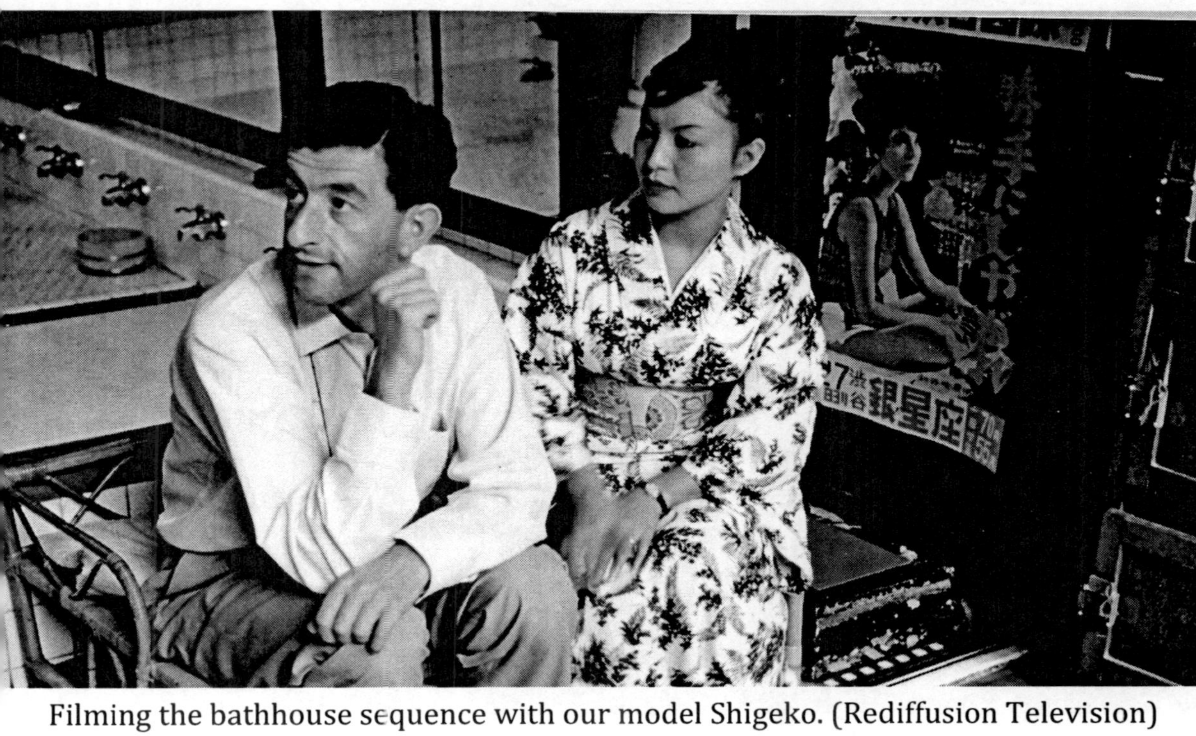

Filming the bathhouse sequence with our model Shigeko. (Rediffusion Television)

The Heartbeat of France, 1960

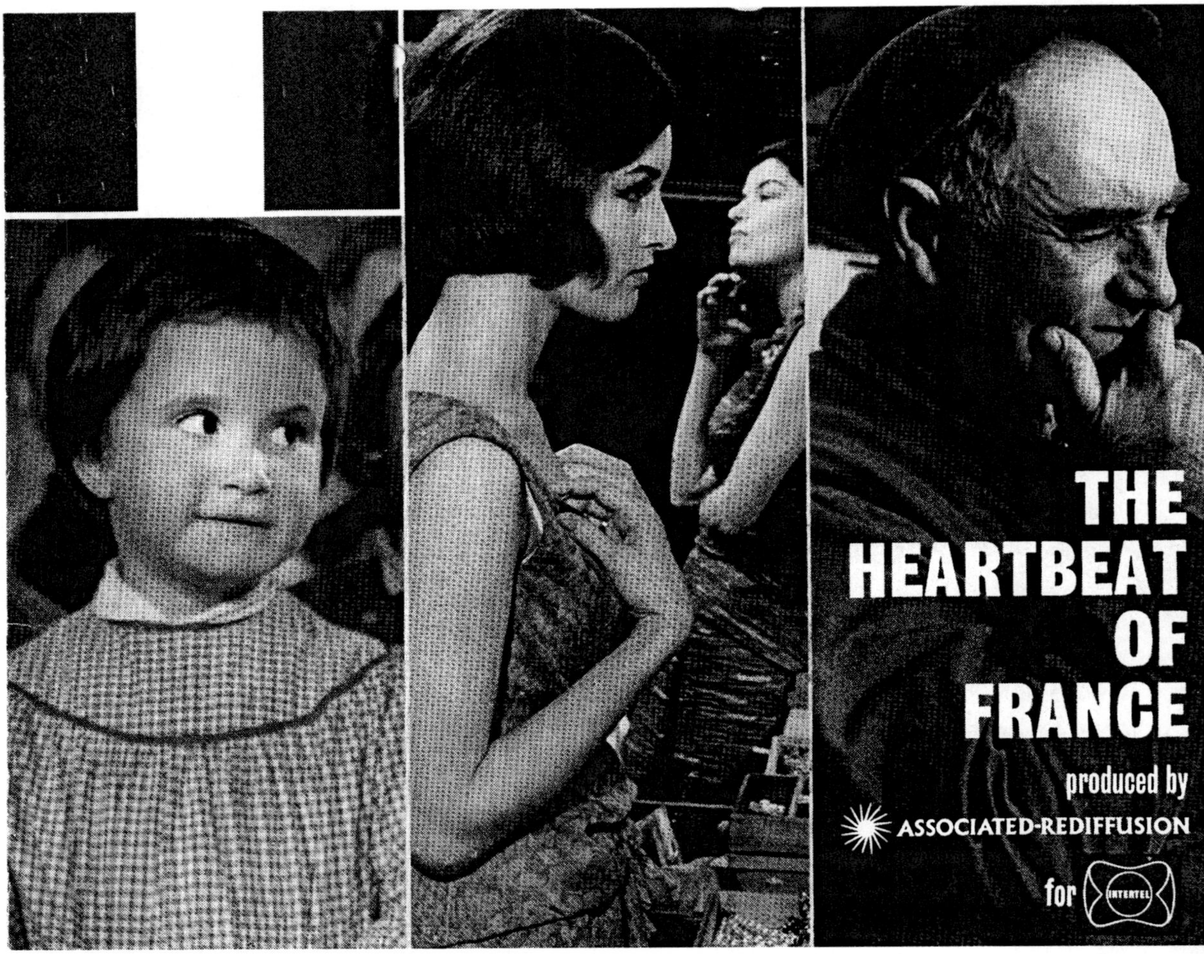

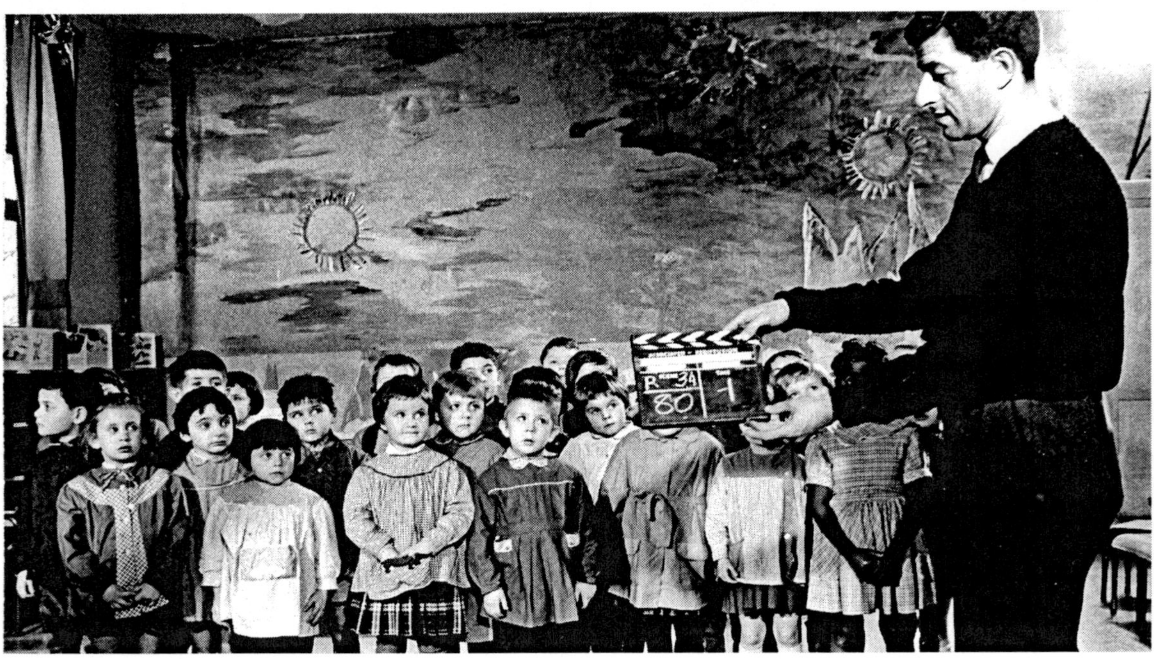

A cast of thousands! (Rediffusion Television)

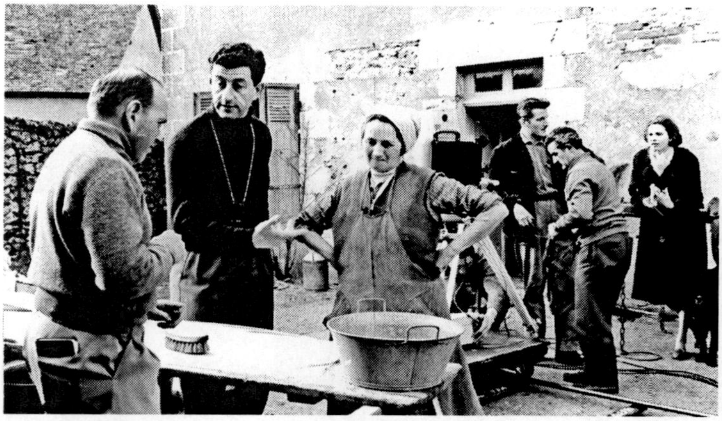

Shooting on Mme Furtain's farm. (Rediffusion Television)

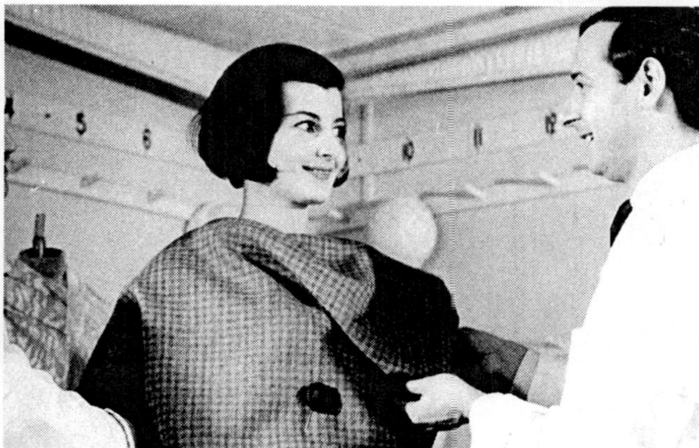

Christian Dior designer Marc Bohan dressing Gail, his favourite model. (Rediffusion Television)

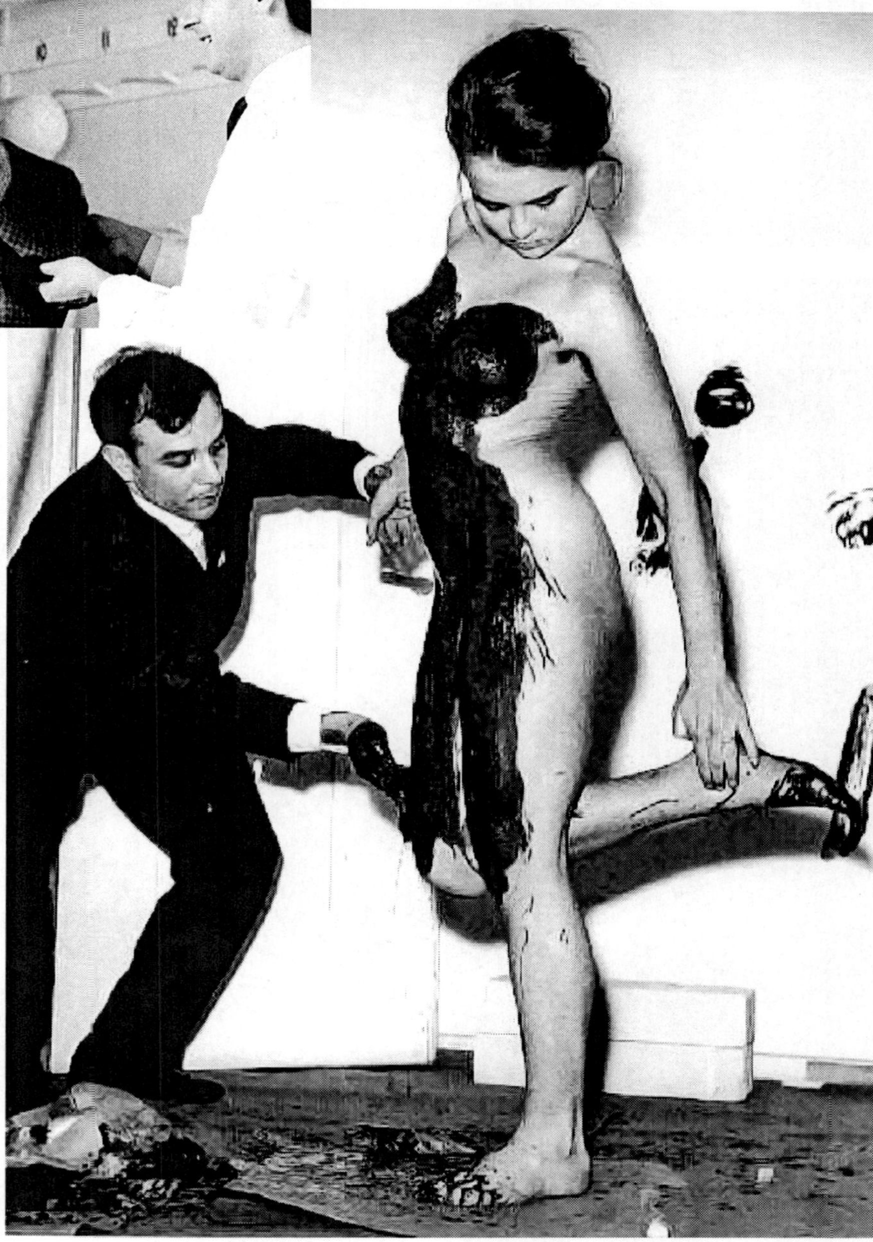

The artist Yves Klein applying the blue pigment he invented to his 'living' paint brush. Rediffusion Television)

This Week, 1961–63

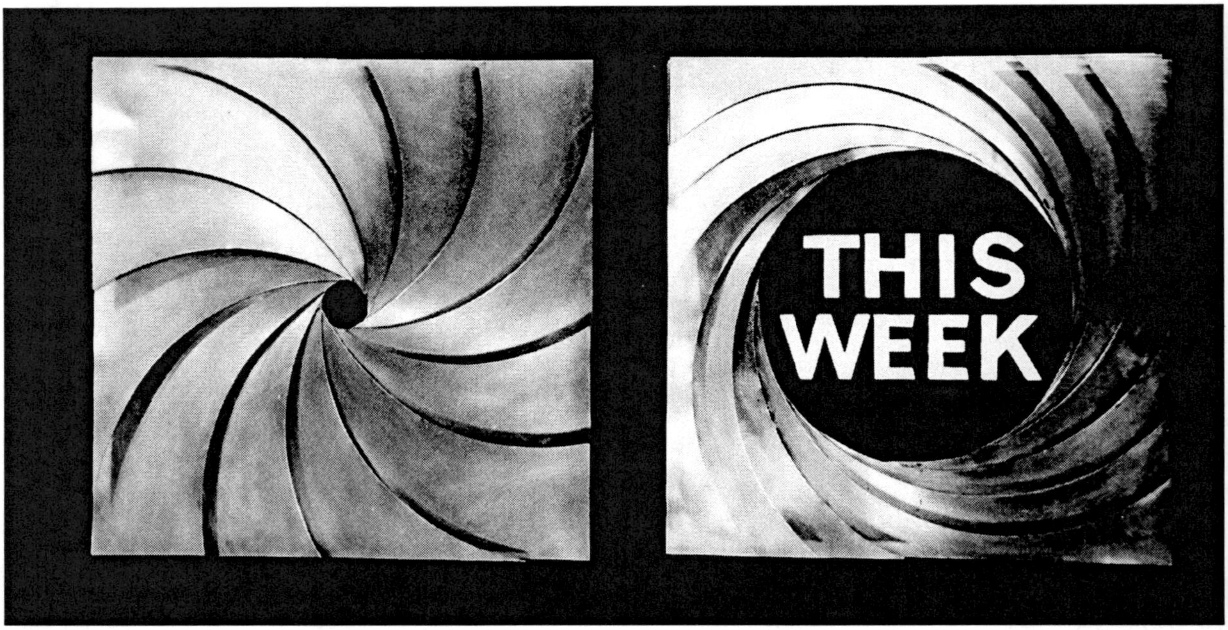

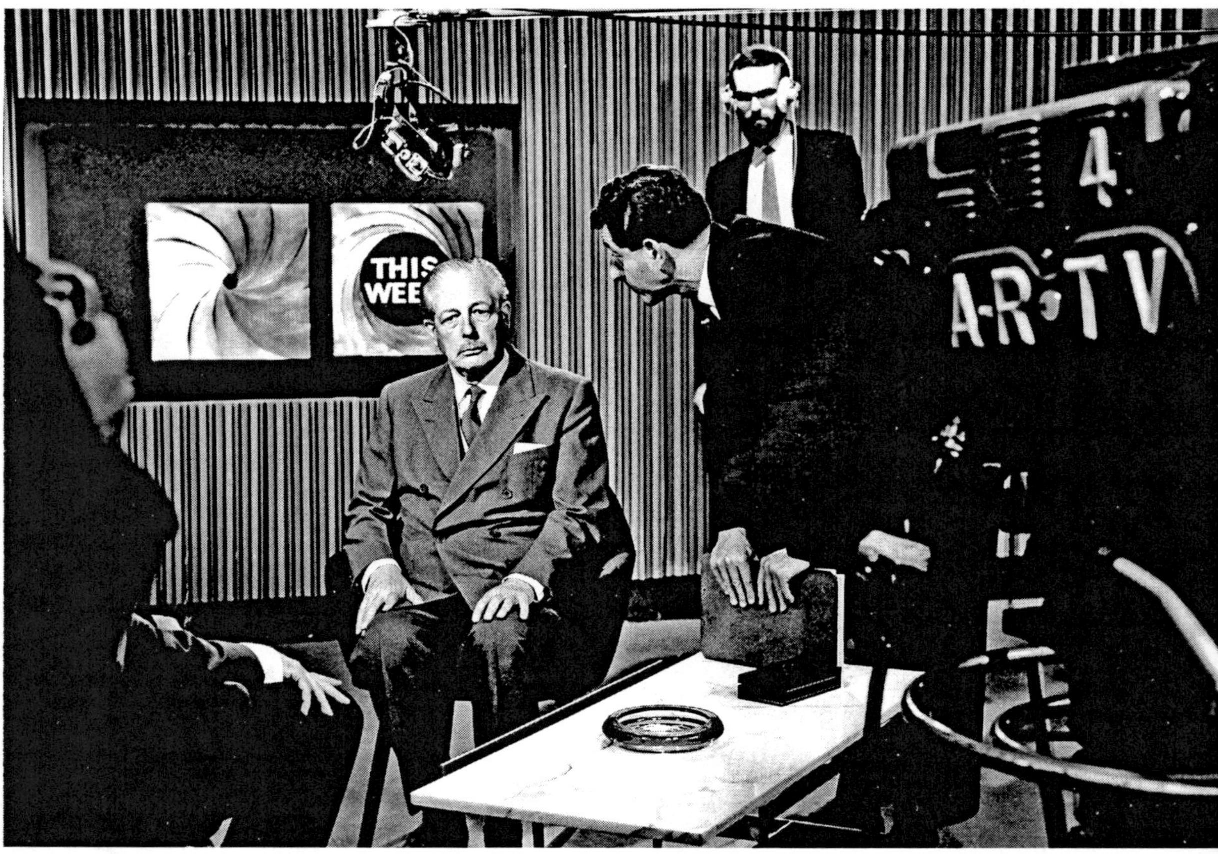

Prime Minister Harold Macmillan in the *This Week* studio for a live thirty-minute interview with Kenneth Harris. (Rediffusion Television)

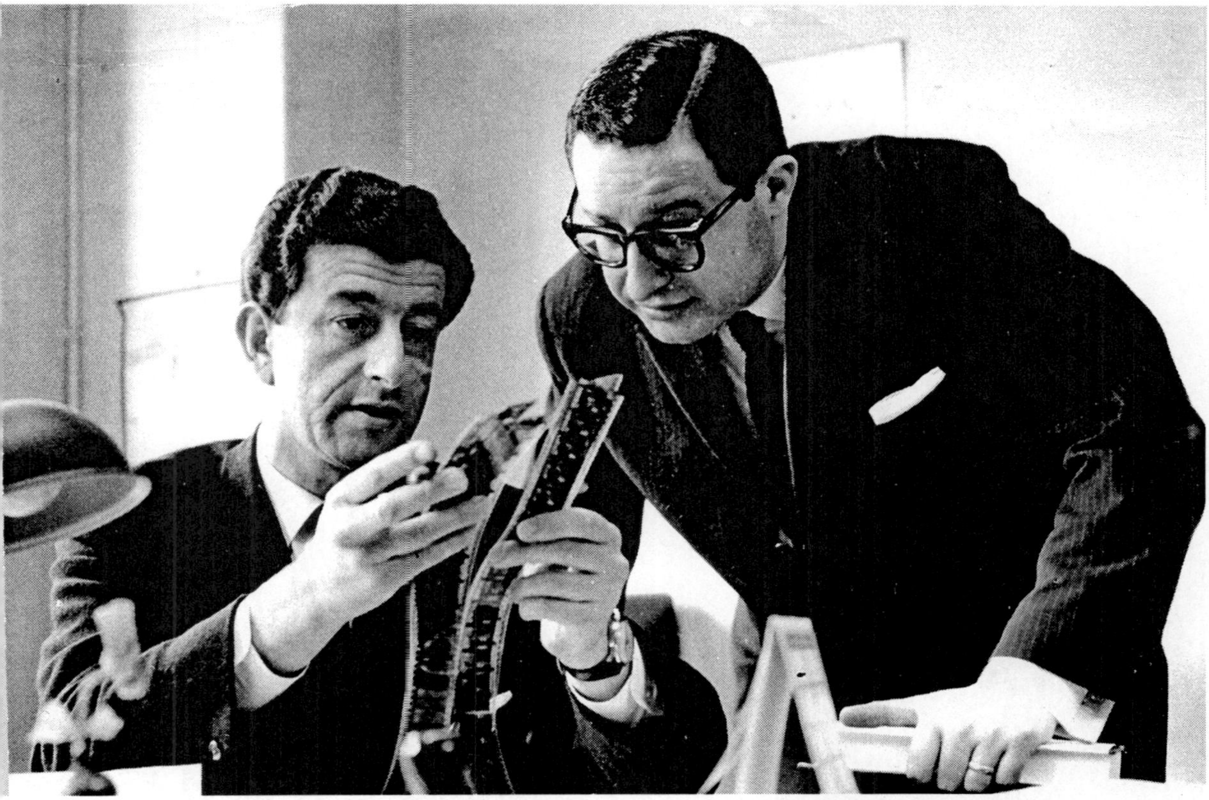

Cyril Bennett and I take over *This Week.* (Rediffusion Television)

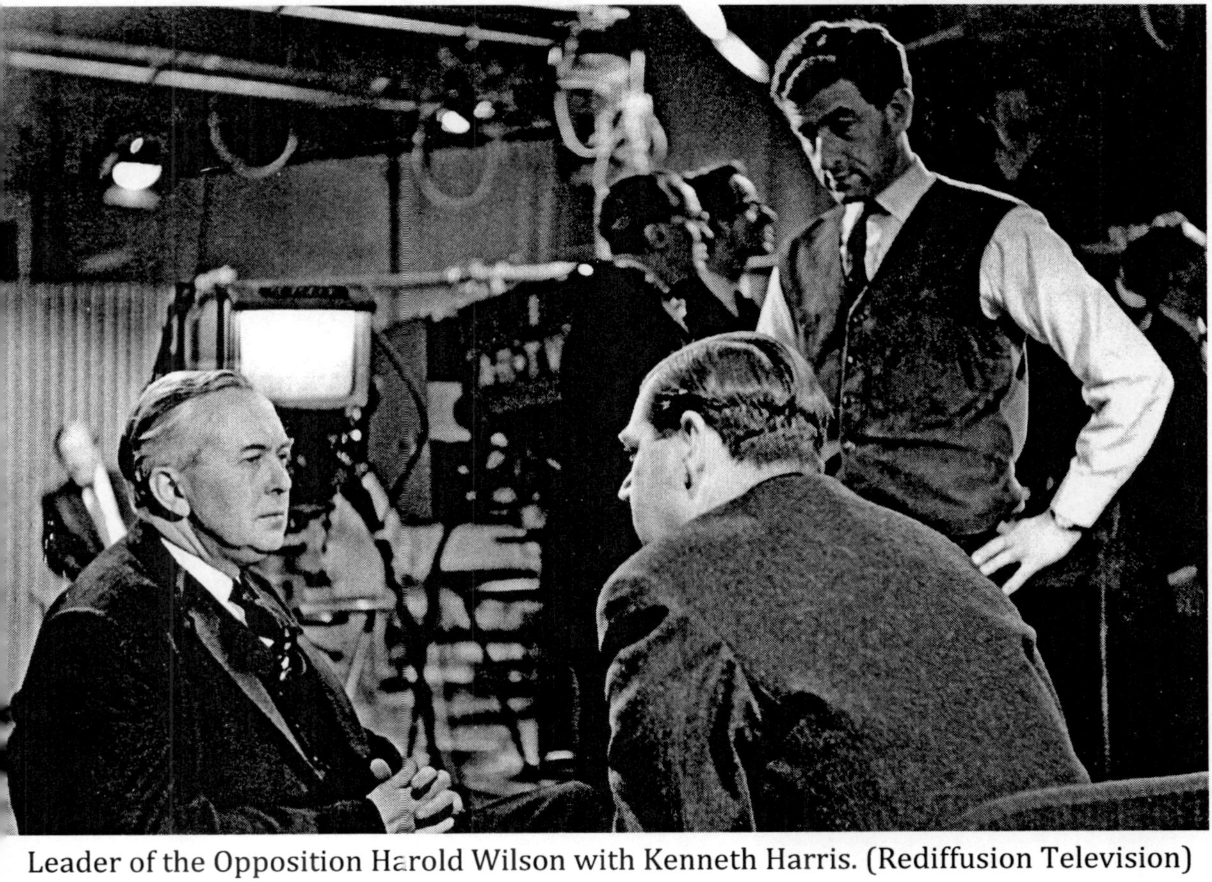

Leader of the Opposition Harold Wilson with Kenneth Harris. (Rediffusion Television)

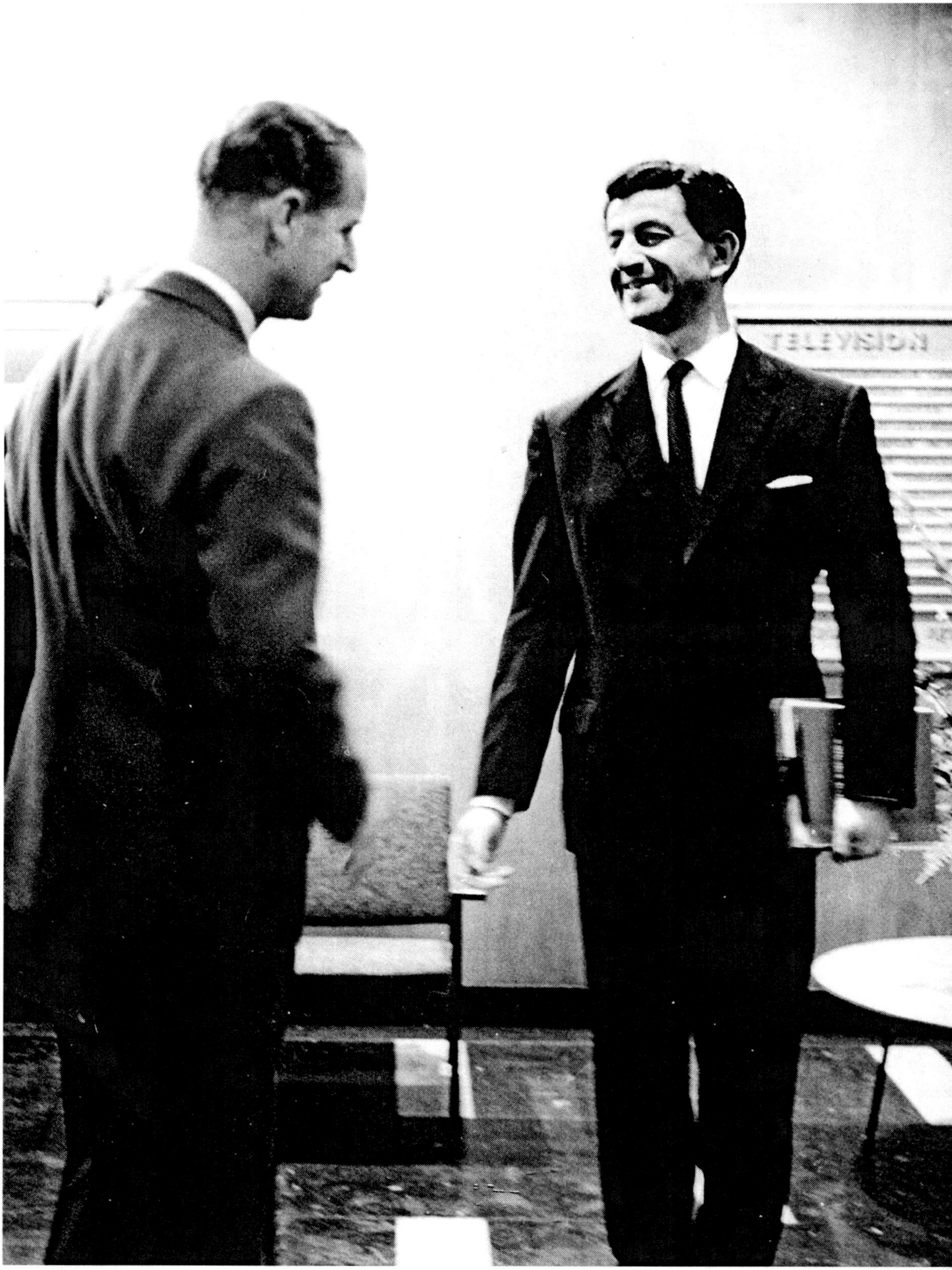

Prince Philip arrives at Television House. It was his debut on ITV.
(Rediffusion Television)

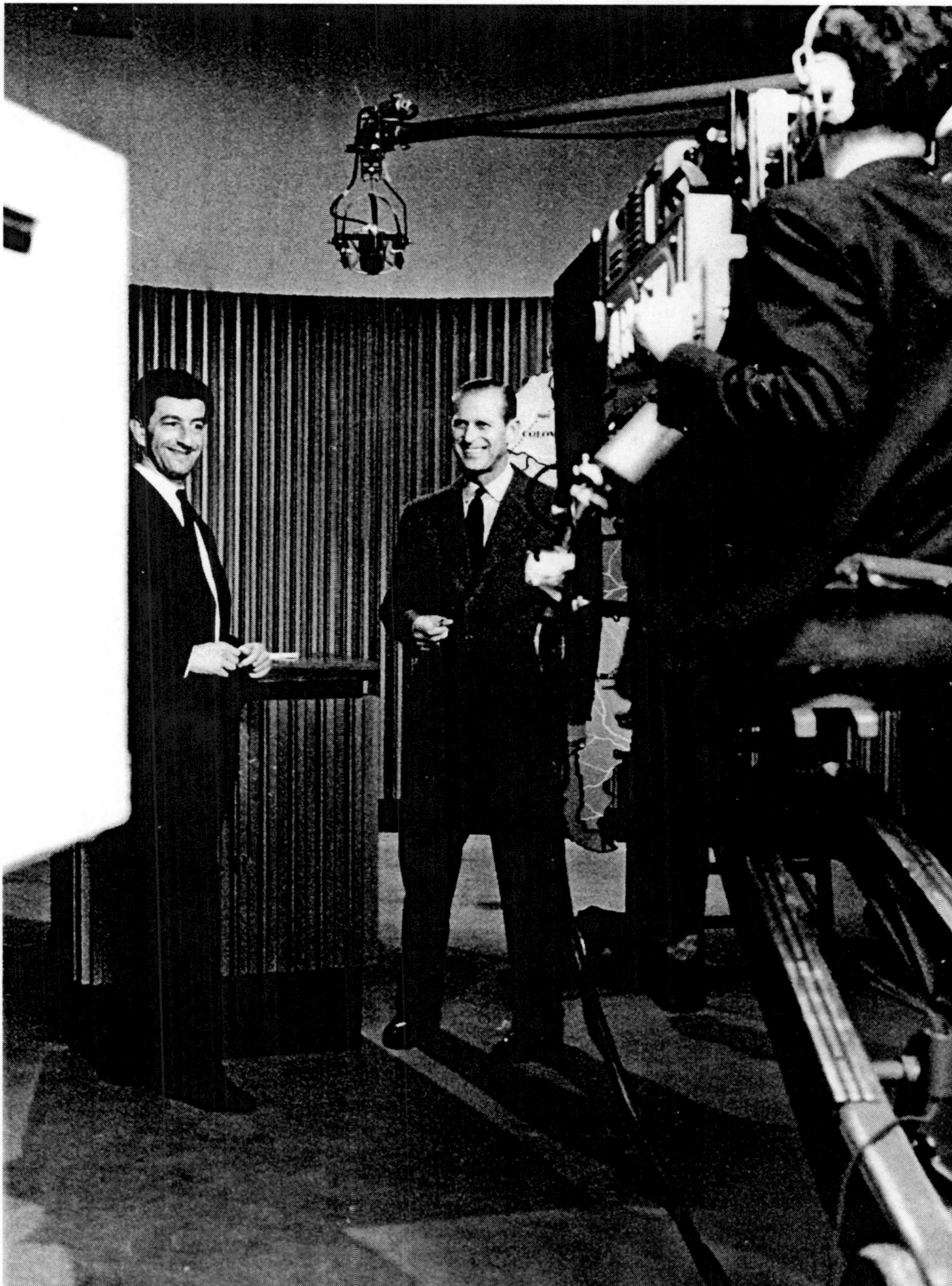

Prince Philip meets the studio crew. (Rediffusion Television)

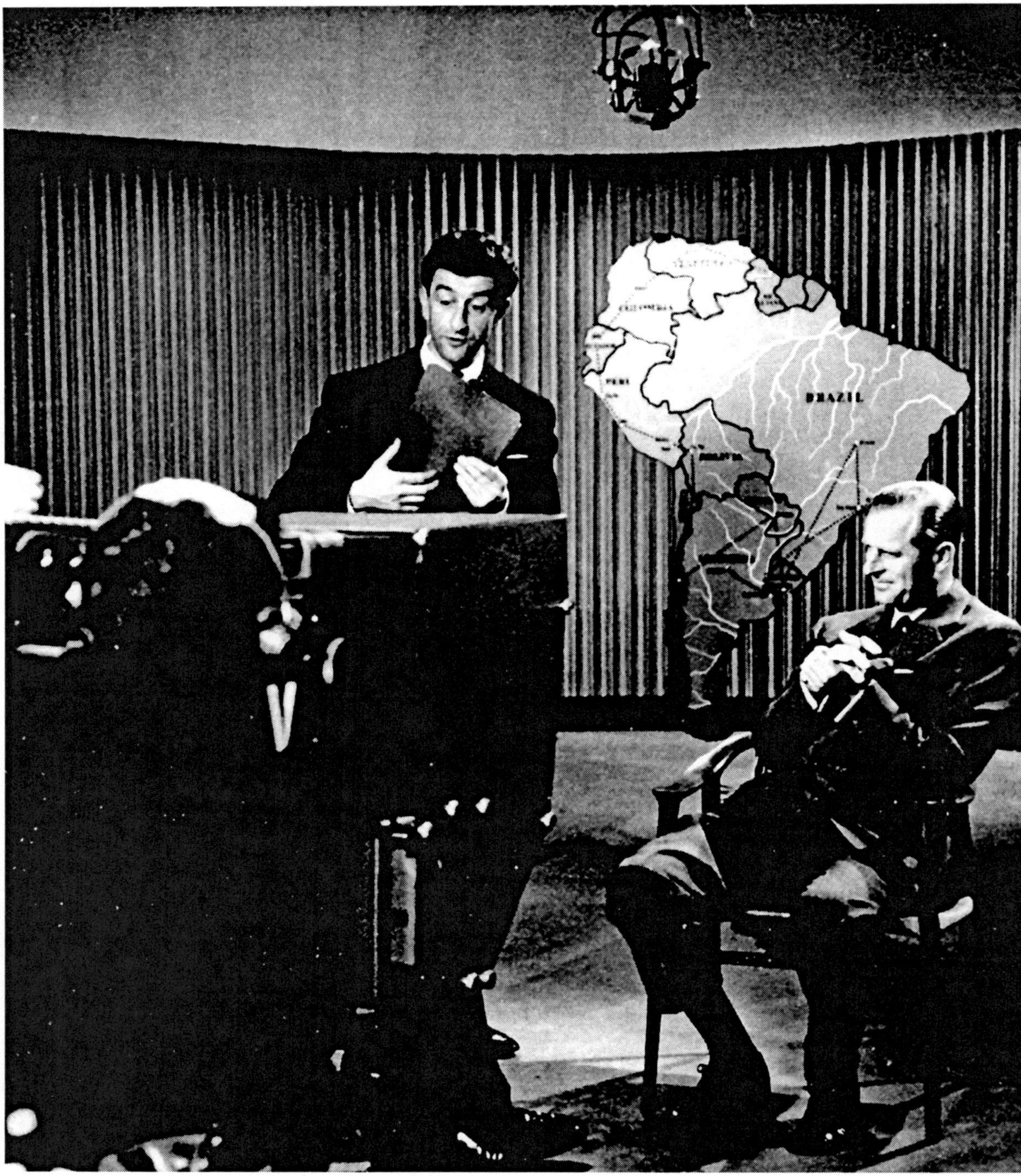

Learning the finer points of using Autocue.
(Rediffusion Television)

16: Black Marries White

Jane and I were celebrating our second year in our small house in Canonbury. She was a busy A-R production assistant; her director, John Frankau, was responsible for a prolific output of television dramas. She was enjoying her work as much as I was mine: it was a good time for both of us. In the mornings we usually set off together to Television House, where I had established an unorthodox parking routine: the uniformed gatekeeper at Somerset House allowed me to enter the splendid inner courtyard, and for a small consideration let me leave the car there. How things have changed.

My desk diaries for 1963–4 remind me of the extramural activities I had taken on and which kept me on my toes. The BFI had invited me to serve on their Television Selection Committee, which was chaired by Ernest Lindgren, the BFI's curator. From a long list of programmes that was handed to us at our monthly meetings the committee had to decide which should be recommended for preservation. Our yardstick was not the quality of individual programmes but their historical value to future students of television, so absolutely dreadful creations like *Double Your Money* or *Take Your Pick* were just as essential as, let's say, a Dennis Potter play. Continuing strands, like *Coronation Street*, always presented a problem – how many episodes should be kept? Maybe one a year? And how about news bulletins or episodes of *This Week*? The meetings were held over lunch in the BFI boardroom, in their then headquarters building in Dean Street, Soho. They usually lasted a couple of hours, with about twelve of us sitting round the boardroom table – sandwiches and wine at the ready. It was an interesting assembly of 'experts', including critics, writers, historians and programme makers. Ernest Lindgren (and later the television critic Philip Purser) often had quite a job keeping us in order as we argued about the merits of individual programmes. The banter was always light-hearted, often very funny – especially when committee members like comedian Barry Took and playwright Philip Mackie got going – but we always had to be reminded of the criteria. Of course, in a perfect world one would simply keep everything, but the reality was that the originating companies had to be willing to donate the selected programme to the archives – and pay for the cost of making copies. The BBC had its own archives, and strove to keep everything (with glaring deletions, which were to come to light years later). ITV supported the BFI's preservation policy and made annual grants available for it.

I had served on this committee for just over twenty years when, in 1984, technology took over in the form of video recording, and we were no longer required to make painful decisions. A deal was struck that allowed the BFI's National Film and Television Archives to record, off-air, the major output from the ITV companies, and some years later the NFTA came to a similar arrangement with the BBC. The possibility of preserving everything became a reality, but needless to say another problem surfaced: the permanence of videotape as a storage medium. After all, we are still not absolutely certain how long paper lasts, and it's been around for quite a while. Even when stored in ideal conditions by the BFI, with meticulously monitored temperature and humidity, there have been cases where videotape's magnetic coating has been known to peel away from its backing. Nothing is forever and, no doubt, the next task will be to transfer this mass of material onto a solid state digital system, which will in turn have to prove its longevity.

Over the years I have enjoyed my association with the BFI and, especially, with the National Television Archives. I was made an honorary member many years ago, and thanks to this relationship I have been able to magpie VHS cassette copies of dozens of my programmes, many of which I have used for lectures and presentations – *The Turn of the Screw* being my prize possession.

Another activity that made fair demands on my time was the Society of Film and Television Arts. I was on the council of SFTA, but its parents, the British Film Academy and the Guild of Television Producers and Directors, still retained their separate councils – the difficult marriage of the two media being only fully consummated in 1975 when it became BAFTA. The Guild's council met frequently, sometimes in our homes. Apart from organising Guild evening sessions for the membership 'to further the arts and crafts of television', we were perpetually engaged in organising and fine-tuning the annual award ceremonies, usually held at the Dorchester Hotel – long before they became a televised annual ritual. It was valuable to have the opportunity to keep in touch professionally with fellow programme makers at the BBC and the other ITV companies.

The year 1964 signalled the start of lobbying for fresh ITV franchise allocations, and there were changes for Associated-Rediffusion. Associated (Newspapers), which had helped to fund A-R when it first started broadcasting in 1955, recognised that they were now no longer a significant shareholder, so A-R dropped the 'Associated' and adopted Rediffusion Television as its new name.

* * * *

It was time to make another documentary, hopefully on film. I relished the idea of working on my own again, away from the relentless pressure of weekly programmes and the tyranny of topicality.

In 1964 I was not aware that 'race relations' was a burning issue; in fact, I can't remember seeing any television programmes on the subject. I knew little about mixed marriages, which at the time seemed to be a taboo subject – maybe too hot to handle. This was all the more reason to make a film about them.

I observed that people in the street were more likely to take notice of couples if the man was black and the woman white; the other way round hardly caused comment; so I decided right from the start that I would concentrate on black male/white female marriages. It was important to avoid imposing an outsider's thoughts and feelings on this tricky subject, but I knew that to make an impressionistic film of what it is like to be in a mixed marriage was bound to evoke an unspoken subtext: 'Would you let your daughter marry a black man?'

My researcher was the splendid Joan Hill, and on her first day she was able to unlock a rich source of information. Her very helpful contact was the Rev. Clifford Hill, who had officiated at many mixed marriages in his church in north London; he put us in touch with several couples.

I wanted to make sure that my final choice of participants came from different social backgrounds, and to use a style of film-making that would allow them to reveal what I expected to be a rich mixture of attitudes, without the intrusions of an interviewer or commentary from a narrator. With Joan Hill I spent over three months meeting many couples, and after I had picked several for the film I got to know them really well, visiting them in their homes. I slowly gained their trust, and finally they became enthusiastic about appearing in the film. I took reams of notes, and learnt a lot about mixed marriages that most of the couples had never previously discussed. Now, in front of me, they openly talked about them for the first time. The observational technique I finally decided on was for the cameras to observe and listen to couples speaking to each other. I used two cameras, one focused on each partner, so that I could capture every word they were saying and at the same time film their reactions as they listened. I sat between them – out of shot – and acted as a prompt, suggesting topics that I knew they had feelings and opinions about. It worked. They were aware of the cameras at first, of course, but soon they became so engrossed in their prompted conversation that inhibition and embarrassment disappeared. Although some of the dialogue sounded slightly stilted, it produced an astonishing and often emotional spontaneity, generating topics that were entirely new to me. The shooting ratio was unusually high, and I knew that editing would be quite difficult – but that is the price one has to pay for this type of film-making.

I was very open about the effects their exposure on network television might have on them and their families, and also the possible reaction of the press, especially the tabloid papers. It is hard to remember today that to be on the telly was still relatively rare: nowadays people are streetwise about the medium, and know pretty well what to expect. I also offered the couples the opportunity to come to Television House to see the final version before transmission and to give their agreement to go ahead. I was surprised that none of them felt it necessary to take me up on this.

I called the film *Black Marries White – The Last Barrier*. From my large clutch of press cuttings I have selected these excerpts, as they seem to echo very clearly what the film was about and the variety of reactions to it.

The *TV Times* asked me to write this promotional piece:

> When I started the research it was like entering a new world. There is no handy reference book to give the facts about mixed marriages. Obviously the only ones who can know anything about it are the partners of a mixed marriage, and I have tried to recreate on film the impressions I got during the many hours of conversation with them. That is what the programme is, an impression of attitudes and emotions about all the things that make and break a marriage. And in this case, marriage complicated beyond measure by racial prejudice.
>
> The couple that was living reluctantly in appalling conditions spoke as frankly and freely as the professional couple in their delightful mews house in Marylebone. Everyone taking part, even those families where the tensions are unbearable, gladly exposed their most private thoughts and feelings because they believed that an understanding of mixed marriage is an integral part of the understanding of the whole problem of colour.
>
> I deliberately chose situations where the husband is coloured and the wife white, because these are the extremes that evoke the maximum reactions. We largely regard an Englishman marrying a coloured girl as a romantic eccentric, a situation that doesn't kindle the deep prejudice of a coloured man invading our society and 'taking' one of our girls.
>
> There is no typical marriage. A union of two people is unique. Therefore, it is unthinkable to make a definite statement about so complex a union as a mixed marriage. That is why I have dispensed with the narrator and the interviewer, even the prepared script. All three might have imposed a different and irrelevant set of attitudes that could have come between the viewer and the people in the film and it might have blurred the fundamental issue. Do we believe in the desirability – even the inevitability – of the ultimate merging of the races? If we do, then the mixed couples in the world today must be regarded as the pioneers who have crossed the 'last barrier' to total integration.
>
> On Wednesday you can see this disturbing programme, and as one of the Jamaicans in the film said to me: 'You're dealing with human dynamite.' He was right.

The morning after transmission:

Shaun Usher – *Daily Sketch*: The dynamite exploded on ITV last night with an extraordinary documentary called *Black Marries White – The Last Barrier*. Its theme: the brutal, biting, loaded question: 'Would you let YOUR daughter or sister marry a coloured man?' There was strong reaction even before the programme went out. Phone calls flooded into Rediffusion's office. The callers were white AND coloured, but their message was the same – 'Take that programme off'.

Marsland Gander – *Daily Telegraph*: *Black Marries White – The Last Barrier* on Independent television last night was the most remarkable documentary that I have seen for a long time. It contained no interviews and no narration; there was no script and there were no names used. No commentator intruded his views or bullied his victims. It was poignant and pungent; quintessentially human and sometimes unconsciously funny.

Peter Morley, of Rediffusion, had taken a roving camera to Tottenham and to Stoke Newington to inquire into the provocative and delicate subject of mixed marriages. He recorded the conversations of husbands, wives and parents. How he managed to find four couples who spoke so naturally, fluently and candidly is a mystery. Says Morley: 'Remember, I'd been talking to these people for months on end. But with the cameras beside me, they came out with things they'd never said before. Take one couple, the wife suddenly asked her husband what he'd do when their little girl came home from school asking why she was called 'nigger'. You could see the husband wince at the thought – he'd obviously not faced it before. And the grim thing was that he had no answer.'

Monica Furlong – *Daily Mail*: Racial intolerance was a tough nut for television to crack, and Rediffusion deserve our thanks for exploring it so honestly in *Black Marries White*. They left nothing out. Every shade of prejudice, conscious and unconscious, every kind of ignorance, every sort of insensitiveness – stone by stone they showed us the huge monument of embarrassment, misunderstanding and human grief. There were the damaged, obsessive couple in their dismal lodgings talking with Pinteresque inconsequence, finding it hard to say the words 'black' and 'white' to each other. There was the girl who had had too much to drink and would not shut up, contriving with ghastly well-meaningness, to say more wounding things than a dozen Fascists. There were people, small, simple people who wanted to do the right thing who had found themselves or their children caught unwittingly between the grindstones of public opinion and still could not endure the knowledge of it. Two couples, however, showed unforgettably that there is a way to break down the racial barriers, a way that involves facing all the facts, knowing all about the myths and the drawbacks and the rude words. A Nigerian doctor and his English wife demonstrated it best. For them racial prejudice had become so thoroughly defeated that it was part of their private joke-world. They enjoyed teasing each other about Negroes being specially virile or about intolerant landladies. They shone with love and understanding for one another. The technique of this programme, which had dispensed with interviewers and experts and relied entirely upon the conversation of black and white people to open up the subject, must be put down as a brilliant success.

These quotes give a pretty good flavour of the film. The Rediffusion telephone operators were kept very busy the next day, with just about an equal number of pro and con callers. The reaction from my colleagues at Rediffusion was different. Apart from my immediate soulmates in the features department there was almost total silence. In our club bar in Television House at lunchtime, where normally the previous night's delights (or otherwise) were the main topics of conversation, mixed marriage was definitely not on the menu. I got the feeling that the programme had touched some raw nerves, because it forced one into a spell of self-examination – the outcome I had hoped for – so I was not disappointed.

The viewing figures were staggering: the *Daily Telegraph* reported: 'The controversial documentary *Black Marries White* was seen by more than 7½ million homes. These audience figures were issued by the TAM ratings organisation. This is a remarkably high figure for a documentary particularly as it did not start until 9.40 p.m. Only the Cup Final and *Coronation Street* had bigger audiences during the week.'

I received a lot of mail, ranging from the complimentary to the vitriolic. Etched permanently in my memory is the parcel I received. I removed the wrapping and found a blood-soaked Bible with an almost illegible scruffy note, putting a curse on my family and me. It remained on my Television House windowsill for a long time, and acted as a constant reminder that programme makers must never ignore their audience.

Plastic soft cover book
Covers

18cm x 25.5cm x
1.5cm.

Mag: Sulph: / Hyd Perox 20vols

Collect trousers

Haircut.

5/5 5/5 5/5

7" x 10" x 1/2"

17: Churchill's Funeral

It was in 1964 that I marked my fourth year planning – with my other hand – a programme with an unknown transmission date.

In 1960 the Queen had officially given her consent for Sir Winston Churchill to have a state funeral, and the BBC and the Independent Television Authority were informed that detailed plans for the great event were about to be made available to the broadcasters. It was decided that, regardless of the day of Churchill's death, the funeral would take place on a Saturday. Rediffusion was the London weekday contractor, with ATV taking over at weekends, but the ITA instructed Rediffusion to handle this complicated outside broadcast. My boss, John McMillan, asked me to take charge of the project as producer and controlling director on behalf of the whole ITV network, shortly after the 1960 outside broadcast I directed of Princess Margaret's wedding.

I gladly accepted the assignment. I was one of millions to whom Churchill was a hero; his Second World War leadership saw to that. I had felt some pride when, after nearly four years' wartime action in the army, I was picked from my regiment to be one of his guards at the Potsdam Conference. Fifteen years later, by a strange coincidence, I had been chosen again, this time to take a more active role. Little did I realise what a mammoth task it was going to be. It was certainly very odd to be involved in producing a programme with an unknown transmission date. The Duke of Norfolk, the Earl Marshal in charge of all major state occasions, gave the project the codename Operation Hope Not, and as the plot thickened I heartily approved of that name.

Soon an army despatch rider appeared in my office in Television House and made me sign for a package that was going to be both my taskmaster and Bible for the next five years. It was a heavy, purple-bound, loose-leaf book entitled *Special District Order, issued by The Major-General Officer Commanding London District and the Major-General Commanding The Household Brigade*. Looking up the distribution list, I noted that I was in receipt of Copy 96. Copy 1 was assigned to the Queen and Copy 302 went to the control officer at Regent's Park Barracks. There were fourteen sections that dealt in the most minute detail with the route, procession, street liners, minute guns, bands, ceremonies at Westminster and St Paul's, rehearsals, administration and so on. And in the back of this 150-page tome was a pocket containing fifteen large folded maps, underlining both the huge scale and the painstaking preparation.

Outside broadcasts require three sorts of expertise: production, engineering and logistics. Rediffusion had some excellent people on the staff to take charge of the last two – the brilliant engineer Basil Bultitude and the ultra-efficient administrator Robert Everett, to name but two. I assembled a very modest production team, recruiting Graham Watts, a Rediffusion staff director, to take charge of finding and negotiating camera positions, and to assist me during the actual transmission. A couple of years or so later Brian Connell joined the team as commentator;

I had got to know him well when he was the anchorman for *This Week*. He was an immensely knowledgeable and erudite journalist, and was very supportive when it came to deciding the style of the broadcast. Helen Littledale, an experienced staff researcher, joined me a bit later.

In ploughing through the *Special District Order*, I became more aware of the scale of the enterprise. It was going to be the largest state funeral since the Duke of Wellington's in 1852, and over 7,000 military personnel were to participate. In comparison the monarch's funeral ceremony is modest; it was prescribed at the death of Queen Victoria and has not changed since. This was quite different. For a start, commoners don't qualify for state funerals – but this was Sir Winston Churchill, and he had made sure that he would be given a grand send-off. I was told that once or twice, as time passed, he requested yet another marching band.

The day's events were to start with the bearer party lifting the coffin off the catafalque in Westminster Hall, where it had lain in state for three days so that the public could pay their last respects. The coffin would then be carried out into New Palace Yard and placed on a gun carriage, the one that was first used at Queen Victoria's funeral. With Big Ben striking 9.45, coinciding with the firing of the first of the ninety minute-gun salutes – one for each year of Churchill's life – the gun carriage and its 140-strong Royal Navy gun crew would move off. And that was the start of the procession. I gleaned all this from the amazing *Special District Order*, and lots more besides. Did it matter that the total length of the procession was 1,394 yards, comprising 2,299 personnel marching in slow time at 65 paces to the minute? It mattered – and how. Without this detailed information it would have been impossible to plan this unique outside broadcast, which, as it turned out, would be seen five years later by many millions worldwide.

I asked Graham Watts to join me in walking the processional route. With the purple book under my arm as a guide, we spent a whole day trying to come to grips with the hurdles we had to overcome. With our starting point at New Palace Yard, we stepped out into Parliament Square, up Whitehall to Trafalgar Square and on to the Strand, Fleet Street and up Ludgate Hill to St Paul's. Here the procession was to be brought to a halt for the funeral service, which would be attended by the world's leaders. After the service it would continue through the City of London, via Cannon Street, Eastcheap and on to Tower Hill; then to Tower Pier, where the bearer party would carry the coffin onto the Port of London's launch, *Havingore*, for the start of the river procession. On reaching Festival Hall Pier, the coffin would travel by motor hearse the short distance to Waterloo station, then by train to Bladen for the private burial service in St Martin's, the parish church of Blenheim Palace.

We calculated that to achieve detailed coverage of all the events of that day, we would need to employ forty-five cameras. It was a tall order – but we got the enthusiastic co-operation of eight other ITV companies from the regions, and the pooling of hardware and crews made it all possible. This meant, of course, that at very short notice studios would be stripped of their cameras, so they could be shipped to London with their directors, crews, engineers and back-up personnel. About three hundred people would have to be fed and watered, and hotels booked for a minimum of five days – and no one knew the date. Mercifully other colleagues took on this logistical nightmare.

The search for camera positions now began. I was particularly keen to find one particular vantage point. As the funeral service in Bladen's village church was going to be private, with only Churchill's immediate family in attendance, the train's departure from Waterloo station – bearing the coffin to its final destination – marked the end of the outside broadcast. I wanted my last shot to symbolise Churchill's exit from his beloved London and the whole nation, and envisaged a scene where the train got smaller and smaller as it disappeared into the distance. I had also learnt that British Rail would take an old steam engine out of retirement to pull the train. It was to be a Battle of Britain-class locomotive, named *Winston Churchill*. With a bit of luck it would puff out lots of smoke from its stack so that the camera could follow its progress to the very last. We searched for a really high camera position – and found one.

The Shell Centre, on the south bank of the Thames close to Waterloo Bridge, was under construction; it was to be one of London's highest office blocks. At this time it was about two-thirds complete, with just the top third showing the bare steel structure. I spoke to the clerk of works, and he told me that the whole complex was due to be completed in just over two years. I asked him whether he realised that he was constructing the tallest and most expensive camera platform ever, and after some more banter he agreed to take me to the top in one of those scary cages running up the outside of buildings for workmen and materials. The view that presented itself was stunning, just what I had hoped for. Churchill had reached a good age (he was now eighty-five): could he possibly wait until all this was ready?

On our holidays Jane and I were always accompanied by my small transistor radio just in case the magic transmission date for Operation Hope Not became a reality. It is hard to believe now that all this planning for the state funeral took place while I was fully involved with other programmes, including my long stint with *This Week*. The stylistic and technical aspects of such a mammoth enterprise were a constant preoccupation.

I was certainly able to keep an eye on the progress the engineers were making. The *This Week* studio was designated as the outside broadcast control centre, and every Thursday evening as I walked into the control gallery to direct the live transmission of *This Week* I was struck by the gradual increase in the number of television monitors. As time went by their number grew from a modest six in 1960 to a frightening array of twenty-five, serving forty-five cameras. The studio was in Television House, and its location in Kingsway was just about half-way along the processional route. All the signals, vision and sound, plus control and communication lines from all the sub-units along the route, had to terminate there, which was a huge engineering effort. It meant a massive digging up of London's streets to bury the cable ducts underground. The Post Office was responsible for this; in fact, they owned these lines, and ITV had to pay a fortune to keep them booked for an indefinite period. Nowadays, of course, all these remote signals would be squirted up to a satellite and linked back to a dish on the roof of Television House.

I was beginning to have thoughts about the overall style of the programme. Right from the very start of the project I wondered what the mood of the nation would be on that day; it was quite hard to discuss and share ideas about tone and style at first: it all seemed so remote. I suppose it was my documentary background that instinctively made me think that this unique occasion demanded more than the straight reportage of 'actuality coverage'. I thought it was important to impose an informative element on the event, and invest the occasion with a clear summary of what Winston Churchill had stood for and stood against. To this end I decided that in addition to Brian Connell's commentary we would use quotations from Churchill's speeches and writings to highlight his character, his beliefs and his achievements, to remind viewers of what this nation and the world owed to him. On the day, therefore, we were to hear the pre-recorded voice of Sir Laurence Olivier reading short excerpts, interpolated with the appropriate matching live pictures as they unfolded in front of the cameras. For instance, as the sailors pulling the gun carriage progressed round the Aldwych and past St Clement Danes, the Royal Air Force church, I would cue the cameraman for a slow zoom-in on the single file of surviving Battle of Britain pilots, slow-marching behind the coffin, and then cue Brian Connell: 'With these men, and with this church dedicated to their gallant comrades, surely this is the moment to remember the great ringing phrase that Winston Churchill spoke in those autumn days of 1940, when they were young and we were all in mortal danger.' And then we would hear Olivier speak these famous words: 'The gratitude of every home in our island, in our Empire, and indeed throughout the world, except in the abodes of the guilty, goes out to the British airmen who, undaunted by odds, unwearied in their constant challenge and mortal danger, are turning the tide of the world war by their prowess and by their devotion. Never in the field of human conflict was so much owed by so many to so few.'

I also felt that we should hear Churchill's own voice at his funeral, to remind ourselves of his stirring rallying calls to the nation during its darkest time. Some of my colleagues thought this a bit risky, a question of taste and all that, but in the event it added hugely to the broadcast, matching its tone and style.

Just over four years into this long period of preparation I had some troubling misgivings. Both the BBC and ITV were spending time, resources and, of course, huge budgets on Operation Hope Not. We did not choose to be in competition with the BBC, but they realised that for the first time their monopoly for covering a major state occasion was being challenged. For obvious historical reasons they assumed ownership of these national events and deeply resented this, heightened by the fact that their rival was a commercial network. I remember with some relish the first briefing meeting early in 1960. The Earl Marshal, the Duke of Norfolk, called the broadcasting organisations to a grand room which he had commandeered in a government building in Northumberland Avenue, and about fifty people attended, sitting round a massive table. By tradition the Earl Marshal is the coordinator – the ringmaster – of state ceremonies, and the Duke of Norfolk was brilliant at the job. He was also blessed with a witty, dry sense of humour. He welcomed us and, looking round the huge gathering, announced: 'Hands up all those from the British Broadcasting Corporation.' A huge forest of arms shot up. 'Hands up all those from Independent Television.' Graham Watts and I raised our hands. 'Now there's a surprise,' said the Duke. It was a good start.

As time went by I became aware how seriously the BBC was taking our challenge, despite their great advantage over us. Their producer, Anthony Craxton, working closely with that genius Richard Dimbleby, had established an unsurpassed track record; they were, with no doubt, world leaders in this field of broadcasting. And here were these upstarts from the commercial world, whom they considered to be beyond the pale. This caused problems. For instance, Graham Watts alerted me to the difficulties he was having with the Ministry of Works in getting permission for some of the camera positions we had requested. We realised that the BBC was leaning on some of its old contacts, so that when we came up with a really good camera position that they had not thought of you could bet that the Ministry would shortly inform us that the BBC had already booked it.

I resented this rivalry, and felt that for this special occasion British television should speak with one voice. It was now April 1964, and I put these thoughts to John McMillan. I said that I felt so strongly about this that I would hand over all my plans and make all the cameras available to the BBC. I had already invested four years of planning, but I would, with sadness, give up my role and leave Anthony Craxton to take control. McMillan decided to call a top-level meeting with the BBC, not only to discuss the coverage of the Churchill funeral but also to explore future plans for the two organisations to take it in turn to cover national events. The meeting took place in Television House chaired by McMillan and attended by Stuart Hood, the Controller of BBC Television, Peter Dimmock, Head of Outside Broadcasts, his assistants, Harry Middleton and Rex Moorfoot, and Anthony Craxton, the producer.

I was asked to present my case, and with mixed feelings I stated that I was prepared to hand over everything; and that ITV would simply take the BBC feed for the broadcast. There was a long discussion, but nothing was decided and they went away to report to their hierarchy. Later they replied by letter. The upshot was that they considered the broadcasting of all national events to be the BBC's duty and would therefore never relinquish this responsibility. In other words, goodbye ITV. I had done my bit, felt better for it, and now got on with the job in hand.

Everything was now in place thanks to our Bible, the *Special District Order*. We knew precisely the position at any given time of the many elements making up the long procession. All the excerpts to be spoken by Olivier had been chosen, as well as Churchill's own contributions. The camera position had been allocated to the nine ITV companies and everyone knew what their role would be on the day. Even the new Shell Centre was ready and waiting for the broadcast's final moments. We also knew that we had a mere six days from the announcement of Churchill's death, inevitably named D-Day, to the funeral on D+6. On D+1 the cameras with their personnel would have to descend on London and work round the clock to get everything rigged in time. The only element that I still had to consider was the choice of opening music, and that led to a very strange experience.

After *Black Marries White* I started to research background material for my next documentary – what it was like to be a musician in the London Symphony Orchestra. And it so happened that on 15 January 1965 I was driving up to Wembley Town Hall to meet the LSO, where Colin Davis was rehearsing and recording Elgar's *Enigma Variations* for Philips. As usual my car radio was tuned to the BBC Third Programme. The music that morning struck me as being exactly what I was searching for. It sounded familiar, but I couldn't name it. I pulled into the kerb, and with pen poised waited for it to finish. 'You have been listening to the symphonic poem *Also sprach Zarathustra* by Richard Strauss.' What a huge relief – at last I had solved the problem of my opening music. Incidentally, this was two years before Stanley Kubrick famously used the same music in *Space Odyssey – 2001*. As I continued my drive a new piece began to play, but it came to an abrupt halt to make way for the announcer: 'We interrupt this programme for a news flash. It has just been announced that Sir Winston Churchill has suffered a stroke.' Uncanny!

I rapidly made my way to Rediffusion's Wembley Studios less than half a mile away, where I knew the weekly management meeting was in session. I burst into the room, gave them the news and asked for Operation Hope Not to be set into immediate operation. The balloon had now gone up. My sense of relief was mixed with doubts. Were the plans robust? Was it all going to work? Had we allowed enough time?

The announcement of Churchill's death was expected at any moment, and that would precipitate D-Day. While we waited we fine-tuned our arrangements. The engineers checked all communications, and the ITV companies started to reschedule their studio commitments so that cameras could be released for shipment to London. An engineer said to me, 'I bet the old boy is making sure that he gives us enough time to give him a decent send-off.' And all of us began to believe it: he hung on for an extra eight days, and died on Sunday 24 January. The state funeral would take place the following Saturday, the 30th. At last, after five long years, we knew the date, and we had just five clear days to mount the operation. I am convinced that had it not been for the extra eight days between stroke and death we would have been dangerously stretched. But because of this hiatus cameras were in position and ready to go on D+4.

Sitting in front of the huge bank of monitors in Television House, five years of planning would now be put to the test. The excitement started as each of the forty-five cameras was switched on and the monitors came alive with the most stunning views of London – as the city had never been seen before. It was snowing and quite magical: the bird's-eye views from the very top of St Paul's Cathedral and the Shell Tower in particular took my breath away.

During that week I asked Laurence Olivier to come to Television House to record the Churchill excerpts. Paul Scofield recorded the prologue, written by James Cameron. And Joseph C. Harsch, the great journalist and commentator, recorded his moving American tribute to coincide with the river procession. All these voices were recorded on audiotape, so that I could cue them to be played in during the live broadcast at pre-planned points during the procession.

Altogether there were twelve outside broadcast camera units covering the route, each one with its own director who was controlling his unit's cameras. I had an omnibus talkback button in front of me, and when I pressed it all the directors and the forty-five cameramen could hear my instructions. We were now able to rehearse, especially the voice-overs. I could decide on the precise shots I was after, work out the pans, zooms and timings, and the point where the tapes had to be cued. The meticulous planning minutiae listed in the much-thumbed *District Orders*, issued five years before, were tested when on D+5, and in the dark, the procession started its rehearsal at 4.45 a.m. All the details of timing and distances were spot on. It was toughest for the bearer party, provided by the Grenadier Guards: they had to lift the lead-lined coffin from the gun carriage onto their shoulders, all 8 cwt of it. For the rehearsal it was filled with sand to the exact weight. We all held our breath, especially when they climbed the many steps up to the west door of St Paul's.

Saturday 30 January 1965, D+6, arrived. It was a bitterly cold and windy morning. The 300-strong ITV team were at their posts at 5.30 a.m. to warm up the equipment and test all lines, and at precisely 8.30 a.m. we went on the air. The broadcast was to last five hours and five minutes. Everything went exactly as planned, except for one moment which took us all by surprise, including the Earl Marshal, who had certainly not planned it as part of the ceremony. London's dockers had secretly decided to man their huge cranes on the south bank of the Thames. And as *Havingore* cast off from Tower Pier bearing Winston Churchill on his last journey, they dipped the big jib arms of their cranes down to the water's edge in salute. I think it was the most moving moment that morning, adding to the high emotion of the day.

My wish for the last shot from the top of the Shell Building was fulfilled. We watched the train on its journey to Bladen disappear into the far distance, with the old locomotive bravely belching plumes of white smoke. Brian Connell finished his sparse commentary with these words:

> So Britain's capital and the great world say farewell to Sir Winston Leonard Spencer Churchill, Knight of the Garter, Order of Merit and Companion of Honour. Now that great voice is stilled. The incomparable services he rendered his country under six reigns for seven decades become part of the history he wrote. Now he will lie in a

> little leafy Oxfordshire churchyard next to his mother, father, his brother and his family. Not far away there stands in the park of Blenheim Palace, the home of his great ancestor the Duke of Marlborough, the column of victory erected in memory of his great forbear. The inscription at the base rings across nearly 250 years of surely unequalled endeavour by two members of the same family, as true of the one as of the other: '. . . when exerted the most rescued the Empire from desolation. Asserted and confirmed the Liberties of Europe.'

Then I cued the end music, from Copeland's *Fanfare to the Common Man*, as Olivier read a final tribute, written in the seventeenth century by Joseph Hall, Bishop of Exeter, entitled 'Character of a Valiant Man':

> His power is limited by his will; and he holds it the noblest revenge, that he might hurt and doth not. He commands, without tyranny and imperiousness; obeys, without servility: and changes not his mind with his estate. The height of his spirits overlooks all casualties; and his boldness proceeds neither from ignorance nor senselessness: but, first, he values evils and then despises them. He is so balanced with wisdom that he floats steadily in the midst of all tempests. Deliberate in his purposes; firm in resolution; bold in enterprising; unwearied in achieving; and, howsoever, happy in success: and, if ever he be overcome, his heart yields last – The Valiant Man.

When we came off the air I pressed my talkback button to thank everyone – and then the last five hours, indeed the last five years, must have caught up with me. The huge relief of a successful broadcast mixed with the strain, the fatigue and, above all, the emotions rendered me literally speechless. Geoffrey Cox, the Editor-in-Chief of ITN News, appeared in the gallery, having come down from his office on the top floor of Television House to congratulate me. He shook my hand and I just stood there with my body and face frozen. I could not speak. I was not crying, yet the tears were rolling down my cheeks. It must have been a good ten minutes before I was able to relax. What a day.

The doyen critic Maurice Wiggin wrote this piece in the *Sunday Times*:

> As the procession moved away a gun was fired in St. James's Park, the first of 90 minute-guns that were to span the lifetime, and the ceremonial of a lifetime. A gun shot that reverberated with the voice of doom. Now it was afoot, at 65 paces to the minute, the slow march of the emperors that measure off the last public moments of the greatest. Now it was permissible, and right, for the camera eyes to leapfrog along the route, and this they did. For no one can bear to march behind the bier save those who must. And here the particular genius of television entered and made us free. Shifts of focus, like a change of rhythm, both rested and enlarged the watcher. And so did the subtle changes of voice and prose when, here and there along the route, at such moments and places that were most apt for it, the commentator paused in his particularity, and other voices took over, the splendid voice of Sir Laurence Olivier and the unforgettable voice of Churchill himself, speaking his own words. These historic echoes made a counterpoint to the commentary which deepened the sense of being present at a culmination of human aspiration and achievement which was already taking on, both here and now, the mysterious dimension of myth and legend. This was the fruit of planning and organisation. This was what is meant by creativeness in television. This it was that

> helped to turn an 'actuality' into a work of art. This was Television's finest hour too.

The next morning there was a telegram of congratulations from CBC's Fred Friendly (Ed Murrow's partner) in New York: 'CBS was richer because of what you and your colleagues did today. We were certainly honored to share it with the American people.' The networks had set up recording facilities at London airport, and as the broadcast progressed they flew the BBC and ITV tapes across the Atlantic for immediate screening. CBS, after a little while, switched from the BBC's version to ours.

Looking back on it, I realised that luck had also played its role on that day – good luck as it happened, with some of my colleagues convinced that somehow Churchill had had a hand in it. The state of the tide on the Thames was one instance. A.P. Herbert wrote:

> None of the knowing scribes who wrote so much about Sir Winston Churchill's funeral observed how great a part was played by the tide. He had planned it all they say, including the river passage from Tower Pier to Festival Pier, long before. But, unless we like to think that the great genius's ghost was still at work, he could not have planned that, on that destined Saturday, January 30th, it should be high water in King's Reach at 1.00 p.m. with the river full and the floating pontoons almost level with the banks. The Saturday before at that time, it would have been dead low water, and the Saturday after, not far from it. The bows at the piers would have been at an angle impossible even for those gallant Guardsmen carrying the coffin. At a chance encounter with the Duke of Norfolk, the Earl Marshal and brilliant master of the ceremonies, I put the point to him, and he confirmed my humble opinion. 'The week before', he said, 'we couldn't have done it.' Thus even the Thames, even the Moon, we may like to think, conspired together to give grace and good order to that great departure.

Later that same year I was made aware of yet another strange twist to this story. I had been asked to make the television series, *The Life and Times of Lord Mountbatten,* and when I first met him he asked me to spend a weekend at his home in Broadlands, 'to get to know each other', as he put it. He had asked to see a telerecording of the state funeral, so I brought down with me and we watched it in his private cinema. As Chief of Defence Staff, Admiral of the Fleet, Lord Louis Mountbatten had walked the length of the procession immediately behind the gun carriage. Being an inveterate stickler for detail, he wanted to know all about it, and when I told him that for five long years I could never go anywhere without my pocket transistor radio, just to keep in touch with the state of Churchill's health, he said, 'I wish we had met before, because I could have given you the exact day of Winston's death; not the year, but the day.' I had been alerted to Mountbatten's famous boasts, and this was going to be my first encounter of one that had all the makings of a tall story. But I was wrong. He told me, 'Some years ago I visited Winston at Chartwell after he had forgiven me over my role as the last Viceroy, when I oversaw the transfer of power in India.' He then explained that, as they were walking round his famous walled garden, the topic of conversation centred on death. 'Dickie, I know the day I am going to die,' Churchill said. 'I am going to die on the same day that my father died.' And he did — on 24 January. Was that why he was able to hang on for those extra eight days after his stroke? What a pity that I didn't meet Mountbatten a few years earlier.

After the event the ITA asked Rediffusion to enter the broadcast for the Grand Prix du CIRAD in Cannes, an international competition for outside broadcasts, organised by ORTF, the French State Television Service. One of the rules stipulated that each entry must not run longer than sixty minutes. I spent the next two weeks reducing my outside broadcast to one hour; we were not allowed to re-edit, and I found myself deleting huge sections; in fact, I had to throw out just over four hours – a very painful task. I heard from contacts at the BBC that Anthony Craxton was going through the same agony with his programme. His coverage with Richard

Dimbleby had also received excellent press reviews, and now the competition between us, which a year before I had tried so hard to avoid, was hotting up again.

Both of us were invited to Cannes to serve on the international jury. There were twenty-four competing programmes from seventeen countries, and the jury was made up of the directors of these programmes. The first day was spent devising procedures to ensure that we could not vote for our own entries. During the following two days we viewed all the programmes, and then came voting day. Victory. ITV won the Grand Prix by a landslide; the BBC's version was not even in the first ten.

This was my first international TV award, and at the celebration luncheon M. Jacques-Bernard Dupont, Director General of the ORTF, presented me with it. The ITA was represented by Bernard Sendell, its Deputy Director General; also present was a crestfallen Peter Dimmock, together with his BBC entourage. This occasion marked a real triumph for all the ITV companies and my Rediffusion colleagues, especially Graham Watts, my brilliant assistant director, who had devoted so much enthusiasm and professionalism to make our broadcast such a success. I was thrilled with the award, and felt great pride and relief that I had not let Churchill down; I must also own up to feeling some *Schadenfreude* concerning the BBC, as they had made life so difficult for us 'commercial boys' for five years. And to add to the BBC's disappointment, later that year I was awarded the Guild of Television Producers and Directors' Outside-Broadcast Award – the BAFTA mask.

18: The London Symphony Orchestra

In February 1965 I resumed my London Symphony Orchestra project, which had been so dramatically interrupted after I had heard the announcement of Churchill's stroke on the car radio. The idea for this emerged the year before, when David (Lord) Windlesham, who was running Rediffusion's feature department, asked me to come up with a proposal for a film about the orchestra. I jumped at it.

I knew what was motivating Rediffusion: it was brownie-point time, as ITV franchise renewals were pressing hard. In its increasing philanthropic pursuit of the arts, the Rediffusion Board of Directors had sponsored the LSO and also the Hallé Orchestra, with donations to a 'Grants to Arts and Sciences' scheme at that time totalling £59,000 – a large slice of money. Now, with the franchise renewal date coming up fast, the Rediffusion Board felt that this largesse required a higher profile.

This was an exciting time. It reminded me of my early documentary days when I was directing sponsored films; here was a 'client' asking me to make a film, with the simple but enticing brief that it should promote the good name of the LSO. What an ideal opportunity to do something different from the predictable orchestral outside broadcasts, many of which could be seen on both the BBC and ITV. I told David Windlesham that I would have to spend some weeks with the orchestra before I could decide what sort of film I wanted to make.

As this was going to be a programme about an orchestra, and because I knew very little about the subject, I found myself going to rehearsals, recording sessions and concert performances – above all, I used the time to get to know the musicians really well; to find out what made them and the LSO tick. It was also important to learn about the continuing logistical, financial and administrative problems faced by the orchestra's management. This was a fact-finding exercise and, as usual, I only settled on the film's form and style once I had assembled the necessary ingredients. I have come across some of the research notes I made at the time:

> A terrible clanging as the bells are lifted over the tailboard . . . a grating screech as £400 worth of timpani in its heavy crate is slid across the pavement . . . the clatter of 90 music stands as they pursue the instruments . . . these are the sounds that are as much part of the orchestra as the music it lives by.
>
> A recording session at Wembley Town Hall in the morning; an orchestral rehearsal at Duke's Hall in the afternoon; a concert in the Royal Festival Hall that evening. Nine hours of music-making, three hours of travelling and, more often than not, for seven days every week. The pre-occupation with their own artistic standard is so intense that the critical moment when overwork and exhaustion must impinge

> on it is cautiously held off at arm's length – though it can never be far off. These aspects, apart from the sheer joy of the sound the LSO makes when they play, must somehow be included. I wonder how many who go to concerts, let alone those who don't, think of an orchestra in terms of individuals? Collectively, they are regarded as musicians, hardly ever as people and never as the workers of this world, and that is what must be highlighted. Should we care that their home lives barely exist? That they get no sick-pay or pension? That they are deeply disturbed by the failure to recruit new orchestral blood of the right standard? To begin to understand their problems, and there are many, the film must reflect this sense of belonging to an orchestra, of being proud to belong, dedicating your whole existence to corporate music-making to the exclusion of almost everything else.

I did not intend this to be a musical film, although we would hear a lot of music. The accent was not on how music is made, but what it feels like to make it – and I called the film *LSO – The Music Men.*

The LSO suggested that it would suit their hectic schedules to concentrate on two activities for the film: a recording session and a concert. And that is how the Philips session with Colin Davis, conducting Elgar's *Enigma Variations* and the *Cockaigne Overture* at Wembley Town Hall, became the backbone of the film, with the film's climax an exciting rendering of the last movement of Beethoven's *Seventh Symphony* at the Festival Hall, conducted by István Kertész.

Shape and style now emerged, and I decided, once more, to make a film that was largely observational, eschewing the services of an outside narrator. Then I searched for the one player through whose eyes I could tell this story, and he soon emerged – the man who became the point of focus; the individual with a corporate LSO identity. I chose Stuart Knussen, the brilliant principal double bass, because his professionalism was typical of each individual player. He spoke with a rich Mancunian voice that reflected the great variety of accents in this multi-class group. Another reason was that he had a twelve year-old son with great musical talent (Oliver Knussen is today one of our leading composers), and with young Ollie, it was possible to explore the grave shortcomings of musical training in this country – the supply of the next generation of LSO players, which was of great concern. I got to know Stuart Knussen really well, and during many sessions with him, some in pubs, some in his home, I amassed a huge amount of detail that would later provide the narrative for the film. By focusing on this one player, the feeling of satisfaction and pride of belonging to and working with a top orchestra would be firmly established.

I also felt that it was just as important to combine the marvellous noise these men make, with all the little human details that we take for granted in ourselves, but never credit a musician to indulge in. For instance, during the *Enigma Variations* recording session in Wembley Town Hall, Colin Davis picks up the rostrum telephone and checks the balance of the brass with the recording engineer, and during this sixty-second conversation the third cello picks up his crossword; the contra-bassoon the *Sunday Telegraph;* the trombone his yachting magazine; the second clarinet his new camera fresh from the Japan tour; the fourth horn examines the sandwiches his wife has packed; matches flare; cigarettes are lit; world tour snapshots are passed from desk to desk. Then in a flash they are playing Elgar again like never before. This facility to relax totally the moment playing stops and to concentrate immediately it starts is essential to the orchestral player's temperament – without it, he would go out of his mind.

I well remember the recording of Variation Seven, short, fast and very furious. After the last note Colin Davis and the orchestra froze for three seconds – a moment of total silence essential to a recording – and then all hell was let loose as they stampeded recklessly out of the hall to be first in the coffee queue, like a classroom emptying when the end-of-lesson bell rings, and with the same excited babble and laughter. The tension of making music was switched off and the batteries were recharged. Ten minutes later they were back at their desks – professional music-makers again – and Colin Davis was back on the rostrum. A retake of Variation Seven was called for, as a jet flying overhead spoilt the last one. He put his hand into his lightweight conductor's jacket, pulled out a crumpled piece of paper and announced, 'Good God, I've found a cheque for £34!' The orchestra burst out laughing. Five seconds later the red light came on – and off they went again.

The next day, sandwiched between two sessions, there was a shareholders' meeting. Each member of the LSO was obliged to take on this extraordinary role – a personal stake in the artistic and financial affairs of this non-profit-making company (even if there was a profit to make). It was an all-male enterprise; the only time a female musician could be seen behind a music stand at this time was when the score demands a harpist. A board of directors, all players, was elected by the members; their outstanding principal horn, Barry Tuckwell, was chairman. They met to make a historic decision: to appoint a new principal conductor to fill the vacuum left by the late and dearly loved Pierre Monteux. Jealous of their independence, they decided that cameras were not to be allowed to record their deliberations. Arriving for the meeting, yes; Barry Tuckwell calling the meeting to order, yes; and then the doors were bolted, with the outsiders where they belonged – outside.

After the vote my crew and I joined Barry Tuckwell and Ernest Fleichmann, the LSO's dynamic general secretary, in a mad dash to Cologne to confront the orchestra's new choice, István Kertész. No, he did not realise that the orchestra retained full artistic and financial control. 'Exactly how much power will I have as principal conductor?' he asked, as the cameras recorded the making of the principal conductor. This much-admired musician performed the function very successfully for three years. Tragically, in 1973, at a young age, he died in a swimming accident.

And so to a milestone in the history of the LSO: the memorial concert to mark Monteux's retirement on his ninetieth birthday, and Kertész's first appearance since his new appointment. In contrast to the shirtsleeves, hacking jackets and jeans of the Wembley sessions, out came the platform uniforms. The only outward sign that reflected the players' individuality was the ninety different ways of knotting a white tie. There was a last drag on yet another cigarette before the march onto the platform, as a packed house eagerly anticipated Beethoven's *Seventh Symphony*.

And then, after the last note has been played, the rapturous applause has died down and the orchestra's fans have poured backstage, the LSO broke up to snatch a night's sleep. At 10 a.m. next morning it was back to Elgar, the glamour of the concert forgotten and replaced by the discipline of yet another recording session. It is tough being an orchestral player, and it is this dedication that I wanted to capture.

It was only after all the filming had been completed and David Hodgson, the film editor, and I had assembled the first rough cut, that I started to concentrate on the spoken word. Armed with an audio tape recorder, I spent many hours getting Stuart Knussen to tell me in his own words what I had learnt from him over the past weeks. This had to be disciplined so that after careful editing it would become the 'information' soundtrack. The technique of eliciting statements from people, as opposed to recording answers to a series of questions, was being used by a handful of documentary makers by now. When I first used it in the 1950s I did not realise that it would evolve into such a useful style. Then I set about recording the other voices: Colin Davis, the young Oliver Knussen, Barry Tuckwell and Danny Liddington, the driver in charge of the orchestra's instruments.

I used three (16mm) cameras to film the orchestra for the Philips' session and the concert at the Festival Hall. For the latter I was keen to put cameras right amongst the players to capture intimate close-ups of the musicians 'at work' – but this was impossible during a public performance. Therefore I asked István Kertész and the orchestra to put on their white ties and tails for their final rehearsal, and we filmed it in such a way that the empty auditorium was never in shot. This material was then intercut with the footage of that evening's performance with the Festival Hall full to bursting point. Stuart Knussen's ecstatic facial expressions as he sawed away on his double bass stole the show. And with shots of the audience applauding this masterly performance, we heard Stuart's final thought: 'This is what makes our life worth living.'

LSO – The Music Men was transmitted at peak time on 22 September 1965. These are excerpts from some of the press cuttings:

Nancy Banks Smith – the *Sun*: Rediffusion last night gave us *The Smashing Sandie Shaw* and *LSO – The Music Men*. Music pop-pop. Music top drawer. Still music. Maybe they had no moral in mind. Maybe there is none. Sandie shown like this, cold, without an audience, was like a conductor without an orchestra. She's hardly a singer, more a symbol; those bare toes and that voice in her nose. But the point about popsters is – isn't it? – that they conduct their audience. Give Sandie a room full of kids and with a movement, a sidelong look, she'll bring the audience thundering in, as the London Symphony Orchestra responded to Colin Davis's baton. I don't suppose Davis would care for the comparison. He explained what it's like to be part of an orchestra with all the flash and fluency of, surely, a Welshman. Almost everything he said about making music *en masse* is worth repeating. 'This extraordinarily exciting noise, like living one hundred times faster. You cease to be just yourself. You become a part of something that is happening. A corporate attempt to produce something marvellous.' It was extraordinary to see. This shirtsleeved sweat shop in Wembley Town Hall, which is the LSO in rehearsal. That craggy man with the fag glued to his lower lip – the principal double bass player. Somehow you felt there should have been something to distinguish conductors from bus conductors, musicians from just men. Nothing. Seventy-five men. One on the rostrum – and suddenly they explode. Like athletes off the starting block. Or a cavalry charge or an aircraft taking off, propellers turning, pistons pumping. Like seeing 75 men go magnificently, mutually mad. Or all falling in love together or all getting religion at the same moment. But, of course, it is a kind of love and a sort of religion. Sandie raises her eyes, and the kids scream. Davis his arms and 75 instruments scream in tune. And both for joy.

The Times: Peter Morley succeeded by judicious cutting and clever camera work in presenting the ethos of an orchestra through the personalities of its individual members and its conductors. Here was a programme about people rather than about music, but one might add a rider and say that it was about why certain people must make music and must make music practically to the exclusion of all other interests. The shapelessness of this documentary derived from the happy fact that the director had not tried to impose a form on what is in reality a sprawling activity. There is nothing more desultory than an orchestral rehearsal; the wonder is that the end product, record or concert, should often be so thrilling. Just why was revealed in the study of the rapport between one conductor, Colin Davis, and his players – an unspoken relationship of *primus inter pares*.

Lynda Dyson – the *Birmingham Post*: When ITV is prepared to devote an hour to a film about the London Symphony Orchestra there is no doubt that televised music has arrived. And to my mind a documentary like this one is worth ten recordings of the Proms. It is a credit to Peter Morley's direction that the anonymous white ties of the symphony orchestra came alive during this film and left me determined to attend a concert by the LSO at the first opportunity.

Hastings Evening Argus: There are times, when a TV piece on classical music falls right on its feet, when the action adds to an appreciation of the music. Last night was another such occasion when Rediffusion sacrificed (for them) an hour of precious programme time to a documentary on the London Symphony Orchestra. *The Music*

> *Men* was a very large peep into the lives of the men who made music professionally, and to do this cameras never attempted to create nor to interpret, but recorded faithfully without ever getting in the way. Peter Morley's film will do more for the cause of classical music on TV than any last night at the Proms.

A journalist from the weekly *Television Mail* (alas, there is no byline on the cutting) took this opportunity to interview me for a lengthy piece, looking back on my first ten tears in TV:

> . . . I didn't ask him – though I admit it was on the tip of my tongue – what sort of viewer he had in mind for *LSO – The Music Men*, when Morley got in first saying that when he first started working for Rediffusion ten years ago, that fact was a constant pre-occupation. It took him two years, he said, to rid himself of an absolute fallacy, which causes a producer to categorise viewers. There is no such person, he said, as an average viewer, any more than there is a man in the street. These are myths. His programme standard, he said, is his own. He makes it, so to speak, for himself and hopes that there are enough viewers who get out of it what he put into it. If a programme is well made then viewers will watch – almost irrespective of the subject. Peter Morley's ten years in Television House are distinguished years by any standards. Soon after he joined Associated-Rediffusion, first in the ITV field, he produced Benjamin Britten's *The Turn of the Screw*, the only full-length opera on ITV. His list is like a telephone directory page. But for all his successes, a professional's career is still precarious. Like an actor, he is still only as good as his last programme. But it keeps him (like them) ever alert. And as well as a number of awards like the Grand Prix for the Churchill funeral he also got himself Jane, a senior production assistant, who has been Mrs Morley for coming up to four years. So there is a lot to be said for Independent Television in the Morley home.

I couldn't help but agree.

19: Lord Mountbatten

Admiral of the Fleet the Earl Mountbatten of Burma was due to retire from active service in the summer of 1965. Early in the Second World War he had been a dashing (some say reckless) destroyer flotilla commander, with his beloved HMS *Kelly* being sunk by German Stuka bombers in the battle of Crete; he was the first Chief of Combined Operations; defeated and cleared the Japanese out of Burma as Supreme Allied Commander South East Asia; as the last Viceroy of India masterminded the controversial transfer of power that split the sub-continent into India and the new Pakistan; returned to the navy, rose to First Sea Lord; and ended his career as Chief of Defence Staff. He was murdered by the IRA in 1979.

In 1922 Mountbatten married the immensely rich heiress Edwina Ashley, granddaughter of Sir Ernest Cassels. They had two daughters: the eldest, Patricia, married the film producer John Brabourne, the 7th Baron Brabourne of Brabourne; her younger sister Pamela married the designer David Hicks.

John Brabourne was on the council of the British Film Academy when we first met during the early Academy merger talks with the Guild of Television Producers and Directors. As a result, since 1958 we had been fellow council members of the newly formed Society of Film and Television Arts. In 1975 it was renamed the British Academy of Film and Television Arts (BAFTA), and we were appointed fellow foundation trustees. And that is how I became involved with the Mountbatten family. In 1964 Brabourne had persuaded his father-in-law – known as Dickie to his large family – to tell the story of his life and times on television, knowing that he was unwilling to authorise an official biography while he was alive, let alone write his autobiography. John put the Mountbatten TV series idea up to the BBC, and a dinner for Mountbatten was hosted by Hugh Carlton Greene, the incumbent BBC Director- General, and a very sumptuous affair it turned out to be. Mountbatten was wined and dined and flattered, and by the time the brandy and port was passed round agreement had been reached for the BBC to make a television series; but it was understood that Mountbatten could only get involved after his official retirement the following year. I was totally unaware of all this when in the spring of 1965 John McMillan once more called me to his office and told me that he had been approached by the Mountbatten family, offering Rediffusion the opportunity to make a series about Mountbatten's life and times, with the proviso that I would be made available to produce and direct it. Was I interested, he asked. I confessed that I knew very little about Mountbatten, but that it sounded like an intriguing idea.

Next I had a meeting with John Brabourne, and the first thing I asked was why the project had been offered to Rediffusion and not the BBC. I was told a bizarre story. John had written to the BBC shortly after Mountbatten's retirement to tell them that he was now ready to embark on the TV series. He had to wait quite some time for a reply, and when it came it simply stated that the BBC had decided not to go ahead with the project. No details were given, and I believe that to this day no one has ever discovered what brought about this volte-face.

So that is how I came onto the scene. Little did I realise that with all the inevitable ups and downs of film-making this assignment was to last three extraordinary years. And in recalling it all now, more than forty years on, I must give due warning that, because of the nature of the project, I will not be able to avoid some fairly outrageous name-dropping.

Early in September 1965 John Brabourne arranged my first meeting with Lord Mountbatten – a lunch at the splendid Knightsbridge headquarters of the Royal Thames Yacht Club, of which he was Commodore. I was unsure how to prepare myself for this day – there was little time to bone up on Mountbatten's unique career – so I thought I might as well parade my ignorance, as that would be less of a risk than pretending otherwise. I arrived with John, and as we approached the bar Mountbatten came over, we shook hands, and he said, 'Do you know what a horse's neck is?' I shook my head. 'It's a navy drink, brandy and ginger ale with ice, and as we are going to work together you might like to get used to it. By the way, I am going to call you Peter.'

'And what shall I call you, sir?' I asked.

'I will answer to anything you like, but I would prefer Lord Louis.'

That was a typical example of his ice-breaking technique. Lord Mountbatten (I will refer to him as LM from now on) had this knack of making every one he met, regardless of rank or stature, feel immediately at ease. I was able to observe this at first hand many times for the next three years. Over lunch he checked out some of the information that John had given him about me. He was particularly interested in my army service, and the sort of programmes I enjoyed making.

'What makes you want to tell the story of my life, and how are you going to do it?'

'Lord Louis, I'm afraid I'm hopelessly ignorant about your life, and at this point I must keep an open mind on how to proceed'.

I soon realised that I had learnt my first essential lesson, which stood me in good stead: with LM you told it 'as it is'; you didn't flannel or bullshit, you made sure of your facts, and you always had to justify your reasons and decisions.

'Right,' he said, 'you'd better come down to Broadlands for a weekend so that we can get to know each other. I'll get John Barratt, my secretary, to arrange it.'

Broadlands is a splendid Georgian Palladian mansion, just outside Romsey in Hampshire. I was to get to know it well. The house, with its magnificent grounds overlooking the river Test, dates back to 1780, when the owner, Henry Temple, 2nd Viscount Palmerston, engaged Capability Brown and Henry Holland to transform it from its earlier incarnation as a Tudor and Jacobean manor house. It was the home of Lord Palmerston (the 3rd Viscount) who became Prime Minister in 1855, and it came into the Mountbatten family when Edwina (Lady M) inherited Broadlands just before the Second World War.

On 27 September 1965 I drove up to the estate's elaborate wrought-iron main gates, which displayed the Mountbatten monogram: the lodge keeper was expecting me, and he waved me through. Along the drive through the park, leading up to the main house, I spotted LM galloping towards me. He pulled up his horse, waved me down and told me where to park. 'Charles will look after your luggage. I'll be with you shortly to show you to your room.' Charles, the butler, who had clocked up many years of service with the Mountbattens, was waiting for me outside the east portico. He took my case, and Evans, one of the stewards, drove my car away, to park it near the stables. This was a different world, and there was a lot for me to take in.

LM appeared, still in his jodhpurs and polo shirt, and gave me a quick conducted tour on the way to my room. There were two grand, sweeping staircases meeting on the landing of the first floor, the one on the left displaying large and small portraits of his ancestors, and the other one, equally impressive, Edwina's ancestors. 'We've put you in the Portico Room. I think you'll find it quite comfortable.' Needless to say it was a magnificent room, the windows overlooking the vast lawn sloping down to the river Test, and a huge four-poster bed; there were two steps down to a sumptuous bathroom. 'Do you see anything special in the wallpaper?' he asked, so I looked hard at the very attractive pattern of climbing roses. Then the penny dropped – the outlines of the stems and petals traced the profiles of Victoria and Albert looking at each other. He congratulated me, as most of his guests had to have it explained to them. I felt that I had scored a minor triumph. 'By the way,' he said, 'this settee belonged to my great-grandmother, Queen Victoria.' He picked up a cushion and gave it to me to hold. 'And this was placed on her lap when she held me for my christening.' Then he said that he would go and change, and come back to take me downstairs for a drink before luncheon was served.

There were more surprises to come. Charles appeared from nowhere with my case and started to unpack it. He took my toilet bag into the bathroom and hung up my dinner jacket in a huge wardrobe, then placed shirts, socks and pants neatly in a chest of drawers, the like of which I had only ever seen in the Victoria and Albert Museum. 'Sir, if I may be permitted to say so, you must be highly regarded by his Lordship to be put up in this room.' I asked him about the room's significance. 'Did his lordship not tell you, sir, that this is the room Her Majesty stays in when she comes down for her annual weekend at Broadlands?' This was a typical example of the Mountbatten style, and I felt that I could now claim that I have slept in the Queen's bed – and sat on her throne. The fact that the Queen and Prince Philip spent their honeymoon here was just one of the many fascinating details that came thick and fast, and somehow had to be absorbed.

Past the array of paintings of his forbears, with their eyes following our every step down the staircase, LM turned our walk to the drawing room into my first genealogical tour that weekend – a swift history lesson going back all the way to Charlemagne, peppered with anecdotes that I tried hard to remember. We went through the Wedgwood room to the drawing room, stopping off at the grog tray. It was not difficult to get to like a pre-lunch horse's neck, and I was then shown intriguing memorabilia, priceless furniture and an eclectic collection of paintings, ranging from a brilliant de La Tour to Canaletto, de László's portrait of Edwina Mountbatten and – in the dining room where Charles was waiting to serve luncheon – some gigantic Van Dycks. Although I was somewhat overwhelmed I enjoyed it all, including the simplicity and excellence of the food.

Coffee was served in the drawing room, and LM announced that he would forgo his constitutional nap to show me the grounds and park. As we strolled through Capability Brown's handiwork, the questions came thick and fast: 'How do you begin to try and discipline the story of my life and tell it in a set of television programmes? Where do you start?'

'Lord Louis, this is the start,' I replied. 'Until I know your story I must simply keep an open mind. The first task is to find and engage an historian and writer, and only then, together with him, can I begin to come up with a plan. At the moment I'm sure that in order to tell the story of your life we must explore the times you lived through. It'll be a major task to get the correct balance. There's a lot of research to be organised.'

'But what do you expect me to do on the screen? Are you going to interview me, or am I just going to be the narrator?'

'I must keep an open mind about that too. I know you'll agree that the primary task is to establish first of all what it is we want to achieve, and only then to decide the best way of achieving it. As always it has to be contents before technique.'

And so it went on, and the more we talked the easier he made it for me to converse with him. By teatime, as we got back to the house, I felt that we had established an atmosphere of candour that was going to prove of immense value in the future. Over tea he described his way of coming to decisions, a style and a technique that he had used right through his career. He called it 'the spirit of the hive': 'I like listening to the buzz of lots of bees inside a hive, freely airing their opinions, making frank contributions to the topic in hand, and then allowing me to make up my mind. I hope you realise that this is the first time since my retirement that someone else is in charge – and I wish you well.' Of course I knew that meant 'You had better bloody well not let me down.'

Soon it was time to change for dinner. I went upstairs to the Portico Room to find my dinner jacket spread out on the bed, with the fresh dress shirt carefully unfolded, its buttons undone and the cufflinks in position. The folded handkerchief, black socks and shoes were also on parade. The last time I had seen such symmetry was in the army, when we had our weekly kit inspection. Charles knocked on the door, came in and asked whether he could draw my bath. I really felt I had arrived. 'His Lordship has asked me to tell you that when you are ready and care to come down to the drawing room, you are to help yourself to the grog tray and that he will join you there.' I thought that I could get used to this. 'Will you take tea in the morning, sir? May I suggest seven forty-five? I will bring the tray to you with the morning papers.' This turned out to be a clutch of all the papers, with the *Daily Mirror* on top; according to Charles, that was a royal family tradition.

After dinner, back in the drawing room over coffee, brandy and cigars, I listened to an avalanche of fascinating anecdotes, and soon came to the conclusion that, as ever, the question of what to include and what to leave out in the telling of LM's life and times was going to be a horrendous problem. LM's 'You must include this story, whatever we do . . .' became a familiar mantra over the next three years. At one point, looking at his watch, he walked over to his desk and picked up the telephone. 'I must just make a quick call to Windsor.' He spoke to the Queen almost daily, and I soon became aware of their very close relationship. I remember him saying: 'Lillibet, I've got the producer, Peter Morley, staying here at Broadlands. We're discussing my television series.' He kept her abreast of all his activities, and when we started the filming for the series, no matter where we were in the world, he would write to her almost daily.

Breakfast the next morning was yet another agreeable experience. The sideboard groaned with an array of Mountbatten silverware dishes, and on lifting the heavy domed covers the full gamut of English breakfast fare was on display.

LM told me that he had invited Ronnie Brockman over for luncheon, as he thought it would be very helpful for me to meet him as he had worked closely with LM for the past twenty years. I learnt that Vice-Admiral Sir Ronald Brockman had been the Secretary to the Viceroy, and was associated with LM's subsequent appointments right up to his retirement.

After lunch LM said that he had some work to do and suggested that Admiral Brockman and I might go out and explore the grounds. The drift of our conversation, as we walked along the Test with the salmon rising, soon changed from vice-regal anecdotes to my role in the enterprise. I realised that the purpose of Brockman's visit to Broadlands was to vet me, and he did this in a searching and most pleasant manner. Looking back on it now, I am sure I must have been vetted by a number of people, but I was unaware of it. After all, I did have access to the Mountbatten archive, and he had only recently retired from his position as Chief of Defence Staff; quite apart from the fact that he had a reputation of being delightfully indiscreet.

Back to London, and there was a great deal to ponder over. LM's first question, 'Where do you start?', was now a reality. On that Monday morning I rang a few friends and colleagues, some at the BBC, to help me compile a shortlist of potential writers. I had watched with admiration the recent BBC series The *Great War*, and I was not surprised when the name of John Terraine, one of its writer/producers, came top on my list. I phoned him and suggested that we might have lunch. He lived in Notting Hill and we made a rendezvous at his favourite watering hole, the Uxbridge Arms, an establishment that was to become a regular venue for us for the years to come. The Ark, a small and rather quaint restaurant nearby, became our eating establishment, and that is where many a plot was hatched.

We immediately hit it off. John was a highly regarded and very successful military historian, with a prolific output of publications covering both world wars. He had a dry and wicked sense of humour that I found very appealing. His involvement with the BBC and *The Great War* series had given him a taste for archive film and its exploitation for good visual storytelling; when I said that we would combine that with a great deal of original filming with Mountbatten, he did not need much persuasion to come and join me. And so began what was to become a unique piece of programme-making. Our pairing for this venture combined the erudition and the intellectual and analytical approach of an historian with my capacity to 'think with my stomach', as I have always liked to describe it. It balanced our strengths and weaknesses and it worked extremely well. It was a case of mutual respect and mutual liking – and as a bonus we never fell out. What luck.

I phoned LM and asked whether I could bring John Terraine down to Broadlands so that they could meet, and that is what happened. I noticed that LM was much impressed by John's immense knowledge and his fresh approach to the interpretation of history for a large television audience. That was a good start. John and I relished the stream of unstoppable stories, and I suggested that in order to get the whole enterprise off the ground we should spend a considerable number of days at Broadlands with a sound recordist, to capture not only the story of LM's life but also the style of his language. I proposed that the three of us would come armed with an inventory of topics and questions, and would go on recording until we had nothing left to say. LM jumped at this notion. A month later this was achieved, and when these recordings were transcribed – producing hundreds of pages – they became the foundation document that enabled John to map out the first outline treatment for thirteen programmes.

It was the convention in the '60s, established by the American networks, that television series ran for thirteen weeks, and Rediffusion reckoned on thirteen half-hour programmes for the Mountbatten series. Minus the time allowed for commercials, this left a mere twenty-six minutes per episode to grab viewers' attention and develop the story. The lesson I had learnt from the clutch of one-hour documentaries I had made over the last ten years was that a programme length of only thirty minutes limits the amount of information that can be communicated and also comes across as being rather lightweight; somehow not as serious as a sixty-minuter. Now, faced with that mountain of transcripts, it was obvious that even if they were one-hour programmes we were going to be very pushed to squeeze the past sixty-five years of LM's life and the times he lived through into thirteen episodes. I kept quiet about this: there were major political and budgetary implications, so it would have been unwise to raise the issue at that point. I was certain that further down the line, when we had reached the stage of assembling one episode on film, the one-hour concept would speak for itself and the powers-that-be would not be able to argue against it.

* * * *

We set to work. It didn't take long for John to come up with a chronology, breaking down the twin threads of the series – the life and the times – into what three years later ended up as twelve hour-long episodes. We were now able to plan the contents of each one, decide on the locations for filming and begin to organise the research for archive film. We also had to decide the most effective way for LM to make his on-screen contributions. There were three options. First was to put his 'to camera' pieces onto a teleprompting device, which ruled itself out because the Autocue equipment was heavy and cumbersome, and the thought of carting it round the world to difficult locations like a Burmese jungle was simply not on. In any case, the cost of an operator and freight charges would have been prohibitive. The second option was to film short and carefully prepared location interviews, but that ruled itself out because LM's style of speaking, verbose to say the least, would have required a series of at least twenty-six episodes! The answer, therefore, was for John to write LM's contributions, for him to learn them off by heart and then speak them directly into the camera. That's where our Broadlands recordings were so valuable, because John could compose these pieces based on LM's own language, and he would feel at home uttering his own, albeit highly condensed version of events. Although I felt that this was a risky solution, not knowing how easy it would come to our star to learn his words or how he would 'perform' them, there was really no alternative. This approach certainly gave us some headaches later on.

At this stage I gave John McMillan a progress report, and spelled out the various recce and shooting trips that we were likely to undertake; also that the royalty costs of archive film were still unknown. And as far as I could tell I would need a three-year production period, two researchers immediately, and one cutting room allocated to me immediately, with another two in about eighteen months' time. He did not demur, so I asked him about the budget. For the second time in five years I heard these halcyon words: 'Let that be my worry – just go ahead.' (The first time it was for *The Turn of the Screw* – what a man.) Despite this encouragement, it was still too early to mention my belief that we would end up with one-hour programmes.

John and I visited Broadlands quite frequently, discussing scripts, eliciting yet more details and generally keeping LM on side. He was an absolute stickler for detail, always probing to find out exactly how we were going to handle it. We were quite glad not to have served under him! But both of us enjoyed these sessions very much – and each time we learnt more about him. He insisted that we should get to know him, warts and all, and we did. LM willingly confessed to being a show-off: he loved being flattered; enjoyed dressing up in his many different uniforms; was intolerant of those who hid their weaknesses; was impatient with his personal staff. 'Good leadership,' he explained, 'is a mixture of arrogance, ruthlessness and vanity, while retaining one's sense of humour.'

What soon became apparent to us was LM's rather disarming way in laying claim to the ownership of all ideas, strategies and inventions. He soon realised that we were well aware of this trait, and had a good laugh when I told him that John and I wanted to call the series *The Life and Times of Lord Mountbatten*, and congratulated him on thinking up such a brilliant title.

Coming under his spell, so to speak, we realised the danger of creating a hagiography. We had to keep that in mind, and make sure we found the right balance between the facts and LM's charming and persuasive 'the great I am' syndrome. Not easy.

Like all members of the royal family he was a great movie fan, and the Broadlands 'period' cinema was luxurious, to say the least. It boasted a fine fireplace with a magnificent Grinling Gibbons carved woodwork chimneypiece of fruit, flowers, small animals and cherubs' heads. On one of my very early visits to the house I screened my Cannes Grand Prix one-hour version of the Churchill funeral – LM was, after all, the principal pallbearer, walking immediately behind the gun carriage. That was when he told me the story about Churchill confiding in him the date of his death.

It was also on this occasion that I learnt about LM's film collection. He was the founder of the Royal Navy Film Corporation, and introduced projection equipment and films to the fleet in the 1920s; and he told me that hundreds of cans of 35mm film were stored in the basement – a collection that over the years he had been presented with or had 'acquired'. 'You should really spend some time going through them, as you may wish to use some of the material in the series.' I listened with horror, fearing that most of this material was bound to be on nitrate film – highly volatile with age, and presenting a real danger to Broadlands. It has been known to combust spontaneously, causing the most fearsome explosions and fires: my early projection days at the Dominion and my close connection with the BFI had taught me that. LM took me down to the basement, and when we entered the storeroom the familiar pervading acrid smell of nitrate film hit me. There were piles of rusty film cans with all manner of titles, although the labels on most of them were difficult to decipher. I picked up a can with the title *Nice and Friendly*. 'Good God, I knew this would be down here somewhere. You must use it in the series.' Indeed we did. It was a one-reeler directed by and starring Charlie Chaplin, Lord and Lady Mountbatten and the child actor Jackie Coogan. Chaplin made it in 1922 as a wedding present to the Mountbattens when they visited Hollywood on their honeymoon. The Mountbatten acting was pretty awful, which adds to the charm of it, and it also shows rare footage of Chaplin as himself.

Decisive action had to be taken. I knew that the Henderson Laboratory in North London specialised in rescuing nitrate film by transferring it onto safety stock. LM agreed immediately for me to organise the removal of this highly dangerous archive, and the next day Henderson's collected all the cans, using special trucks. What a relief.

John Rowe, a Rediffusion film researcher who had been armed with detailed briefings from John Terraine and me, now started to scour the world's archives for the series. I knew London's Imperial War Museum archive pretty well, having used footage from it on several of my productions, and we were bound to use a fair amount of it for the Mountbatten series. I went to see Dr Noble Frankland, the museum's director, to try and do some sort of deal with him regarding royalty fees for an unspecified amount of footage. He suggested that if the museum were to be presented with a 35mm colour print of the whole series on completion he would waive all payments. This was too good to be true, and I happily agreed. He then said that he would like to make one further condition: that I would use my best endeavours to persuade Lord Mountbatten to attend the première of the series, to be staged in the museum's cinema. That evening I rang up LM and explained the situation to him. His immediate reply was, 'Of course I'll be there, but tell Frankland that I'll not be alone, as I will have the Queen and the whole royal family with me – what I call the royal flush.' Three years later that is exactly what happened.

By the beginning of 1966 John had made rapid progress with the outlines for each episode, and we fine-tuned these during frequent sessions at the Uxbridge Arms and the Ark. Because we were creating a novel mixture of history, biography and autobiography, it seemed logical to start with the birth of LM in 1900 and follow chronologically with the rest of the programmes. We told him that we were very grateful to him for having been born in 1900; it eased the mathematics when working out his age during any given year in this hectic twentieth century.

We had now decided upon the contents of each episode, and soon the locations we wanted to take LM back to produced a formidable list of far-flung countries: Ceylon, Malaya, Singapore, Bangkok, India and Malta. Of course there were going to be many locations in the UK: apart from Broadlands, amongst others we wanted to shoot at 10 Downing Street, Christ's College, Cambridge, Buckingham Palace, Greenwich College, the Admiralty, the underground Cabinet War Rooms and the Ministry of Defence. As the outlines developed an impressive list of eyewitnesses had to be approached, and their participation had to be sought.

At the start of 1966 there were additional events occupying my mind. Jane was highly pregnant, having resigned her drama PA position at Rediffusion the previous autumn to prepare for this great event. Unexpectedly I was asked by John McMillan to produce a special live programme to be networked on 8 February. It was called *Pay and Prices – the CRUNCH,* and it was all about the Wilson government's deep economic crisis, during which George Brown, his colourful bon viveur Chancellor of the Exchequer, was trying to combat runaway wages and prices. I was asked to be the show's producer, with an editorial team made up by Alastair Burnet, George Ffitch, Geoffrey Hodgson, George Scott and Andrew Shonfield. A formidable cast had been assembled for the studio: George Brown MP, Reginald Maudling MP, Jo Grimond MP, Aubrey Jones, John Davies, Desmond Donnelly MP, Clive Jenkins, Thomas Kilpatrick, William Rees-Mogg, Lord Sainsbury and George Woodcock. These were the leading players in politics, economics and the trade unions, and I clearly recall the tense atmosphere in the green room as they arrived for transmission. We had to lay on a separate room for George Brown, with a request by his minders only to have soft drinks on parade.

The network agreed to Rediffusion's unique request to allow the programme, once on air, to run its natural length, regardless of the published programme schedule that followed it. It was to be ITV's first 'open ended' programme, and this decision took many by surprise.

I had a surprise of a different kind. I came up from Broadlands early on the morning of transmission day and went straight to the studio, only to be told that a friend had taken Jane to the maternity unit of University College Hospital. As luck would have it I was able to call a break in my studio rehearsals early that evening, dashed up to the hospital and was present at the birth of our son Jonathan. Jane and the baby were both in very good form, and it was with mixed feelings that I had to leave them and tear back again to continue the rehearsals for the next evening's show. The programme came off well, but the London *Evening News* blamed me for what they thought was a mistake in the programme's timing:

> WHY MR MORLEY LET THE TV SHOW RUN
> I talked to-day to ITV producer Peter Morley, the man who annoyed some viewers last night by allowing a live programme, *Pay and Prices – the Crunch* to over-run by 33 minutes. Mr. Morley was a tired man to-day – for personal as well as programme reasons. His wife had had their first child a week early. So Mr. Morley had to divide his time planning the programme and visiting his wife and day-old son. It meant that a James Bond hour, which followed, started at 10.58 instead of around 10.25 p.m. as expected. 'My instructions' said Morley, 'were to let it run as long as the subject justified it. When I thought all that could usefully be said had been said, then I could wind up.' He did not even know a Bond programme was next on the screen.

This cutting earned pride of place in Jonathan's first baby-photograph scrapbook. I received a very nice letter from LM congratulating us on Jonathan's arrival – and soon it was back to the coalface, concentrating on the series. John Barratt, LM's secretary, was doing some great staff-work for the project, writing dozens of letters dictated by his master to his contacts in the countries we wanted to film in. And by contacts I mean the kings, presidents, prime ministers and dictators who were asked to smooth the way for our visits. I took the opportunity to declare him the best-connected unit manager in the business, and he enjoyed that.

Filming started in the spring of 1966, and we finally put the cameras away in October 1968 – the end of an exhausting, eventful, sometimes turbulent, but always highly enjoyable three years. John wrote the 'Mountbatten to camera' pieces based on the hours of recordings we had, and when LM read them for the first time he usually said, 'I didn't know that I could be so succinct.' Learning them off by heart was a different matter. It is not easy when you have never had to do it before, but he was such a perfectionist that he never minded how many takes were required. If I remember correctly our record was fourteen, in the middle of a Burmese jungle with leeches crawling up our legs. But just as taxing as being word perfect was the actual delivery – with the right stresses on the words and at the same time a relaxed demeanour. LM never took naturally to that, and we had to rehearse each piece many times over, with Jonathan Avery, our unit manager, acting as prompt.

In between our shooting dates in the UK in 1966, I went on recce trips to all our foreign locations with Vicky Miller, my PA, not merely to finalise the details of where and how I would shoot this mass of material, but also to organise the many social events LM would wish to attend. Huge demands on his time (and ours) were going to be made in each of the countries – everyone who had met him in his previous incarnation wanted a piece of him – and I found myself having to decline on his behalf a number of requests, even some state banquets and ceremonial parades in his honour.

I also had to make final filming arrangements for the many eyewitnesses that I called on during these hectic visits. It was a cast to conjure with: the Duke of Edinburgh, the Duke of Windsor, Harold Wilson, Lady Asquith of Yarnbury, Anthony Eden (Lord Avon), Clement (Lord) Attlee, Air Marshal Sir John Baldwin, Lord Brabourne, Vice-Admiral Sir Ronald Brockman, The Maharaja of Bundi, Noël Coward, Sir Alec Douglas-Home, Tom Driberg, General Dwight D. Eisenhower, Mrs Indira Gandhi, Mrs V.L. Pandit, H.V. Hodson, Vice-Admiral John Hughes-Hallett, The Maharani of Jaipur, Lee Kuan Yew, Malcolm MacDonald, Harold Macmillan, Donald McLachlan, Dr Noble Frankland, C.R. Rajagopalachari, Major-General Sir Hubert Rance, Duncan Sandys, Sir Geoffrey Shakespeare, Field Marshal Viscount Slim, Vice-Admiral Sir Gilbert Stephenson, General R.T. 'Speck' Wheeler, Brigadier Peter Young and Sir Solly Zuckerman. In addition there were numerous 'other ranks', including crew members who had served with LM in HMS *Kelly*, soldiers from his Burma campaign, survivors of Japanese prison camps and so on.

My mind, when allowed to roam, is packed with all sorts of anecdotes reflecting the many months of filming. I will recall just a few of them – otherwise these jottings are in danger of running to a second volume.

We started the main Far East shooting trip in January 1967. Sri Lanka, then still Ceylon, provided an early laugh for us all. On my recce trip I was asked to make arrangements for LM to be free to attend the première of a new Raquel Welch movie. A few months later, on our arrival in Colombo, the morning headline in the *Weekend* proclaimed 'Supremo to act with sex bomb'. It went on to report that 'Mountbatten was to co-star with the most talked of woman in the film world, sex symbol Raquel Welch, in a film that is to be produced by a top-ranking organisation in Britain. It is expected to be the most authentic war film ever to be made.' A couple of days later LM received a telegram from John Brabourne: 'As requested have signed contract for you to co-star in Life and Times of Raquel Welch.'

Singapore chalked up a personal triumph for me. Prime Minister Lee Kuan Yew threw a huge reception and dinner to honour LM's visit in the gardens of the Istana. We had just finished filming an eyewitness report, with Lee Kuan Yew talking about LM receiving the surrender of the Japanese in 1945, and his role in overseeing Singapore's independence. The whole crew had been invited to this feast. There must have been at least twenty tables, each seating ten guests and hosted by a minister or high-ranking official. There were innumerable courses of delicious Malay food, and as custom dictated the hosts frequently swapped tables so that all of us could meet the Singapore hierarchy. Lee Kuan Yew settled at my table together with his Minister of Education, just as beautifully decorated bowls of quail's eggs were placed in front of each of us. 'Mr Morley,' said the Prime Minister, 'this will be a real test to show how adept you have become with chopsticks, as these eggs usually confound our visitors to Singapore.' He was right: a quail's egg is as slippery as a bar of wet soap. With all eyes on me I had a go – what was there to lose? – and I holed in one, thanks more to luck than good management. Lee Kuan Yew congratulated me, picked up his chopsticks, homed in on an egg, and managed to squirt it across the table straight into the lap of his minister. *Touché*.

Burma was a closed country. With the exception of dealers in timber who were occasionally granted four-day visas, it was virtually impossible to get in; and foreign film crews were totally banned. But as the victor who freed Burma from Japanese occupation, and with the title of Earl Mountbatten of Burma, LM was always welcomed there with open arms. But getting John and me in with the crew called for an extra dose of the Mountbatten arm-twisting technique. Luckily General Ne Win, Burma's despotic ruler (who had established his dictatorship by military *coup d'état* in 1962), paid an annual visit to the UK for medical treatment and usually stayed as LM's guest at Broadlands. I was asked down for the weekend in the late '60s during one of these visits to meet Ne Win and help to soften him up. A despicable man, he was accompanied by Katie, his charming wife. It was a treat to watch LM's technique, which resulted in Ne Win almost believing that it was his own idea to invite me with the crew to his country. He also presented me with a huge box of Burmese cigars, which lasted for years.

On our recce trip arrival in Rangoon Vicky Miller and I were met at the airport by a colonel and a captain, who had been allocated to me as my liaison officers for the filming trip. They had obviously been told to co-operate fully with my requests, and were very friendly and helpful. When they took us on a sightseeing tour of Rangoon I remarked that all the shops seemed to be shut, with no one around. I was told that it was Poya day, when everything always shuts (as used to be the custom here on our Sundays). Sadly I noted that the following few days must all have been Poya days, as everything seemed to be permanently closed up and abandoned. Most men in Rangoon were wearing army uniform and it was depressing to see this rich, lush country in such a desperate state. We were booked into the Inya Lake Hotel – a huge Russian-built edifice with a cavernous dining room. We were the only guests.

When we returned for filming the following year the official reception accorded to LM was very cordial and generous. Our locations were in Rangoon and up country in Pagan, Mandalay, and at the very point where the 14th Army made its famous river crossing of the Irrawaddy in pursuit of the Japanese forces in 1945. We discovered that getting to these locations presented Ne Win with his own set of problems. Burma's socialist dictatorship was fighting internal guerrilla wars with minority groups, such as the Kachins and Karens, and there was a permanent state of tension. It was considered too dangerous for LM and the team to go by rail to Pagan; in addition, Ne Win insisted on accompanying us to these spots. The elaborate plan he had made involved the booking of a plane to fly us to Pagan (the old city of 5,000 pagodas), where he met us on arrival. But Ne Win was not alone: his whole Revolutionary Council was on parade to receive Earl Mountbatten of Burma. The First Secretary of our embassy had also come up from Rangoon, and he told me that Ne Win dared not risk leaving his Revolutionary Council behind in the capital, as he feared plots against him.

We stayed in Pagan filming for two days and then went on board a 1926 Glasgow-built paddle-steamer for the overnight river trip to Mandalay. This was large enough to accommodate the whole Revolutionary Council, LM and his daughter Patricia (Lady Brabourne, the future Countess Mountbatten of Burma), who had joined the party. This ancient steamer had been made moderately comfortable. When John Terraine and I explored the huge engine room we discovered a line of ten large domestic refrigerators that had been purchased and installed for the trip. The whole enterprise must have rocked the Burmese treasury.

After a late on-board dinner it was too hot to go to sleep. John and I shared a cabin, and we decided to spend most of the night on deck. Gunboats fore and aft escorted the steamer down the Irrawaddy, their searchlights sweeping the riverbanks. The full moon's reflection followed us in the calm water; it was very beautiful. I asked John whether he thought that Kipling might have made the same journey on his road to Mandalay, when both of us suddenly spotted several flying fish alongside, gracefully leaping in and out of the water. It was a memorable night.

In the morning Ne Win and his cohorts left for Rangoon, and we resumed our shooting schedule – having been given the use of one of the gunboats.

India stirs up rich memories. Our first call was New Delhi. LM and Patricia had been invited to take up the same quarters they enjoyed twenty years earlier – the Lutyens-designed majestic red sandstone and marble Rashtrapati Bhawan, formerly the palace of the Viceroy and now the presidential residence. LM's old barber and other retainers were called out of retirement to serve their old master, the Viceroy. Wherever we went with him massive, cheering crowds gathered. The vestiges of the British Empire, the pomp and the grandeur, shrieked at you – it was very impressive.

Probably LM's most controversial event of his career was the hurried transfer of power, splitting that 'jewel in the crown', to create an independent India and the new Pakistan. We called that episode 'The Last Viceroy', and to recall those momentous few months in 1947 we met and interviewed some remarkable people who had good reason to remember the dramas of that period, including Nehru's sister, the politician Mrs V.L. Pandit, C.R. Rajagopalarchari, India's first Governor-General, and Prime Minister Mrs Indira Gandhi. In Rajasthan we stayed with and filmed the Maharaja and Maharani of Jaipur, all key players in the transfer of power.

Further south, near Kota, we stayed with the Maharaja of Bundi. He had served under LM in the 14th Army in Burma, and like many of the princes who had to give up power and influence as part of the 1947 settlement for the new India, he lost a great deal of his wealth. On my recce trip, when I went up to Kota to meet him to organise the shoot and make detailed arrangements for the last Viceroy's visit, I offered to pay a facility fee for his generous invitation to put up the crew in his palace, which was some distance away from the only hotel in that area. India was in a parlous economic state, and the use of foreign currency for imports was strictly prohibited. Rather sheepishly, he asked me whether it would be possible for me to obtain a certain piece of machinery in England and somehow bring it into the country when I returned with LM and the crew; he then explained that he was after an Evinrude outboard motor. Back in London I got Rediffusion's agreement to this novel way of paying for location expenses, and LM was delighted to be part of the plot, of course. So we shipped the motor (at vast expense) to customs in Delhi, clearly marked 'to await the arrival of the Earl Mountbatten of Burma'. It worked like a charm. When we arrived I cleared it out of customs and it became part of our camera equipment. On arrival at the Maharaja's palace I got four of his bearers to carry it into my bedroom. Late that night, after a very long day, I was glad to put out the light and get some sleep. Shortly after I had put my head down I heard my bedroom door being slowly pushed open, and an excited Maharaja said, 'Have you been able to grant my request?' Before I could reply he clapped his hands to summon the four bearers who had waited outside to carry away his spoils. He followed them, and half an hour later the door opened once more and two bearers brought in a large bowl of fruit and some flowers with a thank-you note. The Maharaja was a happy man.

Wherever we went in this fascinating country LM was applauded, often mobbed, and the affection shown to him twenty years after independence was manifest and rather touching.

We returned to London from this three-months shoot in March 1967, and discovered that in the world of television great changes were afoot.

Lord Hill, Chairman of the ITA, and his council precipitated a dramatic upheaval, altering the face of ITV. In London Rediffusion was kicked into the long grass by having to merge with ABC from the Midlands and form a newly created Monday to Friday London franchise holder, called Thames Television. The ITA announced this in 1967 and shortly afterwards, in September, Harold Wilson cynically appointed Lord Hill, ITA's chairman, as the new chairman of the BBC's Board of Governors, and gave his ITA job to his old political ally Bert Bowden, now Lord Aylestone.

So here I was, in the middle of making an important (and expensive) television series for Rediffusion, which was about to disappear from under me, and the unfinished *Life and Times of Lord Mountbatten* was to be handed over to the new Thames Television. There were problems.

In 1966 I had set up three cutting rooms in Television House with film editors Alan Afriat and Johnny Zambardi, dubbing editor Rosemary MacLoughlin, and five assistants. By the autumn of 1967 they were making very good progress with assemblies and rough-cuts of the first few episodes. There was still a lot of shooting to be done, with our second four-week session at Broadlands in September and other UK locations to visit. But all the material, including archive film, was at hand to complete episode two. I wanted to finish this as soon as possible, so that I could show it to LM and especially John Brabourne, in order to prove to them both that half-hour episodes were a non-starter. They were easily persuaded, and saw the point immediately that these programmes had to be one hour long.

As the months passed the brand-new Thames TV made its presence felt. Howard Thomas, its new managing director, was making difficulties. He had run ABC Television, noted chiefly for its excellent dramas and light entertainment programmes, but had made little contribution to the network's documentary output. I believe he rather resented being forced to take me and my production on board – 'not a good fit' was the expression used at the time. He wanted to transfer production to his people in Elstree Studios (owned by ABC) and find a way, if possible, to reduce the series to six half-hours.

I persuaded John Brabourne that we should have a showdown with Thames, and arrange a screening to make them aware of what the Mountbatten series was all about. With John McMillan's blessing (he was by now taking a back seat in Rediffusion's affairs), that is what happened. It took place in our preview theatre in Kingsway, and Howard Thomas brought his chairman, Sir Philip Warter, and Brian Tesler, ABC's talented light entertainment producer, who had just been appointed Thames Television's first Controller of Programmes. The two Johns, Brabourne and Terraine, and I represented Rediffusion.

I knew that screening episode two was a good choice for this particular audience, as there was a rich mixture of both the life and the times. It opens in 1917, when the story of the Mountbattens could be said to have started, as the family changed its name from Battenberg to Mountbatten as a result of anti-German hysteria. Russia was swept by revolution, and the imperial family, LM's uncle and aunt, the Tsar and Tsarina, and his five cousins, were murdered by the Bolsheviks; while other members of the family lost their ancient thrones. After the war, in 1920, LM accompanied the Prince of Wales on two spectacular Commonwealth tours (I filmed the Duke of Windsor's eyewitness account of this), and the Prince was then LM's best man at his wedding to Edwina Ashley at St Margaret's, Westminster. They spent their honeymoon in Hollywood, and the episode ends with excerpts from the Charlie Chaplin one-reeler I have already mentioned.

When the lights went up there was hushed silence. Howard Thomas turned to me and uttered these memorable words, 'It's a bit documentary, don't you think?'

Tesler looked embarrassed, but said that he quite liked what he had seen.

'How long did that run for?' Thomas asked. When I told him it was fifty-two minutes, he replied, 'We've been told that we would be taking on half-hour programmes.'

'Yes, originally I was commissioned to make thirteen thirty-minuters,' I said, 'but the moment I met Lord Mountbatten and our research began it became obvious that we would have to go for twelve one-hour network slots.' I felt that I had to risk taking a firm, if somewhat pompous, line. 'It's simply that in certain fields of programme-making content dictates the length required to do the subject justice. In any case, Mr Thomas, which 50 per cent of what you have just seen do you suggest should be junked?'

Howard bristled, and said that Rediffusion could not expect Thames TV to pick up the extra costs for hour-long programmes.

John Brabourne saved the day by saying that it was really a financial rather than a programme problem, and that he was sure Thames TV could resolve it with Rediffusion.

Luckily I then remembered the première at the Imperial War Museum – LM's 'royal flush'. Howard's instinct of sniffing out good publicity took over, and he became friendly. He agreed the one-hour concept, and also that I could finish the series at Television House, even after Rediffusion had pulled out for good, and that my whole team (except for me, as I was a freelance) would be invited to join Thames Television.

Surprisingly, as a parting gesture Brian Tesler turned to me. 'Peter, I'll bet you that the series will never get into the "Top Ten", that it will never be networked, and that Rediffusion will not get an on-screen credit.' I wish I had taken him on, as he lost handsomely on all three counts, but I could understand his attitude. He was a brilliant light entertainment producer, who was later to rise to the highest positions in ITV. But in 1969 both Howard Thomas and Brian, having successfully launched Thames Television, must have found it pretty galling to be obliged to broadcast this inherited prestige series from Rediffusion.

* * * *

I had to complete and deliver the series by the end of 1968. The cutting rooms were going at full pelt, and every spare moment I could find was spent there. But there was still the filming with LM to complete, and woven into all that were extramural activities that demanded attention. The most important was the birth of Benjamin in March – and now there were two sons to come home to in the evenings. Again I was able to be present at the birth, this time without having to rush back to a studio. Much later that year, when we had finished our last LM filming at Broadlands on a Thursday, I was asked to stay over as the Queen and Prince Philip were coming down on Friday for their annual weekend visit and LM wanted me to be there for tea, as the Queen had taken a great interest in the filming for the series. When LM introduced me, he boasted that I was the person who had produced twelve television programmes about his life and times as well as two sons, all in the space of three years. I wished that Jane could have been there. Prince Philip was out in the park riding, so for tea it was just the Queen, LM and me. She was 'mother', and poured the tea and cut the Dundee cake. She was very well informed about all the fun and problems we had had in the Far East, having received the details in LM's numerous letters. I told her that the previous day we had held a special investiture for the man who had more decorations than he could ever wear at any one time, including the Order of the Garter, the Order of Merit, PC, GCB, GSCI, GCVO, DSO and many more. To mark the very last shot for the series I had taken the opportunity to invest him with the CDM and bar. This was a medal made out of tin. I had placed it on one of the priceless drawing room cushions, made a short speech and congratulated the recipient on never having to appear in front of the camera again. I explained that the CDM was given away with every bar of the new Cadbury Dairy Milk chocolate. We were amused! It was all very informal, and very relaxed.

Later in 1968 the Mountbatten family was at Broadlands to entertain the whole production team and their wives for an elaborate and very generous end-of-series luncheon party. The big dining room, which I had got to know so well, was transformed into a banqueting room, seating thirty-six people. I still have the seating plan, drawn up in pencil by LM – as always, a stickler for detail – and there were speeches and reminiscences covering the past three years. I presented LM with the much-travelled clapperboard, showing the last slate number with its date. This was later installed in the Broadlands 'cinema', hanging above the fireplace close to one of Grinling Gibbons' carved masterpieces.

There was one major political hurdle to overcome. I had been tipped off that Thames was finding it difficult to persuade the other ITV companies to network the series, some saying that Thames TV was not trying hard enough. I felt powerless over this, but remembering Brian Tesler's bet I was determined to have a go. I phoned up Lord Aylestone, the ITA's new chairman, and when told his secretary that I was representing Lord Mountbatten (this always worked!) I was put through. 'Lord Aylestone, I'm the producer of the Rediffusion Mountbatten series, which Thames TV is inheriting. I have a real problem and I need your advice. Unfortunately it won't make much sense unless I can show you a completed episode. Do you think that might be possible?'

He thought for a moment. 'I'll try and help, but I don't think it would be wise to screen it here in Brompton Road [ITA Headquarters] behind the backs of Thames TV executives, and I shouldn't really be seen coming to you in Television House without the ritual of being received by your Board of Directors.'

'There's a very grotty entrance here at the back of the building shared with the London School of Economics, and I could smuggle you up to our preview theatre on the fourth floor, with my team holding the lift door open for you, and I'm sure no one of importance will see you.'

'All right, I'll risk it. But I must make one condition. I want to bring my wife, who's doted on Lord Mountbatten all her life.'

And it worked. I greeted them both on arrival, whisked them up to the fourth floor and screened the second episode. Lady Aylestone clapped her hands when the lights went up, and the Chairman of the ITA asked, 'Now, what's your problem?'

I explained that there was a threat that the series would not be networked, and I felt that ITV would be accused of insulting Lord Mountbatten and all his achievements, including the three years he had devoted to the making of this series.

He thanked me for alerting him, and said, 'I'll do my best. We must make sure that it gets a decent time slot.' And that is what finally happened. I must say that playing politics is not my scene, but I relished that particular moment.

The closer we got to the completion of the twelve programmes, the more intense grew the various aspects of publicity and promotion. This was a tough time, as I had to make sure that Thames, in their ignorance of the project, didn't screw up. Luckily I was able to get their agreement to have everything passed through my office (with my team, I was the last occupant remaining in Television House). This ranged from press releases to press conferences, interviews and television appearances, and above all to the intricate arrangements for the Imperial War Museum royal première. This was now scheduled for 19 December 1968.

Howard Thomas's enthusiasm for this occasion knew no bounds. Thames Television, his new company, exploited the prestigious publicity event with gusto and spent considerable sums on the decking out of the IWM's cinema, with a special publication to mark it all and the most extravagant champagnes, wines, canapés and floral arrangements I have ever seen. They mounted a live outside broadcast covering the whole event, with LM, John and me being interviewed. All thoughts about the series being 'a bit documentary' and the row over the running time for each episode had been buried.

The guest list, apart from the whole royal family (other than the Duke of Gloucester who was too frail to attend) included Harold Wilson and the surviving past prime ministers, senior ministers, service chiefs, Church leaders, senior civil servants, court officials, newspaper owners and so on – a total of 230 of the great and the good, including, the extended Mountbatten family and close friends and, of course, Jane, and John Terraine's wife Joyce. There was the usual well-orchestrated line-up for those who were to be introduced to the Queen and her immediate family, and John and I took up our prescribed positions. LM arrived, presenting each of us with a small parcel, gift-wrapped with Woolworth's best Christmas paper and gold ribbon. 'Just a small gift. Open it when you get home. It's just to say thank you to you both.' The hand-written label simply said, 'Peter Morley, Happy Xmas, Mountbatten of Burma 1965–1968.' Much later that evening all was revealed. A plush-lined leather case displayed the most exquisite circular silver gilt presentation box, 3 inches in diameter and 1½ inches deep, and inset into the lid the last remaining Viceroy's medal bearing the Mountbatten coat of arms. Inside the lid was a facsimile engraving in LM's hand: 'Peter Morley from Mountbatten of Burma 1965–1968.' The whole thing was specially created by his son-in-law, designer David Hicks. It was a generous and highly valued memento.

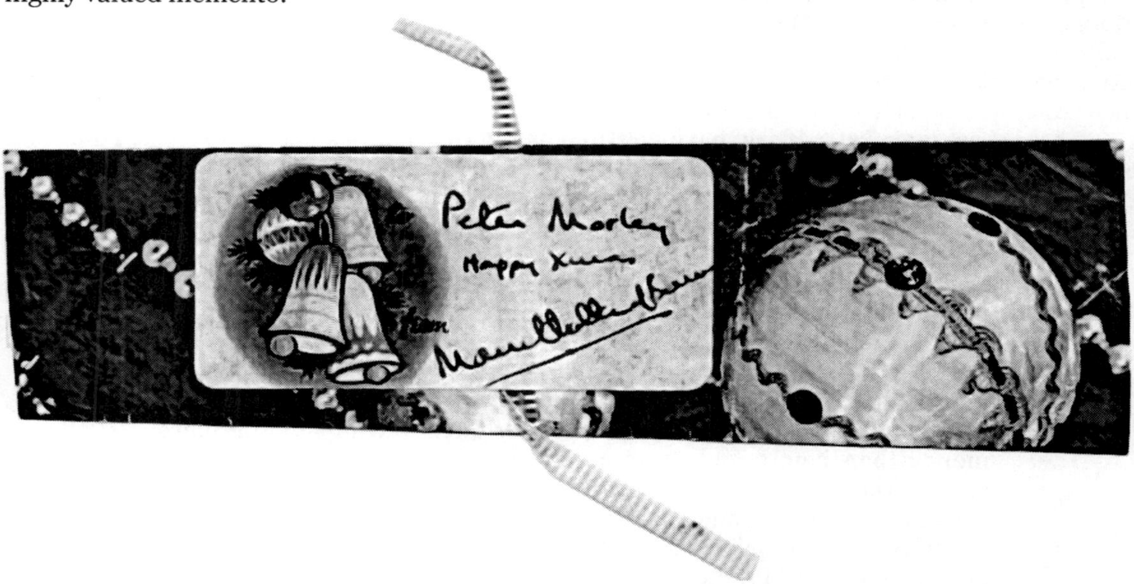

All the arrangements for that evening worked without a hitch, apart from a small delay right at the start, as everyone had to wait for the Queen Mother's traditional late arrival for functions of this kind. Nobody seemed to mind. The Queen and Prince Philip spent quite a lengthy period talking with John and me – we were the 'tail-end Charlies' at the end of the line-up – while the rest of the royals slowly progressed along the long line.

The film was introduced with a short speech by Noble Frankland, and when the end credits rolled there was warm applause; I can't remember either John or me ever needing a drink so desperately, and when we and our wives mixed with this exalted audience after the screening it was with great relief that we felt that somehow we had rung a bell with them. LM was as pleased as punch, and made a point of introducing us to a host of VIPs. It was a good launch for the series, which started its weekly transmissions on 1 January 1969.

LM told me later that the Queen cleared her evening engagements on the days of transmission, because it was 'Dickie Time'.

* * * *

In February 1969, halfway through the weekly transmissions, I was coming to the end of my stint as chairman of the SFTA, and as I was also chairman of the Guild of Television Producers and Directors, I had to officiate at our February Awards Ball at the Dorchester. By this time Prince Philip had persuaded his uncle to take over from him as president of the Society of Film and Television Arts, and so I was sitting next to LM at the top table at the Dorchester, with Jane on his other side. I found myself having to follow the president's speech with my chairman's speech – a daunting task, as LM was such a brilliant speaker. Kenneth Horne, who kept the nation in stitches with radio's *Round the Horne*, and who was the master of ceremonies for the awards presentation, sat opposite me.

In those days these events were not televised – thank goodness. LM and I had checked out each other's speeches in advance: I felt I needed his opinion as I was determined to take the opportunity to comment on the controversial new franchise allocations. Both their lordships, Hill and Aylestone, were at the top table. Before the banquet started there was my chairman's reception of VIPs in another suite, and I warned Lord Hill that I was going to be critical about his franchise decisions that had killed off Rediffusion. The old wartime radio doctor put his arm on my shoulder and said, 'Dear boy, you can be as rude as you like about me, I have a thick skin. All I can tell you is that I have made the changes because I simply don't believe in perpetuity.' End of conversation.

In the banqueting hall after dinner, as coffee was being served, the toastmaster introduced the president. LM's speech went down extremely well. He made some jokes about the production, and sent John Terraine and me up rotten, saying that during those three years he had occasionally referred to us as those two wizards but most of the time as those 'two four-letter men'. Soon it was my turn. Kenneth Horne leaned across the table and whispered, 'Follow that!' And, with some trepidation, I did.

Three years later Peter Black, having retired as the *Daily Mail*'s television critic, published his *The Mirror in the Corner*, based on twenty years of close observation of the early years of BBC TV and the effect ITV had on broadcasting when it came into being in 1955. This is what he said about Lord Hill's franchise reshuffle:

> Encouraged and applauded by almost all public opinion, Lord Hill presided over a non-event that added nothing significant to programmes in number, quality or regional flavour. It probably cost £20m in new equipment, in the writing off of existing equipment, in redundancy payments to staff – some of whom, far from needing this consolation, had already gone to work for the new companies at more money than before and in some cases without even vacating their offices. The cost in morale is not measurable, but Peter Morley (one of Rediffusion's best men, the documentary maker responsible for Rediffusion's last major series, *Mountbatten*), tried to put it into words at the Guild of TV Producers and Directors 1969 Ball. Lord Hill, seated among the guests, heard him say: 'When producers and directors think about their work, they think not only about the end-product on the screen. Programme-making is a team job; so we think and care about the many people with different skills who make the programmes with us. For the first time, the reality of working in an insecure industry has been dramatically demonstrated. And with it have come problems of which some have yet to be solved: problems which are not easily understood; problems which affect the heart and soul of an industry. To erase old loyalties, to sever long friendships, to lose identity, is

> painful. To build all these things up again from scratch is very, very difficult. To make people feel aware that they again belong to something really worthwhile takes an extra amount of enlightened leadership and above all takes time. Those who expected great things from the night of July 29 1968 [when the new franchises commenced] have failed to take this simple human factor into account.'

After my speech the toastmaster announced the start of the awards ceremony and introduced Kenneth Horne. He started off in great form, and then disaster: he collapsed on the dais in mid-sentence. A heart attack. LM leant over to me and whispered, 'You're the chairman, you're in charge. Good luck.' I helped carry Kenneth out and then came back onto the dais. I announced that I was sure that Kenneth Horne would wish us to carry on, and then took on his role of presenting the awards. He died before he had reached St George's Hospital, and at the end of the evening I had to make that sad announcement. What a night.

* * * *

I had to persuade Howard Thomas to let me stay on in my office with my PA, Jenny Over, for the three-months transmission period, as there was no one at Thames who could handle the flood of phone calls, letters and press queries. In any case, Jonathan Avery had to return hundreds of photographs to their owners, and with one of the cutting room assistants catalogue many thousands of feet of film for storage in the archives. Howard readily agreed, but I had to point out to him that I expected to be paid for this period, which rather surprised him. Very odd.

The reaction to the series could not have been more positive. There was an avalanche of press cuttings; the viewer ratings were excellent; it was never out of the top ten; and I know that my ex-Rediffusion colleagues were glad to see the Rediffusion credit conspicuously well displayed on the screen.

I was awarded the Royal Television Society's silver medal for the production, and that was particularly gratifying because the RTS was a television engineering society (John Logie Baird being one of its founder members); at that time they only gave one annual award to a programme maker. It is a beautifully engraved coin, 1½ inches in diameter and set in a velvet-lined case. I kept it propped up on a bookshelf out of reach of Jonathan, now nearly three-years old, who thought that he could take it round to our local newsagent and buy some sweets with it.

I kept in touch with Lord Louis. We frequently corresponded, and I was able to provide an informal after-transmission service for the many letters and requests he received as a result of the series. There was also the close connection with John Brabourne and our joint interest in the SFTA, soon to be known as BAFTA.

* * * *

In 1979 the IRA murdered Lord Louis – and that was the end of an era. I attended his Westminster Abbey funeral service with Jane, and spotted a great number of the eyewitnesses we had filmed for the series, which reminded me of the extraordinary life of an extraordinary person, and the luck I had had in getting to know him and working with him for three privileged years.

20: Investiture

All my close colleagues, in fact, the whole staff of Rediffusion, had by now been given new jobs, either with the newly merged Rediffusion/ABC contractor Thames Television, or with the new London Weekend contractor LWT. They had all been awarded handsome redundancy payments, finally vacating their old jobs on a Friday and starting their new jobs on the following Monday. But I did not envy them their security: I still felt, as I had done in 1955 on entering television, that I wanted to protect my independence and take pot luck with my work.

John McMillan also had a new role; he was now chairman of special events for the whole ITV network. When he vacated Television House in 1968 he mentioned that once I had cleared my Mountbatten commitment he hoped to put some work my way. 'Pete,' he said, 'how would you like to produce and direct a major outside broadcast for the ITV network?'

'Another funeral?'

It was, in fact, the Investiture of the Prince of Wales in Caernarvon Castle, which was to take place in July 1969.

During those first few months of that year, while the weekly Mountbatten series was on the air, John Terraine and I thought about another historical series. We felt that it was high time for a television history of Europe in the twentieth century – a century that saw Europe twice tear itself apart in two major conflagrations, with the Cold War now centre stage. I remembered only too well that during my stint producing *This Week* in the early 1960s there was constant pressure on us to give vent to the great controversy at the time – whether we should join the EEC (the European Economic Community) or not. We had many programme items covering Britain's application to join in 1961, only to be exceeded by even more items when in 1963 de Gaulle uttered his famous '*non*'. John and I felt that we should find a way of using television to put the momentous events of the twentieth century into their historical context, and try to find out what it means to be a European – exploring the continent's history, politics and culture, and giving some depth to the running controversy about 'joining Europe', which, as I write this almost forty-five years later, is as passionate today as it was in the late '60s and '70s.

After several of our constitutional sessions in the Uxbridge Arms in Notting Hill, and meals in the Ark, John began speculatively to write thirteen outline treatments. Also, at that time, my old friend and colleague, Cyril Bennett, who was now installed as controller of programmes at the new London Weekend Television headquarters, said that he would find a place for me later in the year.

I felt that there might be life after Mountbatten.

* * * *

In January 1969 Denis Forman, managing director of Granada Television, took over the role of chairman of special events, and he contracted me to produce and direct the Caernarvon Investiture on behalf of the ITV network. Although this was on a much smaller scale than Churchill's funeral, it again required the cooperation and pooling of resources from several ITV contractors.

As usual I embarked on an intensive planning period, and in the middle of it, in May, an official cream-coloured envelope popped through our door. It was from 10 Downing Street, stating that 'The Prime Minister had it in mind on the occasion of the forthcoming list of Birthday Honours, to submit your name to The Queen with a recommendation that Her Majesty may be graciously pleased to approve that you are appointed an Officer of the Order of the British Empire.' This was a surprise.

On Saturday 14 June the Birthday Honours List was published, and at 7 a.m. that morning my bedside telephone rang, I picked it up and an unmistakable voice said, 'I know you will find this difficult to believe, but I had absolutely nothing to do with it. Very many congratulations.' And Mountbatten hung up. This was typical; and he followed it up with a very warm handwritten letter. All his life he had made sure that those who had served successfully with or under him received recognition – and he was well known for 'promoting gongs'. In my case, though, I later learned that it was the ITA, on the dissolution of Rediffusion, that had put my name forward – for my contribution to the ITV network, including both Churchill's funeral and the Mountbatten series. Apparently this was the first time that a practising television director had been recognised in this way. There was an avalanche of letters and telegrams of congratulations from friends and colleagues, including Sir Robert Frazer, chairman of the ITA, and the chairmen and managing directors from many of the ITV network companies.

The investiture was held in Buckingham Palace on 25 November 1969. Moss Bros supplied all the gear for the occasion: morning dress, stiff shirt, black shoes, top hat – the works. Jane and Jonathan were in the car, and as I pulled into the forecourt of the Palace, Jonathan, then almost four, asked, 'Daddy, do you think the Queen has finished the breakfast washing-up?'

We were shown up a sumptuous staircase, flanked on each side by dismounted soldiers from the Household Cavalry. I felt sure that our son would happily have taken one of them back home. We were then separated, the recipients being schooled in the investiture rituals that had to be learned. I was in good company, which included Bernard Miles, Anna Neagle, John Betjeman, Arthur Askey, Bobby Charlton, Robin Knox-Johnston and several others whose faces were familiar.

We were all seated in the huge ballroom, and waited our turn to be called to walk up to the dais to face the monarch, while all our families and guests sat in the gallery overlooking the action. The Coldstream Guards band was playing medleys from *My Fair Lady* and other current West End musicals. Jane had to cope with Jonathan; always rather short on patience, he had discarded his brand-new velvet-collared coat and his jacket, and said he felt hungry. Jane told me later that after consuming a very noisy rusk, and just some minutes before the Queen's arrival, he desperately needed the royal loo! They were both back in their seats in time to see me walk up to the dais to be invested with my gong. The Queen told me that she had enjoyed all twelve episodes of the Mountbatten series.

We came back to our Canonbury home in Grange Grove, where family and friends were waiting for our return – bottles of champagne at the ready. It was truly a day to remember.

* * * *

In May of that year I made several trips to Wales with Pam Humphries, my temporary and very efficient Welsh PA, to meet the technical people for the outside broadcast of the Prince of Wales's Investiture at Caernarvon. There was also a meeting with Lord Snowdon, the castle's Constable and designer of the ceremony, whose transformation of the castle's open-to-the-sky interior was remarkable, especially the focal point of the ceremony, which was the royal dais, made of Welsh slate with a spectacular perspex canopy.

Once again ITV was in competition with the BBC; nothing had changed since Churchill's funeral – except that this was going to be the BBC's first major outside broadcast in colour. Their first colour transmissions had been the 1968 Wimbledon championships, but now they had acquired many more colour cameras. I had again recruited Brian Connell to be the main commentator, and we invited that master of journalism and broadcasting Wynford Vaughan-Thomas to join Brian in the commentary booth to provide the intricate and magical element which only that Welshman knew how to project.

For these national state occasions television outside broadcasts call for an appropriate prologue before the events of the day unfold. The one I devised for the Churchill funeral in 1965 worked really well, and now it was a question of 'follow that'. It was Wynford who triggered the idea. He told me about the Welsh redoubt, an array of keeps and castles built by Edward I after he had conquered Wales by defeating Prince Llywelyn, killed in battle in 1282. I felt that these castles could make an appropriate visual background to a short history of Wales, ending with Caernarvon Castle – the focal point for this royal occasion.

Wynford wrote a beautifully crafted ten-minute narration, describing the iron ring of fortifications which Edward I had built around Snowdonia, using quotations and poetry of the time. The one person whose rich Welsh voice would do justice to these words was Richard Burton. I felt that the most graphic way of portraying Edward's grand strategy was from the air, and I chose to shoot the whole sequence from a helicopter, illustrating the complete sequence with shots of Snowdonia, the Menai Straits and the six castles of Rhuddlan, Conway, Beaumaris, Caernarvon, Criccieth and Harlech.

Normally this would have been done with a film camera, but I was reluctant to use film. No matter how well it is shot, processed and transmitted, it brings with it a textural quality that makes it unmistakably look like film, quite different from the texture created by the electronic camera. As I was going to use twenty-eight of these I wanted to avoid mixing these two media. And here I had a bit of luck. I was able to use that astonishing new portable video-tape recorder and camera, the Ampex VR 3000. The electronic camera was not much larger than a home movie camera, but the recorder was the size of a suitcase. The picture quality was so remarkably good that when experienced engineers played back tapes recorded on this machine they could hardly believe their eyes.

I must repeat part of the answer to a written interview I gave to the editor of *Film* magazine, Derek Knight, eight years before, in 1961, when he asked about the future of electronic cameras: '. . . who knows what future video-tape holds for the film-maker. Is film out? Will the amateur cinematographer with a small electronic camera be able to strap a pocket video-tape recorder round his waist, shoot, go home and play it back on a TV monitor? I am looking forward to reading *Film* in 1965, I think by then we may have the answer.'

Well, eight years later we had the answer in spades. This new Ampex camera was first used at the 1968 Mexican Olympic Games. ATV, the Midlands ITV contractor, purchased one of the cameras, and when I heard about this I persuaded them to let me borrow it, plus its ace cameraman, Jim McCutcheon. It was the first time I had seen this equipment, which recorded picture and sound onto 2-inch wide videotape, using small spools, and weighed a ton. Jim had to wear it on his back in Mexico!

I made a rendezvous with Jim and the helicopter pilot in Kidlington, near Oxford, and we flew up to RAF Valley, on Anglesey. A small modification made it possible to have a 9 inch monitor on my lap in the helicopter, so I could see what the cameraman was seeing in his viewfinder and could 'direct' the shooting; What's more, I could call for instant playback to assess what had been recorded. An intercom between the pilot, cameraman and myself converted the helicopter into a flying one-camera studio. It was an exhilarating experience. Probably because of the shaking it was getting from the helicopter, the recorder broke down several times, and we had to land high up on a flat bit of Snowdonia, where we had stationed an Ampex engineer with a full tool-kit, to effect running repairs.

The next day, with shooting completed, we flew back. A car was waiting for me at the Hammersmith heliport to rush me to Shepperton Studios for my recording date with Richard Burton, who was filming there. Then it was off to Manchester to edit all this material. Electronic video editing had by now also made huge strides; it was technically not available to me ten years earlier when I directed *The Turn of the Screw*.

Early in June the ITV construction team started work on building the control rooms and commentary booth, right up against the castle's outside walls, and the vastly complicated engineering tasks began. The BBC's similar complex had been erected next to ours.

Anthony Craxton, who had been my rival producer/director for Churchill's funeral, was once again in charge for the BBC; I had not seen him since we were on the Cannes jury together three years before. He was very friendly, and offered to place a colour monitor into my control room so that I could see what the BBC's output looked like. I was very grateful, and when we first got pictures up two days before transmission, I was much impressed by the colour quality – and looked forward to the time when all programmes would be in colour.

I started my first camera rehearsal and run-through, including playing in my pre-recorded prologue and historical sequence, when, unannounced, a BBC engineer burst in and removed the colour monitor. I was later told by one of Craxton's assistants that Peter Dimmock, BBC's head of sports and outside broadcasts (I last saw him outside the Cannes jury room after Churchill's funeral had won the Grand Prix, for which he had never forgiven me), had somehow got a feed of my prologue rehearsal, must have felt that we had something special going for us, and reacted in this curious way.

The big day was 1 July 1969. The ITV contingent of cameramen, engineers and the production team, totalling 200, were on parade and ready. The four-hour broadcast went off without a hitch, and Brian and Wynford excelled themselves. Well, there was one hitch. I can't remember at which point during the ceremony this happened, but quite close by there was an almighty explosion and my array of thirty-two monitors leapt in unison an inch off their seating, luckily without sustaining any damage. Mercifully the explosion, courtesy of some Welsh Nationalists, was not heard within the castle's walls, and the show went on.

As usual on these occasions, when the BBC and ITV show their separate interpretations of the same event the natural instinct of a majority of viewers is to switch to 'Auntie', making ITV ratings look pretty sick. But in spite of it being in glorious black and white, the ITV version of that day's ceremony got an extremely good press – and once again the ITV bosses, whose companies contributed to its success, sent letters of congratulations.

* * * *

London Weekend Television was now in deep trouble. Having won their franchise and started operating in 1968, it soon became clear that some of the company's promises, stipulated in their franchise application prospectus, could not be met. They had promised a regular, well-funded output of documentaries and current affairs programmes, but the advertising revenue for a weekend-only TV station could not sustain them. There was also resistance from the rest of the ITV network to screen a lot of this programming. Michael Peacock, who had torn himself away from the BBC, was the managing director, with Cyril Bennett his controller of programmes. They offered me a year's contract to make occasional features and documentaries of the type that they hoped would be a regular contribution. On the very day that I arrived in Station House, LWT's temporary headquarters on the North Circular Road, Michael resigned, together with a number of his key executives, leaving Cyril for the time being to run the show more or less on his own. It was not a brilliant start for me.

I only made one programme for LWT, which was transmitted at the very end of 1969. Cyril had met a bright and amusing twenty-one-year-old student, Gyles Brandreth, and they came up with an idea: to investigate the effect of a decade's television on a boy who was aged ten at the start of the '60s – someone who had been brought up on a rich daily diet of television. After several sessions with Gyles I decided to narrow down his ten years of viewing to news and current affairs programmes, and to explore the effect on a young mind of the drip-drip exposure to the outside world through the small screen.

It turned out to be a ninety-minute programme (probably a bit too long), with lots of newsreel clips of the decade chosen and annotated by Giles, and an intriguing quartet of 'experts' in the studio to analyse his comments and put forward their ideas of the effect of television on young viewers. They were Michael Foot MP, Iain Macleod MP, Fred Friendly and Lady Longford.

I called the programme *A Child of the Sixties*. It was transmitted on 27 December, between Christmas and New Year, and pretty well sank without trace. There was very little press reaction, but LWT seemed to be well satisfied. In the following years I often spotted Gyles Brandreth's name popping up in the press. He eventually became a Conservative MP, author, after dinner speaker and journalist, and his many accomplishments include winning the National Scrabble championship.

It was two years after this short stint with London Weekend Television that Cyril tragically died – far too young. I had lost a true friend.

* * * *

For me, the end of the '60s also marked the end of a fascinating chapter in my early programme-making adventure. I had had the great fortune to be in at the very beginning of ITV, and although we did not realise it at the time I belonged to a small gang of people who are now labelled the pioneers of the medium. As a freelance director (unique at the time), I had been on contract to Rediffusion, a contract that had somehow renewed itself every quarter since 1955. This had now come to an end, and I was about to experience great changes.

For the first time I began to realise how precarious a freelance existence really is, and what amazing good luck I had enjoyed up to that moment.

21: Thames Television

The start of 1970 was curious, to say the least. My contract with LWT still had nine months to run, but they had no room in their schedules for the sort of programmes they had hired me to make. Stella Richman had taken over as controller of programmes. She expressed little hope for further assignments, although she asked me to work up some programme ideas in case the company's fortunes changed. I thought that I would have a lot of time on my hands, but all sorts of interesting things were happening – and now I had to adapt to a new regime that called for having several balls in the air at the same time.

Soon I found myself taking part in the debate concerning a future second channel for ITV. ITV2 had been mooted by the government, and the ownership, structure and financing of an additional television service became a controversial issue. Should it be complementary to ITV or be its competitor? Should it be a non-profit-making channel and still carry commercials? 1976 was to be a watershed year for television, with both the BBC charter and the ITV franchises due for renewal. And for the next few years those of us who cared about the future of television got deeply involved.

In my capacity as an ex-chairman of the Guild of TV Producers and Directors, and its successor, the Society of Film and Television Arts, and also as a freelance programme-maker, I attended meetings and made speeches. There were sessions with Brian Young, the ITA's director general, and after seeing Harold Evans, editor of the *Sunday Times*, I wrote a lengthy piece for his paper stressing the importance of the channels being complementary, and possible ways of achieving this. At the time both the ITV contractors and the advertising industry lobbied for a competitive role for ITV 2, with both channels scrabbling for a maximum audience – dealing a fatal blow to the idea of public service broadcasting. What we did not know at the time was that it would take many more years for a second channel to emerge, in the shape of Channel 4, which was launched in 1982. It was independent, non-profit-making, ran its own commercials and was partly subsidised by the ITV companies – with a special remit to preserve the public service broadcasting ethos. It proved to be a great success.

* * * *

At the same time our History of Europe project was shaping up nicely. There were many sessions with John Terraine, who was making good progress with the outlines. But then we had another new idea. It came about because I felt that it would take so very long to find a backer for this major project that we should also have a one-hour project up our sleeve, one that it might be easier to sell to the BBC or an ITV company. John readily agreed, as he also felt the distinct need to stave off hunger. Over a drink in the Uxbridge Arms the idea for this 'one-off' was born.

Experience over the past few years had shown again and again that documentary television programmes, especially those with a rich story to tell (however well made, however attractive), when compared with the written word suffer from an element of superficiality imposed on them by the medium. There is just so much that the viewer's eyes and ears can absorb at any one time: the demands made on the senses are formidable, and as so often happens there is the danger of an information overload. I think of a single programme being like a moderately sized painter's canvas. To retain the viewer's attention one must tell the story using broad brush-strokes. With the luxury of twelve hours, as with Mountbatten, thereby increasing the size of the canvas by a factor of twelve, one is still obliged to use the same broad brush.

Our single programme idea was based on the frustration John and I felt while making the Mountbatten series. It centred on a traumatic event in Mountbatten's early life; an event that had a profound effect on him and shaped his career. It was the rise and fall of his father, to whom he was devoted. Prince Louis of Battenberg left Germany in 1868, aged fourteen, to join the Royal Navy. He settled in England, became a naturalised British subject and had a brilliant service career, rising to the very pinnacle of the Senior Service – First Sea Lord, the professional head of the Royal Navy.

On the eve of the First World War, in July 1914, there was a test mobilisation of the Reserve Fleet, with its start and end dates having been posted to other nations – as demanded by international convention. On the weekend of 26 July Prime Minister Herbert Asquith, First Lord of the Admiralty Winston Churchill, the Foreign Secretary and the rest of the cabinet had, as usual, gone away for the weekend. But the next day, Monday, the tens of thousands of men who had been called up for the test mobilisation were due to be paid off – not to do so, not to demobilise, could be construed as an act of war. Prince Louis, the First Sea Lord, alone in London, took the momentous decision not to demobilise and ordered the fleet to stand fast. As a result, with the outbreak of the First World War a few days later, on 4 August, the Royal Navy was ready and at action stations. He was lauded for his wisdom and courage. But almost immediately intense anti-German feeling, fuelled by the most poisonous propaganda, caused anyone with a German name to be called a traitor. Even dachshunds were kicked in the street! This made it impossible for Prince Louis of Battenberg to stay in office, and he was forced to resign – hounded out of office. For Mountbatten, now a fourteen-year-old cadet at Osborne Naval College, it was shattering news. He felt deeply humiliated, and swore that as an act of vindication he would climb to the top of the navy, as his father had done, and one day attain the rank of First Sea Lord. Which he did.

Sadly, in the twelve-hour-long Mountbatten television series we could only devote about six minutes to this event, even though it had such a profound effect on him. This illustrates the limitations in this type of programme-making: the evergreen problem of how much to put in and how much to leave out.

So we developed our idea: we would take these six crucial minutes from the Mountbatten series and expand them into a one-hour programme, investigating the effect of the hysterical anti-German propaganda during the First World War. We took these thoughts to Jeremy Isaacs, who was now head of features at Thames Television. He was very interested, but he put us on hold until he had finished some forward planning for Thames. We kept our fingers crossed.

And then the plot thickened. I got a call from John Grist, head of the BBC's talks and features department, asking me out to lunch. He told me that for some time his department had tried to persuade Paul Fox, who was Controller of BBC1, to give the go-ahead for the BBC to produce a follow-up to their very successful *The Great War* with a new television series on the Second World War. As John Terraine had been one of the two writers of *The Great War*, and together we had made the Mountbatten series, he thought that we would be the ideal pair to take on this task.

The reason he gave why Paul Fox was in two minds about the idea was understandable. Only a couple of years before the BBC had launched colour television, and Paul feared that to sink a huge sum of money and valuable air-time into programmes that for obvious reasons had to be in black and white might slow down the spread of colour receivers. Grist felt that a decision was imminent, and told us that Derek Amore, number two in his department, would keep in touch with us.

So there we were, with a series on Europe bubbling away in the background, a real prospect of a programme on propaganda for Thames, and now the possibility of a long stint with the BBC on a subject that we were both extremely interested in, especially John – a highly regarded military historian. We were wined and dined by Derek Amore every few weeks, eagerly awaiting for white smoke to rise from Paul Fox's office.

I will always remember the next phase. I was at home in Canonbury when I heard a motorcycle courier stopping outside the house, and a letter landing on the door mat. It was from Jeremy Isaacs, saying that he wanted me to know before I heard it on the evening news bulletins that Thames Television was announcing the start of work on a twenty-six one-hour episode television history on the Second World War. A blow if ever there was one! He added: 'I regret having had to be so secretive about this, especially as you confided in me. But I knew before talking to you of the possibilities at the BBC. (Indeed it was partly being approached myself and then left dangling which made me realise that Thames could do this on its own.)' He then went on to say that this should make no difference to my making a programme on propaganda for Thames, together with John.

I phoned John to break the bad news to him. He was deeply shocked, almost speechless, as he had really set his heart on the BBC venture; and we decided to speak in the morning. I sensed that he would be off to the Uxbridge Arms in Notting Hill to drown his sorrows. I waited till the evening and called Paul Fox at his home, knowing that he would be equally distraught. Betty Fox answered the phone and told me that she had heard the news, but that Paul had taken their boys up to Birmingham for a football match; she would tell him to phone once he got back. The call came about midnight and there was Paul: 'I'm not prepared to talk about it, Peter. Give me a few days and then try again.' He could not have relished the thought of going to his office in the morning with a great deal of egg on his face – also, the BBC was bound to get stick from the press.

I luckily recalled a piece of advice from Lord Mountbatten when he listed one of the elements of good leadership: 'the art of making good news out of bad news'. And it worked. The next morning, when I spoke to John, I said that as the BBC had been caught with its trousers down, we had a new pair for the corporation – namely *A History of Europe in the Twentieth Century*. Both of us got rather excited at the thought, and I decided that I would ignore Paul's 'few days' and call him. I waited till about 11 a.m., said to his secretary that it was an urgent call, and she put me through. Before he could protest I said: 'Paul, you've really been caught out, and I think I have the perfect project for you to take the place of the ambushed Second World War idea.'

'Right,' he said, 'meet me at my usual Notting Hill restaurant at 1 p.m.' I have always admired those who can make instant decisions.

Before setting off to Paul's favourite watering hole, John and I spent an hour on the telephone, marshalling our thoughts and fine-tuning our presentation. On arrival I could not help noticing that two tables away, of all people, Roy Jenkins MP, deputy leader of the Labour Party, was entertaining a lady to lunch. Renowned for his knowledge of good claret, he was even better known as the great advocate for Britain's future in Europe (later he served as president of the European Commission from 1977 for four years). I thought this might turn out to be a good omen for us. And it was. Paul was taken by our proposal; he even said that he wished he had thought of the idea himself. We recalled the early '60s, when he was editor of BBC's *Panorama* (and I was producing *This Week*), and the numerous filmed items and studio discussions we screened on the running controversy of Britain's role in the European Community. Paul agreed that a major television series providing an essential background to the history of this complicated continent would be of great value, and fitted the BBC's public service role really well.

He asked us to be patient for a month or so, as he could not commit the BBC to such a vast project without consulting his programme board first, but he was keen to go ahead, and said he would probably place it with Dick Cawston's documentary department. This was good news, as Dick and I knew each other well: we were both council members (and past chairmen) of the SFTA, and quite soon we were to be fellow foundation trustees of BAFTA.

* * * *

In May 1971 I got a call from Thames Television. Jeremy Isaacs was keen for us to go ahead with the propaganda programme. I was given an office in the Thames headquarters in the Euston Road, and came across many ex-Rediffusion colleagues who had joined Thames at the demise of the old company. We took on Kate Haste (now Lady Bragg, married to Melvyn), as our general researcher and Maurice Raine as film researcher. They started digging up anti-German propaganda material, and such was the wealth of what they found that we realised doing justice to this fascinating subject would really require at least two one-hour programmes – but we had to make do with one. As usual the broad brush principle ruled, with the agony of having to spike a great deal of valuable evidence.

The words 'anti-German hysteria' were only used once in the Mountbatten series; now we were able to expand on it, and we realised it was no wonder that Prince Louis of Battenberg was hounded out of office. The virulent and grotesque utterings in the press beggar belief. Here are some choice examples:

> *Weekly Dispatch*, September 1914 – The truthful war picture would present Belgium as a slaughterhouse with the peace-loving, unarmed inhabitants being killed in thousands by the Germans. Rivers of blood, mountains of innocent dead, sacked towns and villages – these have marked the advance of the Germans. The wild orgies of blood and debauchery, the atrocities, outrages, murders and mutilations, the ruthless violation and killing of defenceless women, girls and children of tender age, have been, it is now admitted by Germans themselves, carried out with their full knowledge, and even as part of the actual plan of campaign of their War-Lords. The civilised world stands aghast at the Kaiser's atrocities. Humanity cries aloud for vengeance.
>
> *Weekly Dispatch*, September 1914 – The Germans bayoneted a Belgian child to death for calling '*Vive l'Angleterre*.' They killed their own wounded to save time, and cut off the hands of British medical orderlies. Some of the British wounded and killed, says a correspondent, were placed on a hayrick by Germans, who then set the hayrick on fire.

Horatio Bottomley was the founder and editor of the scurrilous weekly magazine *John Bull*, which enjoyed a huge circulation. He also attracted large audiences to his frequent public meetings. Here is an example of his nauseating style: 'Every German, old or young, naturalised or not, is a potential spy. The time has surely come when the nation must force the Government to take a strong and decisive line. Our naturalisation laws are a scandal. We want men to loathe and despise the Hun. Yes, we must have that League of Hate. The Kaiser and his hellish horde are possessed by the soul of Satan. You cannot naturalise, an unnatural beast – a human abortion – a hellish fiend. But you can exterminate it.' Bottomley had a habit of inserting small boxes into the middle of his *John Bull* newspaper columns with messages like these:

> Refuse to be served by an Austrian or German waiter.
> If your waiter says he is Swiss, ask to see his passport.
> If by chance you should discover one day in a restaurant that you are being served by a German waiter, you will throw the soup in his foul face; if you find yourself sitting at the side of a German clerk, you will spill the inkpot over his vile head.

Bottomley was at one time the richest man in England. A swindler, twice bankrupt, and an expelled MP, after the war he spent seven years in prison. He died in 1933 – a penniless drunkard.

But there was another thriving medium making appeals to the public: the cinema. While we were making the programme we learnt from film historian John Huntley that during the First

World War there were 5,000 cinemas in this country, serving an audience of 20 million a week, compared with only 4 million a week today. And the opportunity to exploit film as a propaganda medium was not lost on the Ministry of Information. It sponsored live action 'shorts' that were quite outrageous. The one we included in our programme shows two German soldiers in a Belgian town, confronting a woman who is holding her baby wrapped in a shawl. They tear the baby away from its mother, knock her to the ground and then throw the baby onto the pavement. Then there were the first animated cartoons for the big screen. Lancelot Speed, G.E. Study and Bruce Bairnsfather were the brilliant pioneers in this new art form, and they too took every opportunity to provide the vitriol of propaganda.

We called our programme *The First Casualty* – a quote from Hiram Johnson, who was Governor of California during the First World War: 'The first casualty when war comes is truth – and the assassin of truth is propaganda.'

The programme, transmitted later that year, was well received. Without doubt it was an eye-opener, and the contribution from one of our experts was very much to the point. Cecil Harmsworth King, a press lord himself, spoke eloquently about his two illustrious uncles, Lord Northcliffe and Lord Rothermere, who between them owned *The Times*, the *Daily Mail*, the *Daily Mirror*, the *Glasgow Herald* and the *Leeds Mercury*:

> In wars it is said, no holds are barred. To interest the ordinary man in the street, it was not enough to talk about the military menace of German armed forces, it had to be made an emotional subject, and I'm sure that it was with this in mind that my two uncles rather stepped up the propaganda, in the form of stories of terrorist acts by German troops, which subsequent investigations have shown to be quite false. I'm not sure whether they deliberately concocted these stories, but if they didn't they certainly seized on them when they presented themselves. It's just the material to provide an emotional basis for an anti- German war.

John, who spoke his own narration, brought the programme to a conclusion with these words:

> In the end, of course, it all back-fired. In 1918 the British people arrived at peace in a mood of hatred and revenge – and the peace they helped to make, enshrined in the Treaty of Versailles, faithfully reflects the conflict between their bad emotions and their good intentions. Soon afterwards it began to be apparent that most of the war-time propaganda had been lies – sheer, downright lies. People were sickened to learn how they had been deceived – how they had allowed themselves to be deceived; wanted to be. Many now became distinctly cynical about 'devilry' in any form. And this proved to be a pity, because, by a stupendous irony, a regime came to power in Germany in 1933 which did, indeed, deliberately cultivate brutality, mass-murder, torture, genocide. The slow reaction of so many people against the Nazi threat must, at least in part, be attributed to the excesses of propaganda to which they had been subjected during the First World War.

What we tried to show in our programme was that propaganda had secured its own defeat. Truth had, indeed, become a casualty.

TEA BREAK IN THE DUAL MONARCHY

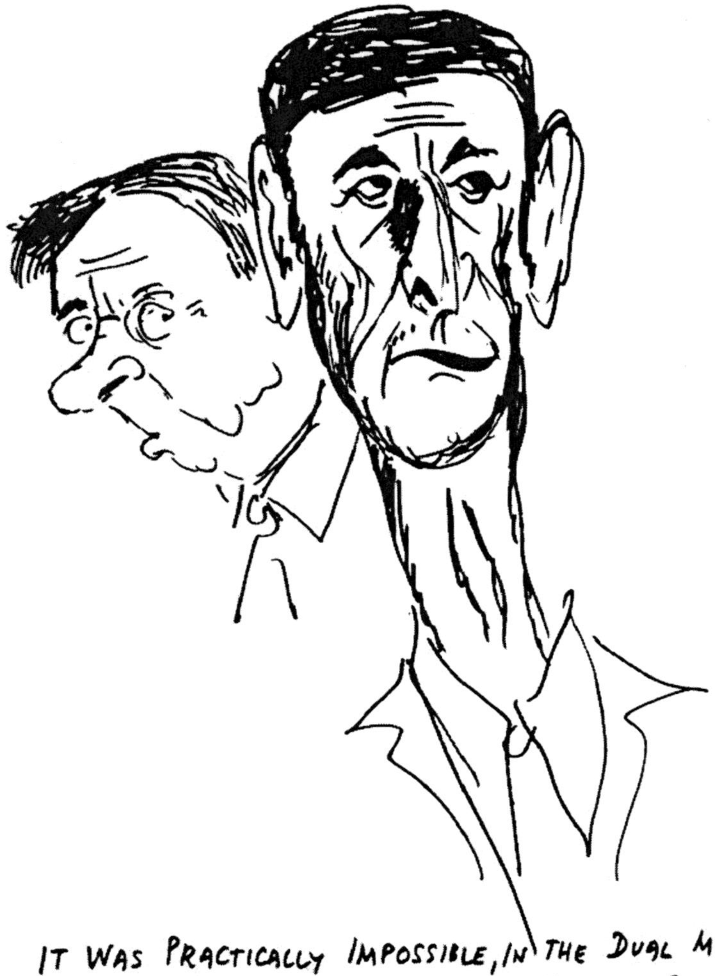

IT WAS PRACTICALLY IMPOSSIBLE, IN THE DUAL MONARCHY, TO CROSS THE CONSTITUTIONAL TEAS OR DOT THE CONSTITUTIONAL ICES. IT WAS POSSIBLE TO BE TERRAINE WITHOUT BEING MORLEY. IT WAS POSSIBLE TO BE MORLEY WITHOUT BEING TERRAINE. IT WAS EVEN PROBABLE TO BE NEITHER, BUT IT WAS AWFULLY HARD TO BE BOTH. HOW LONG COULD THESE TENSIONS LAST? DO NOT MISS PROGRAMME 13 : FROM SARAJEVO TO DALLAS

22: The History of Europe

In October 1971 John Terraine and I signed our contracts with the BBC – an adventure that was to last almost four years. For me it was a moment to savour. In my very early days in television I came under the influence of people like Grace Wyndham Goldie (who pioneered the coverage of politics by the BBC) and Huw Wheldon, and I cherished an ambition that one day I would have the opportunity to make programmes for the BBC. And now it was to be a major assignment, with a budget of over half a million pounds.

At the time it was almost unheard of for a couple of outsiders to bring a large project to the BBC, and we had many meetings with Paul Fox (Controller of BBC1), Dick Cawston (head of the documentary department) and the BBC's legal people to find a formula to accommodate this novel situation. We insisted on retaining some of the copyright to this project, but historically the BBC never granted residual rights to producers or directors. Therefore we asked a much-respected showbusiness lawyer, Laurence Harbottle, to handle the negotiations on our behalf; and he picked up and dusted off a dormant company called Casterbridge Productions (from then on jointly owned by John and me) which enabled the BBC, by contracting Casterbridge, to accept (somewhat reluctantly) our demands.

But there were more important details we had to agree before we could start, such as John's view – the historian's view of Europe in the twentieth century – of the contents of the series, and my ideas of the style we should adopt once the contents had become clear. The treatments John had worked on the previous year now came into their own. What was emerging was that this was going to be a European look, rather than a British look, at Europe; and it would deal not merely with politics and major events but would cover the whole spectrum of social, cultural and artistic change during the first seventy-five years of the twentieth century. We wanted the essence of this television history to be its internationalism, its international approach to themes that are often too narrowly treated. We hoped that it would appeal to viewers not only in Europe itself but wherever European influence has been felt.

It seemed to make good sense both for political and commercial reasons to ask a German television station to come in as a co-production partner, and Paul Fox had little problem in getting Süddeutscher Rundfunk (SDR) from Stuttgart to get involved. As usual at that time, for major projects such as this, the BBC recruited Time-Life Films as a co-production partner, which more or less guaranteed an American sale of the series. Sadly the term co-producer turned out to be a misnomer – co-financer more accurately described the role. I sent scripts across the pond to Time-Life, and to this day I have still not had a reply. SDR showed some interest; at least they provided a German academic, a professor of history, to be one of our consultants. I had hoped for much more.

I persuaded Paul that as this was John's view of European history he should be seen and heard delivering it. Apart from a clear speaking voice, he had a very good screen presence, and

Paul, who had seen *The First Casualty*, agreed. But then he called us back for another meeting: Time-Life had stipulated that they wanted a 'name' to front the series, as without one they would have problems selling it to the networks in the States. John and I were appalled. The thought of an actor delivering John's words was totally unacceptable; and giving that role to a well-known television presenter would be equally bogus. It was a serious dilemma. Reluctantly we came up with a solution: Peter Ustinov. We felt that if we had to have a name it needed to be a true 'European', and if ever there was one it was Ustinov, whose immediate family tree had branches reaching out to France, Germany, Russia, Switzerland and Italy, with a small twig even pointing to Ethiopia.

The next step was to nail down the two distinctive roles for Terraine and Ustinov, the historian and the raconteur. It was easier said than done, and we embarked on our first trip to one of Ustinov's homes, hidden in its own vineyard on the shore of Lake Geneva. He was most hospitable, very funny, pleased to be asked to take part in our series, and most willing to co-operate in any way we desired. He appreciated that a clear distinction had to be drawn between the two roles, and although he felt that he knew a fair bit of European history he was certainly not an historian, and would leave all that to John to avoid any possible clashes. But Ustinov felt that he could colour in some of the 'drier' bits of history, and I suggested then and there that his role could well be described as the 'embellisher'. That went down well. Over dinner that night he paraded a whole string of colourful, even hilarious, anecdotes of the sort that he thought we might find helpful, and readily agreed to read John's scripts and write his proposed contributions for our consideration. We came back to London feeling moderately optimistic about our solution to this unwelcome stipulation. The words we chose in order to give the curious dual role a certain amount of logic were embedded in the opening titles of each of the thirteen episodes:

> The Mighty Continent
> A View of Europe in the Twentieth Century
> Written and Narrated by John Terraine
> With personal comments by Peter Ustinov
> Produced by Peter Morley

And to make sure that the audience was kept in no doubt, Ustinov introduced himself at the start of the very first episode with these words: 'This series of programmes is the story of the thorny road which Europe has travelled in the last seventy-five years, as seen by one British historian, John Terraine, who will tell the story in his way, and embellished by comments from a mongrel with antecedents in most of the countries described – myself – a collaboration, in other words, between a professional and an amateur.'

* * * *

I was given a suite of offices high up in the East Tower of the BBC's White City Television Centre, which housed Dick Cawston's documentary department, and put together my team. In the final year of production this grew to over twenty. My unit manager was Chris Berry, who masterminded the budget and the schedule, and I was lucky with Annie Hewitt, my very experienced PA, who knew how to circumnavigate the 'BBC system' and how to get things done quickly. My associate producer was Brian Lewis; in the film business he would be called second unit director. He did a magnificent job, using a second BBC film crew to shoot some of the material that I simply could not include in my heavy schedule. Jane Ades handled the elaborate picture and documents research, while Maxine Baker scoured the world's film archives. Colin Reed was the historical researcher who worked very closely with John Terraine. In the cutting rooms Alan Tyrer, the senior film editor and arguably the best in the BBC, with two other editors and their assistants, had their work cut out with daily rushes and masses of archive film flooding in from the laboratories.

John and I, sometimes with my PA, went on several extensive recce trips all over the Continent, which for me was a fascinating learning experience thanks to John's expert, witty and thought-provoking tutelage. Periodically we visited Peter Ustinov to discuss details with him, and to make him aware of the way the programmes were shaping up. These were always highly entertaining sessions, and he lived up to his reputation of being a most generous host.

But then we made a worrying discovery. To our surprise, Ustinov did not really show the interest in John's scripts that we had expected. What he really wanted was to come on location with us once we started shooting, make up his contributions on the spot and deliver them to the camera. Had we been making a series named *Peter Ustinov's View of Europe in the Twentieth Century* that might have worked extremely well – giving total freedom to his exceptional talents as a raconteur. But that was not the purpose of the exercise. It was a big problem.

We started filming in Vienna, and after the first day's shoot Ustinov and I had dinner together at Sacher's restaurant. I began to realise the very essence of our problem. We were discussing John's scripts in general when he said the trouble was that John believed in total clarity – the academic's approach – and that he had an aversion to this. 'The moment you have clarity,' he said, 'you're lost.' Here spoke the master of improvisation. His convoluted style of storytelling with its clever, elaborate use of language, his thinking on his feet and his playing to and with the audience, all conspired against clarity but made him one of the world's great raconteurs. This multi-talented man, a genius if ever there was one, should, in fact, never have agreed to play second fiddle to the main creator of the project – a project that he knew would not be under his control.

I began to realise that this European 'mongrel' might turn out to be a serious liability. John and I had to make doubly sure that his contributions, on which we had pinned so much, would not undermine John's view of European history. Luckily we were alerted to this early on, and although occasionally it caused great friction we managed to contain him. As a result there were many last-minute script alterations to accommodate Ustinov's contributions, many of which we knew we would not be able to use. Often I had to go off and shoot extra scenes to create a fall-back position, to make sure that we could 'adjust' things in the solitude of the cutting rooms months later. And on the whole we got away with it.

The atmosphere on location with our star occasionally became prickly, but on the whole once a day's shooting finished we managed to maintain a friendly and light-hearted atmosphere. Peter Ustinov really was wonderful company, never at a loss for a good story, and he often got out his pen to doodle caricatures of John and me, sometimes on paper table-cloths when we were enjoying an evening meal – his way of getting his own back on us.

I had almost forgotten the extent of our filming and the heavy schedule we set ourselves. We criss-crossed the continent, shooting in a rich mixture of locations: Paris, Brunete, Dachau, Versailles, Rome, Belsen, Arromanches, Sermoneta, Remagen, Oradour, Monte Cassino, Vienna, Brussels, Berlin, Blaenau, Strasbourg, Munich, Budapest, Geneva, Heidelberg, Warsaw, Madrid, Nürnberg and Leningrad.

Being on location is one thing, but the real magic only happens in the tranquil atmosphere of the cutting room. That is where one sees the results of all the hard location and research work – and that is where one gets one's comeuppance. As we had three cutting rooms on the go at the same time, it was an exciting and concentrated exercise in programme making. I spent most of my time with the editors, with John coming in periodically to see our progress, to discuss alterations and to hone his final narration scripts.

I screened the first three rough cuts to Dick Cawston, and that was always rewarding. He came to each viewing fresh, and as he was a very successful documentary maker himself it was valuable to use him as a sounding board: one gets so close and involved with the job in hand that an outsider's view, especially Dick's, was most helpful.

* * * *

The series finally went on the air at peak time on BBC1 in November 1974. The BBC instigated a great deal of publicity, and the press coverage was huge. On the whole it is fair to say that *The Mighty Continent* enjoyed mixed reviews. There were those who thought the series too superficial; others could not see the logic of Ustinov's involvement; some said that with the recent transmissions of Thames's *The World at War* series and the BBC's *Empire* series there was a surfeit of historical programming. On the other hand there were also some excellent reviews, but the most telling, as always, were the viewing figures. After all, these ambitious series are made for the viewing public and not the press. The BBC was satisfied not only with the viewing figures – on average over 5 million, which was high for documentaries – but also with the BBC's Audience Reaction Index, which showed a 77 per cent approval rating, with a huge mailbag of approving letters from viewers. These figures were sustained for all thirteen episodes, with the last being aired in February 1975. Süddeutscher Rundfunk (SDR) transmitted a German language version later that year, where it was very well received and gained some excellent press reviews; then in 1976 it was shown in America on PBS, where I collected the Documentary Award from the Columbus Film Festival.

When it was all over I had mixed feelings about my longed-for stint at the BBC. I was never made to feel that I was member, albeit only a temporary one, of this great organisation. I had hoped that I would feel part of it, but tucked away, high up in the East Tower with my splendid team, I might just as well have been in a suite of offices in the West End. I missed the camaraderie of fellow programme makers. As time went by I could understand my disappointment; it was no one's fault. After all, I was a freelance, that rare breed almost unknown in the BBC at the time: nearly all their producers and directors were staff people, and I think that I must have been looked upon as a visiting stranger. Not only that, but the department's jealously guarded traditional Tuesday night documentary slot was handed over to me, pre-empting for thirteen weeks its regular output, and that probably did not make me the most popular visitor. It was also unfortunate that not long after I started my contract Paul Fox, who had championed this series, left his post as controller of BBC1 in 1973, to take over as managing director of Yorkshire Television. His successor was Brian (Ginger) Cowgill, and I never knew whether he approved of Paul's work in progress that he had inherited – in fact there was no contact with him at all, although John and I got a note of thanks from him six months after we had left.

One other strange memory of that time is the astonishing fact that apart from the first episode, which was shown to the press, and three other programmes seen by Dick Cawston in their rough-cut state, the series went on the air unseen and unchecked by anyone else from the BBC. I have never understood how that was allowed to happen.

I have a digest of viewers' letters that the BBC compiled, and to this day they make gratifying reading. *The Mighty Continent* was shown in many countries, and together with the solid video cassette sales of the series in America, especially in the educational market, it makes me look back on the three years with the BBC as well worthwhile; an experience that I am glad not to have missed.

It was now April 1975, and back to my normal situation: what next?

The Ratline

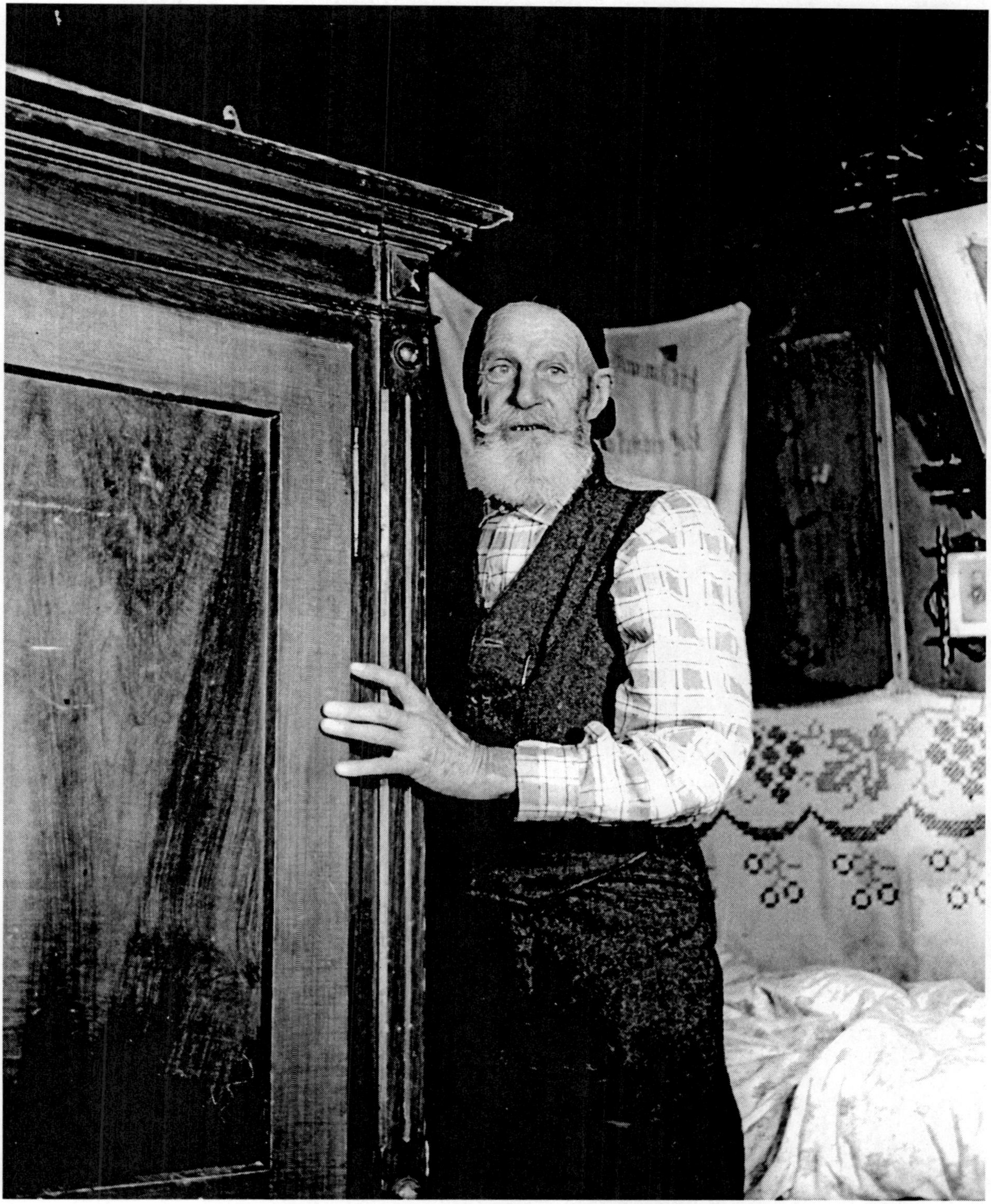

The Austrian mountain guide known as 'The Smuggler'.
(Rediffusion Television)

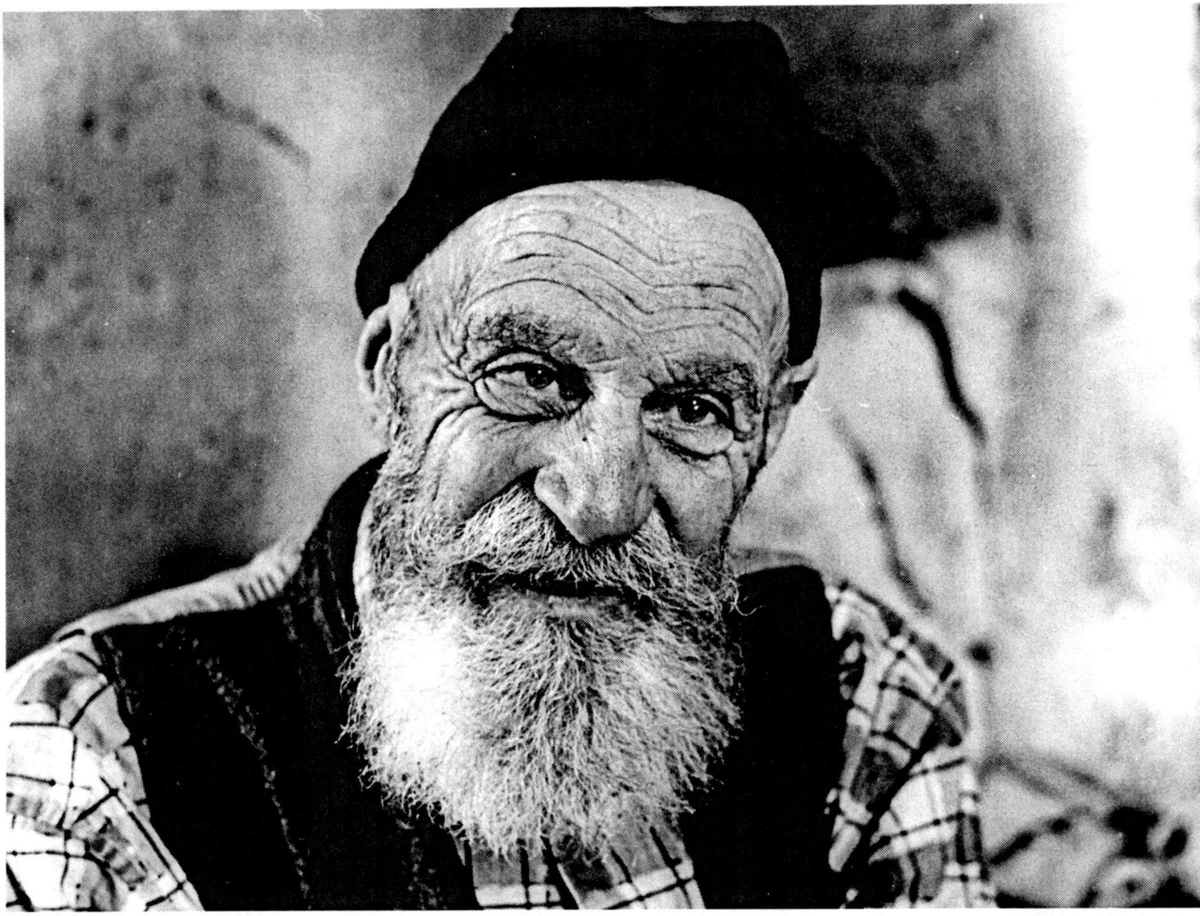

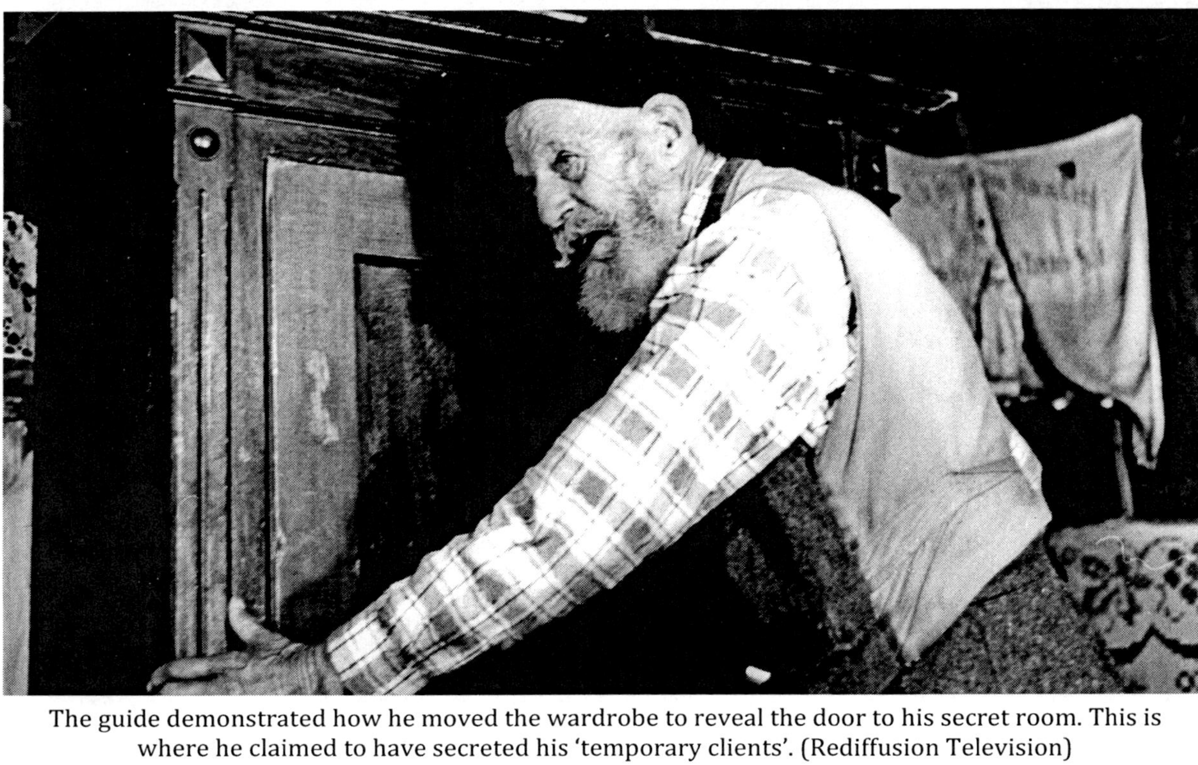

The guide demonstrated how he moved the wardrobe to reveal the door to his secret room. This is where he claimed to have secreted his 'temporary clients'. (Rediffusion Television)

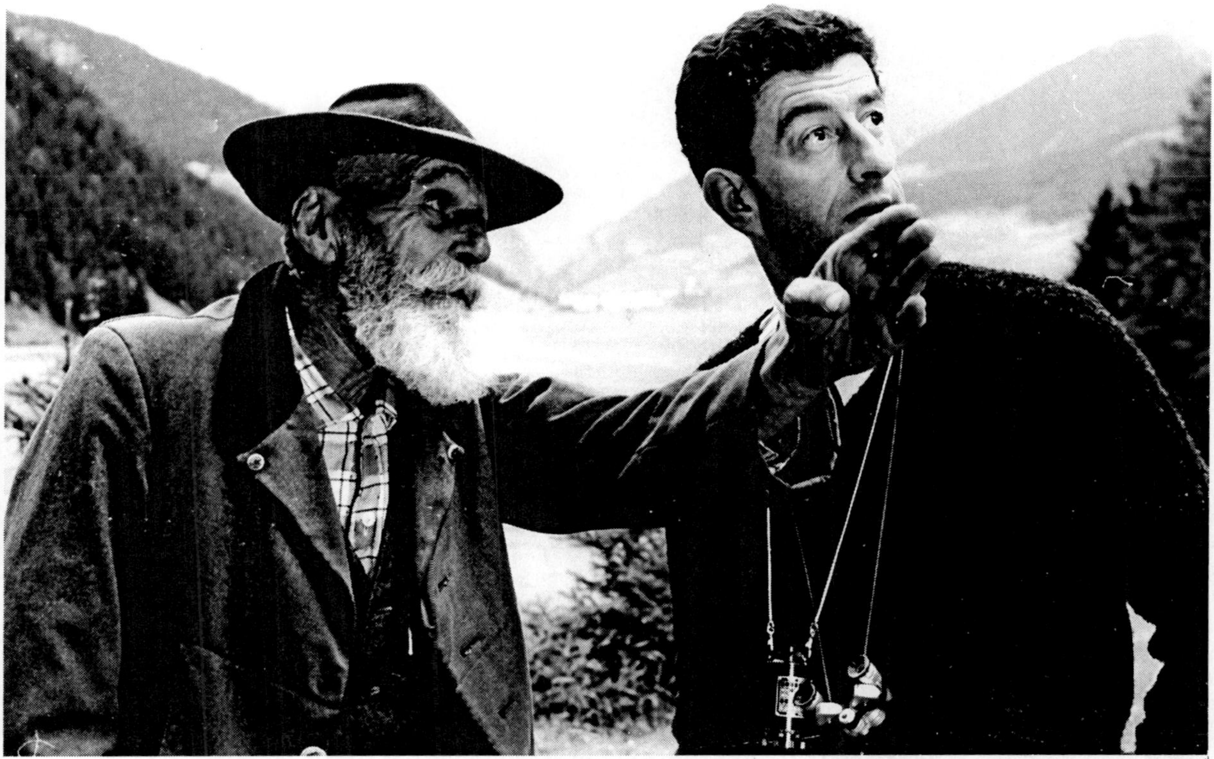

He took me up the mountain to where the borders of Austria, Switzerland and Italy meet. (Rediffusion Television)

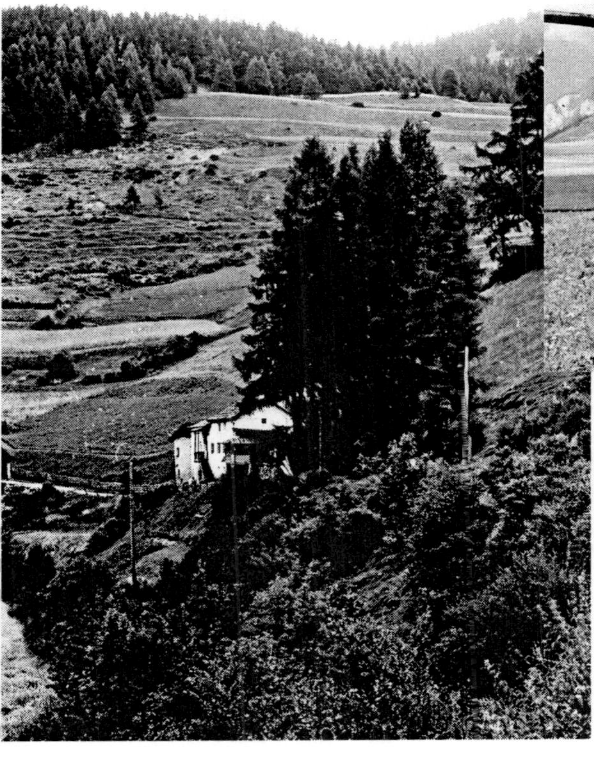

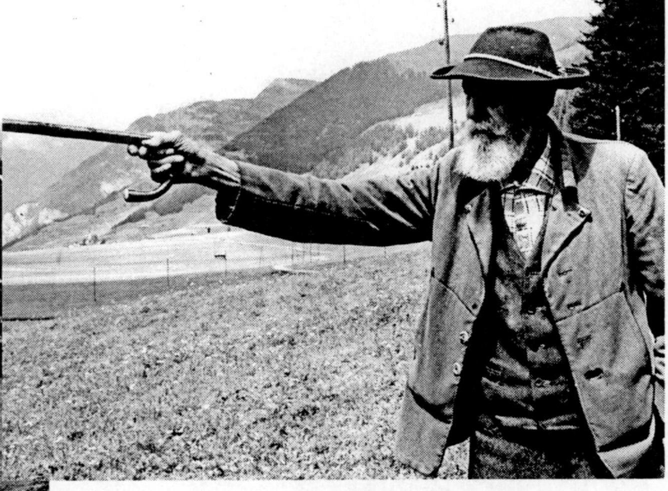

'That is Italy.' (Rediffusion Television)

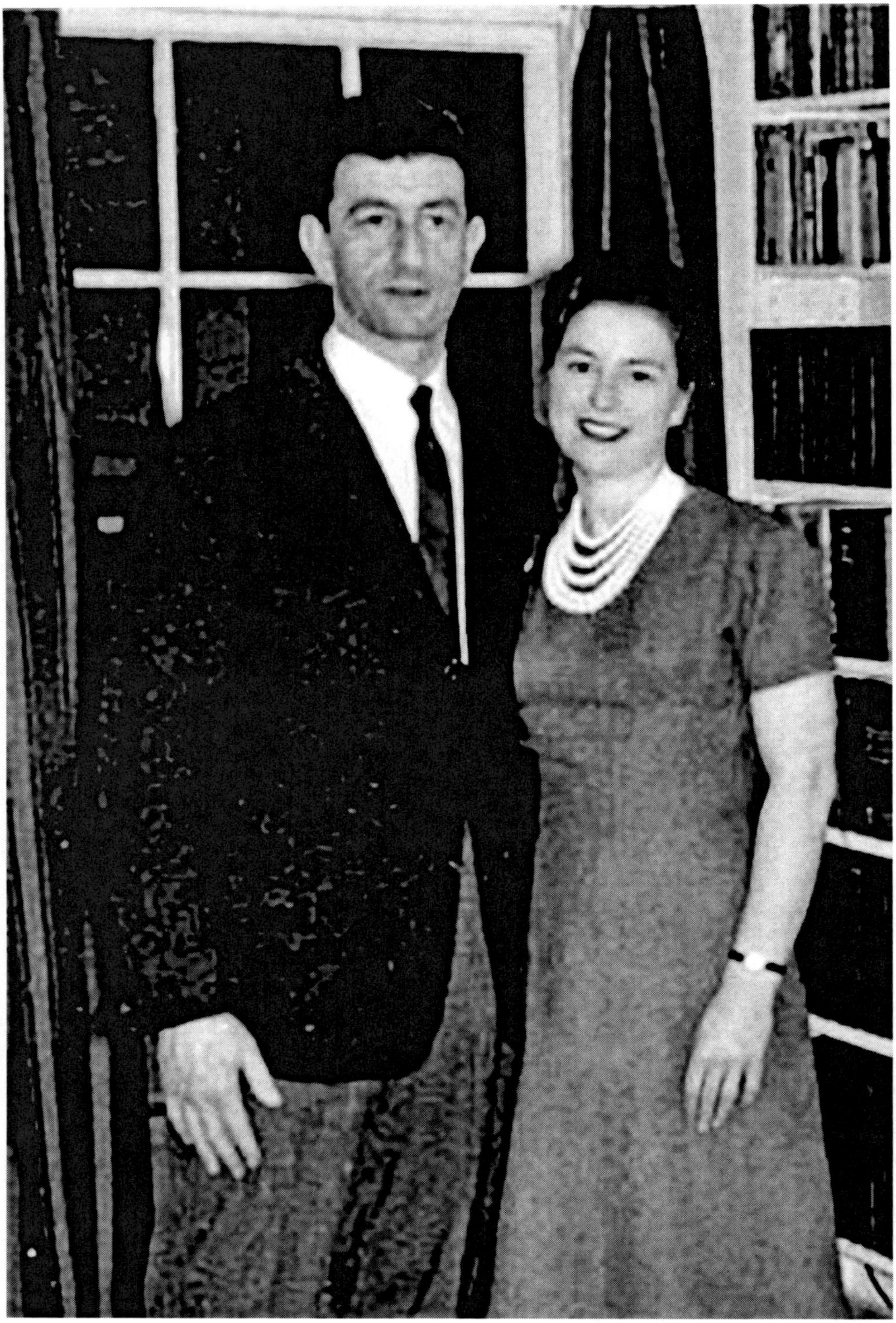

Our wedding day, 26 January 1962. (PM)

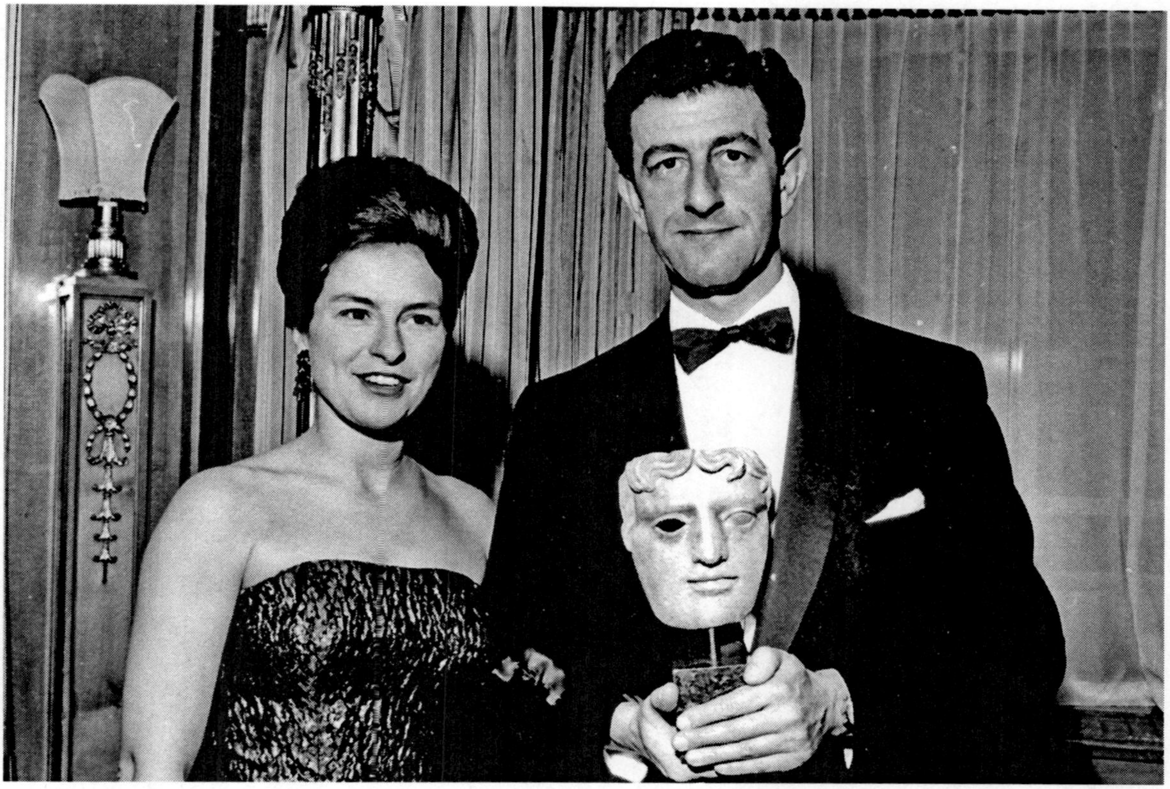

Our first 'do' at the Dorchester: ITV's first current affairs award for *This* Week, beating BBC's *Panorama*. (Rediffusion Television)

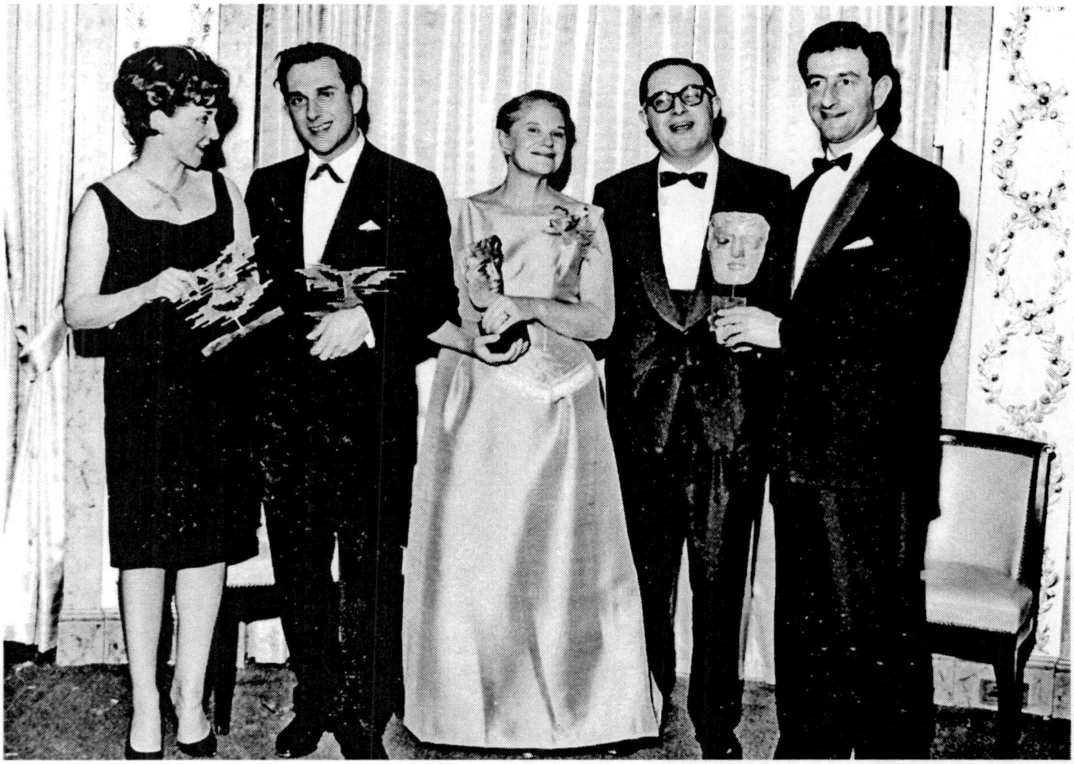

We were in good company that evening. Left to right: Vivian Merchant, Harold Pinter, Joan Kemp-Welch, Cyril Bennett, Peter Morley. (Rediffusion Television)

Black Marries White, 1964

Black Marries White—The Last Barrier

An Impression of Mixed Marriage
Most people, even those who profess to have no colour prejudice, shy away from the prospect of 'my daughter marrying a Negro.' There are no facts and no statistics about mixed marriage. There are only experiences and attitudes to what is a profound human dilemma. This is a frank programme about a disturbing subject, and the people taking part are the only people who can possibly know anything about it—those who are partners in a mixed marriage. There is no narrator to explain the tensions and pressures that both the white and coloured societies impose on those who have dared to cross the colour line in marriage. There is no interviewer whose own attitudes could diffuse the issues. There is only the stark dialogue of human experience, which come spontaneously from the mixed couples themselves. *Black Marries White* is a challenge to re-examine our attitudes in the light of these experiences

CAMERAMAN MICHAEL RHODES
SOUND STAN CLARKE FREDDIE SLADE
FILM EDITOR DAVID HODGSON
PROGRAMME ASSISTANT JOAN HILL
DIRECTED BY PETER MORLEY

Rediffusion Network Production

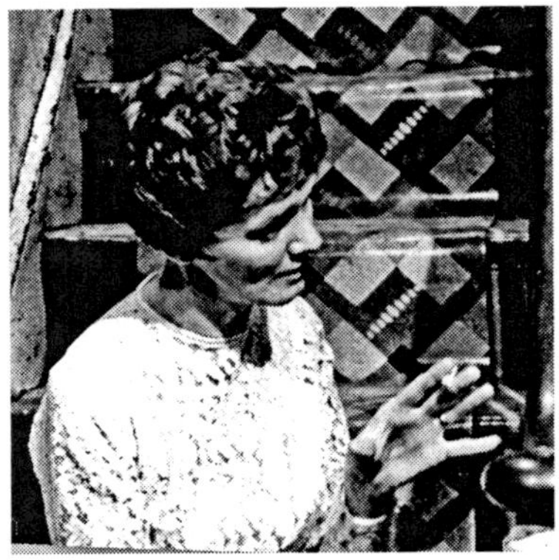

'If God didn't want us to mix he would have separated us.' (Rediffusion Television)

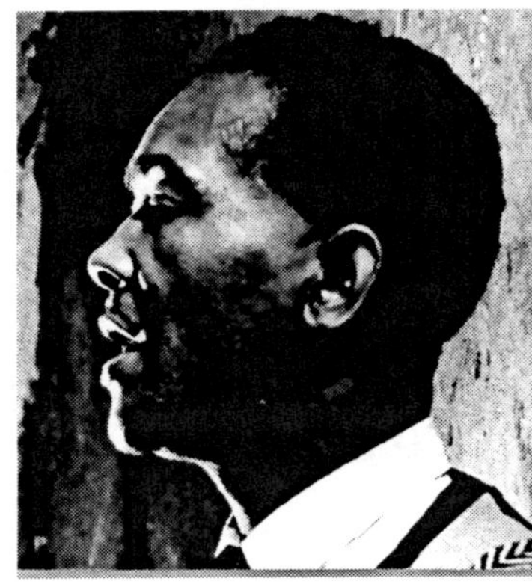

'It doesn't matter what outsiders say as long as we're happy.' (Rediffusion Television)

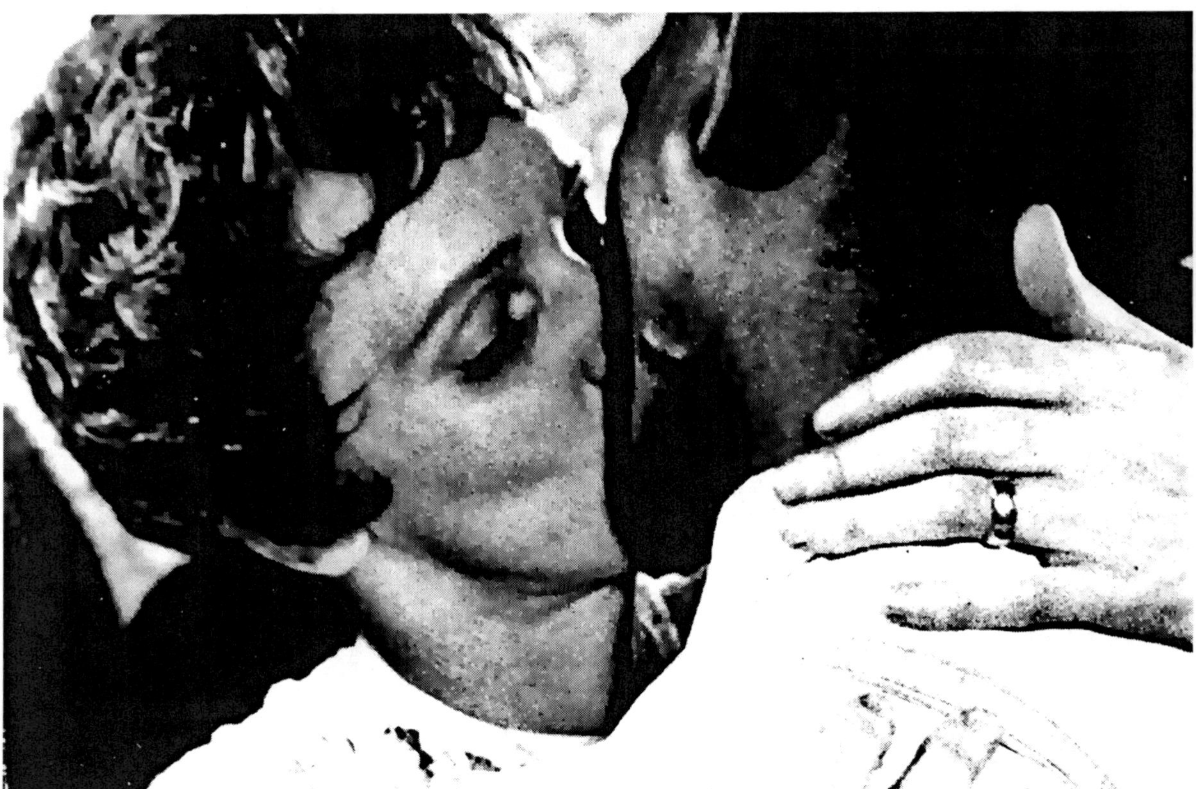

'If one day Beverly comes home from school and says to you, "Daddy, why do they call me a nigger girl?" what would you say to her?' (Rediffusion Television)

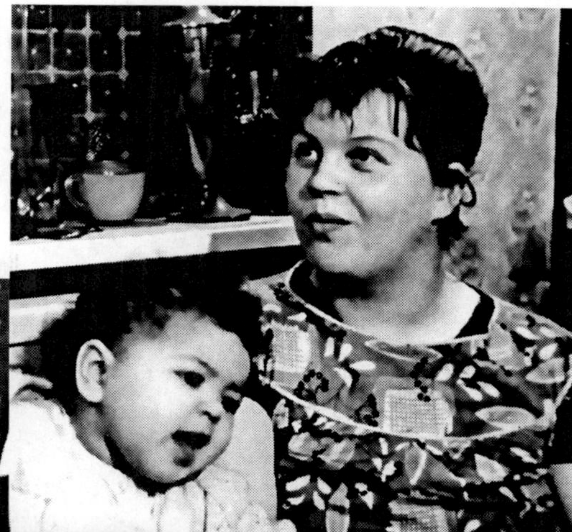

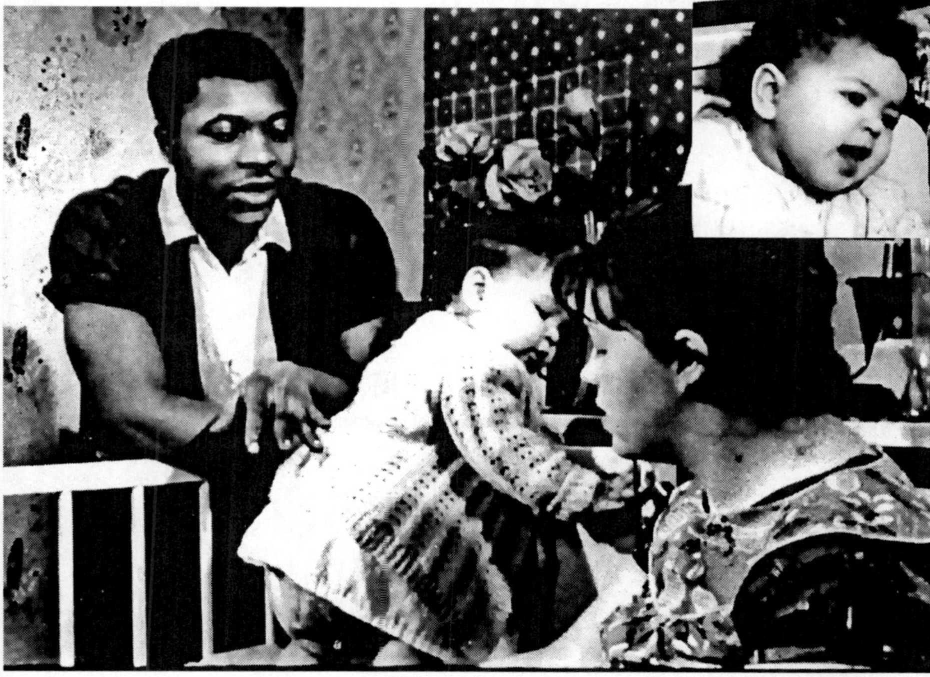

Sometimes I think about it.' (Rediffusion Television)

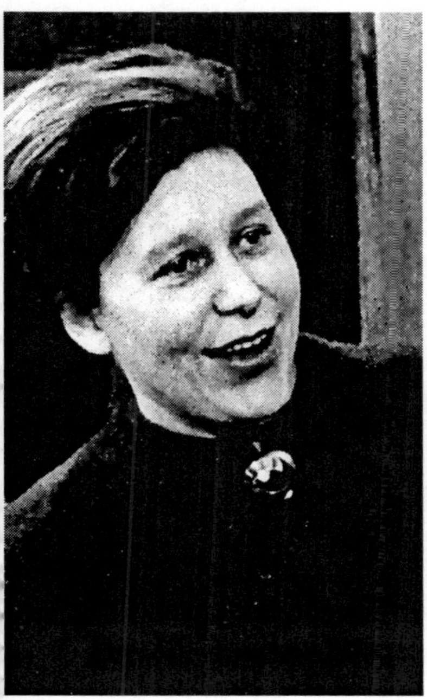

'. . . and in our case with a mixed marriage it is obviously more important that we should have been well adjusted and happy together before we started introducing children into it.' (Rediffusion Television)

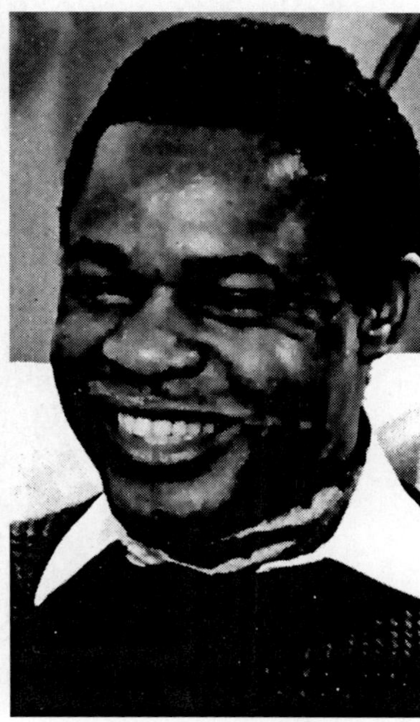

The State Funeral of Sir Winston Churchill
30 January 1965

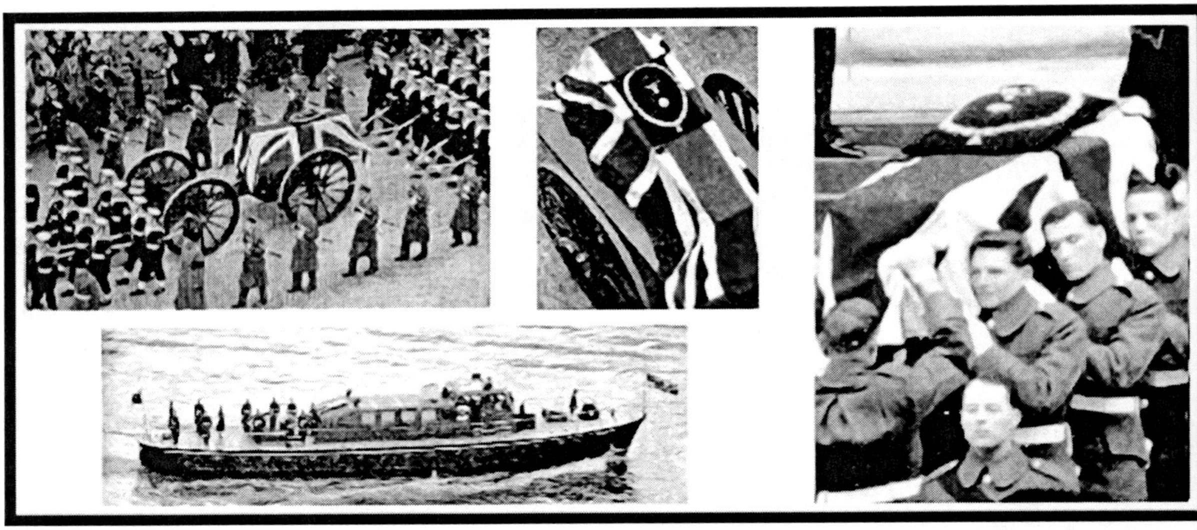

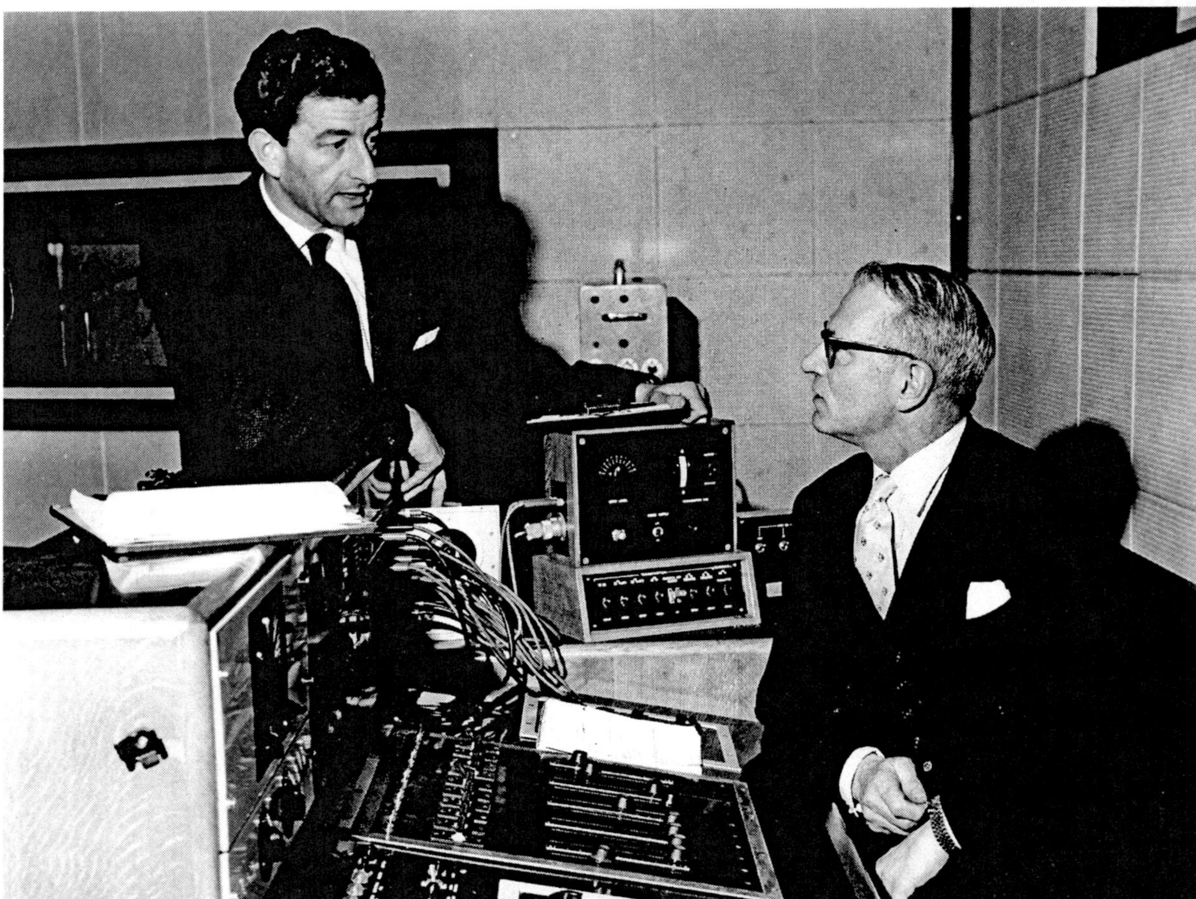

D+2: four days to go. Pre-recording the Churchill quotations with Laurence Olivier.
(Rediffusion Television)

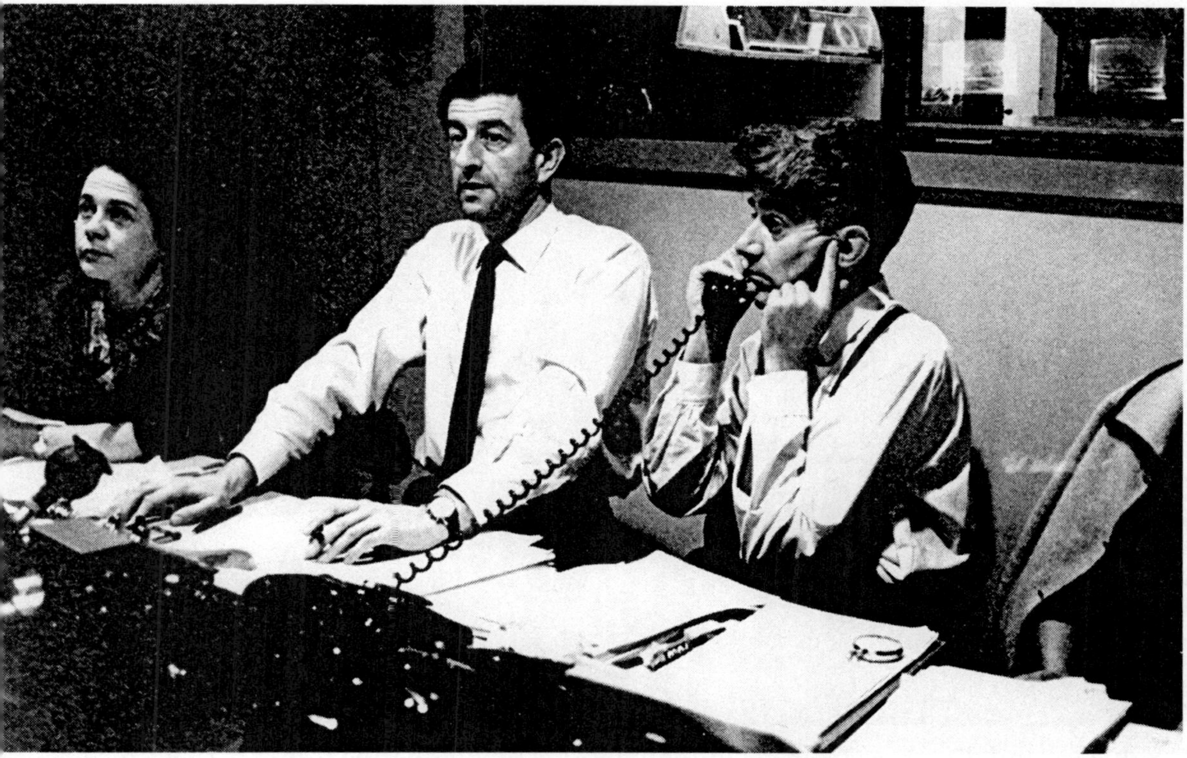

D+5: the 4 a.m. rehearsal one day before transmission. I am flanked by vision mixer Bridget Booth and assistant director Graham Watts. (Rediffusion Television)

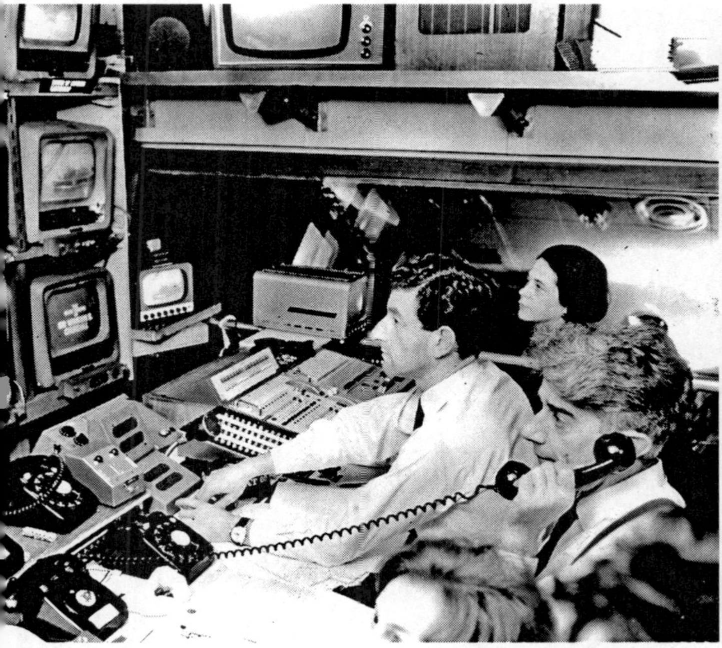

D+6: on the air for five hours, with my finger on the 'omnibus talkback' button – so that I could speak to forty-five cameramen. (Rediffusion Television)

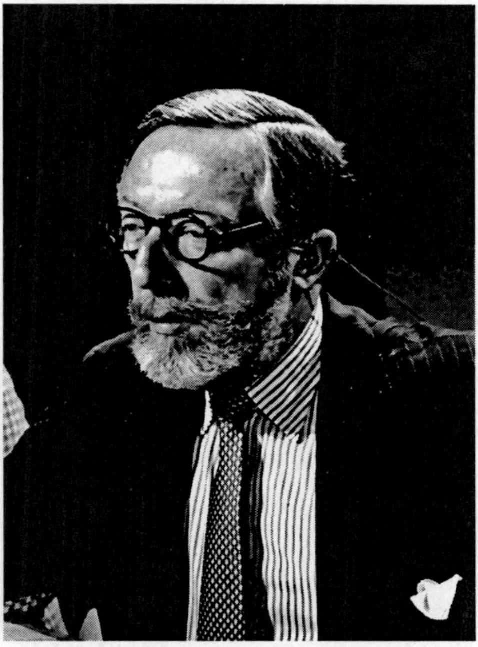

Brian Connell faces his own monitors for his live commentary. (Rediffusion Television)

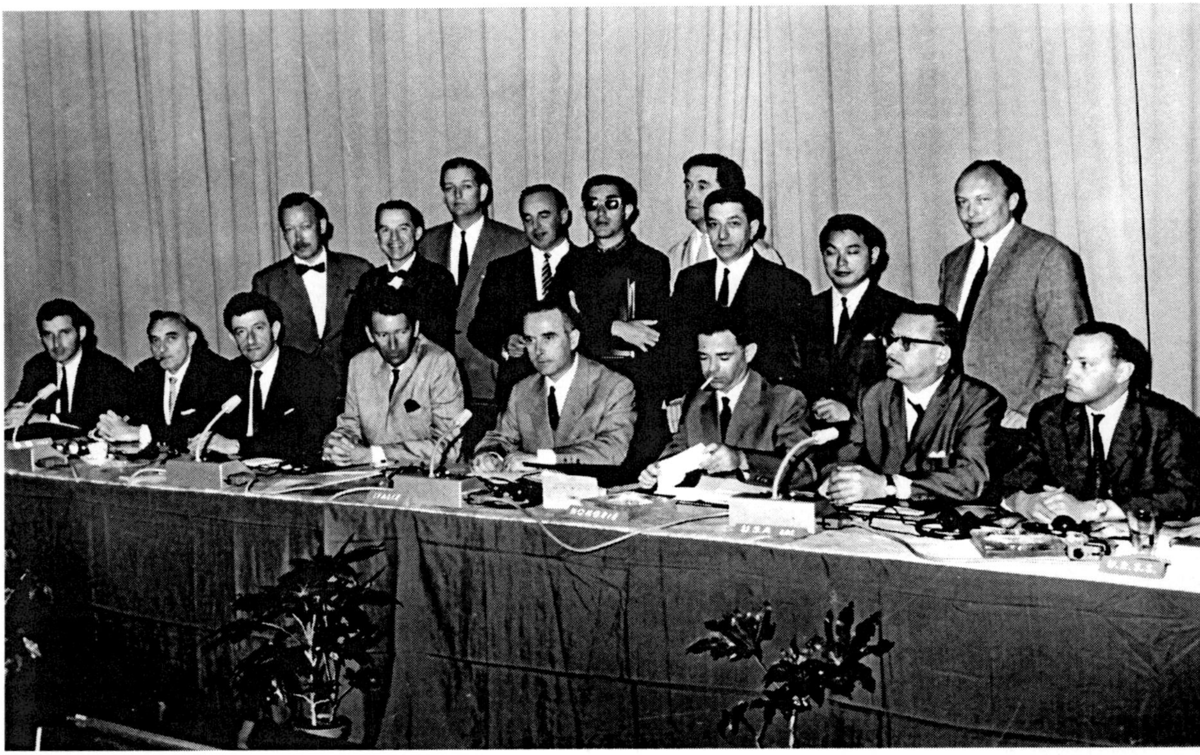

Producers and directors from seventeen nations made up the Cannes jury with rival BBC producer Anthony Craxton next to me, fourth from left. (Rediffusion Television)

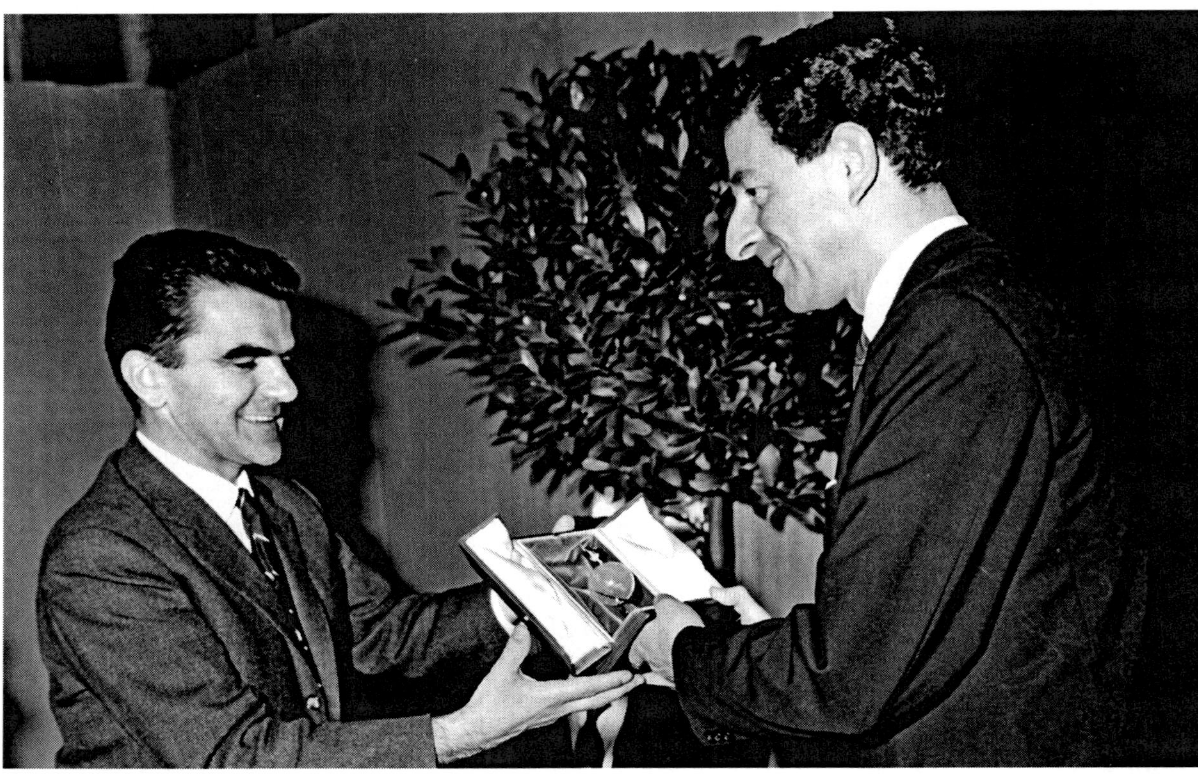

The Cannes Grand Prix, presented by Jacques-Bernard Dupont, Le Directeur Général de l'Office de Radiodiffusion-Television Française. (Rediffusion Television)

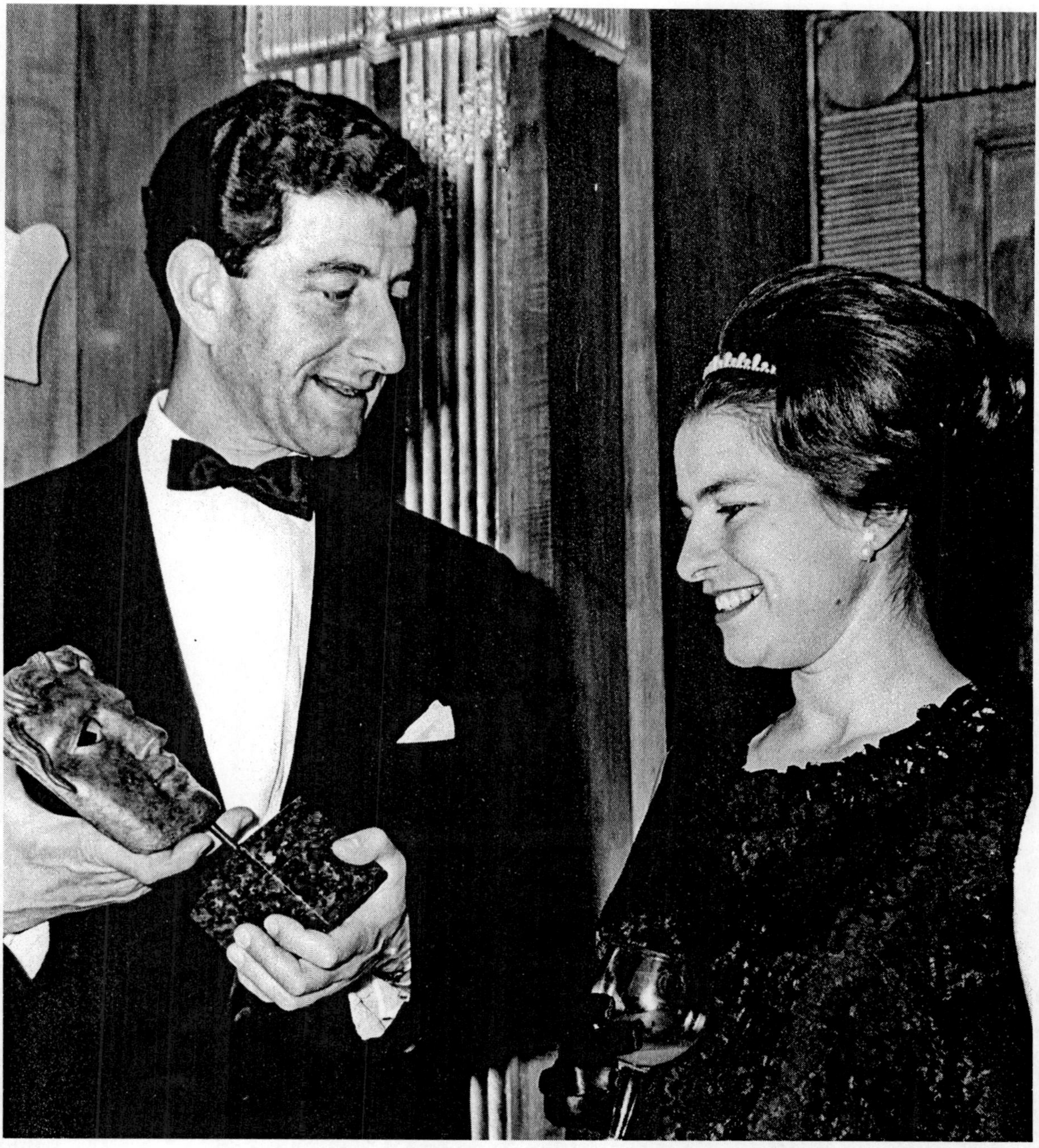

The 1965 Television Ball at the Dorchester Hotel with Jane, the BAFTA mask and Jonathan, due in two months. (Rediffusion Television)

LSO – The Music Men, 1965

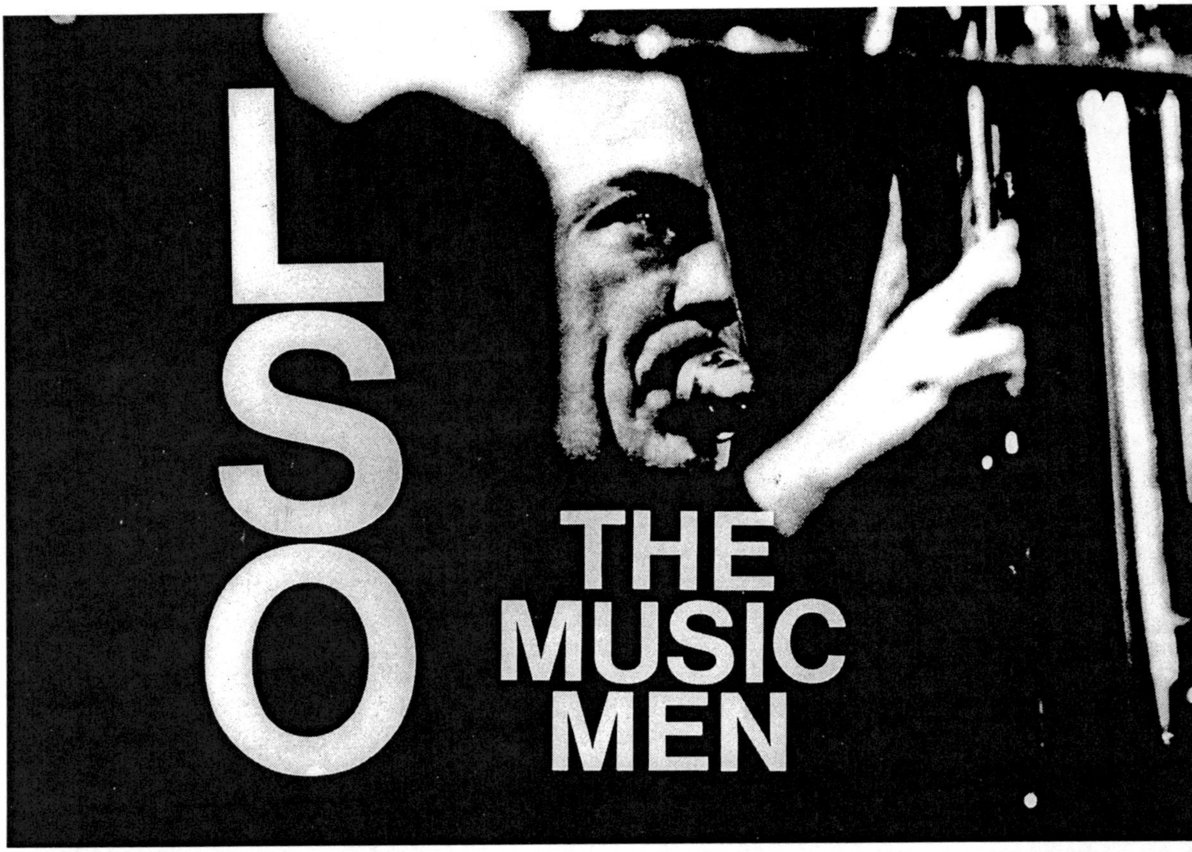

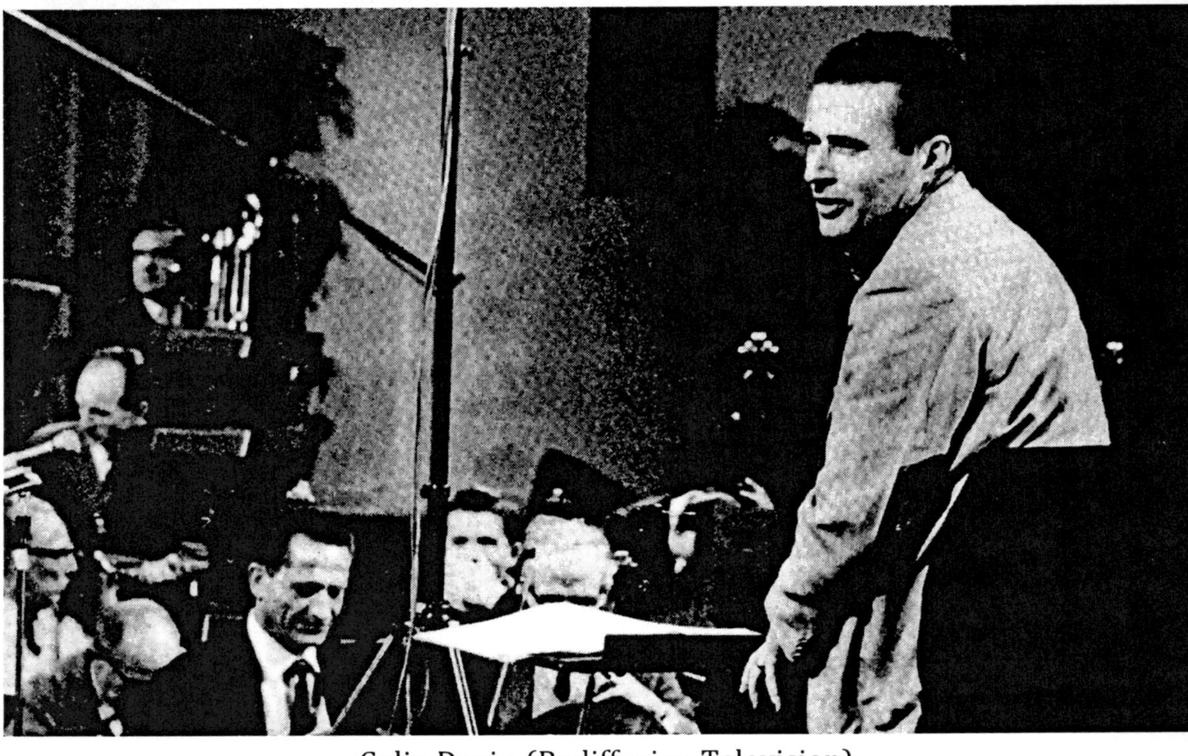

Colin Davis. (Rediffusion Television)

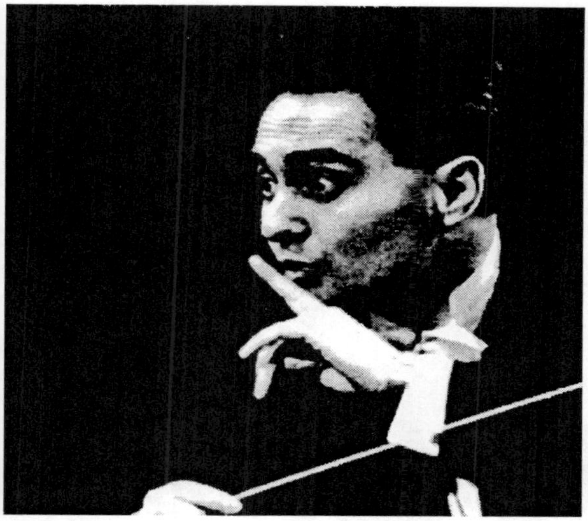

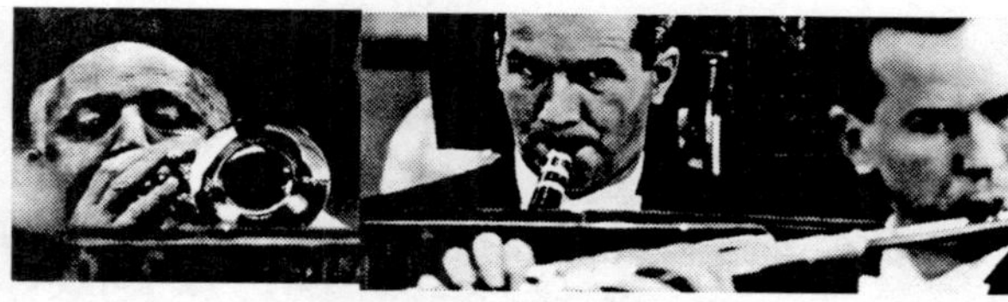

'Seventy-five men. One on the rostrum – and suddenly they explode, like athletes off the starting blocks.' (Rediffusion Television)

István Kertész. (Rediffusion Television)

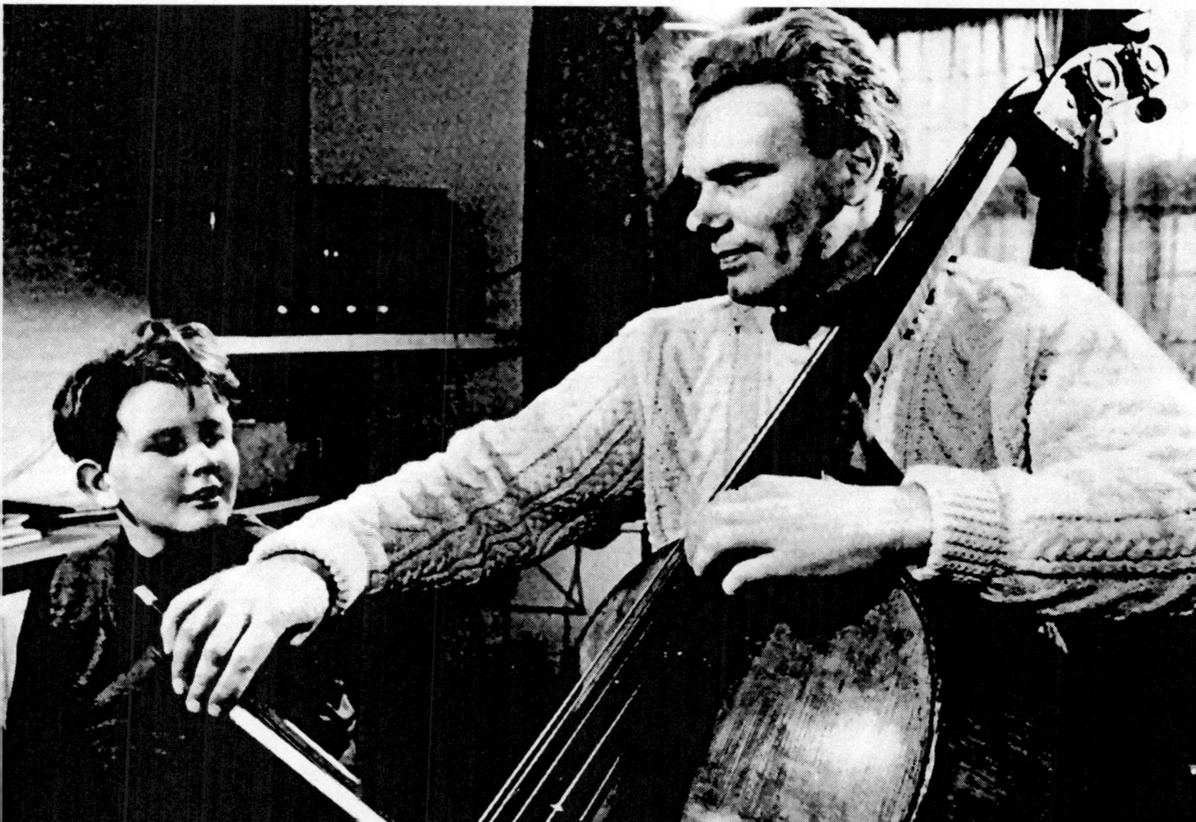

Stuart Knussen and his twelve-year-old son Oliver, a budding composer. (Rediffusion Television)

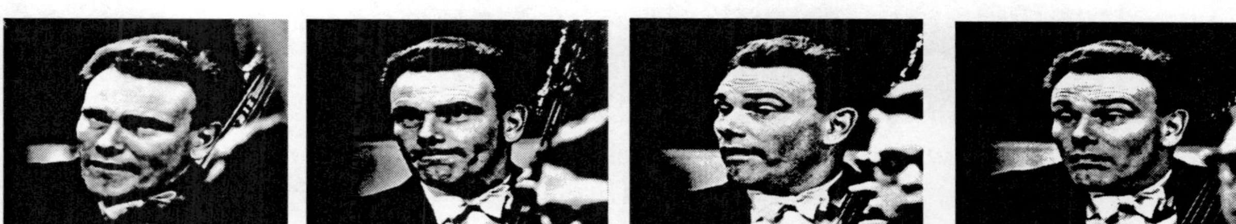

The Life and Times of Lord Mountbatten 1956-68

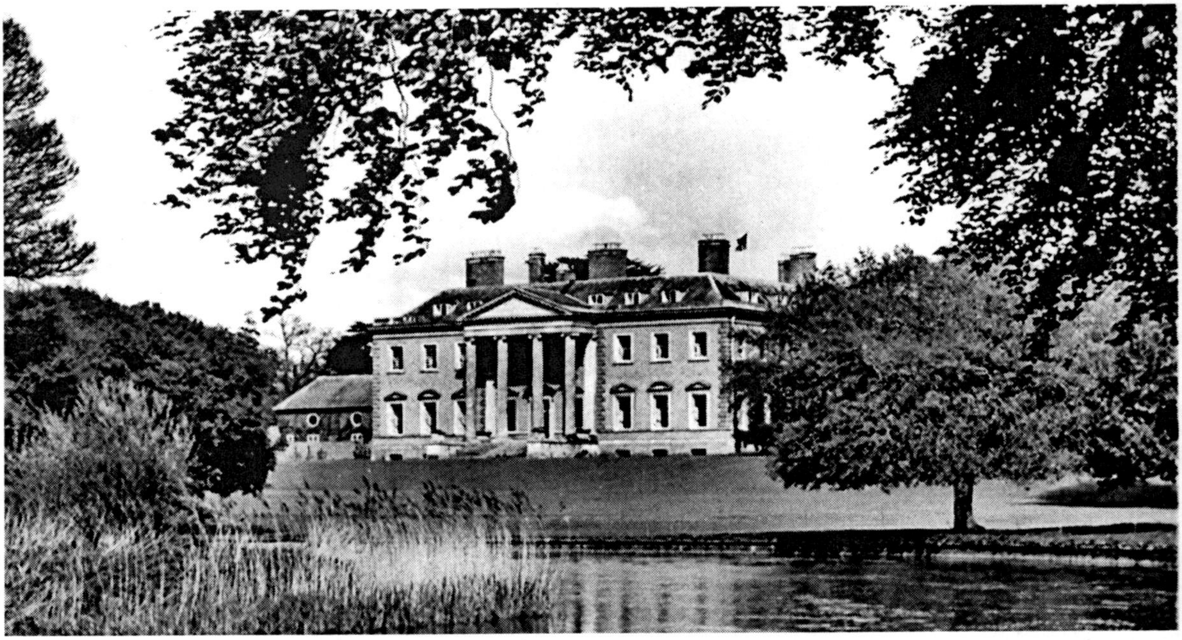

Broadlands. (Broadlands Archive)

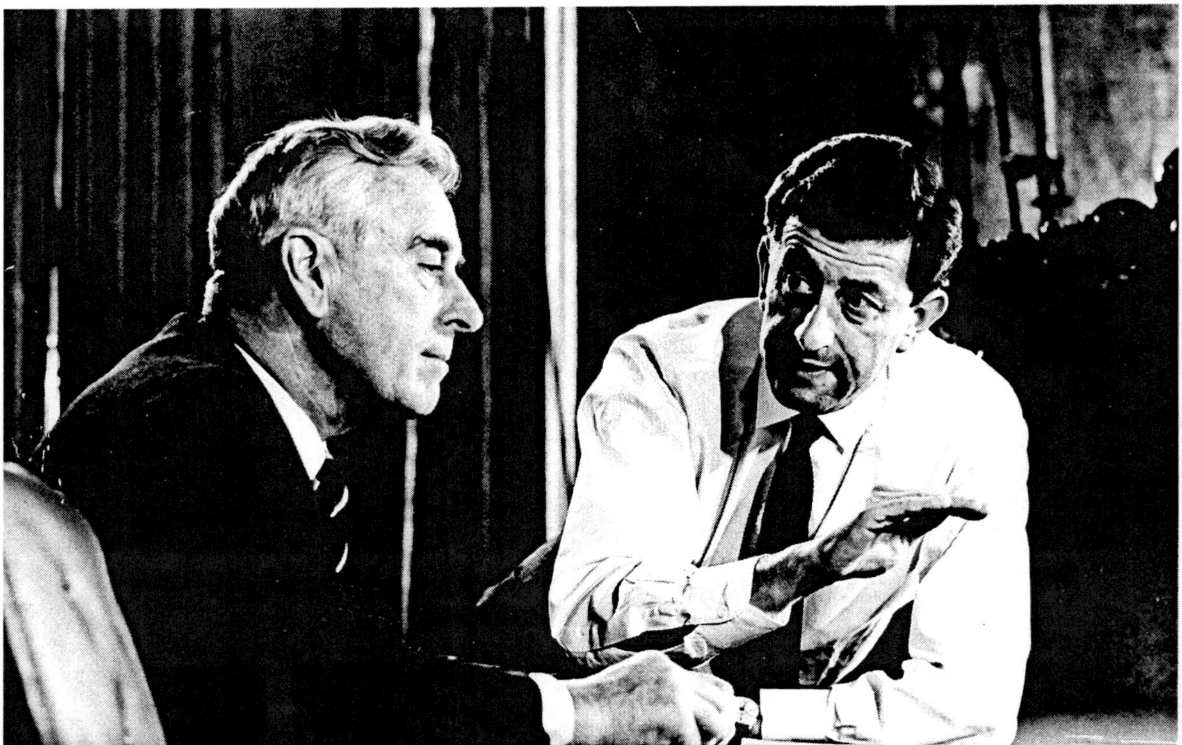

Coming to grips with the problem of deciding on the contents and style of twelve hours of television. (Broadlands Archive)

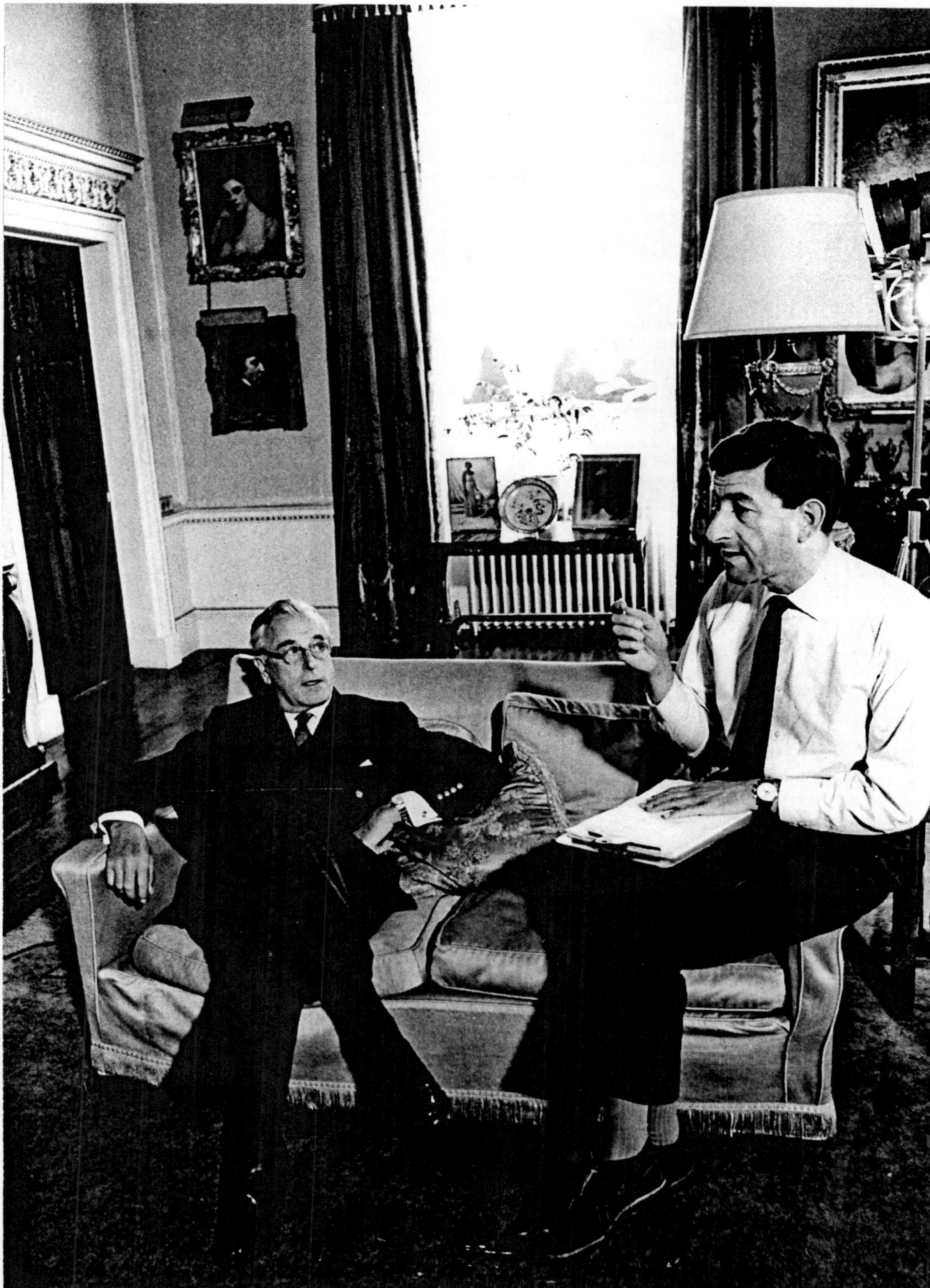

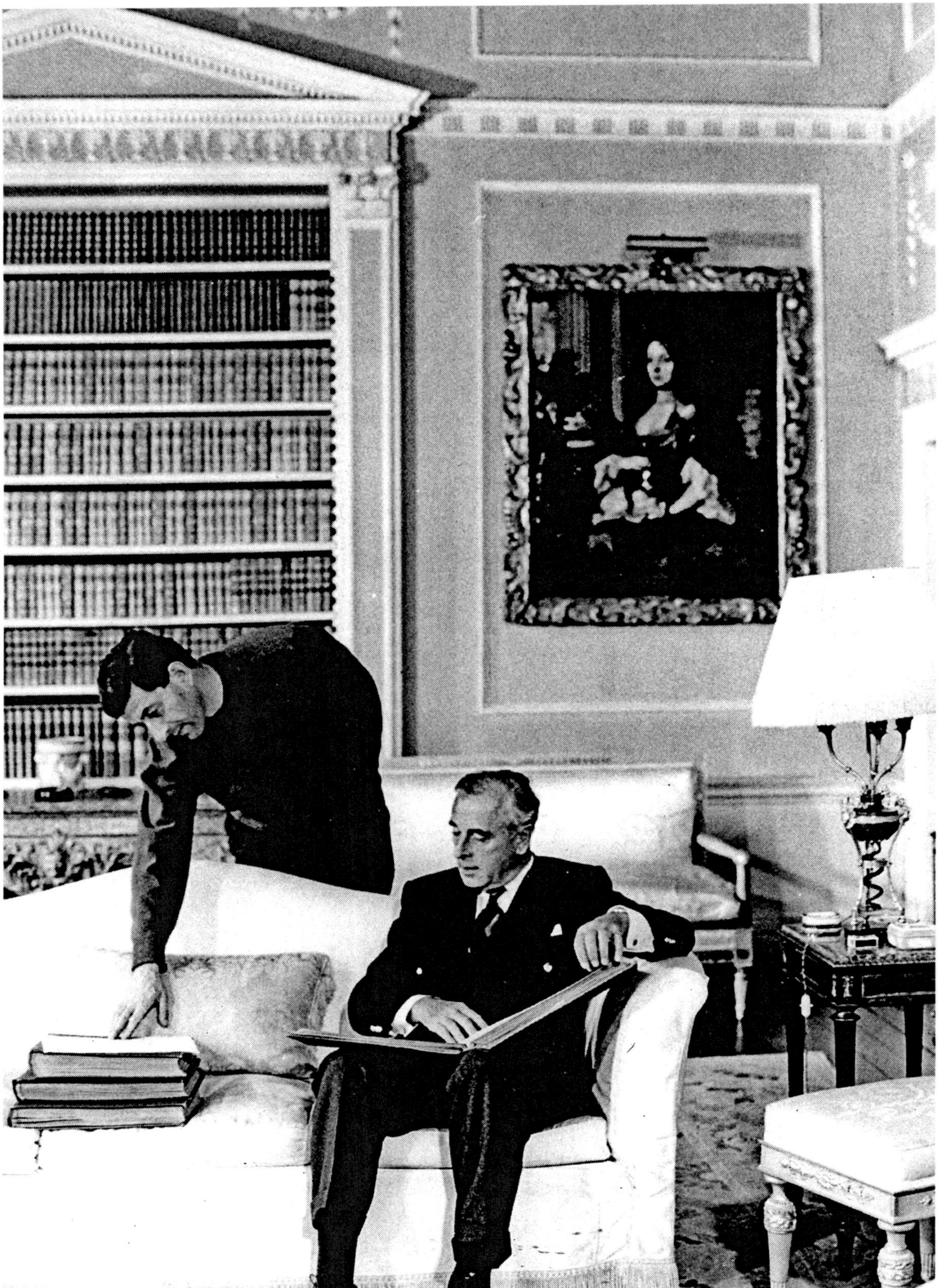

The Wedgwood Room: an introduction to the massive photographic collection. (Broadlands Archive)

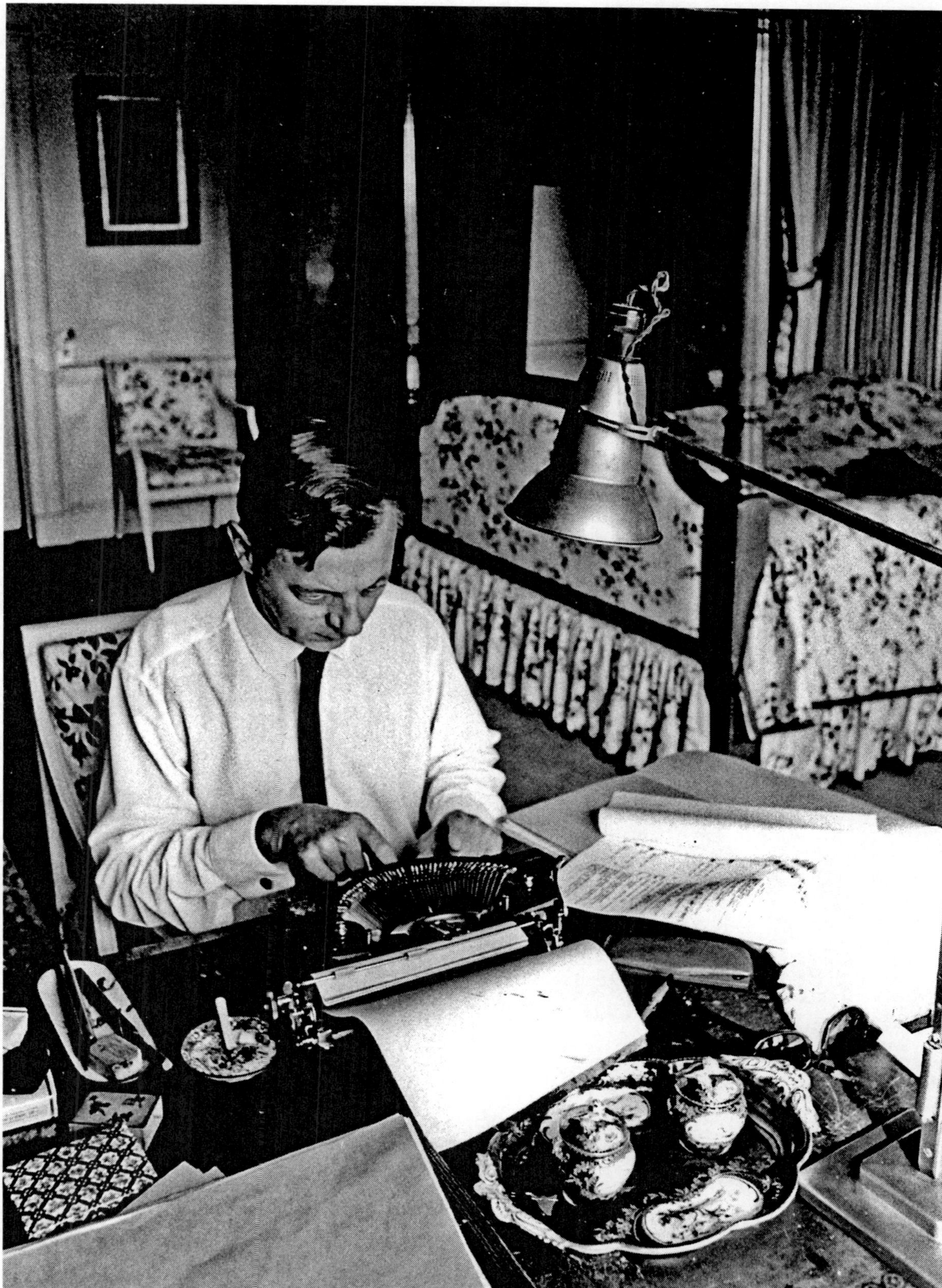

The first week in Broadlands with John Terraine. (Broadlands Archive)

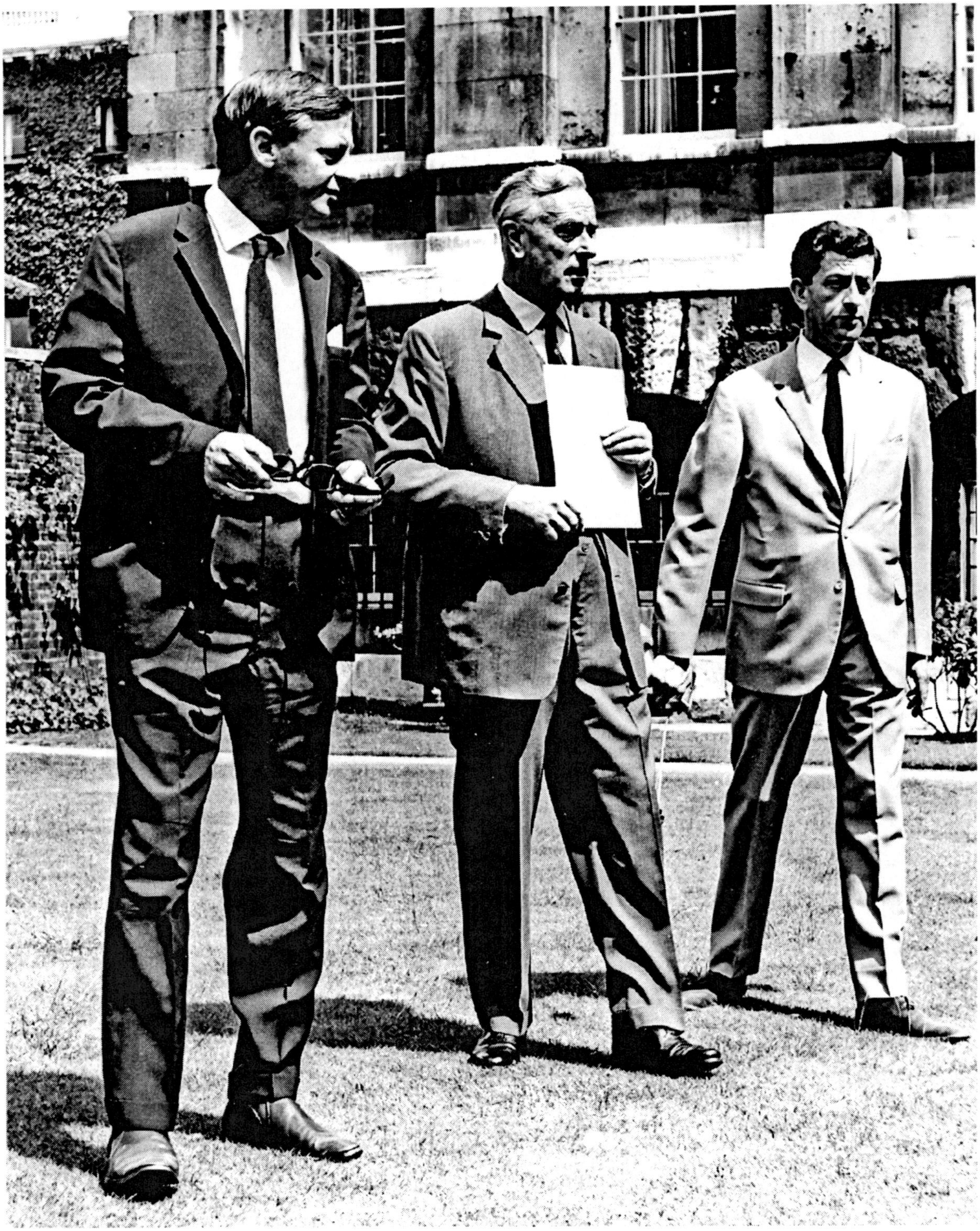

With John Terraine and Lord Mountbatten filming in the garden of 10 Downing Street. (Broadlands Archive)

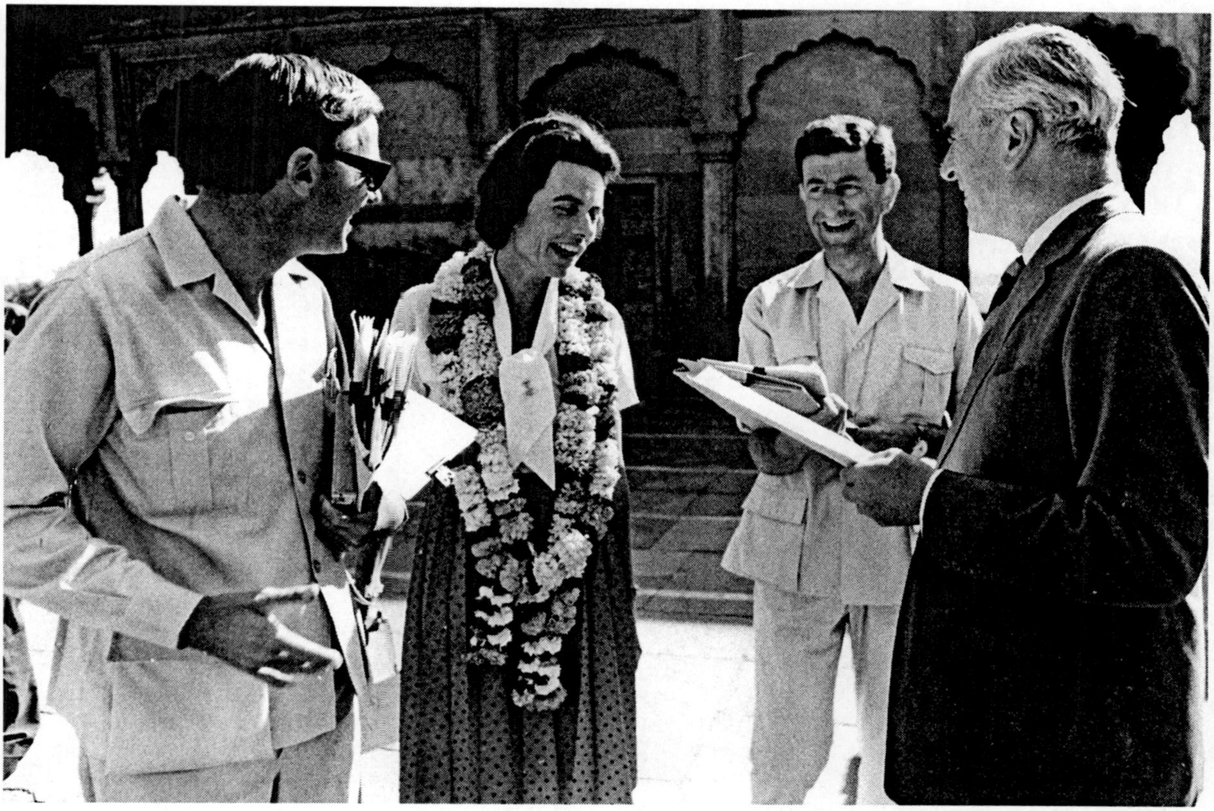

Patricia (the Countess Mountbatten of Burma) joins us in Delhi. (Broadlands Archive)

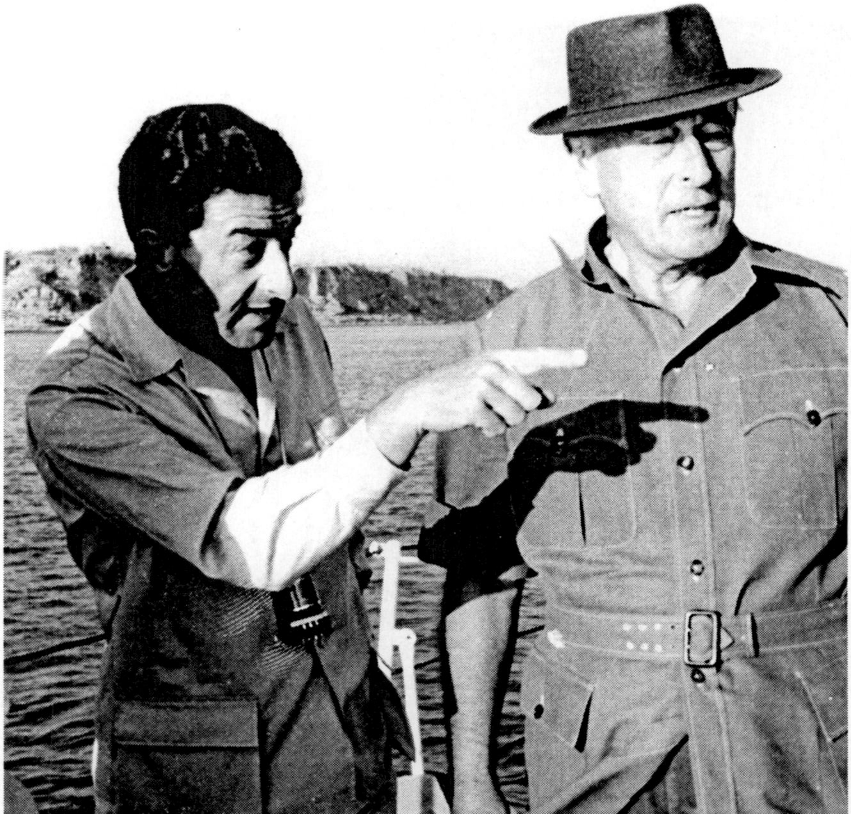

On the Irrawaddy on our way to Mandalay, I spot a flying fish. (Broadlands Archive)

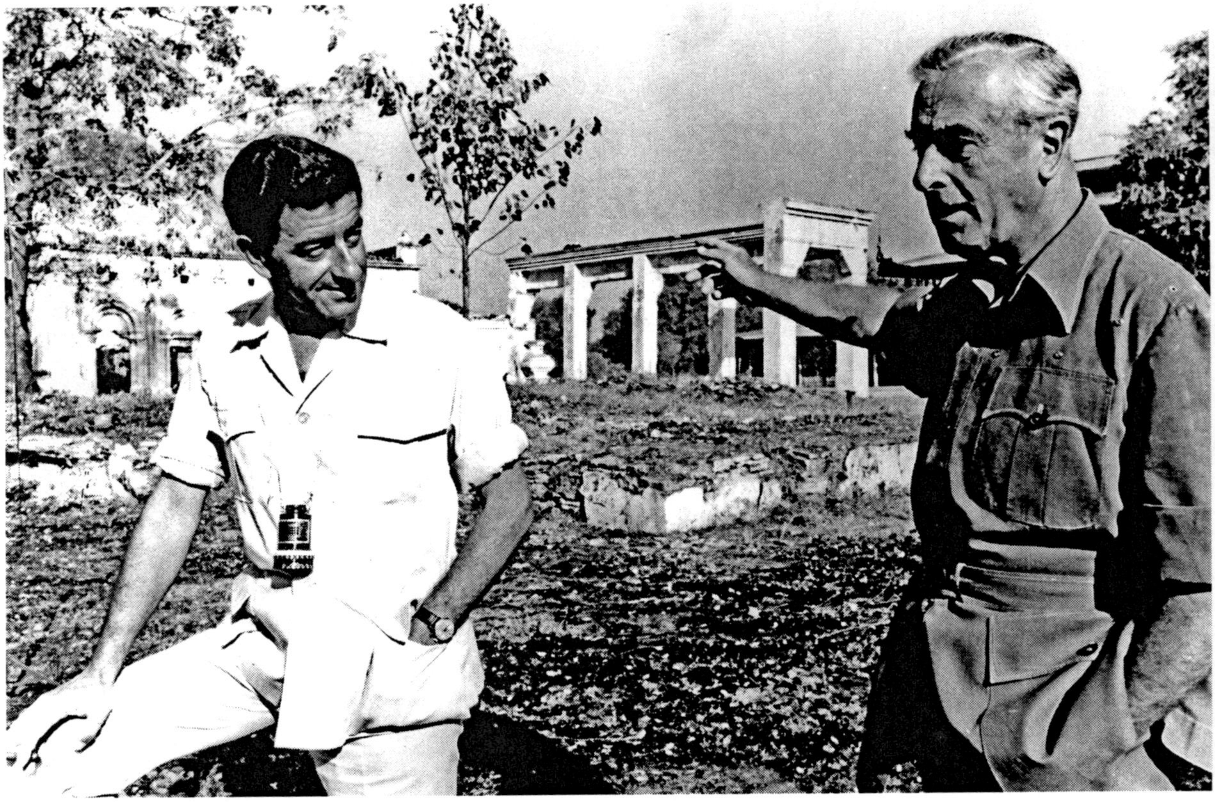

Mandalay: Supreme Allied Commander South East Asia explains the capture of Fort Dufferin. (Broadlands Archive)

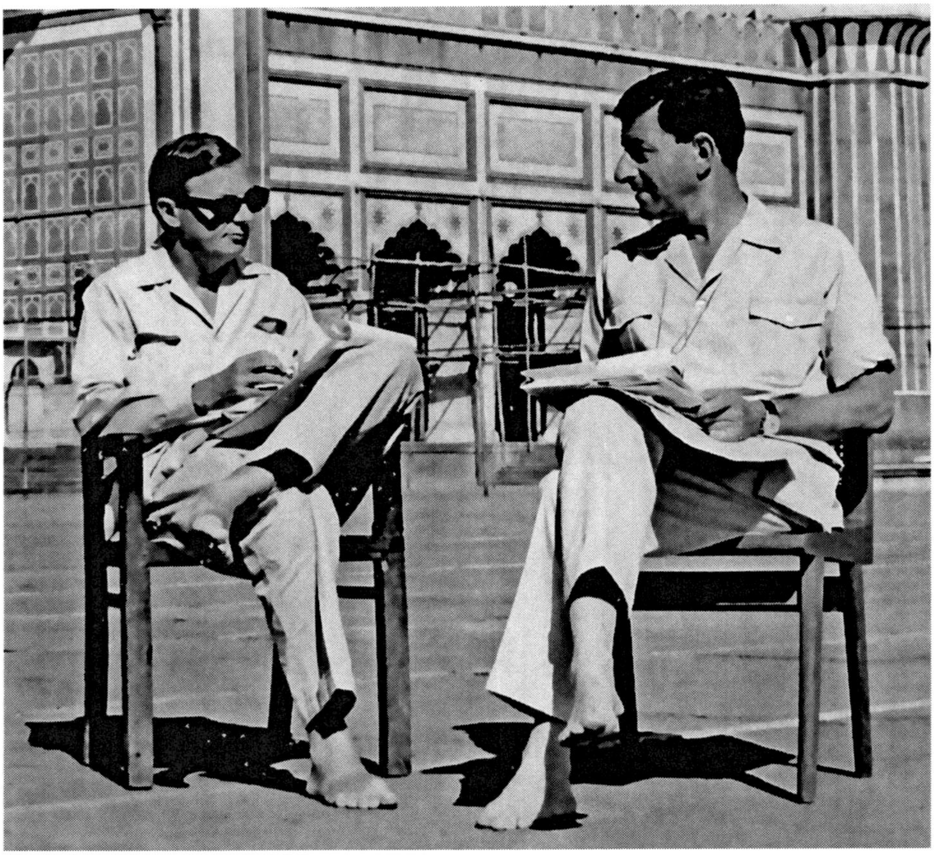

LM occasionally referred to us as 'the two wizards', but most of the time as 'those two four-letter men'. (Broadlands Archive)

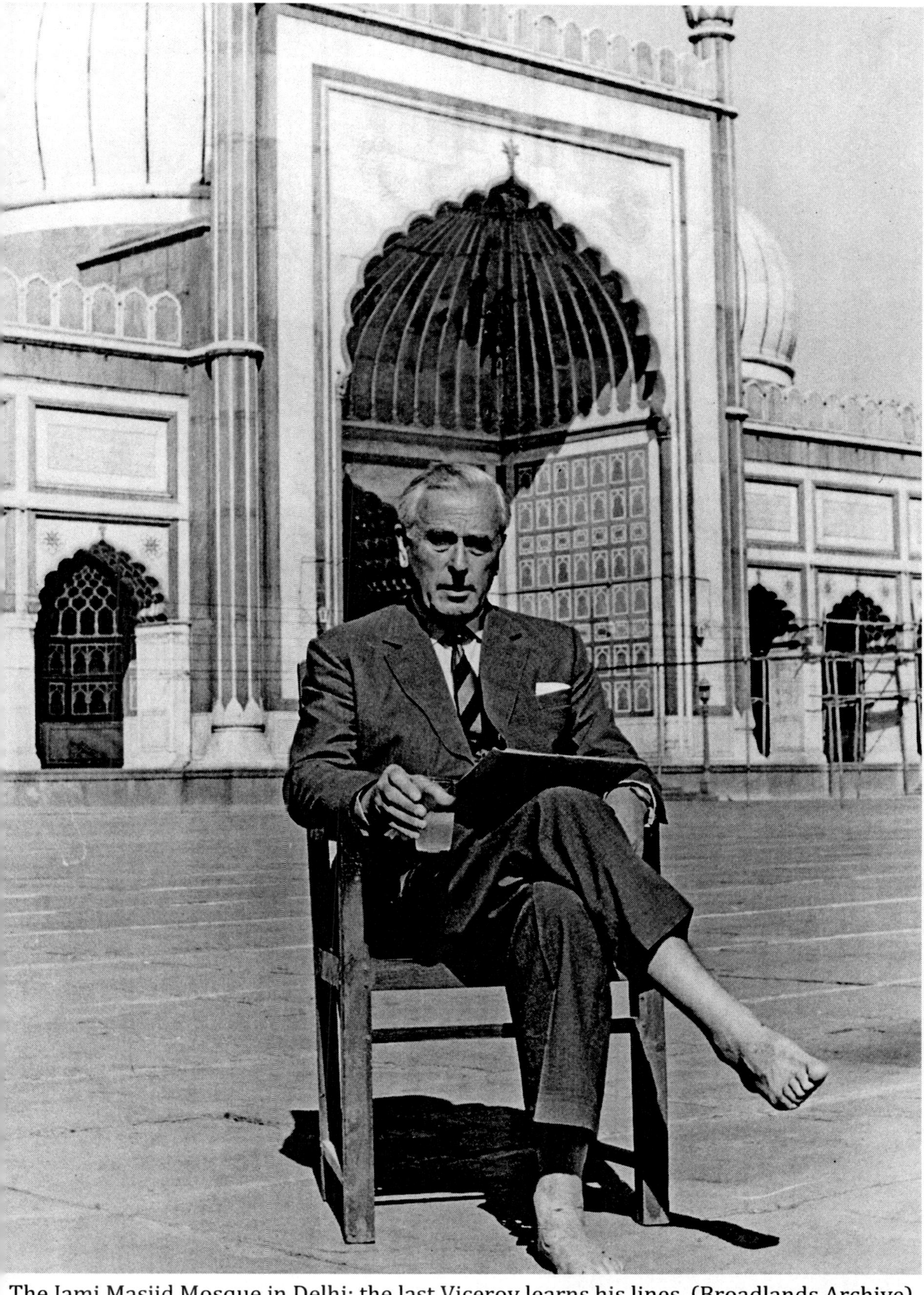

The Jami Masjid Mosque in Delhi: the last Viceroy learns his lines. (Broadlands Archive)

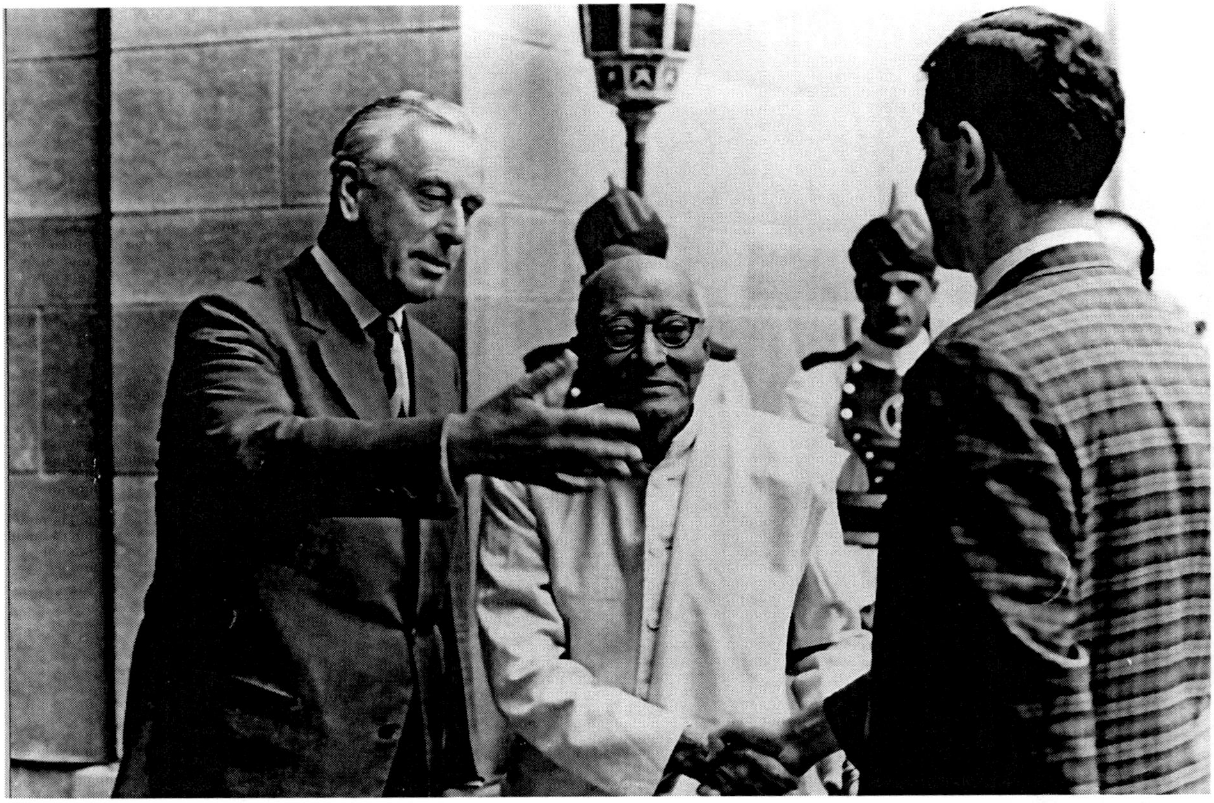

C.R. Rajagopalachari, India's first Governor-General, who took over from the last Viceroy. (Broadlands Archive)

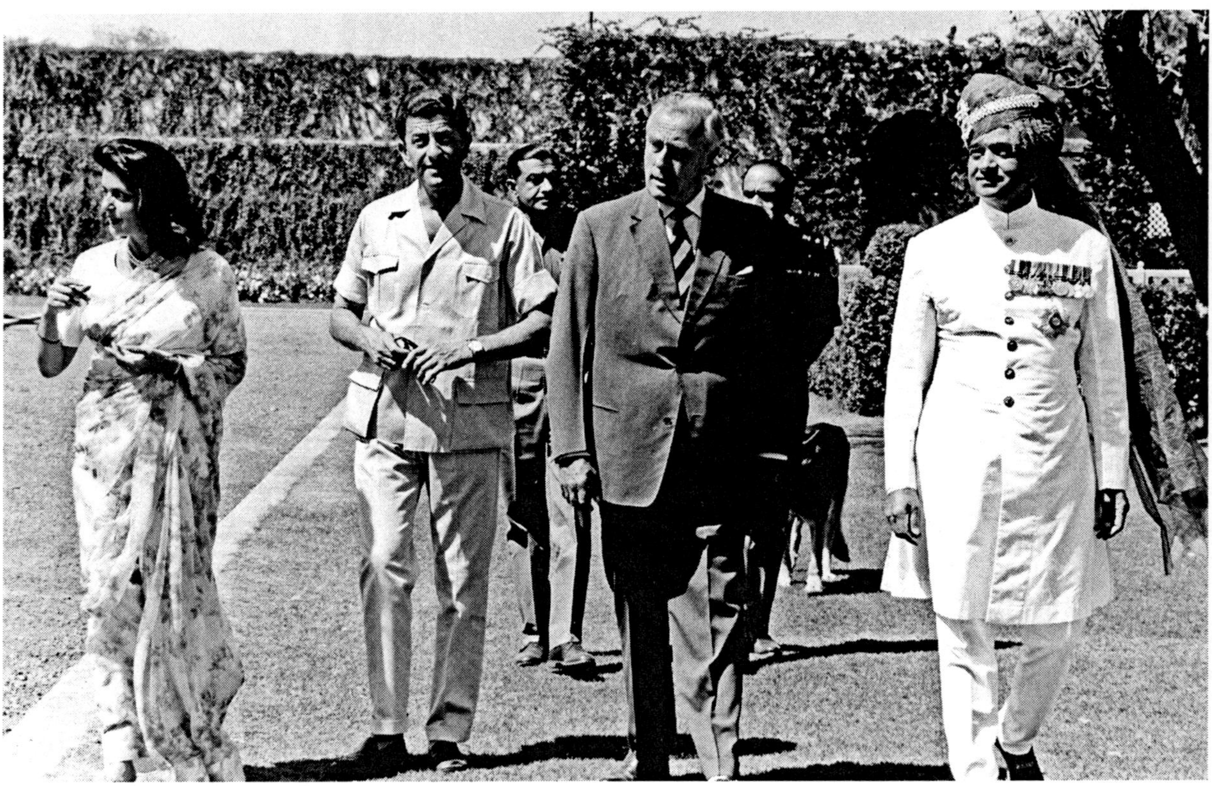

The Maharaja and Maharani of Jaipur in their palace grounds. (Broadlands Archive)

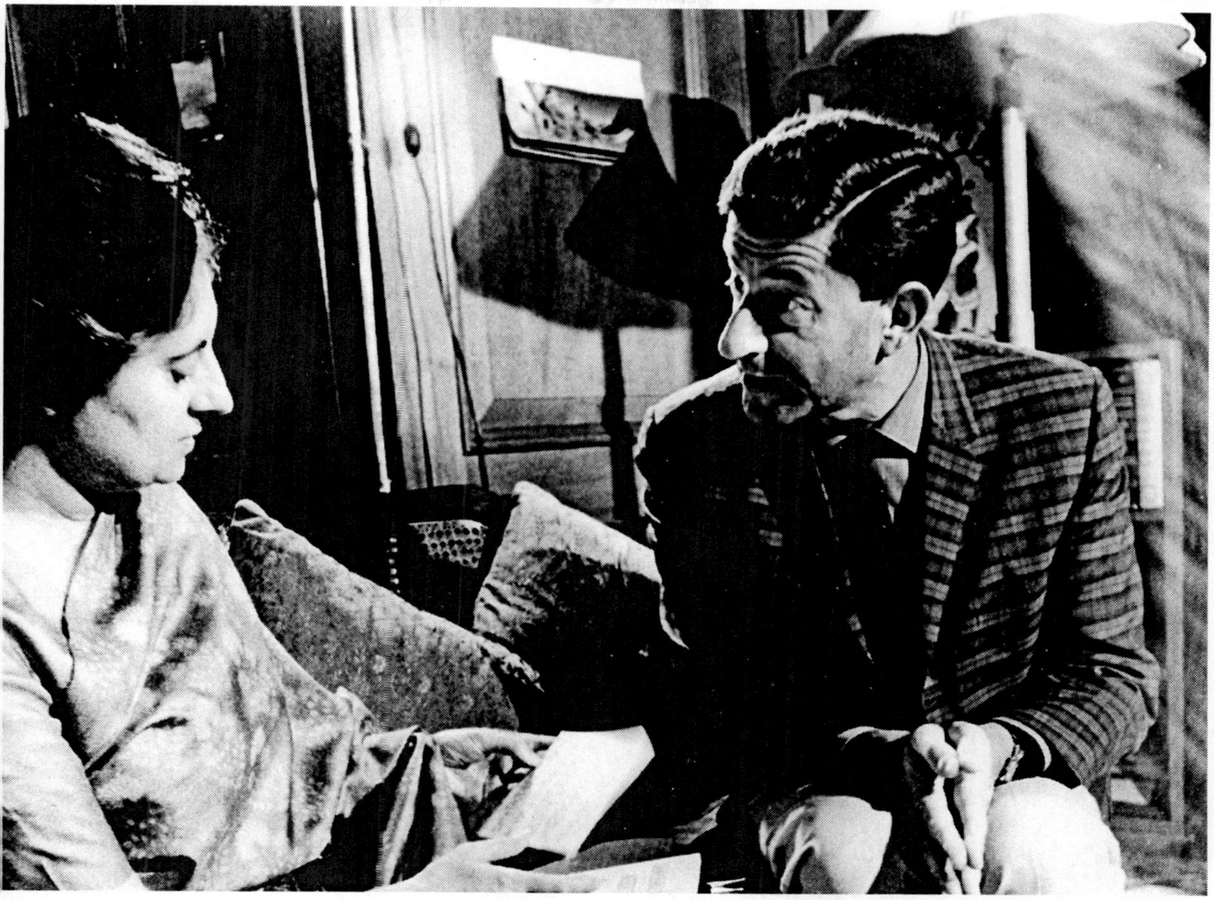

Prime Minister Indira Gandhi. (Broadlands Archive)

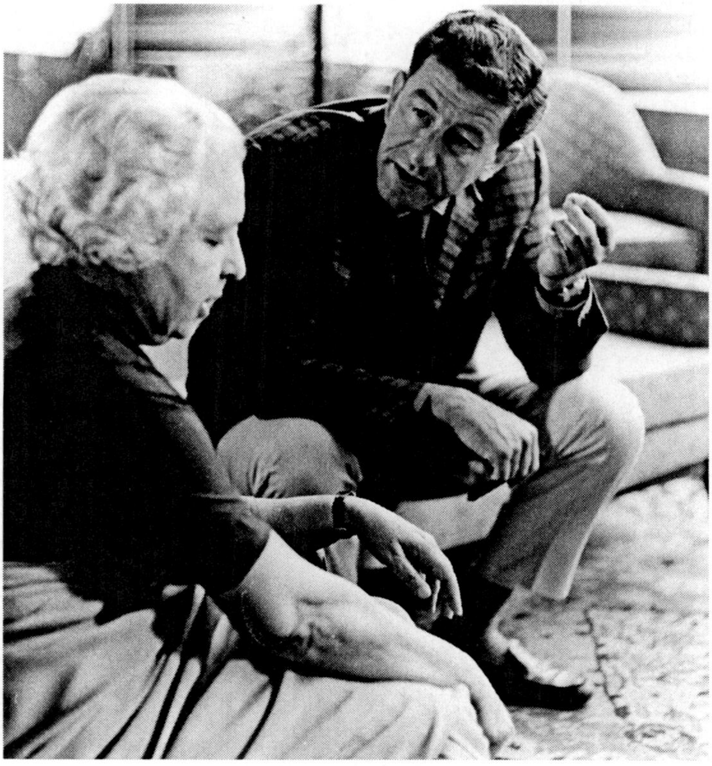

Mrs V. L. Pandit (Nehru's sister), ambassador to America. (Broadlands Archive)

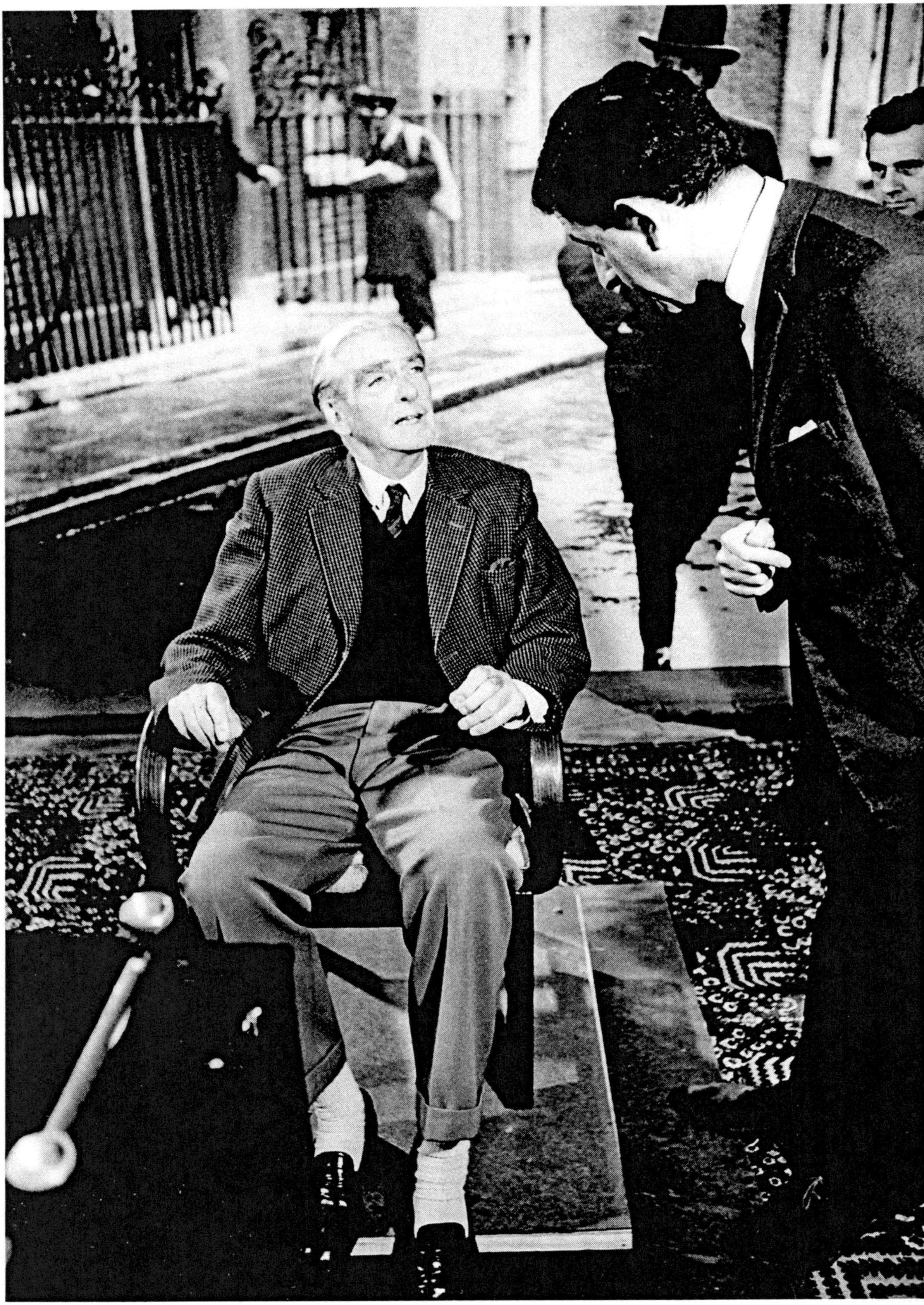

Anthony Eden (Lord Avon). (Broadlands Archive)

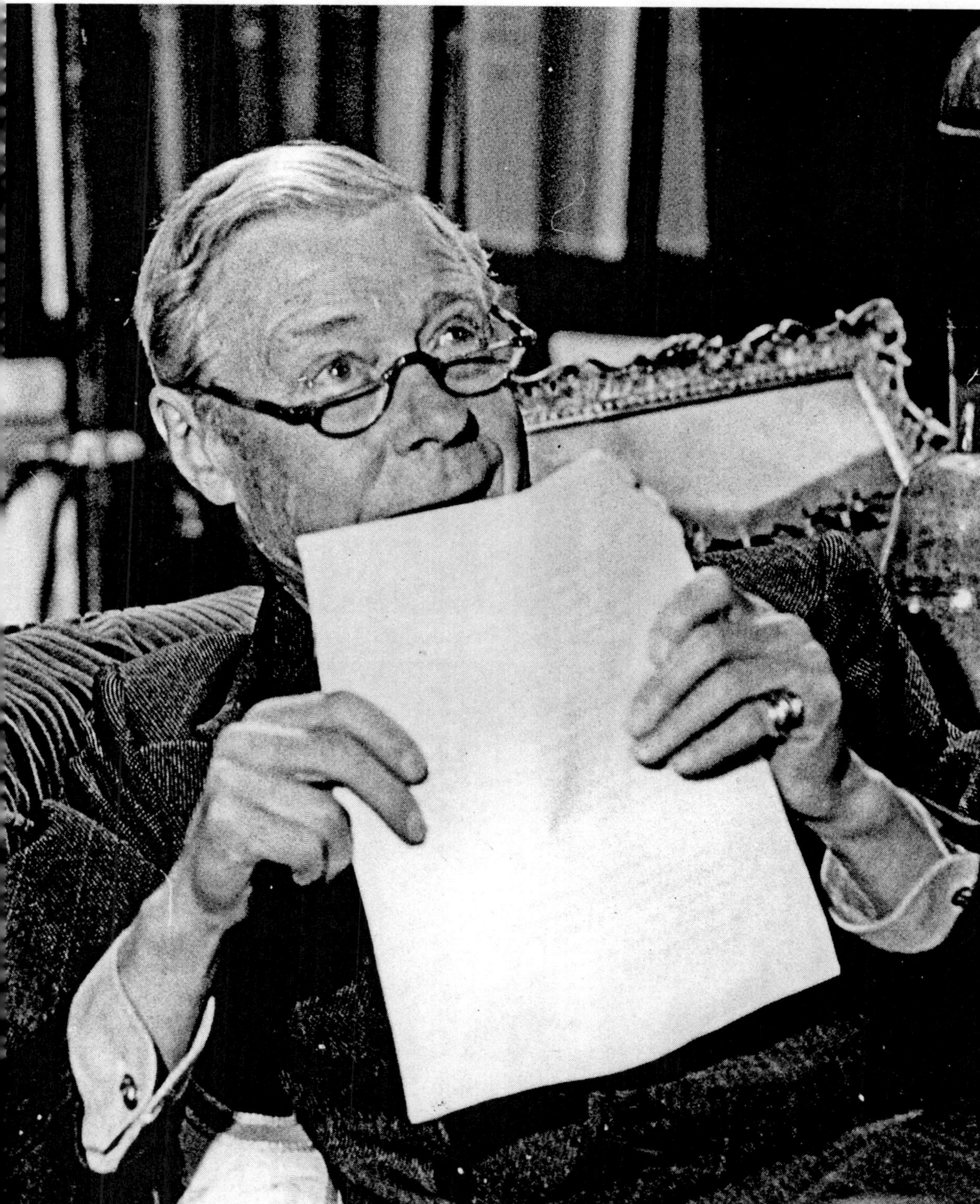

We filmed the Duke of Windsor in his Paris home. (Broadlands Archive)

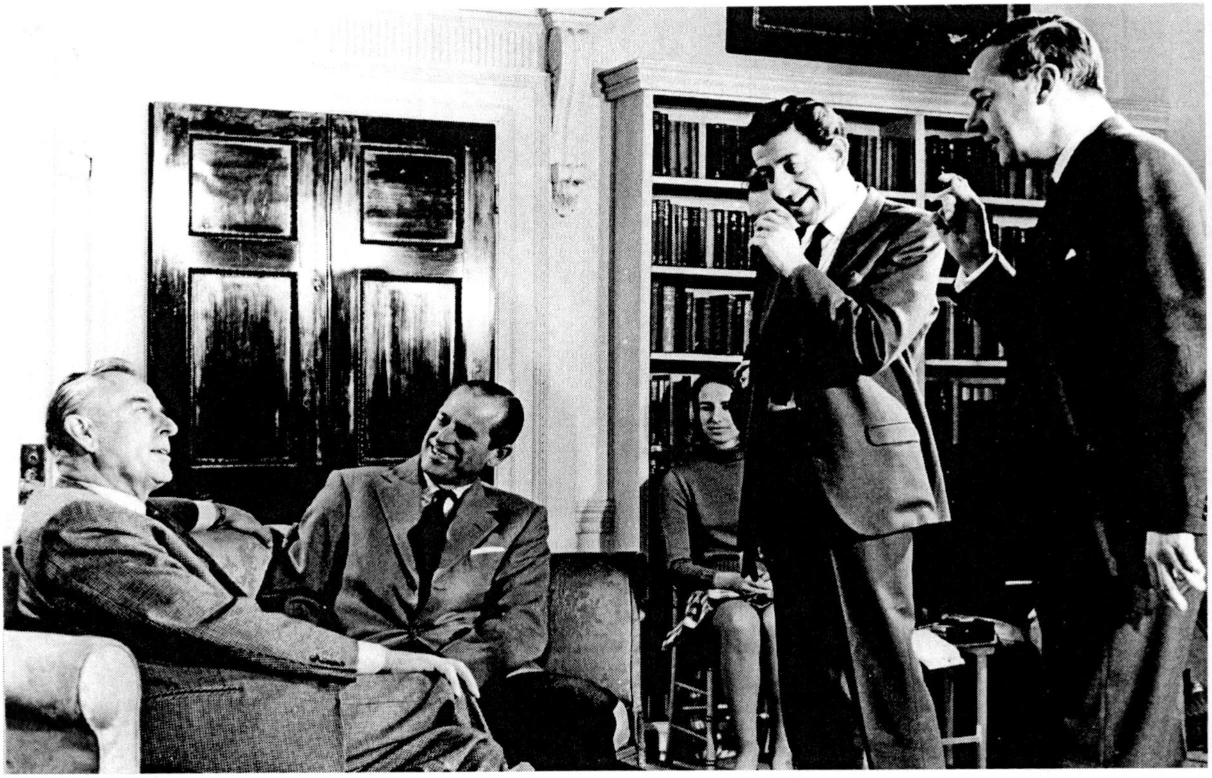
LM with his nephew Prince Philip at Broadlands. (Broadlands Archive)

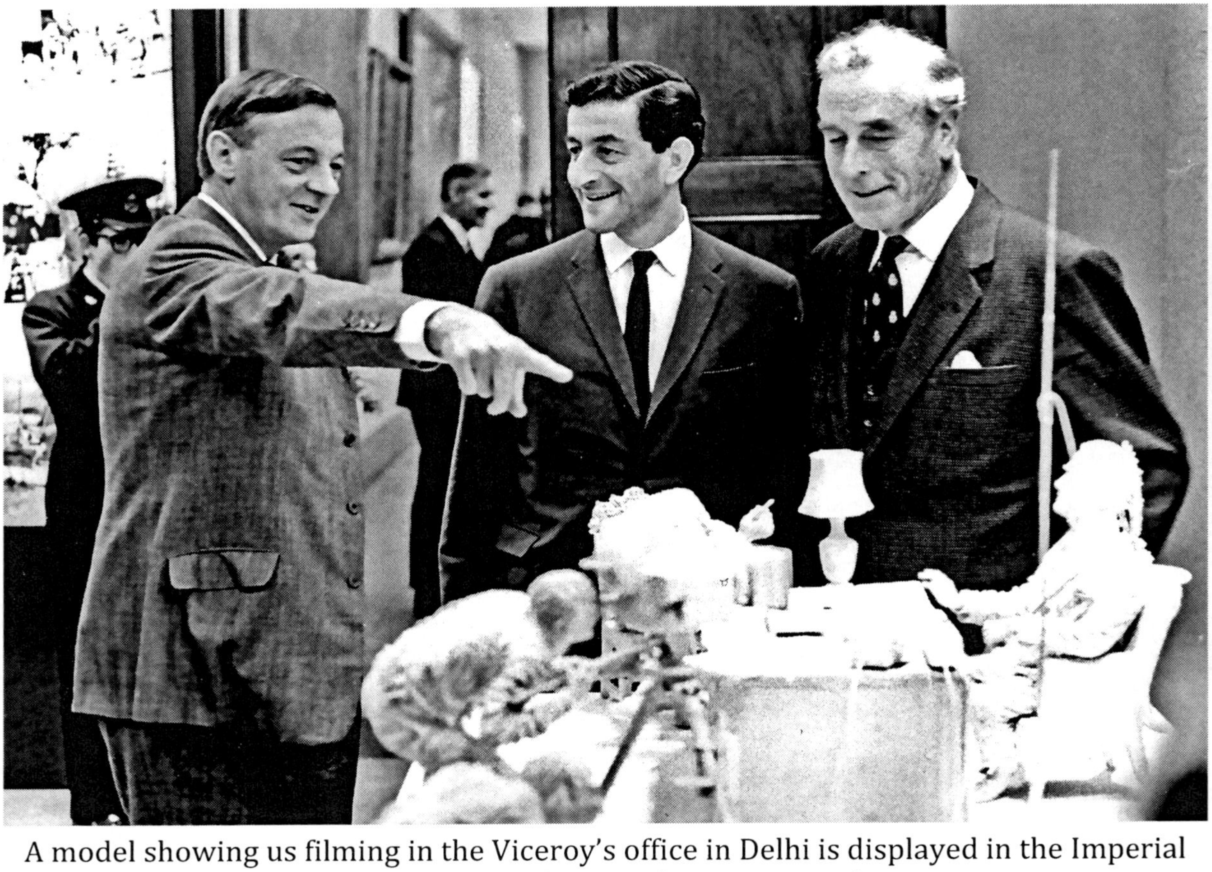
A model showing us filming in the Viceroy's office in Delhi is displayed in the Imperial War Museum. (Imperial War Museum)

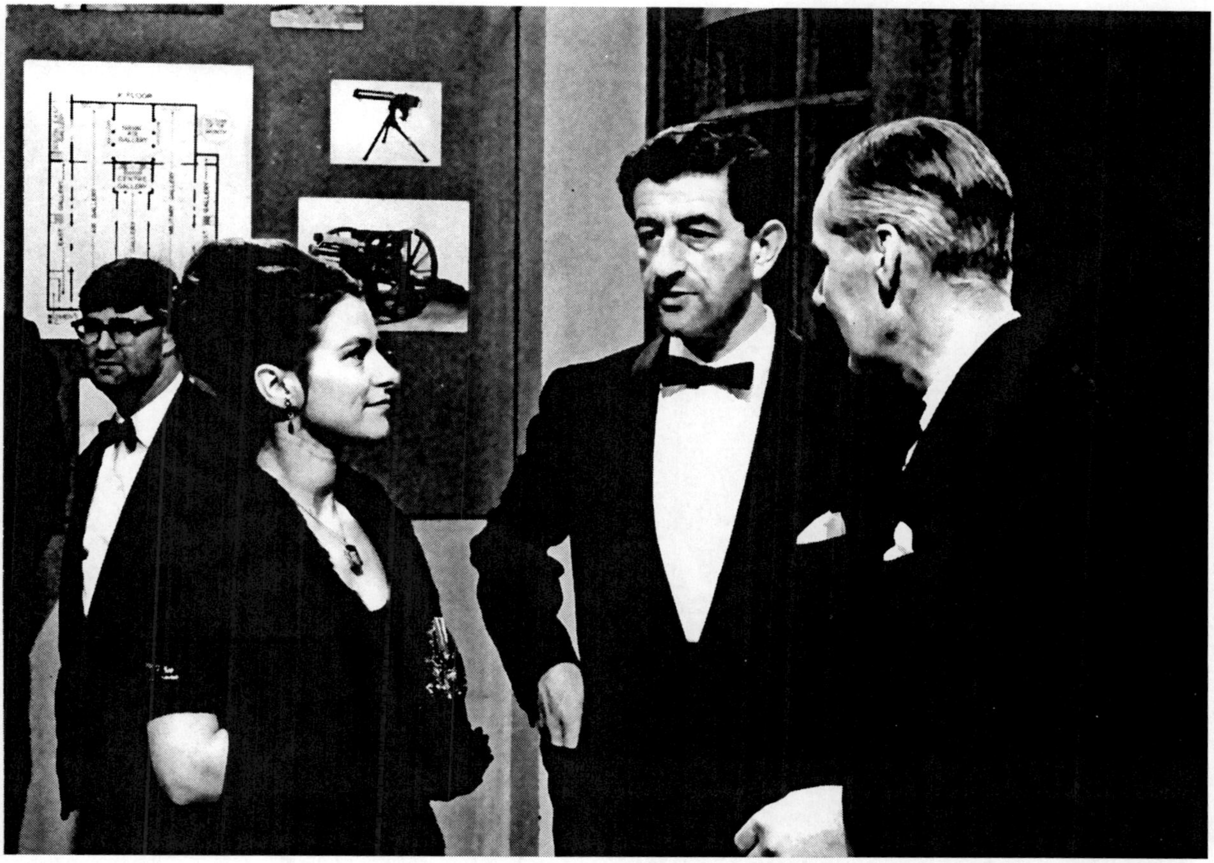

Noble Frankland, Director of the Imperial War Museum, greets the Morleys. (Imperial War Museum)

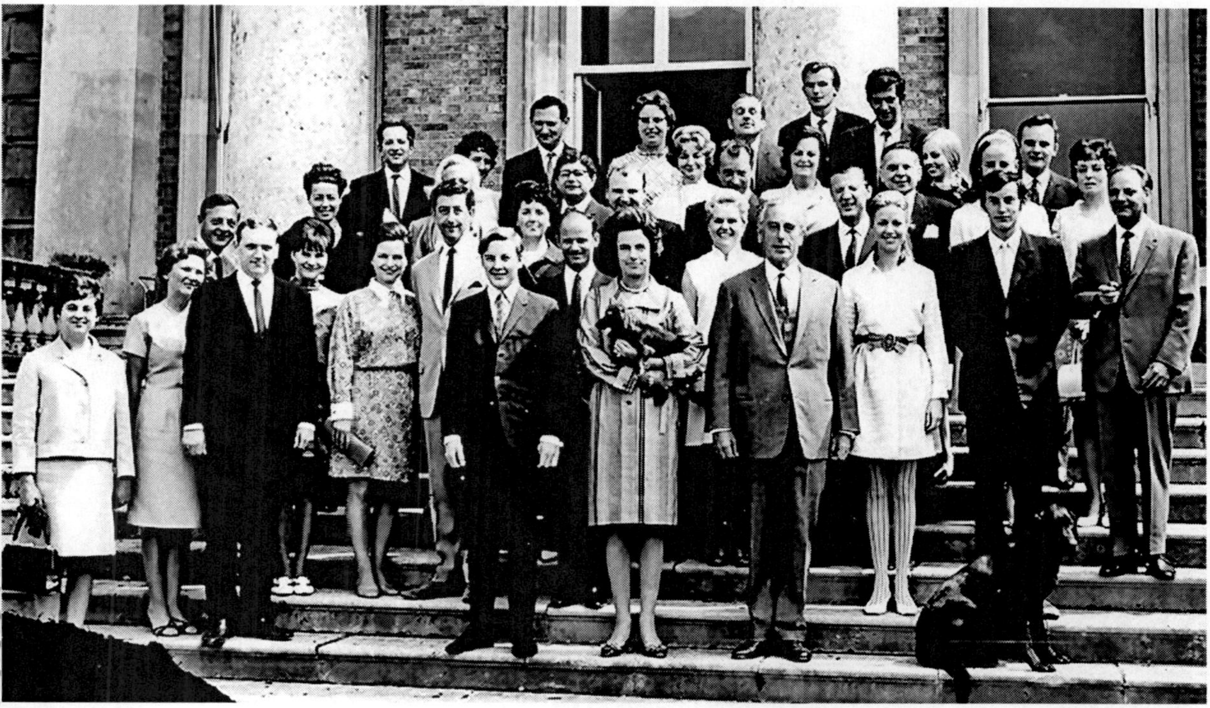

The Mountbatten family throws a farewell party at Broadlands for the whole team, including wives. (Broadlands Archive)

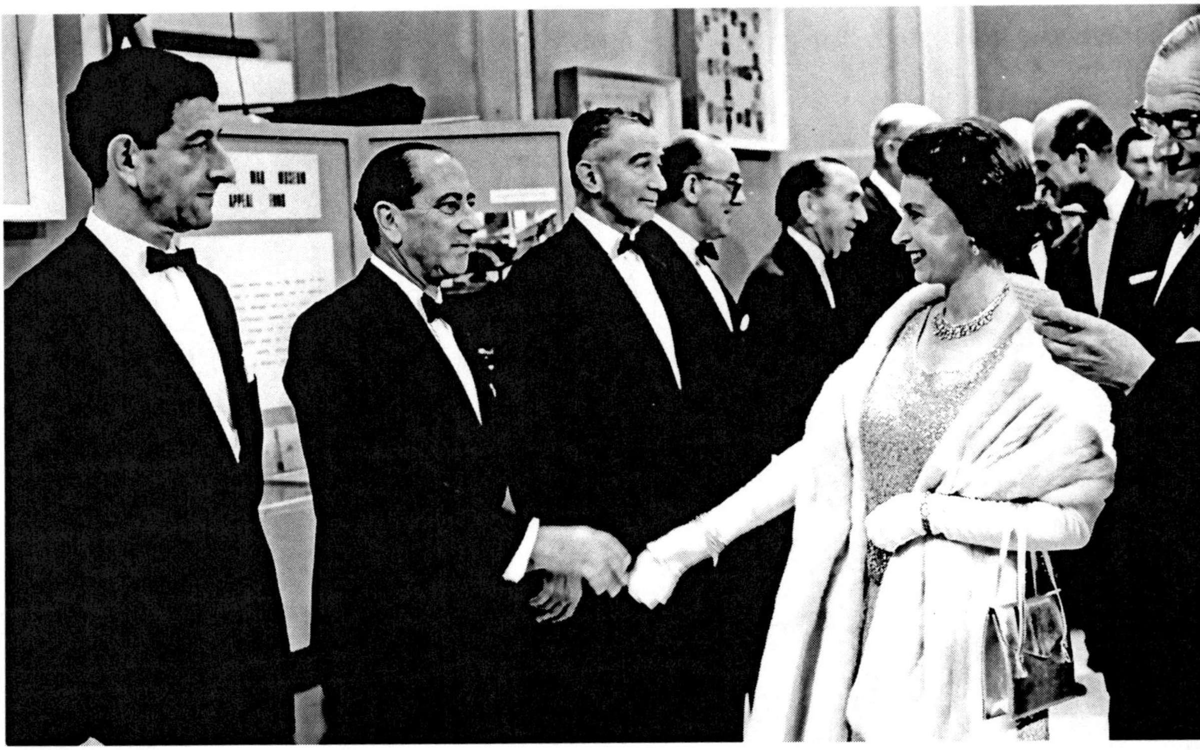

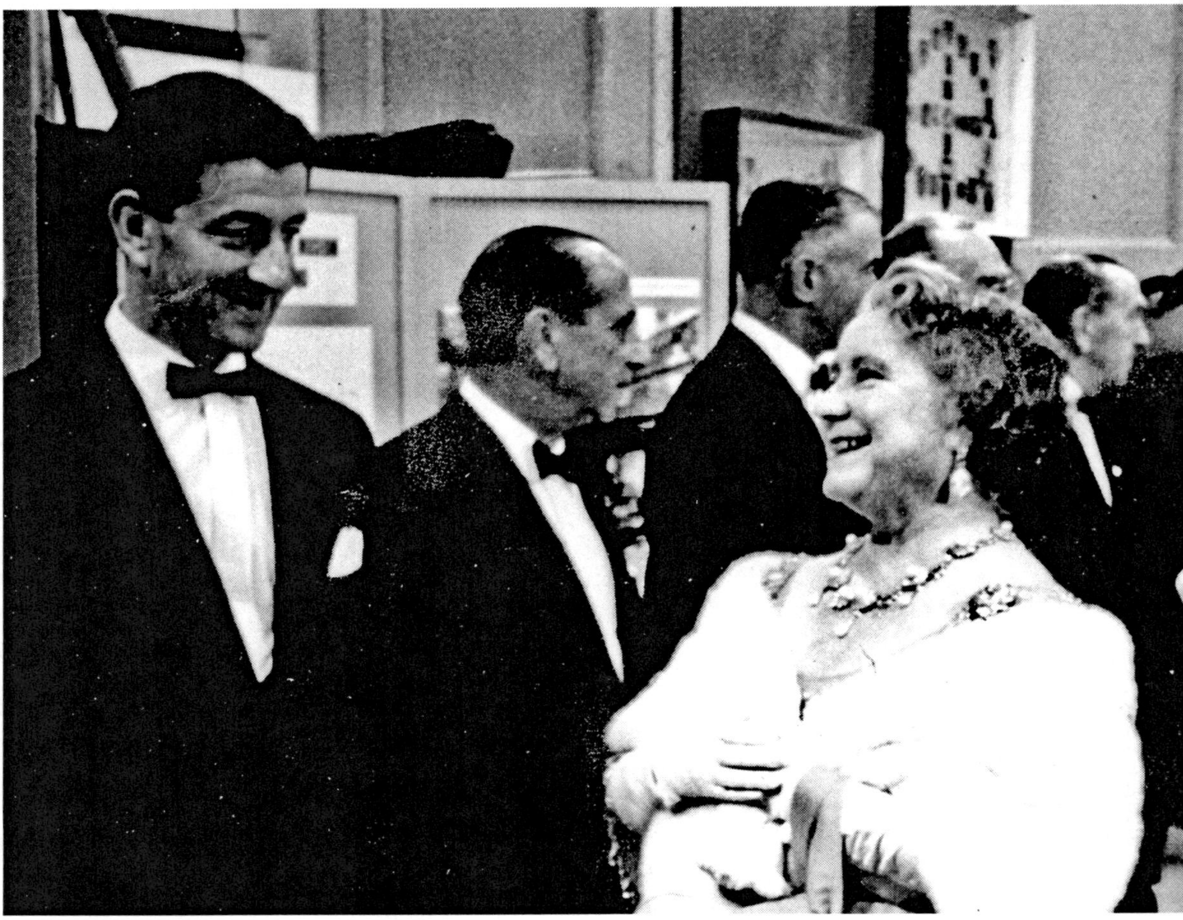

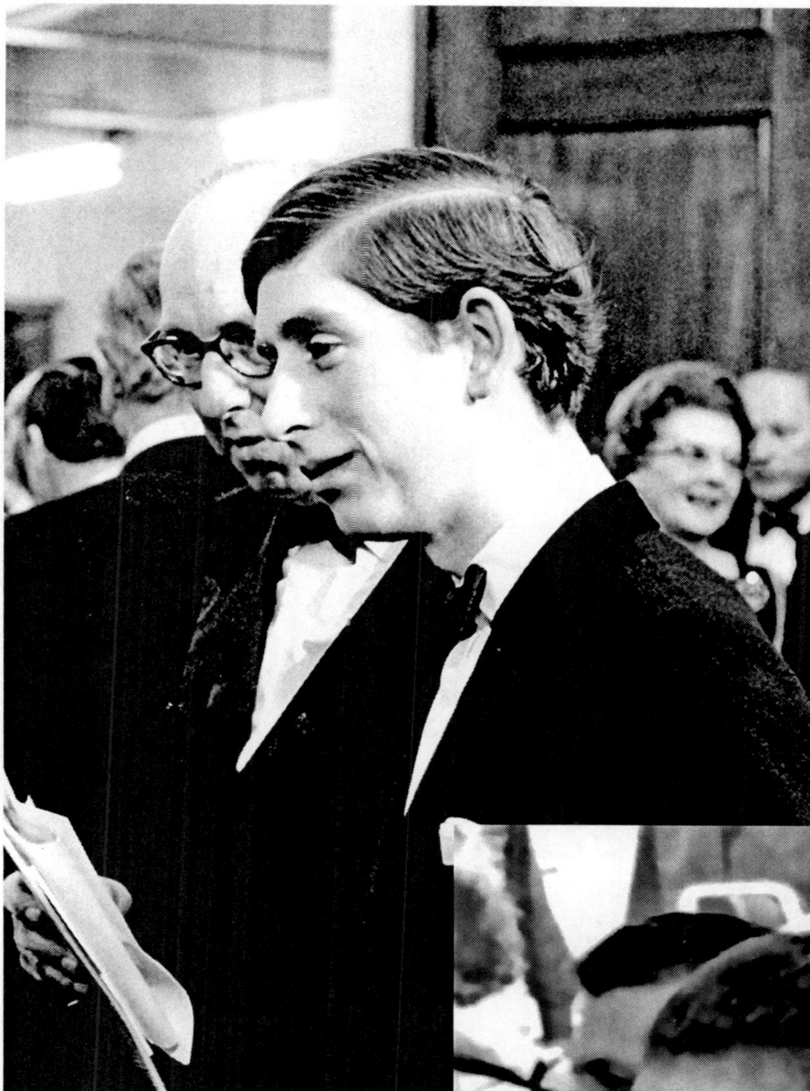

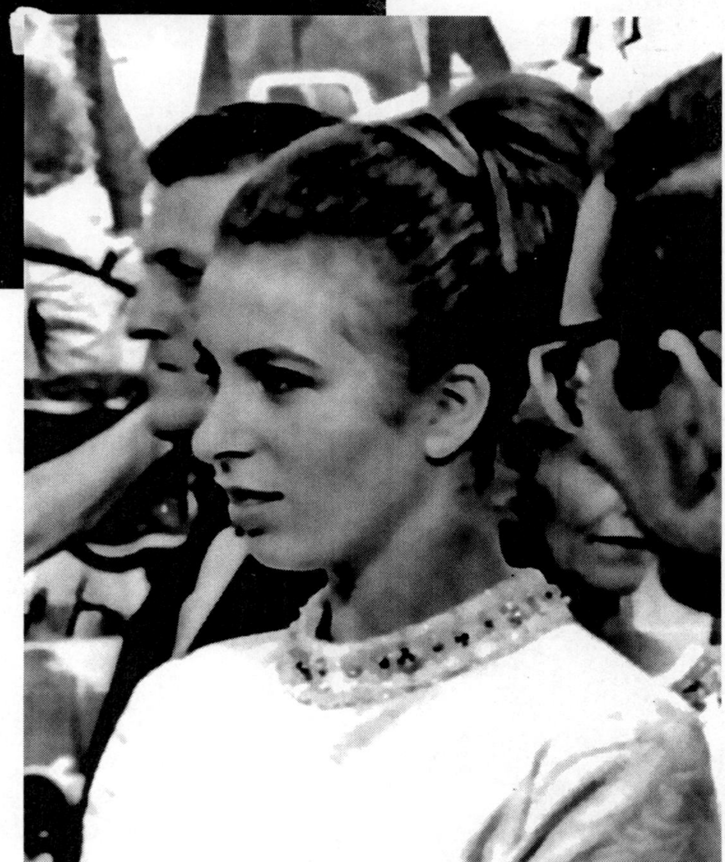

The 'Royal Flush': Imperial War Museum, 19 December 1968. (Imperial War Museum)

The Investiture of Prince Charles, 1 July 1969

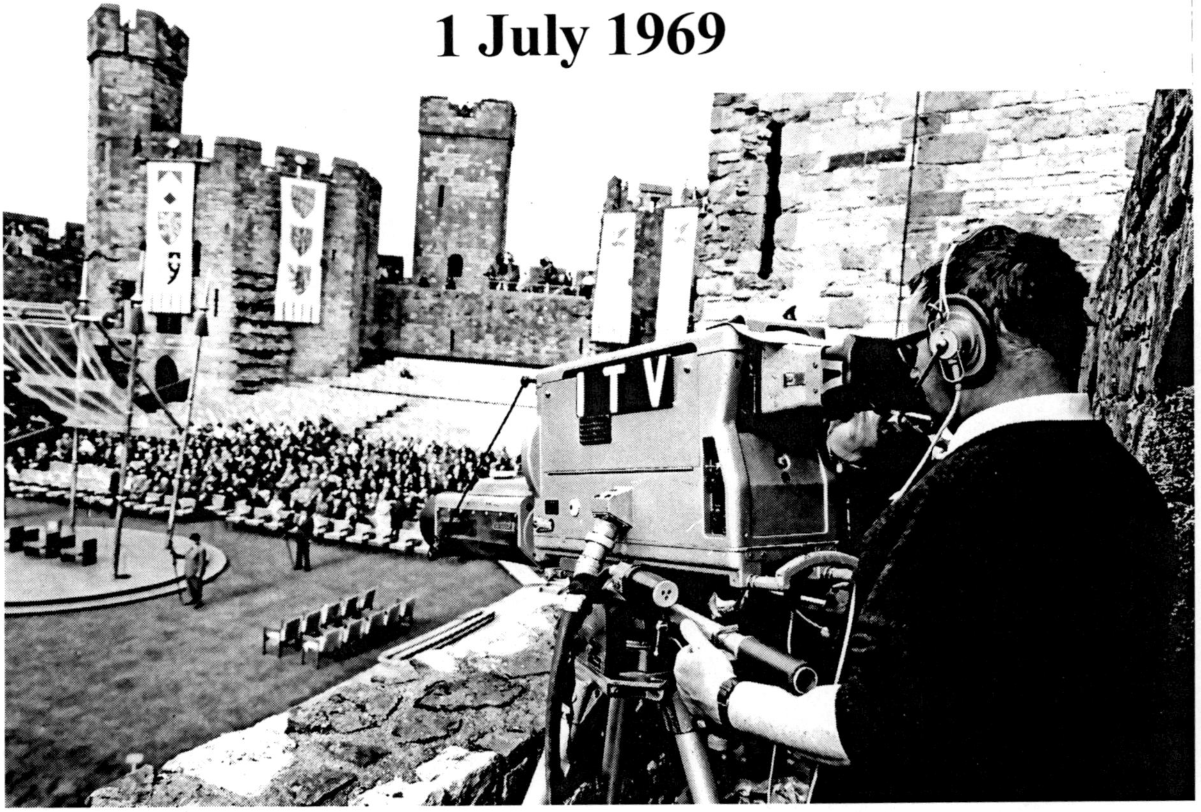

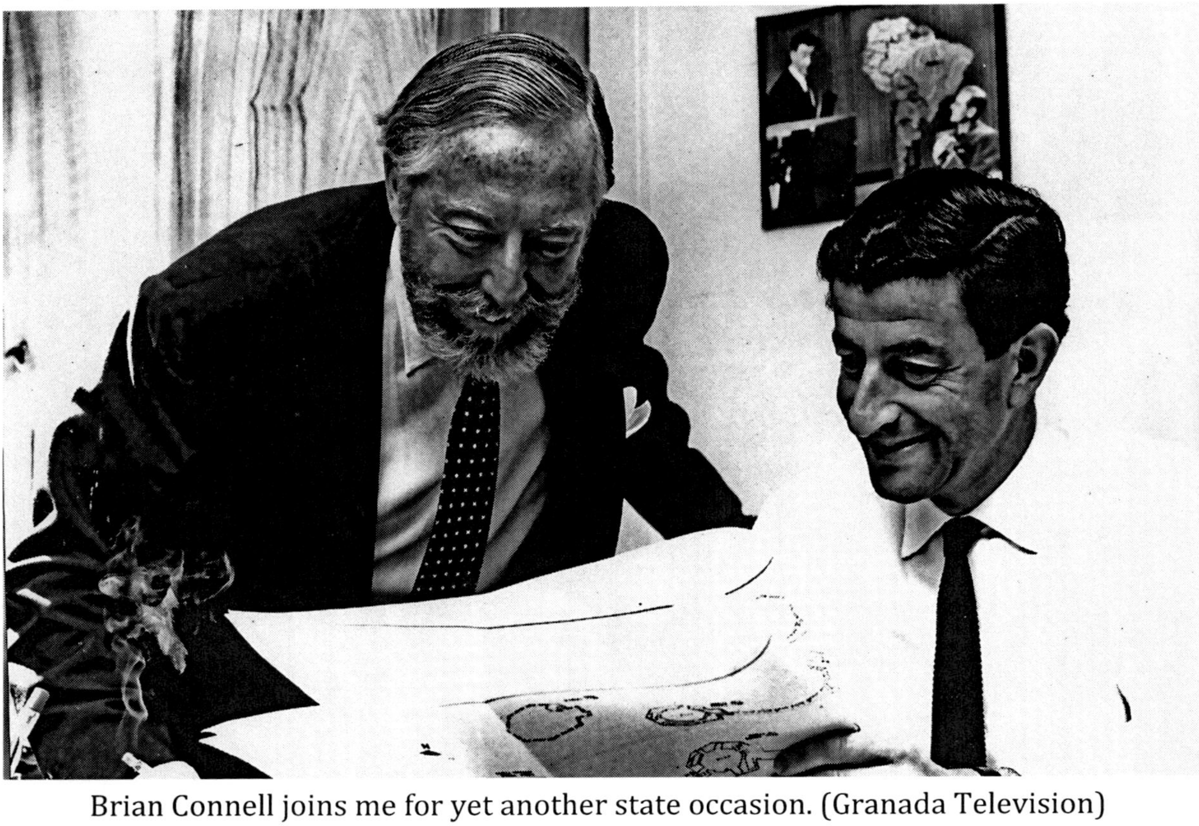

Brian Connell joins me for yet another state occasion. (Granada Television)

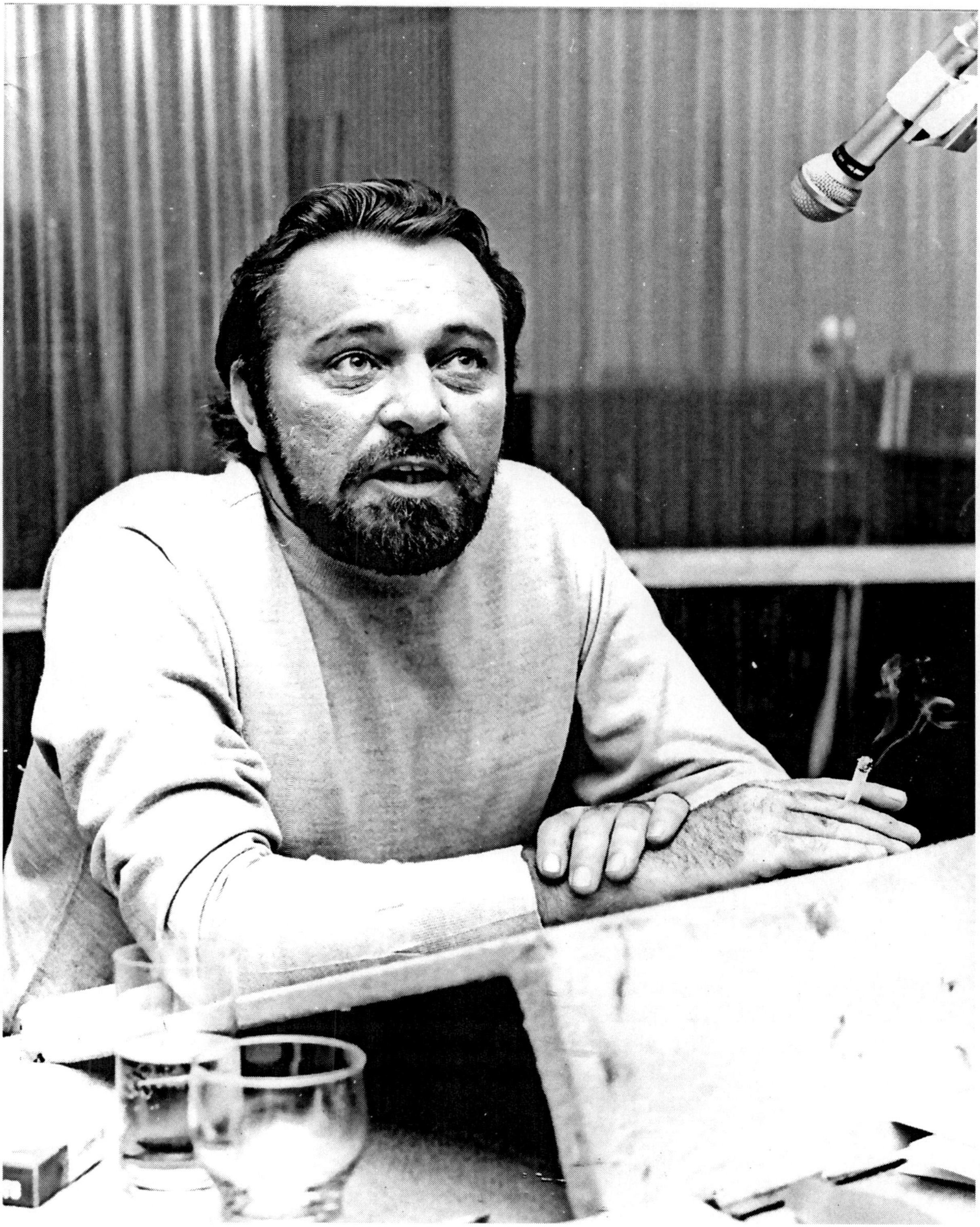

Richard Burton recording the prologue. (Granada Television)

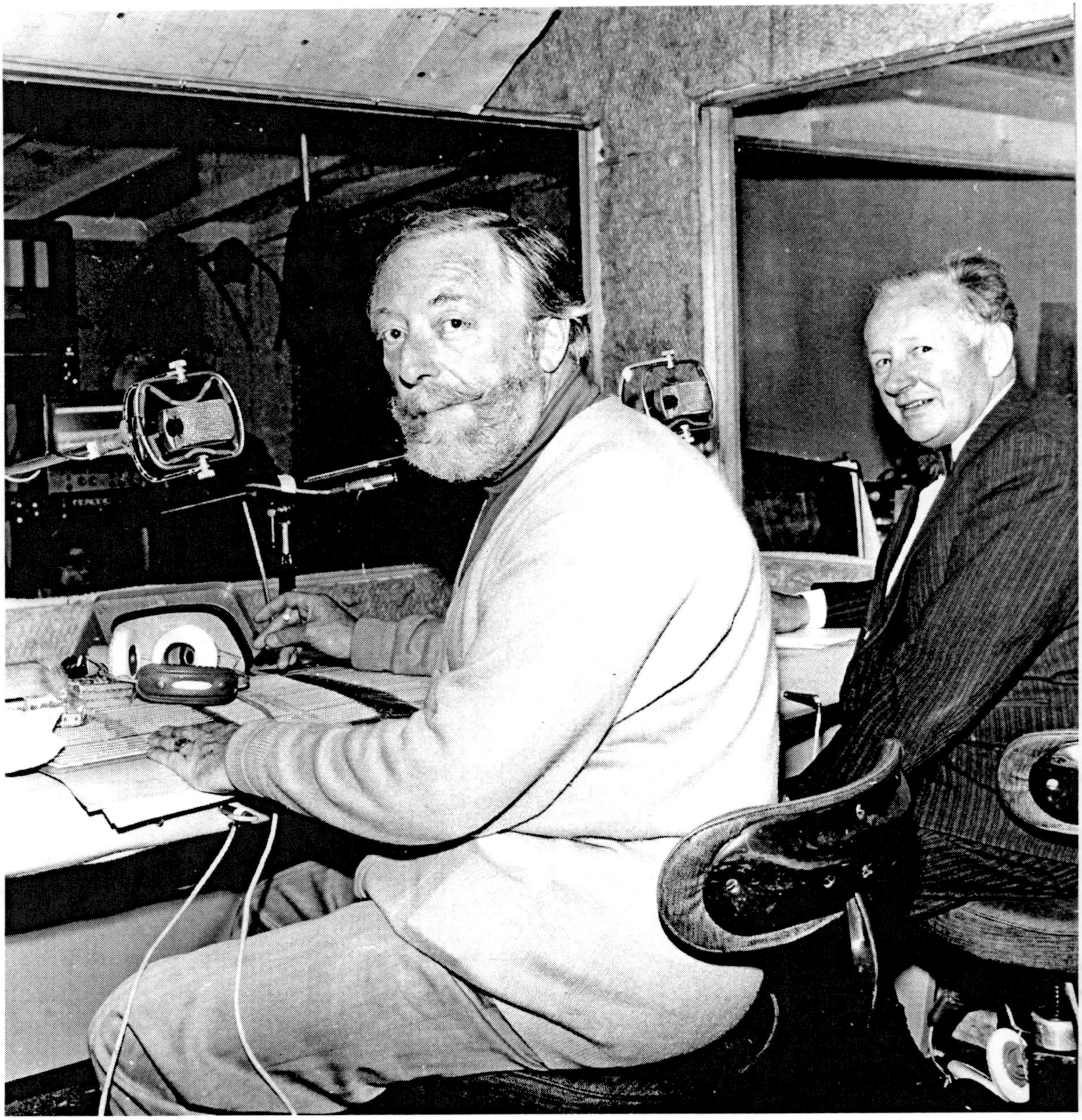

Brian Connell in the commentators' booth with Wynford Vaughan-Thomas.
(Granada Television)

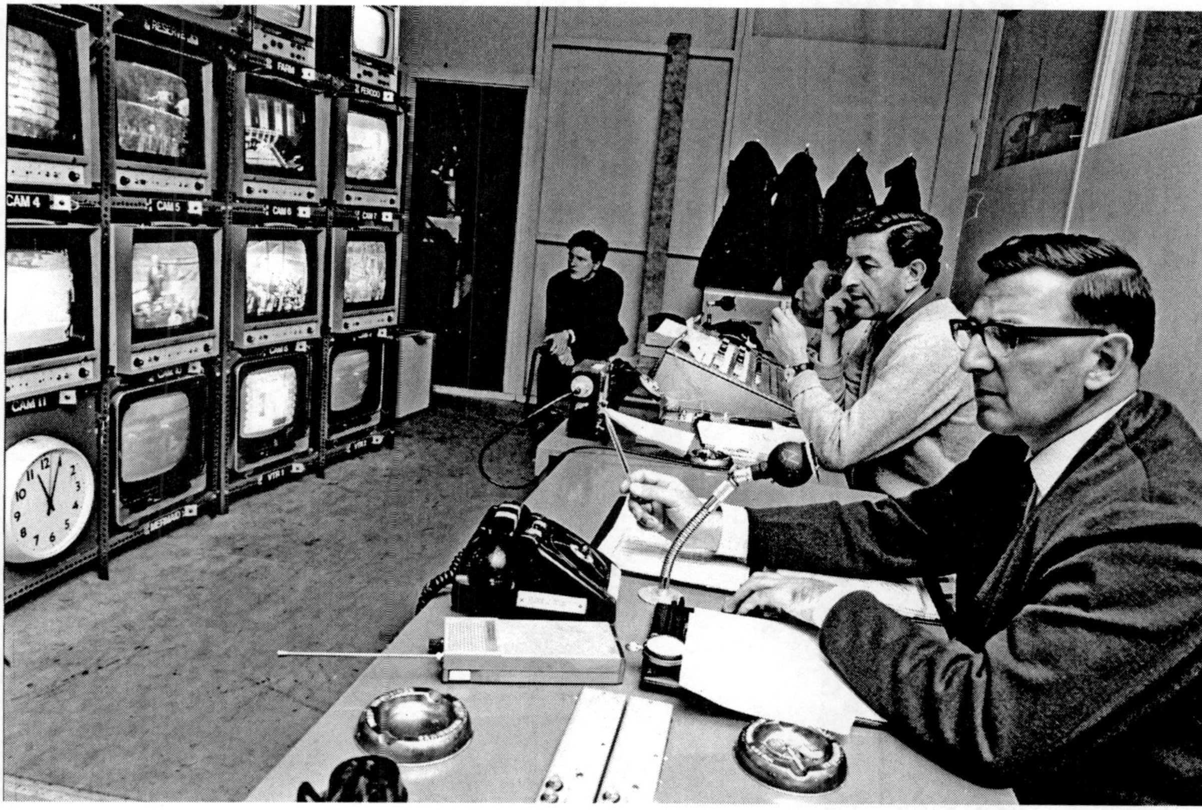

On air with twenty-eight cameras. (Granada Television)

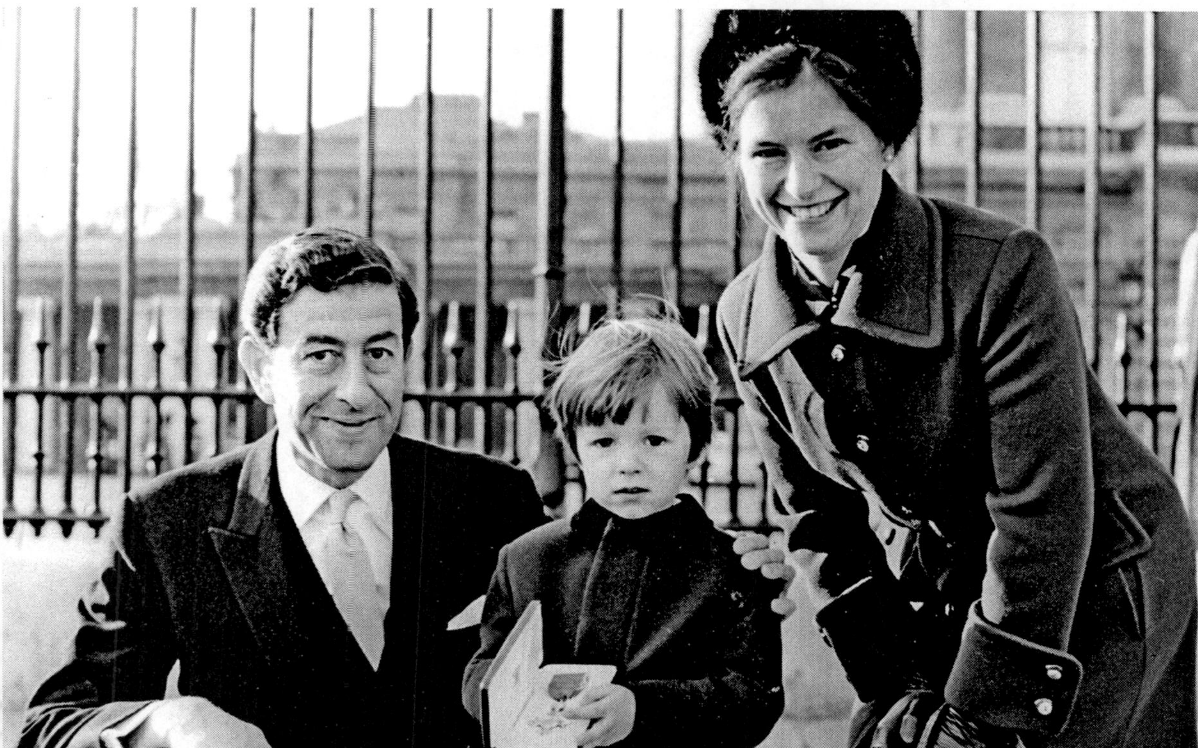

At Buckingham Palace – for my second investiture that year. Jonathan, aged three, shows off the OBE. (Rediffusion Television)

The Mighty Continent, 1971–75

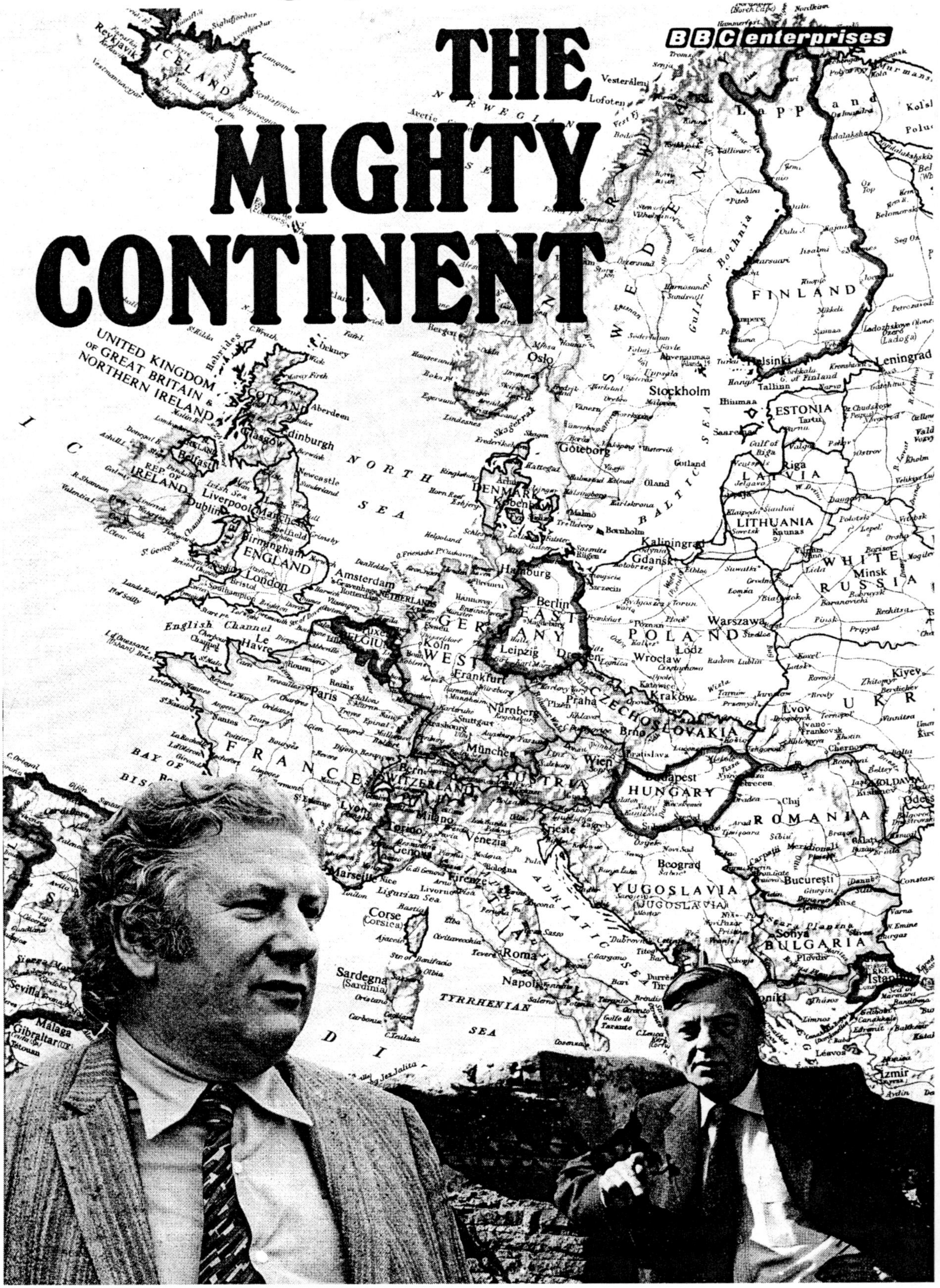

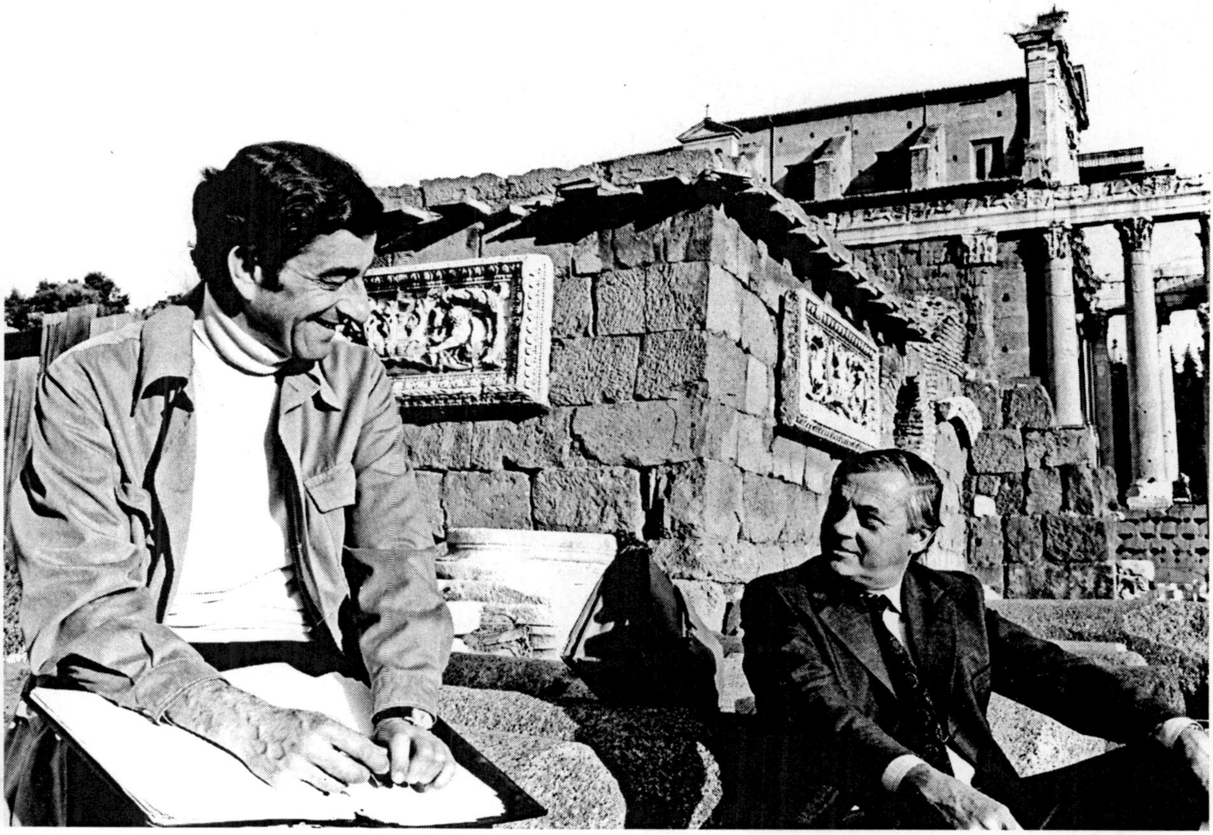

In the Forum in Rome. I teamed up with John Terraine again for another three-year stint. (BBC)

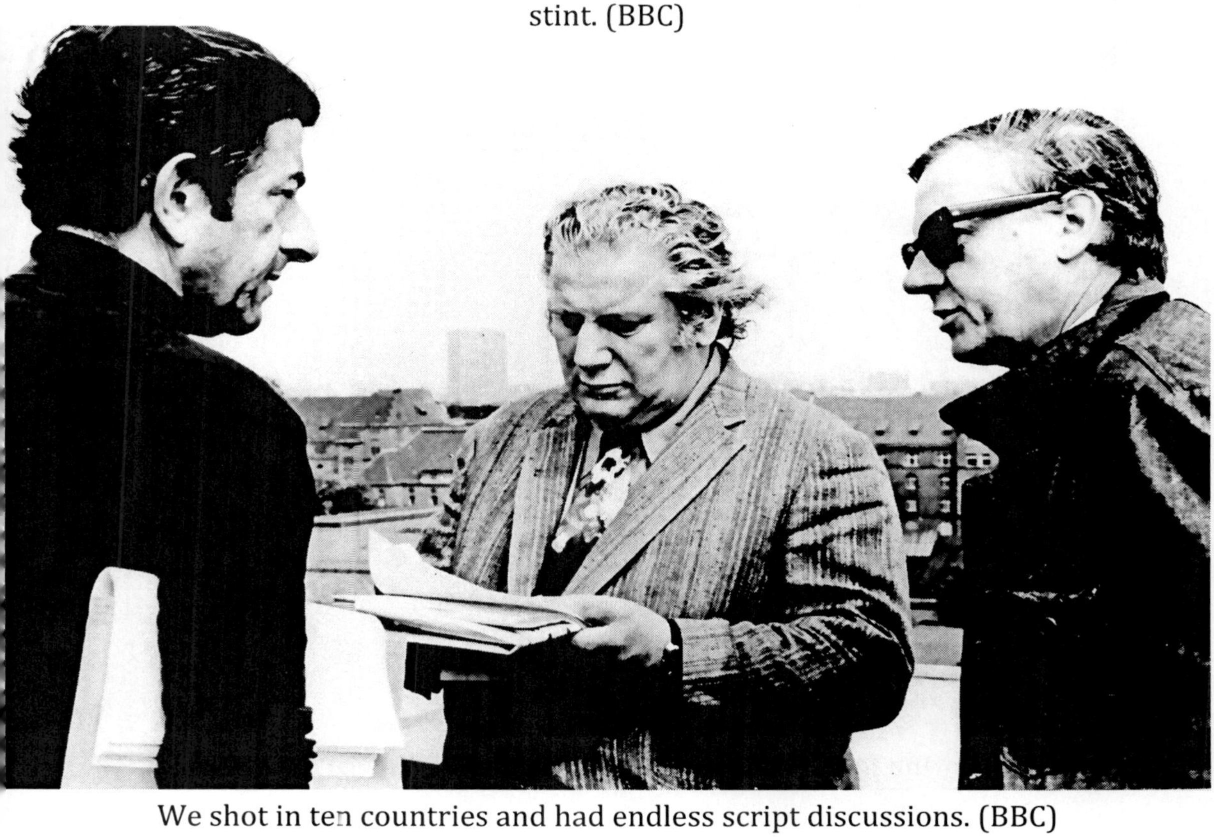

We shot in ten countries and had endless script discussions. (BBC)

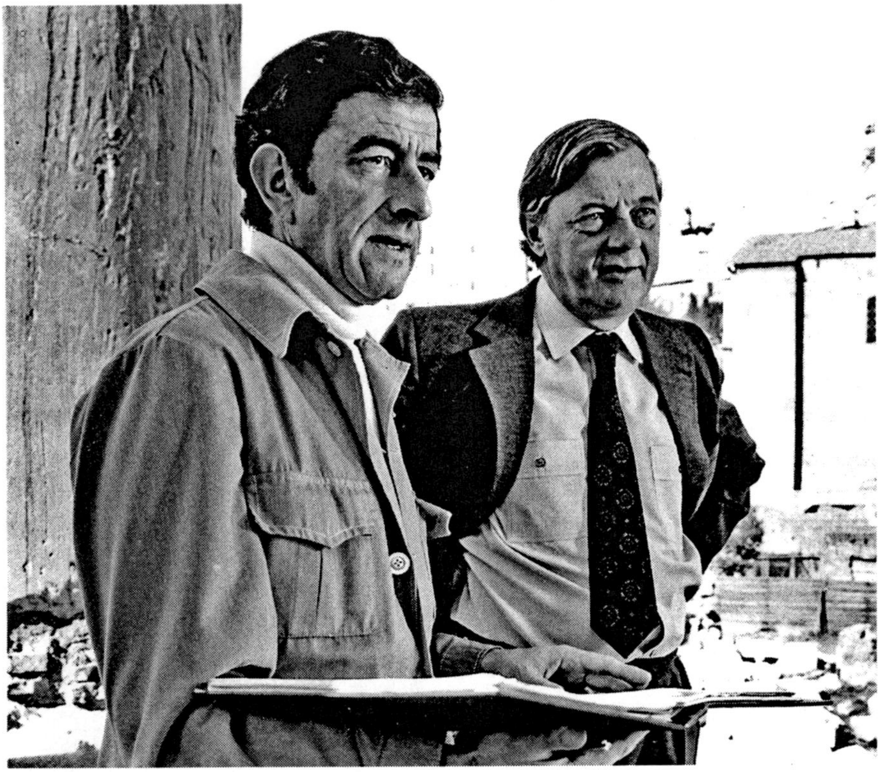

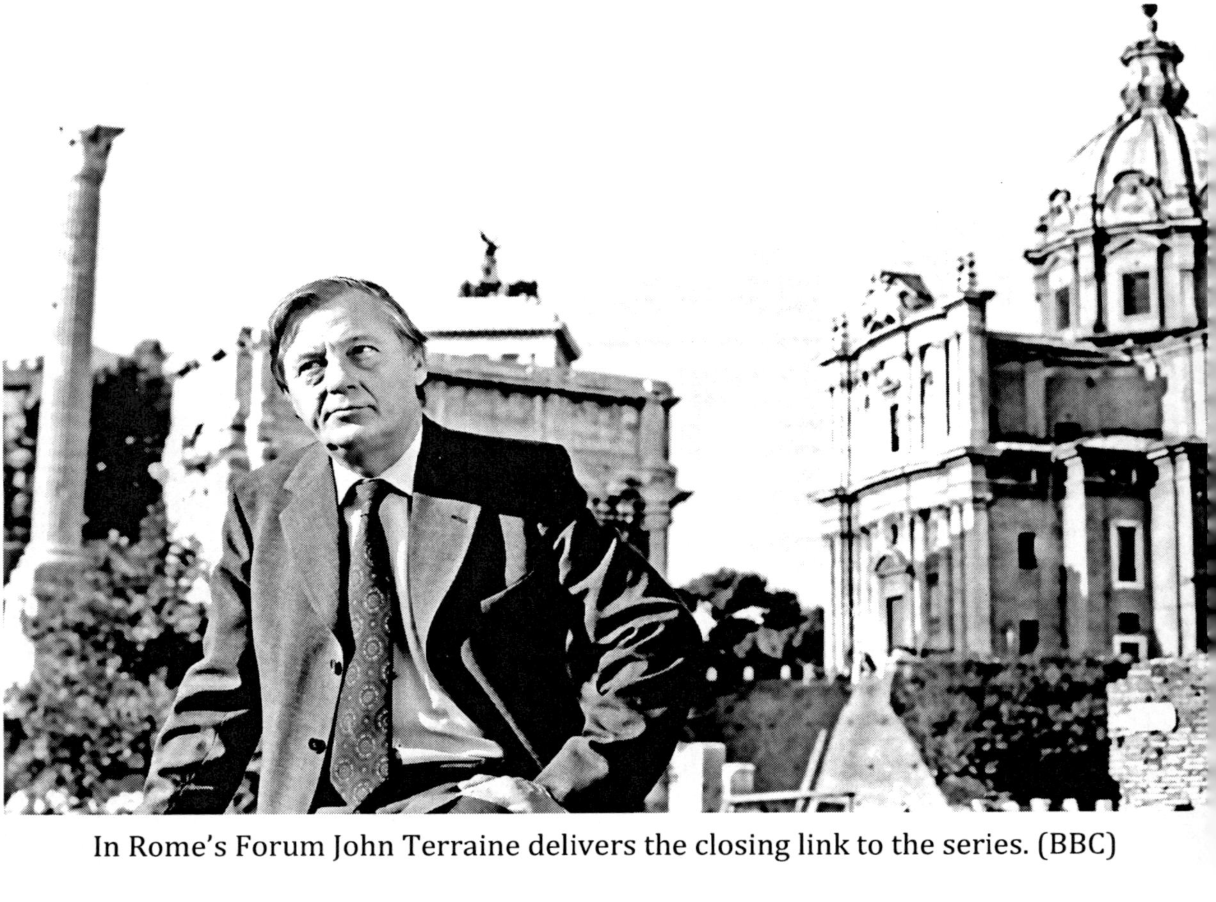

In Rome's Forum John Terraine delivers the closing link to the series. (BBC)

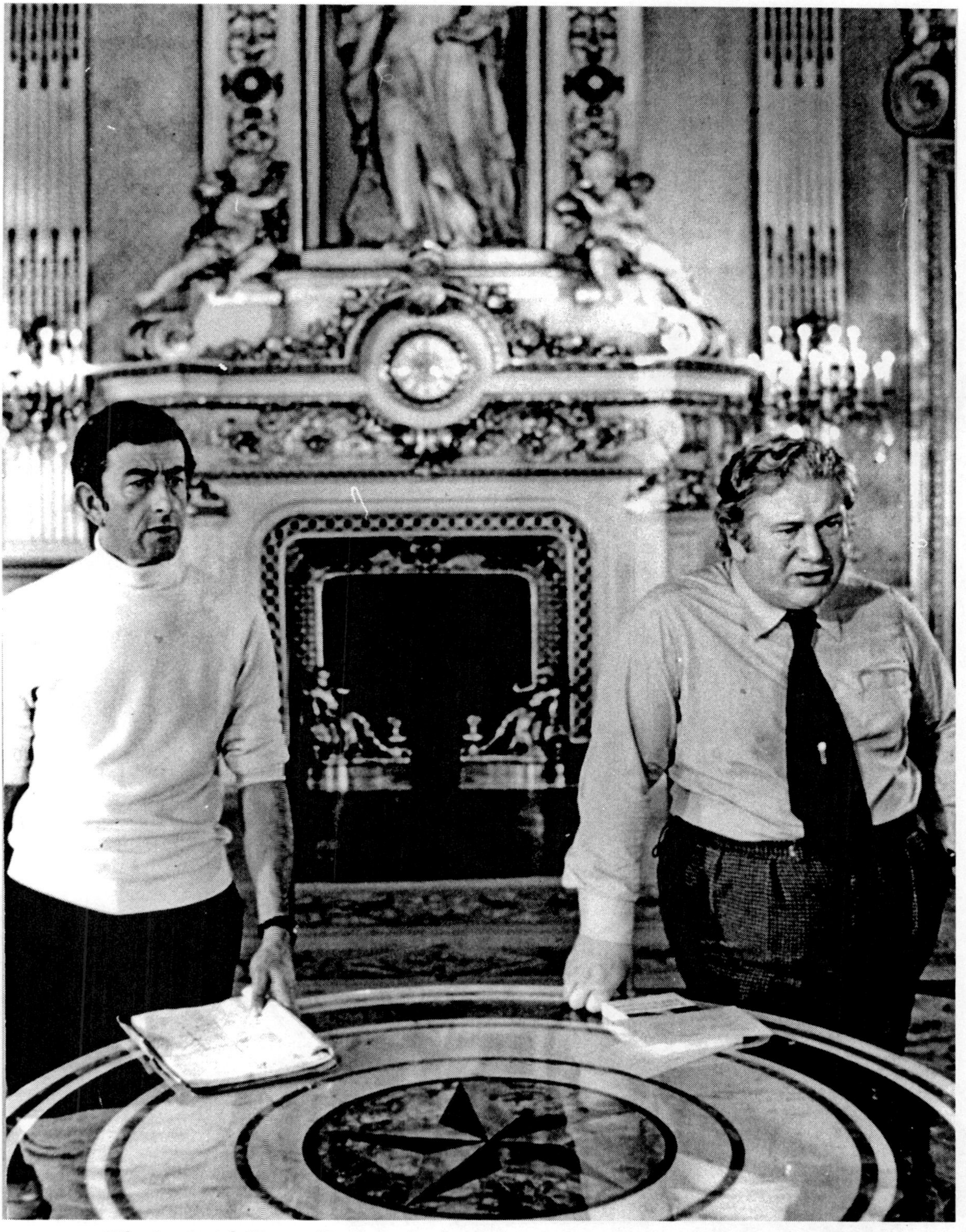

Filming with Peter Ustinov in the Schönbrunn Palace, Vienna. (BBC)

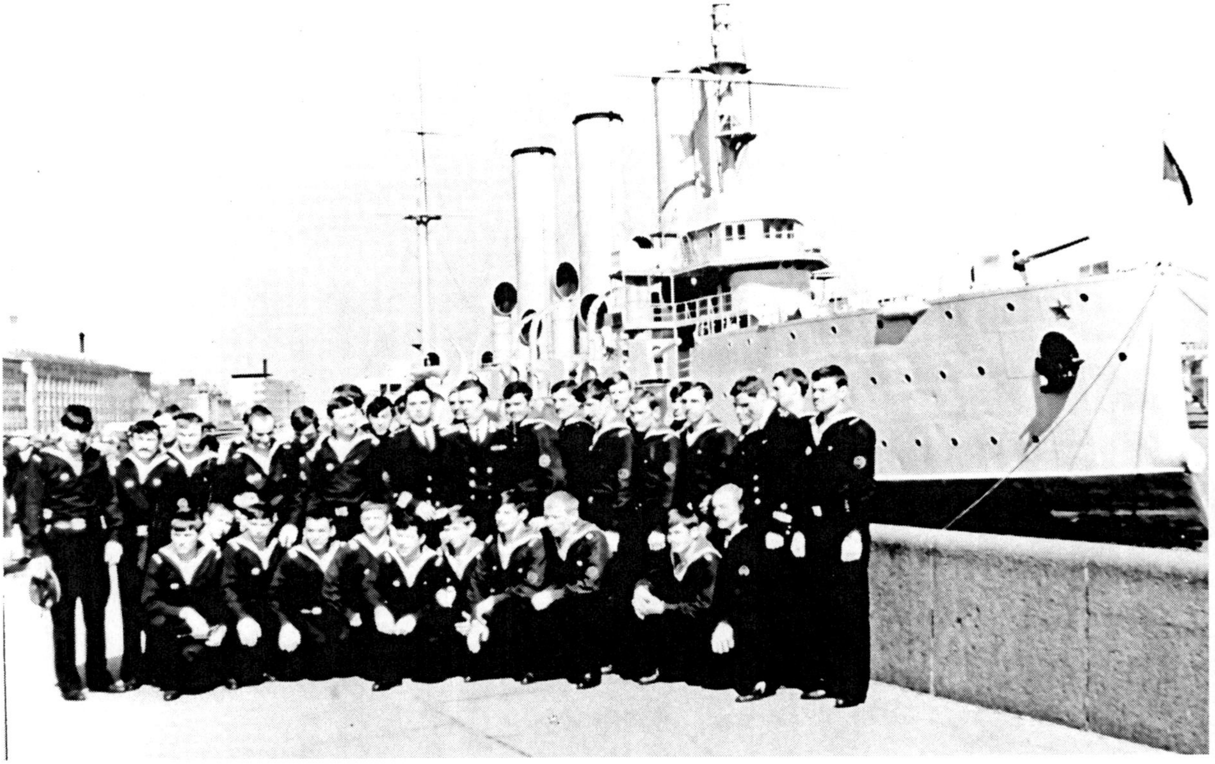

Naval cadets in Leningrad visit the cruiser *Aurora*, which fired the first shot in 1917, marking the start of the Russian Revolution. (BBC)

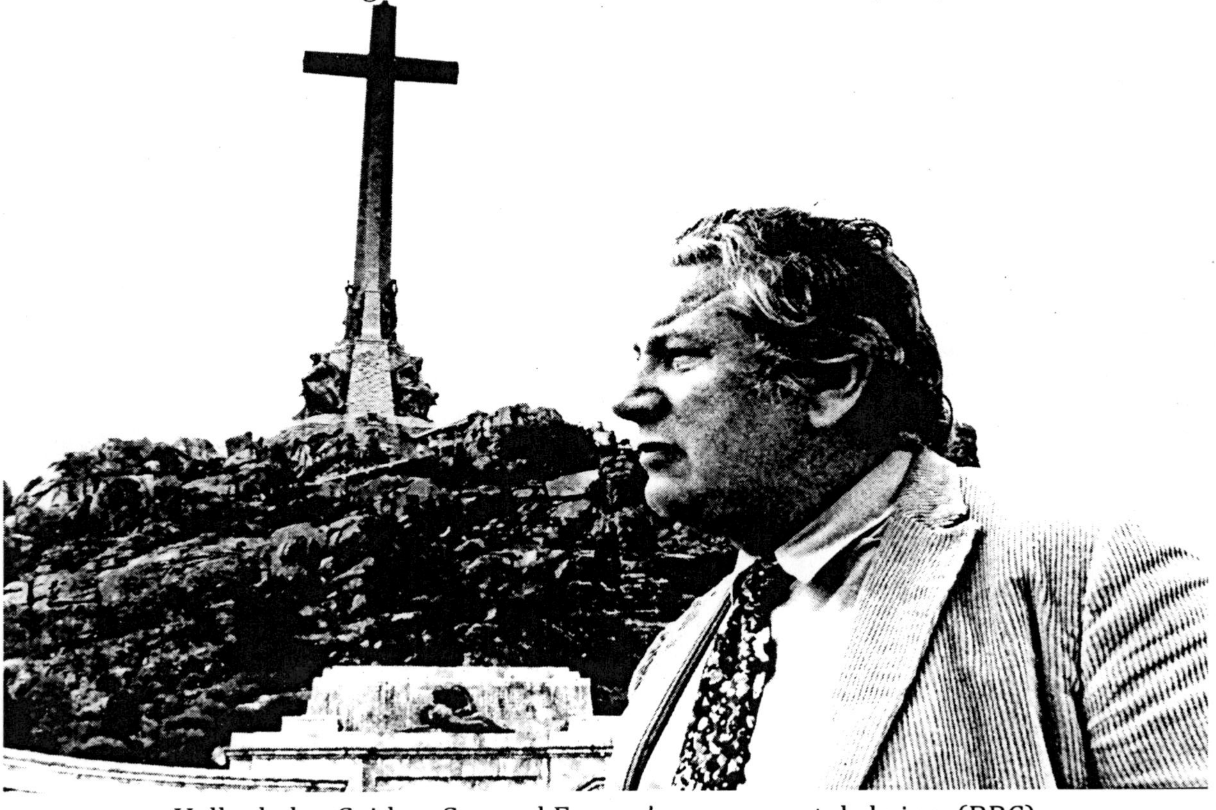

Valle de los Caidos, General Franco's monumental shrine. (BBC)

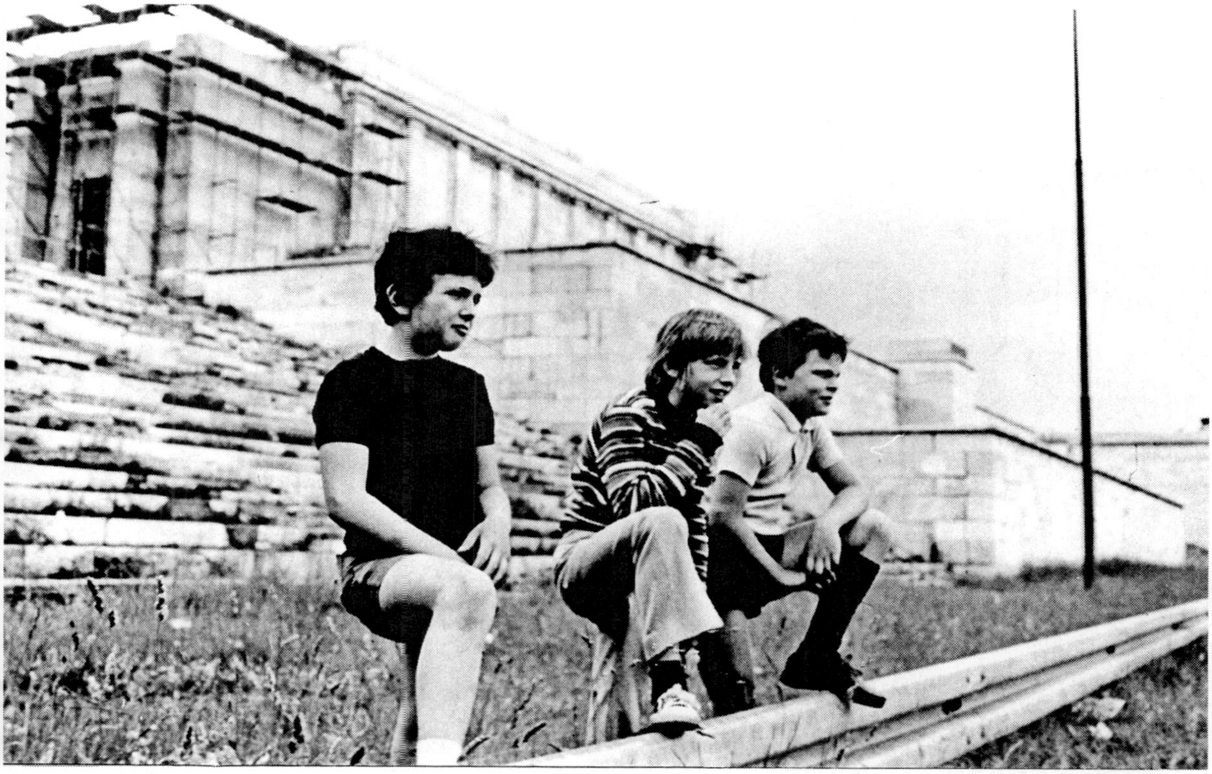

Built by Speer, the massive focal point of Hitler's Nürnberg rallies – and a good skateboard venue for today's children. (BBC)

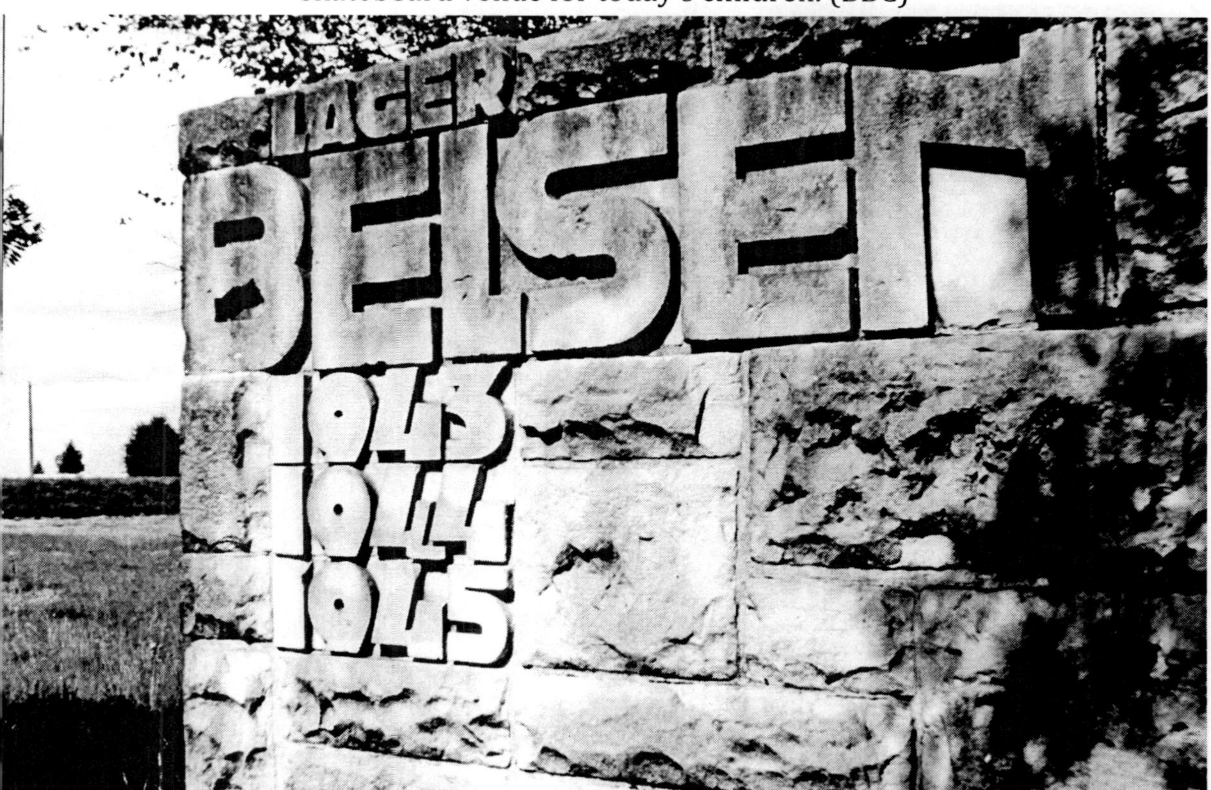

A monument to millions of Nazi victims. (BBC)

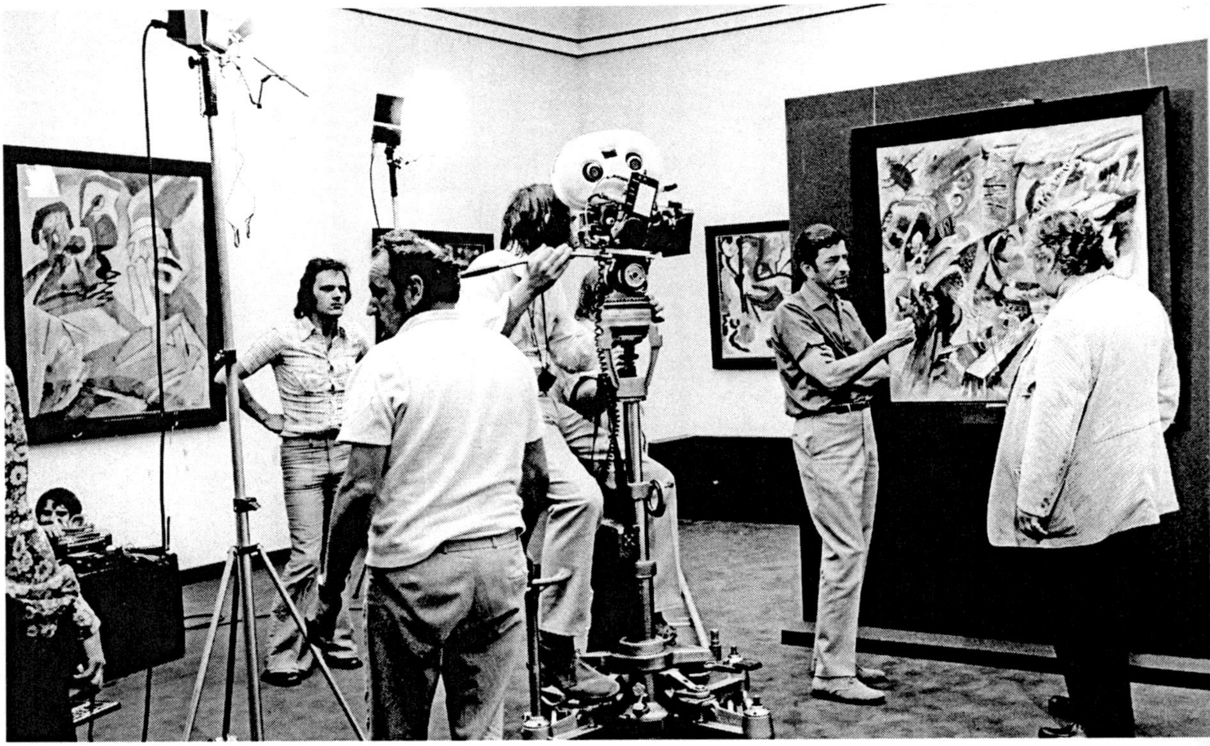

The Blaue Reiter Gallery in Munich with Kandinsky, Paul Klee, Franz Marc and many others. (BBC)

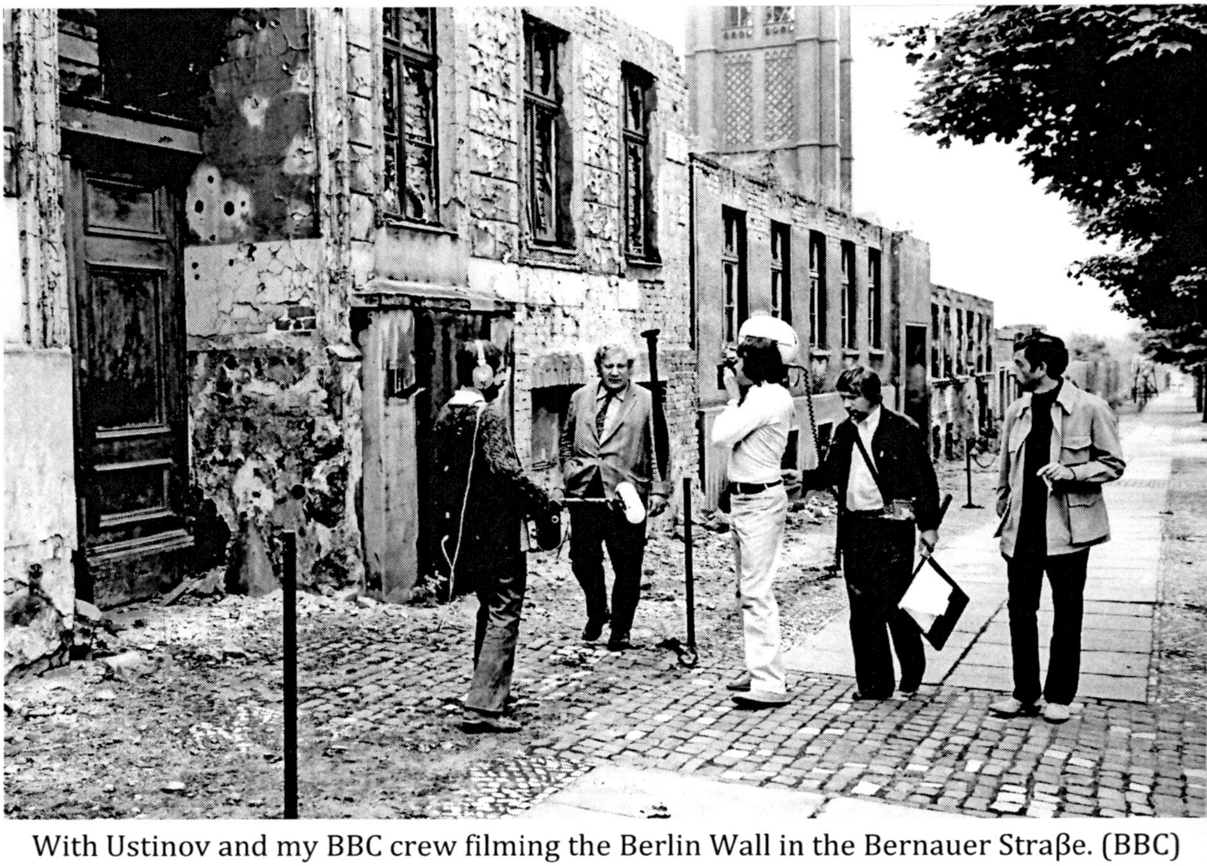

With Ustinov and my BBC crew filming the Berlin Wall in the Bernauer Straβe. (BBC)

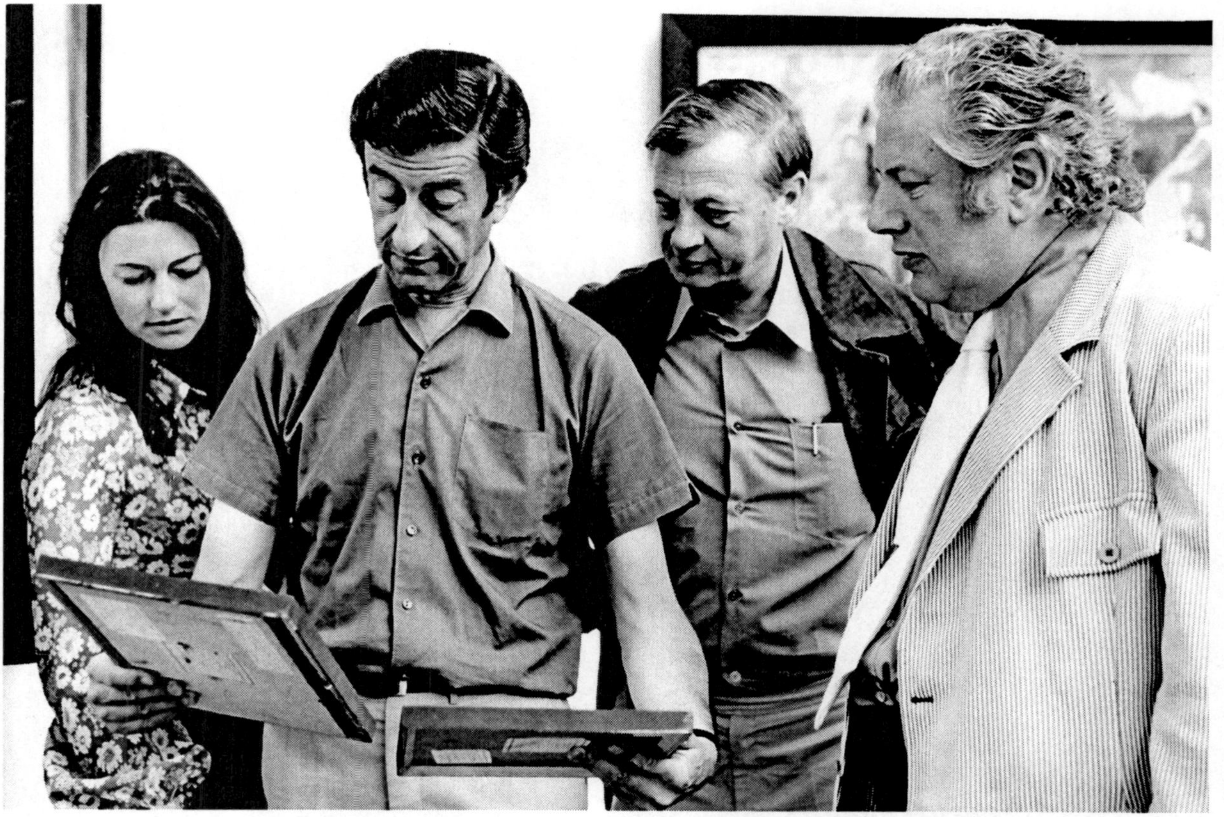

Annie Hewitt, my BBC PA, joins the selection committee. (BBC)

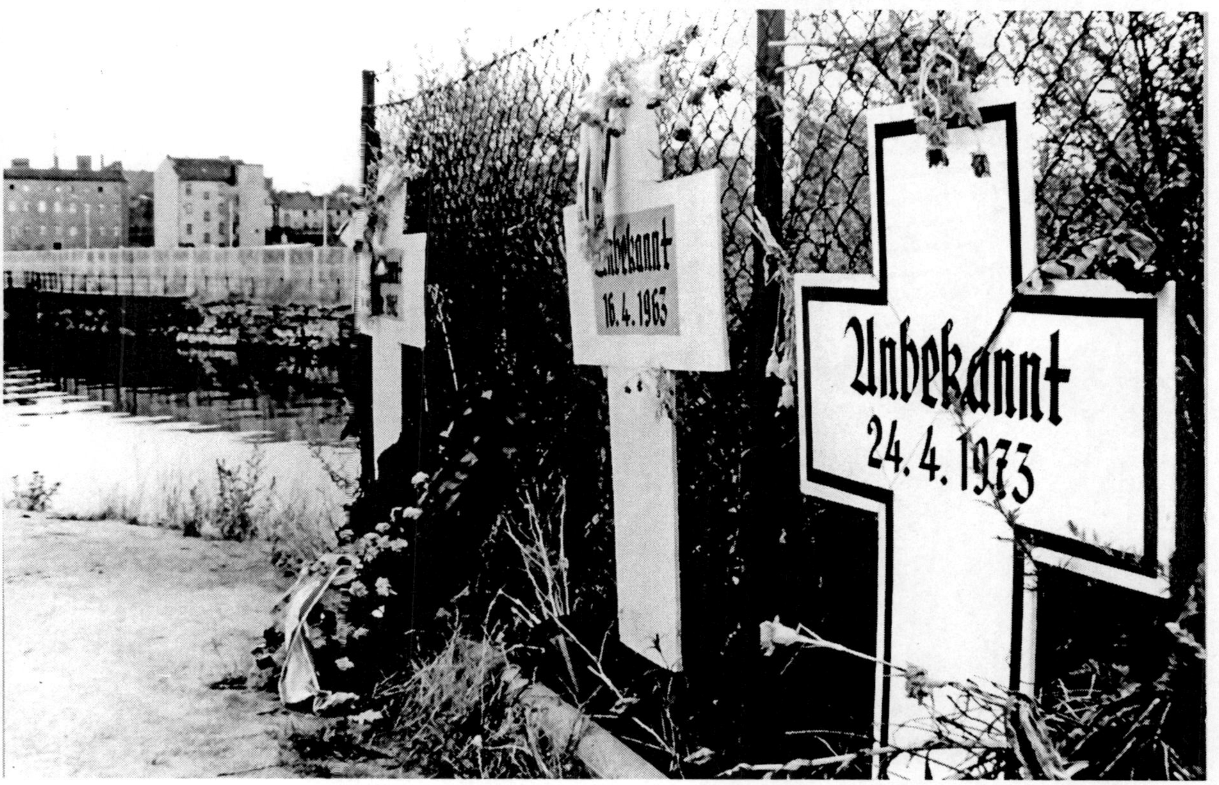

A newly erected memorial to unknown victims who were shot fleeing across the river Spree. (BBC)

BAFTA's royal opening, 10 March 1975

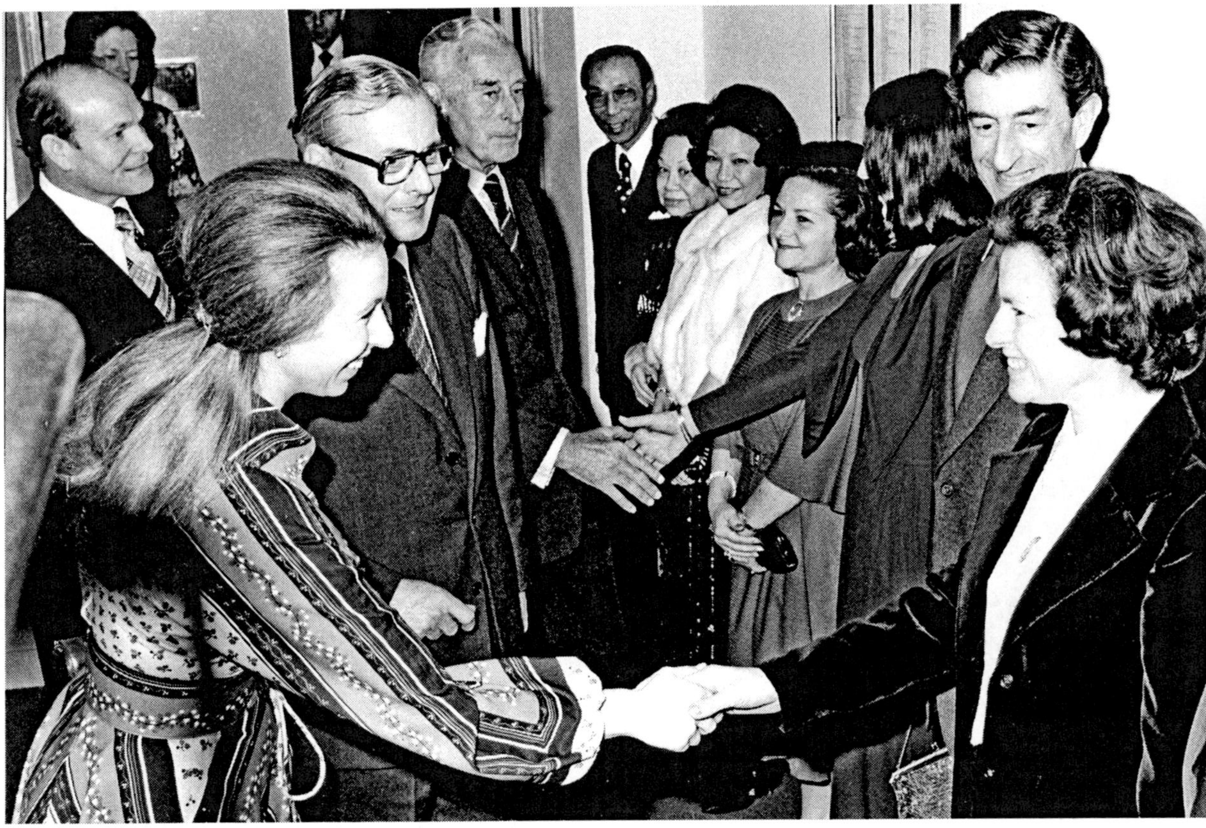

Jane greets BAFTA's new president, Princess Anne. Facing her are Sydney Samuelson, Dick Cawston and Lord Mountbatten. (BAFTA)

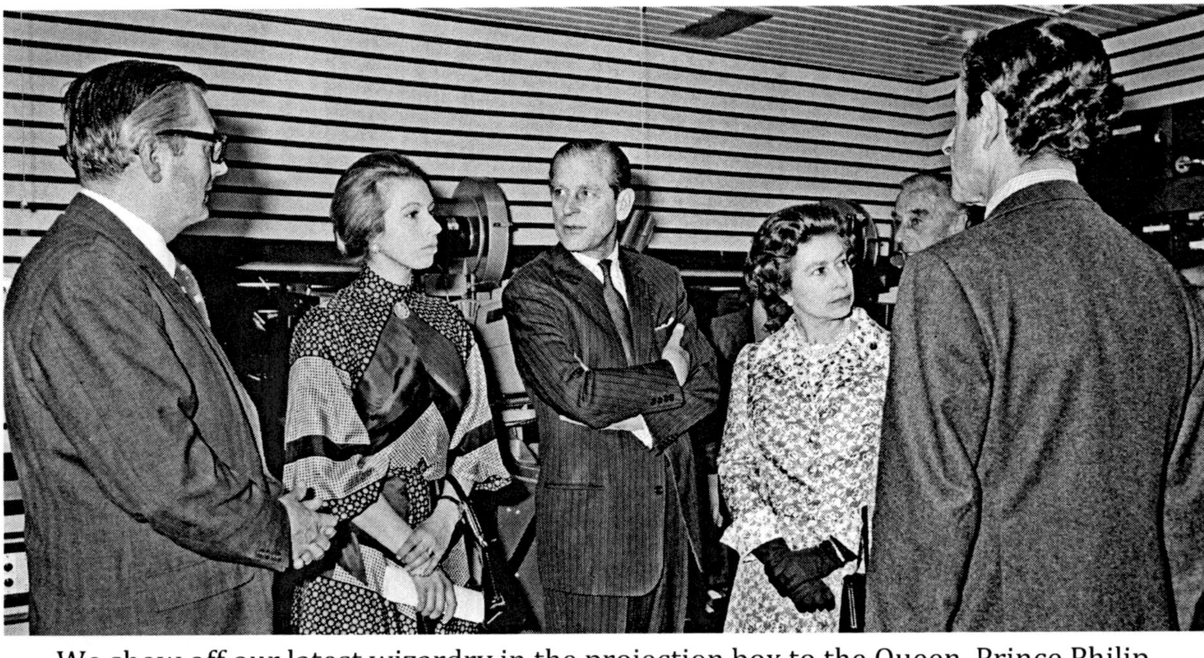

We show off our latest wizardry in the projection box to the Queen, Prince Philip, Princess Anne and Lord Mountbatten. (BAFTA)

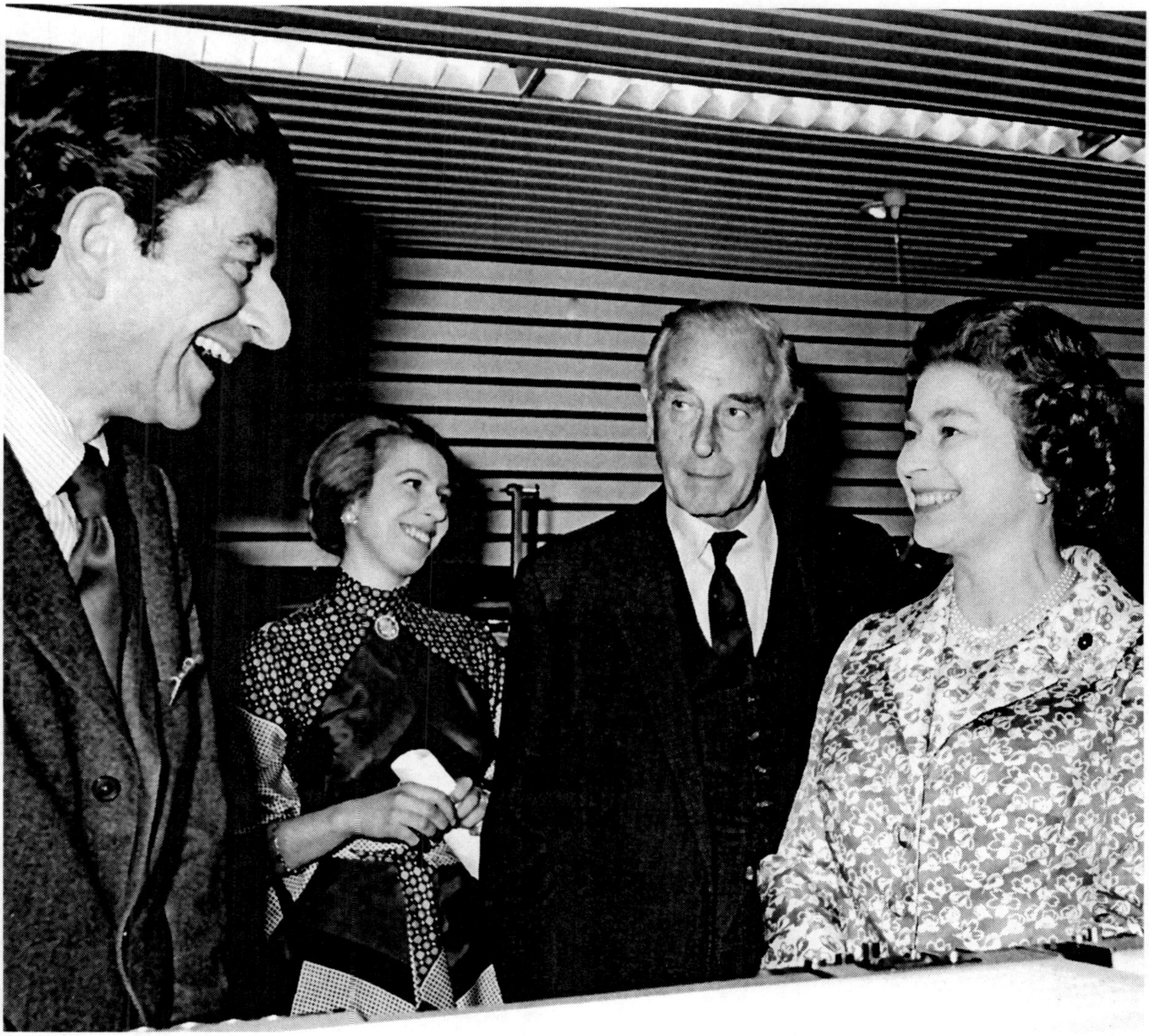

The mood was, to say the least, very relaxed. (BAFTA)

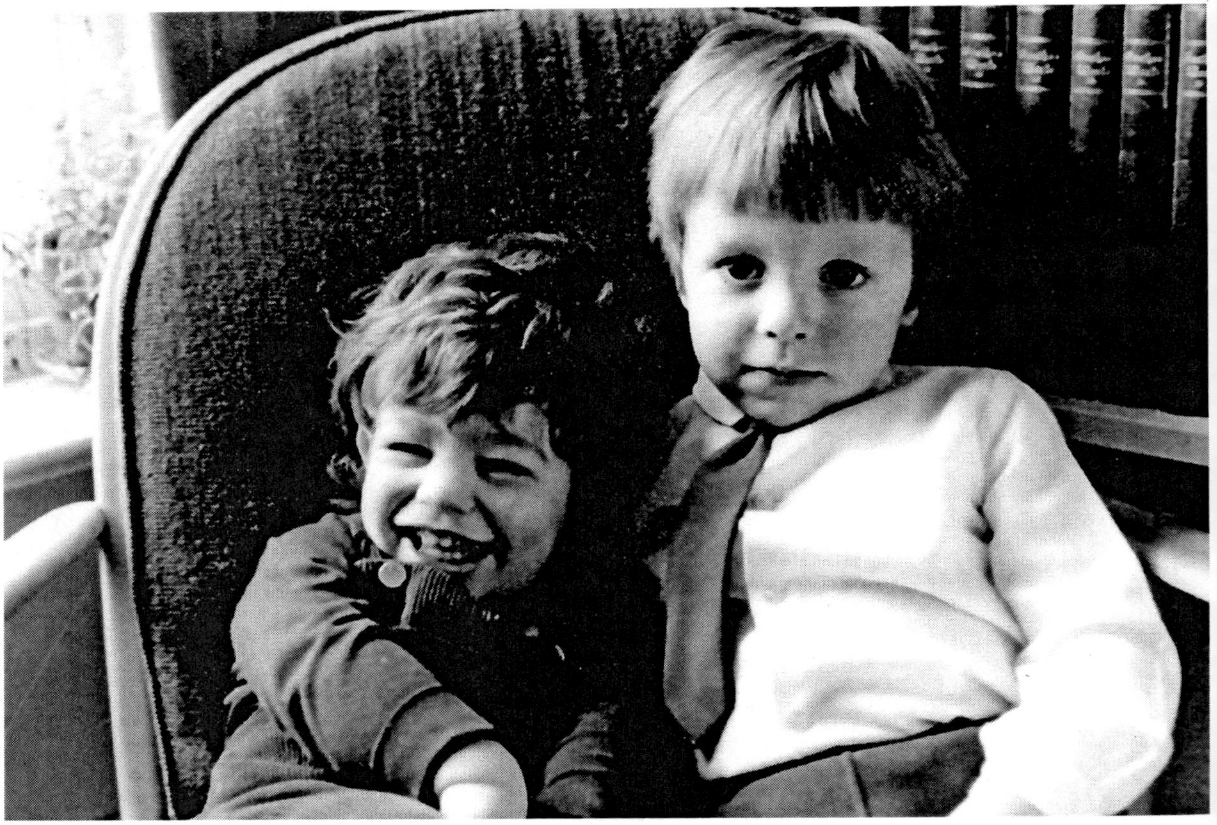

Jonathan and Ben outgrew our small house in Canonbury. (PM)

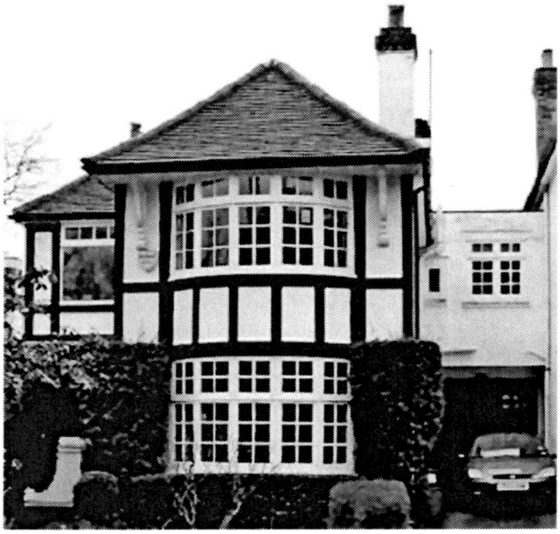

We settled in Highgate. (PM)

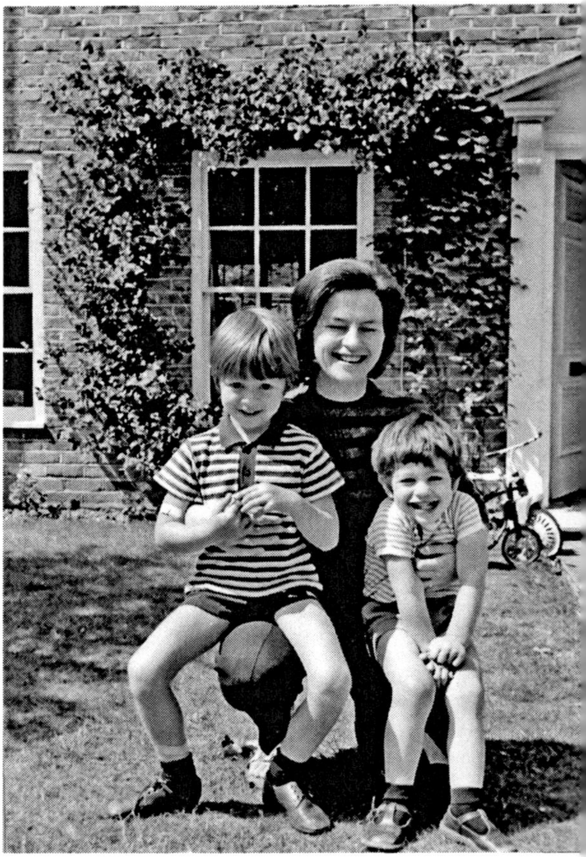

Jane with the boys. (PM)

23: BAFTA

The editor of the *Shell Times*, a monthly publication for the many thousands of Shell staff employed in the oil industry worldwide, told me that his paper had kept a pretty close eye on the development of television programming in the UK, and invited me to write an article for his paper on the role of the producer. 'For instance, why did you think that anyone would want to watch seventy-five years of European history in thirteen hours?' It was a good question. 'Could you write a piece on programme standards and generally answer the question: Producers – who do they think they are?' I accepted, because I felt that maybe after twenty-one years of programme-making under my belt it was time to indulge in a bit of navel-gazing. Here is an edited version of that *Shell Times* article, written in 1975:

> PRODUCERS – WHO DO WE THINK WE ARE?
> Television comes like water out of a tap – we take it for granted. It is almost inconceivable to do without it. But unlike water, we have opinions about it; we have our likes and dislikes, we are amused, entertained, informed, enthralled, maddened, outraged and often plain bored by it. And the responsibility for provoking any one of these reactions must be faced fairly and squarely by the TV producer. 'Who does he think he is?' is a good question. Our names appear briefly at the end of a programme, and with so much television on three channels I wonder whether, apart from my wife, children and mother-in-law, you, the viewer, have the time or indeed the interest to read and absorb that name, let alone reflect on the indisputable fact that this should be the target of your anger or applause? So 'who do I think I am' to be in a position to inflict my work on you, the public?
>
> In the same way that a tax inspector is a taxpayer, a traffic warden a motorist, a customs officer a holiday traveller, so a TV producer is a viewer. And as a viewer, what do I make of this 'tap in the living room', and how does it influence me when, periodically, I help to top up the reservoir at the other end?
>
> My approach to viewing is simple enough. I try to satisfy my curiosity and taste, knowing that a programme I go out of my way to avoid is appreciated in many homes, and vice versa. So let me declare my tastes: News; documentaries; current affairs; history in any form; arts programmes; cricket; *The Sky at Night*; *The Magic Roundabout*. With two small sons prepared to look at almost anything, our diet at home also includes Jimmy Savile, pop programmes and a rationing of Westerns. Typical? No, of course not. Is there such a thing as a typical

viewer – indeed, an average viewer, let alone an average person? I consider it to be an insult to be labelled average. It is a term that stifles individuality, denying its very existence. Yet, this is how the media often brands us. This is one of the dangers that afflict the communication industry, because by implication, the next step after working out the average is to arrive at the lowest common denominator, and that, of course, wildly underestimates the intelligence of the viewing public.

I believe that broadcasting organisations attempt to cater for most individuals and tastes, and try to resist the temptation to pitch their sights so low as to turn an evening's viewing into something that merely goes in one eye and comes out the other.

In the UK, we, the viewers, are lucky (so we are told) because according to world opinion, we have the finest television service; fortunately, there are many, in and out of the industry, who never cease to question this status.

The '50s and early '60s were the pioneering years when it was much easier than it is now to be original, to create a sense of occasion, to try something new, not simply for the sake of it, but because so much had never been attempted before. Novelty, innovation and unpredictability brought surprise and excitement to viewing. How then does a producer square up to his audience; what yardstick can he use to measure his target? As I have said, I don't believe that there can be an average viewer, and this mercifully rules out the arrogant notion that I could possibly judge what you, the viewer, likes and dislikes. I can only know the tastes and prejudices of one viewer – myself – so that the yardstick of communication that I apply, finds its measure in my own highly subjective judgement, and how I look at TV programmes. You may think this to be a symptom of congenital conceit, but I simply could not operate any other way. Of course, this needs to be qualified, and I will try and do this by giving an example. *The Mighty Continent* is a television history spanning seventy-five years of Europe in this century, in twelve one-hour episodes. The series expresses the personal views of historian John Terraine, TV writer and presenter, and took three long years to make. When I started off, should I have second-guessed the degree of knowledge of European history of a BBC1 peak-time audience? Of course not, it would have been the height of arrogance. Instead, I just knew that European history had always fascinated me and, rightly or wrongly, I hoped that it might interest and stimulate others. That was my yardstick.

I am not an historian, and my knowledge was, to say the least, superficial and sketchy. So, in the course of making this series, I was enjoying a three-year history seminar; my mentor was John Terraine, my teaching aids were millions of feet of archive film, historical locations all over Europe, books, paintings, music, photographs and cartoons. You may think that twelve hours of TV, covering seventy-five years of history, is a lavish amount of screen time. But it isn't – one is still forced to be highly selective, and naturally, one man's choice is as good, or bad, as another's. The problem of successful communication, as every editor knows, is not deciding what to put in, but what to leave out.

What you finally saw on the screen was the result of three years of acquired knowledge, distilled, visualised and finally presented in such a way that, hopefully, those who watched the series got as much illumination and interest out of it as we endeavoured to put into it.

In other words, all the time I was making the series I tried to see the programmes as a viewer – this viewer – and as they would strike me within my own family circle on my own television set at home. I just don't know what other standards a producer can apply.

And what did the audience make of it all? Naturally, some people were bound to have disliked it, disagreed with it, been bored rigid by it. The press response ranged from predictably hostile reviews to very friendly ones. We had an average audience size of 5 million (the BBC consider this to be very large for Tuesday nights) but more satisfying, a very high audience appreciation index. And the only reaction which had any real meaning was a large bag of viewers' letters, and I am going to be immodest enough to quote an extract from my favourite: 'I am taking my History "A" levels. Thank you for *The Mighty Continent*, you have made history live for me.' There were a lot of letters like this, and apart from doing one's ego a power of good, they manage to put flesh onto the dry bones of viewing figures and statistics. This is the only feed-back of any value to a producer. So the next time that you turn on that tap in your living room, and see a programme you don't much care for, or possibly like very much, at least you have the advantage of being able to identify the programme-maker, whereas the producer, even if he 'knows who he thinks he is', will never know who you are.

* * * *

Our two boys, Jonathan and Benjamin, were now nine and seven, attending Canonbury Primary School, and the move up to secondary schooling was going to be a major problem – at that time secondary education in Islington was considered by many parents to be a wasteland. Jane and I had come to the conclusion that it was too risky to contemplate privately funded education – my lack of confidence in my freelance status, with its unpredictable see-saw income, saw to that. Our bijou neo-Georgian house in Canonbury was beginning to burst at the seams, so in any event a move to something larger was on the cards.

We knew that the William Ellis Grammar School in Highgate was well regarded. Grammar schools were about to lose their status (Wilson's Labour government's education shake-up has a lot to answer for), and we hoped that in its new role, as a state secondary school, it would inherit its high standing. We went house hunting in Highgate to be within the school's catchment area: it was called voting with our feet. We finally took possession of a five-bedroom house on Highgate's Holly Lodge Estate. This was in a terrible state, and needed just about everything doing to it. This is where being a freelance had an advantage. I took 'time out' for eight weeks, acting as clerk of works and carpenter, with a crew of two builders, an electrician and a heating engineer for what is now known as a complete make-over. In October 1975 we moved in – and Jane and I are still here.

The boys went to St Michael's, a Church of England primary school in Highgate village, and then both were accepted by William Ellis. Mission accomplished – or so we hoped. I remember saying to Jane at the time that it's only when the boys are in their thirties that we will begin to realise what mistakes we might have made with their education.

* * * *

During the early days of the '70s the Society of Film and Television Arts (SFTA) was growing fast, and the council had ambitious ideas for it. We rented a pokey little office in Great Portland Street, almost too small to hold council meetings, let alone for the membership to meet. It was obvious that unless we acquired our own premises with the necessary facilities the SFTA would wither.

In 1969 Dickie Attenborough (now Lord Attenborough) had taken over from me as chairman, and for the next two years this dynamo of a man got things moving together with

John (Lord) Brabourne: they were both ace fundraisers. They discovered that a majestic nineteenth-century Classical building in Piccadilly, created for the Royal Institute of Painters in Watercolours, had been empty for some time. It was derelict and the lease was up for grabs. This was an ideal building for our purposes, with an excellent address, close to Fortnums and opposite the Royal Academy, but we would have to raise a massive amount of finance. The first positive idea for funding this ambitious scheme came from Dick Cawston, who directed the joint BBC/ITV groundbreaking documentary *The Royal Family*, screened in 1969. This was the first time that the Queen had agreed to cooperate in a film that showed her family at work and play, and it was a huge success. The Queen had stipulated that any profits generated from its sales should be distributed to charities, and soon the profits had accrued to £50,000. Dick suggested at a council meeting that we should try and persuade the Queen to nominate the SFTA as her preferred charity, so we consulted Lord Mountbatten, our president, and he promised to help. He used his enormous powers of persuasion, coupled with his closeness to his niece, and he got her agreement. The Palace stipulated that the SFTA would first have to appoint a board of trustees to ensure that the agreed terms of the royal donation would be safeguarded, and that the new headquarters would be used solely to further the arts and crafts of film and television. In other words, the trustees' responsibilities included a guarantee that the old Royal Institute of Painters in Watercolour would not be used as a blue-movie house! And so in 1971 the SFTA trustees were established; they were Dickie Attenborough, John Brabourne, Dick Cawston and myself.

To get final approval from the Palace before purchasing the lease, Lord McLean, the Lord Chamberlain, had to vet the building, and in July 1972 Dick and I met him in Piccadilly and conducted him round the pitch-dark interior, with a clutch of torches provided by the agent's representative. Lord McLean liked what he saw and we were given the go-ahead, but it took many more months before we acquired the lease of what is now 195 Piccadilly. Dickie and John set out on a furious fund-raising campaign: we required £250k to rebuild the inside of the building to create a 230-seat cinema, plus a smaller one, catering facilities, meeting areas with bars and all the necessary office accommodation. It was a very tall order, but we opened the doors to the membership in 1975.

We now called ourselves the British Academy of Film and Television Arts – BAFTA. It had been a long haul from the late 1950s, when the British Film Academy and the Guild of Television Producers and Directors began their tentative and difficult merger talks. Lord Mountbatten persuaded his great-niece, Princess Anne, to take over as BAFTA's president, and she played a very active part supporting all our activities. The BAFTA council decided to name our main cinema 'The Princess Anne Theatre', and on 10 March 1976 the Queen and Prince Philip were on parade for the grand opening of the BAFTA Centre. Sydney Samuelson (now Sir Sydney) was reigning chairman of BAFTA at the time, and he and I staged this historic event. The great and the good filled the theatre, and after the Queen had declared our headquarters officially open, Princess Anne announced the presentation of BAFTA's first fellowship. At this point an extremely well-kept secret was revealed. Earlier that evening Charlie Chaplin, now very old and very frail, had been smuggled into the building in his wheelchair and hidden, if I remember correctly, in one of our large stationery cupboards. On cue, the doors to the theatre opened and to the audience's great surprise our vice-chairman, Johnny Goodman, wheeled him into the auditorium, where our president presented him with the BAFTA mask. The Queen then rose and walked over to him to congratulate him. That picture made the front page of *The Times* in the morning.

Then it was our opportunity to show off all the latest technical innovations we had installed, demonstrating BAFTA's ability to project images ranging from Wide Screen, Cinemascope and Panavision to off-air TV and the latest innovation – the video cassette.

Sydney Samuelson was on the stage, making the presentation, and I was up in the projection box, cueing the projectionist – it was like doing a complicated live outside broadcast. We changed the screen masking for each format and played movie clips to demonstrate them all, ending with the huge Panavision screen size and clips from that year's Innsbruck Winter Olympics. As a planned afterthought, Sydney held up a video cassette and said, 'For those who have not seen one of these, you just slot it into the recorder, press a button – and sometimes it can work miracles.' And on the array of television monitors suspended from the theatre's ceiling a picture of a hand holding a film clapperboard popped up, with a voice announcing, 'Take One – and I sincerely hope it will be in one take.' And with the clap, the camera panned up to show Prince Charles holding the board in a television studio. I was looking through the projection box porthole and saw the Queen as surprised as the rest of the audience. The week before I had flown up to Glasgow to shoot this piece. At the time Charles was a lieutenant in command of the minesweeper HMS *Bonnington*, moored in the Firth of Clyde, and so could not join his family at BAFTA. He directed his message to the Lord High Admiral, the Queen, and went on: 'Knowing of the presence of at least three other Admirals at the Centre today, I would like to pay my humble respects to the Academy's paternal first president, to the Academy's avuncular second president and to the Navy's most attractive admiral, the present president.'

This all went down well. Afterwards the royal party came up to the projection box, where we introduced them to the crew and showed them round. We had a good laugh when I told the Queen about my trip to Prince Charles in Glasgow; it really was a secret that had been successfully kept from her.

I frequently see Sydney Samuelson, who became a fellow trustee and a good friend in the '80s, after Dick Cawston's sad and totally unexpected death. Both of us started in this business as projectionists early in the war, and we often look back on BAFTA's royal opening night with relish – staged, as it was, by two ex-'projies'.

24: Silver Jubilee

Early in 1976 I was approached by that great impresario Bernard Delfont to have lunch with him. He was, among many activities, the boss of EMI Films, based at Elstree Studios. Because of my 'royal connections', as he put it, he offered me the prospect of making a documentary film for general cinema release in 1977 to celebrate the Queen's Silver Jubilee. I readily accepted: the thought of making a film for the big screen was irresistible. That was the good news; and then I discovered the not so good news.

Delfont had a limited budget (I understood that he was financing the film himself) and I had to observe Eady Fund rules, a government-regulated system for subsidising British films. This stipulated that 75 per cent of the film had to be newly shot footage – a tall order for a film that, because of its subject matter, surely had to be based on archive footage; how else could one tell the story of the first twenty-five years of the monarch's reign in a feature-length movie? But I was prepared to have a go, and with the co-operation of the Palace I thought it might be possible to construct a film based on new material I would shoot with the Queen during this current year.

My first port of call was Ron Allison, the Queen's press officer, whom I had met when I was making the Mountbatten series. I went to see him at Buckingham Palace, and soon discovered that I was asking the impossible. The Queen's diary is finalised at least a year in advance, and to ask for facilities for some special filming simply was not on. Ron was most sympathetic, and appreciated the hole I was in. He said that he would do his best to get approval for me to tag along with a film crew to cover some of the royal engagements and activities that are normally 'out of bounds' to the press. I crossed my fingers that I would get sufficient material, hopefully of a more intimate kind, to make the film for EMI. Because of my close relationship with Lord Mountbatten, I was able to ask him whether he could put in a good word for me, and the outcome of this was a message that the Queen would try to fit in a session especially for my film possibly later in the year; but at that point there were no promises.

It was premature to think of the shape and style of the film until I had gathered together all its ingredients. This was familiar territory for me, as twelve years earlier I treated *LSO – The Music Men* and *Black Marries White* in a similar way. I asked the Palace to let me have the scripts and recordings of all the Queen's public speeches and Christmas broadcasts back to 1952; I felt sure that they would provide the underlying themes of her reign, and form the backbone for the film. And that is how it finally worked out. Once again I did away with a narrator; instead I used extracts from these speeches, including one from Prince Philip, to achieve an impressionistic picture of the first twenty-five years of the reign.

I set up office in Elstree Studios, and found working in a movie-making atmosphere hugely enjoyable. I had a production manager, production secretary, unit manager, accountant and publicist on my team, plus two fully fledged 35mm camera crews and two cutting rooms. We filmed in a great variety of locations, highlighting the busy and often taxing royal duties. Of all these locations, it was the trip to Canada and America in 1976 that is firmly embedded in my memory. It combined the Queen's Commonwealth visit to Canada with the opening of the Montreal Olympic Games, followed by her visit to Boston to join the 1766 bicentennial celebrations of America's independence.

In June I went on an advance recce starting in Boston, and with the enthusiastic organisers of Boston 200 set out to find locations, camera positions, boats to film from and all the other small details for a successful shoot. The 'natives' were extremely friendly, and we all relished the irony of the Queen's visit to Boston – the cradle of American Independence – to join Bostonians who were celebrating her forefather's overthrow and defeat two hundred years earlier.

Then it was on to Ottawa, where I had to seek approval and co-operation from Canadian government officials who were in charge of protocol and procedures for the royal visit. They were relieved when I made it clear that I was not going to Montreal to film the Olympics opening ceremony, but wanted to limit my locations to Halifax, Nova Scotia, where she would arrive in *Britannia*, and New Brunswick. I was then due to leave Ottawa for Fredericton, capital of New Brunswick, to organise the filming there, and go on to Halifax to do the same; then return quickly to London for the next UK shoot – the State Visit of the French President, Valéry Giscard d'Estaing. And so to the first unforeseen adventure: the Canadian pilots union had called a nationwide strike, and air traffic was about to come to a standstill. The colonel in charge of the royal tour came to my rescue. He drove me out to a small airfield, where on my behalf (and at huge expense) he had persuaded the owner of a small single-engined plane to fly me from Ottawa to Fredericton.

The pilot lent me a fur-lined flying jacket, and we collected a flask of hot coffee and mugs, stowing them under my seat. It turned out to be a hair-raising 400 miles. As we took off I could see that the cloud base was only a few hundred feet, and as we climbed we were soon swallowed up inside a thick and turbulent cloud. For the next few hours all I could see were the instruments showing altitude, speed and our direction. The pilot had given me a headset to wear, 'to keep my ears warm', as he put it, but it enabled me to listen to his occasional calls to control points along the route verifying our position, and that was quite reassuring. After being tossed around in what looked like the same cloud we had entered in Ottawa over three hours earlier, the pilot pushed his control column forward and, with huge relief, I saw Fredericton airport less than 1,000 feet below us. I admired the pilot's skill, thanked him and reminded him of the untouched coffee under my seat.

I checked in at the Lord Beaverbrook Hotel, and then went to the Beaverbrook Art Gallery, the focal point of the Queen's visit, to meet its curator and finalise camera positions for her visit. On my way to his office I spotted Graham Sutherland's portrait of Churchill, and works by Turner, Stanley Spencer and Salvador Dali, to name but a few. Back at the hotel I was told that there might be a chance in the morning of hiring a private plane to take me another 200 miles east, to Halifax. I was very glad to crawl into bed.

Just after midnight I was woken up by frantic banging on my door; it was the assistant manager telling me that I had ten minutes to get to the airport for the last flight to Halifax. Apparently the pilots of Maritime Airlines were the last to take strike action, and this particular pilot, who lived in Halifax, wanted to get home before the deadline. In a panic I put on my shirt and trousers over my pyjamas, threw everything else into my case and made for the airport, where they were holding the plane for me. Three hours later I was sound asleep in a Halifax hotel bed. What a day.

I had only one call to make in the morning. It was to the harbour master to organise my coverage of the Queen's arrival in the Royal Yacht *Britannia*. When I told him that I had to find a way to get out of Canada to fly back to London, he contacted a friend who could fly me across the border to Bangor, Maine, where I could pick up a Delta flight to Boston, and thence back to London. I spoke to the owner of the six-seater on the phone, and his hugely inflated fee for the flight was way above my Jubilee film budget. I told him I would have to find five passengers to share the cost. So off I went to my hotel. It was now lunchtime, and I went up to the bar, ordered a drink and tapped my glass with some ice tongs. This momentarily stopped the chatter round the bar, so I asked in a loud voice, 'Anyone for Bangor?' Immediately I became the most popular man in Halifax, as at least twenty American citizens stranded in Canada crowded round me, desperate to fly home. I picked five candidates, and in two taxis we drove to the flying club; then off we flew to Bangor. In spite of everything I arrived back in London as per my schedule. Some recce – some trip.

* * * *

On 11 July the Queen was due to arrive in Boston. I flew there three days in advance with my two camera crews, and a mountain of equipment as we were shooting in 35mm. Bearing in mind the limited ratio of archive film I could use in the final cut, we took the opportunity to shoot quite a long sequence of Boston girding itself for this historic visit. There were one or two choice moments we captured on camera, including the telephonist at the Boston 200 headquarters fielding an enquiry: 'Good afternoon, this is Boston 200. Yes, I can connect you with someone who can handle the Queen.'

The royal address to the people of Boston was delivered from the Old State House, still bearing on its frontage the proud sculptures of the Imperial lion and unicorn. It was well received, and the Queen brought the house down with this remark: 'It was not many miles from here, at Lexington and Concord, that the first shots were fired in the war between Britain and America 201 years ago. If Paul Revere, Samuel Adams and other patriots could have known that one day a British monarch could have stood beneath the balcony of the Old State House from which the Declaration of Independence was first read to the people of Boston – well, I think they would have been extremely surprised.'

Later that day I attended a reception for Boston's dignitaries on board *Britannia* and at the same time made sure that half of our camera equipment was stowed safely below decks, ready for the Canadian leg of the tour. The next morning the crew and I flew to Halifax to get ready to film *Britannia*'s arrival due the following day. And now for an unexpected adventure. I had arranged with the harbour master to get a lift in the pilot boat together with one of my cameramen and sound recordist. This was due to sail at 4 a.m. to meet the royal yacht several miles out in Halifax waters. We were then to climb on board *Britannia* and film the arrival from her deck, while the other camera crew covered the scene from the quay. The forecast was for severe gales, and when we met the pilot at that unearthly hour he was not at all sure whether he would have to cancel his trip. I was rather hoping that he would, because I am such a lousy sailor and can barely cope with the sea when it is dead flat. We climbed on board what looked like a miniature trawler. I was told that this pilot boat had an extremely powerful engine in order to handle the notoriously heavy seas in Halifax waters. We set off, and within minutes I was looking for something to hang onto. I stayed with the pilot in the wheelhouse, and when the skipper lit up a foul-smelling pipe even the pilot turned green. I went down below, threw up, and felt better for it.

Visibility was almost nil, and the skipper was in constant radio contact with *Britannia* to achieve the planned rendezvous. One hour after setting out her hull loomed up out of the darkness, when we were about 50 yards away. We drew up alongside. *Britannia*'s sailors dropped a very long rope ladder over the side and the experienced pilot grabbed it, then like a monkey clambered up and disappeared from sight. It was my turn. I tried hard to remember the skipper's strict instructions, telling me that because of the heavy swell of the sea the pilot boat would rise and fall about 20 feet, so I had to make a quick grab for the rope ladder at the exact moment when the boat reached her highest point in the water, then climb like mad. I did this as the boat disappeared from under me, and had managed to climb just one rung when she came up again on her next rise. I realised that I might be knocked back into the water, and survival instincts took over. After what seemed like an endless climb the welcoming strong arms of two of *Britannia*'s sailors helped to pull me onto the deck. I made sure that my other two crew had followed me, then the duty officer welcomed us. A voice behind me said, 'That was a bit hairy,' and when I turned round it was Prince Philip, in a heavy raincoat, who had come out on deck at that early hour to watch the fun.

Sailors brought up our camera equipment, and although the weather was foul we were able to capture on film the preparations for docking, with a very soggy Royal Marines band on the deck of *Britannia* to announce her arrival in Halifax.

The only other journey we were able to cover was a state visit to Finland. We also filmed a fistful of engagements in the UK, including the royal family at Balmoral Castle and Trooping the

Colour. Then in the autumn I was told that I could have half a day for some exclusive filming. I wanted some linking sequences in the final cut, so I asked to film the Queen riding on her own in Windsor Home Park, and planned a series of tracking shots taken from a camera car alongside her. The Queen was very understanding and helpful, and didn't seem to mind a bit being asked for several takes. She wanted to know how I was getting on with the film, and regretted that that it had not been possible to allocate more of her time to the project.

In November I went to Buckingham Palace to screen the rough-cut to the Queen. She liked the Boston sequence best, and said that she hoped to see the final version before she and Prince Philip embarked on their Jubilee Commonwealth Tour early in 1977.

A few months later, on 4 February, I was asked to report to Windsor Castle at 8.45 p.m. to show the finished film, *25 Years – Impressions*, to the Queen and Prince Philip. The venue was the magnificent St George's Hall. There were just four chairs facing a screen, which is normally secreted in the floor. The projection box is at the far end of this very long hall; when not in use, its portholes are obscured by large paintings.

The fourth chair was for the Queen's private secretary, and I sat between the Queen and Prince Philip. I kept my fingers crossed that they would like the film, and when the lights went up there was a short silence, broken by Prince Philip: 'Well, if nobody is going to say anything, I am going to clap my hands.' He turned to me and said, 'I like it very much.' The Queen, too, looked pleased, and asked some interesting questions about the difficulty of deciding what to put in and what to leave out. She then invited me to join them for a nightcap, and we walked along corridors to her private quarters, where Prince Philip told me to choose from an array of at least ten malt whiskies. There was also a tray of finely cut smoked salmon sandwiches, and the Queen offered me a plate and asked me to help myself. It was all very relaxed. She wanted to know more about the opening Boston sequence, which she said she had really enjoyed. It shows Boston getting ready for her visit, the camera capturing a rich moment in which workmen were erecting the dais from which the Queen made her speech. A very pretty black girl from Boston 200 called Virginia was supervising this, and she told the elderly foreman in no uncertain terms that she was not satisfied with the dais position but wanted it swivelled round a bit to face the audience. 'OK, we'll do as the lady says,' he reluctantly said to his gang. After moving the dais, and as the open sides of its base were nailed up, there was a loud yell – upon which they discovered that they had nailed in one of their mates. I now witnessed a side to the Queen that the public never sees – she launched into a word-perfect impersonation of Virginia. It was very funny.

We talked a lot about the Mountbatten series (it was seven years since its transmission). She remembered very clearly the technical problems we had had in Ceylon, and remarked how 'Uncle Dickie' thrived on problem solving. I left Windsor Castle after 11 p.m., with fond memories of a remarkable day.

The gala première was at the EMI cinema in Shaftesbury Avenue on 16 February 1977. The Queen and Prince Philip had departed on their Commonwealth Tour, so Prince Charles officiated. There was the usual line-up in the foyer and it was all very jolly.

The film was shown in selected cinemas in Britain. I think I just about got away with it. Reviews were mixed, and only one or two critics mentioned the restrictions imposed by the Eady Plan on the use of archive material. It felt like a sabbatical from television, and was an enjoyable experience.

25: RCA

Going through my appointments diaries, which I luckily still possess, for 1976 and 1977 produced such a range of diverse activities that over thirty years later they make me wonder how I ever had any time to see my young family grow up. We were now well settled in our new home in Highgate, and in spite of a hectic life away from home I still somehow managed to find time for a certain amount of do-it-yourself to complete all the many targets we had set ourselves. The biggest and most rewarding of these was the Douglas fir tongue and grooving covering the whole of our newly created combined kitchen and living area – clear proof that the less time you have at your disposal the more time you are somehow able to find to achieve the tasks that seem impossible.

While I was editing my Jubilee film I was, at the same time, pursuing a new and novel way of communicating. My close friend Richard Sonnenfeldt, room-mate from our schooldays at Bunce Court when we were in our early teens, was now a big noise with RCA, in charge of a large team of experts developing a revolutionary videodisc technology called SelectaVision, and he asked me over to New York several times to suggest what sort of programming they ought to publish on RCA's new gadget. We first started talking about this when I stayed with him on Long Island. When he took me sailing in Long Island Sound, I remember, we explored my first ideas about how to make and present programmes that could be released from the tyranny of the broadcast time-slots that dictate their running time. As I stated earlier, the lesson learnt from making documentaries, whether single programmes or long series, is that the amount of information one can impart has to be rationed to avoid mental overload; and in any case the retention of details by the viewer is immediately compromised by demands made on the poor overworked brain by the programmes that follow it. Maybe new technology, a new means of imparting information, might now come to the rescue. It was an exciting prospect and I felt that I wanted to be part of it.

On one of my brief visits to RCA, in New York's Rockefeller Centre, I was being given a demonstration of a prototype of the disc player when Dick told me that he had arranged for me at short notice to attend the RCA board meeting – which was that morning. The developing SelectaVision technology was on the agenda, and he thought that it would be very useful for me to give my views on 'software' – a new name in the communications vocabulary. At the appropriate moment, when SelectaVision was about to be discussed, I was wheeled into the inner sanctum and confronted by a boardroom table as long as a football pitch, with about twenty RCA executives sitting around it. Robert Sarnoff, President of RCA and a name to conjure with, was in the chair. Everyone was sporting a diamond-studded tiepin. Dick's had a cluster of diamonds on his pin, each one confirming a patented invention. I was now in the company of America's finest engineers.

'Welcome, Mr Morley,' said Sarnoff. 'Mr Sonnenfeldt has told us about you, and that you might have some suggestions for exploiting our new videodisc system.' A sea of faces turned towards my end of the long table and I had to think fast, as I was totally unprepared.

'Mr President, RCA has set itself the problem of how to deposit high-quality colour pictures and stereo sound onto a round, flat object, and then be able to play it all back on a domestic machine. I have just had a demonstration of the disc player and I am bowled over by it, and think it is very exciting. But it leaves me with a question: what motivated this engineering triumph in the first place?' I could feel the piercing stares of the assembled engineers focusing on me. 'With great respect, I do hope that this isn't a case of new technology being invented for its own sake, looking for an application. I'm very glad that Mr Sonnenfeldt has invited me over to New York, wearing my "software" hat, to help identify some of the benefits your new technology might offer.'

I felt I had shot my bolt. After all, I was only a visitor, and I felt that I might be shown the door. Instead I was asked to elaborate on my ideas for the 'interactive' use of their new technology, and there followed an interesting discussion. Sarnoff thanked me for my contribution, and I left. Shortly afterwards Dick called me, and asked me to be a software consultant for RCA. That meant visits to Holland and Germany, where Philips, Grundig and Decca were all developing their separate systems. I had to write long reports on what I learnt, and also put forward concrete ideas for what they called their 'RCA's opening night catalogue'. I didn't realise it at the time, but it was to lead to an important change in my work a few years later.

* * * *

At about this time, completely out of the blue, I received an invitation to join the European Audiovisual Committee. Being one of just two UK representatives I was quite flattered, although I had never heard of this group. Terry Hughes, a journalist, was the other member, and when we met at our first session in Brussels we discovered what we had let ourselves in for: 'The Audio-Visual Division of the European Commission is responsible for a wide range of activities including the supply of radio and TV and film material to developing countries, the supply of information to local and regional radio stations, the production of audio-visual material for the Commission offices in member and non-member states.' Alan Watson (later Lord Watson), previously a television anchorman, was the committee's chairman. One of his minions (there were many) sent out the agenda for this session, including hotel details and expense claim forms for reimbursing travel and overnight expenses.

After checking in at a very posh Brussels hotel, we were escorted to an up-market restaurant, where we met committee members from other EEC countries over drinks. It was all very jolly, and the dinner that followed was magnificent. When coffee was served Alan Watson made a speech of welcome, followed by several other speeches in different languages. I enjoyed the Italian one best, because the speaker had imbibed enough to make it difficult for him to keep his balance.

I was glad to get back to my room. The next morning we assembled for the official committee meeting, chaired by Alan Watson. The main item on the agenda was the Commission's desire to establish an EEC television festival to award prizes to the best programmes from the nine member states, promoting interest in the first European direct election, which was to be held in 1979. With the translations into French and English, and the first vague thoughts by some of the delegates, we were asked to come up with some firm ideas at the next meeting, probably in six months' time. It was time for lunch. Again we were shipped to one of Brussels' superior watering holes, and after a splendid meal there were more speeches, largely of a political nature, with several of the delegates offering their services to be put in charge of the proposed festival. I recall looking at Terry Hughes opposite me, wearing the same 'What the hell are we doing here?' look on his face as I was. And that was it. We flew back to London early that evening, and not only waited for the date of the next meeting but also about five months to have our not inconsiderable expenses reimbursed.

Wearing my BAFTA trustee hat, I asked Reg Collin, our chief executive, to write an outline proposal for a TV festival, which I presented at the next session in Brussels. After a lot of opposition from the French, who wanted to run the show, it was agreed that BAFTA should do a study and submit a detailed plan with costings for the next meeting. Once again the same gastronomic procedures were observed, as was the maddening withholding of travel expenses. And so it went on for the following year, with more meetings and a lot of work by BAFTA to produce a detailed document. It all ended in tears when I got a letter of apology from Alan Watson, who said that the Commission could not afford the funding for a television festival. I finally received my expenses – and never heard from Brussels again. To this day I don't know whether I am still a member of the audiovisual committee, or, indeed, whether it was disbanded or not; but what I do know is that the burdening bureaucracy, the sheer incompetence, the waste of taxpayers' money and the strong whiff of political infighting made my Eurosceptic juices rise.

26: Prime Ministers

In August 1976 Paul Fox called me. As managing director of Yorkshire Television he had put the company on the map with a very successful drama and documentary output. He said, 'I need you to carry out a rescue mission.'

He had done a deal with David Frost's company, David Paradine Productions, to make a series of thirteen programmes called *Prime Minister on Prime Ministers*. Harold Wilson, now in retirement, had readily agreed to this, especially as it was going to be closely tied to a book of the same title that he was writing; and the first three episodes had already been filmed: Pitt, Peel and Disraeli.

I met Paul in YTV's preview theatre in Old Burlington Street, where he screened all three. They were dire. Both Wilson and Frost had stipulated that they did not want to go to locations outside London, and as a result the programmes consisted of static, boring interviews with a painting or sculpture of the relevant prime minister in the background. I well remember when the lights went up: Paul looked at me and I made a thumbs down gesture. 'A re-shoot?' he asked. I nodded.

The next step was for me to attend a luncheon in a private room at Kettners restaurant in Soho. Present were Lord Blake, the great historian and biographer; Michael Deakin, YTV's executive producer; Anthony Jay, David Frost's script consultant; Harold Wilson; and Lady Falkender.

I had been warned about Lady Falkender who, as Marcia Williams, became Harold Wilson's political secretary in October 1956 and was ennobled by him as Baroness Falkender in the notorious 'lavender honours list' of 1974. There was a flood of stories about her – *Private Eye* thrived on them. Some say that she ruled her boss with an iron fist and ran No. 10. 'Marcia can't see you for two weeks but the prime minister can see you straight away' was an often-quoted barb by the press. I was told to be very careful: she was foul-tempered and likely to eat me alive.

On arrival we had drinks at the bar and I was introduced to everyone. Lady F. took me to one side, and I thought to myself 'Tally Ho'. Then she totally disarmed me. 'I'd like you to call me Marcia – may I call you Peter?'

'Of course. But I've been warned that you might eat me!'

'People always say the most terrible things about me – all lies! But, please, be absolutely frank and tell me what you really think about Harold's first three programmes.'

'I'm afraid they won't do. They're boring to watch. David reels off questions, which sound as though they were provided by Harold Wilson in advance. They really need to be re-shot.'

'What a relief! That's just what I think – but I've kept my mouth shut.'

'Who'll tell him – you or me?'

'You'd better leave that to me. Harold will take it from me.'

We sat down to eat, and Wilson asked me what I thought about the three programmes. I said that they lacked colour and that it would really be more interesting if he and David could film the interviews at appropriate locations – for example, in the Palace of Westminster and Walmer Castle for Pitt, Broadlands for Palmerston, Chequers for Baldwin, Caernarvon for Lloyd George, and the Cabinet War Rooms for Churchill.

Everyone seemed to agree and Marcia, sitting next to me, whispered, 'Thank God for that. I'll tell him about scrapping the first three when I'm in the car with him.'

From that moment she and I got on famously. She turned out to be a great help and ally when filming started again later that year, and accompanied Wilson to every location. We were to stay in contact for many years afterwards, meeting sometimes for lunch.

The production routine that I inherited was, to say the least, odd. Each programme, that is each prime minister, triggered a Café Royal luncheon, attended by the same group. Wilson arrived with his drafted or finished chapter on that particular PM. A lively and very informative discussion took place, which highlighted the areas that the programme should explore. Wilson, himself a well-qualified historian, had many an altercation with Lord Blake, and it was fascinating to observe this high-powered intellectual shadow-boxing. There was one occasion when Wilson apologised for arriving a bit late, saying that he had been up all night 'writing the Disraeli chapter'!

David Frost was never in attendance as he was commuting weekly by Concorde to New York for his coast-to-coast television show, so he missed out on what would have been a valuable briefing session. But Tony Jay, who made valuable contributions to these discussions, was responsible for bringing David up to speed. It sounds quite crazy now, but Tony used to meet him at Heathrow as he came off his overnight flight, and they would travel in a chauffeur-driven car to the location at which we were shooting, David being fully briefed for the interview *en route*. He had a talent for assimilating a lot of information very quickly, and by the time he arrived and had been to make-up to remove the telltale signs of the flight he was well prepared to face Wilson.

YTV had agreed to let me set up an office and two cutting rooms in Wardour Street, staffed by YTV film editors and assistants who travelled down from York every Monday and returned home for the weekend. I must say that this was my least favourite way of making programmes. I felt frustrated that I could not provide my usual input, as the method used to harness Wilson and Frost relegated me to the role of the 'rescuer', as Paul Fox put it.

Towards the end of the year the programmes trickled out weekly on the ITV network without fanfares. I was not proud of them. Sadly, such a good idea went out almost unnoticed. To hear someone who has been a prime minister – and knows what he is talking about – expound on twelve of his predecessors could have been fascinating and historically very valuable. But there were compensations, as in the following year Paul was to offer me the opportunity for an adventure that was really worthwhile.

When Wilson's book was published he kindly sent me a copy with this inscription: 'For Peter with warm thanks and deep appreciation – always tyrannous but nice with it.'

* * * *

In 1977 the domestic video cassette recorder arrived, opening up a potential rental market for movies and the newly named videograms: programmes made specially for this new technology. A new name had to be invented because new agreements – videogram agreements – covering copyright, performance, royalties and so on had to be negotiated for a product that the public could purchase and own for ever.

There were three competing cassette systems vying for a huge potential market: Sony's Betamax, Philips' VCR and JVC's VHS. VHS came out on top and won the world's markets. Also looming up fast was the prospect of videodisc technology.

In the autumn of 1977, while I was still cutting *Prime Minister on Prime Ministers*, I got an interesting call from EMI – at the time the largest manufacturers of audio discs in the world. They set up a small company called EMI Videogram Productions to work out how best to package and market videos for this new rental market, and also produce experimental audio-visual material for the approaching videodisc market. They invited me to make their first production for the new technology. They probably approached me having come across the following article which I wrote for the Royal Television Society (many years before the appearance of CD, CD-ROM and DVD, let alone solid state technologies):

> A New Grammar – First Steps
>
> Recently it was said that the weakness of the videodisc is not in its technology, but in the imagination of those who create programmes for it. The temptation to put technique before content is as old as broadcasting itself – the videodisc makes this temptation almost irresistible.
>
> If brilliant innovations such as still-frame, random access, rapid search, chapterisation, dual audio information and all the other marvels are put at our disposal, why not exploit them? The challenge is plain: to develop a style using this amazing new technology in an entertaining and informative way – but avoiding the danger of doing so for its own sake.
>
> Thus, for those who have spent years making films and TV programmes – with a beginning, middle and end – there is as much to learn as there is to 'unlearn'. A new visual literacy beckons.
>
> The videogram is not designed to fill a slot in a television schedule. It must stand on its own, unsupported by programmes either side of it, and what is more, earn its keep from its first day of publication. It is not a memory of last night's TV. Videograms must be able to stand up to the test of time and repetition. They must be able to survive close scrutiny over many years; that is why I like to label them 'evergreen' programmes. Unlike the ephemeral TV programme, the videodisc will carry its contents as though it has been set in concrete. And because of the ability to speak to the disc-user, unfettered by the strictures of TV programme scheduling and the accidental but inevitable collisions with programmes on competing channels, new and exciting possibilities present themselves.
>
> The main one is a welcome opportunity to provide a much greater information density than even the most carefully crafted TV documentary is able to achieve. At last, programmes like *Life On Earth*, *World At War*, *The Life And Times Of Lord Mountbatten* can, if published on videodisc, carry footnotes and appendices, encompassing a huge array of extra information which the programme maker has been forced to exclude, as the amount of detailed information which can be absorbed in one viewing is so limited. Similarly, a TV drama such as *Gossip From The Forest* could be much enhanced by the addition of complementary videogram reference chapters detailing the historical context which inspired the writer in the first place.
>
> The videogram maker will be inviting the disc-user to participate in an act of communication that is outside the prescribed time-frame of broadcast TV and its inherent passivity. 'What is the running-time of a disc?' will become an irrelevancy. The question is 'how much information can be crowded into a disc?' And if we can develop this new grammar successfully, time will not be the yardstick. The 'non-linear' approach will be measured by something else: involvement, enrichment, entertainment, repeatability and above all, participation. Not a million miles from traditional publishing!

EMI told me that they had got the approval from King's College, Cambridge, to record on video their traditional Service of Nine Lessons and Carols on Christmas Eve. It was quite a coup, and when I was invited to direct this first videogram I grasped the opportunity with both hands. I was asked to direct in such a way that the programme could be transmitted in traditional manner on broadcast television, but at the same time in a way that allowed some of the interactive properties of the videodisc to be exploited.

I realised that to make it 'timeless', the traditional service had to undergo a fundamental change in presentation. The BBC outside broadcast units cover this splendid event every year, and an integral part of it alongside the choir's carols is the lesson readers walking down the aisle to the lectern and returning to their pews. The readers are usually chosen from various walks of Cambridge life, and the fashion of the ladies' hats and coats alone would have made it difficult to create a sense of timelessness – leaving aside the risk taken every year regarding the quality of delivery of the lessons. There had to be some changes.

With enthusiastic support and invaluable help from the Dean of King's College, we transformed this annual event from a religious service into *Christmas Carols from Cambridge*. The first decision was to do away with a congregation, giving me the space and rare opportunity to display the magnificence of some of the chapel's features: the fan vaulting, Tudor heraldry, stone and wood carvings, door and ceiling bosses, paintings and tapestries. In addition I now had the freedom to place the choir in many different locations within the chapel against a variety of rich and unusual backgrounds – and, as it turned out, discover acoustic qualities that had never been put to the test before.

But the most telling transformation was brought about by asking Sir John Gielgud to pre-record the lessons. His reading was of an extraordinary beauty, and his 'evergreen' voice had never sounded better. My recording session with Sir John took place at the EMI Abbey Road Studios. He told me that he was delighted to work in Studio One, made famous by the Beatles.

I illustrated the lessons with appropriate details from the chapel's stained glass windows. As these are totally inaccessible, they had to be reproduced from transparencies taken some years before, when the interior of the chapel was being restored and scaffolding allowed photography. As I have always tried to avoid mixing electronic pictures with film, the textural difference being so jarring, I persuaded Ken Morse, the ace film rostrum cameraman, to replace his film camera temporarily with one of the first relatively small EMI video cameras. This resulted in rostrum camera work of a quality that is so remarkable that it really does look as though the windows were recorded on location.

Since *The Turn of the Screw* eighteen years before, I had not enjoyed and got so much pleasure out of a production. It started with my first planning trip to Cambridge. As I entered King's College Chapel I could not help looking up at that stunning fan vaulting, and it literally took my breath away. No wonder that Sir Christopher Wren is reported to have said, when he first stepped inside, 'I wouldn't know where to place the first stone.' And I was going to work here for five days. I remember thinking that not only was this a great privilege, but that I was actually going to be paid for it.

A video facility company, Trillion Video, provided the crews and hardware for four cameras, plus the small EMI camera. I had asked for a big camera crane, and by the time all the lighting gear was in place this glorious chapel looked like an expensive film set. It was now one week before Christmas, and the director of music, Philip Ledger, appeared to conduct his immaculately rehearsed choir. I was only allowed two two-hour recording sessions a day, so that some of the very young choirboys didn't keel over with fatigue. In fact they were so excited that my floor manager had his hands full preventing them from climbing all over the cameras. Now, nearly forty years later, some of these gifted young rascals may well have their own offspring in the choir.

The original stereo sound was recorded by EMI's senior sound recordist, Christopher Parker, who after many years of making audio records of concerts, operas and indeed carols from King's found himself for the first time in company with cameras, cranes and lights. In spite of that the final sound on this videogram could easily have gone onto audio disc and no one would have been any the wiser. The video and sound editing was carried out at Trillion. We had to develop untried techniques, and as a result pushed forward the art of video editing with stereo sound by a considerable margin.

EMI's courage in commissioning an expensive production such as this on a purely experimental and speculative basis was admirable. From my point of view, the experience gained was immense. I shipped a final version of the videogram to Dick Sonnenfeldt in New

York, and with EMI's blessing he had some experimental SelectaVision discs pressed. Five years later I was able to produce an early 'interactive' disc on the Japanese VHD system and exploit the chapterisation possibilities, with instant access to individual carols and lessons.

I invited a contingent of BBC decision-makers, including Humphrey Burton, to BAFTA and showed them *Christmas Carols from Cambridge* in the Princess Anne Theatre. As a result they transmitted my version twice the following Christmas, replacing their normal outside broadcast. It got good reviews – ensuring that 1977 ended on a high note.

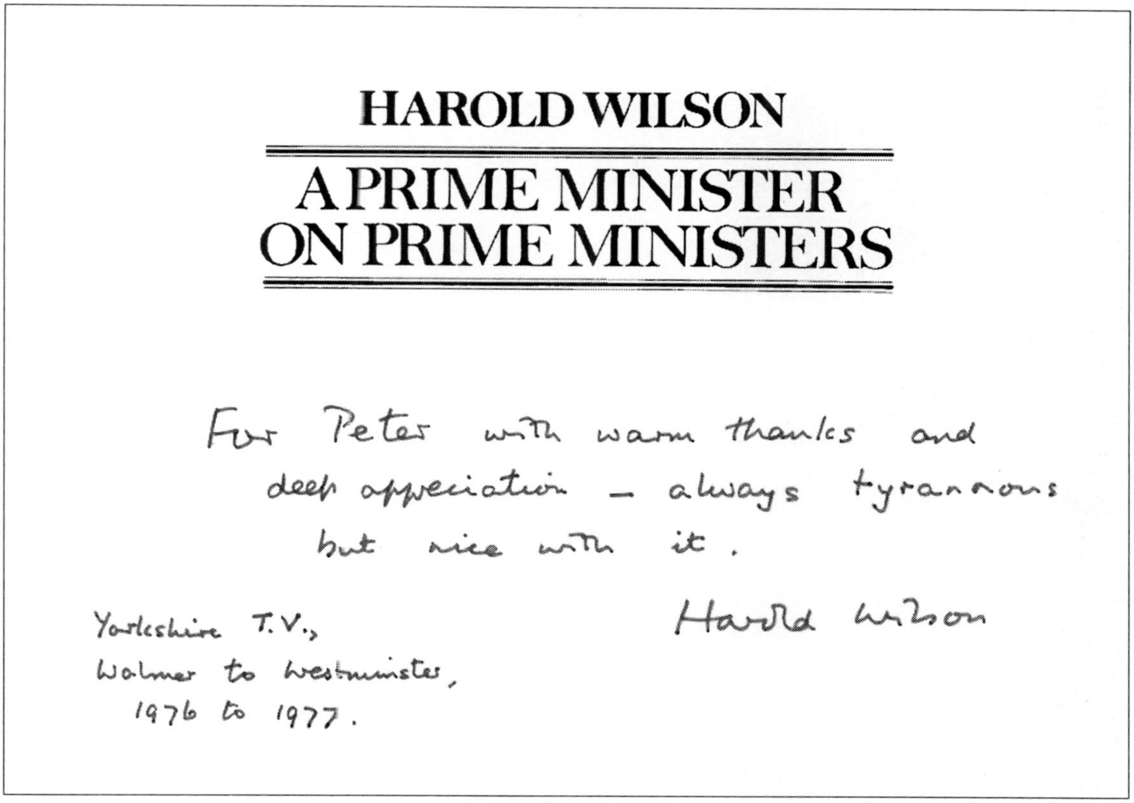

HAROLD WILSON

A PRIME MINISTER ON PRIME MINISTERS

For Peter with warm thanks and deep appreciation – always tyrannous but nice with it.

Harold Wilson

Yorkshire T.V.,
Walmer to Westminster,
1976 to 1977.

27: Kitty - Return to Auschwitz

While I was still cutting *Prime Minister on Prime Ministers* and preparing for the King's Chapel shoot, Paul Fox sounded me out about producing and directing a clutch of six one-hour documentaries for Yorkshire television, telling the stories of acts of extraordinary courage displayed by women during the Second World War. Each one of these was to focus on an individual's lone fight against Nazism and all it stood for. I thought this was a good idea and gladly accepted. We agreed that my contract would start as soon as I had finished my current commitments. The series was to be called *Women of Courage*.

The YTV research team allocated to this project came to see me in my Wardour Street cutting rooms. We established the criteria for the choice of people and their experiences, agreeing that ideally we would focus on untold stories. The chosen women had to be able to speak English and be willing to travel back to the relevant locations. Kevin Sim, who was later to join me as YTV's co-producer on the series, led the research team, assisted by Barbara Twigg. They set off around the world to find and compile a list of potential candidates, and mailed me with progress reports and short synopses.

By May 1978 I had finished editing *Christmas Carols from Cambridge* and started on the new YTV project. The successful research had produced a long and very impressive list of candidates, which had to be whittled down so that I could set off on my travels and meet those who were shortlisted. As I went around the various countries, it became more and more difficult to choose. Each and every one of these women deserved to be included, thanks to their courage and heroism in pursuit of a common cause. Sadly television schedules are not that accommodating.

One of the women was Kitty Hart, a radiologist who lived in Birmingham. The researchers were deeply impressed by the story of her survival in Auschwitz, and begged me to include her on my short list – urging me to go to Birmingham to meet her. I was reluctant to do this as I could not see how her story, although quite extraordinary, could possibly match the criteria we had laid down. All the other candidates were mature women who had made conscious decisions to fight evil regimes, while Kitty Hart was an immature twelve-year-old who was simply engulfed by events.

Kitty came from a Jewish community in the small town of Bielsko in Poland, and after the German invasion was on the run with her mother. In his despair Kitty's father made a courageous and selfless decision: by bribing some officials with the remnants of his wealth, he procured false Aryan papers for his wife and daughter, and had them smuggled onto a train transporting Polish slave labourers to work inside Germany. He hoped that as immigrant workers their chances of survival might just increase. They never saw him again.

Four years later, in 1943, Kitty and her mother were betrayed while working as labourers in Dresden, and their false identities were discovered. They were arrested, tried and dispatched to Auschwitz, not because they were Jewish but because they had committed a serious crime:

‘endangering the security of the Third Reich . . . had illegally entered Germany with forged papers . . . herewith sentenced to hard labour for life’. Kitty was aged sixteen. She and her mother faced an entirely new challenge as they arrived in Auschwitz-Birkenau – only a stone’s throw away from their home town of Bielsko.

Kitty’s was a complex story of courageous self-preservation and ultimate survival. If we were to go ahead and tell her story, I realised I would have to ask YTV to let me make the film as a one-off documentary, not part of the series – and I doubted very much whether they would increase the budget for this extra programme. Nevertheless, at the researchers’ insistence I reluctantly agreed to take the train up to Birmingham.

I bought some flowers for Kitty at the station. When she opened her front door to greet me she placed them on a chair in her hall before showing me into her sitting room. I very soon realised that she was counting on being taken back to Auschwitz, and that the researchers had given her to understand that this was likely to happen. I was a bit alarmed, because of my initial concerns about the project.

Kitty took me over to the mantelpiece and handed me a small transparent Perspex presentation stand. Mounted inside it were two separate pieces of human skin, each one bearing a camp number: one was hers, the other her mother’s. They had them removed from their arms when they finally settled in England after the war, and their display on the mantelpiece served as a visible and constant reminder of their time in Auschwitz. Kitty had prepared a light lunch, and when we sat down she produced a small loaf of bread that she had baked, and ceremonially cut off one slice. As she held it up for me to see, she said that it represented ‘life or death – the daily Auschwitz bread ration’, used by the inmates both for sustenance and for bribing and bartering. Every day since she had settled in Birmingham after the war she had observed this ritual.

After lunch we sat down in her living room and I got the full impact of her fight for survival, delivered with an unstoppable eloquence that left me speechless and exhausted. I made my excuses to return to London in the early evening, with another visit planned for the following week.

On the train home I tried to analyse the situation. Here was a survivor with an almost unbelievable story to tell, and a most persuasive way of telling it. Kitty appeared to ‘live’ Auschwitz every day, surrounded by memorabilia that recalled her experiences. She told me that right through the post-war years she had felt completely detached from that particular part of her life and had refused to get involved emotionally in the past, pretending that it didn’t happen. ‘I didn’t allow my brain to take it in – I couldn’t go on living if I did.’ And yet she had surrounded herself with Auschwitz artefacts to remind her, every day, of the very events she had refused ‘to take in’. I was confused. Was this how she was able to cope with memories? Was she burdened by a feeling of guilt? What effect would a return to Auschwitz have on her? Could it be damaging? Was I prepared to accept the responsibility of taking that risk, quite apart from possibly having to face accusations of media manipulation? Would Yorkshire TV concur? It was a troubled journey.

On my next visit I learned a great deal more about Kitty. She had little time for what she called the trivialities of life. For instance, when I arrived at her house the flowers from my previous visit were still in place, unwrapped, on the hall chair. I took her out for lunch in her local pub. On the way there the heavens opened and I suggested that I would run back to fetch an umbrella. ‘Don’t be daft,’ she said. ‘So it rains and we get wet – so what?’

We got on very well and I was able to ask many questions. I got the impression that she not only wanted to but really needed to go back – maybe to find tangible and convincing proof that she had, in reality, lived through that hell thirty-three years before, and survived it.

I discovered that Kitty’s eldest son, David, a young doctor working in Vancouver, was very keen to see Auschwitz. Kitty phoned him, and when I spoke to him he said that he would gladly fly over from Canada to accompany his mother; he felt that the time had come for her to make the return journey. I felt reassured that accompanied by her doctor son she would be in safe hands, and this finally persuaded me that it was a risk worth taking.

I consulted Paul Fox and explained the situation to him. I was keen to make the film, and suggested that as a first step I should go on a recce trip to Auschwitz before reporting back to him with a proposal.

Now I was free to go ahead and get ideas on how to translate Kitty's story into a film. The story was becoming clear, and now the film's style had to be decided in the light of the locations and all the obvious logistical problems that were bound to arise. I flew with Kevin Sim to Krakow, and from there we took a taxi to the camp. The emotions stirred by my arrival at Auschwitz-Birkenau are hard to describe. None of the films and programmes I had made touching on the Nazi period prepared me for what I experienced. As far as the eye could see from the top of the main building's watchtower loomed this vast camp. It had never occurred to me to consider its physical size; Auschwitz statistics are measured in a headcount of people, not in acres. It became painfully obvious that taking in millions of people at one end and reducing them to ashes at the other required facilities on a massive scale. The few films I had seen on the Holocaust had not made this clear to me, and now there was an opportunity to film Kitty and David in a way that would convey the obscene size of Birkenau. This, then, would be a story of survival, seen through the eyes of one person and set against this immense and horrendous site.

Some of my YTV colleagues had suggested that a reporter should accompany Kitty to interview her. I could not accept this, as I was certain that this would stifle her natural, eloquent delivery; it would blunt the impact of a mother telling her son what she and his grandmother had endured. In any case, I felt that the intrusion of a questioning outsider in a very private and highly emotional situation was unacceptable.

With this in mind the style for the film became clear. I had got to know Kitty well enough to be fairly certain that once she entered Auschwitz-Birkenau she would take control of the situation and pour out her recollections to David, peppering them with anecdotes. This, no doubt, was going to be a very raw film, and its style would have to reflect this. I felt this was a unique opportunity to add fresh insight into the infamy of Auschwitz.

I explained to my colleagues that restraint was the order of the day. The style was going to be purely observational – a technique I first used in the late '50s, of course – as it was imperative to capture the truth. This style relies on an element of luck, as it depends on the people being filmed becoming so preoccupied that they are oblivious of the camera.

On my return I went up to York to put my plans to Paul Fox, who needed reassurance that Kitty really wanted to go on this pilgrimage. I was able to convince him and he was very supportive, even though I warned him that the main risk was Kitty's reaction on arriving at the camp. If she took one look and decided she could not, after all, go through with it, an expensive YTV crew would be left high and dry on location, with no film to bring home and a blown budget. Typically Paul backed the project despite this, and wished me luck.

Then I suggested that YTV should consider Kitty's story as a one-off television film. That is what happened, and the film, now known as *Kitty – Return to Auschwitz*, became a ninety-minute documentary. The *Women of Courage* series was reduced to a quartet of one-hour films that told the stories of four remarkable women from Norway, Poland, England and Germany. All these five films were shot over a period of six months.

* * * *

It was November 1978, and the filming of *Kitty – Return to Auschwitz* was about to start. I arrived with the crew in Krakow, about 50 miles from Auschwitz and the closest town to it. We were all booked into the Holiday Inn – an inappropriate name if ever there was one. Kitty and David arrived the following day, and over dinner I was able to brief them. I explained that very early in the morning they would travel to Auschwitz in a taxi, and that the sound assistant would wave them down about a quarter of a mile from the camp's main gate. He would wire them up with radio microphones, and send the taxi on its way. The driver would be instructed to drop them at the gate, as I was keen to capture Kitty's reaction to seeing the outside of the camp for the first time after so long. I explained that the crew and I would be inconspicuous: we would keep our distance, simply observing them with the camera, and would follow her wherever she chose to go. I would not offer any suggestions or instructions, and there would be no prompting or cueing; in fact, I would not be speaking to her at all. From the moment the taxi stopped and dropped them off they would be on their own. At this point Kitty confessed that she was worried about how she would react on seeing the camp again. I crossed my fingers.

It was 18 November – a bitterly cold morning – and we were ready. I knew that we might have to walk huge distances and could be miles away from the camera truck, so to ensure uninterrupted filming the cameraman, Frank Pocklington, his assistant, the sound recordist and I weighed ourselves down with as many film magazines as we could carry. In order to hear every word spoken by Kitty and her son, Frank and I wore cans, with short cables plugged into the recordist's mobile equipment. By keeping very close to Frank I could whisper instructions into his ear. We were a small, mobile and compact unit.

As Kitty and David approached we started filming, and I held my breath as they got out of the taxi. Kitty paused for a moment, and then took her first tentative steps through the main gate of Auschwitz-Birkenau. I felt now that we stood a fair chance of bringing back a unique film.

We followed them into the camp, keeping a distance of about 20 yards; I did not want to intrude. When she was inside the camp Kitty stopped, looked and sobbed. I had to fight back my tears. Later Frank warned me that these opening shots might be slightly out of focus, as the eyepiece of his camera had filled with tears.

When Kitty had composed herself, she said, 'I've come to speak for all the people who died here . . .' and from that moment she took command of the situation, never drawing breath. It was as though a bottle of rare vintage champagne had been uncorked and its contents were unstoppably gushing out. I sensed that she felt herself under great pressure to prove to herself that the memories she had lived with all these years were really true. She was in a great hurry. Kitty explained to David that she was there because some people were denying that the Holocaust had ever happened, and as there would soon be no one left who survived Auschwitz she owed it to future generations to explain what had happened before it was too late. 'You're here just to see that it's true. Thirty members of your family have died here. Your grandfather, your grandmother, my family, all my school friends, everybody out of our home town. Everybody's ashes are here.'

And so for three long and freezing days we followed Kitty with the camera running, not knowing where she was taking David next. Time and time again she surprised him, and us, with the most dreadful revelations.

I noticed quite early on that a curious change was taking place between mother and son, as though their natural relationship had been temporarily suspended – his mother had become a sort of stranger to him. On the few occasions when Kitty broke down in the middle of some poignant recall, David appeared to find it awkward to come close to her, and was hesitant in putting his arm round her shoulder. His few questions were quickly put down; she found it hard to tolerate interruptions to her flow of recollections. She seemed to resent his presence, but conversely appeared to be glad that there was someone who was listening to her. There was just one occasion when Kitty put a question to her son, wanting to know whether she should feel any guilt about the actions she took in order to survive:

> . . . you see, I realised one very important thing. That one of the best things to do in this camp was to do nothing. Just . . . just . . . be invisible . . . just, you know . . . hide, hide. I mean there were fifty thousand . . . hundred thousand people here, so you could hide behind people if you were small, insignificant, invisible as I tried to be. But the other thing I found is that one of the best things to do was to carry bodies. Why? I mean, it was very hard work but (a) you worked inside the camp – you didn't do external work, you see; and (b) the dead body had a bread ration; a piece of bread! The dead body had one change of clothes, and it wasn't any good to this dead body, was it? I mean, I don't have to feel guilty about this, do I?'

Kitty looked as though she gladly accepted her son's reassurance – and I learnt something about the guilt of surviving.

On the first day we filmed continuously for six hours. Bad light and total exhaustion brought the shooting to an end. I purposely did not contact Kitty after we had returned to the hotel that night, and the next morning we continued exactly where she had left off. By the end of the third day the essential footage was in the can – and I had not spoken to her once.

There was one particular event during the filming which troubled me at first. Kitty had found the block where thousands of women at a time were herded in for their almost waterless ablutions. It was dark inside and there were no windows, so we could not follow the two of them in. But I whispered to Frank to keep the camera running, and then heard David exclaim that he had found a shoe.

'Oh my God!' said Kitty. 'Leather shoes . . . that meant life or death for somebody. To have a pair of leather shoes meant fifteen days' bread ration – so either you ate or you had your pair of leather shoes.' As she walked out into daylight, caressing this battered object, I thought that no one would believe this. I had seen a mountain of many thousands of similar shoes in the Auschwitz museum. What was a single one doing in this pitch-dark block? How did it get there? Had it languished there since 1945 when the Russians liberated the camp? Later I queried it with the curator of Birkenau, and he too was baffled. The fact that there was no light inside the ablution block may have allowed the relic to escape detection for thirty-four years – but its presence has remained a mystery to this day.

I had to think twice whether to include this sequence in the final cut. If someone thought that I had planted the shoe in advance, for the sake of 'good television', might it not undermine the honesty of the whole film? The same could also have applied to the moment when Kitty led us to the pits where people were burned alive. With a stick she dug around in the ashes and found a human bone. 'This represents a small proportion of the 4 million,' she said to David, 'and perhaps your grandparents – perhaps.' Had someone planted this small bone fragment? Should this end up on the cutting room floor? I believe, though, that if you don't have complete faith in the veracity of your own material and embark on a course of dubious self-censorship, you should not be making this type of film.

I spent another day filming in Birkenau, picking up linking and atmospheric footage. Although I had finished with Kitty and David they came back to the camp on their own, as she wanted to relive and retrace the last three days. When I came across them walking along the infamous railway track, leading to the crematoria, we spoke briefly, for the first time inside the camp. The next morning they returned to London, where David caught his flight back to Vancouver.

We had one more day in which to film essential links. The most important was a very long tracking shot inside a latrine block, with an array of over sixty holes that served the bodily functions of over 2,000 inmates. Only a small amount of light filtered into this block, so we had to find a mains supply for the small number of lights we had brought with us – and I recruited the help of the camp's resident maintenance man. He ran a long cable to the rusted barbed wire fencing about a hundred yards away and connected it to the perimeter lighting circuit, which, to our absolute amazement, was still live and functioning.

For me, this tracking shot turned out to be one of the most telling and most painful in the whole film. It plays in total silence for one minute, slowly exposing hole after hole in this obscene, endless concrete slab. Barbarity revealed.

The maintenance man then told me that on the previous day he had seen Kitty and David disappear into one of the blocks nearby, and had overheard her telling him that she was going to write her name and camp number on a wall, as she had spent many nights there. I was determined to find the inscription. Darkness had set in, so I went off with the cameraman and one of our battery lights. Going inside several blocks to find Kitty's message was eerie beyond words. I was about to abandon the search when I found it. We took one shot, seconds before the battery in our lamp died – and that became the very last shot in the film. It simply stated:

> Kitty-Felix Hart 39934
> 18.11.1978

* * * *

I travelled to Warsaw with the crew to shoot one of the *Women of Courage* documentaries, and arrived back in London eight days later. I was very keen to phone Kitty to find how she had reacted to the trip, and I got my biggest surprise yet. Tearfully she said that she felt terrible because she had let me down, let the crew down, let YTV down. I asked what she meant. 'All the trouble you've taken, all that expense of flying everyone to Auschwitz, and I never opened my mouth once.' And she had never stopped talking for three solid days!

When I finished the cut Kitty came up to London and I screened it for her. She was dumbfounded, and could hardly believe that it was her speaking, non-stop throughout the whole film. I ran it again, and slowly she began to realise how much the return to Auschwitz had affected her.

* * * *

Reactions to the initial ITV network transmission in November 1979 were very positive, with huge press coverage. YTV was delighted with the exceptionally high viewer rating of close on 13 million. Kitty was inundated with letters – they came by the sackful. Even those optimistically addressed to 'Kitty, Birmingham' reached her.

I was intrigued by a few telephone calls from viewers who wondered where I had found that old black and white footage I used in the film. I had deliberately not used a single frame of archive film: the word pictures that Kitty painted in people's minds were far more graphic than old newsreel film. Extraordinary.

The film was subsequently shown on television around the world, including in Germany, and produced my largest collection of press cuttings:

> *Sunday Telegraph* – Philip Purser: The only pictures of Auschwitz were as it is today: vast, desolate, blank: not a single frame from the appalling historical material available. Yet Peter Morley's rigorous self-limitation made this one of the most vivid and complete evocations of the infamous extermination complex I have encountered, certainly much more so than the fictional reconstructions.
>
> *New York Times* – Richard F. Shepard: *Kitty – Return to Auschwitz* is probably unlike any other program you have seen in the welter of television in fact or in fiction with the extermination-camp horror. This is a documentary that might be called a testamentary. Mrs Hart is the narrator, and she and her grown son are the only ones seen as they wander over the vast, rather bucolic and silent land known as Auschwitz in the plains of Poland. It is an extraordinarily touching program. So many others have tried to recapture the evil spirit of Auschwitz. It is eloquent in its restraint.
>
> National Catholic News Service: The British documentary, directed by Peter Morley, not only adds to our understanding of the Holocaust but is also a sensitive portrait of a survivor of mass hatred who can never forget the experience, but knows that living cannot be based on hatred and revenge.
>
> *Newsday*: This a documentary? No. It's too moving. This is non-fiction drama, a one-woman show, unaided by standard footage from the archives. Peter Morley has made a work of art. Restraint!
>
> *Indelible Shadows* by Holocaust historian Annette Insdorf: To see Kitty testifying in the physical context of the now silent death camp results in a uniquely cinematic event, as historically significant as it is emotionally wrenching.
>
> The historian Jon Toland: To my surprise, her oral history turned out to be at least as effective as any written record I've read, if not more so.

The film attracted a clutch of national and international awards: the Royal Television Society's Documentary Award, the Commonwealth Documentary Award, and in 1981 a particularly poignant award: the Berlin Prix Futura.

YTV generously paid for Jane to accompany me to Berlin to attend the Prix Futura Festival, as *Kitty* had been short-listed. This was Jane's first visit to Germany. I was able to introduce her to Berlin and take her to the locations that were so much of my past. My sister, with her phenomenal memory, provided the details of locations, such as the site of the family apartment where I was born, the bakery round the corner where, apparently, I was sent to buy doughnuts, and my primary school – all rebuilt. I had become fairly familiar with the city while researching and filming for *The Mighty Continent* and other documentaries. I took Jane to the observation platform in the notorious Bernauer Straße, making it possible to look over the Berlin Wall. A typical swathe of the 'Iron Curtain' was revealed, with its tank traps, minefields, barbed wire and snarling Alsatian guard dogs tethered to long leads. It was all so grey and depressing, as were the memorial crosses, permanently adorned with fresh flowers, that marked where East Germans had been shot during their attempts to flee to the West.

The next day the international jury announced that I had won the Prix Futura, and I savoured the irony of the situation – an irony that did not escape many of those who attended the presentation ceremony. This was held in the orangery of the rebuilt Charlottenburg Palace, the old town palace of the Kaiser. The last time I had seen it was in 1945, when it lay in ruin and ashes, as I drove past it in my tank. And now, thirty-six years later, as Dr Guido Brunner, the Burgomaster of Berlin, presented me with the prestigious Berlin Prix Futura, he shook my hand and said, 'I believe your film makes this a very special award.' He was right.

Earlier that year *Kitty* had been shown twice on the American PBS network, and I was subsequently invited to the Banff Television Festival in the Canadian Rockies to show it to delegates and speak at a seminar on its production. There were a great number of American television people present, and I believe that this was what sparked off the interest shown by the three big US networks. But it was Pamela Hill, a brilliant documentary producer who was in charge of ABC Television's prestigious monthly peak-time documentary slot, who approached YTV for the screening rights for the USA. She stipulated that the programme should be cut down to sixty minutes, and wanted a transcript from YTV for this purpose. When I heard about this I phoned her and offered to make the cuts myself, explaining that it was my baby and I would hate anyone else to do the butchery. She agreed, and said she would come over to London to look at the proposed cut-down version. The following week she arrived in my Soho cutting room, where she saw the film and agreed to my cuts. After dinner at the Savoy, where she was staying, Pamela said that she would like to invite Kitty and me to New York for the screening.

A week later the invitations from ABC arrived: tickets for Kitty and me to fly over on Concorde, with reservations for two suites in the fabulously lush Helmsley Palace Hotel. Both of us enjoyed the adventure! The flight was memorable, especially the devilled kidneys for breakfast. We were met at Kennedy airport by Pamela's secretary, who escorted us in a stretched limousine to the hotel. Kitty's sitting room was piled to the ceiling with flowers, and mine was suitably stacked with champagne and wines of all descriptions. What a welcome, what an extravagance, how delightfully over the top and how very American. It would all be much more frugal today.

The next morning we appeared on ABC's *Good Morning America* and took part in two press conferences. I said to Pamela that it was almost an 'Un-American Activity' to pre-empt one of her own peak-time shows in order to make room for a British documentary – this had never happened before. We were wined and dined, and that evening's transmission sparked off another round of press interviews the following morning. Soon afterwards I received through the post the American Clarion Award for the best Network TV Program in the Human Rights Division.

Four years on, in 1985, Japan staged what they rather innocently termed the first International Television Festival. The organisers combed the world for what they considered to be the best documentaries ever made and selected a long list of international productions as their nominations for the Tokyo Prize, inviting the directors of each one to Tokyo. From the UK they selected a BBC documentary about the making of the H-bomb and also *Kitty*. At the time I was involved in videodisc production and had close associations with JVC in Tokyo, and when they discovered that I had been invited to this Japanese festival they invited 'Mrs Morley' to accompany me. At last, after all these years, Jane was able to join me on one of my exotic trips to the Far East, and we were able to fly out first-class, in style. Ever since I had made *The Two Faces of Japan*, over thirty years earlier, I had hoped that one day I would be able to show her Japan. And now it was happening.

But first came the festival. Each director of the nominated programmes had to address the festival jury, made up of 150 Japanese television producers and directors, before the screening of their film. There was instantaneous translation for all, and I saw some really excellent documentaries from other countries, including a dramatisation from Holland of the Wannsee Conference of 1942, at which Heydrich presented the 'Final Solution', using the verbatim dialogue from the minutes taken at the time. I felt that this was certain to get the prize.

Then came the result of the jury's vote, and to my great surprise *Kitty* triumphed. The chairman of NHK (the BBC of Japan, which had sponsored the festival), presented me with the Tokyo Prize. Two weeks later *Kitty* was shown on the Fuji Television network. Reaction to this foreign documentary by the press and the viewing public was so overwhelming that a repeat was transmitted almost at once.

JVC took over after the festival, putting us up in the grand Imperial Hotel for a week and providing one of their bright young executives to take us to Kyoto, where we stayed for a few days. I had kept in touch with Ian Mutsu, who had given me all the technical and other support in 1960 for *The Two Faces of Japan*, and when we got back to Tokyo I made contact with him, so we had another guide to show us around. It was a memorable trip.

* * * *

But what puts all these awards into the shade is the most valuable reward of all – the lasting effect that the return to Auschwitz had on Kitty herself. The film totally changed her attitude to her incarceration and to her survival. Over twenty-five years have now elapsed but we have kept in close touch, and I have witnessed, with admiration, the new lifestyle that Kitty has chosen since her cathartic return trip. She faced those unspeakable experiences in a new light, and my early misgivings about the great risk of taking her back have faded. When I first got to know her I felt that she probably needed to return, but I had no inkling that her pilgrimage would result in such profound changes. Gone is the mantelpiece display of the preserved camp numbers, gone is the ritual of baking the Auschwitz loaf, gone are the memorabilia that cast such a negative spell on her past. Instead there has emerged a new and positive attitude to life in general, and to her experiences and survival in particular.

Ever since the film's transmission in November 1979 Kitty has been in huge demand. She has lectured in dozens of schools on the Holocaust. She has visited Bielsko, where the Jewish community, which included thirty members of her family, perished. She has taken student groups on numerous trips to Auschwitz, and has played an active role in countering those who have denied that anything ever happened.

The raw style of the film, eschewing cold statistics, interviews and conventional film-making, managed to establish a truth about the camp that is unchallengeable – and thanks to her courage and her eloquence Kitty gave the word Auschwitz a new meaning.

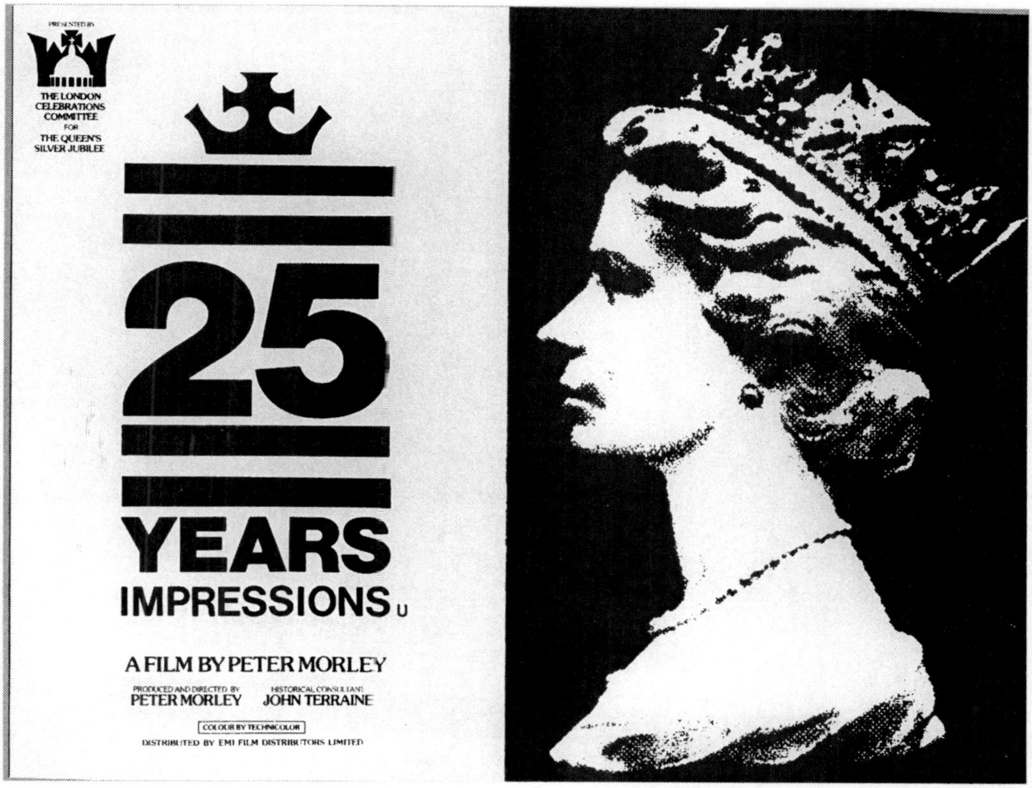

My film about the Queen's Silver Jubilee was made in 1976. (EMI Films)

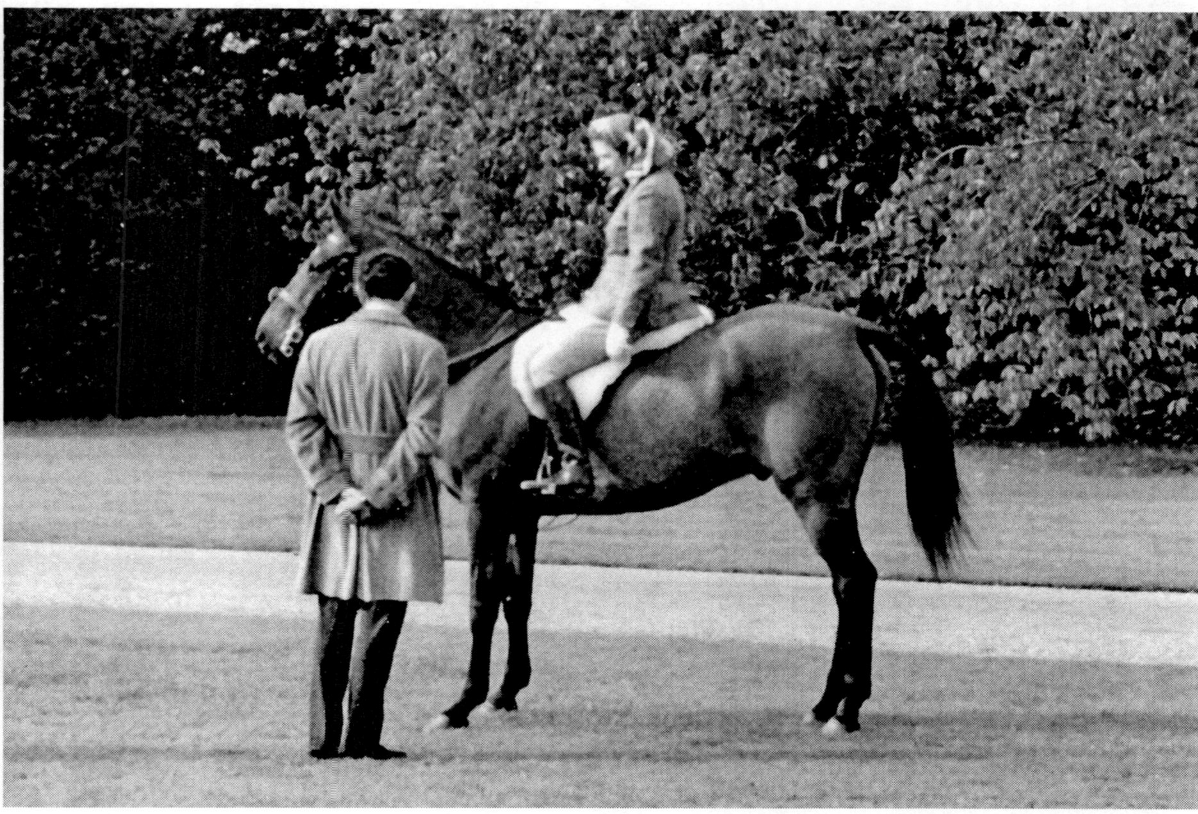

With the Queen, planning and filming the riding sequences in Windsor Great Park. (EMI Films)

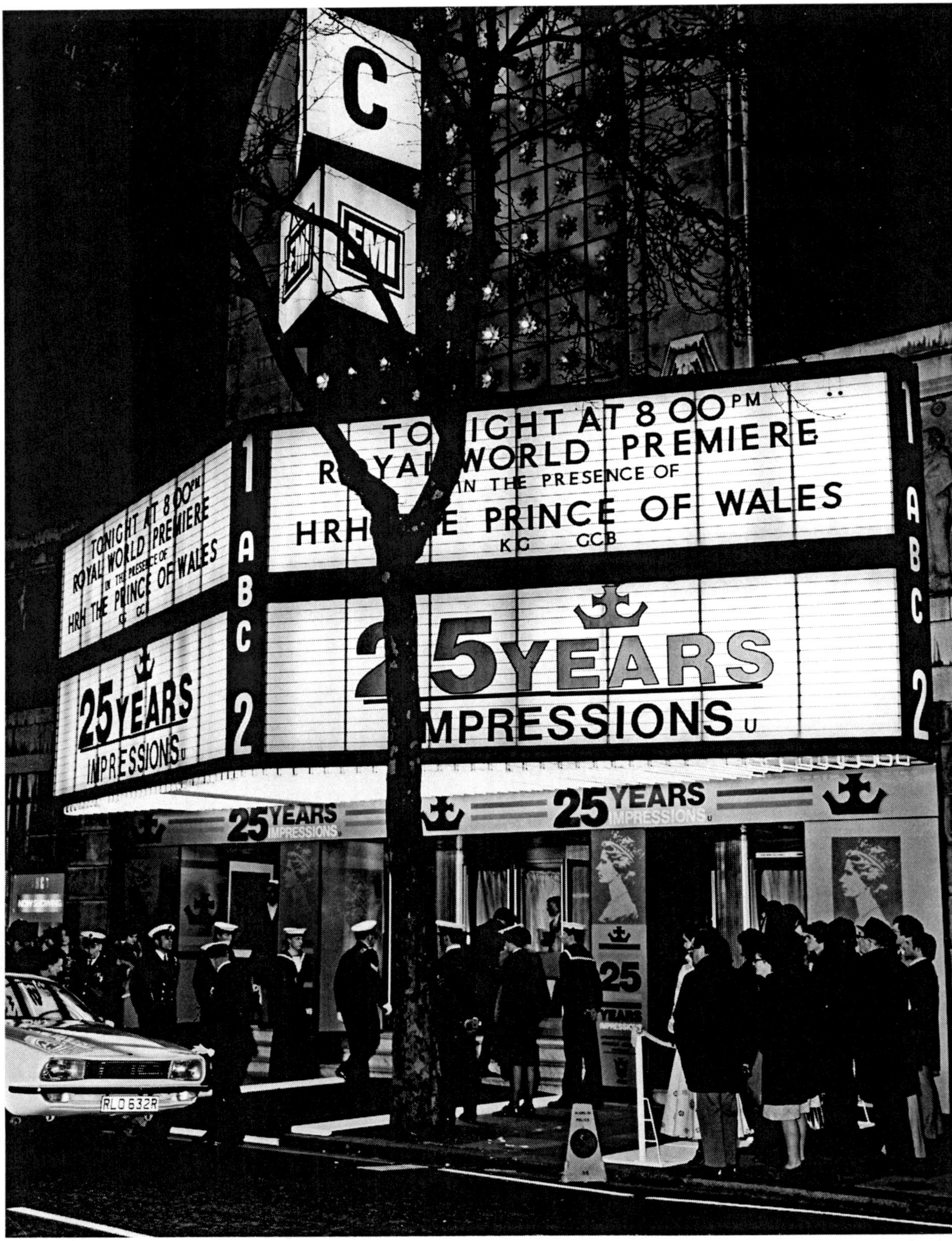

The West End première of EMI's *25 Years – Impressions* at the ABC Cinema in Shaftesbury Avenue, 16 February 1977. (EMI Films)

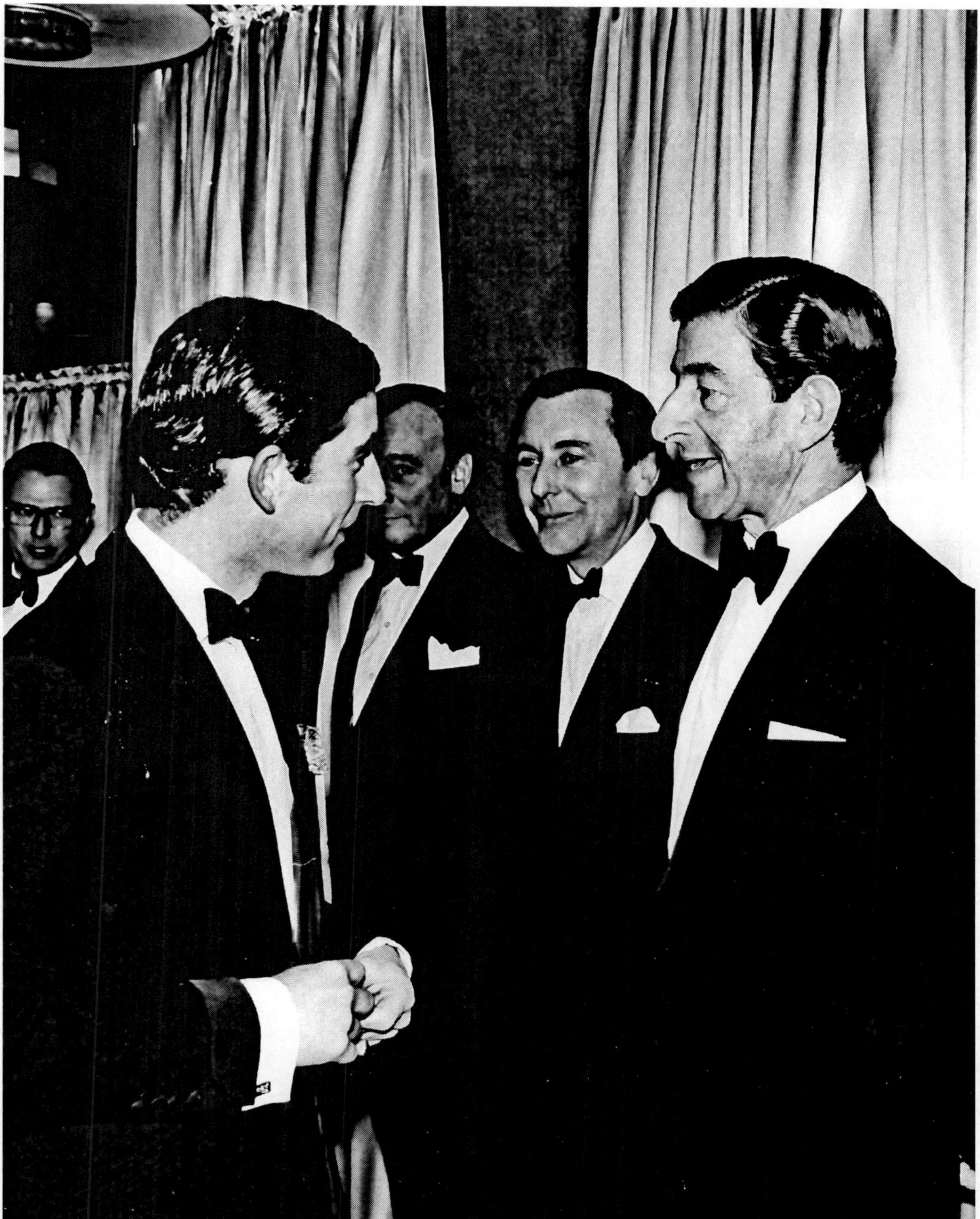

Prince Charles stands in for the Queen, who was on her Silver Jubilee Commonwealth Tour. (EMI Films)

Christmas Carols from Cambridge, 1977

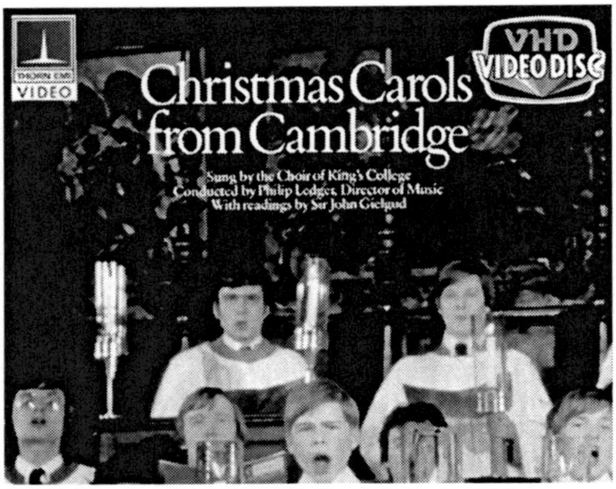

The sleeve for the VHD videodisc. (EMI Films)

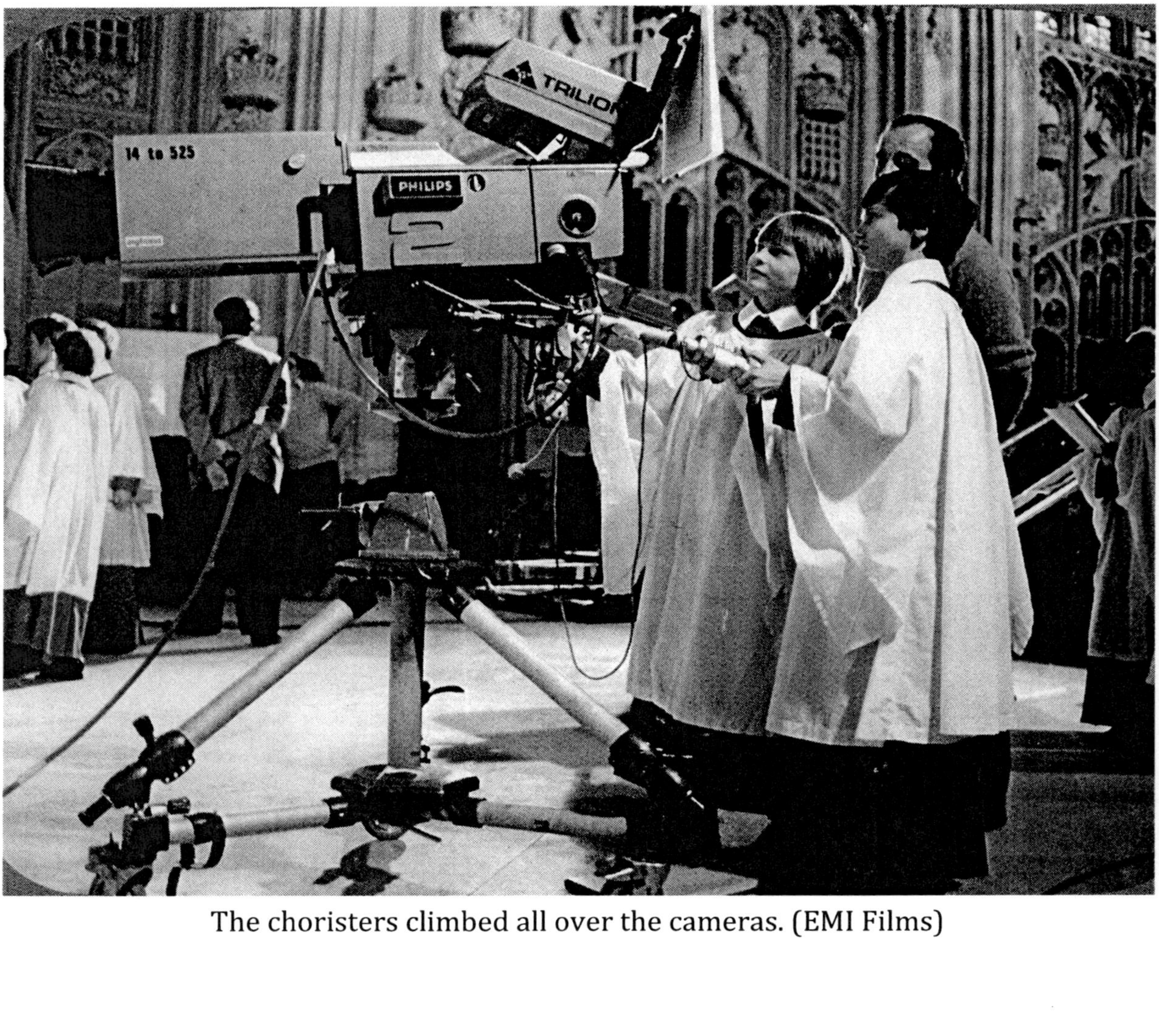

The choristers climbed all over the cameras. (EMI Films)

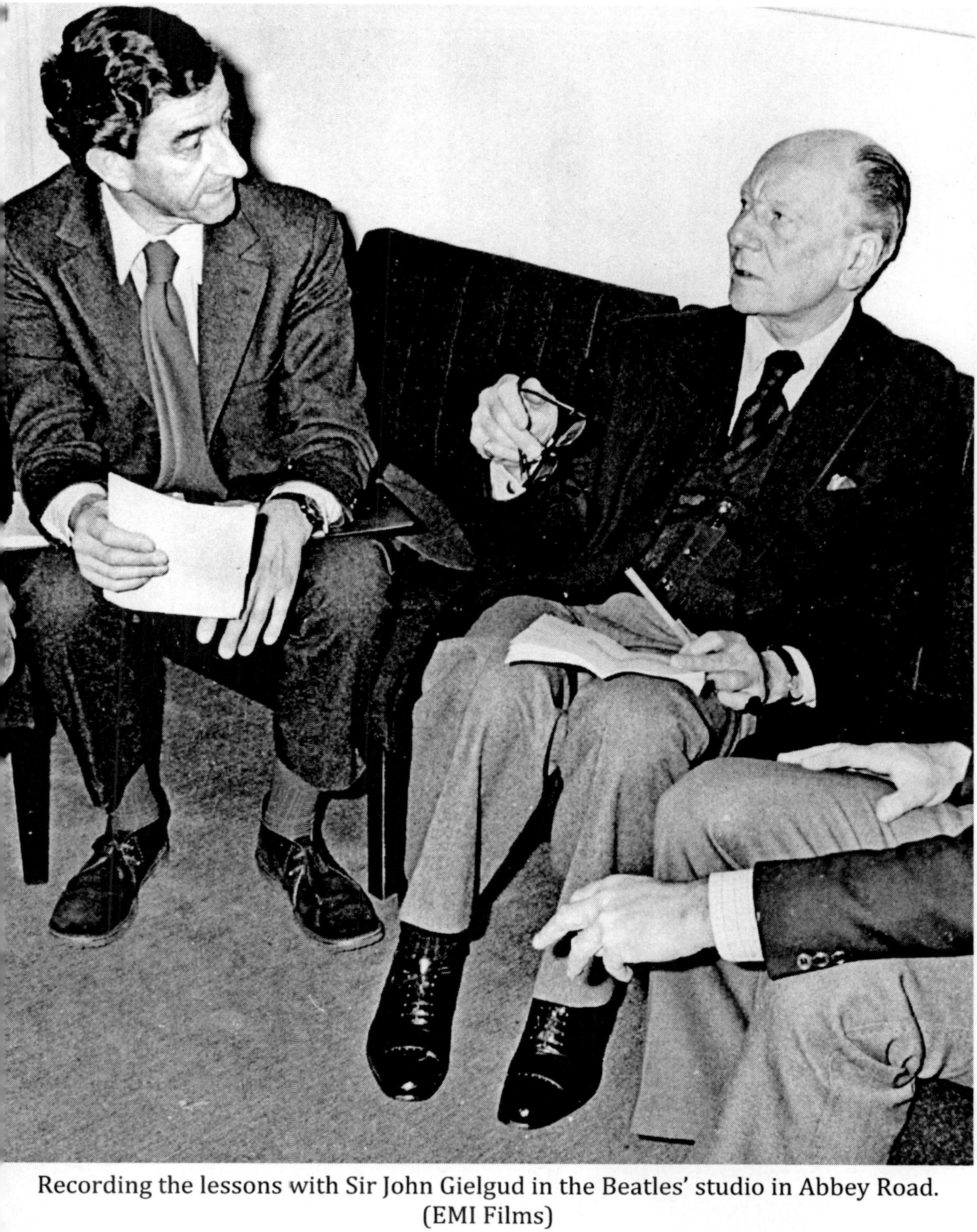

Recording the lessons with Sir John Gielgud in the Beatles' studio in Abbey Road.
(EMI Films)

Kitty – Return to Auschwitz, 1978

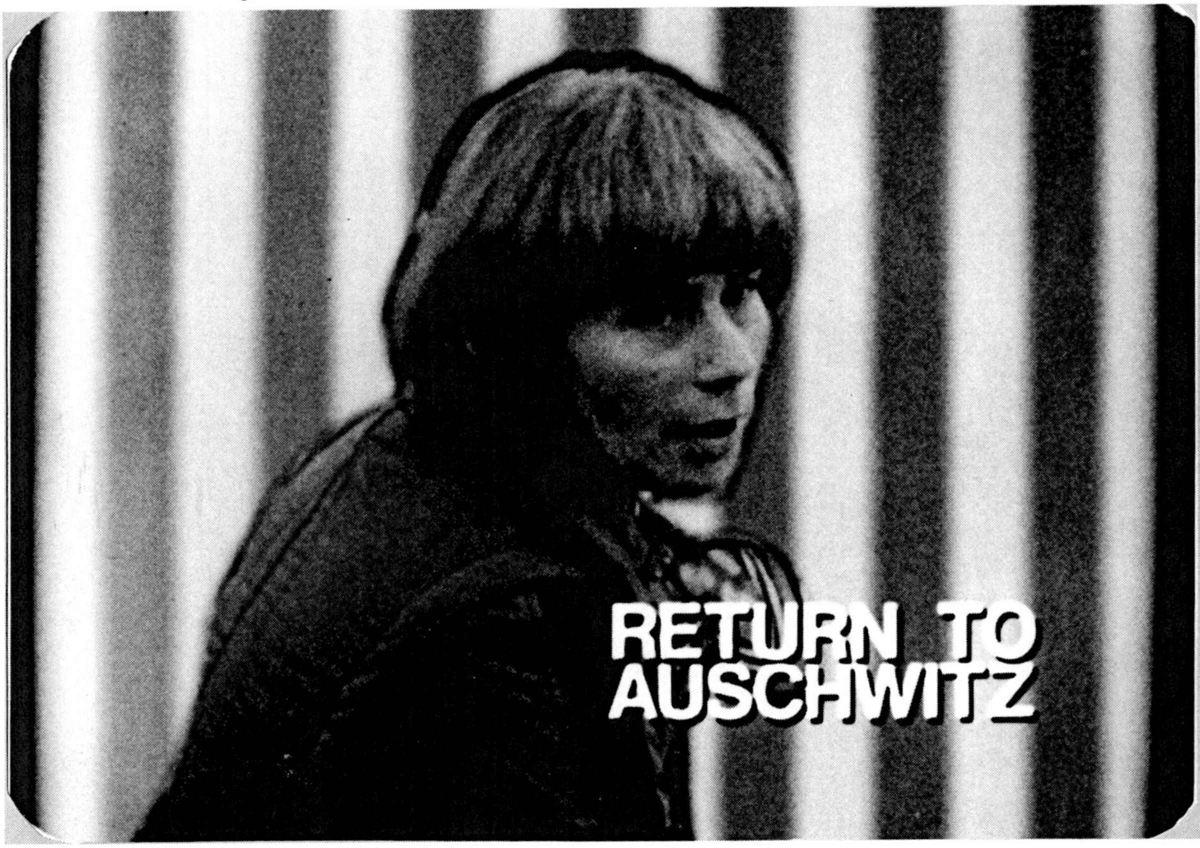

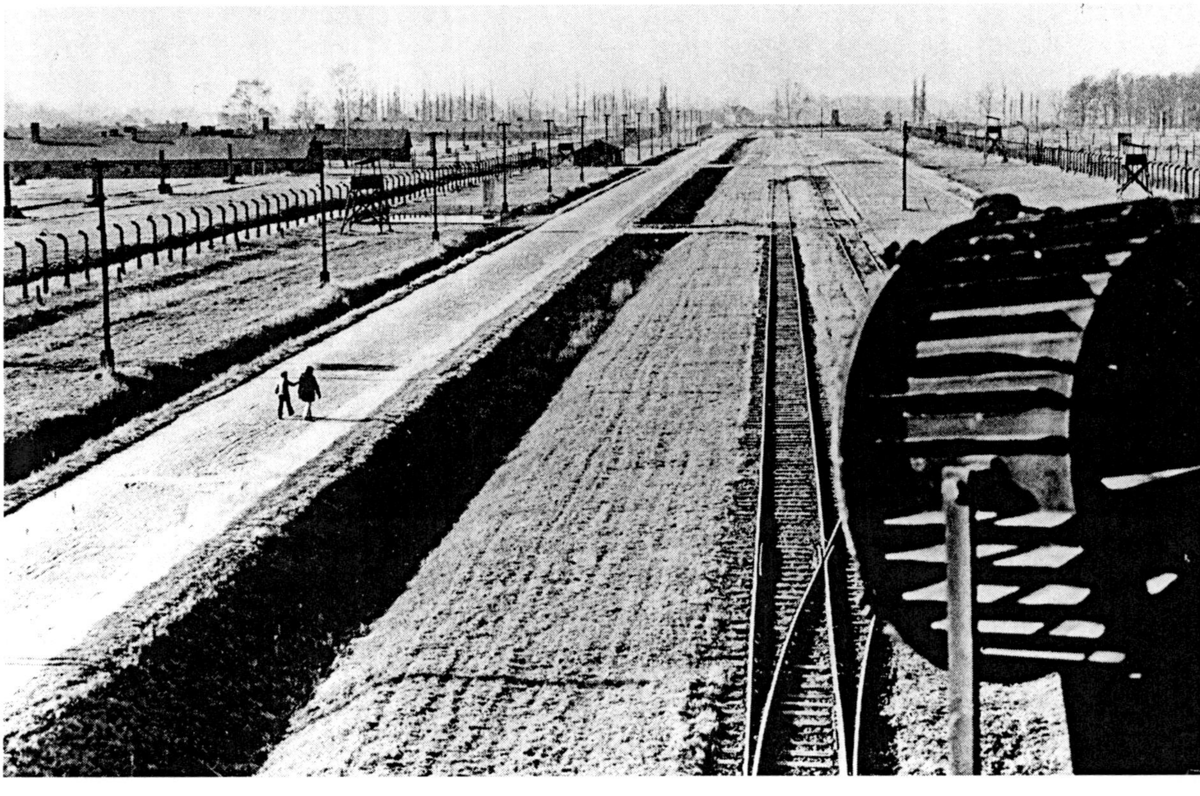

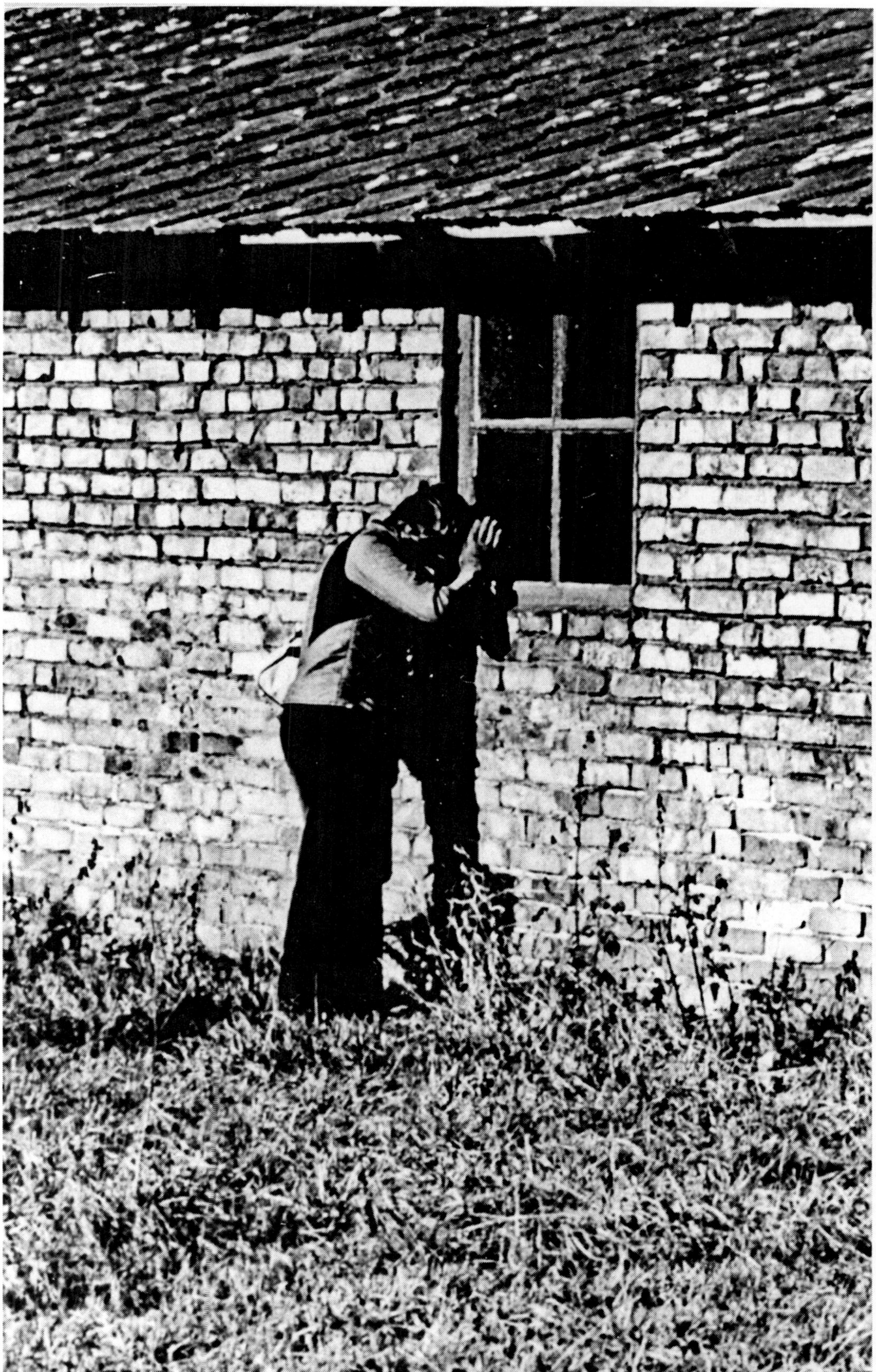

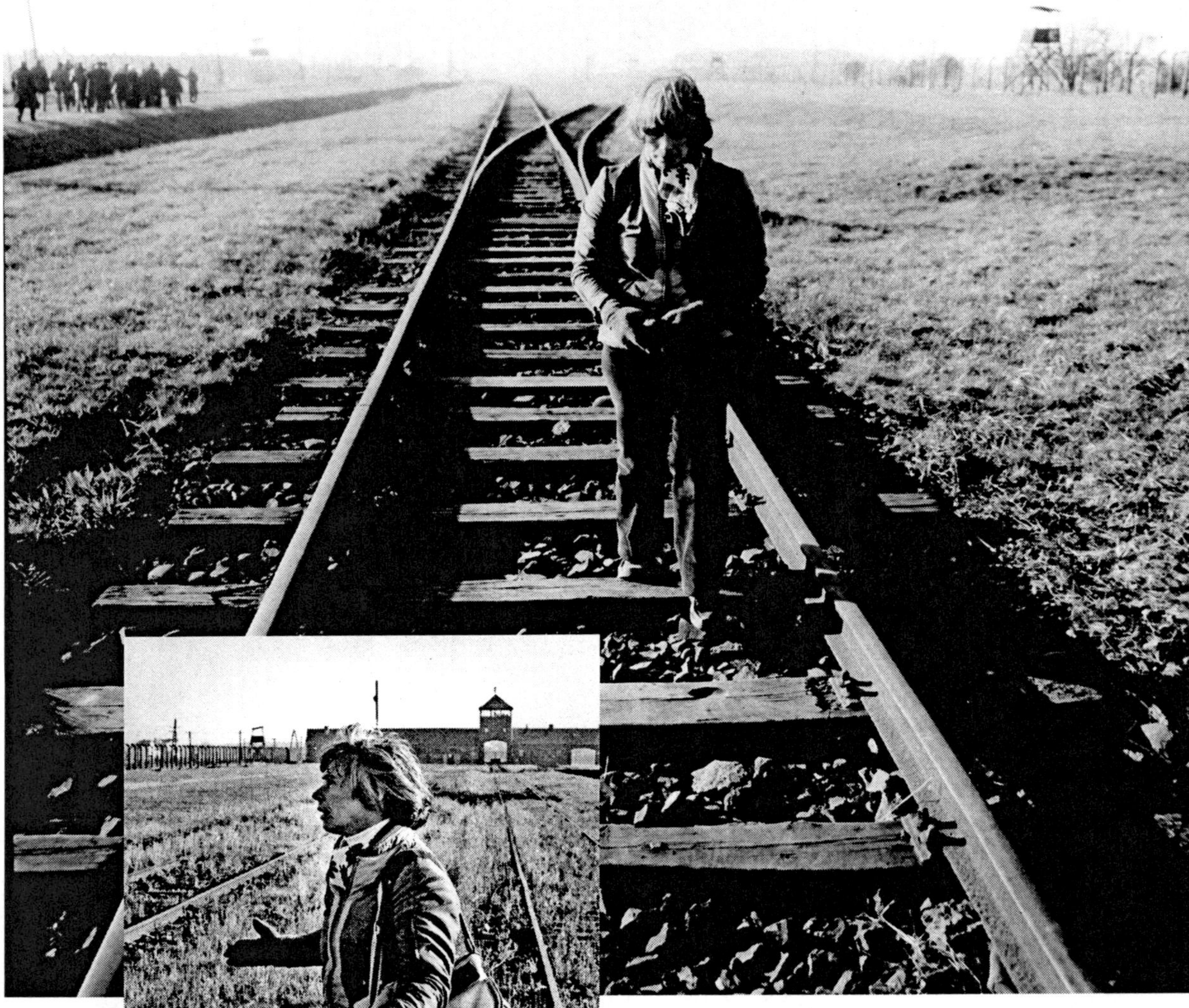

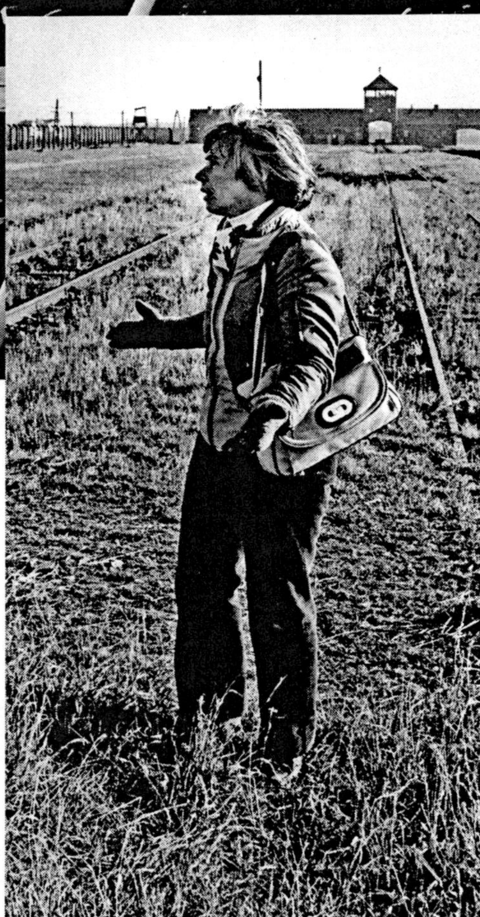

Kitty Hart returned to Auschwitz-Birkenau thirty-three years later to show her son David what it was like to live and survive there. (PM)

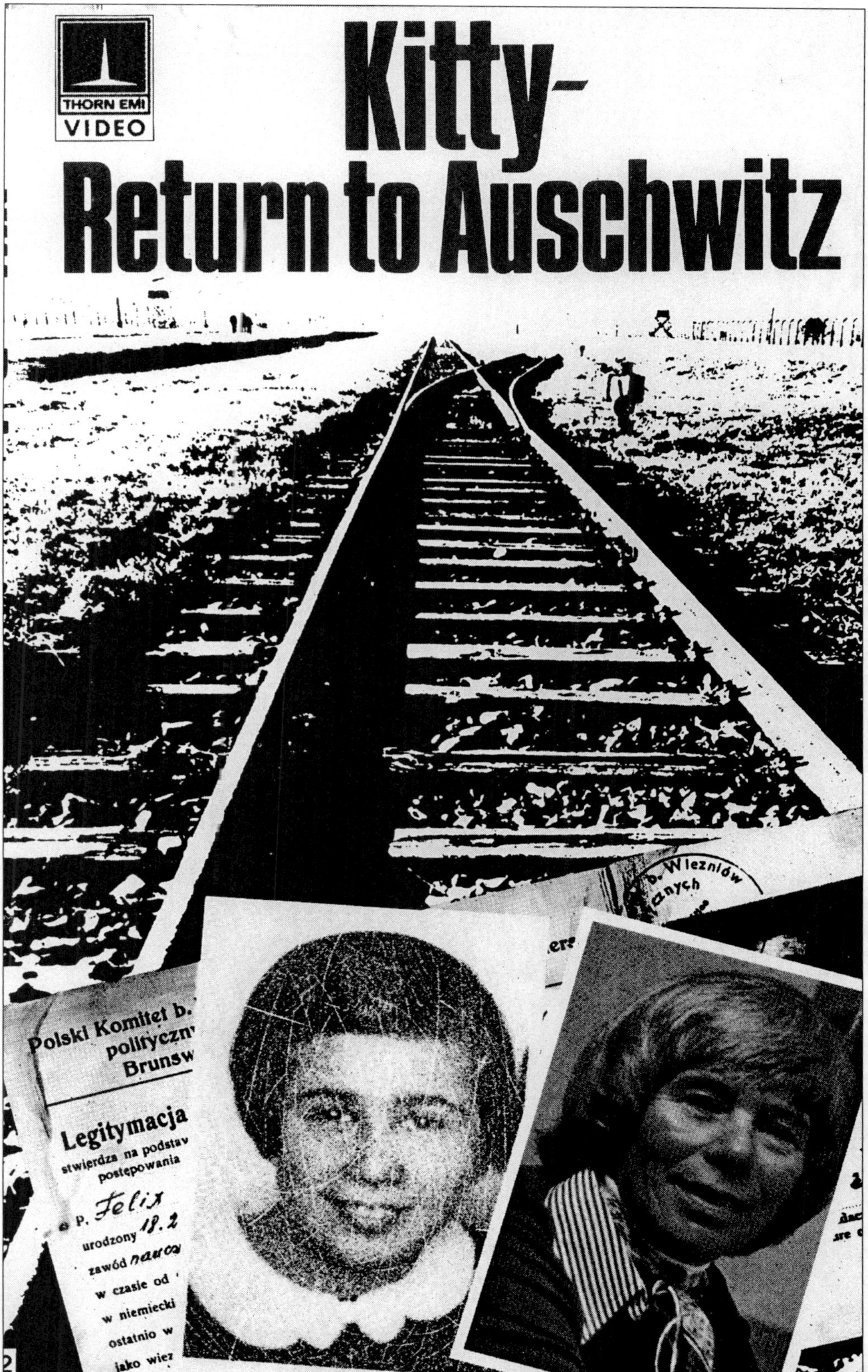

The cover for the VHS cassette. (EMI Films)

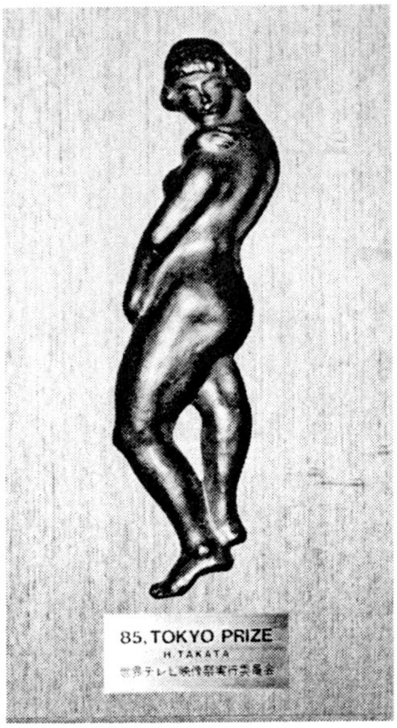

The Tokyo Prize.
(PM)

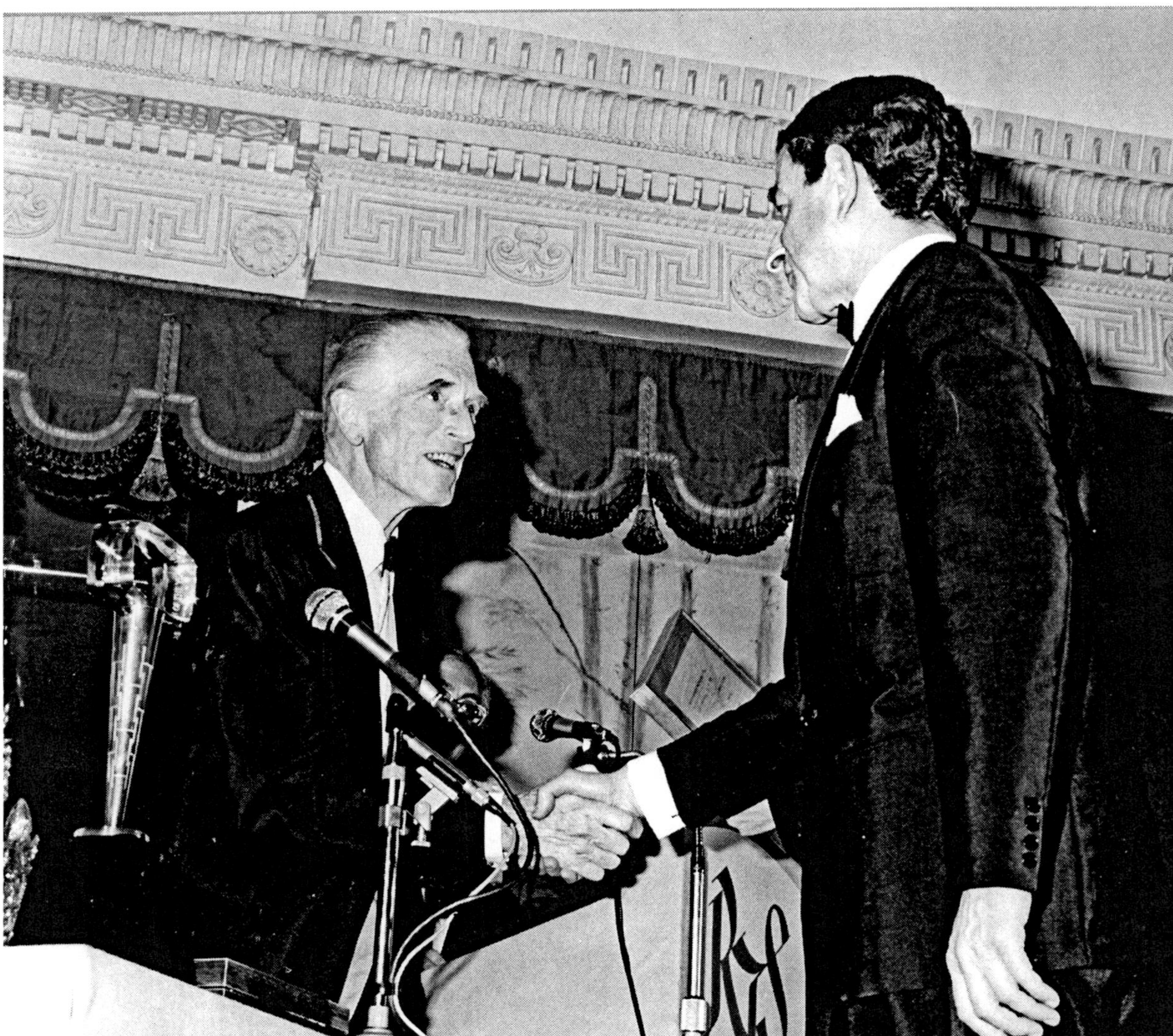

The Royal Television Society's Documentary Award presented by John Freeman, President of the RTS. (Royal Television Society)

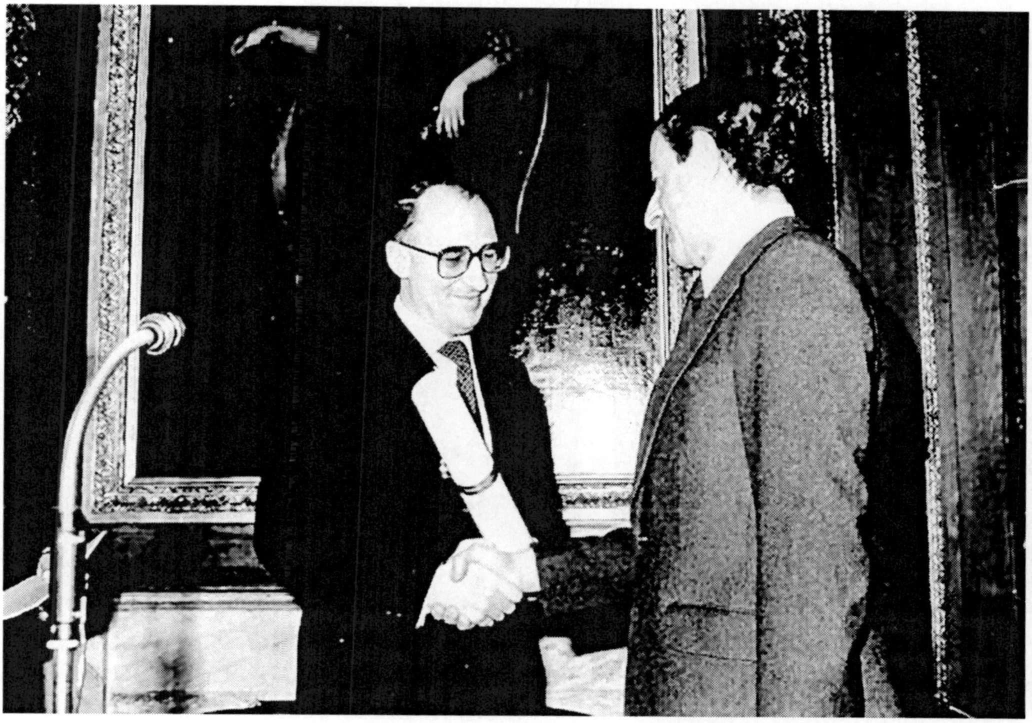

Dr Guido Brunner, Burgomaster of Berlin, presents the Berlin Prix Futura in the Orangery of the rebuilt Charlottenburg Palace. (PM)

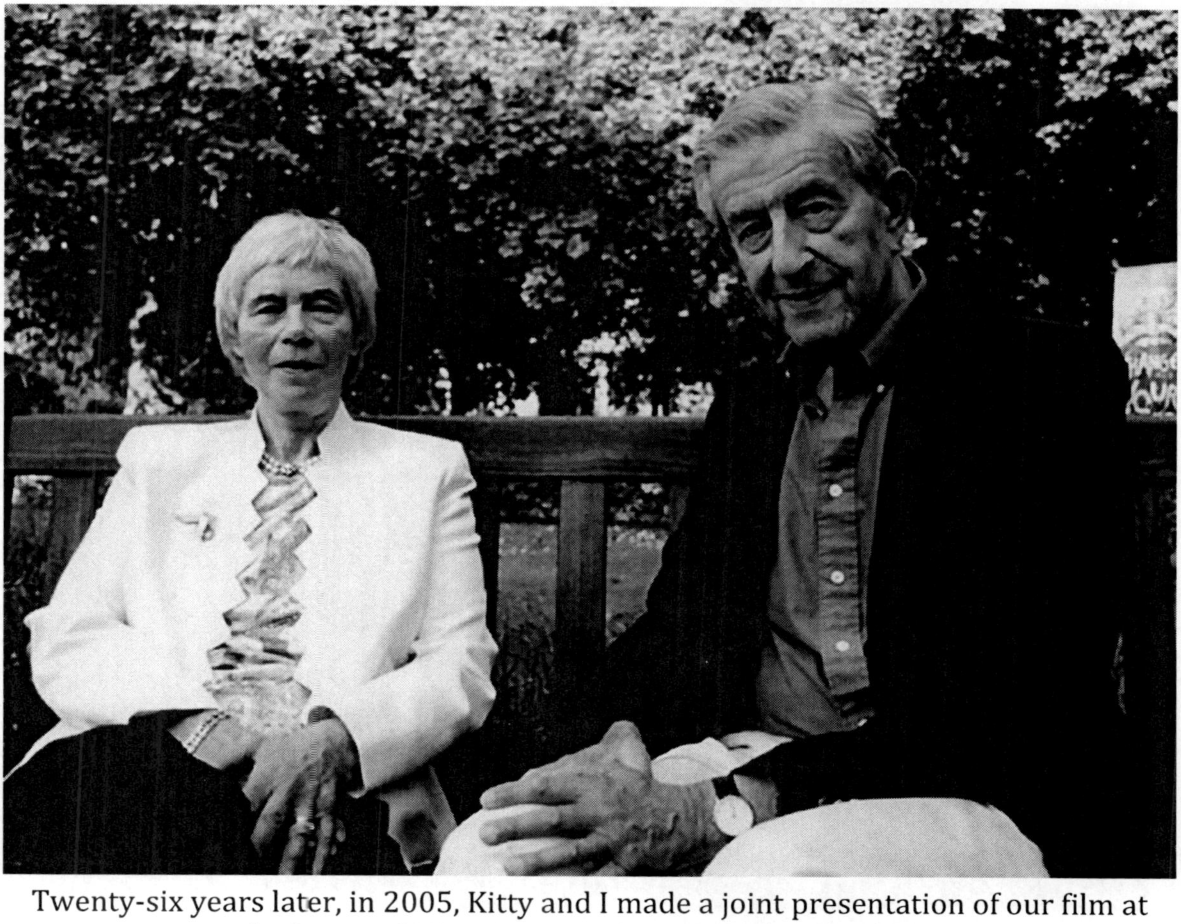

Twenty-six years later, in 2005, Kitty and I made a joint presentation of our film at the Imperial War Museum. (Imperial War Museum)

Women of Courage, 1979–80

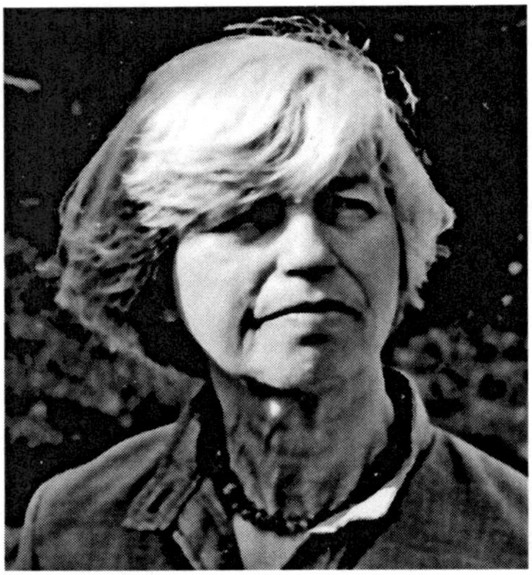

Hiltgunt Zassenhaus. (Yorkshire Television)

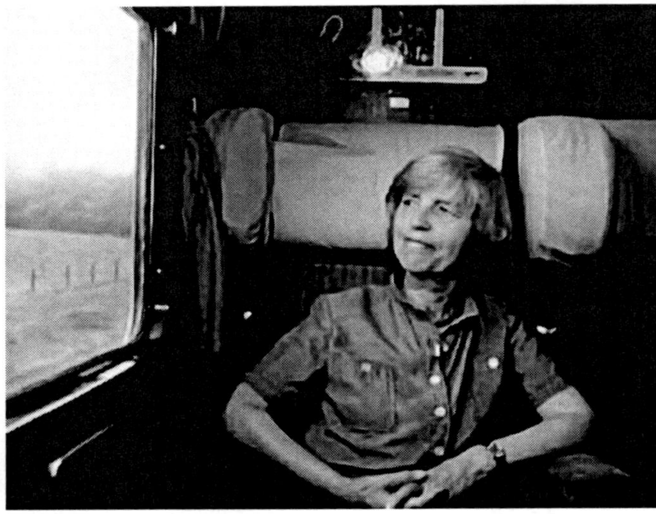

Hiltgunt relives the hazardous train journeys she made smuggling vitamins, bread and news from home to Scandinavian prisoners in Germany. (Yorkshire Television)

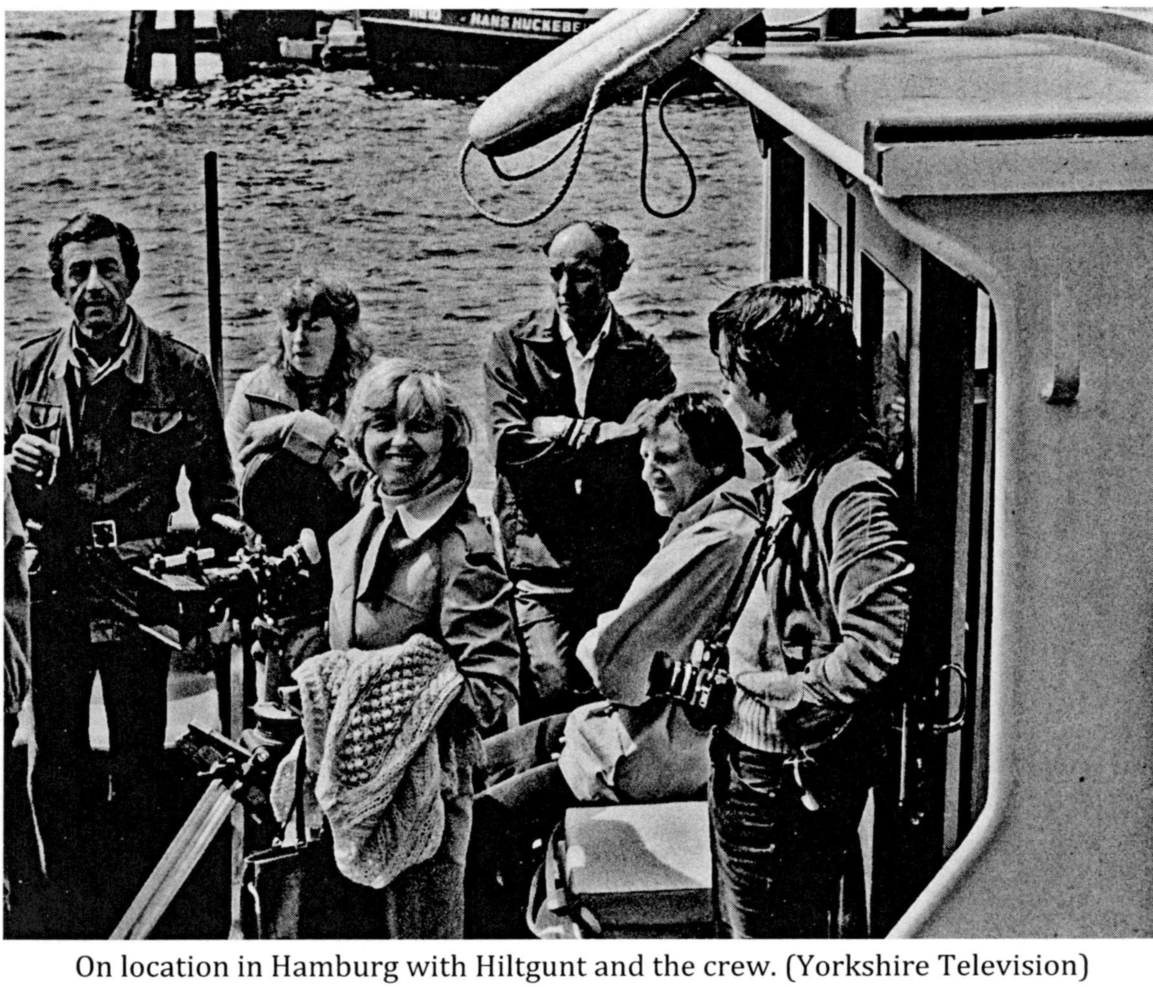

On location in Hamburg with Hiltgunt and the crew. (Yorkshire Television)

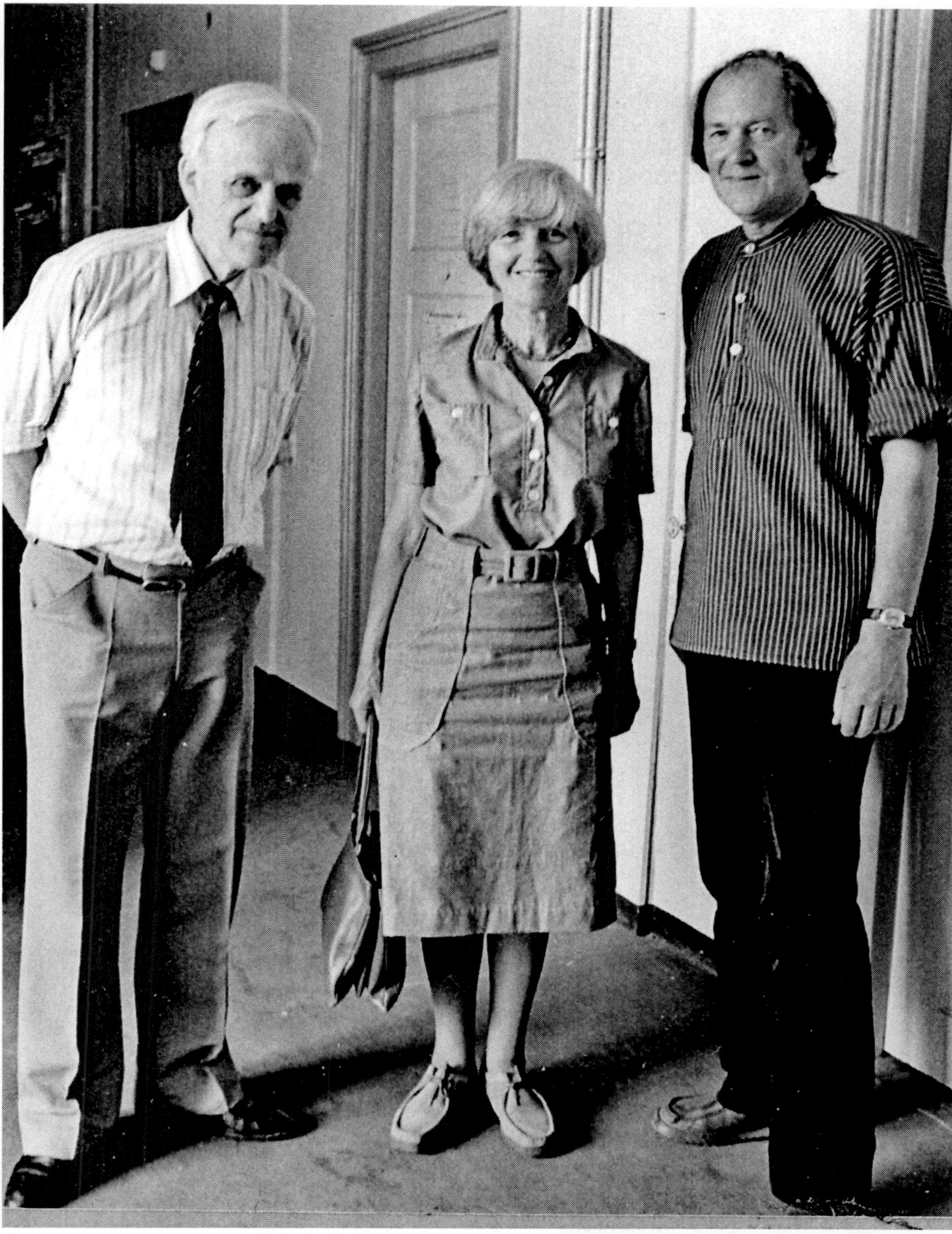

A reunion in Hamburg's Fuhlbüttel Prison with two of the Norwegian inmates. (Yorkshire Television)

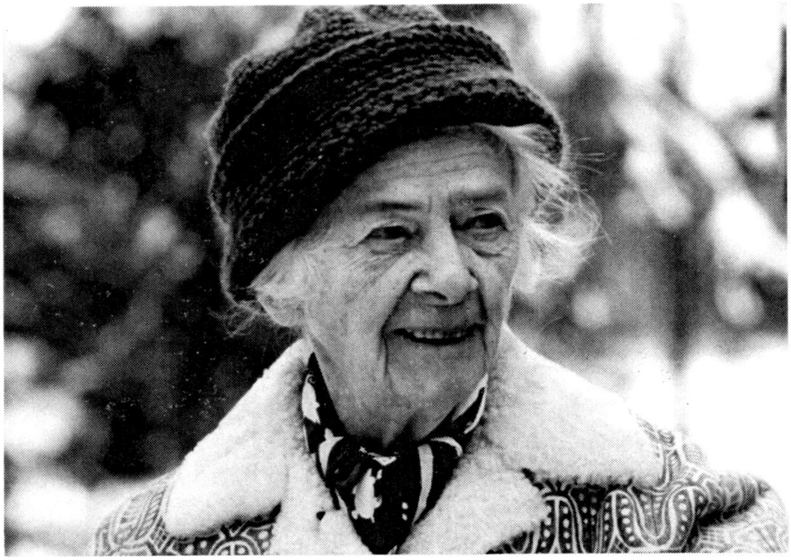

Sigrid Lund.
(Yorkshire Television)

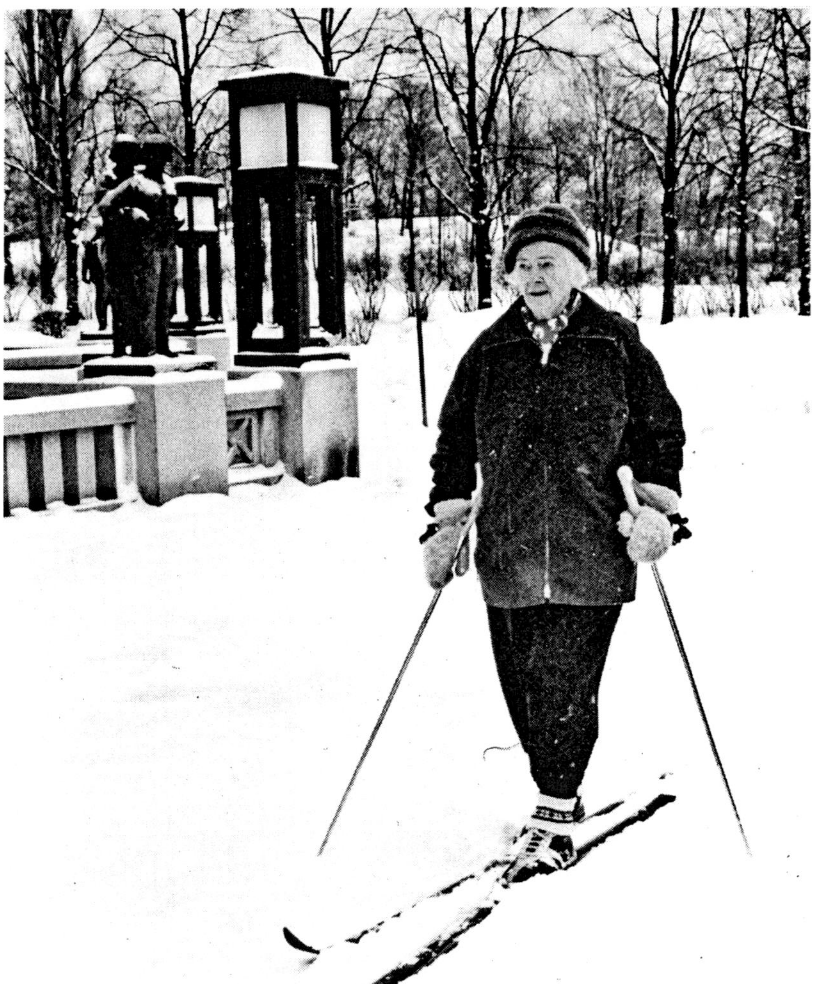

Sigrid Lund, aged eighty-eight, joins us on location.
(Yorkshire Television)

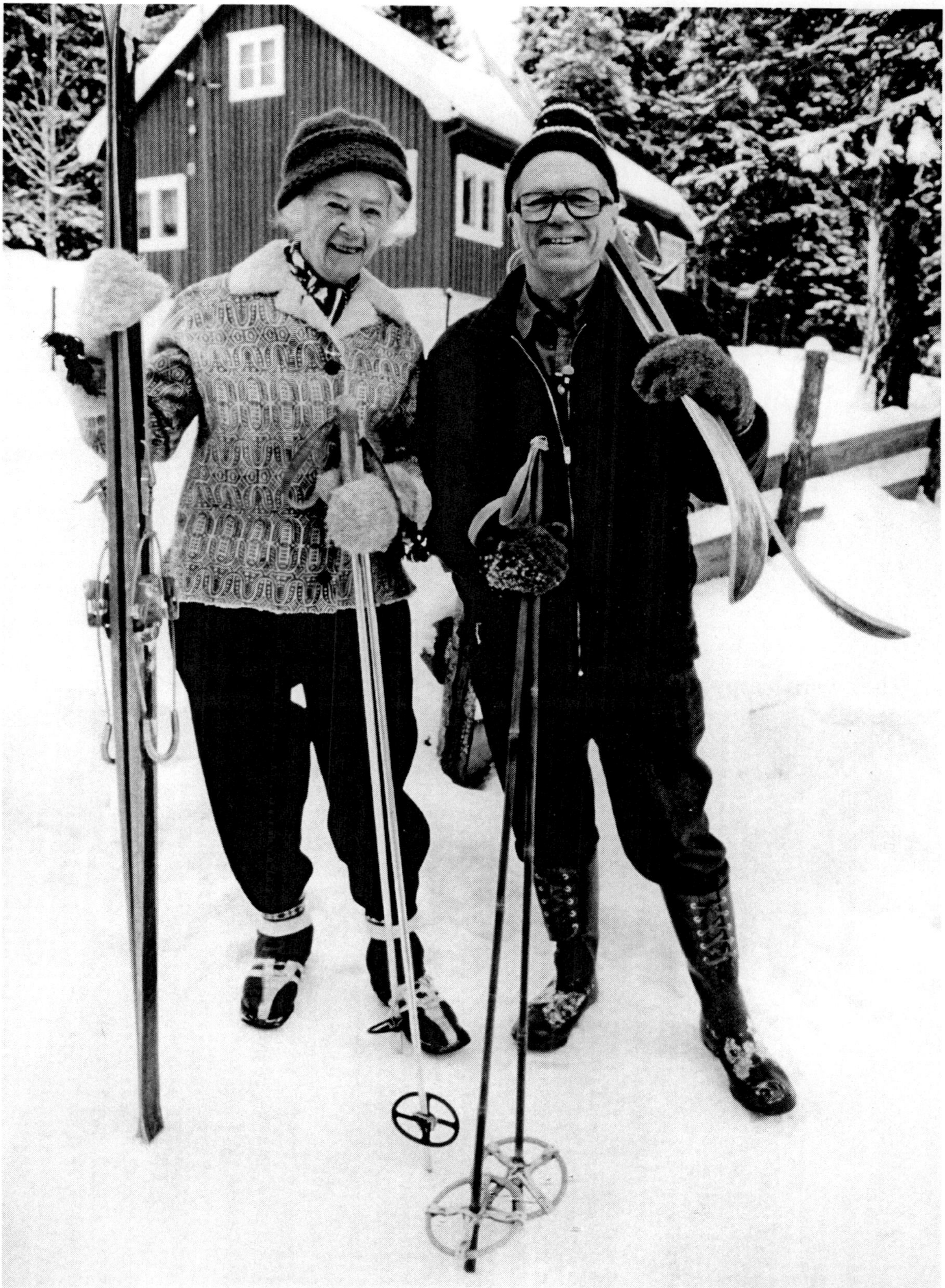

Thirty-seven years earlier the woodcutter Torkel Fornessis had guided Sigrid Lund and Jewish children across the lake to Sweden and to safety. This was their first meeting since that hazardous operation. (Yorkshire Television)

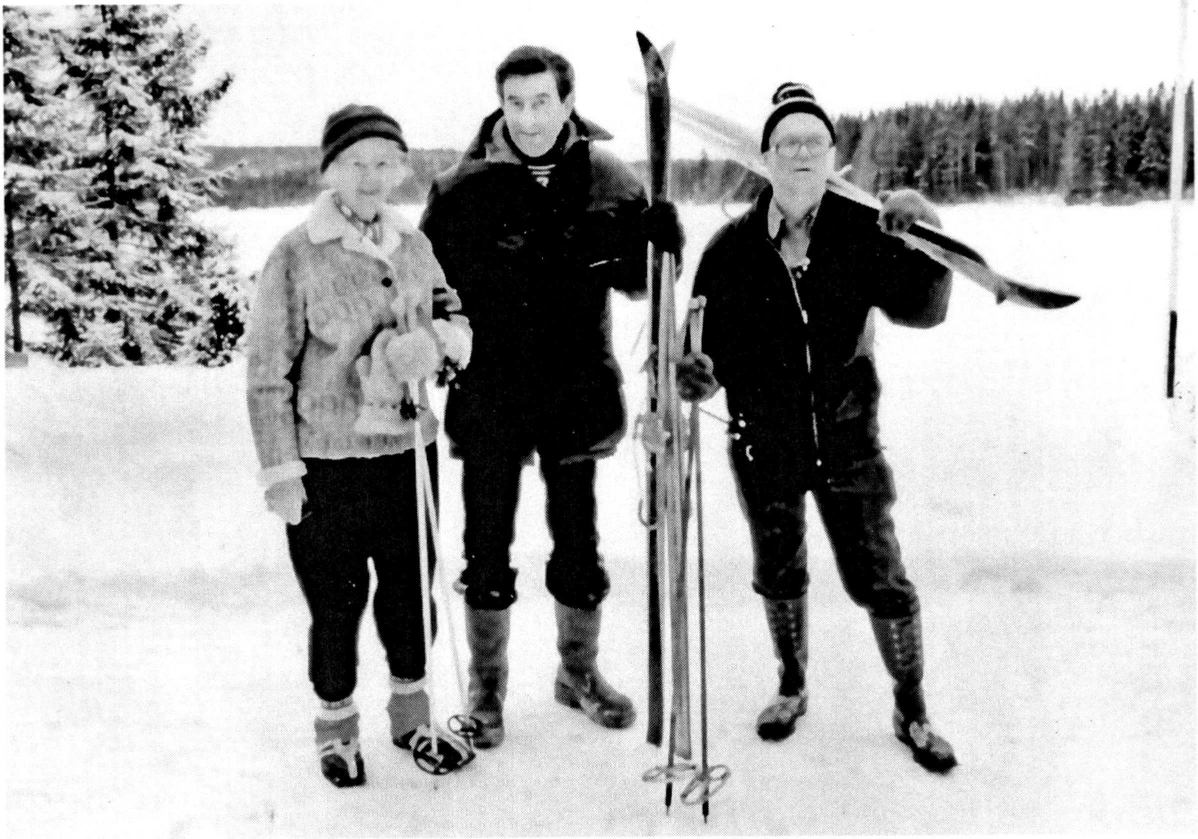

They were happy to cross the lake again for the camera. (Yorkshire Television)

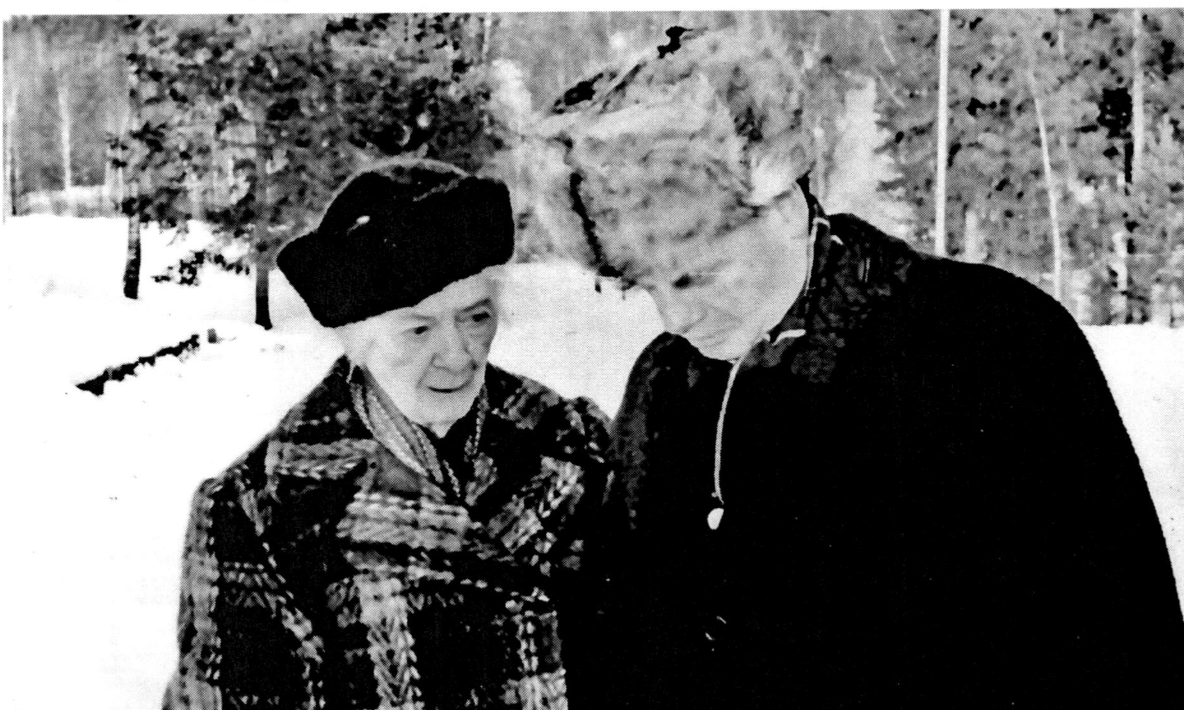

Sigrid's teenager son Bernti, caught red-handed for his clandestine work in the resistance movement, survived Sachenhaus concentration camp. (Yorkshire Television)

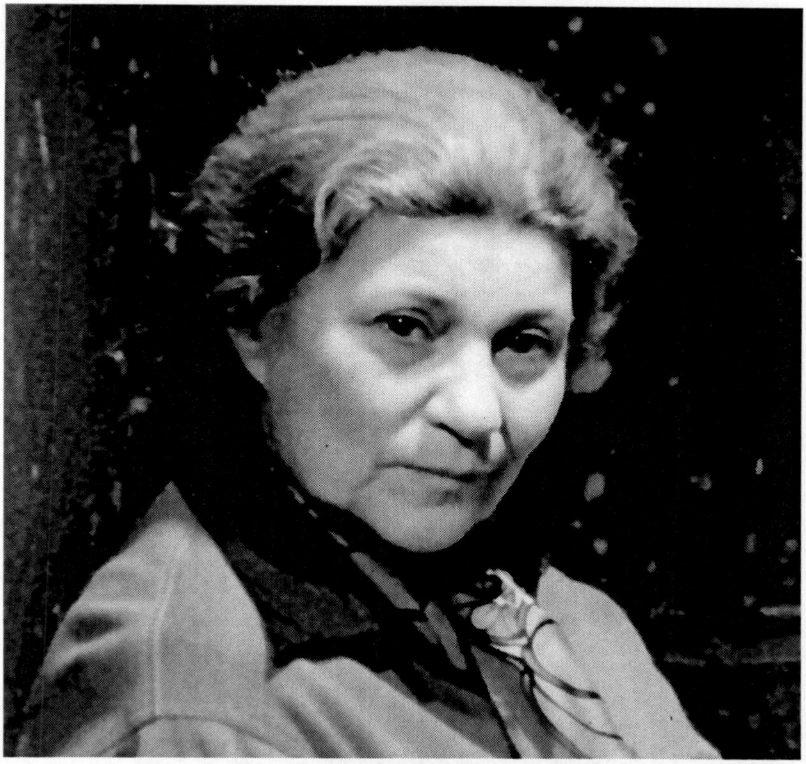

Maria Rutkiewicz. (Yorkshire Television)

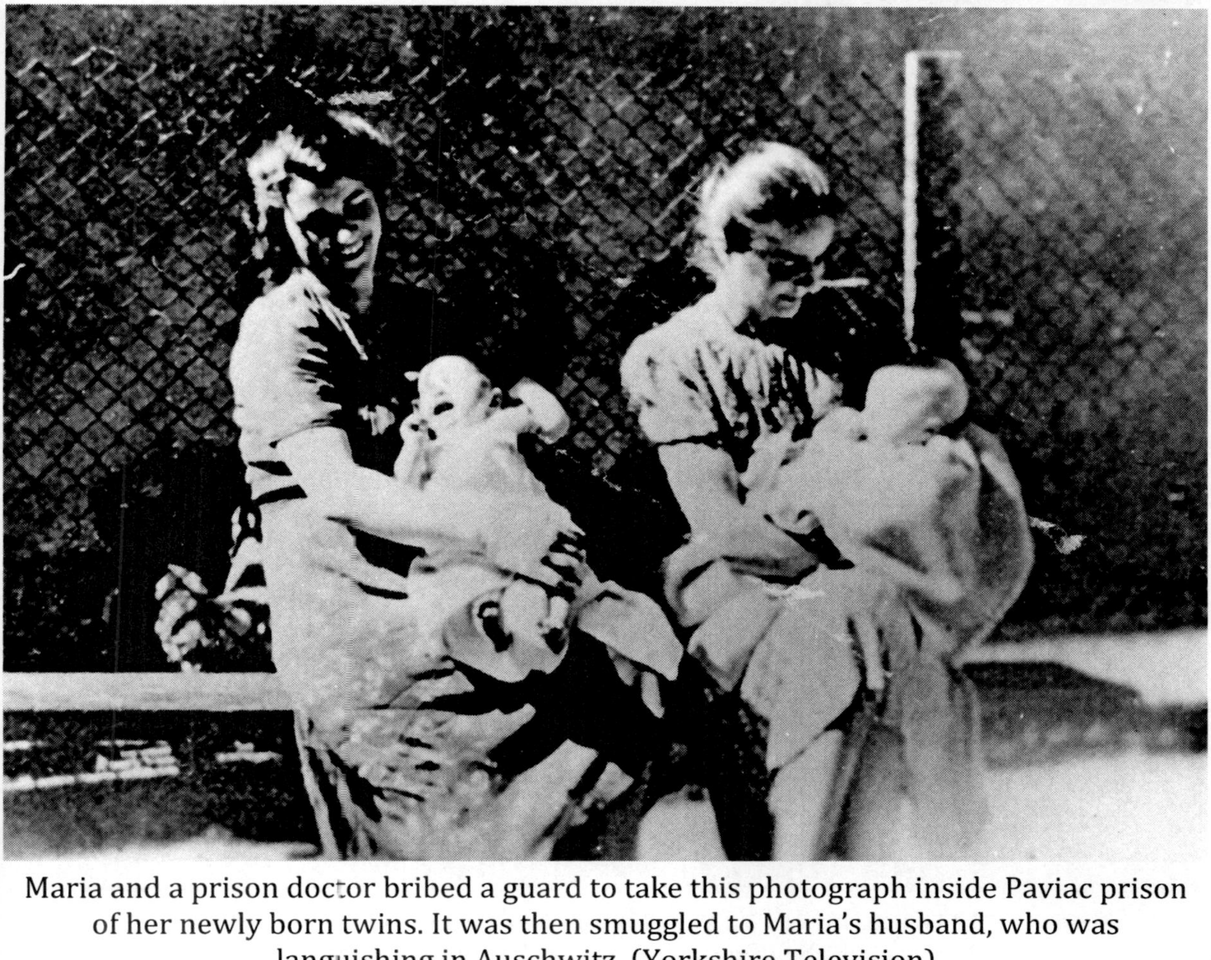

Maria and a prison doctor bribed a guard to take this photograph inside Paviac prison of her newly born twins. It was then smuggled to Maria's husband, who was languishing in Auschwitz. (Yorkshire Television)

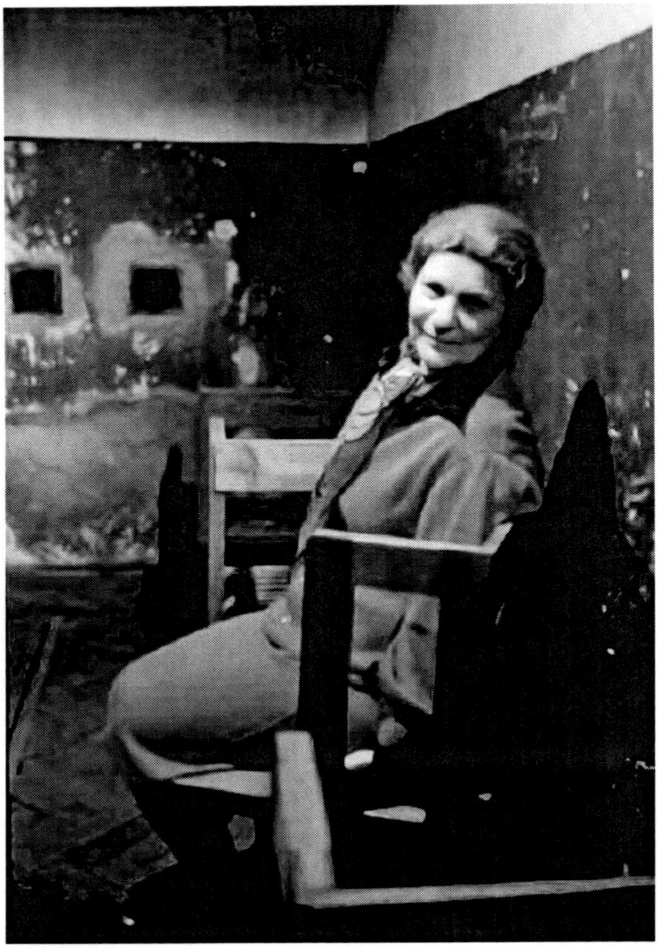

We filmed Maria in the torture chamber of the Gestapo headquarters in Warsaw, now a museum. (Yorkshire Television)

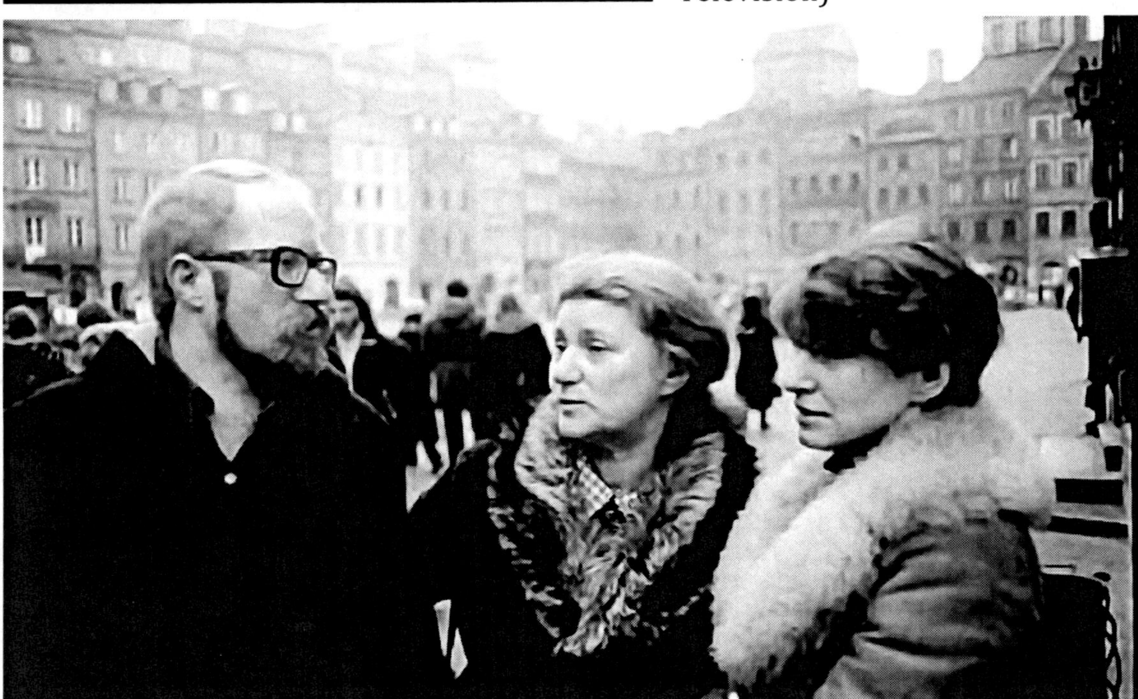

Maria and her twins thirty-five years later in Warsaw. Wicek is an architect, Malgosia a theatre designer. (Yorkshire Television)

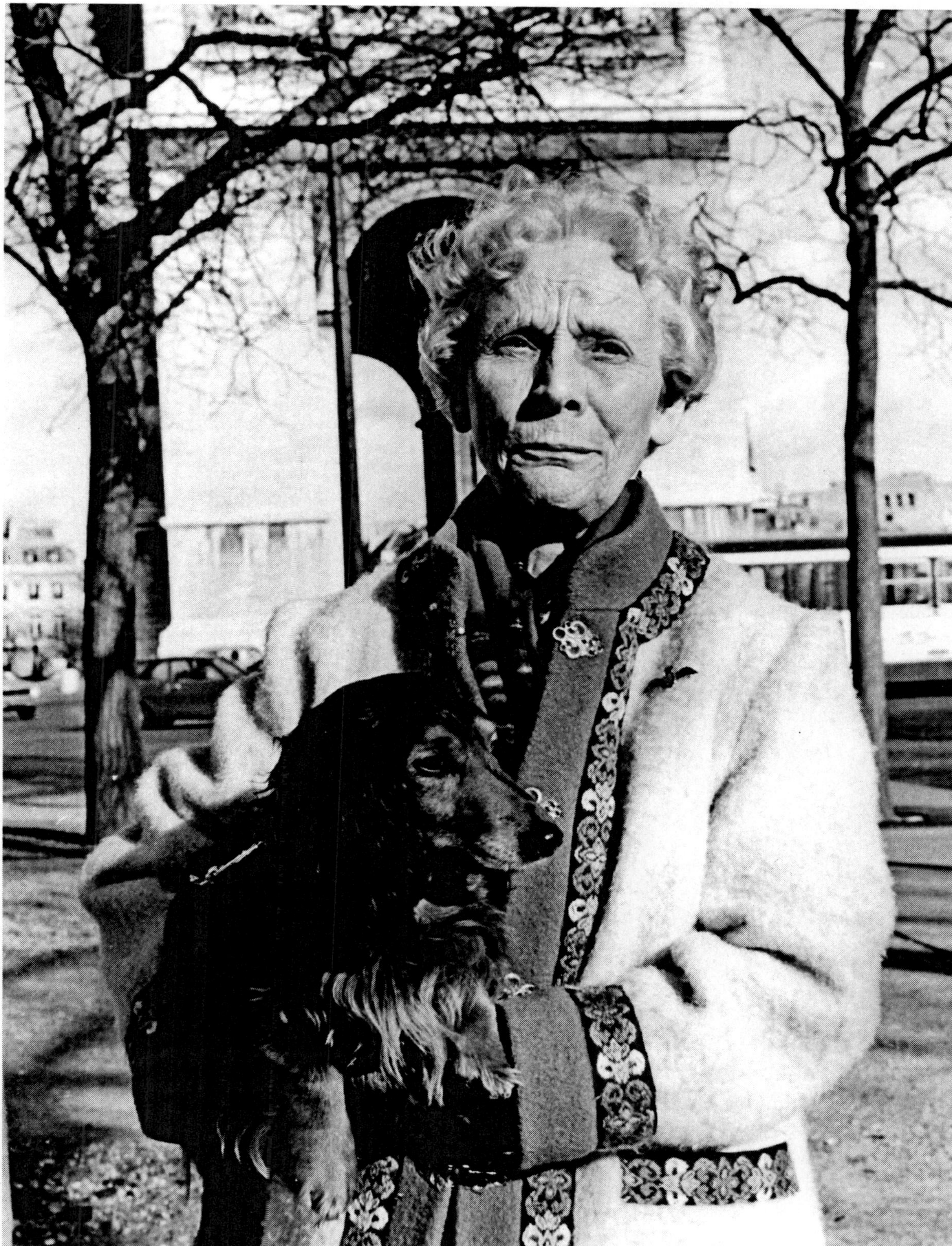

Mary Lindell aged eighty-six with Tommy, her companion for filming.
(Yorkshire Television)

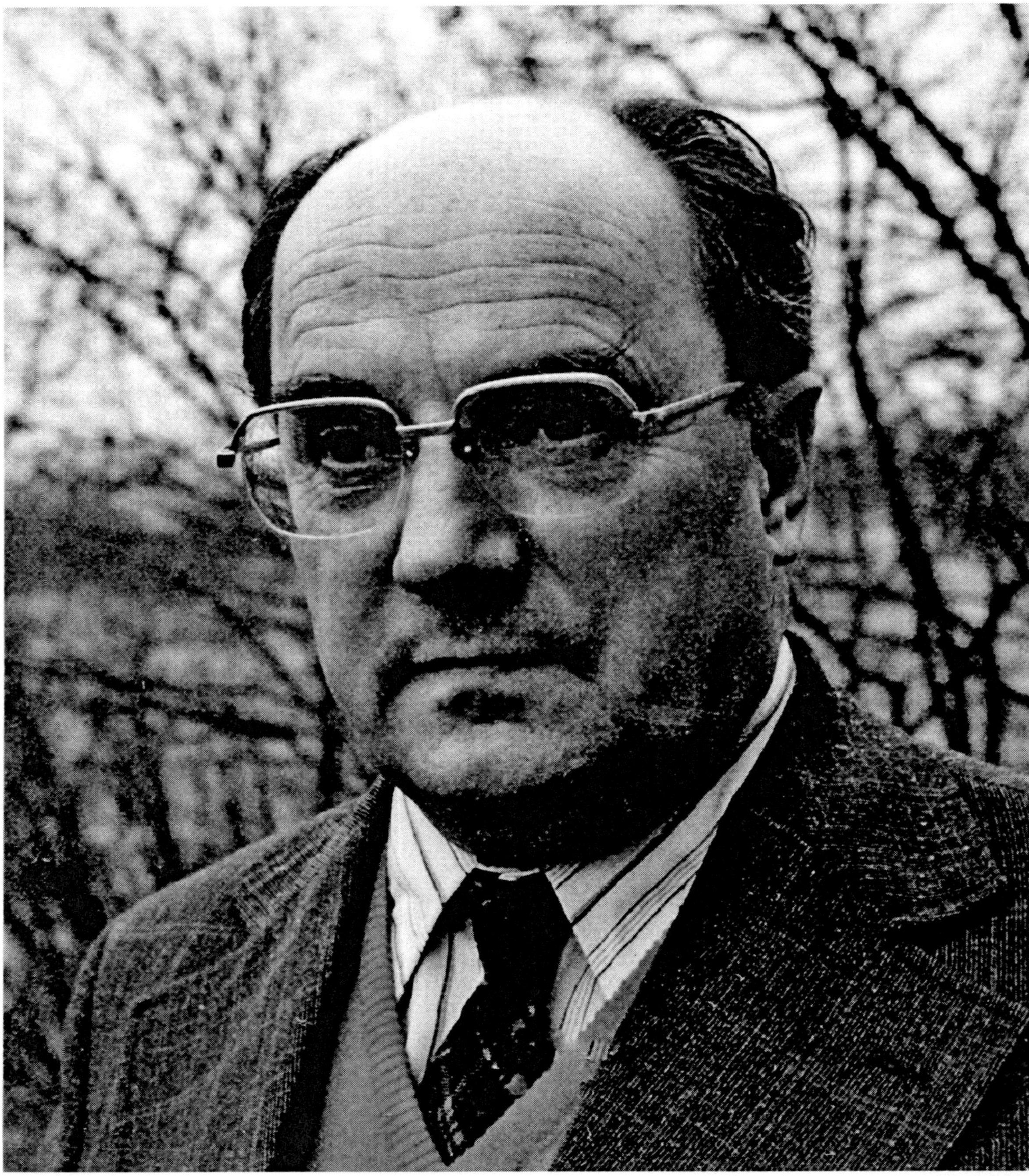

Mary's son Maurice, captured, incarcerated and tortured in Lyons. The Nazis failed to beat the whereabouts of his mother out of him. (Yorkshire Television)

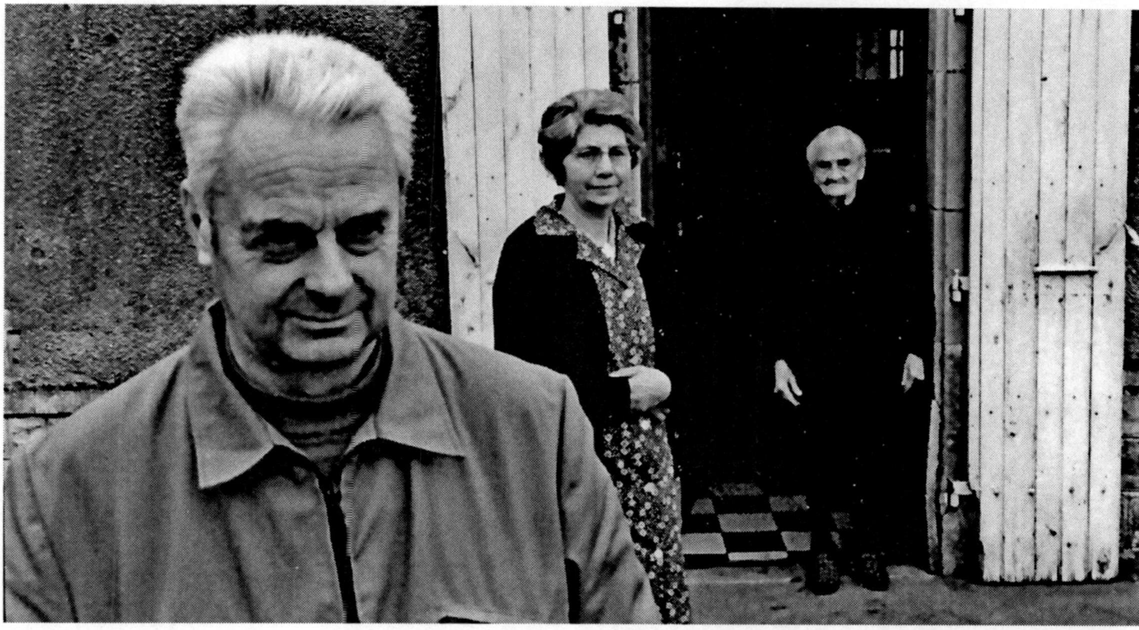

Four brave men at the 'Toque Blanche' in Ruffec. The *patron*, the forger, the village baker and the farmer took huge risks running Mary's highly successful Marie-Claire Line through Vichy France to the Pyrenees. (Yorkshire Television)

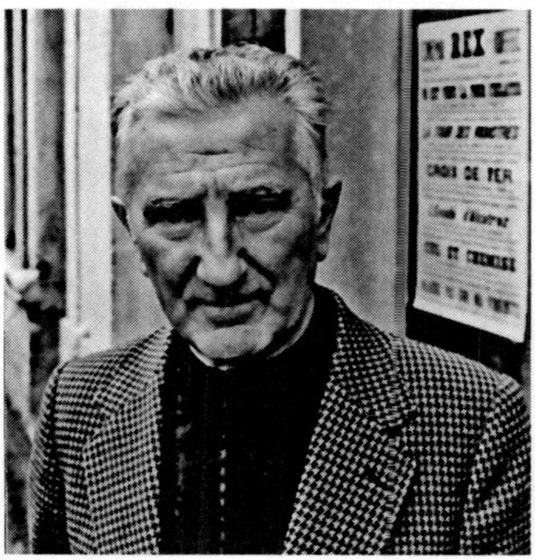

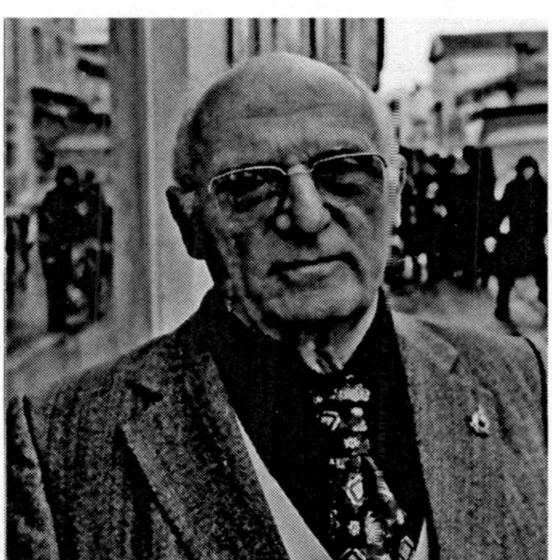

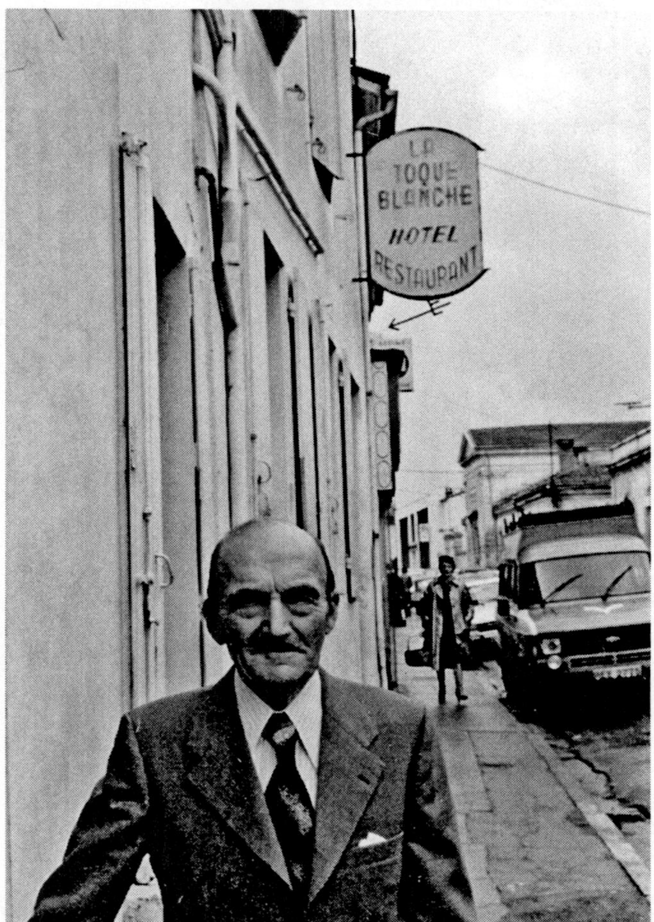

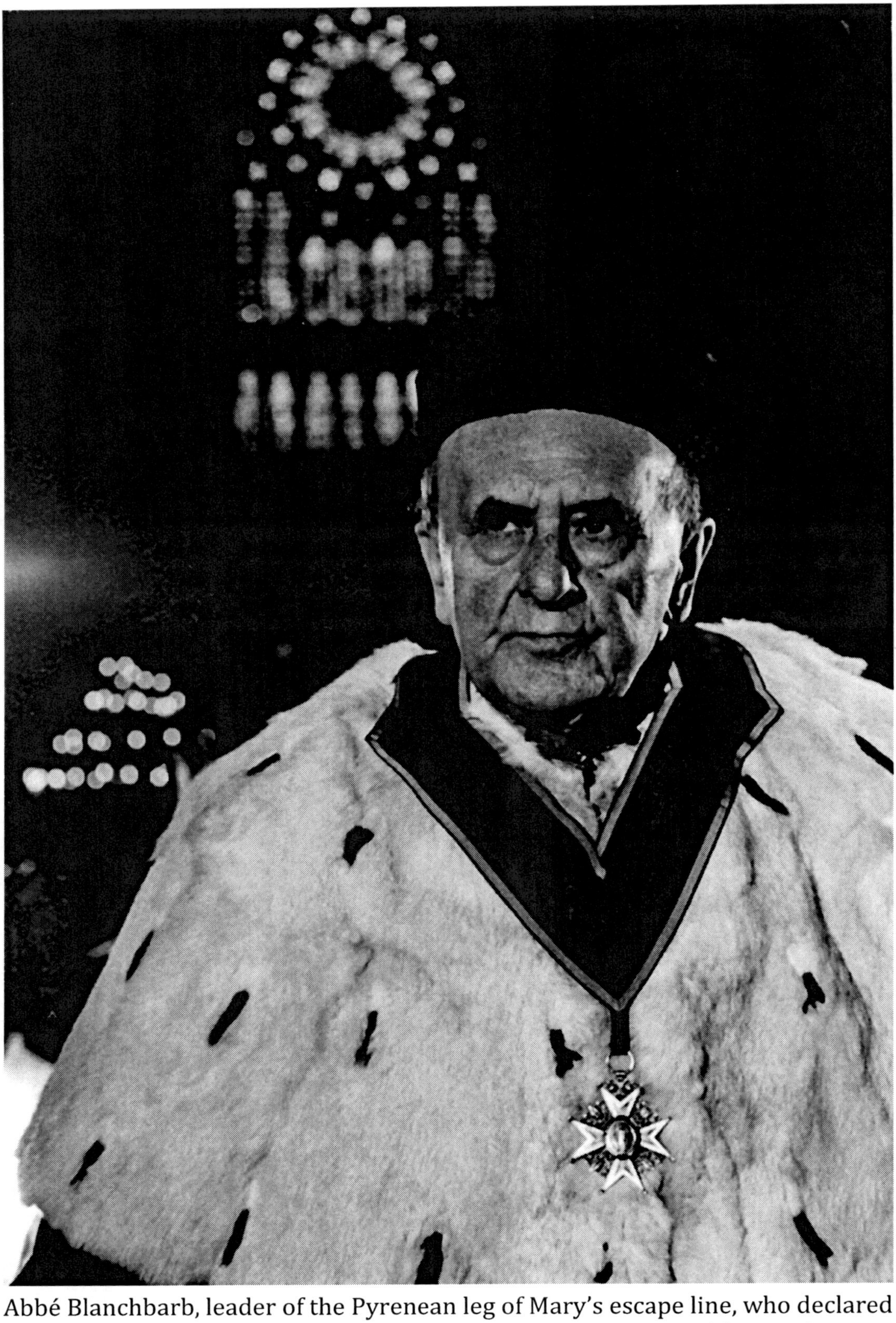

Abbé Blanchbarb, leader of the Pyrenean leg of Mary's escape line, who declared triumphantly, '*Pour une femme, Marie Claire est un grand homme.*' (Yorkshire Television)

28: Women of Courage

For *Women of Courage* we chose, out of many examples of individual acts of courage displayed during the Second World War against Nazism, four women who gave the words idealism, belief and humanity a special meaning. They shared an instinctive compulsion to fight the Nazi regime, and the films set out to throw light on what inspired them to respond in this way; why they were ready to take appalling risks and to sacrifice themselves and their families when the end result was so very uncertain. At the start of the Second World War Kitty Hart was only twelve years old, whereas these four women were mature enough to realise what was happening in Germany, and single-handedly took up the challenge. Here were a German, a Norwegian, a Pole and a Brit, with different backgrounds and different motivations – a rich mixture of political ideals, religious beliefs, pacifism, patriotism and sense of duty – but with an unshakeable faith in what they were fighting for and fighting against in common. They took it upon themselves, in spite of the odds, to take a stand.

The experience of working with these four women was quite different from working with Kitty. The style I used for that film was not appropriate now. These four films told largely unknown stories and had to be treated in a more conventional way, with eyewitness contributions from those involved in these extraordinary adventures and a narrative – expertly written by Kevin Sim – to provide factual, personal, historical and geographical information. Archive film was also an important ingredient.

Hiltgunt Zassenhaus

I first met our German participant when I visited Baltimore on my 1979 travels to choose potential candidates. Hiltgunt Zassenhaus was well known and much admired at that time for belonging to that rare breed of family doctors who spend a great deal of time visiting people in their own homes. There was absolutely no outward sign of the extraordinary and perilous double life she had led in her home town, Hamburg, during the Nazi years. I was well briefed about her by the research team, and now, in her comfortable house, I got to know her, and persuaded her to come over to Germany to film her story.

Hiltgunt was seventeen when Hitler came to power in 1933. Her father was a Lutheran minister and headmaster of the Girls' High School; her mother was an active supporter of the Social Democratic Party. Her liberal upbringing ensured an instant revulsion against everything the National Socialists stood for, and in 1934 she 'fled to Denmark to inhale free air', as she put it, and studied Scandinavian languages. She mastered both Danish and Norwegian, and when war broke out in 1939 she was called up for war work and ordered to report to the Nazi Department of Justice as a censor. After the invasion of Norway in 1940 she was not only responsible for censoring mail passing to and from Scandinavian prisoners and resistance fighters, who were incarcerated in jails and camps all over Germany, but, at the insistence of the

Gestapo, she also had to visit these very prisoners to spy on them. Not only that, she was ordered to spy on their jailers too, and report back to her masters in Hamburg.

The risks that Hiltgunt took on these spying missions were extraordinary. She carried weighty suitcases of food, medication, vitamins, books and writing materials to the prisoners, with letters from their families that she had intercepted in her censor's office. Above all she brought hope and inspiration. Crucially, Hiltgunt kept a detailed record of all the prisoners and their locations. She carried a gun on these perilous journeys, to use on herself if she was caught. Although she constantly feared being denounced by informers, the prison officials feared her in turn, thinking that she was working for the Gestapo. As she said, 'It was a question of who feared the most.'

Hiltgunt survived the Hamburg RAF firestorm that had killed so many, including some of the friends with whom she was studying medicine in her precious spare time. And these words give a measure of her true feelings at the time: 'It really came to this, that at least in my family we had to hope that we would be bombed, although it was almost suicidal to think this way. But how could we otherwise hope for it all to come to an end? But as a German, continuously I had to hope for the demise of Nazi Germany.' I will always remember this quote – because I had seen the devastation of Hamburg for myself in 1945.

Having been nearly caught out several times, and summoned for interrogation to Gestapo headquarters, the final blow fell when Hiltgunt was arrested during one of her secret mercy missions to a prison in Bautzen, very close to Dresden. It was February 1945, and that massive raid by Allied bombers, which caused huge devastation, coincided with her being taken by train to the city. Everyone had to get off the train and walk the last few kilometres because of the destruction. Amongst the panic and confusion she managed to free herself and eventually find her way back to Hamburg. The Dresden raid had saved her life.

In Hamburg Hiltgunt heard from a prison guard that all political prisoners were to be executed, as the Nazis did not want any witnesses to their crimes. Himmler, to save his skin, had started negotiations with Count Bernadotte, President of the Swedish Red Cross, who had flown to Berlin; his mission was to save all the Scandinavian prisoners. A fleet of Red Cross buses arrived in Germany to collect them together and get them home. Many of those outside Hamburg could not be found, but Hiltgunt intervened: her ultimate achievement was to save the lives of 1,200 Scandinavian captives in the closing weeks of the war, because she had kept a detailed record of their exact locations. She was named the 'German Angel'. 'My task was to help 1,200 people to maintain their hope and somehow to last out until they could come home. Now you might say, what does it matter 1,200 people, there were millions of people who died. Well it mattered to me.'

Thirty-five years later I filmed this sequence with Hiltgunt on a platform at Hamburg's main railway station as a train departed for Dresden, in what was then East Germany, with relatives waving goodbye to loved ones they were not allowed to visit in the DDR:

> I saw people saying goodbye to each other and it suddenly reminded me of how many times in my life I had to say goodbye. I had to say goodbye to many Germans, whom I had hoped would rise to the occasion and who did not, who just failed. I had to say goodbye to my prisoner friends who got their freedom, who left me behind, and I had to say goodbye to a brother whom I loved very much, who died in Russia. I had to say goodbye to a Germany where I could no longer live. Somehow my trust in people had been taken for ever and ever. Somehow I could never be the same in my relationship with other Germans. It was just as if you had had a friend who had somehow disappointed you so much that it could never be the same.

After the war Hiltgunt looked after war orphans in Hamburg, who were roaming the streets. She made an appeal to her ex-prisoners in Scandinavia, and they responded with supplies of food and clothing for these children. In 1947 Hiltgunt was the first German to be invited to Norway and Denmark after the war. By this time her story was well known in Scandinavia, and she was welcomed in both countries as a heroine. She resumed her medical studies, first in Bergen and then Copenhagen. In 1952, now a qualified doctor, she left Europe with her mother to start a new life in America. I visited Hiltgunt again many years later, in 2001, again in Baltimore. She was now eighty-two, having retired only two years before – a remarkable and admirable person, revered by her patients and, of course, by her surviving Scandinavian ex-prisoners.

Sigrid Lund

So little had been told about the Nazi occupation of Norway that I welcomed the chance to go to Oslo and meet our 'woman of courage'.

Filming Sigrid Lund, aged eighty-eight, in her Oslo home, I was fascinated by her early recollections – and was in awe of her eloquent and very moving use of the English language. Born in Oslo in 1892, Sigrid and her siblings were brought up in a religious, liberal and strictly pacifist atmosphere. In 1913 this twenty-one year-old well-educated woman experienced her first contact with early Nazi ideas. She was studying singing, and with her teacher grasped the opportunity to go to Bayreuth to stay at Wahnfried, the villa belonging to the Wagner family. Eva Wagner (daughter of Richard Wagner) and her son, Siegfried, were their hosts. There they met Eva's English husband, the writer Houston Stewart Chamberlain, a naturalised German since 1916. Noted for his anti-Semitic views, expressed in his *Foundations of the Nineteenth Century,* he proclaimed the superiority of the German people, asserting that they were descended from superior Teutonic or Aryan stock. Sigrid had a lot of discussions with him and returned to Oslo utterly appalled. This set her on a course that, twenty years later, challenged her strong pacifist beliefs.

When the Nazis came to power in 1933 Sigrid was taking an active part in the Women's International League for Peace and Freedom, helping refugees flee from Germany. By the time the war started there were several other organisations helping refugees, and she became involved in Nansenhjelp, headed by Odd Nansen, the son of the famous Arctic explorer. He sent Sigrid to Prague, in Nazi-occupied Czechoslovakia, to attempt to bring out a group of thirty-seven Jewish children. Tears came to her eyes when she began to describe this mission and the emotions she had felt forty years before: 'It was a very moving moment when the children said goodbye to their parents. They did not know that they might never see them again. And to see these parents carrying these old suitcases with the clothes, small toys and all the things that could help to give some joy and support to the children – and how they stood there alone back on the station – was a very, very sad moment.'

With two Norwegian helpers, Sigrid travelled with her charges by train to Berlin, where they had to change railway stations for their journey further north. She told of the dreadful experience when they tried to get onto a bus to take them to the other station, and the conductor would not let Jewish children aboard. So they had to cross Berlin, and total strangers spat on them.

They finally made it, first to Sweden and then to Oslo. Sigrid then found foster homes for the children all over Norway. They were safe at last, but not for long. Norwegians counted on their neutrality to keep them out of the war – it had kept them out of the First World War – but this hope was shattered in 1940, when they were invaded and occupied by the Wehrmacht.

Sigrid, her husband and her teenage son now became very active in the underground resistance movement. All three knew that the others were involved, but to protect their security they kept their activities from each other. It was two years later, when the Gestapo came and arrested their son, that she discovered he was editing an underground newspaper – aged sixteen. He spent two years in an Oslo prison and was later shipped to Sachsenhausen concentration camp in Germany: he survived. Her husband, who was a resistance organiser in the north, was betrayed, escaped arrest and fled to Sweden. In spite of her strong pacifist upbringing, Sigrid decided to continue the struggle: 'What inspired us was the absolute belief in the value of the human being.'

In 1942 Quisling, the Norwegian Nazi installed by the Germans as Norway's minister president, ordered the arrest of Jews throughout the country. Sigrid summoned her group of resistance fighters to work out how to bring her thirty-seven children from their dispersed foster homes to Oslo, then set a well-planned escape line into motion, smuggling them to neutral Sweden.

Finally, after many communication problems, the children Sigrid had snatched from German-occupied Prague made it to a secret hiding place in Oslo, except for three. Sadly they had been betrayed by their foster parents to the Gestapo, and were shipped to Poland where they perished in concentration camps. Sigrid was tipped off that she, too, was about to be betrayed to the Gestapo, and was forced to join the children and seek refuge in Sweden.

We shot the hazardous journey that Sigrid and her team organised to smuggle her small charges across the frontier to Sweden, travelling in two open lorries, loadbeds covered with tarpaulin sheets, for several hours in pitch darkness – and only just avoiding German patrols. I drove the car, while the cameraman in the passenger seat filmed Sigrid and Sverre Sigordson (who had been in charge of the Oslo end of the escape line) in conversation on the back seat. They recalled with great clarity every moment of that hair-raising journey, reliving their experience for the first time since that bitterly cold winter of 1944.

My researchers had found the spot, about 50 miles to the east of Oslo, where there is a large lake near the Norwegian/Swedish frontier and where Torkel Fornessis, a woodcutter, had lived all his life, in a small cottage on the edge of a huge forest. Thirty-six years earlier he had acted as a fearless guide, escorting refugees on skis and sledges across the frozen lake to the far side, then through the snow up a forest track to a cairn that marked the frontier with neutral Sweden. He then returned home to get ready for his next secret crossing.

I arranged in advance for one of the team to flag us down a few hundred yards inside the forest, so that the cameraman and I could walk on ahead to the woodcutter's cottage. I wanted to catch on camera the meeting between Torkel and Sigrid – their first meeting since he escorted her and the children across the ice to safety in Sweden.

This remarkable eighty-eight-year-old woman had put on her skis, and now came down a small track from the edge of the forest to join us. When she saw Torkel she threw her arms around him, and we all felt lumps in our throats.

> We were very sad all of us to leave Norway. We didn't feel freedom as something that we were looking forward to, but something that we had to take because we were forced to leave the country. When we came to the broad open gate in the forest which showed what was the border line with a cairn in the middle, stones laid upon stones, and there we stood, all of us, and without actually thinking about it or reflecting anything, we all began to sing our national anthem, until we couldn't do it any more, because we actually, I think, wept, all of us. And then, Torkel, we said goodbye to you and wished you all the best and thanked you for what you had done for us and you turned your back to us and went home – alone.

Maria Rutkiewicz

I looked forward to filming in Warsaw, intrigued to find out how freely people could talk about their recent past – Stalin's hatred of all Poles, including members of the Polish Communist Party, the purges, the Katyn massacre and so on.

In 1978 the Cold War was still with us, and Maria Rutkiewicz, now a widow, had lived through the worst of this period – although her elegant Warsaw flat gave no clues about the extraordinary wartime experiences and the cruelties that its owner had endured.

Maria was most welcoming. Her command of English was fairly good, which was not surprising when we discovered that after the war she had married a diplomat. Her second husband was Arturo Stanewicz, who in 1971 was appointed Polish ambassador to the Court of St James; they had lived in London for seven years. Those invited to the numerous Embassy receptions she must have hosted could never have guessed the story behind this remarkable woman.

In 1919, as a result of the First World War, and after 130 years of foreign domination by her two neighbours, Russia and Germany, Poland's independence was restored. Maria, born in Warsaw in 1917, was to witness the internal conflicts that freedom brought to the new Poland.

Maria came from a well-educated, liberal family, and was much influenced by her sister and elder brothers, who early in their lives became part of a group of young Socialists and

Communists. By the time she was seventeen Maria had joined in with their activities. Marshal Piłsudski, the nation's hero who had fought for and won Poland's freedom, was now in charge. By 1926 he had taken on virtually dictatorial powers and cracked down heavily on Communists and their activities. Maria's sister and brothers were arrested, as was Maria herself for a short time. At the age of twenty-one she married Wicek Rutkiewicz, an active Communist Party member, and they faced a bleak future. Stalin distrusted Polish Communists, and as part of his purges during the '30s he summoned their leaders to Moscow and had them executed.

In 1939, a mere twenty years after Poland regained her freedom, it took just thirty-six days for her to lose it again when Hitler invaded. Thousands of Polish soldiers, including Maria's husband, were marched off to an uncertain future in German prisoner of war camps. Maria saw the German troops march through the streets of Warsaw. There was no doubt about their intention: they were there to smash the Polish nation once and for all. The order went out to liquidate the educated classes, as clarified by Berlin in this spine-chilling memorandum: 'The term Polish intelligentsia covers primarily Polish priests, teachers, lecturers, doctors, dentists, veterinary surgeons, officers, executives, businessmen, landowners, writers, journalists, plus all persons who have received a higher or secondary education.'

Maria had no choice, and like many of her Communist friends she fled east to that part of Poland which was now occupied by Russia – thanks to the infamous pact between Hitler and Stalin. And two years later, when the Germans invaded Russia, it was time for her to flee once again, this time to Moscow. She was recruited into the Polish underground movement: the Russians now found use for some Polish exiles to strike back at the Nazis. Maria, trained as a radio operator, joined an underground cell of Polish Communist activists to galvanise Communist opposition to the Nazis inside Poland itself.

After just one practice jump, on a December night in 1941, the cell parachuted into Poland, just outside Warsaw. Maria recalled that moment:

> What was it like to be for the first time flying into Poland? We were very happy that we were back in our country, but I'll tell you something very intimate. I would be a bit embarrassed to repeat it in other circumstances, but I think that it will be enough to understand that when we landed with our parachutes and we were together because it was some minutes to find each other, and we all came together with Marcelli Nowotko, our leader of the cell, who was a huge man, and we stand with him for a moment, and our first words for all of us, for all of us, it was the same one word, it was Poland, Poland, Poland.'

Maria's husband had escaped from a POW cage, and joined his wife in Warsaw to work alongside her in the Communist underground. Transmitting intelligence reports back to Moscow meant that Maria had to move her radio equipment around Warsaw to escape detection, and that is how she witnessed many atrocities being committed in the streets by the Nazis. She talked most movingly about the Warsaw ghetto, where she saw Jews dying in the street: 'We knew that this was the end of some part of our Polish population, Jewish origin but Polish, and it was a tragic experience, because the most difficult moment is when you can't help.'

In May 1943, after the heroic uprising of the surviving Jews, the SS were able to report to Berlin that the ghetto no longer existed. Then they intensified their search for members of the underground movement. They caught and shot all but one of Maria's cell, including its leader, Marcelli Nowotko. In July Maria's husband was arrested and shipped to Auschwitz, and two months later she was caught in the act of transmitting messages to Moscow. 'I remember that the door opened and many Gestapo men ran in, and I managed to smash my apparatus. And then they asked me questions and tried to find out everything connected with my work. They started to beat me, and then they found in my bag a letter from a doctor stating that I am pregnant, and they said now you will be shot.'

Maria was taken to Poland's notorious Paviak prison, the holding centre for political prisoners of the Nazis, and her interrogation took place in the cells of the Gestapo headquarters. The remains of both have been restored and now feature as a museum in Warsaw.

We had some difficulty at first getting permission to film there. Probably some over-sensitive official thought that Maria might air views about Russia's attitude to Polish Communists, but in the end we were able to take her back to that evil place – thirty-six years after the event.

> In a room of interrogation like this happened awful things, you see all these tools for beating, for beating to death sometimes. They told me that they would 'bring my husband here and we will beat him to death in front of you and then you will tell us everything'. When I was beaten, they told me that they are very humane, because they beat me only in my face and not all over as I was pregnant, so they were very humane. I was beaten very hard, so when I was sent back to the prison, the woman supervisor said she can't recognise me, and she didn't know to what cell to send me, and then I told her my name and the number of my cell.

Maria was under sentence of death, and now discovered that she was going to have twins. Polish prison doctors, who had befriended and looked after her, used all their influence to persuade the Germans to postpone carrying out the death sentence at least until the birth of the babies. They agreed: twins triggered a special medical research interest for the Germans.

On 16 February 1944 it was reported from Paviak that five women and three children had been shot. On the same day in the prison hospital Maria's twins, a boy and a girl, were born. 'Suddenly I was not alone. I had the responsibility for two little human beings. I thought of my husband who wanted so much to have the children and now he has the children, but not knowing about them. In Warsaw it was an event. In the underground press there was a notice that twins were born in Paviak.'

I would have had doubts about the next part of Maria's story, had she not handed us tangible proof. Through the prison underground a message reached her from Auschwitz that her husband desperately wanted to know what had happened to her. Wicek was oblivious of her incarceration, let alone of the twins. She befriended a German criminal prisoner, who had a camera that he used to take portraits of the SS guards, which they sent home to their families. Maria persuaded him to take a snapshot of her with the twins, which the underground would then smuggle to Auschwitz, in the hope that her husband would receive them. To prevent him guessing that she was in Paviak, Maria and one of her doctor friends posed in front of a nondescript fence with some trees in the background, happily holding the twins. Amazingly, the photograph was in Wicek's hands quite soon afterwards. He was overjoyed, but he showed it to a friend who had been to Paviak and recognised the fencing in the background. Wicek now knew the worst. He survived Auschwitz, but died at the very end of the war in Sachsenhausen.

Maria then presented me with a copy of the photograph.

In the summer of 1944 the main Polish underground movement, the Home Army, was preparing for its most important action of the war. With Russian forces fast approaching from the east, they were waiting for the order from London to liberate Warsaw. On walls throughout the city the slogan 'Paviak will be revenged' appeared. The Germans, sensing that the end was near, began to deal with the problem posed by the remaining inmates of Paviak. The lucky ones were evacuated to concentration camps, but many were executed, including the last survivor of Maria's cell who had parachuted with her into Warsaw. Maria now waited her turn. Soon there was talk that something dramatic was about to happen, and the Gestapo began burning all documents. The SS guards were disorganised and in a panic. It was rumoured that children might be allowed to go free, and Maria smuggled out a note in the hope that it would reach her brother's family: 'My dears, the last days have brought us so much news, and given us new hope, but our situation is extremely poor, we could be executed at any moment. So after long hours of thinking I've come to the conclusion that I must send the babies to you now. There is no chance of all three of us escaping. I know I am putting you in a difficult situation but only you, my dearest ones, can save them.'

A brave woman from an organisation that was helping prisoners arrived with horse and cart at Paviak's gates to collect the children:

> 'Mothers together, mothers together with the children' – so we went together. It was so unexpected that I didn't feel that it was so marvellous to be free; I didn't feel it because I wasn't prepared. And my sister-in-law waited for me expecting me to hand over the babies, and she was so astonished when I told her, 'I am going with you'. After three years of imprisonment, and suddenly we were to be free. It was another kind of freedom, it was not the real freedom, but we were free. At that time, a time of war, a time of Nazis, everything could happen, everything in the world could happen and suddenly there happened something very good but unexpected.

The last scene in the film showed Maria sitting on a bench in Warsaw's ancient square, with the twins each side of her: Wicek (named after her husband), an architect, and Malgosia, a theatre designer. They never knew their father, and like millions of other Poles the war had devastated their family. Maria's mother was shot by the Germans, her husband died in a concentration camp, her eldest brother had joined the army, and was killed in 1939 when Germany invaded Poland, the other brother fought with the French resistance, and after capture perished in Auschwitz. This is how she summed up her feelings:

> How to forget all my relatives; all my close friends who were killed; how to forget over six million people killed in my country? Impossible. I don't want to remember who did it – of course, I remember quite well. But it is not a matter of who did it, but why it happened, why it was so. We must only remember that we have a duty not to allow it to be repeated. My generation must remember that something so cruel happened that we must protect others from this awful experience.

Mary Lindell

When the research team discovered this fiercely patriotic, eccentric, arrogant, and very amusing eighty-five year-old, I agreed at once that she simply had to be one of the four in our *Women of Courage* quartet. Her story was, to say the least, bordering on the bizarre, and filming it became irresistible.

Meeting Mary for the first time in her smart apartment in Paris merely confirmed that her story had to be told. All of 5 feet tall, slightly built and elegantly dressed, Mary Lindell greeted us, holding her dachshund Tommy in her arms: 'Oh, thank God, some Englishmen! Can't stand the French, you know – come in.' Although she had lived in Paris for the past sixty-one years – since the end of the First World War – she considered her apartment to be on British soil, and she never let us forget it.

In her living room the well-known Karsh portrait of Churchill glared down, and on display beneath it was an impressive array of medals and decorations, including a Croix de Guerre awarded to her in the First War and a Croix de Guerre from the Second. It was now sixty-two years since the *Daily Mail* broke the news of her death on the Western Front, and thirty-six years since notices appeared on the streets of Paris declaring that she had been shot by the Nazis.

Mary Lindell was born in Surrey in 1895 into a wealthy English family. I am going to quote liberally from the film, because it is through her use of the English language that you will get a true flavour of this extraordinary woman:

> My mother was a Colls of Trollope and Colls. It was her father who was a very well-known architect. I think he'd built the Mansion House, and God knows what he didn't build, and of course he was stinking with money – made absolutely millions. I mean he was a very wealthy man. My mother was a very wealthy bit of works too, although nobody would ever have thought of it, and because she had the necessary I was lucky. My godfather died and left me quite a nice little lot of money too, so I was really quite independent. That I suppose is why I've

> become arrogant and independent now, because from fifteen onwards I never knew what money was, do you see what I mean? It just was there.'

After this first take I knew that we had struck gold.

Aged nineteen at the outbreak of the First World War, Mary immediately volunteered for the VAD nursing service, but left after a run-in with her superiors. She went over to France and volunteered for the Secours aux Blessés Militaires, the aristocratic division of the French Red Cross. Joining the French troops in the trenches on the Western Front, she worked for the next four years in forward dressing stations and hospitals, where she was known to the wounded as the '*Bébé Anglaise*'. There were many recorded acts of sheer bravery, when she went with small medical teams to tend the wounded only a short distance from the German trenches, and she once experienced a gas attack. This heroism was recognised by the Croix de Guerre awarded to her in 1918.

After the war Mary remained in France. She had married a French count, so now she was the Comtesse de Milleville and had dual nationality. She and her husband had three children. In the '30s Mary closely followed the rise of the Nazis, and dusted down her old French Red Cross uniform with its rows of medal ribbons 'in case the balloon went up'. The Comtesse was ready for all eventualities.

She did not have long to wait. In 1940 the demoralised French army suffered the greatest defeat in its history, and the country's British allies were scurrying back home from Dunkirk. Many were left behind and taken prisoner. Those still free had little hope of escaping from occupied France by themselves, and it was to help them return to England to fight again that galvanised Mary into action.

> Well, to be quite honest, we weren't really proud of the French – we were sick to death of them – and we knew that some of us had to stay here who could stand up to the Jerries and could help the people through. The French wouldn't have done it. What gave me the idea was what Edith Cavell had done in the last war, and it was therefore necessary that something had to be done in this war. Who? There was nobody in Paris, nobody who could do it. And so I said, 'There you are, darling. It's you. You'd better do it'.

And she did. With the help of her son Maurice she organised an escape route to ferry soldiers and refugees past the heavily guarded checkpoints that marked the demarcation line between German-occupied France and Vichy France. Mary put escapees up in her flat, and when the coast was clear she ferried them in her car across the border. She flaunted her Red Cross uniform, and managed to intimidate high-ranking officers in charge of the German army in Paris, declaring that she was an officer of the Red Cross and demanding petrol coupons for humanitarian reasons. She was fearless, and they simply did not know what to make of her. She said that 'the Jerries simply loved titled people, especially in uniform with lots of medal ribbons'.

Soon the Secret Service chiefs in London heard from an officer who, thanks to Mary, made it back to England, that there were an extraordinary English woman and her son who ran an escape line from her flat in Paris.

> I had a very special ceremony here because I had to sort out the people who were genuine and wanted to go over. And so I had a tray with English earth, which I'd dug up from the Embassy garden. Although the Germans had closed the Embassy down, I managed to get in – you can always get in with a bit of you know what. Now this tray with the earth on it – they had to put their hand on the earth and swear an oath; I think we brought God into it and things like that, and they had to swear that they wanted to go over to England to fight, otherwise if they didn't, well they were simply shoved out and that was the end of it.

As early as Christmas 1940 the Germans were getting suspicious of Mary's many car journeys, as well as the traffic of people in and out of her flat. In the New Year Nazi security police arrived to arrest her. 'The bell rang. My daughter answered it and she just looked back and said 'It's the Huns.' I said 'Oh, well, bring 'em in.' And they were extremely polite and extremely co-operative. And the first thing we did, we had tea. It was tea-time, so we had tea and they loved it.'

They left, unable to prove that Mary was helping escapees; but she was found guilty of insulting the German army, and was given a nine months prison sentence, which she served in Fresnes prison outside Paris. This diminutive figure threw her weight around, demanding special treatment for imprisoned British officers, and the Germans were only too glad to get rid of her at the end of her sentence.

Paris was now too dangerous for Mary: the Gestapo had her number, and she knew that she could not resume her people-smuggling activities. Afraid that she might be arrested at any moment, she decided to escape back to England. After a difficult and dangerous journey, which took almost six months, she arrived in London in 1942 and reported her clandestine freelance activities to Colonel Jimmy Langley of M19, the unit which organised escape lines.

He and his assistant, Colonel Airey Neave, who had recently escaped from Colditz, found Mary rather hard to take, and certainly disapproved of having such a loose cannon doing her own thing in France, thereby putting at risk their organised and disciplined escape plans. She had fierce arguments with them, hating the thought of being controlled by someone from London, but in the end she agreed to their demands. After training Mary for her new assignment, they arranged for her to be flown back to Vichy France in a Lysander, to set up an escape network for shot-down British airmen – thereby breaking their rule of never sending anyone back to the Continent who was known to the enemy. They were much relieved to see the back of her.

We filmed Jimmy Langley, long retired and living in Bawdsey on the East Coast. With the cut-glass voice of a professional soldier, he ended his interview thus: 'Mary is a very brave and courageous woman who always, and still does, I think, wanted to have it her own way. From the moment she arrived in England, she was, to put it mildly, difficult. She made it clear that she wished to go back and she was absolutely fit so to do, but she did get across people, there's no doubt about that. A lot of the high-ups in M19 came away with an impression that she was all right in very small doses.'

On her return Mary discovered that during her absence the Germans in Paris had sentenced the Comtesse de Millville to death; but she now had a new name: Marie Claire. She set up the Marie Claire Line, centred on the small town of Ruffec, just inside Vichy France. Escaping Allied pilots were contacted over a wide area of Northern France, collected at Ruffec, smuggled into Vichy France, then escorted (normally by train) to Foix. Pyrenean guides then led them over the mountains to Spain; and most of them finally got back to England. Each of these journeys was hazardous, to say the least, and Mary got into many scrapes, once being badly wounded by French collaborators. During this time her son Maurice had been betrayed, caught and imprisoned in Lyon. He was severely tortured to make him reveal the whereabouts of his mother, her new name and the names of all her contacts. When Mary heard about this she immediately went to Lyon, and paid a huge ransom for his release.

> He looked just like God's Wrath. He was so thin, the poor little devil, and as he came forward to kiss me his glasses dropped off and to my horror he went down on his knees and was feeling about for them and I said, 'What's the matter?' And then he told me that they'd tried to make him talk, and they'd beaten him with these chains across his eyes, you see, and well, we thought he was going blind. He did have a very, very cheap time there, he really was tortured. But they didn't get anything out of him, I will say that for him.

In November 1943 Mary's luck finally ran out. On one of her many trips south to Foix with escaping airmen, she too was betrayed and arrested at the railway station by German security police who were operating in Vichy France. They put her on a train bound for Paris with an escort, to face the death sentence.

> As I didn't want to go to Paris, I thought the best thing to do was to get off the train and I chose my spot, and when I got there I told my guard that I usually felt sick on the train and when I'm going to be sick, I'll just hit him on the knee so as not to do it in his lap. So I hit him on the knee where I got where I wanted to get off the train and went in the corridor. Unfortunately, I walked a bit too quickly because I wanted to get a move on, you see. He followed me, and he immediately began shooting. I thought, oh, the bastard, he's shooting. As I turned to go through, he got me in the cheek. I didn't even feel it. And I opened the door on to the rail and there, when you do that, you can't jump at once because you have to be careful of the telegraph poles, because if the telegraph pole hits you it's nasty. And as I jumped he fired. He got me twice in the head, which, of course, helped me getting along a bit. It really was a hell of a jump.

Amazingly, when the train stopped the guards found her body, still alive, on the embankment. She was taken to a military hospital, and against all odds survived. When she was well enough she was taken to Dijon jail for interrogation. In September 1944 she was transported by rail to Ravensbrück concentration camp, north of Berlin, a camp for women from all over occupied France. Amongst them was a group of British prisoners who were SOE agents who had been caught working with the French Resistance.

> The conditions in Ravensbrück were pretty dim for the general public. But you must remember I got there in a British uniform, with a couple of rows of British decorations, with my identity papers proving my title, which you know the Germans love. The political officer was completely lost from the very beginning, and, of course, when I realised this I threw my weight about, as you can imagine. They used to call me the arrogant English woman, '*Die arrogante Englanderin*'. I'd say, 'You're a lot of bastards.' I was arrogant and I consider we had the right to be arrogant, don't you? After all's said and done, we were winning the war, and if ever there were any discussions with them I used to say right at the beginning, 'You've lost it, you know perfectly well you've lost the war.' And they knew they had too. It didn't stop them. They were beastly. The weaker the people the more beastly they were.

Mary was more fortunate than the others; because of her nursing experience she got a job in the Revere, the camp hospital. Taking great risks, as usual, she was able to steal some precious medication from the Revere, and saved the lives of several British prisoners, including some of the SOE agents. But she was powerless to stop the Germans from executing Violette Szabo, Lilian Rolf and Danielle Williams.

Count Bernadotte who, thanks to Hiltgunt Zassenhaus, had saved the lives of Scandinavian prisoners, also negotiated with Himmler the release of some of the foreign women inmates of Ravensbrück. Mary Lindell was one of them, and that is how she finished her war. She was taken to Sweden, and then returned to her old apartment in Paris. Mary was now separated from her husband, who had gone to live in South America. Maurice also survived, and was a great help to us in the making of this film, as were her Marie Claire Line team in Ruffec, who risked their lives many times over to help Allied airmen. When we went to Ruffec to film them they were sad that we couldn't persuade Mary to come with us. ('I hate those beastly trains,' she said.) All of them idolised their leader. And when we filmed the eighty-five year-old Abbé Blanchbarb, the canon of Metz Cathedral and leader of the Pyrenean leg of Mary's escape line, he declared triumphantly, '*Pour une femme, Marie Claire est un grand homme.*'

We finished the film with this statement from Mary – which said it all:

When they say I'm a heroine I am most embarrassed and I think it's ridiculous. I mean, after all said and done, one does a job – it's a job. A lot of people say, oh, how courageous, how brave, and I say, no. Luck. I was lucky. And I was wounded three times and they all said, you'll never recover. Luck. My number wasn't up. But a heroine? All twiddle rot. What is a heroine? Joan of Arc? I'm certainly nothing like that. Edith Cavell? Phew. When people say that it makes me mad. I'll tell you, in my little tupenny-ha'penny mind I represented Great Britain, who was standing up against the world and fighting for it, and I wasn't going to let Great Britain down. It just didn't enter my head. And I wasn't frightened. I mean to say, if you're shot, well, you're shot, and that's the end of the story, isn't it?'

* * * *

These four films exemplify the triumph of the human spirit, and in getting to know these four exceptional people I learnt that courage breeds a special form of modesty – a reluctance to admit that they had done anything out of the ordinary. Instinctively they took it upon themselves, in spite of all odds, to make a stand against an evil regime. It would have been unthinkable for them to have acted in any other way.

In recalling these four stories of sixty years ago, I have an additional reason to appreciate the remarkable courage displayed, because, by a strange coincidence of place and time, it so happened that in May 1945, as Germany was collapsing and as I entered Hamburg in my tank with the 8th Hussars, Mary Lindell came through the city on her way from Ravensbrück to Sweden; Hilgunt Zassenhaus had just arrived in Hamburg, her home town, escaping arrest in Dresden; and Sigrid Lund's son, having been released from Sachsenhausen, had arrived in Hamburg on his way home to Norway.

My memory of that time brings into sharp focus the crucial difference between a soldier and the lone resistance fighter. While these women had to face the enemy on their own, make their decisions on their own, take personal responsibility for every action, large and small, on their own, we were protected and cosseted by a well-organised military machine acting in unison with thousands of others. This memory alone underlines my unbounded admiration for these four Women of Courage.

29: Videodiscs

In 1980 my three-year contract with Yorkshire Television came to an end, and I felt that I wanted a change of direction. It was *Kitty – Return to Auschwitz* that provided the final push. I feared that the opportunities to have the freedom to make films like that were receding fast. For *Kitty* I had asked for a ninety-minute slot and got it. I asked for the suspension of commercial breaks and got it. It was the only time in all those years that I worked in television that I could sit back, look at the final cut and not face the age-old problem of what to put in and, worse, what to leave out. For once I was not forced to compromise – the contents and style saw to that. What chances were there for future projects of that nature?

The exciting pioneering days had long gone. For a freelance to hawk around programme ideas to BBC1 and 2, ITV and Channel 4 in the '80s was much harder, with an abundance of challenging younger talent competing for attention. I was also conscious of the first signs of the 'bean counters' taking over the management and decision-making from senior programme people. This development made me anxious about the future of broadcasting, and I felt that the moment had come to draw a line.

At first, of course, I feared that I might miss directing films and TV programmes – but not a bit of it. I relished the opportunity to be in on something new for the second time in my life. My interest in videodisc development had increased over the last few years, after *Christmas Carols from Cambridge* in 1976, and my continuing association with the RCA system in the States whetted my appetite for a different sort of programme-making. What finally tipped the balance was an irresistible offer from Thorn-EMI.

It was EMI who had contracted me to make the *Christmas Carols* 'videogram', and the powerful Thorn Group had now gobbled up EMI. Thorn, with their rental clout in the UK and abroad, was well on the way to making VHS the world standard home video system; and the purchase of EMI gave them ownership of a very large movie catalogue to prime the new video cassette market.

VHS was invented and manufactured by JVC in Japan, and the Thorn technology agreement with JVC meant that they were obliged to back their next home video gizmo, namely the brand-new VHD videodisc technology. This is when the EMI executives, who had hired me in 1976 and knew about my RCA involvement, made an attractive offer for me to come and develop and produce videodiscs for the VHD system. There were many Soho lunchtime meetings and I finally negotiated a satisfactory contract. I was to be Thorn-EMI's Controller of Programmes, and to my surprise they accepted my insistence on an eight-year contract. I was able to persuade them that it would take that long to develop and produce the quality and quantity for a sustainable videodisc market. With a splendid office in Thorn House, Upper St Martin's Lane, and a small team of enthusiasts, I started an unfamiliar and intriguing new life. As in the early days of television, there was no yardstick to go by: so-called interactive videodiscs were talked about in the abstract, and you just made it up as you went along. It was exhilarating, once more, to start with a clean slate.

The next three years were frantic. Thorn had announced a launch date for VHD, and I was responsible for producing an inventory of interactive videodiscs for their opening night catalogue. They were spending a fortune in acquiring more movie rights, while I was in charge of a £2 million budget and creating something entirely new. By using narrower 'brush strokes', it was now possible to invite the active user of the videodisc to interact with a richness of information that was denied to the passive television viewer. Here was the escape from the tyranny of the broadcast time-slot that I had been looking for, and the release from the medium's limitations in communicating detailed facts and figures, let alone ideas.

Today this sounds like old hat, but in the early '80s it was entirely new. The whole panoply of technological magic, now taken for granted, simply did not exist. Home computers, CD-ROM, mobile phones, the Internet, CD and DVD had yet to find their roles.

Thorn-EMI felt that the 'how to' market should be their first target, and so I found myself producing discs on fishing, car maintenance, dress-making (so help me), cooking and subjects of that ilk. What intrigued me was not the subject matter but designing methods of manipulating the contents and finding ways to exploit the new, but still primitive, functions of the videodisc player, such as chapterisation, indexing, automatic picture stops, still frame, slow motion and dual sound tracks, allowing two comprehension levels – all this controlled by the user's handset.

JVC sent over a large team of technicians to oversee the building of a VHD disc manufacturing plant in Swindon, and I found myself making many trips to Japan to persuade JVC to implement technical functions for their player that had not occurred to them. To visit Tokyo, with its new skyscrapers, brilliant underground train service and all the other outward changes that had transformed the city since my early documentary *The Two Faces of Japan* in 1960 was always an exciting experience. And I was about to learn something about the way large corporations conduct their business.

It was customary for Thorn to dispatch a large team, consisting of senior engineers, technicians, corporate business affairs experts, lawyers and publicity people, to negotiate, finalise and sign off agreements with JVC. And I arrived in Tokyo on my own.

On the first morning I was met by a JVC representative, who picked me up at my hotel and escorted me in a chauffeur-driven car to the plant. About a mile before reaching our destination he stopped the car and got out to make a phone call; I realised that he was alerting his superiors of my imminent arrival. When we pulled into the drive of their huge head office I was greeted with an array of Union Jacks fluttering in the breeze. I was nearly as surprised as the baffled JVC high-ranking welcoming group, who expected to greet the usual army of Thorn people.

Tea was served in an ante-room to the board room, and the conversation was very formal but friendly. My hosts were all wearing identical smart light blue uniforms, sporting the JVC logo. I explained that I was a producer and director, and their international sales director, who spoke good English, declared that he would from now on call me 'Mister Peter Morray Softwarosan'.

I sat on one side of a very long board room table, facing twelve JVC executives and an interpreter. As was normal practice, I had telexed an agenda for the meeting from London, but the JVC managing director announced that he had to put an extra item at the top of it. This did not surprise me. He felt that he needed an explanation of how decisions could be arrived at without the presence of the usual Thorn representatives. I explained that the UK launch date for their splendid system meant that there was great urgency to settle some purely technical matters, and that Thorn-EMI had given me full plenipotentiary powers to do this. I said that agreement had to be reached that day or the launch date would be jeopardised. There was a big sucking-in of breath, but it worked.

In order to exploit some of the VHD player's tricks I had requested some additional player functions, and I had redesigned, and made a cardboard model of, the remote handset to accommodate them. I handed the model to the chief engineer across the table. He and two of his assistants went into a huddle and studied my proposed changes. After a lot of discussion between them and their other colleagues, they requested another meeting the following day to announce the result of their deliberations – which surprised me: normally when technical alterations were accepted it took about six weeks for JVC to come up with a prototype. To my astonishment, the following morning they successfully demonstrated the redesigned remote control, implementing all the functions I had asked. They must have worked flat-out all night. It was very impressive.

Back at Thorn House I had got to know the Group chairman. I had invited him to some early demonstrations of the first clutch of discs we were making, and we got on well. He asked me to lunch and I was able to hold forth about the early VHD launch. As Thorn-EMI was creating a world VHS video cassette market using a video player that could also record programmes, would not the VHD videodisc system, without recording capability, create unwelcome competition? He told me I was not the only person who had nobbled him on this.

Thorn-EMI Videodisc, as we were now called, moved to new premises in Tottenham Court Road (up the road from the old Dominion Theatre!), and there I continued to spend huge chunks of production money on all manner of titles. I contracted Colin Mably, a senior science lecturer, onto my team, and between us we created a rich science resource for primary schools. This six-disc set would, we believed, stimulate a videodisc market in the UK. We persuaded Thorn to make their VHD players available at a reduced price to schools, and started a marketing operation. The desktop computer was now making itself known, and we started to investigate the possibility of putting the videodisc player under computer control. It was an interesting time and I enjoyed it, little realising that rampant and unstoppable technology was consigning videodisc to rapid obsolescence. As it turned out, a year later the VHD launch was aborted (which was no surprise to me) and the disc plant in Swindon was shut down. The write-off cost Thorn-EMI over £12 million. And yet, in spite of that, I was told to soldier on and develop more titles, and was asked to find new accommodation. I set up shop in Dean Street, right in the middle of Soho. My contract had four more years to run, and Colin Mably and I, now good friends, were able to continue to make and market our science series of discs for schools.

Thorn decreed to set up a new company that did not carry their name, and I thought that Evergreen Communications Ltd would fit the bill. We instigated an independent evaluation of school users, and the reaction was enthusiastic – but as always schools were underfunded, and they found it almost impossible to finance the new technology. They were happy with their video cassette players.

We now changed over to the competing Philips laserdisc technology, as their optical disc looked like becoming the world standard. It was even more expensive than the VHD player, but the discs could be pressed in Germany. I had to convert all our material to make it play on laserdisc. Little did any of us realise that this large, shiny laserdisc, with its optical reading technology, was the grandfather of all the emerging disc systems, such as CD, CD-ROM and DVD.

In 1989 Thorn said that enough was enough and decided to close us down. One of their main board directors, Marshall Young, who had monitored our progress and signed off our accounts, called me on the phone and asked whether I would like to consider an MBO. After I asked what on earth MBO meant, he explained that he was offering a management buy-out. Not only that, he was so enthusiastic about our efforts that he resigned from Thorn, became the chairman of Evergreen and then persuaded Thorn to loan us the money for the buy-out. We had a couple of months to vacate our Dean Street offices, and the three new directors of Evergreen Communications, Marshall Young, Colin Mably and myself, set an early trend by deciding to work from our respective homes. It was the best move I have ever made. I set up all the technical video editing equipment, acquired a computer, a fax machine, a copier and an answer-phone. I was self-contained and self-sufficient – it felt good.

Jonathan and Ben had flown the nest by now, so I converted the boys' old playroom into my office/studio, and taught myself word processing and desktop publishing. With Marshall's overseas contacts we got an American publisher excited about our science discs, and after several trips to the States clinched a distribution deal with Simon & Schuster. After two years they admitted that they had failed in their marketing effort and wanted to get out of the tough contract Marshall had negotiated. It cost them dearly, and the money we received from them easily (and thankfully) enabled us to pay off our MBO debt from Thorn.

Colin, in the meantime, had struck up a friendship (culminating a few years later in a very happy marriage) with Anne Benbow, educational chief of the American Chemical Society, who sponsored a run of science programmes on laserdisc and video cassettes for American schools, and Colin and I were contracted to make them. All the rushes were shipped back here, and I enjoyed the prospect of being, once again, an editor, using my own equipment in my own home. Every so often I popped over the pond to Annapolis to do all the post-production work; it was always a pleasurable experience.

And then in 1996 – disaster. Something totally unexpected occurred. It just proves the old saying that all of us are only inches away from the unknown. Jane suffered a spontaneous prolapse of a disc half-way down her spine, and after hospitalisation and two years of physiotherapy she was classed as an incomplete paraplegic. What this means is that to this day she is confined to a wheelchair, although with enormous effort and support she manages to take a few steps, such as going into a restaurant or theatre where there is no disabled access. She is amazingly agile in water, and I take her swimming every week. I can't begin to describe Jane's great courage, her stoicism, and above all her wonderfully positive outlook. We decided from day one of this new regime that we would retain a healthy sense of good humour, and we have. My 'caring' duties could have been so onerous, but they are not. Working from home means that my new and unexpected duties don't interfere with my work. I reckon that we make a good team, cheerfully facing the realities of this situation. Long may it last.

* * * *

In 1998 I was asked by the United States National Archive and Records Administration, based in Maryland, to lecture on and then screen *Kitty – Return to Auschwitz.* Suddenly I found myself in demand in the States, because a senior staff member from the United States Holocaust Memorial Museum was in the audience. Thus started a series of lecture/presentation engagements in America, lasting four years. The bulk of these were sponsored by the Holocaust Museum, with gigs in New York, Washington, Chicago, Florida, Los Angeles, Denver and San Diego. In addition to *Kitty,* I also showed the four *Women of Courage* films to an interesting variety of audiences, a mixture of Holocaust survivors and their families, Jewish groups, Catholic groups, university students, teachers, and sometimes whole classes of young pupils from the local schools. I enjoyed all this very much, and felt it was worth doing. I always get a kick out of visiting the States, and at the end of each trip, on my way back to London, I managed to stay with my old friend Dick Sonnenfeldt and his wife Barbara, in their Port Washington home on Long Island. Jane, too, looked forward to my short absences: she enjoys being independent and copes wonderfully well. These gigs dried up after 2002 because of America's economic climate: sponsorship funding became very difficult. Back here, however, I made similar presentations that now included the *Churchill Funeral* and *The Turn of the Screw* at the National Film Theatre on the South Bank, the Imperial War Museum and Christ Church, Oxford.

In the summer of 2004 I retired from BAFTA, together with my fellow trustees the Lords John Brabourne and David Puttman. John and I had been trustees from the very first day and had now served for almost thirty years. It was time to make room for fresh blood, and I also hoped that I could win more time to do other things – including this attempt to rewind my life by putting it down on paper. I embarked on the task several years ago – and of course it took much longer than I had imagined. The demands made on my time, as I get older, evoke the old cry, 'How on earth did I ever find the time to go to work?'

30: Afterthoughts

In this chronology I have listed the output of a fairly eclectic range of programmes by just one practitioner – but I was not alone: there were many others who could equally claim similar experiences in this shared adventure that started more than fifty years ago. Now, with hindsight, I am going to step back for a moment and briefly record some thoughts about television, then and now.

No one could guess, when faced with competition from the launch of ITV in 1955, how the BBC would react. History tells us that the BBC was confident that its broadcasting ethos was secure, and there was no need to fear the challenge from the 'commercial upstarts'. Fierce public arguments in the press and in Parliament broke out, focusing on opposing theories: 'giving people what they want' versus 'giving them what you think is good for them'.

But this controversy was not the talking point in Rediffusion's club bar – we were much too busy satisfying the voracious appetite of a brand-new national network, helping to sustain its daily schedule of programmes.

There have been many learned books tracing the history of those first ten or so years of the two-channel service, and they make interesting reading today, especially in the light of the fairly recent, and in my view rather frightening, revolution in broadcasting technology. Historians and media experts tell us about the BBC's early shock discovery of an entirely unexpected, indeed exploding, mass audience for television, which was clamouring to be 'entertained'. It is worth recalling that within the first year of ITV the number of homes able to receive television went up from 188,000 to a staggering 1,550,000. By the winter of 1956 this number was increasing by 50,000 every week, and by September 1957 ITV, now two years old, reached 4.8 million homes; and the viewing ratio was 79:21 in favour of ITV. The BBC monopoly had been well and truly broken. This turned out to be very good news, because within a short time the advent of ITV, acting as a powerful stimulant, transformed the BBC into the best and most respected broadcasting organisation in the world. The standard was set for public service broadcasting.

It was in this climate that I started making programmes – in a way, ploughing my own furrow, oblivious of the changes that would sooner or later affect programme makers. I consider myself to have been fortunate to have had the chance to make, in those early few years, both mass and minority audience programmes that some thought could only be made by the BBC. *The Turn of the Screw* and *Tyranny – the Years of Adolf Hitler* exactly fitted that category.

I have often wondered what made me tick. There was no yardstick to compare myself with; there was hardly any time to watch other people's programmes; the documentaries I had been making before 1955 suddenly seemed dated. The immediacy of this new medium was going to change everything. There was precious little thinking time to develop concepts, ideas and styles; there was no one around to ask for help or advice. The pressures were such that you just went ahead and somehow made it up as you went along. The chances were that you achieved something entirely new – such was the primitive state of the medium. I was quite unaware of the bigger picture. I certainly never thought about the role of television, let alone its duty to the public – I had seen so little of it – and like many others I was conscious only of its novelty value. It is difficult for today's viewers to realise that video recording in the home had yet to be invented, and if you were not able to see a programme as it was being transmitted – well, that was your bad luck.

I got to know fellow programme makers from the BBC (through the Guild of Television Producers and Directors) and was impressed and obviously influenced by their approach to broadcasting, admiring the commitment to the very broad spectrum of programming that made up the BBC broadcasting philosophy. I became aware that programme-makers at the BBC belonged to an all-embracing broadcasting organisation, dedicated to 'speak to the nation', whereas ITV, as set up by Parliament, was a network of regional companies – with the major competing players providing the bulk of the programmes. The prospect, therefore, of establishing cohesiveness – ITV speaking with one voice, as the BBC was able to – was illusory. In spite of that, new ground was being broken in many fields of programming: ITV's contemporary dramas were beginning to have an effect on the BBC's output, as were the current affairs programmes, starting in 1956 with *This Week,* soon followed by Granada's *World in Action*. Most memorable was the contribution made by ITN. They introduced the role of the newscaster, and put television journalism firmly on the new medium's map. And at Rediffusion we also were contributing to a new grammar in programme-making.

The only tangible feedback of our endeavours was from the press. Of course it was always warming to bask for a few moments in a good review, but very few critics had the experience (or column inches) to indulge in detailed constructive criticisms. I consider Philip Purser, Maurice Richardson, Maurice Wiggin and Peter Black to have been my distant mentors. I feel that they conducted a gentle, continuing dialogue with me over many years, and I learnt more from their columns about television in general, and my programmes in particular, than from anywhere else.

As the years passed and as television evolved from being a grand adventure, as I used to call it, into a communications industry, I was able to develop my thoughts about the medium and my belief in the public service broadcasting ethos as practised by the BBC. My involvement in the arguments for a future second channel for ITV was motivated by this belief, and I was much relieved when the new Channel 4 remit came into being.

During these years I felt great loyalty to Rediffusion, although I was not on the staff. It was a lucky mixture, both of belonging and yet keeping a certain distance, which gave me as a freelance an element of freedom to pick and choose the sort of programmes I wished to make. Apart from producing and directing, I got satisfaction from my involvement firstly with the Guild and then, for over thirty years, with BAFTA and the Royal Television Society. I never felt any ambition to shin up that greasy pole to an executive position, as a number of friends and colleagues managed to do. Lord Mountbatten said to me after the three-year production period with him that I should put my name forward to become a head of department or channel controller, and he found it difficult to understand that I was happy with what I was doing. Promotion for him was part of the game, but I did not feel like playing it.

When I decided to put active programme making to one side in the early '80s, some colleagues found this difficult to take. In a way I had had my fill. I had been lucky to have been in at the start, and the time had come for a change of gear. It was a chance, once again, to be in on something new. What finally persuaded me, in effect it became my swansong, was *Kitty – Return to Auschwitz.* As I have indicated, the film's emotional impact left its mark on me. The support I received from YTV, and especially from Paul Fox, to go and make this film 'my way' was remarkable, but I feared that this enlightened attitude to programme making was likely to undergo changes in the '80s and beyond. The culture of television at the end of the first quarter-century of ITV's existence was showing these signs, and I didn't much like the direction it was taking. Profit motivation was to become a driving force. Those of my colleagues who had made it to the top of the tree were in danger of being outnumbered by others whose broadcasting philosophy was a million miles away from the more idealistic years which I had the good fortune to experience.

* * * *

The year 2005 signalled both the sixtieth anniversary of the end of the Second World War and the fiftieth of the start of independent television in the UK – two landmarks, nostalgia aside, that cause me to reflect on these past eighty-five-plus fairly active years of my life. The first recalls a bizarre irony – that when I finished my war my brother Tommy and I stood to attention in the gun turrets of our tanks as we passed Churchill in Berlin – of all places. The second event marks the great good luck I had when, over fifty years ago, my television career took root. But there is an even more important reason for celebrating – because that was the moment when, in 1955, I met Rediffusion's production assistant Jane Tillett – my wife to be.

Over seventy years have elapsed since I started as a rewind-boy in the projection box of the Dominion, Tottenham Court Road. Needless to say, it never occurred to me at the time that one day I might sit down, put pen to paper and chronicle these events. I have now definitely done with rewinding.

Credits

1955–56	***Fan Fever***
	Members' Mail (17 programmes)
1957–58	***On Stage*** (6 programmes)
	Salute to Show Business
	Conflict (13 programmes)
	Only Yesterday (13 programmes)
1959	***Tyranny – The Years of Adolf Hitler***
	Israel Rises – The Birth of a Nation
1959	***The Turn of the Screw***
1960	***Princess Margaret's Wedding***
	Alcoholism — Study of a Disease
	The Two Faces of Japan
1960	***The Heartbeat of France***
1960–63	***This Week*** (130 editions)
	The Rat Line – banned by the ITA
1964	***Black Marries White — The Last Barrier***
1965	***The State Funeral of Sir Winston Churchill***
1965	***LSO – The Music Men***
1965–69	***The Life and Times of Lord Mountbatten***
1970	***The First Casualty***
1971–75	***The Mighty Continent***
1976	***25 Years – Impressions***
1977	***Prime Minister on Prime Ministers***
	Christmas Carols from Cambridge
1978	***Kitty – Return to Auschwitz***
1978	***Women of Courage***

Index

Lightning Source UK Ltd.
Milton Keynes UK
177998UK00002B/72/P

9 781904 408772